HP Certified
HP-UX System Administration

ISBN 0-13-018374-1

90000

9 780130 183743

Hewlett-Packard® Professional Books

OPERATING SYSTEMS

Fernandez	Configuring CDE: The Common Desktop Environment
Lund	Integrating UNIX® and PC Network Operating Systems
Madell	Disk and File Management Tasks on HP-UX
Poniatowski	HP-UX 11.x System Administration Handbook and Toolkit
Poniatowski	HP-UX 11.x System Administration "How To" Book, Second Edition
Poniatowski	HP-UX System Administration Handbook and Toolkit
Poniatowski	Learning the HP-UX Operating System
Poniatowski	UNIX® User's Handbook
Rehman	HP Certified, HP-UX System Administration
Sauers, Weygant	HP-UX Tuning and Performance
Stone, Symons	UNIX® Fault Management
Weygant	Clusters for High Availability: A Primer of HP-UX Solutions

ONLINE/INTERNET

Amor	The E-business (R)evolution
Greenberg, Lakeland	A Methodology for Developing and Deploying Internet and Intranet Solutions
Greenberg, Lakeland	Building Professional Web Sites with the Right Tools
Ketkar	Working with Netscape Server on HP-UX

NETWORKING/COMMUNICATIONS

Blommers	Practical Planning for Network Growth
Lee	The ISDN Consultant
Lucke	Designing and Implementing Computer Workgroups

ENTERPRISE

Blommers	Architecting Enterprise Solutions with UNIX® Networking
Cook	Building Enterprise Information Architectures
Pipkin	Halting the Hacker: A Practical Guide to Computer Security
Pipkin	Information Security: Protecting the Global Enterprise
Sperley	Enterprise Data Warehouse, Volume 1: Planning, Building, and Implementation
Thornburgh	Fibre Channel for Mass Storage

PROGRAMMING

Blinn	Portable Shell Programming
Caruso	Power Programming in HP OpenView
Chaudri, Loomis	Object Databases in Practice
Chew	The Java™/C++ Cross-Reference Handbook
Grady	Practical Software Metrics for Project Management and Process Improvement
Grady	Successful Software Process Improvement
Lewis	The Art & Science of Smalltalk
Lichtenbelt, Crane, Naqvi	Introduction to Volume Rendering
Mellquist	SNMP++
Mikkelsen, Pherigo	Practical Software Configuration Management
Norton, DiPasquale	Thread Time: The Multithreaded Programming Guide
Wadleigh, Crawford	Software Optimization for High Performance Computing

IMAGE PROCESSING

Crane	A Simplified Approach to Image Processing
Day	The Color Scanning Handbook
Gann	Desktop Scanners: Image Quality

OTHER TITLES OF INTEREST

Kane	PA-RISC 2.0 Architecture
Markstein	IA-64 and Elementary Functions

HP Certified

HP-UX System Administration

Rafeeq Ur Rehman

www.hp.com/go/retailbooks

Prentice Hall PTR
Upper Saddle River, New Jersey 07458
www.phptr.com

Library of Congress Cataloging-in-Publication Data

Rehman, Rafeeq Ur.
  HP Certified : HP-UX system administration / Rafeeq Ur Rehman.
    p. cm.
  ISBN 0-13-018374-1
    1. HP-UX. 2. Operating systems (Computers) I. Title.

  QA76.76.O63 R435 2000
  005.4'469—dc21   00-024274

Editorial/Production Supervision: *Mary Sudul*
Cover Design Director: *Jerry Votta*
Cover Design: *Talar Agasyan*
Manufacturing Manager: *Maura Goldstaub*
Acquisitions Editor: *Jill Pisoni*
Editorial Assistant: *Justin Somma*
Marketing Manager: *Bryan Gambrel*
Series Design: *Gail Cocker-Bogusz*

Manager, Hewlett-Packard Retail Book Publishing: *Patricia Pekary*
Editor, Hewlett-Packard Professional Books: *Susan Wright*

Published by Prentice Hall PTR
Prentice-Hall, Inc.
Upper Saddle River, NJ 07458

Prentice Hall books are widely used by corporations and government agencies for training, marketing, and resale.

The publisher offers discounts on this book when ordered in bulk quantities. For more information, contact Corporate Sales Department, Phone: 800-382-3419; fax: 201-236-714; email: corpsales@prenhall.com or write Corporate Sales Department, Prentice Hall PTR, One Lake Street, Upper Saddle River, NJ 07458.

HP and HP-UX are registered trademarks of Hewlett-Packard Company. Other product or company named mentioned herein are the trademarks of their respective owners.

Printed in the United States of America

10 9 8 7 6 5 4 3 2 1

ISBN 0-13-018374-1

Prentice-Hall International (UK) Limited, *London*
Prentice-Hall of Australia Pty. Limited, *Sydney*
Prentice-Hall Canada Inc., *Toronto*
Prentice-Hall Hispanoamericana, S.A., *Mexico*
Prentice-Hall of India Private Limited, *New Delhi*
Prentice-Hall of Japan, Inc., *Tokyo*
Simon & Schuster Asia Pte. Ltd., *Singapore*
Editora Prentice-Hall do Brasil, Ltda., *Rio de Janeiro*

To my parents.
Everybody in the world may wish to have such a family.

CONTENTS

vii

2

Working with Files and Directories   *21*

3

Environment Variables   *41*

6

Regular Expressions   *87*

7

File Permissions   *99*

8

UNIX File System Hierarchy *119*

13

Installing HP-UX 215

14

System Startup and Shutdown 243

15

Software and Patch Management   *271*

16

Reconfiguring the HP-UX Kernel   295

17

Peripheral Devices   *317*

18

HP-UX File Systems and Logical Volume Manager   *337*

19

User and Group Management   *373*

22

Memory and Swap Space Management   *427*

29

Configuring LAN Interface Adapters   *543*

28

Introduction to the TCP/IP Protocol *523*

32

Configuring and Managing NIS   *617*

35

Network Time Protocol 669

36

System and Network Administration: Final Thoughts 679

FOREWORD

HPEducation has a long-standing tradition of making sure their customers have the highest quality skills to perform complex tasks in the work environment. Now HP Education has come up with a method to help you prepare to validate your knowledge and skills in HP-UX system and network administration. HP Certified's new book, *HP-UX System Administration* is designed to help you prepare to take the HP-UX System Administration exam (3H0-002). With a variety of concept descriptions, examples, and practice test questions, this book will help provide the final review to preparing for this challenging exam.

Certification is becoming the standard for identifying competence in the workplace. Many IT professionals now have several credentials to show they understand and can use the latest systems, tools, and techniques in the IT environment. Preparation materials such as tutorials, Web-based practice tests, and self-paced study guides all aid the candidate in preparing for these all-important exams. Because of the time crunch we all face, we need these tools to validate readiness and boost self confidence.

More and more, candidates are asking for self-paced materials to help them learn, study, and grow. HP Education is determined to provide you, the IT professional, with a variety of learning formats to help you keep up with the fast pace of technology while meeting your demanding schedule.

Jamie Mulkey, Ed.D.
HP Certified
Worldwide Certification Program Manager
HP Education

Rob Adams
Worldwide Program Manager—UNIX
HP Education

PREFACE

I have tried to write a book that covers all HP-UX system and networking administration concepts. The book is divided into three parts. The first part consists of Chapters 1–11. It covers general UNIX concepts, user commands, and shell programming. The second part of the book covers HP-UX system administration and consists of Chapters 12–25. The third part consists of Chapters 26–36 and is dedicated to computer networking concepts and HP-UX network administration tasks. The book is divided into these three parts according to requirements of the HP-UX certification examination. This is also quite a logical way to present the material to a UNIX system administrator. At the end of each chapter, you will find chapter review questions to check your understanding of the material presented in the chapter. There are some sample test questions under "Test Your Knowledge," which will provide you an idea of which type of questions are going to be asked in the actual exam. I have tried to use a combination of simple and difficult questions in this part. Answers to the review questions are provided in Appendix A, and answers to the sample test questions are available in Appendix B.

While writing this book, I have tried to explain all system administration concepts in reasonable detail. Many examples are presented in each section of a chapter to help the user understand what happens when a particular command is executed. Commonly used command-line switches are also listed wherever appropriate. You will also find many screen shots showing what happens when you select a menu or press a button in the GUI windows. I have also tried to explain each system and network administration task using both command-line utilities and System Administration Manager (SAM). Most "old-fashioned" people would like to carry out many tasks using the command-line interface, which is also very important for passing the HP-UX certification examination.

The book is organized such that it progresses from simple-to-understand concepts to more-difficult and complicated ones. The same strategy is also implemented in each chapter. Figures, tables, and examples are presented wherever helpful to communicate the concept. The first few chapters contain more examples than the later ones to give a user a good start.

Another consideration in the organization of the book is logical relevance and order of the chapters. If an idea or concept depends on another concept, it is placed later in the book.

This book is intended to be the most comprehensive book on HP-UX. It not only covers the HP-UX certification exam, but it also serves as a reference book for even the most experienced HP-UX system administrators. The first part is designed with the most basic concepts so that anybody who is new to HP-UX can get the full benefit. The next two parts cover more-complicated system and network administration tasks. Both novice and experienced users will find interesting things here.

Part 1: Fundamentals of UNIX Systems

The first part is an introduction to the UNIX system. This is a more-general UNIX part and consists of login and logout procedure, file and directory manipulation, file editing, an introduction to the POSIX shell, and file security/permissions. This part shows the concepts of users and groups, which are common to all UNIX systems. UNIX commands related to all these topics are presented and the more commonly used options of these commands are discussed. This part also throws light on standard input/output and I/O redirection. Chapters 10 and 11 introduce shell programming concepts. Here you will find a number of shell programs, up to elaborate shell variables and flow control structures.

Part 2: HP-UX System Administration

The second part is the core HP-UX system administration part of the book. It fully covers all issues from the installation of HP-UX to managing devices, security, and system performance. The part starts with an introduction to System Administration Manager (SAM), which is a comprehensive HP-UX tool meant for system administration. Installation of HP-UX on a server or workstation is presented next. After that, you will gradually progress from basic to more-complex system configuration tasks, building a kernel, managing devices, adding/removing users, and concepts of the HP-UX file system.

Part 3: HP-UX Network Administration

The third part covers HP-UX network administration. It also contains general networking concepts such as the ISO-OSI reference model and TCP/IP networking. One chapter is dedicated to ARPA/Berkeley services. Then NFS, NIS, DNS, and NTP are covered.

How to Register for the HP-UX Certification Examination

You can register for the examination by calling Sylvan Prometric at 1-800-755-EXAM or directly at Website `http://www.2test.com`. You can also visit an authorized Sylvan Prometric Testing Center to get more information. A list of authorized testing centers is available at `http://www.2test.com`. More information is available on the HP Education Website `http://education.hp.com`.

Strategies for Taking the Test

You should take a practice test to estimate the time needed to answer all questions. Stay relaxed and have a good night's sleep before the test day. Keep the following things in mind for a successful examination:

- Reach the testing center at least 15 minutes before the scheduled starting time. You have to sign a few papers and show identification before you start the test.
- Have with you at least two pieces of personal identification: One of these must contain your photograph. For example, valid identification documents might be your driver's license and a credit card.
- You don't need to carry any paper or pencils with you.
- Carefully read each question before answering it.
- Try to answer the easy questions first. If a question is taking a long time, just mark it and move to the next question. You are allowed to go back to review your answers and answer any leftover questions. The first target should be to go through all the questions from start to finish.
- When selecting an answer, try to rule out some of the options. This will help you select the right answer.
- While reviewing your answers, try to read the question very carefully: You may have chosen a wrong answer because you have misunderstood the question.

ACKNOWLEDGMENTS

I have been lucky to get help from many people during the manuscript writing. There is a great contribution from Gary Labeau from Hewlett-Packard Corporation who reviewed this book. He did a great job and a put a lot of effort in reading each and every word and providing a wealth of suggestions.

Susan Wright at Hewlett-Packard Corporation arranged meetings to discuss all matters about the book. I was able to get feedback from others during these meetings. This helped a lot to plan and arrange book contents.

Jill Pisoni at Prentice Hall PTR coordinated this production. She planned goals and pushed all people involved in the production process to meet these goals. Without her effort, it would have been difficult to carry out the job. Thanks Jill.

Jim Markam and Mary Sudul at Prentice Hall PTR was extremely helpful in proper organization of manuscript and figures right from the beginning of the project. He provided all sort of help in production matters.

Special thanks to Patricia Lickliter, Christopher Paul, and Victor Zhiltsov at Dedicated Technologies Inc. for their suggestions and continuous encouragement.

I learned a lot from the experience of Karen Lintala and Randy Mather at Honda of America Mfg. Inc. Randy has a rich experience of HP-UX system administration and I learnt a lot from him.

I am thankful to my wife for bearing with me during the last seven months. She gave me full support and tried to provide the best environment at home to help complete the book. I am also thankful to Afnan for his nonstop entertainment activities that kept me fresh.

Nothing is complete without mentioning Dr. Shahid Bokhari of the Department of Electrical Engineering, University of Engineering and Technology, Lahore, Pakistan. He is the source of all my UNIX knowledge and the most incredible person I have met in my life. He has established a well-maintained UNIX laboratory where people like me are able to experiment.

January 15, 2000

Fundamentals of the UNIX System

Getting Started with UNIX

UNIX systems, unlike their counterpart single-user systems, are multiuser systems designed for many people to use one computer simultaneously. In fact, larger UNIX machines serve thousands of users simultaneously.

The two most commonly used standards for the UNIX systems are *Berkley Distribution* (BSD) and *AT&T System V Release 4 (SVR4)*. Most vendor-specific versions of UNIX are based on one of these distributions. Although UNIX vendors have different brand names for their particular system, most features are common. The main vendor differences are in configuration and system administration utilities. The UNIX system used by Hewlett Packard is called HP-UX, which is modeled after SVR4. This chapter will bring you up to speed on the login and the general concepts of HP-UX system administration, covering the topics listed in the chapter syllabus.

1.1   UNIX Shells

The core of the UNIX operating system is the *kernel*. It can be thought of as a piece of software that handles all the communications between user software and computer hardware. It is the kernel that decides how to communicate with peripheral devices, how to share time among users of the system, how to allocate memory for different programs running, and how to utilize the processor and other resources. The kernel keeps records of all programs (commonly called *processes*) running on the system and shares time among these processes according to a well-defined policy.

Users of the UNIX system don't have a direct interaction with the kernel. Instead, the user always works with a program called the *UNIX shell*. A shell can be considered a command interpreter. The shell takes user commands, interprets them, and takes the necessary action to execute them. It also provides the output of these commands to the user.

The most commonly used shells are listed in Table 1-1. All of these shells are available on HP-UX.

Table 1–1 *Most Frequently Used UNIX Shells*

Name	Description
Bourne shell	Available on all UNIX platforms. It is the oldest and most widely used shell.
C shell	It uses a C language-like syntax for shell programming.
Korn shell	It has more complex and advanced features than the Bourne or C shell and takes more time to master.
POSIX shell	IEEE POSIX (Portable Operating System Interface) compliant shell. It is the default and primary shell for all users on HP-UX.

Each of these shells has its own capabilities and limitations. The default shell used on HP-UX systems is the POSIX shell, although the user is free to choose any of the available shells.

Throughout the book, whenever I refer to "shell," it means the default HP-UX POSIX shell. The capabilities of the other three shells will be discussed as we move forward to Chapter 9.

1.2   Logging In and Out of HP-UX

All HP-UX users are assigned a user name or login name and a password to access the system. Each user name is unique. When users want to start using the system, they enter the user name and password assigned to them. The process of entering this information is called the *login process*. Similarly to end a user session, the user issues a command (exit), and this process is called the *logout process*. The login and logout processes are necessary for system security so that only those authorized can use the system.

The Superuser

There is a special user in the UNIX systems called **root**. This user is created during the installation process of HP-UX. The **root** user has privileges to do all system administration tasks, such as adding and deleting users, administration of printers, and other routine system maintenance tasks. Usually, the systems administrator uses the **root** user name. It is a common practice to call the **root** user the *superuser* to show the power associated with the name.

Each user in the UNIX system has a unique number associated with the user name, called a *User ID*. The **root** user has ID 0; therefore, any user with that ID has superuser privileges.

Logging In

When logging in, you'll see a login prompt on your terminal screen similar to the one shown in Figure 1-1.

```
GenericSysName [HP Release B.11.00] (See /etc/issue)

Console Login :
```

Figure 1–1   *HP-UX login prompt.*

This prompt shows that the system is waiting for a user to enter a login name and password. At the login prompt, the user should enter the login name. The system then prompts for the password assigned to the login name. The user then enters the password. If the login name and the password match one of the users on the system, the user is allowed to log into the system. If the login name and password do not match an existing user, then access to the system is denied and the error message, Login incorrect, is displayed. Figure 1-2 shows an example of a complete login session where a user named **boota** logs into HP-UX.

Once the user sees the $ symbol, the login process is complete.

Shell Prompts

As soon as a user logs into HP-UX, the shell assigned to the user starts and displays the *shell prompt* (also called the *command prompt*). Superuser and common user command prompts differ: $ represents a common user, while #

```
GenericSysName [HP Release B.11.00] (See /etc/issue)

Console Login : boota
Password:
Please wait...checking for disk quotas
(c)Copyright 1983-1997 Hewlett-Packard Co.,  All Rights Reserved.
(c)Copyright 1979, 1980, 1983, 1985-1993 The Regents of the Univ. of California
(c)Copyright 1980, 1984, 1986 Novell, Inc.
(c)Copyright 1986-1992 Sun Microsystems, Inc.
(c)Copyright 1985, 1986, 1988 Massachusetts Institute of Technology
(c)Copyright 1989-1993  The Open Software Foundation, Inc.
(c)Copyright 1986 Digital Equipment Corp.
(c)Copyright 1990 Motorola, Inc.
(c)Copyright 1990, 1991, 1992 Cornell University
(c)Copyright 1989-1991 The University of Maryland
(c)Copyright 1988 Carnegie Mellon University
(c)Copyright 1991-1997 Mentat, Inc.
(c)Copyright 1996 Morning Star Technologies, Inc.
(c)Copyright 1996 Progressive Systems, Inc.
(c)Copyright 1997 Isogon Corporation


                     RESTRICTED RIGHTS LEGEND
Use, duplication, or disclosure by the U.S. Government is subject to
restrictions as set forth in sub-paragraph (c)(1)(ii) of the Rights in
Technical Data and Computer Software clause in DFARS 252.227-7013.


                  Hewlett-Packard Company
                  3000 Hanover Street
                  Palo Alto, CA 94304 U.S.A.

Rights for non-DOD U.S. Government Departments and Agencies are as set
forth in FAR 52.227-19(c)(1,2).
$
```

Figure 1–2 *Login session for user* **boota***.*

represents a superuser. When you see either of these command prompts, you can issue any command for which you are authorized.

> **When you log in as the `root` user, be careful, as by your actions you can accidentally damage the system integrity.**

Logging Out

Once you have finished working on HP-UX, you need to log out of the system. The logout process finishes your session. To log out, use the `exit` command at the shell prompt. The system will terminate your session and display the login prompt. A typical logout process is as follows.

```
$ exit
logout

GenericSysName [HP Release B.11.00] (See /etc/issue)

Console Login :
```

Study Break

Logging In and Out as a Super- and Common User

Practice logging in to HP-UX with your own login name. Notice your command prompt. It must be a dollar ($) symbol. Use the `exit` command to log out of the system. When you see the login prompt again, log in as `root` (*superuser*) using the root password. The superuser prompt will be a pound symbol (#). Again log out with the `exit` command. Try the same procedure on another terminal.

1.3   Home Directory

Just after the login process, a user goes into a default directory set for that user. This default directory has a special significance and is called the user's *home directory*. Every HP-UX user has a predefined home directory that is created at the time of creating the user. Usually users' home directories are the same name as the user name and are placed in /home. For example, the home directory of user **boota** is /home/boota.

1.4   Using HP-UX Commands

Once you see the shell prompt, you must use HP-UX commands. Enter the command name and then press the Enter key to execute it. If the command is valid, the shell executes it and displays the result produced by the command.

The simplest command to use is the date command, which shows the current date and time on the system. For example, the date command will be used as follows.

```
$ date
Thu Aug 29 15:36:23 EDT 1999
$
```

If you enter a wrong command, the shell will display an error message. For example, the result of a misspelled date command is as follows.

```
$ daet
sh: daet: not found.
$
```

Now it is time to use some other simple commands like pwd, whoami, and uname.

Remember: A common user is not allowed to use the commands related to system administration tasks such as creating a new user or changing the system date and time. Only the superuser has the privilege to use such commands.

Extrinsic and Intrinsic Commands

Some of the commands that a user issues are *intrinsic* commands, which are built into the UNIX shell being used. Other commands, stored as separate files, are called *extrinsic* commands. When a user issues a command, the shell first checks if it is an intrinsic command. If it is not, then extrinsic commands are checked. The command for changing a directory (cd) is a typical intrinsic command, and the command for listing files (ls) is a typical extrinsic command. The extrinsic and intrinsic commands are also called *external* and *internal* commands, respectively.

Changing Your Password

Perhaps the first command every user should know is how to change the password. When the superuser or the system administrator creates a new account for you, your initial password is typically (but not always) set. When you log into HP-UX for the first time, you should change your password to secure your account. The password is changed with the passwd command. When you issue this command, you will be asked to enter the current password. For security reasons, this password will not be displayed on the screen. If you enter this old password correctly, you are prompted to enter the new password. Once you enter the new password and press the Enter key, the system will ask you to reenter the new password. Now you enter the new password again. A typical password changing session would be like the following.

```
$ passwd
Old password :
New password :
Re-enter new password :
Password changed
$
```

Please note that you must have a password between six and eight characters long, and it must be a combination of characters and numbers. At least two characters of the password must be letters and one must be a number or a special character, such as a dash (-), underscore (_), or asterisk (*). If you use a password of length greater than eight, any characters after the eighth character are ignored. For security reasons, it is better not to use any dictionary word as a password.

Shell History and Repeating Commands

The HP-UX shell keeps the last executed commands in a shell history. The shell history is used for future reference to the same commands or reexecuting the commands without retyping them. The command history is saved in a file called .sh_history (in which an underscore separates the characters .sh and the word history) for each user. This file is kept in the user's home directory. Users can set the number of entries in the history through a control variable, which will be discussed later in Chapter 3.

To repeat a previous command, a user presses the `Esc` – `k` key combination. The previous command appears on the command prompt. If the user wants to go another step backward, simply pressing the `k` key again moves one step back. Similarly, you can go back as far as you want until the history is finished. When the correct command is displayed, just press the `Enter` key to execute it.

For example, consider you have used the following three commands in sequence.

```
$ date
Thu Aug 29 15:36:23 EDT 1999
$ whoami
boota
$ pwd
/home/boota
$
```

Now you want to execute the date command again. Just press `Esc` - `k` once and you shall see that pwd command appears on the command prompt. Now press the `k` key again and whoami will appear. Pressing the `k` key for the third time, the date command will appear on the command prompt. Now you can execute the command by pressing the `Enter` key.

The history command is designed to recall commands which have been used previously. For example, the following command shows the last three commands.

```
$ history -3
date
whoami
pwd
$
```

Command Aliases

An alias is a different name for a UNIX command. Aliases can also be used to remember commands by assigning them more meaningful names. They can be set using the `alias` command at the command prompt. For example, the `ls` command is used to list the file and directory names in HP-UX. If you want to use `dir` instead of `ls`, you can use an alias for that purpose as follows.

```
$ alias dir=ls
$
```

If after that you use `dir` command, it will function the same as the `ls` command does. Aliases are very useful for situations in which a user has to repeatedly issue a complex or long command.

1.5 Shell Startup Files

When you log into HP-UX, some commands are executed automatically and the environment is set for you (e.g., setting of variables that control the behavior of your shell). As an example, the history length is set at the login time. Similarly, it is possible to set how your shell prompt should appear, which printer should be used for your print requests, in which directories the shell should look for extrinsic commands you issue, and so on. All this is done through shell startup files. If you have a DOS or Windows background, these files can be considered as the AUTOEXEC.BAT file in DOS or the Startup Group in Microsoft Windows.

There are two types of startup files: the *system startup file* and the *user startup files*. The system startup file is common for all users of the system, while user startup files can be customized for every user.

System Startup File

The system startup file is used for tasks that are common to all system users. Examples of these tasks are setting your time zone (`TZ`), and the global search path for extrinsic commands. The system startup file is called `profile` and is present in the `/etc` directory of HP-UX. It is the responsibility of the system administrator to manage this file and make it more useful, keeping in mind a particular UNIX environment. The system startup file can also be used by a system administrator to send messages that are displayed to users as soon as someone logs into the system.

User Startup File

The user startup file is called .profile ("dot profile") and is placed in a user's home directory. This file is used for user-specific tasks, such as setting shell aliases, and for executing any programs that a user wants to start soon after login. A typical example of such a program is a customized environment used for database operators in which a form is displayed for entering data into the database. This file can also be used to change or modify some of the environment settings made by the superuser in the system startup file.

The system startup file is executed first in the startup procedure, and then the user startup file is executed. In addition to these two files, an HP-UX user can execute another file pointed to by the ENV variable if it is set in either of the two startup files.

Study Break

Using HP-UX Commands

Log in using the user name assigned to you and change your password. Try a new password fewer than six characters. Also try using a password containing all letters. Check if the system date and time are correct. Find out the name of your home directory using the pwd command. List files in your home directory with the ls -a command and write down the names of files that start with a dot (.) character. Create an alias for this command. Before logging out, use the history command to list all of the commands you have used.

1.6 Some Simple HP-UX Commands

In this section, I will describe some simple HP-UX commands. Some of these commands are very useful and handy, even for complex system administration tasks. These commands are useful for getting information about your system and users. This basic information can be utilized for system administration tasks. The man command is used to get help on all HP-UX commands, and you will need to refer to it often.

Where Am I?

In the HP-UX environment, it is always important to know what directory you are in before you move to another directory else. You can use the pwd (*print working directory*) command at any time to find out the current directory name.

```
$ pwd
/home/boota
$
```

What Is the Current Date and Time?

The date command tells you the current date and time set on the HP-UX system clock.

```
$ date
Thu Aug 29 15:36:23 EDT 1999
$
```

The date command is also used for changing the date and time. This feature of the command is accessible by the superuser only. So if you are logged in as user **root**, you can set a new date and time, in case the displayed date or time is incorrect. Please note that there is another HP-UX command, time, which is used for another purpose (not for displaying or setting system time).

Who Are Others and Who Am I?

What if you see an unattended terminal to which a user is logged in? You can use the whoami command to identify who is logged in. When you use this command, you are actually asking the system to tell "you" about "yourself."

```
$ whoami
boota
$
```

There are some other interesting uses of this command. For example, if you write a shell program that will do something different depending on which user executes the program, this little command does a great job of detecting who initiated the program.

There is another useful command that is even shorter than this one. This is the who command, which tells you the login names of all users logged into the system, along with their login time and the terminal line they are using. The output of the who command may vary depending on how many users are logged in.

```
$ who
operator   pts/ta     Aug 30 16:05
boota      pts/tb     Aug 30 15:59
$
```

It is interesting that an even shorter command exists in HP-UX, which is w, and it does a similar job. Additionally, the w command tells how long the system has been up, what the current time is, and what the logged-in users are doing.

```
$ w
4:27pm  up 1 day, 12:10,  2 users,  load average: 0.07,
0.08, 0.09
User       tty            login@  idle   JCPU   PCPU   what
operator pts/ta           4:05pm   12                   -sh
boota    pts/tb           3:59pm                         w
$
```

In HP-UX, some commands are linked to other commands such that the result of these commands is the same. For example, the w command is linked to the uptime -w command and both have the same output. Command linking is done to provide a short name for a frequently used command.

What Is the Name of My System?

Every HP-UX system has a system name. If you are curious to know what the system name is or which version of HP-UX is running on the system, use the uname command.

```
$ uname -a
HP-UX myhp B.11.00 E 9000/800 71678 8-user license
$
```

Here the command output shows that it is an HP-UX system. The system name is *myhp* and it is running HP-UX version 11.00.

Printing Banners

Banners are very useful for printing welcome messages at login time and for separating printed pages of different users when many users are using a common printer. You can print a fancy design of your name using the `banner` command.

```
$ banner BOOTA
######  ####### ####### #######    #
#     # #     # #     # #     #    # #
#     # #     # #     # #     #   #   #
######  #     # #     # #     #  #     #
#     # #     # #     # #     #  #######
#     # #     # #     # #     #  #     #
######  ####### ####### #        #     #
$
```

The Calendar

A calendar is displayed by `cal`, which is a short and handy command for printing the calendar of a particular month. In the simplest case, the `cal` command prints the calendar of the current month, but you can use the command in a number of ways to print the desired calendar.

```
$ cal
    August 1999
 S  M Tu  W Th  F  S
 1  2  3  4  5  6  7
 8  9 10 11 12 13 14
15 16 17 18 19 20 21
22 23 24 25 26 27 28
29 30 31
$
```

Getting Help with Manual Pages

UNIX systems provide a very powerful and useful feature that provides detailed help on all of the commands. This tool is called *manual pages* or *man pages*. You can use the man command to get help for any UNIX command as follows:

```
$ man cal
cal(1)                                              cal(1)

NAME
      cal - print calendar

SYNOPSIS
      cal [[month] year]
```

```
DESCRIPTION
     Cal prints a calendar for the specified year. If a
     month is also specified, a calendar for just that
     month is printed. If neither is specified, a calen-
     dar for the present month is printed. Year can be
     between 1 and 9999. Month is a decimal number be-
     tween 1 and 12. The calendar produced is a Gregorian
     calendar.

EXTERNAL INFLUENCES
   Environment Variables
     LANG determines the locale to use for the locale
     categories when both LC_ALL and the corresponding en-
     vironment variable (beginning with LC_)do not specify
     a locale. If LANG is not set or is set to the empty
     string, a default of "C" (see lang(5)) is used.
       . . .
       . . .
$
```

How would a user get help on the man command itself? Just as man cal provides help on the cal command, the man man command helps with the man command. We shall describe the manual pages in more detail in Chapter 8.

Executing Multiple Commands on One Line

The shell allows users to enter multiple commands on a single line. In this case, each command is separated by a semicolon. See the result of the command execution as given here.

```
$ cal;date
     August 1999
 S  M Tu  W Th  F  S
 1  2  3  4  5  6  7
 8  9 10 11 12 13 14
15 16 17 18 19 20 21
22 23 24 25 26 27 28
29 30 31
Mon Aug 30 17:57:51 EDT 1999
$
```

Options and Arguments

Options and arguments are used to enhance a command feature. Anything typed after the command name is either an option or an argument. A minus (-) symbol precedes any option. *Options* change command behavior as shown with the `history` command where you used -3 as an option. *Arguments* provide additional information to a command. You used the `man` command with argument `cal`, which provided information to the `man` command to show manual pages for the `cal` command.

■ Chapter Summary

In this chapter, you learned some basics of the UNIX operating system. This included login and logout procedures, the superuser account, introduction to the UNIX shell and its startup files, and running UNIX commands. You also learned how to get help with UNIX commands and how to run multiple commands simultaneously. Options and arguments are used with most of the UNIX commands, and you know the difference between the two and how they are used.

Concepts and commands learned in this chapter are the most basic ones for UNIX users. Commands like `uname`, `date`, and `who` provide you with basic system information. The `uname` command shows the system name and operating system version installed on the system, while the `date` command shows system date and time. You use the `who` command to find out who is currently logged into the system. The `w` command provides additional information about how long the system has been running. You learned the use of command aliases and how you can use aliases to save time when typing long commands. The `man` command provides help whenever you need it. To list commands you have issued, you use the `history` command. From a system administration point of view, you learned about the system startup file, `/etc/profile`. Configuration of this file is an important task when adding users and setting an appropriate environment for them.

▲ CHAPTER REVIEW QUESTIONS

1. What is the role of the shell in a UNIX system?

2. What is the difference between intrinsic and extrinsic commands?

3. What restrictions apply to an HP-UX password?

4. What are shell startup files? Is it possible for a user to have no startup file?

▲ TEST YOUR KNOWLEDGE

1. *The system startup file for a UNIX shell is invoked:*
   A. when the system boots up
   B. whenever a user issues a new command
   C. when a user logs into the system
   D. any time a user starts a subshell

2. *The default POSIX shell prompt for a common user is:*
   A. #
   B. %
   C. $
   D. current directory name followed by #

3. *When a user logs into HP-UX, the initial directory is:*
   A. the root directory
   B. the home directory for the user
   C. the user directory
   D. any directory chosen by the system at random

4. *What is the difference between intrinsic and extrinsic UNIX commands?*
   A. Intrinsic commands are built into the shell, while extrinsic commands are separate programs.
   B. Extrinsic commands are built into the shell, while intrinsic commands are separate programs.
   C. The superuser runs extrinsic commands, while any user can run intrinsic commands.
   D. A user logged in on the console runs intrinsic commands, while a user logged in from other terminals runs extrinsic commands.

5. *What is true about the superuser?*
   A. The superuser has user ID 100.
   B. Any user whose user name starts with words `root` or `admin` can be a superuser.
   C. Any user with user ID 0 is a superuser.
   D. A user with the name `super` is a superuser.

6. *The default shell for HP-UX users is:*
   A. Bourne shell
   B. C shell

      C. POSIX shell

      D. Korn shell

7.   *To log out of the HP-UX session, you use command:*

      A. `logout`

      B. `exit`

      C. both of the above

      D. `quit`

Working with Files and Directories

As a user of a UNIX system, dealing with files is a routine task. A considerable proportion of time is consumed working with files. To make the best use of your time, you always need to reduce time spent on file handling. This can be accomplished through efficient use of commands related to file and directory operations. HP-UX provides a simple and powerful command mechanism. Other uses of file handling commands are for grouping these commands and passing output of one command to another. Operations can be performed on single files or a group of files at the same time. When preparing for the HP-UX certification examination, knowing these basic file operations is important. There are some questions on the certification exam that are directly related to file handling. Other than that, many other questions have implicit application to the commands presented here.

Most of this chapter is devoted to the use and explanation of file handling commands. You will

21

learn very basic operations on files. These operations include creating, listing, deleting, and displaying contents of a file. Then you will learn some rules that apply to file names, and you will see which file names are legal in HP-UX. After that, basic operations on directories will be presented, where you will find commands for creating, deleting, and changing directories. Copying and moving files are routine tasks, and commands for these are presented next. For simultaneous operations on multiple files, wildcards are used, and you will see the uses of each of them. Searching text files for a particular string and finding files with a particular name on a system will be the next topic. At the end of the chapter, you will learn more commands for file manipulation.

2.1 Basic Operations on Files

The most common operations on files are creating new files, deleting unnecessary files, listing file names, and displaying the contents of a file. After login, you can perform all of these operations in your home directory. Let us see how we do it.

Creating a File

A file is a named area on the disk(s) where you can store information. The cat command is a basic command used for creating new files containing text. For example, if you want to create a file with the name newfile, containing three lines, the process is as follows:

```
$ cat > newfile
This is first line. <ENTER>
This is the second line. <ENTER>
This is third and last line. <ENTER>
<CTRL-d>
$
```

Note that you press the Enter key at the end of each line. When you have finished entering the text, you press CTRL - d (pressing the *Control* and *d* keys simultaneously) to end the text entry process and save the file.

Please note that use of the cat command for creating a new file is not very common but it is the simplest way to do so. Most of the time you will be using the vi editor to create or modify files. The vi editor is discussed in more detail in Chapter 5.

Listing Files

Now that you have created a file, you can verify it by listing it using the ls command.

```
$ ls newfile
newfile
$
```

The ls command shows that our newly created file, newfile, does exist and that the file creation process was successful. What if you want to see a list of all other files? This is very simple; you use the ls command without any argument.

```
$ ls
FORMAT    FORMAT.ZIP    myf    newfile    rafeeq.zip
$
```

Now the ls command shows that there are five files with the names shown above. Please note that UNIX is case sensitive, meaning it differentiates between lowercase and uppercase letters. So the file name myfile is different from MyFile.

HP-UX has another popular command to list files. This is the ll (long listing) command.

```
$ ll
total 350
-rw-r-----   1 boota    users    104230 Aug 27 19:04 FORMAT
-rw-rw-rw-   1 boota    users         0 Aug 30 20:47 myf
-rw-rw-rw-   1 boota    users        72 Aug 30 20:47 newfile
$
```

This command shows that there are three files, with the names displayed in the last column of the output. If you are wondering what the -rw-rw-rw- characters displayed in the first column are, just leave these for the time being. These are the file permissions showing who is allowed to read, write, and execute a particular file. We will be discussing file permissions in more detail in Chapter 7. If you remember from the first chapter that some commands are linked to other commands, ll is another example. This command is linked to the ls -l command. The ls command has many options, and you can have a look at these using its manual pages.

Now we try to figure out the other columns in the file listing. The second column shows how many links are associated with this file. A 1 (numeric one) means there is no other link to this file. The next column shows the owner of the file. The **users** is the group name of the user **boota** who owns this file. The next column shows the file size in number of bytes. Then we have the date and time of last modification to the file, and in the last column the file name is displayed.

Deleting Files

To keep the system clean, you need to delete unwanted files from time to time. The files are deleted with the rm command.

```
$ rm newfile
$
```

 Warning

The rm command has no output in the normal case. You need to be careful when deleting files, as the deleted files cannot be undeleted. An error message is displayed only if the file you are deleting does not exist.

Displaying Contents of a Text File

We already have used the cat command for creating new files. The same command is used to display contents of text files.

```
$ cat newfile
This is first line.
This is the second line.
This is third and last line.
$
```

We have just omitted the ">" symbol from the command line. The cat command displays the entire contents of a file in one step, no matter how long the file is. As a result, the user is able to see only the last page of text displayed. There is another useful command with the name more that displays one page of text at a time. After displaying the first page, it stops until the user hits the spacebar. The more command then displays the next page of text and so on. Figure 2-1 shows a screen shot of the more command while displaying the .profile file.

```
$ more .profile

# @(#) $Revision: 72.2 $

# Default user .profile file (/usr/bin/sh initialization).

# Set up the terminal:
        if [ "$TERM" = "" ]
        then
                eval ` tset -s -Q -m ':?hp' `
        else
                eval ` tset -s -Q `
        fi
        stty erase "^H" kill "^U" intr "^C" eof "^D"
        stty hupcl ixon ixoff
        tabs

# Set up the search paths:
        PATH=$PATH:.

# Set up the shell environment:
        set -u
        trap "echo 'logout'" 0
.profile (76%)
```

Figure 2–1 *Use of the* more *command.*

2.2 File Naming Rules

When you create a new file, there are some rules governing the naming of the file. These rules are related to the length of the file name and the characters allowed in naming a file.

General Guidelines for File Names

Generally a file name in UNIX can be as long as 256 characters. The rules that apply to the file names are as follows.

1. A file name can be a combination of letters, numbers, and special characters.

2. All letters, both upper- (A–Z) and lowercase (a–z) can be used.

3. Numbers from 0 to 9 can be used.

4. Special characters like plus (+), minus (-), underscore (_), or dot (.) can be used.

5. As mentioned earlier, UNIX is case sensitive, and uppercase and lowercase letters are treated separately. So file names `myfile`, `Myfile`, `MyFile`, and `myfilE` are different names.

6. There are no special names for executable files in UNIX; the file permissions show which file is executable and which is not.

Hidden Files

Any file that starts with a dot (.) is not displayed when using the `ll` or `ls` command. These are hidden or invisible files. Usually these files are used to store configuration information. If you remember the user startup file with the name `.profile`, it is a hidden file. To display the hidden files, use the `ls -a` command.

```
$ ls -a
.profile   newfile    testfile.zip
$
```

Hidden files are more protected against the `rm` command when used to delete all files in a directory. This command does not delete hidden files.

2.3 Working with Directories

Basic operations on directories are creating new directories, deleting directories, and moving from one directory to another in a directory hierarchy. Commands used for these operations are presented in this section. As far as names of directories are concerned, rules that apply to ordinary files also apply here.

Creating Directories

A directory can be considered a special type of file used as a folder to contain other files and directories. Directories are used to organize files in a more logical and manageable way. A directory can be created with the `mkdir` command.

```
$ mkdir newdir
$
```

After creating a directory, verify its existence with the `ls` or `ll` command. Note that when we use the `ll` command for the long listing, the first character in the file permissions is "d" instead of "-", showing that it is a directory, not an ordinary file.

```
$ ll
total 3
-rw-rw-rw-  1 boota   users     0 Aug 30 20:47 myf
drwxrwxrwx  1 boota   users    96 Aug 27 19:04 newdir
-rw-rw-rw-  1 boota   users    72 Aug 30 20:47 newfile
$
```

Using the `ls` command without the `-l` option shows all names of files and directories, and you are not able to distinguish between them. If you don't want to display the long listing and still need to distinguish between files and directories, you can use the `lsf` or `ls -F` command. These are equivalent commands, and the screen output just appends a "/" symbol at the end of the directory name.

```
$ lsf
mydir/   newfile    testfile.zip
$
```

Here you can see that `mydir` is a directory, whereas the other two are ordinary files.

Deleting Directories

Directories are deleted with `rmdir` command. This command deletes only empty directories. If the directory contains another file or directory, first that file or directory must be deleted. In case a user needs to delete a directory that is not empty, it is possible to use `rm -rf` command, which can delete a nonempty directory.

Be careful in using `rm -rf`, as it removes the entire directory tree without any warning to the user.

Understanding Directory Structure

The UNIX file system is composed of directories and files. The top-level directory is called the *root directory* and is represented by "/" symbol. All other directories and files may be considered *inside* the root directory. A directory one level above is called a *parent directory*, while a directory one level below is called a *child directory*. For example, the root directory "/" is the parent directory for home directory, and boota is a child directory of home directory (see sample directory tree in Figure 2-2).

Parent and child directories are just relative to each other. For example, home directory is a child directory of the root directory but it is a parent directory for the boota directory.

The directory names are referenced relative to the root directory. A complete reference name to a directory is called a *path name*. For example, the path name of the home directory is /home. Similarly, the path name of directory boota is /home/boota. It is easy to judge from the path name that boota is a child directory of home, which in turn is a child directory of the root directory. Files also have path names similar to directories. For example, a complete path name for a file created in directory /home/boota with name myfile is /home/boota/myfile. A path name that starts with the "/" symbol is called the *absolute* path name. We can also use *relative* path names, which start from the current directory. For example, to refer to a file with the name alpha in the parent directory of the current directory, we may use a path name ../alpha.

Whenever a new directory is created, two entries are created in the new directory automatically. These are "." and ".." where "." is a reference to

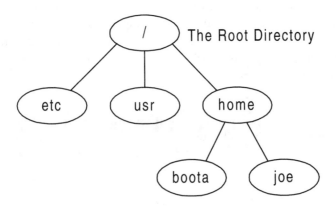

Figure 2–2 *A sample directory tree.*

the current directory and "`..`" is a reference to the parent directory of the current directory.

Moving Around in a Directory Tree

You used the `pwd` command in Chapter 1. This command was used to check the current directory. The `cd` (change directory) command is used to move to some other directory in the directory tree. This command, like other UNIX commands, can be used both with absolute and relative path names. You already know that a user automatically goes to the home directory just after the login process. We again consider the example of user **boota** who has just logged in and is in home directory, `/home/boota`. To confirm that she is indeed in her home directory and then move to the `/etc` directory, the user issues the following commands.

```
$ pwd
/home/boota
$ cd /etc
$
$ pwd
/etc
$
```

The last `pwd` command showed that the user has moved to the destination directory `/etc`. In this example, we used an absolute path. In an example of using a relative path, consider the user **boota** is in her home directory `/home/boota` and wants to move to the `/home` (the parent) directory. She can use the `cd ..` or `cd /home` command, and either will have the same effect. In `cd ..`, she asked the shell to move to the parent directory of the current directory. What if you use `cd ../..`?

Study Break

Basic Operations on Files and Directories

Having learned how to create and delete files and directories, create a new directory with the name `topdir`. Use the `cd` command to go into this directory and create a file with the name `file1`. Go back to the parent directory with the command `cd ..` and try to use the `rmdir` command to remove the `topdir` directory. You will see an error message showing the directory is not empty. Use the `cd` command to move to this directory and delete the file using the `rm` command. Now again go to the parent directory and delete `topdir` with the `rmdir` command.

Once again create the same directory and the same file inside it. Now use the `rm -rf` command to delete the nonempty directory.

Use the `cd /var/adm` command to move to this directory. Now again use the `cd` command, using both absolute and relative paths to go to the `/etc` directory. For the absolute path, you need to use the `cd /etc` command, while for the relative path the command will be `cd ../../etc`.

2.4   Copying and Moving Files

Many times you will be copying or moving files from one place to another. These two operations are similar except that the old file is deleted in the move operation.

Copying Files

The files are copied with the `cp` command. The source and destination file names are supplied to the `cp` command as arguments. The first argument is the source file name, and second argument is the destination file name.

```
$ cp myfile anotherfile
$
```

This command copies `myfile` from the current directory to `anotherfile` in the current directory. It is possible to copy files from any directory to any other directory using the path names of the files. For example, if you want to copy `profile` from the `/etc` directory to the current directory with the name `myprofile`, the command line will be as follows.

```
$ cp /etc/profile myprofile
$
```

As another example, if you want to copy the file in the above example with the same name in the current directory, you just use "." in place of the destination name. Note that the "." character is a relative path that refers to the current directory. For example, to copy `/etc/profile` with the name `profile` in the current directory, the following command can be used.

```
$ cp /etc/profile .
$
```

Two or more files can be copied simultaneously using the `cp` command. In this case, the destination must be a directory name. The following command copies two files, `file1` and `file2`, from the current directory to the `/tmp` directory.

```
$ cp file1 file2 /tmp
$
```

Moving and Renaming Files

The `mv` command is used for renaming files and moving files from one place to another in the directory structure. Like the `cp` command, it takes source and destination file names as arguments. If both source and destination names are specified without any path (absolute or relative), the file is renamed. On the other hand, if any or both of the file names contain a path name, the file is moved from the source location to the destination location.

RENAME A FILE

```
$ mv myfile newfile
$
```

Make sure that the operation was successful by using the `ll` command.

MOVE A FILE

```
$ mv myfile /tmp/myfile
$
```

Two or more files can be moved simultaneously using the `mv` command. The destination must be a directory name. The following command moves two files, `file1` and `file2`, to directory `/tmp`.

```
$ mv file1 file2 /tmp
$
```

You must be careful with the `mv` command, as it will overwrite any existing file if the destination file name matches any source file. And it will do it without any warning. To make sure that existing files are not overwritten, always use the `mv` command as `mv -i`. In this case, if the destination file already exists, the `mv` command will ask you to confirm the move or rename operation.

2.5 Wildcards

When you want to use many file names in one command, such as the one where grep is used to search a pattern in many files, it is very inconvenient to type all these names at the command line. Wildcard characters are used as a shortcut to refer to many files. Two wildcards are used in UNIX, the asterisk character (*) and the question mark (?). The * matches zero or more characters, whereas ? matches only one character. There is a third type of character matching mechanism that checks a range of characters. This is the [] pattern, and a range is specified inside the square brackets. Sometimes this is called the third wildcard.

Use of *

Suppose you use the ls command to list files and the following list appears.

```
$ ls
myfile   myfile00   myfile01   myfile010   myf   xyz
$
```

Now we can use the * character to list files we want to be displayed. If we want to list all files that start with myfile, the command is:

```
$ ls myfile*
myfile   myfile00   myfile01   myfile010
$
```

To list all files that start with my, we use:

```
$ ls my*
myfile   myfile00   myfile01   myfile010   myf
$
```

Use of ?

The ? matches only a single character. For example, if you want to list all files that start with myfile0 and the last character may be anything, the result is:

```
$ ls myfile0?
myfile00   myfile01
$
```

Now try to figure out why myfile010 did not appear in the list.

The wildcard characters can be used wherever you need to specify more than one file. For example, if you want to copy all files from the current directory to the /tmp directory, the command will be:

```
$ cp * /tmp
$
```

Similarly, if you want to search for the word root in all files of the /etc directory, you can use this command.

```
$ grep root /etc/*
```

The wildcard characters are very useful, and if you master these, you can save a lot of time in your daily computer use.

Use of [ ] Wildcard

This wildcard matches a range of characters given inside the square brackets. Only one character from the range is taken. For example [a-m] means any one character between "a" and "m". Similarly [a,c,x] means character "a", "c," or "x".

```
$ ls /etc/[w,x]*
/etc/wall   /etc/whodo   /etc/wtmp   /etc/xtab
$
```

The above command lists all files in the /etc directory that start with a "w" or "x" character.

2.6 File Types

You have been using commands like cat and more with text files. How do you know which file is a text file, which contains binary data, or which is a C program? The UNIX file command is used to determine the type of file. See the following examples.

A Text File

```
$ file /etc/profile
/etc/profile:   ascii text
$
```

A Directory

```
$ file /etc
/etc:      directory
$
```

An Executable File

```
$ file /bin/ls
/bin/ls:    PA-RISC1.1 shared executable
$
```

A Shared Library

```
$ file /lib/libc.1
/lib/libc.1:  PA-RISC1.1 shared library -not stripped
$
```

A Shell Script

```
$ file abc
abc:       commands text
$
```

Similarly, the file command is able to detect a number of other file types. The file command uses the /etc/magic file to determine different file types by finding a *magic string* inside the file. A detailed discussion on magic numbers is out of the scope of this book, but you can see man pages for /etc/magic for further information on magic numbers. The file command is very useful in situations where you want to determine the type of file before performing an operation on it. It is quite possible that your display would be garbled if you were to use the cat command on a binary file.

Study Break

Copying and Moving Files Using Wildcards and Finding the Type of a File

General syntax of the cp and mv commands is that you specify the source file name first and then the destination file name. Create a directory with the name impfiles in your home directory. Copy the /etc/hosts file into this directory. Also copy all files starting with "m" from the /etc directory to this directory. Now move the hosts file from the impfiles directory to the /tmp directory. Using range characters [a,e,i,o,u], list all files in the /usr directory that start with any vowel.

You can find out the type of a file by using the file command. Try to find a shared executable file on the system by applying this command to different files.

2.7 Searching File Contents

Finding a text string in one or multiple text files is easy using the grep (*global regular expression print*) command. It does the job in a number of ways. You can search for text strings in one or many files. You can also specify additional criteria for the string, such as whether it occurs at the start or at the end of a line. If you are using multiple files for a search, grep also displays the name of the file in which the string is found. It can also display the location in the file where the string is found.

Searching a Word

Here we show how you can find whether a particular user exists by applying the grep command on the /etc/passwd file.

```
$ grep Mark /etc/passwd
mstyle:elBY:2216:125:Mark Style,,,:/home/mstyle:/usr/bin/sh
mgany:iF5UeWQ:2259:125:Mark Gany,,,:/home/mgany:/usr/bin/sh
mbuna:tQfwUNo:2318:125:Mark Buna,,,:/home/mbuna:/usr/bin/sh
mblack:ipCg:2388:125:Mark Black,,,:/home/mblack:/usr/bin/sh
$
```

This command shows that there are four users on the system with the name Mark. If you want to make a search case insensitive, you may use grep -i instead of grep. If you are interested to know how many times the string occurs in the file, without displaying the lines containing the string, use grep -c. You can even reverse the selection of lines by grep -v. In this case, all lines that *don't* match the string pattern are displayed.

Searching Multiple Words

If you want to search using a string of multiple words, enclose the words with double quotes. For example, if you want to search for "Mark Black" in /etc/passwd, you will use the grep command.

```
$ grep "Mark Black" /etc/passwd
mblack:ipCg:2388:125:Mark Black,,,:/home/mblack:/usr/bin/sh
$
```

For a case-insensitive search of "Mark Black," use the following command.

```
$ grep -i "mark black" /etc/passwd
mblack:ipCg:2388:125:Mark Black,,,:/home/mblack:/usr/bin/sh
$
```

Searching a String in Multiple Files

As I mentioned earlier, the grep command can be used to search multiple files for a matching string. You need to specify all file names in which you want to search for the text string. For example, if you search for the word root in the /etc/passwd and /etc/group files, the following result is displayed.

```
$ grep root /etc/passwd /etc/group
/etc/passwd:root:8JgNSmFv806dA:0:3:,,,:/home/root:/sbin/sh
/etc/group:root::0:root
/etc/group:other::1:root,hpdb
/etc/group:bin::2:root,bin
$
```

The command shows that the word root occurs once in the /etc/passwd file and three times in the /etc/group file.

2.8   Finding Files

The find command is used to search for a file on a system. For example, if you want to find all files that start with my in the /etc directory and all of its subdirectories, the command is:

```
$ find /etc -name "my*"
/etc/profile
/etc/protocols
$
```

In a similar way, the find command can be used to find files that are newer versions of a certain file. The search can also be made on file types and file permissions. Please refer to man pages for more information on the find command.

2.9   Miscellaneous File Handling Commands

Here are some other useful commands related to file handling.

The Head and the Tail

Sometimes you need to view only the first or last few lines of a text file. By default, the head command lists the first ten lines of a text file, and the tail command lists the last ten lines of a file. For example, if you want to see the first ten lines of the /etc/passwd file (used to store user names and passwords), the command and its output will be:

```
$ head /etc/passwd
root:8JgNSmFv806dA:0:3:,,,:/home/root:/sbin/sh
mmsecad:ETxUQ5wSQZCAk:0:3::/:/sbin/sh
daemon:*:1:5::/:/sbin/sh
bin:*:2:2::/usr/bin:/sbin/sh
sys:*:3:3::/:
adm:*:4:4::/var/adm:/sbin/sh
uucp:*:5:3::/var/spool/uucppublic:/usr/lbin/uucp/uucico
lp:*:9:7::/var/spool/lp:/sbin/sh
nuucp:*:11:11::/var/spool/uucppublic:/usr/lbin/uucp/uucico
hpdb:*:27:1:ALLBASE:/:/sbin/sh
$
```

Additional parameters can be used with both the head and tail commands to view any number of lines of text. A tail -n 3 /etc/passwd will show the last three lines of the file. If you want to see what is being added to a text file by a process in real time, you can use the tail -f command. This is a very useful tool to see text being added to a log file.

Counting Characters, Words, and Lines in a Text File

Many times, you want to know how many characters, words, or lines there are in a file. In the /etc/passwd file, for example, there is one line for every user. You can count the number of users on the HP-UX system if you count the number of lines in the file. We use the wc (*word count*) command for this purpose. It displays the number of lines, words, and characters, respectively.

```
$ wc /etc/profile
171 470 3280 /etc/profile
$
```

It shows that there are 171 lines, 470 words, and 3280 characters in the /etc/profile file. If you want to count only the number of lines in a file, you can use wc -l. Similarly, for counting words, wc -w, and for counting characters, wc -c, can be used.

```
$ wc -l /etc/passwd
2414 /etc/passwd
$
```

It shows that there are 2414 lines in /etc/passwd, which is an indirect way to find out the number of users on this system.

Link Files

Many times you need to refer to the same file that has different names. You can create a link file that is not the actual file but points to some other file to which it is linked. There are two types of links, hard and soft. Soft links may be established across file systems. The soft link is a special type of file; the first character of the ll command list is "l" for link files. To create a link, the ln command is used. For example, to create a hard link, abc, to a file, myfile, we use:

```
$ ln myfile abc
$
```

To create a soft link, we use the -s option.

```
$ ln -s myfile abc
$
```

■ Chapter Summary

In this chapter, you learned operations performed on files and directories. Creating, deleting, and displaying are basic operations on files. You learned how to create, delete, and change directories. Rules related to file names were also presented in this chapter. Basic rules are that file names are not longer than 256 characters and all letters and numbers can be used. Now you also know that file names in HP-UX are case sensitive. You copied and moved files from one place to another in the HP-UX directories with the cp and mv commands. The mv command was also used to rename files.

Operations on multiple files can be performed using the wildcards asterisk (*) and question mark (?), and square brackets can be used to specify character ranges. You learned how to determine the type of a file with the file command. The grep command was used to find a text pattern inside a text file. During this process, you can also specify search criteria. Based on this criteria, you can use the grep command to find a string at the start or end of a line. You can also perform case-insensitive searches. Finding files in a system with the find command was also covered in this chapter. Other than this, you have also learned how to count characters, words, and lines of a text file with the wc command and how to display first and last lines using the `head` and `tail` commands, respectively. You have also seen how to create link files.

Commands presented in this chapter are very basic and important for handling files and directories on HP-UX and need some practice to get used to. At the same time, you need to be careful about some commands that can delete your files without giving any warning message.

▲ CHAPTER REVIEW QUESTIONS

1. What restrictions apply to UNIX file names?

2. What is the difference between the *home directory* and the *root directory*?

3. Is it possible to create multiple directories with a single command line?

4. What is the difference between the `cp` and `mv` commands?

5. How do absolute path names differ from relative path names?

6. Write a command to list all files that start with `my`, with any characters in the third to fifth positions, and that end with the `e.txt` pattern.

▲ TEST YOUR KNOWLEDGE

1. *The* `cat` *command is used to:*
   A. create a file
   B. display contents of a file
   C. both of the above
   D. not a UNIX command

2. *The maximum length of a file name may be:*
   A. 8 characters
   B. 15 characters
   C. 256 characters
   D. no restrictions on file name length in UNIX

3. *The* `more` *command is used to:*
   A. display the contents of text files
   B. display the contents of any type of file
   C. display all of a text file
   D. get more help on a command

4. *What is the function of the following command*
   grep "Mark Black" /etc/passwd
   A. It searches for the name Mark Black in the /etc/passwd file.
   B. It searches for the word Mark in the Black and /etc/passwd files.
   C. It is an ambiguous command with unpredictable results.
   D. We can use the find command here instead of grep.

5. *Consider a directory with five files in it. The file names are* pg.c, pg1.c, *pg2.c, pg3.cpp, and* pg10.c. *We use the command* ls pg?.?. *The files displayed are:*
   A. pg1.c, pg2.c
   B. pg1.c, pg2.c, pg10.c
   C. pg1.c, pg2.c, pg3.cpp
   D. pg2.c, pg10.c

6. *How can you tell the number of user accounts on a UNIX system?*
   A. by using the number command
   B. by asking the system administrator
   C. by counting the users one by one
   D. by counting lines in the /etc/passwd file

7. *You are currently in the* /home/boota *directory. Which command will bring you the to* /etc *directory?*
   A. cd etc
   B. cd ../../etc
   C. cd /etc
   D. both options B and C

Environment Variables

As soon as a user logs into HP-UX, the shell is invoked and waits for commands from the user. To execute these commands, the shell needs to know some information about the *environment* being used. For example, to correctly display a file, the shell needs to know which type of terminal is attached to the system. Similarly, when a user issues an extrinsic command, the shell needs to know in which directories it should look for the command. In UNIX terminology, we call this type of information the *shell environment*.

The shell stores environment information in *environment variables*. Usually, many types of variables are set in the system startup file (/etc/profile) managed by the system administrator. The users can also set environment variables through the use of a user startup file kept in the home directory (.profile).

Any program that needs environment variables checks the existence and value of these variables at the startup time. For example, the editor program

41

vi needs your terminal information to correctly display and scroll text. When you start the **vi** editor, it will check the **TERM** variable. If it understands the terminal type set by the **TERM** variable, it will start in full screen mode; otherwise, it will start in line editing mode, where you can edit or display only one line of text at a time. Similarly, the `more` command needs the **TERM** variable to display a particular number of text lines, depending on the type of terminal being used.

You can modify and change environment variables set by the system administrator. The system administrator usually sets the **PATH** variable that shows the search path for the executable commands. But as you start using the UNIX system, you also create your own programs and scripts, and you want the shell to look into the directories containing your own programs as well. For this purpose, you can add your own directory names in the **PATH** variable.

In this chapter, you will see the difference between environment and shell variables and how to set and display variables. There are many predefined environment variables, and the most important of these will be discussed. Then you will learn how to increase the visibility of a shell variable by *exporting* it. The default HP-UX command prompt shows little information, and you will see how to add some useful information to it using variables. Since **PATH** is an important variable, you will learn more about it at the end of the chapter.

3.1 Environment and Shell Variables

When a shell executes a command, UNIX creates a process in memory for that command. This process is called the *child process* of the shell. Because the shell created this process, the shell is called the *parent process* of the command process.

You can also invoke a shell within another shell. The newly created shell is the child shell. You will be writing shell scripts when you move to the fourth section of the book. These shell scripts are executed within the parent shell as child processes.

All child processes inherit environment variables from their parent (the shell). On the other hand, shell variables are set locally by the shell and are not visible to any child process. Each child gets a copy of the environment variables and is allowed to make changes to these variables. But it should be kept in mind that these changes are local to the child process and can't reflect back. This means that changes made to the environment variables are lost as soon as the child process finishes. Or you can say that a child process can't make changes to the parent variables. The differences between shell and environment variables are presented in Table 3-1.

Table 3–1 *Comparison of Shell and Environment Variables*

Environment Variables	Shell Variables
Also called global variables	Also called local variables
Inherited by all child processes	Not inherited by children
Usually contain system-specific information	Usually used to keep temporary values in shell programs

3.2 Setting and Displaying Variables

When using the POSIX shell, you can set a variable at the command prompt just by entering a variable name followed by an "=" sign and the value you want to assign to the variable. It is a convention to name all user-created variables with uppercase letters, but lowercase letters can be used if needed. Also, a variable name can start with characters of the alphabet only, not with numbers. For example, VAR3 is a legal name for a variable while 3VAR is not. Below is the process of setting a variable.

```
$ VAR3=TestVar
$
```

The command prompt appears without any message. Note that there is no space character on either side of the "=" symbol. If you place a space around the = sign, the shell interprets it as a command and displays an error message, as no command with the name VAR3 exists on HP-UX.

The echo command is used to view the value of a particular shell variable. To view the value of our newly created shell variable, use the following method.

```
$ echo $VAR3
TestVar
$
```

Notice that we have used a $ symbol to start the variable name. If we don't use the $ symbol, the echo command displays whatever it gets on the command line as is. The $ symbol tells the echo command that the argument is a variable, not a simple text string. The result of using the above command without $ is as follows.

```
$ echo VAR3
VAR3
$
```

As you can see, the echo command has displayed its argument text, not the variable value.

Listing All Variables

If you want to list all variables known to your current shell, use the set command.

```
$ set
EDITOR=vi
EPC_DISABLED=TRUE
ERASE=^H
FCEDIT=/usr/bin/ed
HISTFILE=/home/root/.sh_history
HISTSIZE=400
HOME=/home/boota
INTR=^C
LINENO=1
LOGNAME=boota
MAIL=/var/mail/boota
MAILCHECK=600
MANPATH=/usr/share/man/%L:/usr/share/man:/usr/contrib/man:/
u
sr/local/man/%L:/usr/local/man
NAME=12
OPTIND=1
PATH=/usr/sbin:/baan/bse/bin:/usr/bin:/usr/ccs/bin:/usr/
contrib/bin:/usr/bin/X11:/usr/contrib/bin/X11:/opt/perf/
bin:/u
sr/sbin:/sbin
PPID=26709
PS1='boota on myhp $PWD => '
PS2='> '
PS3='#? '
PS4='+ '
```

```
PPID=26709
SHELL=/sbin/sh
TERM=vt100
TMOUT=0
TZ=EST5EDT
VAR3=TestVar
_=set
$
```

This list will change from system to system. It also depends on what applications are running on the system, as applications also set their environment variables. We will discuss some of the common variables in the next pages.

Variable Containing More Than One Word

Often a variable has a value that contains space characters in it. If you try to set a variable containing spaces in the normal way, you will get an error message as follows.

```
$ NAME=Mike Ron
sh: Ron:  not found.
$
```

The shell thought that you were setting a variable NAME with value Mike while Ron is a UNIX command. The shell then tried to execute this command and failed. To set variables containing multiple words, we use single or double quotes.

```
$ NAME="Mike Ron"
$
$ echo $NAME
Mike Ron
$
```

Single quotes may also be used.

```
$ NAME='Mike Ron'
$
```

There is a slight difference between single- and double-quote characters that I will soon elaborate on.

The echo command can be used to display a variable and additional text at the same time. For example, just after displaying the NAME variable, we want to display the number 7. What if we use command echo $NAME7?

```
$ echo $NAME7
sh: NAME7: Parameter not set.
$
```

The shell actually started looking for a variable name NAME7 instead of NAME but could not find it. To avoid this ambiguity, we use { } to separate a variable from the rest of the text as follows.

```
$ echo ${NAME}7
Mike Ron7
$
```

Many UNIX users put { } around variable names to avoid any ambiguity. The curly brackets must be used any place a shell variable is used with some other text.

Modifying a Variable

Assigning a new value to the same variable name modifies the previous value of the variable. It can be done in two ways. If we just assign a new value, the old value of the variable is destroyed. We can also append to the old value by putting the variable name on the right-hand side of the = symbol at the time of assignment. For example, if we want to add a third part to the NAME variable, it can be done as follows.

```
$ NAME="$NAME Junior"
$
$ echo $NAME
Mike Ron Junior
$
```

This is a very useful way to add your own directories to the **PATH** variable. The **PATH** variable set by the system administrator contains a list of directories where command files are located. When finding a command, if you want the shell to also search in your own directories, you can use the above method to append your own directory names to the **PATH** variable.

Single- and Double-Quote Characters

Now we come to the difference between single and double quotes. Consider the above command example by replacing the double quotes with single quotes and watch the result carefully.

```
$ NAME='$NAME Junior'
$
$ echo $NAME
$NAME Junior
$
```

This is not what we wanted! What happens is that single-quote characters do not expand any variable name inside them to its value. Instead, anything inside the single quotes is taken as is and assigned to the variable. One must be careful when using single quotes! The same rule applies when you use single and double quotes with other commands. See the results of two echo commands.

```
$ NAME= "Mike Ron"
$
$ echo "$NAME Junior"
Mike Ron Junior
$ echo '$NAME Junior'
$NAME Junior
$
```

Removing a Variable

A shell variable can be removed by the unset command on HP-UX. Please note that this command is not available in all UNIX shells.

```
$ NAME="Mike Ron"
$ echo $NAME
Mike Ron
$ unset NAME
$ echo $NAME
sh: NAME: Parameter not set.
$
```

Assigning Output of a Command to a Variable

On most keyboards, the back quote character is displayed when you press the "~" key without the SHIFT key. It is used to assign the result of a command to a variable. If you want to assign your login name to a variable NAME, you can use the following command.

```
$ NAME=`whoami`
$
$ echo $NAME
boota
$
```

You can also use the back quote character anywhere that you want to substitute the result of a command. In the following example, it is used with echo command.

```
$ echo "My login name is `whoami`"
My login name is boota
$
```

3.3 Predefined Environment Variables

There are some standard variables that many HP-UX commands use. These are called predefined because their names are standard. Here are some of these variables and their use by different commands.

- PATH is the most commonly used environment variable. It contains the command search path or name of directories where your shell searches for a command when you issue it. Usually it is set up through the system startup file (/etc/profile) and can be modified by a user to add personal directories through the user startup file (.profile). Each directory in the PATH variable is separated by a colon.
- HOME is automatically set when a user logs into HP-UX. It contains the path of the user's home directory. To refer to the .profile file in your home directory, you can use $HOME/.profile as the complete path to the file. Please note that there is another way to refer to your home directory in HP-UX, and that is the ~/ combination.
- PWD shows the current directory. It is also set automatically whenever you use the cd command. It always has the value of the current directory.
- SHELL shows the absolute path of your login shell. It is automatically set at the login time.

- **TERM** contains the name or type of your terminal. It is usually set through the `/etc/profile` shell startup file using the `tset` or `tty-type` command.
- **PS1** contains the primary command prompt string. This string is displayed in your shell prompt. If `$` is displayed as your command prompt, the value of **PS1** is a `$` symbol.
- **PS2** contains the secondary command prompt string. That is, if you issue a command that is incomplete, you will see a prompt by the shell with a value of **PS2**.
- **MANPATH** contains the list of directories where the `man` command looks for manual pages. A colon separates each directory in the list.
- **TZ** contains the local time zone that was set at the time of HP-UX installation. Commands such as `date` read this variable.
- **EDITOR** contains the name of the editor you want to use for command line editing or for typing mail messages. You can set this variable in your shell startup file with your favorite editor.
- **HISTFILE** contains the name of the history file where your command history is kept. All of the commands you use go to the history file.
- **HISTSIZE** variable shows how many commands are kept in the history file.

Study Break

Predefined Environment Variables

Knowledge of shell variables is very helpful in understanding the behavior of some commands. Use the command:

```
echo "Incomplete command test
```

You will see a ">" symbol in the next line. You get back neither the command prompt nor any other display. You may be wondering what happened to the command. Actually, you issued an incomplete command, missing the closing double quotes. The symbol ">" is the value of the `PS2` environment variable that is displayed whenever you use an incomplete command. Just complete the remaining part of the command and press the `Enter` key at this prompt.

Change this variable so that it gives a more meaningful message, such as "Incomplete command>" and again use the same command to check if it works. Using the `set` command, see which variables are set on your system. To find out more about an environment variable, get help with the `man sh-posix` command.

3.4 Exporting Shell Variables

Earlier I mentioned that the shell variables are not visible in child processes whereas environment variables are. We can *export* shell variables so that they are available in the child processes. The `export` command is used for this purpose. In our previous example of setting the NAME variable, we can export it to make it visible for other processes that our shell creates.

In the next example, I demonstrate the difference between exported and nonexported variables. First we create a variable NAME and then start a child shell by executing the `sh` command. When we use the `echo` command in the child shell for the NAME variable, it is empty. Now we use the `exit` command to return to the parent shell and export the NAME variable. We start the child shell again, and now the variable is visible in the child shell. Finally, we use `exit` again to return to the parent shell.

```
$ NAME="Mike Ron"
$ echo $NAME
Mike Ron
$ sh
$ echo $NAME
$
$ exit
$ export NAME
$ sh
$ echo $NAME
Mike Ron
$ exit
$
```

If you make a change to an environment variable, always export it. This is necessary so that the correct value of the variable is inherited by the child processes.

3.5 Setting the Command Prompt

The PS1 variable controls the appearance of the user command prompt. A user can modify the command prompt by setting a desired value of PS1. If you want to change your command prompt from a simple $ sign to "My Computer =>", you can use the following command.

```
$ PS1="My Computer =>"
My Computer =>
```

As you notice, the command prompt changes as soon as you change the value of PS1. Just to remind you, you also have to export the PS1 variable to make this change visible in the sub-shells.

Adding Useful Information to the Prompt

You can play some tricks with the command prompt to display useful information. For example, it is very handy if the prompt displays the current directory, as it can be hard to remember which directory you are in. We can make a slight change to PS1 to display the current directory path.

```
$ PS1="My Computer \$PWD =>"
My Computer /home/boota =>
```

As you can see, the prompt changes and the current directory is there. Now, whenever you use the cd command to change the current directory, the PWD environment variable changes, and your prompt also changes to show the new current directory. Similarly, it is possible to have your login name and the computer name in the command prompt along with the current directory, as shown in this example.

```
$ PS1= "`whoami` on `uname -n` \$PWD =>"
boota on myhp /home/boota =>
```

This is very useful if you work in a network environment and often log into different machines with different names. It is the command prompt that tells you which machine you are on, which login name you are using, and what the current directory is. Does this seem interesting to you? You can also try to change your prompt to include the date and time, blinking characters, and so on, depending on the type of terminal you are using.

3.6 The PATH Variable

PATH is one of the most important variables a user has to deal with. It contains the names of the directories where the shell searches for commands. These directory names are separated by a colon.

```
/usr/bin:/usr/ccs/bin:/usr/contrib/bin:/bin
```

If you have placed your own commands in your home directory, you can add your home directory to the PATH variable with the following command.

```
$ PATH=$PATH:$HOME
$
```

Although you are free to add the HOME directory at the beginning or end of the PATH variable, it is always desirable to add your own directory names at the end. This is because, if you accidentally use a program or script name, the same as a standard HP-UX command, your program will be executed instead of the HP-UX command, as it will be found first by the shell.

■ Chapter Summary

In this chapter, you learned the difference between environment and shell variables, how to set and change the values of variables, and how to utilize environment variables for some useful tasks. You have seen how to avoid ambiguities when using variables with the help of curly brackets. You also have knowledge of important predefined variables and their uses. You have learned other useful information, such as the difference between single and double quotes and command substitution using back quotation characters. Some useful information was also added to the command prompt with the use of PS1 variable.

In the next chapter, you will see the use of I/O redirection and pipes, where you will be able to use the output of one command as the input to another command.

▲ CHAPTER REVIEW QUESTIONS

1.   What is the difference between environment and shell variables?

2.   What is the role of the time zone (TZ) variable in a company with offices in many countries?

3.   Why do you export a variable?

4.   Name any four predefined environment variables.

▲ TEST YOUR KNOWLEDGE

1. *Just after login, you issue the command* echo HOME. *What will be the output of this command?*

    A. It displays the HOME directory name of the user.

    B. It displays nothing, as the HOME variable is not yet defined.

    C. It displays the word HOME.

    D. none of the above

2. *What is* not *true about the* PATH *variable?*

    A. It shows the path of the current directory.

    B. It shows the names of directories that are checked when searching for a command.

    C. It is usually set in the /etc/profile by the system administrator.

    D. The value of the PATH variable can be changed by a user.

3. *You have a variable "*ABC*" with value "*Alphabets*". You use the following command to change its value.*
    ABC='All $ABC'
    What will be the new value of the variable?

    A. All $ABC

    B. All Alphabets

    C. All ABC

    D. The variable value can't be changed with this command. It remains "Alphabets".

4. *To assign the output of a command to a variable, we use:*

    A. double-quote characters

    B. comma characters

    C. single-quote characters

    D. back-quote characters

5. *The value of the* PS2 *variable on your system is "*>*" (greater-than symbol). You issue an incomplete command. What will be the shell's response?*

    A. The shell will issue an error message showing that the command is incomplete.

    B. The shell will display "PS2".

    C. The shell will try to execute that part of the command that is supplied.

    D. The shell will give a ">" prompt and wait for you to complete the command.

6. *What is wrong with the shell variable name* 3Xyab2?

    A. It is not a legal name, because a shell variable must contain only uppercase letters.

    B. It is not legal, because variables can only have uppercase or lowercase letters, not a combination.

    C. It starts with a digit, so it is not a legal name.

    D. It ends with a digit, so it is not a legal name.

Input/Output Redirection and Pipes

Most UNIX commands are designed to take simple text (alphanumeric) data and punctuation as input. Usually, the output is also of simple text. Whenever you start a UNIX command, it opens three standard data streams: *standard input* (stdin), *standard output* (stdout), and *standard error* (stderr). Every UNIX command takes input data from stdin and sends its normal output to stdout and error messages to stderr. These data streams are often called *standard input/output*. UNIX associates numbers known as *file descriptors* with all open files. File descriptor 0 is used with standard input, 1 with standard output, and 2 with standard error.

Standard input, usually the user keyboard, is normally the place where a program reads its input from. Standard output, usually your terminal screen, is where the results of a command or program are displayed. In normal cases, standard error messages are also displayed on the terminal screen, but it is always possible to separate stdout from stderr. The UNIX shell can redirect any of these streams to a file, a device, or some other command, as required by the user. We call this process *I/O redirection*. You studied one example of output redirection in Chapter 2, when you created a new file with the `cat` command. In its normal use, the `cat` command reads from the keyboard (stdin) and writes to the terminal screen (stdout). We used the ">" symbol to redirect output from the stdout to a file. Similarly, when we displayed the contents of a file with the `cat` command, we redirected input to the `cat` command from the keyboard (stdin) to the file. Figure 4-1 shows the standard location of input, output, and error for any UNIX command or program.

Another useful feature of UNIX is the *pipe*, with which we can send output of one command to the input of another command. This is often used to process and format data produced by a command and make it more understandable. Many commands are

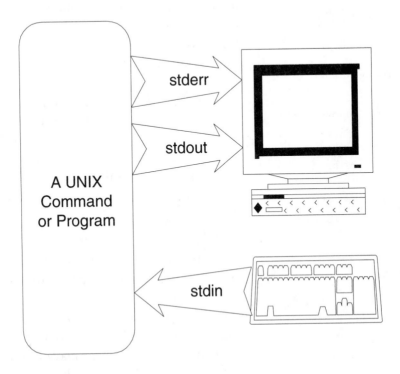

Figure 4–1 *Location of standard I/O.*

used as *filters* in UNIX, which take input from a command, filter the required data, and throw away the garbage. For example, the `cat /etc/passwd` command displays the contents of the password file, but using a filter we can extract only login names of the system users.

Sometimes UNIX is also called a *file-based operating system*, meaning that any type of input or output device can be considered as being a file. All of the devices connected to a system are controlled through device driver files. When you want to print something, just direct it to the printer device file. If you want to send something to the terminal display, send it to the display device file. I/O redirection and pipes are considered very powerful features of UNIX, as any combination of commands can be used to get the desired result.

In this chapter, you will learn how to redirect any type of input, output, and error to another location. You can also redirect all of these at the same time. You will also learn the uses of pipes and tees to filter and redirect data to multiple locations.

4.1 Redirecting Standard Output

Redirection of stdout is controlled by ">" the greater-than symbol. The process of redirecting output is shown in Figure 4-2. The command takes input from the keyboard but sends its output to a file on disk.

Note that error messages still go to the terminal screen. To demonstrate the process of output redirection, we can use the same example of Chapter 2, where we displayed contents of a file as follows.

```
$ cat newfile
This is first line.
This is the second line.
This is third and last line.
$
```

To redirect the output of the `cat` command we use the following step.

```
$ cat newfile > file1
$
```

Now the `cat` command displayed nothing, as the output of the command is redirected to a file. If we check the contents of file `file1`, it will contain the same text as `newfile` (the output of the `cat` command).

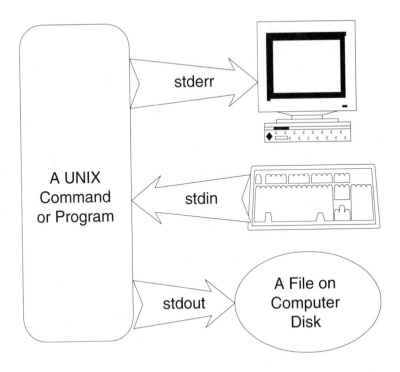

Figure 4–2 *Standard output redirection.*

This is another way of copying text files. As you go through the book, you will find how versatile the UNIX commands are and how many different ways these commands can be used. Until now, you have used the cat command to create a new file, display contents of a file, and copy a text file using redirection. The same command is used for other purposes as well, and you will learn more uses of the cat command later in this chapter.

As another example, consider the who command. We redirected its output to a file with the name whofile. We can verify the contents of whofile with the more or cat command.

```
$ who > whofile
$ cat whofile
operator    pts/ta          Aug 30 16:05
boota       pts/tb          Aug 30 15:59
john        pts/tc          Aug 30 14:34
$
```

If a file with the name `file1` already exists, it will be overwritten by using the above command without any warning.

Joining Two or More Files

Two or more files can be joined into a single file by the use of the `cat` command and redirecting output to a file. Let us suppose there are three files in your home directory, with the names `file1`, `file2`, and `file3`. If you use the `cat` command with `file1` and `file2` as its arguments, it will show you the contents of `file1` and `file2`, respectively. What if we use the `cat *` command? It will display the contents of all files in the directory. Now, by simply redirecting the output to another file, the command will concatenate all of these files.

```
$ cat file1 file2 >file4
$
```

This command created `file4`, which contains the contents of both `file1` and `file2`. The following command creates `file5`, containing all files in the directory.

```
$ cat * >file5
$
```

This is the another use of the `cat` command is for joining two or more files.

Appending to a File

In the case of output redirection with the ">" symbol, the file to which we redirect the output of a command is overwritten. It means that the previous contents of the file are destroyed. We can use the double redirection symbol ">>" to keep the previous contents of the file. In such a situation, the output of a command is appended to the file. Consider the following example.

```
$ cat file1 >>file2
$
```

This command means that `file2` still contains the old contents of `file2`. In addition to this, the contents of `file1` are added to the end of `file2`. If `file2` does not exist, it is created. This is a very useful feature and is used in many situations. For example, if we want to check how many users are logged in every hour, we can ask UNIX to run `date` and `who` commands every hour and redirect (append) the output of both of these commands to a log file. The `date` command will append the current date and time and the `who` command will append a list of users. Later on we can view this log file to get the desired information.

Redirecting Standard Output to Devices

In addition to redirecting output of a command to a file, you can also redirect it to any device, as UNIX treats all devices as files. Just as an example, the device file of the console is `/dev/console`. If you want to send the contents of a file to the console, you can use the following command.

```
$ cat file1 >/dev/console
$
```

The file will be displayed on the console screen. Similarly, if you know the device file name of another terminal, you can send a file to the monitor of that terminal.

Many times, systems administrators use this procedure to diagnose a faulty terminal. If you don't get a login prompt of an attached terminal, try to send a file to that terminal with the above-mentioned procedure to ensure that the cabling is not faulty. If the file is displayed on the terminal screen, you have assurance that there is no hardware fault and that something is missing in the configuration of that terminal.

Sometimes you can use the same redirection method to print simple text files, if the printer is directly connected to the HP-UX machine and you know the device name for the printer.

When redirecting output, keep in mind that sterr is not redirected automatically with the output. If the command you issue generates an error message, it will still be displayed on your own terminal screen.

4.2 Redirecting Standard Input

UNIX commands can send output anywhere when using output redirection, and they can also get input from places other than the keyboard. Figure 4-3 shows I/O locations in the case of stdin redirection.

We use the "less-than" symbol (<) for input redirection. Say that you have already created a text file with name myfile. You want to send this text file to a user **jane** through electronic mail. The easiest way to do this is to ask the mail program to get its input from this file instead of from the keyboard. The process of doing this is as follows.

```
$ mail jane <myfile
$
```

The mail program sends an email message to user **jane** on the current system consisting of the contents of myfile. This is a more convenient way to type messages when you need time to compose them. You just create a file, and when you are satisfied with what you have typed, send it through email.

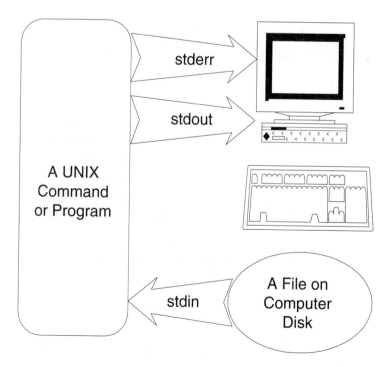

Figure 4–3 *Standard input redirection.*

4.3 Redirecting Standard Error

The stderr stream can be redirected in a similar fashion as stdin or stdout. Figure 4-4 shows what happens when we redirect the stderr.

There is no special symbol for redirecting stderr. The same ">" symbol is used but with the number 2 attached in front of it. If you remember from previous pages, there are three file descriptors opened whenever a command is issued. These file descriptors are shown in Table 4-1.

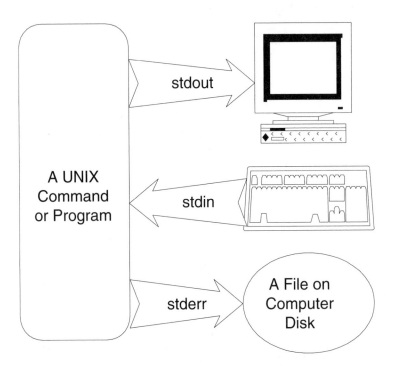

Figure 4–4   *Standard error redirection.*

Table 4–1   *Standard File Descriptors*

File Descriptor Number	Description
0	Standard input
1	Standard output
2	Standard error

We use "2>" for stderr redirection to tell the shell that we want to redirect the error messages instead of stdout (for which the file descriptor value is 0). Consider the following command.

```
$ ll xyz
xyz not found.
$
```

We tried to list a file with name xyz and the command result shows that this file does not exist. This is an error message of the ll command. Now see the following command.

```
$ ll xyz >abc
xyz not found.
$
```

We tried to redirect the output, but still the message is displayed on our screen. The redirection had no effect because we are trying to redirect stdout while the command is generating stderr messages. Now let us see what happens if we change ">" to "2>".

```
$ ll xyz 2>abc
$
```

Now there is nothing displayed because the error message has been stored in a file with name abc. You can use the cat command to verify that the error message was indeed stored in the abc file.

4.4 Redirecting Standard Input, Output, and Error Simultaneously

As you become more and more accustomed to HP-UX, you will often need to run unattended programs that execute at specific times, for example, at midnight. You need the program to take input from some files, such as system log files, and send its output to some other file. You also need to know if some error occurred during the execution of such programs. You can then look over the results of the program and any errors at any convenient time. This is the case where you redirect all of the three types of standard I/O to files. See Figure 4-5, showing where data streams come and go in such a case.

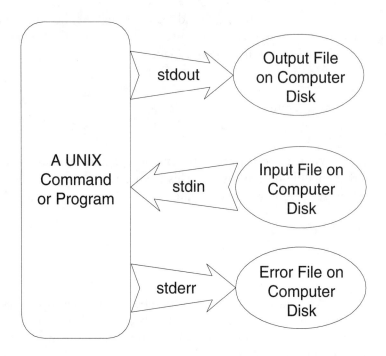

Figure 4–5 *Redirection of standard input, output, and error.*

We shall demonstrate the use of all of the three redirections with the sort command. Let us suppose we have a file with name unsorted with the following four lines in it.

```
$ cat unsorted
This is number 1
This is number 5
This is number 3
This is number 2
$
```

We can use the sort command to arrange (sort) these lines. When we use the sort command with input redirection to this file, this result appears.

```
$ sort < unsorted
This is number 1
This is number 2
This is number 3
This is number 5
$
```

Now we can redirect output of the command to a file named `sorted` and the error to a file named `error` with the following command.

```
$ sort <unsorted >sorted 2>error
$
```

Does this seem complicated to you? Indeed it is not. You can even change the order in which input, output, and error files appear.

Study Break

Use of I/O Redirection

As you have seen, I/O redirection is an important tool for a UNIX user. Until now you have studied all types of I/O redirection. As you have seen, you can use one or all types of redirection with a command. The I/O redirection feature is used by system administrators extensively in scripts used for system maintenance purposes. Most of the time, these scripts are time scheduled and run without any user interaction. It is very useful to record output of these scripts to diagnose any problem occurring during execution. You will see in the next section that the pipe is another very important tool, which, when used with I/O redirection, can filter useful data from system log files.

This is the time to practice with I/O redirection. Use the `date` command and redirect its output to a file named `logfile`. Use the `who` command and append its output to the same file. Wait for five minutes and again use the `date` and `who` commands and append their output to `logfile`. Now use the `cat` command to display `logfile`. You will see that it contains a line for time and date and then a list of users who were logged in at that time. You can use this technique with the UNIX scheduler (`cron`) to create a log for a whole day and study it later.

4.5   Pipes and How They Are Used

Look at Figure 4-6 carefully. It shows another powerful feature of the UNIX shell, using the output of one command as input of another command. We call this process *piping* due to its similarity to the real-world use of a pipe. At the command line, both of the processes (commands) are connected using the vertical bar symbol " | ". This symbol is often called a pipe symbol. When two commands are connected through a pipe, the first command sends its output to the pipe instead of sending it to the terminal screen. The second

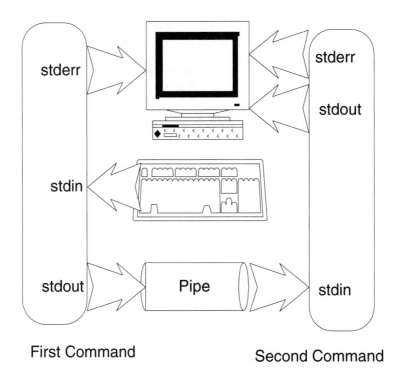

Figure 4–6 *Use of pipes.*

command reads its input from the pipe rather than from the keyboard. Both of the commands still send error messages to the terminal screen, as shown in the figure. The first command takes input from the keyboard (stdin), and the second command sends its output to the terminal screen (stdout). If the second command needs input data but nothing is available in the pipe, it just waits for the first command to send something into the pipe.

Pipes are often used to filter, modify, or manipulate data output of one command. Multiple levels of pipes can be used in one command line. Similarly, pipes can also be used in combination with I/O redirection symbols.

Use of Pipes as Filters

Many times we don't need all of the output produced by a command. In such a case, we can *filter* the desired information from the output produced by a command. Filtering means extracting useful data and throwing away the rest. We have already studied the who command, which is used to see the names of logged-in users. In large systems, where hundreds of users are logged in simultaneously, it is difficult to find out whether a particular user is currently logged in. In this situation, we use the filter to get the desired information. We can use the who command with the grep command, where grep acts as a filter. Consider the next example, where we want to find if a user "**mike**" is logged in. First we use only the who command and then we combine the who and grep commands.

```
$ who
operator    pts/ta        Aug 30 16:05
boota       pts/tb        Aug 30 15:59
mike        pts/tc        Aug 30 15:44
linda       pts/td        Aug 30 14:34
$
```

Now we use a pipe to filter out our required information.

```
$ who | grep mike
mike        pts/tc        Aug 30 15:44
$
```

As you can see, only the line containing the word "mike" is now displayed. We have used the grep command previously to find a string from one or multiple files. The grep commands, at that time, used file names as input. In this example, it did the same thing but took its input from the pipe.

How did grep know that no more data were coming from the pipe and that it should stop processing? Well, this is quite simple. The who command sends an end of file (EOF) character when it has completed sending output to the pipe. The grep command checks the EOF character and stops execution when it finds the character. In case there are no data in the pipe and the grep command has not received the EOF character, it will just wait until it gets more data or the EOF character.

As another example, we can get only login names from the who command by using another filter known as cut. We will discuss the cut command in more detail in the last chapter, but for the time being just see how we use it to extract the first word of each line and throw away the rest.

```
$ who | cut -f 1 -d " "
operator
boota
mike
linda
$
```

The cut command takes its input as fields separated by space characters and picks the first field from each input line. Since the first field of all output lines is the login name, we got the login names only in the output.

You can also use multiple levels of pipes as shown below.

```
$ who | cut -f 1 -d " " | grep mike
mike
$
```

Try to explain what is happening here. We have filtered the output of one command and then again filtered the output of the second command. You can continue this process as far as you want.

Use of Pipes for Data Manipulation

As we have used pipes for filtering data, we can also use them for reorganizing and manipulating data. What if you need to get output of a command in sorted form? Yes, it is quite simple if you pass it through the sort command using a pipe. Consider the above example of using the who command. See how the output changes without and with a sort pipe.

```
$ who
operator    pts/ta      Aug 30 16:05
boota       pts/tb      Aug 30 15:59
mike        pts/tc      Aug 30 15:44
linda       pts/td      Aug 30 14:34
$
```

Now we use a pipe with the sort command.

```
$ who | sort
boota       pts/tb      Aug 30 15:59
linda       pts/td      Aug 30 14:34
mike        pts/tc      Aug 30 15:44
operator    pts/ta      Aug 30 16:05
$
```

The sort command has arranged the output of the who command in alphabetical order. If there are many users logged in, the output of the who command just scrolls up and you see only the last page. In that case, you can use the more command as a filter to stop the scrolling at the end of each page.

```
$ who | more
```

Filters can do many things for you in a very simple way. If you were using some other operating system, you might need to write separate programs!

4.6 The T-Junction

This is a special type of pipe similar to a T pipe junction in real life. This is used to redirect incoming data in a pipe to more than one place. Please see Figure 4-7 to get an idea how the T-junction works.

The tee command is used to form a T-junction. It takes its input from stdin and writes the same thing to stdout as well as to another file at the same time. Consider the same example of the who command. If you want to display the output of the who command at the terminal as well as save it in who-file for future use, the command line and result will be as follows.

```
$ who | tee whofile
operator    pts/ta        Aug 30 16:05
boota       pts/tb        Aug 30 15:59
mike        pts/tc        Aug 30 15:44
linda       pts/td        Aug 30 14:34
$
```

Now if we see the contents of the whofile, it will contain the same data.

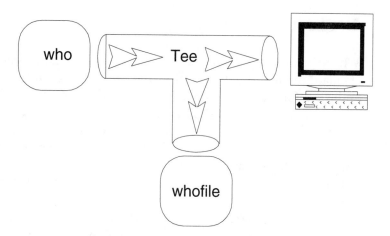

Figure 4–7 *The T-junction.*

```
$ cat whofile
operator    pts/ta      Aug 30  16:05
boota       pts/tb      Aug 30  15:59
mike        pts/tc      Aug 30  15:44
linda       pts/td      Aug 30  14:34
$
```

Like ordinary pipes and redirection symbols, multiple levels of t-junction pipe can be used to send data to many places. Can you use the sort or head commands with the tee command now? How about using the spell command to check spellings of a command output?

Table 4-2 is a summary of the redirection and pipe symbols used in HP-UX.

Table 4-2 *Standard I/O Redirection*

Symbol	Function	Syntax
>	Redirect stdout and overwrite or create a file	prog > file
<	Redirect stdin	prog < file
>>	Redirect stdout and append to, or create a file	prog >> file
2>	Redirect stderr	prog2> file
2>&1	Send stderr and stdout to the same file	prog2>&1 file
|	Pipe stdout of prog1 to stdin of prog2	prog1 | prog2
|&	Pipe stdout and stderr of prog1 to stdin of prog2	prog1 |& prog2

Note: prog, prog1, and prog2 represent a command or executable program, while file is any file

■ Chapter Summary

Whenever a UNIX command is executed, it opens three standard files for standard input and output. UNIX uses file descriptor 0 for standard input (stdin), 1 for standard output (stdout), and 2 for standard error (stderr) messages. In this chapter, you learned the meaning of standard input, output, and error and how to redirect them. You used the output redirection symbol >, input redirection symbol <, and error redirection symbol 2>. In addition, you learned how to append output of a command to a file with the >> symbol. You also used 2>&1 to redirect standard output and standard error to one place.

Use of pipes was the other important matter discussed in the chapter. You used the pipe symbol "|" and also used the tee command to pipe output of a command to more than one place.

▲ Chapter Review Questions

1. UNIX is a "file-based" system. What does that mean?

2. What if we redirect output of a command to a file that already exists?

3. What if we pipe output of a command to another command that expects nothing as input?

4. Can we redirect both input and output to same file?

▲ Test Your Knowledge

1. *What is the file descriptor used for stderr?*
    A. 1
    B. 0
    C. 2
    D. 3

2. *The symbol used to append to a file when redirecting stdout to that file is:*
    A. >
    B. >>
    C. <
    D. 2>

3. *When you redirect both stdout and stderr to the same location, you use:*
    A. 2&>
    B. 2&>1
    C. 2>&1
    D. 1>&2

4. *A pipe is used to:*
    A. send output of one command to the input of another command
    B. filter certain data from the output of a command
    C. reorder output of a command
    D. all of the above

5.   *Which is* not *true?*

A. Pipes can be used with redirection symbols.

B. Pipes cannot be used when stdin redirection is used in a command.

C. It is possible to redirect all stdin, stdout, and stderr at the same time.

D. The tee command sends output of a command to two locations.

Using the vi Editor

Until now you have been creating new files but had no way to edit a file. This chapter builds skill in using the vi editor, which is the most widely used editor on UNIX. The vi editor is available with every distribution of the UNIX operating system. Initially, all users of UNIX find the vi editor difficult to use. But as they become used to it, they start to like it due to its simplicity and power. It is not like common editors found on desktops with menus and screen displays. It gives you the full screen for displaying text. The bottom line is mostly used for vi commands when needed.

This editor is capable of handling multiple files simultaneously. All open files are called *buffers* in vi terminology. You can perform routine editing tasks within one buffer as well as across buffers. You can *cut*, *copy*, and *paste* text, search and replace text, export and import text to and from other files, and spell check. In addition, it is possible to configure the vi editor according to your requirements using a configuration file.

In the beginning, it is difficult to remember vi commands because there are no menus. As you continue using vi, you will soon remember these commands because they are simple. I have seen many experienced UNIX users who use vi, although other GUI-based editors are available, just because of its simplicity and power. In addition to the use of vi for general file editing, it is also used for typing email and editing the command line. You have already learned the EDITOR environment variable in Chapter 3. If you set the value of this variable to vi, all of your command line editing will use the same commands you use in vi.

This chapter does not explain all of the powers of the vi editor but provides sufficient explanation for the commonly used features. You will learn most of the file editing tasks in this chapter. We will start with vi modes and cursor movement and then move toward other text editing features.

5.1   Modes Used in vi

There are three modes used in the vi editor. These are the *command mode,* the *last line mode,* and the *insert* or *input mode.* Command mode is used to issue commands. Commands used in vi are not echoed on the screen and they take effect when you press a command key. Last line mode is also called ex command mode. In this mode, ex commands are used, and these are echoed at the last line of your screen. These commands usually start with a colon character. Some commands also start with a slash character, and these are used for search and replace operations. In this chapter, I will use *vi command* for both vi and ex commands. Insert or input mode means to type or insert text into the active buffer. The insert mode is also called the text entry mode.

When you start vi, it is in command mode. This means that whatever you type is considered a command by the editor. You can switch to text entry mode or insert mode by pressing i at any time in the command mode. After that, whatever you type is inserted into the *file buffer* and is displayed on the terminal screen. A file buffer is an area in memory where files are loaded and edited by vi. When you are in insert mode, you can't issue any command until you return to the command mode. To go back to command mode insert mode, you press the Esc key on your keyboard. During a file editing session, you may switch between command mode and insert mode many times.

If you are not sure at any time which mode you are in, just press the Esc key once or twice. If you are in command mode, you will remain in command mode and if you are in insert mode, you will go into command mode.

5.2 Starting and Stopping vi

The editor is started when you use a vi command and give a file name as its argument. For example, if you want to edit a file with the name myfile, you will use:

$ **vi myfile**

This command starts vi and allocates a memory buffer for file myfile. If the file already exists, text in the file will be displayed on the screen. The bottom line, which is used as a status line, will display a file name, line number, and number of characters in the file. Remember that you can't add any text to the file until you go into insert mode because vi started in the command mode. You will see something like Figure 5-1 when you start vi.

```
This is line number 1.
This is line number 2.
This is another line.
This is the last line in the file.
~
~
~
~
~
~
~
~
~
~
~
~
~
~
~
~
~
"myfile" [Read only] 4 lines, 103 characters
```

Figure 5-1 *A sample* vi *startup window.*

The tilde character (~) you see in the screen shot shows that the file has no text in these lines. To switch to insert mode, you press the i character just after starting vi. After that you can insert any text into the file. One line of text may be up to 256 characters in length. When you press the Enter key, you go to the next line. When you have finished entering text into the file, you press the Esc key to return to command mode. Now you can issue any required command. To save the file, you can use the :w command. You will observe that as soon as you enter the colon character, the cursor goes to the bottommost line (the same line that was used as the status line) and the colon is displayed in the start of that line. This is the line where vi commands are displayed.

After you save the file, you can quit the editor with the :q command. You can also use :x or :wq to save and quit in one step.

Note that you can use the vi command without any file name. In that case the editor will start with an unnamed file buffer in the memory. When you need to save a file, you can use :w filename instead of :w in the command mode. The buffer will be saved with the file name you supplied with the :w command. In the same fashion, you can use the :w filename command to save a file buffer with a new name if you have already opened a named file.

Multiple files can be opened with vi by supplying multiple file names at the command line. If you want to open three files (file1, file2, file3) simultaneously, the command will be as follows.

```
$ vi file1 file2 file3
```

If you made some changes to a file and don't want to save them, you can quit the vi editor with the :q! command. If you try to quit the vi editor after making changes to it with the :q command, it will refuse. The exclamation symbol "!" forces vi to quit even if the file buffer is changed. You can add the exclamation symbol to any command when you want to *force* vi to do something.

Warning

Most vi beginners make mistakes while using vi, resulting in unexpected changes to the file being edited. It is a good habit to use the :w command every few minutes to save the file being edited. Then if you make a mistake and don't understand what has happened, just quit vi with the :q! command and restart it with the saved file. In this case, you will lose only the data typed after the last save.

5.3 Cursor Movement

To move the cursor, you must be in command mode. On most of the modern terminals, you can move the cursor with the arrow keys on your keyboard. If this is not possible with your keyboard, you can move your cursor using other commands, as mentioned in Table 5-1.

Table 5–1 *Cursor Movement Commands*

Command	Effect
l	Move one character right
h	Move one character left
j	Move one line down
k	Move one line up
<space>	Move one character right
G	Go to last line of the file
nG	Go to line number *n* in the file
$	Go to end of current line
^	Go to start of line
w	Go to beginning of next word
b	Go to beginning of previous word
e	Move to end of word
H	Go to first line of screen
M	Go to middle line of screen
L	Go to last line of screen
(	Go to beginning of sentence
)	Go to end of sentence
{	Go to beginning of paragraph
}	Go to end of paragraph

Before using any of these commands, make sure that you are in the command mode by pressing the Esc key. The G command is used to go to a line number in the file. If you want to go to the start of the file, use 1G. To go to end of file, use G. To go to line number 100, use 100G. You can press CTRL-G at any time to find out which line you are on. You can also instruct the vi editor to display the line number with each line using the :set number command.

The start and end of a sentence are considered with reference to the dot "." character. The start and end of a paragraph are indicated with reference to a blank line. In other words, text within two blank lines is considered to be a paragraph.

We can combine vi commands. For example, $ is used to go to the end of a line, and G is used to go to the last line of the file. We can combine these two commands as $G to go to end of the last line of a file. Other commands can be combined in a similar fashion.

5.4   Inserting and Deleting Text

Text insertion takes place only when you are in insert mode. Text deletion tasks are performed in command mode. You already know how to switch between these two modes. Here we will introduce some more commands to switch to insert mode from command mode.

When you use the i command to go to insert mode, new text is entered where the cursor is at the time you press the character i. When you insert new text, the previous text on the right-hand side of the cursor moves toward the right. If you use the a command to go to insert mode, the new text entry takes place *after* the current position of the cursor. You can use the I command to start entering new text at the beginning of a line and the A command to start entering at the end of a line. If you want to enter text at the end of the file, you can combine the G and A commands for this purpose. See Table 5-2 for a list of text entry commands.

Table 5–2 *Text Insertion Commands*

Command	Effect
i	Start inserting text at the current cursor location.
I	Start inserting text at the beginning of the current line.
a	Start inserting text at the next character position relative to the current cursor location.
A	Start inserting text at the end of the current line.
o	Append a blank line just below the current line and start inserting text from the beginning of that line.
O	Append a blank line just above the current line and start inserting text from the beginning of that line.

To delete text, press ⎡Esc⎤ to go to command mode and then use any of the commands described in Table 5-3.

Table 5–3 *Text Deletion Commands*

Command	Effect
x	Delete character at current cursor location.
nx	Delete *n* characters starting at current cursor location.
X	Delete previous character from the current cursor location.
nX	Delete *n* previous characters from the current cursor location.
dd	Delete current line.
db	Delete previous word.
dw	Delete from current cursor location to the end of word.
dG	Delete to the end of file including current line.

5.5 Replacing Text

In addition to inserting and deleting text, you can also replace existing text with new text. You can replace a single character or many lines of the text. The r command is used to replace a single character. When you press r while in command mode, nothing happens, but as soon as you press the next character, it appears on the screen replacing the character at the current cursor location. To replace one character and then go to insert mode, use the s command. You will see a $ symbol and vi will put you in the insert mode just after replacing the current character. You can also replace multiple characters with the R command. These and other replacement commands are listed in Table 5-4.

Table 5–4 *Text Replacement Commands*

Command	Effect
r	Replace current character remaining in command mode.
s	Replace current character and go to insert mode.
R	Replace multiple characters until the ⎡Esc⎤ key is pressed.
cw	Change to the beginning of next word.
cc	Change entire line.
cG	Change to the end of file.

5.6   Undo and Redo

If you make a change by mistake, you can always undo that change. You use the u command to undo the last change. You can also use the U command to undo all changes made to the current line. To redo something changed by undo, you can use the " . " (dot) command. Undo and redo are opposite to each other.

5.7   Scrolling Text

You can scroll text in both the upward and downward directions. Table 5-5 shows the commands to scroll text. Before using any command, press Esc to go to command mode.

Table 5–5 *Text Scrolling Commands*

Command	Effect
CTRL-b	Scroll one screen back.
CTRL-f	Scroll one screen forward.
CTRL-u	Scroll half screen back.
CTRL-d	Scroll half screen forward.

5.8   Search and Replace

Search and replace is a necessary editing feature found in all good editors. If you want to find a text pattern in vi, you can use the /text command, where *text* is the string you want to search. This command searches the text in the forward direction from the current cursor position. You can search in the backward direction if you replace / with ? in the command. To repeat the search once you find a string, just use / or ? without typing the string again.

You can also replace text after a search is made. For example, if you want to replace the word "Atlanta" with "Chicago," you can use the command :s/Atlanta/Chicago/ to search for the next occurrence of "Atlanta" and then replace it with "Chicago." You can use the search-and-replace feature in as many lines as you want or in all of the file. Table 5-6 shows a summary of search-and-replace commands used in vi.

Table 5–6 *Text Searching and Replacing Commands*

Command	Effect
/text	Search *text* in forward direction starting from current cursor location.
?text	Search *text* in backward direction starting from current cursor location.
/	Repeat previous search in forward direction.
?	Repeat previous search in backward direction.
n	Repeat search in the same direction.
N	Repeat search in the opposite direction.
:s/oldtext/newtext	Search *oldtext* in the forward direction and replace it with *newtext*.
:m,ns/oldtext/newtext	Search *oldtext* in the forward direction from line *m* to line *n* and replace it with *newtext*.
:s/oldtext/newtext/g	Search *oldtext* in the entire file and replace it with *newtext*.
/<space>text	If you put a space between the / and the *text* to be searched, only whole words are searched.
/^text	Search *text* only in the beginning of a line.
/text$	Search *text* only in the end of a line.
/(More than one word)	Use parenthesis to search multiple words.

Escape characters have special meaning in vi. For example, the $ character is used to show the end of a line. If you want to search the $ sign in vi, you need to put a backslash (\) in front of it to tell vi that it should be considered an ordinary character and no special meaning of $ should be taken. You will use "/\$" to search for the $ character in a file. Similarly, other special characters (^, *, /, .) must also be escaped.

5.9 Cut, Copy, and Paste

You have already seen commands used to delete text, such as dd and dw. These commands cut the text and put it on a cut buffer. Text from the cut buffer can be pasted anyplace using the p command. The text that you want to copy from one place and paste at another is yanked (copied) first. We use the yy command to yank one line of text. You can also yank multiple lines of text by using the nyy command where *n* is the number of lines starting from the current cursor position. To paste the text at a new place in the file, move the cursor to that place and use the p command to place the text after the cursor position. You can also use the P command to paste the text before the cursor position.

The *cut-paste* combination is the same as moving text from one place to another. You can move text with the m command. The m command moves one line of text from the current cursor position to a new position given to m. For example, m 7 will move the current line to line number 7. You can also move multiple lines of text with the m command, for example, "1,15m76" will move lines 1 to 15 and paste them after line number 76.

The line number method can also be used to copy and paste text. As an example, "7,23t55" will copy lines 7 to 23 and will paste these lines after line number 55. To remind you, you can use the :set number command to see line numbers with each line. Table 5-7 shows commands related to cut, copy, and paste.

Table 5–7 *Cut, Copy, and Paste Commands*

Command	Effect
yy	Copy or yank current line.
nyy	Copy *n* lines starting from current line position.
p	Paste yanked text after the current cursor position.
P	Paste yanked text before the current cursor position.
:m a	Move current line and paste after line number a.
:a,bmc	Move lines from a to b and paste after line number c.
:a,btc	Copy lines from a to b and paste after line number c.

5.10   Importing and Exporting Text

The vi editor lets you deal with files in many ways. We can open multiple files, copy text from an opened file to save it to another file on disk (*export*), or insert a disk file into the editor at a specific location (*import*).

Importing a Disk File into Editor

To insert a disk file into a location in the opened file, we use the :r filename command. The *filename* is the name of a file, with full path. If the path is not specified, vi searches for the file in the current directory. For example, if you have opened a file file1 in the editor and want to insert another file file2 after line number 8, you first move the cursor to line number 8. Then you issue the `:r file2` command. All contents of file `file2` are inserted into the editor after the current line. This is a handy way to combine multiple files.

Exporting Text from the Current File

You can export any number of lines so that they are saved as a new file on the disk. We use the `w` command for this purpose. As an example, if you have opened `file1` in the editor and want to save lines 3 to 47 as `file3`, you can use the command `:3,47w file3`.

If you want to save the opened file as a new file (to make a backup), the same command can be used without line numbers. To save the current file as `file4`, you use `:w file4`.

5.11 Configuring `vi` Options

You can customize `vi` according to your requirements using `vi` environment options. Each option can be set in `vi` with the `:set` option command, where the word *option* is replaced with some valid option name. Options can also be unset using the same command and by adding *no* before the option name, like `:set nooption`.

You have already seen how you can tell `vi` to display line numbers with every line. For this you used the command `:set number`. A list of `vi` options is shown in Table 5-8.

Table 5–8 `vi` *Options*

Option	Effect
`:set number`	Sets line number in front of each line in `vi`.
`:set all`	Lists all available options.
`:set autoindent`	The next line is indented the same number of character as the current line.
`:set readonly`	Sets the current file as read-only. No change is saved.
`:set wrapmargin=n`	Sets the right wrap margin equal to *n*. If we are using 80-column display and the wrap margin is set to 6, every line will be wrapped to the next line after 74 characters.
`:set showmode`	Shows the user when the user is in "insert mode," "replace one character mode," or "replace mode."

You can also use abbreviations for these commands. For example, you can use `:se nu` instead of `:set number`.

The `vi` editor has a configuration file with the name `.exrc`, which is stored in the home directory of each user. You can put `vi` options in this file to make the settings permanent. After creating this file, whenever you start the editor, it will first read the `$HOME/.exrc` file and set the options automatically. For example, if you are writing C programs, you may want to set `autoindent` and `number` every time you start editing a C program. You can create an `.exrc` file with the following two lines in it.

```
se nu
se ai
```

Now these two settings are permanent until you make a change in the `$HOME/.exrc` file manually.

■ Chapter Summary

This chapter was devoted to working with `vi` editor. We studied many features of `vi`, including `vi` modes, text insertion and deletion, searching and replacing text, importing and exporting to `fdisk` files, cut-copy-paste, and `vi` configuration files. We also introduced the character-quoting feature when dealing with special characters.

▲ CHAPTER REVIEW QUESTIONS

1. What is the difference between the insert and command modes of the `vi` editor?

2. How is *cut-paste* different from *import-export*?

3. Is it possible to edit binary files with the `vi` editor?

4. What is the role of the `.exrc` file?

▲ TEST YOUR KNOWLEDGE

1. *You have made changes to a file and want to quit* vi *without saving these changes. What command will you use?*

    A. `:wq`

    B. `:x`

    C. `:q!`

    D. `:w!`

2. *You want to replace* cat *with* dog *in your file at all locations in the* vi *editor. You use:*

   A. /s/cat/dog

   B. :s/cat/dog/

   C. :s/cat/dog/g

   D. :s/dog/cat/g

3. *While in command mode you press "a"; what happens?*

   A. This is an invalid command.

   B. The editor goes into insert mode and starts inserting text after the current cursor location.

   C. The editor searches for character "a" in the open file.

   D. The editor gives a beep sound.

Regular Expressions

All human languages have idioms and phrases. These are made up of combinations of words not used in their ordinary meanings. Regular expressions can be considered as idioms of the UNIX shell. These are used for string pattern matching in many UNIX commands. As idioms and phrases convey a handful of meanings in few words, regular expressions are also very useful where you need to match complex text patterns and ordinary methods are just not applicable.

Regular expressions consist of strings of characters, position specifiers or anchor characters, and meta characters that have special meanings. Each regular expression is expanded into its meaning before the UNIX shell executes a command containing a regular expression. Before we actually use regular expressions in this chpater, we will start with the command execution process. We will then discuss basic meta characters used in regular expressions. You will learn the use of regular expressions with some simple commands. At the end of the chapter, you will be able to use regular expressions to search and replace character strings in files and in stdin and stdout.

6.1   How a Command Is Executed

All HP-UX commands consist of two basic parts. The first one is the command name and the second part consists of options and arguments. Before executing a command, the shell looks for a valid command in the path specified by the PATH variable. If it finds an executable command, it checks for any meta characters or position specifiers used in the arguments. These meta characters and position specifiers are discussed later in this chapter. If the shell finds any of these characters in the arguments, it starts expanding the argument according to predetermined rules. After expansion, the shell then passes the arguments to the command and invokes it for the execution process. The shell then displays any output or error message generated by the command on the user terminal. It also checks to see if the command execution was successful and keeps a record until a next command is executed.

The command execution process is completed in the following steps.

1. The shell looks for a valid command by searching all directories specified by the PATH variable.
2. Options and arguments are parsed and arguments are expanded depending on the special characters used.
3. The command is invoked.
4. The results of the command are displayed back to the user.

As an example, if you issue a command `ls [a-d]ile`, before executing the `ls` command, the shell first expands its argument `[a-d]ile` to `aile`, `bile`, `cile`, and `dile`. After that, the `ls` command is executed, which, in turn, will list any file having any of these four names.

After understanding this process, let us move to the next sections where you will learn the use of special characters and regular expressions.

6.2   Position Specifiers

Position specifiers are characters that are used to specify the position of text within a line. Sometimes these are also called *anchor characters*. The caret character (^) is the starting position specifier. It is used to match a text string occurring at the start of a line of text. The dollar sign ($) is the end-position specifier and is used to refer to a line that ends with a particular string.

Table 6-1 shows the uses of position specifiers.

Table 6–1 *Uses of Position Specifiers*

Position Specifier Example	Result of Match
^Miami	Matches word *Miami* at the start of a line.
Miami$	Matches word *Miami* at the end of a line.
^Miami$	Matches a line containing only one word, *Miami*.
^$	Matches a blank line.
^\^	Matches a ^ at the beginning of a line.
\$$	Matches a $ at the end of a line.

Use of $

The dollar sign $ is used to match a string if it occurs at the end of a line. Consider a file with the name myfile having contents as shown below after using the cat command.

```
$ cat myfile
Finally I got it done. The procedure for adding a
new template is completed in three steps.

1- Create a new template.
2- Assign this template to a node with this procedure.
   Action -> Agents -> Assign Templates -> Add -> Enter
   hostname and template nee -> OK
3- After assignment, the template is still on the ITO
   server. To install it on the required server, the
   procedure is:
   Action -> Agents -> Install/Update SW & Config ->
   Select Templates, Node name & Force update -> OK

If step 3 is successful, a message appears on ITO
message browser showing that update process on the node
is complete.

IMPORTANT
===========
The template will not work if the node name specified
in it is unknown to ITO server. In our template we
specified batch_server which was unknown to ITO server
```

```
node name in the template. Finally I got out the node
name which is more convenient as ITO automatically takes
current node name if the name is not specified in the
template.

Template Options
================
1- It runs every minute. Scans the file only if it is
   modified.
2- User initiated action is specified to run restart.
3- A short instruction is provided to run the script.
   It needs to be modified to make more meaningful.
$
```

Let us use the grep command to find all lines in the file that contain the word *node*.

```
$ grep node myfile
2- Assign this template to a node with this procedure.
message browser showing that update process on the node
The template will not work if the node name specified
node name in the template. Finally I got out the node
current node name if the name is not specified in the
$
```

You found out that there are five lines in the file containing the word *node*. Now let us find only those lines that end with this word by using the $ position specifier.

```
$ grep node$ myfile
message browser showing that update process on the node
node name in the template. Finally I got out the node
$
```

The position specifiers can be used with any command that deals with text-type data.

Use of ^

The caret character (^) matches a string at the start of a line. Using the same example of finding the word *node*, now at the start of a line, enter the following command and watch the result.

```
$ grep ^node myfile
node name in the template. Finally I got out the node
$
```

As another example, you can list all users on your system with login names starting with the letter "m" as follows.

```
$ grep ^m /etc/passwd
```

Getting Rid of Blank Lines

Use of position specifiers is very useful in many cases. To show you one example, ^$ can find blank lines in a file. If you want to count blank lines, you can just pipe output of the grep command to the wc command as in the following.

```
$ grep ^$ myfile | wc -l
5
$
```

This command will scan myfile and tell you exactly how many blank lines there are in the file. You can use the grep command to take out all blank lines from the file as shown below. The grep -v command reverses the selection and shows those lines that are *not* empty.

```
$ grep -v ^$ myfile
Finally I got it done. The procedure for adding a
new template is completed in three steps.
1- Create a new template.
2- Assign this template to a node with this procedure.
   Action -> Agents -> Assign Templates -> Add -> Enter
   hostname and template nee -> OK
3- After assignment, the template is still on the ITO
   server. To install it on the required server, the
   procedure is:
   Action -> Agents -> Install/Update SW & Config ->
   Select Templates, Node name & Force update -> OK
If step 3 is successful, a message appears on ITO
message browser showing that update process on the node
is complete.
IMPORTANT
===========
The template will not work if the node name specified
in it is unknown to ITO server. In our template we
specified batch_server which was unknown to ITO server
node name in the template. Finally I got out the node
name which is more convenient as ITO automatically takes
current node name if the name is not specified in the
template.
```

```
Template Options
================
1- It runs every minute. Scans the file only if it is
   modified.
2- User initiated action is specified to run restart.
3- A short instruction is provided to run the script.
   It needs to be modified to make more meaningful.
$
```

Please note that an "empty line" means a line that doesn't contain any characters. Some lines seem to be empty but actually contain a space or tab character. These lines are not matched by the above command. To match a line that contains space characters, you can use ^ [ ] $, where there is a space character between the two square brackets.

Escaping Position Specifiers

Sometimes the actual string contains one of the position specifiers or meta characters. If you pass this string as-is to a command, the shell will expand the meta character to its special meaning, and you will not get correct results. To instruct the shell not to expand a character to its special meaning, you need to *escape* that character. For this purpose, you use a backslash (\) before the character. For example, if you want to search for the $ character in a file, you will use the grep \$ command instead of grep $. If you don't escape the $ character, this command will display all contents of the file.

Please note that \ is also a special character. To match a backslash, you need to use two backslashes \\ in the string.

6.3 Meta Characters

Meta characters are those that have special meaning when used within a regular expression. You already have seen two meta characters used as position specifiers. A list of other meta characters and their meanings is shown in Table 6-2.

Table 6–2 *Meta Characters Used in Regular Expressions*

Character	Description
*	Matches any number of characters, including zero.
.	Matches any character, one at a time.
[]	One of the enclosed characters is matched. The enclosed characters may be a list of characters or a range.
\{n1,n2\}	Matches minimum of *n1* and maximum of *n2* occurrences of the preceding character or regular expression.
\<	Matches at the beginning of the word.
\>	Matches at the end of the word.
\	The character following acts as a regular character, not a meta character. It is used for escaping a meta character.

Use of the Asterisk * Character

The asterisk character is used to match zero or more occurrences of the preceding characters. If you take our example of myfile, the result of the following grep command will be as shown below.

```
$ grep mom* myfile
name which is more convenient as ITO automatically takes
   modified.
   It needs to be modified to make more meaningful.
$
```

Is this what you were expecting? The grep command found all text patterns that start with "mo" and after that have zero or more occurrences of the letter m. The words that match this criteria are "more," and "modified." Use of * with only a single character is meaningless as it will match anything. For example, if we use m*, it means to match anything that starts with any number of "m" characters including zero. Now each word that does not start with the letter "m" is also matched because it has zero occurrences of "m". So one must be careful when using the asterisk (*) character in regular expressions.

Use of the Dot (.) Character

The dot character matches any character excluding the new line character, one at a time. See the example below where we used the dot to match all words containing the letter "s" followed by any character, followed by the letter "e".

```
$ grep s.e myfile
new template is completed in three steps.
If step 3 is successful, a message appears on ITO
The template will not work if the node name specified
specified batch_server which was unknown to ITO server
current node name if the name is not specified in the
1- It runs every minute. Scans the file only if it is
2- User initiated action is specified to run restart.
$
```

In every line shown above, there is a word containing an "s" followed by another character and then "e". The second-to-last line is of special interest, where this letter combination occurs when we combine the two words "runs every." Here "s" is followed by a space and then an "e".

Use of Range Characters [...]

Consider that you want to list all files in a directory that start with the letters a, b, c, d, or e. You can use a command such as:

```
$ ls a* b* c* d* e*
```

This is not convenient if this list grows. The alternate way is to use a range pattern like the following.

```
$ ls [a-e]*
```

Square brackets are used to specify ranges of characters. For example, if you want to match all words that contain any of the capital letters from A to D, you can use [A-D] in the regular expression.

```
$ grep [A-D] myfile
1- Create a new template.
2- Assign this template to a node with this procedure.
   Action -> Agents -> Assign Templates -> Add -> Enter
3- After assignment, the template is still on the ITO
   Action -> Agents -> Install/Update SW & Config ->
IMPORTANT
3- A short instruction is provided to run the script.
$
```

Similarly, if you need to find words starting with lowercase vowels, [aeiou] will serve the purpose. If such words are desired to be at the beginning of a line, we can use ^[aeiou]. Multiple ranges can also be used, such as ^A[a-z0-9], which matches words that are at the start of a line, has "A" as the first character, and either a lowercase letter or a number as the second character.

The selection criteria can also be reversed using ^ as the first character within the square brackets. An expression [^0-9] matches any character other than a number.

Use of the Word Delimiters \\< and \\>

These two sets of meta characters can be used to match complete words. The \\< character matches the start of a word and \\> checks the end of a word. Without these meta characters, all regular expressions match a string irrespective of its presence in the start, end, or middle of a word. If we want to match all occurrences of "this" or "This" as a whole word in a file, we can use the following grep command.

```
$ grep \<[tT]his\>
```

If you use \\< only, the pattern is matched if it occurs in the start of a word. Using only \\> matches a pattern occurring in the end of a word.

6.4 Standard and Extended Regular Expressions

Sometimes you may want to make logical OR operations in regular expressions. As an example, you may need to find all lines in your saved files in the $HOME/mbox file containing a sender's address and date of sending. All such lines start with the words "From:" and "Date:". Using a standard regular expression it would be very difficult to extract this information. The egrep command uses an extended regular expression as opposed to the grep command that uses standard regular expressions. If you use parentheses and the logical OR operator (|) in extended regular expressions with the egrep command, the above-mentioned information can be extracted as follows.

```
$ egrep '^(From|Date):' $HOME/mbox
```

Note that we don't use \\ prior to parentheses in extended regular expressions.

You may think that this task can also be accomplished using a standard regular expression with the following command; it might seem correct at the first sight but it is not.

```
$ grep '[FD][ra][ot][me]:' $HOME/mbox
```

This command does not work because it will also expand to "Fate," "Drom," "Droe," and so on.

Extended regular expressions are used with the egrep and awk commands. Sometimes it is more convenient to use standard expressions. At other times, extended regular expressions may be more useful. There is no hard and fast rule as to which type of expression you should use. I use both of these and sometimes combine commands using both types of expressions with pipes to get a desired result. With practice you will come to know the appropriate use.

■ Chapter Summary

Regular expressions are very useful in day-to-day work where you need to match character patterns. In this chapter, you learned how a UNIX command is executed. Position specifiers are used to match a pattern at the start or end of a line, and you learned the use of caret ^ and dollar $ position specifiers. Then you studied other meta characters and their use in regular expressions. The asterisk character is used to match any number of characters, including zero. The dot character matches one character at a time, including the new line character. Square brackets [] are used for specifying a range of characters. You also used word delimiters \< and \>. These are used to match a complete word during a text pattern matching process.

Extended regular expressions have some additional features and are used with commands like egrep and awk. They are able to incorporate logical OR operation while matching a text pattern.

▲ CHAPTER REVIEW QUESTIONS

1. Describe the process used by the UNIX shell for command execution.

2. What is the command to find all lines in a file that start or end with the word "an"?

3. What is the result of the following command?

   ```
   grep ^[a-z]$ ?
   ```

4. Write a command that lists all users in the /etc/passwd file whose name starts with a vowel and who are assigned the POSIX shell (/usr/bin/sh).

▲ TEST YOUR KNOWLEDGE

1. *The purpose of the command* `grep ^Test$` *is:*

    A. to find the word "`Test`" in the start of a line

    B. to find the word "`Test`" in the end of a line

    C. to find the word "`Test`" in the start or end of a line

    D. to find a line containing a word "`Test`" only

2. *Square brackets in pattern matching are used for:*

    A. escaping meta characters

    B. specifying a range of characters; all of which must be present for a match

    C. specifying a range of characters; only one of which must be present for a match

    D. specifying a range of characters; one or more of which must be present for a match

3. *A regular expression* `\<join` *matches:*

    A. all words starting with "`join`"

    B. all words ending with "`join`"

    C. all words starting or ending with "`join`"

    D. none of the above

4. *The* `grep` *command can use:*

    A. standard regular expressions only

    B. extended regular expressions only

    C. both standard and extended regular expressions

    D. either standard or extended regular expressions but not both of these simultaneously

5. *Which of these is NOT a meta character?*

    A. `*`

    B. `\`

    C. `$`

    D. `-`

File Permissions

In a multiuser operating system like UNIX, many people are using system resources including disks and files. It is important to keep individual user files secure so that other users are not able to read, modify, or delete them. At the same time, users may be working on the same project and need to share files among themselves. It becomes important that a user be able to grant read or write access to some of the other users. If a group of programmers is working on some software development project, they need to share code and information. They also need to protect this information from people outside the group.

UNIX implements a file security policy by dividing users into three categories. These are the owner of a file, the group of users to which the owner of a file belongs, and all other users of the system. Files and directories can be granted read, write, or execute permissions to one or more user groups. In addition to this file permission scheme, HP-UX also implements another scheme, which is

99

known as *access control lists* (ACLs). Using an ACL, individual users can also be granted specific permissions in addition to group permissions.

In this chapter, we will go through some basic concepts of UNIX file permissions. You will learn categories of UNIX users and how file permissions are managed among them. You will study types of file permissions and how to change them. Here some commands to change or modify file permissions will be introduced. All users can't use all of these commands, and you will see who is permitted to do what. There is a set of default file permissions, and you will see how to deal with it. Many times you need to change the owner or group of a file, and you will learn some commands to do so. You will see what the special file permissions are and how these affect system security. Then there will be a method to find files with a particular set of permissions. In the end, ACLs will be introduced and a method for listing and changing the ACL associated with a file will be presented.

After going through this chapter, you will be able to list and modify file and directory permissions and ACLs. You will also be able to find potential security problems related to wrong file permissions.

7.1 Who Are UNIX Users

The users on a UNIX system are divided into groups. Every user must be a member of one of the groups. The group information is maintained in the /etc/group file. Although a user may be member of more than one group, he or she has a primary group membership. All other groups are secondary groups for a particular user. The file security and permission system is designed on the group information. A user who creates a file is the owner of that file. The owner of a file has the privilege to assign or revoke file permissions to other users. The owner can assign any permissions to the members of any group of which the owner is a member. All other users of the system who don't belong to this group are considered "others" in UNIX terminology. Sometimes these "other" users are also called "world," and permissions granted to them are "world" permissions.

From this discussion, we conclude that there are three types of users in UNIX. They are:

1. the owner
2. the group
3. others

Every file and directory has a permission set that tells which user has what permission. No one except the owner or the superuser can alter this permission set.

The division of users in this scheme provides a lot of convenience for securing as well as sharing files among different users. Multiple group membership for a user is also very useful. For example, an accounts manager may be a member of the accounts group and the managers group. The accounts manager can then share files related to management tasks with other managers, but the files are still protected from other members of the accounts group. Similarly, there may be an applications group, members of which may be able to run or stop applications on the system. Some of these members may also be assigned some of the system administration tasks and in a special group created by the system administrator.

7.2 Types of File Permissions

Every file in UNIX has one or more of three types of permissions. A file may be readable, writable, or executable. A user who has read-only permission for a particular file can only read it and is not able to change its contents or to delete the file. A write permission allows a user to modify the file or delete it. As we mentioned in Chapter 2, there are no special names for executable files in UNIX. Any file can be executable if a user has permission to execute it and if it is a valid executable file or shell script. If a user compiles a program but nobody has the right to execute it, it will not be executed. On the other hand, if you assign execute permission to a file that does not contain anything to execute, UNIX still tries to execute and displays an error message.

File permissions can be displayed using the `ll` (or `ls -l`) command in HP-UX. This command shows the long listing of files. The first field consists of 10 characters. The first character shows the type of the file. File types are explained in Table 7-1. The next three characters (2nd to 4th) show permissions for the owner of the file. These permissions are always listed in `rwx` format. In `rwx` format, "`r`" represents read permission, "`w`" is used for write permission, and "`x`" is for execute permission. If one of these characters is present, it shows that the permission is granted. If the character is not there, a hyphen "`-`" is placed, showing that the permission is withheld. After the file owner permissions, the next combination of `rwx` shows permissions of the group to which the owner belongs. The last combination of `rwx` is for all other users of the UNIX system.

Table 7–1 *File Types as Displayed by the* ll *Command*

First Character in First Field	Type of File
-	Ordinary file
d	Directory
l	Symbolic (or "soft") link file
c	Character device file, like a modem or terminal
d	Block device file, like a disk
p	Named pipe

To understand the file permissions, consider the following example where we use the ll command to list files in the current directory.

```
$ ll
total 28
-rwxrw-r--    1 boota    users     103 Sep  8 18:06 abc
drwxrwxrwx    2 root      sys      8192 Sep  8 18:00 usage
-rw-r-----    1 boota    users      44 Sep  3 20:24 qwe
-rw-rw-rw-    1 boota    users    2078 Jul  2 00:38 sqlnet.log
-rw-rw-rw-    1 boota    users      14 Sep  3 18:28 xyz
-rw-rw-rw-    1 boota    users      68 Sep  3 20:24 zxc
```

Now, you can see from this listing that abc is an ordinary file. It has read, write, and execute permissions for the owner of the file (user name **boota** shown in third column). Other members of the group (group name **users** shown in fourth field) have read and write permissions for the file, but they are not able to execute it. The last set, r--, shows that users who are not members of the group **users** can only read this file.

The next file in the listing is a directory with the name usage. We came to know that this is a directory by looking at the first character of the line, which is "d". You can see from the listing that user **root** is the owner of this directory and that it belongs to group **sys**. Everyone has read, write, and execute permissions for this directory. Then we have a file qwe and we can see that other users have no permission for this file.

Importance of Read Permission

Read permission is the basic file permission. Other permissions are not of much use if someone doesn't have the read permission. If a regular user has no read permission for a file but has execute permission, he or she can't execute the file, as you need to read the file before executing it. Also, having write permission without a read permission will allow a user to delete the file. The user will not be able to edit the file because you need to read the file before you edit it.

For example, `prog2` is a program file having the following permissions. The owner can't execute it because the read permission is denied.

```
---xrw-rw-   1 boota    users     14 Sep  3 18:28 prog2
```

If the owner of the file tries to execute the file, the following message appears.

```
$ prog2
sh: prog2: Cannot find or open the file.
$
```

As you can see from the file permissions for the owner (`--x`), although the owner has execute permission, the shell is not able to read the program file. And if you can't read a program, how can you execute it?

Left-to-Right Rule of File Permissions

In UNIX, the permissions are read from left to right. It means that the first allow or deny that comes to your path is applied. For example, if the owner of a file doesn't have execute permission to a file and the group has the execute permission, the owner will not be able to execute the file. This is because, first of all, owner permissions were analyzed by the shell and it came to know that the execute permission is revoked. The shell did not go further in checking the group or other permissions and stopped any further action on the file with an error message. Consider the same program we used in the previous example with permission set as shown below.

```
-rw-rwxrwx   1 boota    users     14 Sep  3 18:28 prog2
```

Here the owner has read and write permission but all others have execute permission in addition to read and write. When the owner executes the program, the following message appears

```
$ prog2
sh: prog2: Execute permission denied.
$
```

The UNIX way of interpreting file permissions is different from some other operating systems that analyze all permissions applied to a user and take the most allowed or most restricted permissions set.

Directory Permissions

Most users organize files in directories. Directory-related permissions affect all of the files contained in that directory. There are some rules that should be kept in mind when granting or revoking permissions to a directory. For a proper operation, a directory should have read and execute permissions set. The following rules apply to directory permissions in addition to general file permissions:

- If read permission for a directory is not set, no file inside the directory can be listed or accessed.
- If execute permission of a directory is not set, files inside the directory can be listed with names only. This means ls will work but ll will not work. Also, no files inside the directory can be read or executed. Because of this, the execute permission for a directory is also called *list permission*.
- If only execute permission is set and read or write permissions are not set, a user can go into the directory with the cd command and execute a program inside the directory if the program name is known. Also, a file can be viewed with the cat command if the file name is already known. It means you can execute programs but can't see the files.
- If a directory contains a file that a user can't delete (no write permission), he or she can't delete the directory even though write permission is granted for the directory.

We will see an example of how directory permissions affect files inside a directory, but first let us see how we can change file permissions.

7.3 Modifying File Permissions

The superuser or owner of a file can modify its permissions. We use the chmod command for modifying permissions of a file. Permissions can be changed in two ways; you can use either user symbolic modes or octal numbers for modifying permissions.

Modifying File Permissions Using Symbolic Modes

There are four user modes that can be used with the chmod command. We represent different users with these modes. Also, there are file modes which are represented with characters we have studied earlier. User and file modes are listed in Table 7-2.

Table 7–2 *User and File Modes*

Mode	Meaning
u	User or owner of a file
g	Group membership of the file
o	Others (not owner or member of group)
a	All users
r	Read permission
w	Write permission
x	Execute permission

To grant permission to a user, we use the "+" symbol between the user and file modes. To revoke a permission, use "−" between the user and file modes. To exactly assign a permission, regardless of the previous permission, we use the "=" symbol.

For example, to grant execute permission to the owner of file myprog, the chmod command will be used as follows. We have used the ll command to show old and new file permissions.

```
$ ll myprog
-rw-rw-rw-    1 boota    users      103 Sep  8 18:06 myprog
$ chmod u+x myprog
$ ll myprog
-rwxrw-rw-    1 boota    users      103 Sep  8 18:06 myprog
$
```

To revoke write permission of other users, we can use the following command.

```
$ ll myprog
-rwxrw-rw-    1 boota    users      103 Sep  8 18:06 myprog
$ chmod o-w myprog
$ ll myprog
-rwxrw-r--    1 boota    users      103 Sep  8 18:06 myprog
$
```

Now the owner has all read, write, and execute permissions, members of the users group have read and write permissions, and all other users have only read permissions. If you want to grant all users only read permissions, you can use following command.

```
$ ll myprog
-rwxrw-r--   1 boota    users       103 Sep  8 18:06 myprog
$ chmod a=r myprog
$ ll myprog
-r--r--r--   1 boota    users       103 Sep  8 18:06 myprog
$
```

As you have seen, when we use the "=" symbol, the new file permissions are set regardless of the previous permissions.

You can also combine more than one mode in the command line to change multiple permissions simultaneously, as in the following example.

```
$ ll myprog
-r--r--r--   1 boota    users       103 Sep  8 18:06 myprog
$ chmod u+x,o-r myprog
$ ll myprog
-r-xr-----   1 boota    users       103 Sep  8 18:06 myprog
$
```

Changing File Permissions Using Octal Numbers

Each group of rwx can be represented by an octal number. In the binary number system each position has a weight associated with it. These weights double at each step as we move from right to left, the right-most character carrying weight 1. If we map this scheme to rwx, the "x" carries weight 1, "w" carries weight 2 and "r" carries weight 4. We can change symbolic modes with these weights. A file that has all the permissions set can be considered as carrying weight 7 (4+2+1). A file with only read and write permissions will carry weight 6 (4+2). As three binary characters make one octal digit, we add weights of three modes for each user group (owner, group, others) to make an octal number containing three digits. As an example, if we want to grant all three (read, write, execute) permissions to all users, we can use 777 with chmod as follows.

```
$ ll myprog
-r--r--r--   1 boota    users       103 Sep  8 18:06 myprog
$ chmod 777 myprog
$ ll myprog
-rwxrwxrwx   1 boota    users       103 Sep  8 18:06 myprog
$
```

If you want to grant all permissions to the owner (4+2+1=7), read and execute permissions to the group (4+1=5), and no permission for other users (0), the command is:

```
$ ll myprog
-r--r--r--   1 boota    users      103 Sep  8 18:06 myprog
$ chmod 750 myprog
$ ll myprog
-rwxr-x---   1 boota    users      103 Sep  8 18:06 myprog
$
```

If you feel comfortable with octal numbers, this is a quicker way to grant or revoke multiple file permissions.

7.4 Default File Permissions

What will be the permissions of a newly created file or directory? By default, all new files carry rw-rw-rw- and all new directories have rwxrwxrwx permission. We can control default file permissions with the umask command. The umask command sets the *mask* for new files. A mask is three digit octal number similar to the one we used to set file permission. It shows which permissions will be revoked when new files or directories are created. For example, if you set umask to value 022, the write permission for group and other users will be withheld for a new file. New default permissions for files will be rw-r--r--, and for directories these will be rwxr-xr-x. See the following command sequence for the role of umask on new files.

```
$ touch file1
$ ll file1
-rw-rw-rw-  1 boota    users       0 Sep  8 18:06 file1
$ umask 022
$ touch file2
$ ll file2
-rw-r--r--  1 boota    users       0 Sep  8 18:06 file2
$
```

This happened because the octal character 2 represents "w" in the symbolic mode. When this appears in the group and other places, it revokes "w" or write permission from both of these. Also note that we have used the touch command, which creates a zero-size file if the file does not already exist. The touch command changes file update time to the current time if the file already exists.

The current mask value is displayed with the umask command when used without any argument.

```
$ umask
022
$
```

A new mask value can be set at any time. A better place for setting the mask value is the user startup file $HOME/.profile so that the value is set as soon as a user logs in.

7.5   Changing the Owner and Group of a File

When a user creates a new file, it belongs to the user who created it and to the current group of the user. Any user other than the owner of the file can't change ownership of a file, except the superuser. A user can change group membership of a file only if he or she is member of both the old and new groups. In normal circumstances, the system administrator needs to change file and group ownership when copying files to new user directories or when making files available to new users or groups.

In HP-UX, you use chown (CHange OWNer) for changing the owner of a file and chgrp (CHange GRouP) for changing group membership of a file. Let us see what happens when we change the owner of a file from user **boota** to **jim**.

```
$ ll file1
-rwxrwxrwx    1 boota    users       0 Sep  8 18:06 file1
$ chown jim file1
$ ll file1
-rwxrwxrwx    1 jim      users       0 Sep  8 18:06 file1
$
```

Note that the user name is changed in the third field. We don't need to mention the old owner name when changing ownership of a file with the chown command.

A similar method is used for changing the group ownership of file1 from **users** to **root** with the chgrp command.

```
$ ll file1
-rwxrwxrwx    1 jim      users       0 Sep  8 18:06 file1
$ chgrp root file1
$ ll file1
-rwxrwxrwx    1 jim      root        0 Sep  8 18:06 file1
$
```

Multiple file names and wildcard characters can also be used with chown and chgrp. Names of a new owner and group must be present in the /etc/passwd and /etc/group files, respectively. The chown command can also be used to change the owner and group in one step. See the following example, where the owner and group are used together with a colon symbol.

```
$ ll file1
-rwxrwxrwx    1 boota    users      0 Sep  8 18:06 file1
$ chown jim:root file1
$ ll file1
-rwxrwxrwx    1 jim      root       0 Sep  8 18:06 file1
$
```

To change the ownership or group of a directory tree, you can use the -R option with both of these commands and with the directory name as argument. Whenever you change ownership of a link file, ownership of the file to which the link points is also changed. To avoid this, use the -h option with the chown or chgrp commands.

Study Break

Dealing with File Permissions

Up until this point you have studied basic concepts of file security structure used in UNIX. You have seen what the file permissions are and how can these be set and modified. Let's take a short break and use some of these concepts.

First, use the command umask 000 to ensure that the default file permissions are being used. Then, create a new file in your home directory with the name testfile. List the file using the ll testfile command and see what the default permissions are. Check the mask value using the umask command. Now change the value of umask to 222 and create another file with the name myfile. Did you find any difference between the file permissions of testfile and myfile? Now try to change the contents of myfile using the vi editor. When you try to save the file, vi tells you that the file is read-only. This is because you had changed the mask value such that the owner didn't have write permission. Quit the vi editor without saving the file and use the chmod command to grant write access to the owner of the file.

7.6 Special File Permissions

There are three types of special file attributes: *set user ID* (SETUID), *set group ID* (SETGID), and *sticky bit*. In the general case, if a user executes a file owned by someone else, the process created in memory is owned by the user who executes the file. In the case of SETUID, the process created is owned by the owner of the file. A similar rule is applicable in the case of the SETGID bit. The sticky bit is used to protect files in that directory.

SETUID and SETGID

We use the chmod command to set these special permissions to a file. If you are using a symbolic method, use u+s for setting SETUID and g+s for setting SETGID. In case you use octal numbers, add a fourth octal digit on the left-hand side of the file permissions. Digit 4 represents SETUID and 2 represents SETGID. Examples of symbolic and octal number use are given below.

```
$ ll file1
-rwxrwxrwx    1 boota    users      0 Sep  8 18:06 file1
$ chmod u+s file1
$ ll file1
-rwsrwxrwx    1 boota    users      0 Sep  8 18:06 file1
$ chmod 2777 file1
$ ll file1
-rwxrwsrwx    1 boota    users      0 Sep  8 18:06 file1
$
```

As you can see, "x" is replaced by "s" in the file permission representation with either SUID or SGID.

The SUID bit plays an important role when you want to execute a program with higher privileges. For example, when you change your password, you modify the /etc/passwd file. Only **root** has permission to modify this file, so how can every system user modify it? This becomes possible because the command you use for a password change (/bin/passwd) is owned by **root** and has the SETUID bit set. So whenever any user executes this command, the command runs as **root** and has the privilege to modify the /etc/passwd file.

This also causes a great security problem. For example, if you have a program with the SUID bit set, anybody executing that program gets the privileges of the owner of the program during the execution of that program. Now, if by chance you also allow write permission to that program file, someone can change the contents of the program and execute it with the owner privilege. Just imagine if someone has write permission to a file owned by **root** and the SETUID bit is in place, the user can change its contents with some other command to damage the whole file system!

Sticky Bit

The sticky bit is represented by "t" and can be set using the chmod command with the u+t symbolic method or 1 (one) in the fourth digit position of octal numbers. One example is:

```
$ ll file1
-rwxrwxrwx   1 boota    users      0 Sep  8 18:06 file1
$ chmod u+t file1
$ ll file1
-rwsrwxrwt   1 boota    users      0 Sep  8 18:06 file1
$
```

The use of the sticky bit for directories has a significant advantage. If the sticky bit for a directory is set, users can use that directory as a public area for file sharing. Any file present in a directory with the sticky bit set can only be deleted by the owner of the file. It may be useful to set the sticky bit for the /tmp directory where users can safely put and delete their temporary or sharable files.

7.7 Finding Files Having a Particular Set of File Permissions

You have already used the find command to search any file in the file system hierarchy. You can also use the find command to list files with desired file permissions in the file system. For example, if the system administrator wants to list all files for which the SUID bit is set in the /usr/bin directory, the following command is useful. Here I have shown only partial output, as the actual output is quite long.

```
#  find /usr/bin -perm -u+s -exec ll {} \;
-r-sr-xr-x   5 root   bin   49152 Apr   9  1998 /usr/bin/chfn
-r-sr-xr-x   1 root   bin   49152 Nov   6  1997 /usr/bin/chkey
-r-sr-xr-x   5 root   bin   49152 Apr   9  1998 /usr/bin/chsh
-r-sr-xr-x   1 root   bin   53248 Apr   9  1998 /usr/bin/ct
-r-sr-xr-x   1 root   bin   40960 Apr   9  1998 /usr/bin/cu
-r-sr-xr-x   1 root   bin   73728 Feb   2  1998 /usr/bin/df
-r-sr-xr-x   1 root   bin   49152 Nov   7  1997 /usr/bin/login
-r-sr-xr-x   1 root   bin   45056 Jun  15  1998 /usr/bin/lp
-r-sr-xr-x   1 root   bin   40960 Oct  27  1997 /usr/bin/lpalt
-r-sr-sr-x   2 root   mail  45056 Nov   7  1997 /usr/bin/mail
#
```

This output shows that whenever someone uses one of the above commands, he or she will become the superuser during the execution time of the command. You can also use a similar command to check your files in your home directory to find out if some security hole exists due to any mistake in granting permissions. The following command lists all files for which SETUID is set, and anybody from group or others also has write permission to that file.

```
$ find / -perm -u+s,g+w,o+w
```

7.8 Access Control Lists

Access control lists are used to grant or deny permissions to users or groups in addition to those specified with traditional UNIX file access permissions. This mechanism is also called *discretionary access control* (DAC) and is supported under the older HFS file system but not under the modern JFS file system. To grant or deny specific file accesses to a user or group, users are specified as shown in Table 7-3.

Table 7–3 *Access Control List User Specification*

Pattern	Description
user.group	ACL for a specific user and a specific group
user.%	ACL for a specific user and all groups
%.group	ACL for all users and a specific group
%.%	ACL for all users and all groups

Listing ACL

Access Control Lists can be listed using the lsacl command.

```
$ lsacl myfile
(boota.%, rwx) (jim.%,rwx) (%.users,r-x) (%.%,r--) myfile
$
```

This command shows that users **boota** and **jim**, belonging to any group, have all read, write, and execute permissions, all users of the **users** group have read and execute permissions, and all other users have only read permissions.

Changing ACL

The chacl command is used for changing ACLs. You can grant another user mary read, write, and execute (rwx) permissions to myfile.

```
$ chacl "mary.%=rwx" myfile
$ lsacl myfile
(boota.%, rwx) (jim.%,rwx) (mary.%,rwx) (%.users,r-x)
   (%.%,r--) myfile
$
```

7.9 Miscellaneous Commands

Here are few other commands that are not used directly to modify file permissions but are related to this process.

The newgrp Command

If a user is a member of more than one group, all new files created by that user belong to the current group. If the user wants the new files to belong to another group, the newgrp command changes the current group membership temporarily. In the following example, user **boota** belongs to group **users** (default group) and **class**. See how the new files created by the touch command are affected by changing the group membership.

```
$ touch file1
$ ll file1
-rw-rw-rw-   1 boota    users     0 Sep  8 18:06 file1
$ newgrp class
$ touch file2
$ ll file2
-rw-rw-rw-   1 boota    class     0 Sep  8 18:06 file2
$
```

File file1 belongs to group **users**, while file2 belongs to group **class**.

The su Command

The *switch user ID* (su) command is used to change the user ID temporarily just as you used the newgrp command to change the group ID. You need to know the password for the user you are changing to. The following command changes the user ID to **jim**.

```
$ su jim
Password:
$
```

To switch back to the actual user ID, use the `exit` command. After changing the user ID, all new files created belong to the new user. The environment related to user **jim** is not loaded until you use the `su - jim` command instead of `su jim`.

If you don't specify any user name with the `su` command, it will change to user **root**. You can become the superuser temporarily by using this command if you know the **root** password.

Many system administrators work under a user ID other than **root** and change the ID to **root** only if required. This is done to avoid any accidental damage to files with commands like `rm`.

The id Command

The `id` command is used to display the current user and group IDs. A typical result of this command is:

```
$ id
uid=415 (boota), gid=100 (users)
$
```

The command shows that the current user is **boota** having a user ID of 415. The current group membership is **users** and the group ID is 100.

■ Chapter Summary

In this chapter, you learned the concept of file permissions and access control lists. These are very important from a file- and system-security point of view. The following items were presented in this chapter.

- There are three types of user in UNIX; the owner, members of the owner group, and all other users.
- The three types of permissions can be set for every file and directory. These are read, write, and execute permissions.
- A file's permissions can be changed with the `chmod` command.

- The owner and group of a file can be changed with the `chown` and `chgrp` commands.
- Use of the `SETUID` and `SETGID` bits and security problems associated with these.
- Use of the sticky bit and its effect on files and directories.
- Finding files with specific file permissions using the `find` command.
- Use of Access Control Lists (ACLs) with the `lsacl` and `chacl` commands, which are used to list and change ACLs, respectively.

In addition, you have also used some other commands that don't affect file permissions directly. The `newgrp` command is used to change group membership temporarily while the `su` command is used to change user ID temporarily. The `id` command is used to check the current user and group membership.

In the next chapter, we will see the file system structure of HP-UX and how different directories are arranged in the file system. We will also see which directory contains what type of files.

▲ CHAPTER REVIEW QUESTIONS

1. How many types of users are present in UNIX and what is the use of groups?

2. What is the advantage of placing a user in more than one group?

3. What is the use of `SETUID` from the system administration point of view?

4. Write a command to find all files in a directory with the sticky bit set and copy these files to the `/tmp` directory.

5. What if the `SUID` for a file is set but the file is not executable?

6. Why are the Access Control Lists used?

▲ TEST YOUR KNOWLEDGE

1. A file has `rwxr-xr--` permissions. It is owned by a user **mark** belonging to a
    group **users**. You are logged in as user **jim** belonging to group **users**. What
    permissions do you have for this file?

    A. only read permission

    B. read, write, and execute permissions

    C. read and execute permissions

    D. You don't have any permissions for the file, as the file is owned by
       another user.

2. You are logged in as user **jim** and create a file `myfile` and want to give it to a
    user **mark** by changing its ownership. The command for this is:

    A. `chown mark myfile jim`

    B. `chown mark myfile`

    C. `chmod mark myfile`

    D. You can't change file ownership.

3. The `id` command without any argument lists:

    A. user ID

    B. group ID

    C. both user and group IDs

    D. system ID

4. You want to change your group ID temporarily. Which command will you use?

    A. the `newgrp` command

    B. the `chgrp` command

    C. the `id` command

    D. all of the above

5. The system administrator wants a command to be executed with **superuser**
    permissions no matter which user executes it. He or she will set:

    A. the SUID bit

    B. the SGID bit

    C. the sticky bit

    D. the execution bit

6. *A file* `myfile` *already exists. You use command* `touch myfile`*. What will be the effect of this command?*
    A. It will erase the file and create a new file with the same name and zero byte size.
    B. It will rename the file as `myfile.bak` and create a new file with the name `myfile` and zero byte size.
    C. It will change the file modification date and time to the current value.
    D. It will do nothing, as the file already exists.

7. *You are logged in as user* **boota** *belonging to group* **users**. *When you list files using the* `ll` *command, you see the following list.*

    ```
    -rwxrw-r--   1 jim   class   0 Sep  8 18:06 myfile
    ```

    What operations can you perform on this file?
    A. read, write, and execute
    B. read and write
    C. read only
    D. modify and delete

8. *You use the command* `chmod 764 myfile`*. It provides:*
    A. read, write, and execute permissions to the owner
    B. read and write permission to the group members of the owner of the file
    C. read permission to all users of the system
    D. all of the above

UNIX File System Hierarchy

UNIX files and directories are arranged in a systematic way, like a tree structure. The root directory is represented by the slash symbol (/). It serves as the *root* of this directory tree. By *file system layout*, we mean the arrangement of files and directories in a directory tree. It does not mean the actual physical format of the disk drive but shows only logical arrangement. Directories in UNIX are named and arranged in a fashion that have particular meaning for users. Every directory contains a particular set of files related to some defined purpose or task. For example, all files in the /etc directory are related to some sort of system configuration task. Similarly, the home directories of all users are usually kept in the /home directory.

There are two major types of file system hierarchies used in UNIX distributions. One of these is based on Berkley Distribution of UNIX (BSD) and the other is AT&T System V. The file system layout of HP-UX version 10.x and above is based

119

on AT&T system V release 4 (SVR4). The directory structure starts with the root directory. All other directories are named relative to the root directory. There are two major groups of these directories. One is the group in which system files are present and don't change frequently. This is the *static* part of the directory hierarchy. The other group contains those files and directories that are changed on a routine basis and are sometimes called *dynamic* files and directories. An example of this type of file is log files that change on a day-to-day basis. Another division of directories may also be based on shared and nonshared files.

This chapter contains an introduction to the directory tree and the types of files in each directory. We will describe what directories are related to system files and what are used by HP-UX users. Through a careful study of the chapter, a user will build understanding of how to quickly find different files and directories used for particular purposes. As examples, you will learn where files containing manual pages are located and what directory contains files related to network administration.

8.1 Static and Dynamic Files

Static files and directories contain information that usually does not change after system installation. The files that fall into this category are executable files, libraries, applications, and so on. This part contains /sbin, /usr, and the application directories under /opt. As these files are also shared among many systems in a network where diskless or dataless clients are used, they are also called *shared* files. The dynamic files are those that are found in other directories like the /var directory, which holds most of the log files. In fact, the name var also comes from "variable." Similarly, you place temporary files in the /tmp directory. Most of the applications also put their temporary files in the /var/tmp directory and it continuously changes. Contents of the home directory also change whenever a user is created or deleted or whenever a user makes changes to any of his or her files. Figure 8-1 shows the division of a file system into static and variable directories.

To keep the logical division of files and directories, HP-UX keeps all application directories separate from system directories so that these two types of files never get mixed with each other. Similarly, executable and nonexecutable files and directories are also kept separate from each other. In the

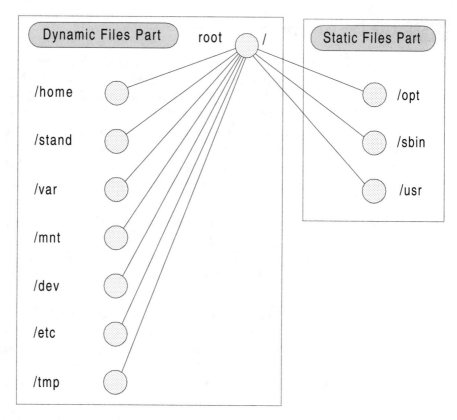

Figure 8–1 *Static and dynamic directories.*

following part of this chapter, you will get a brief introduction to the contents of each directory under the root directory. The directory tree is specific to HP-UX version 10.x and above.

8.2 The Root Directory (/)

All of the file system is viewed with reference to the root directory. The name root comes from the logical position of this directory. This is the top-level directory in the tree structure and hence the name root is used for it. It is represented by a slash character (/). It must be kept in mind that the root directory or any other directory is not related to physical disks in any respect. The directory structure is just a logical arrangement regardless of the number of disks in your system or how these disks are partitioned.

8.3 The Device Directory (/dev)

The *device directory* contains all of the device files. Device files are used to represent devices attached to the system. Each device file has a major and a minor number. The major number of a device file represents a device driver built into the HP-UX kernel, while the minor number represents the device's hardware address and (optionally) certain device-specific options. An instance means a logical numbering of the same type of devices. For example, there may be more than one SCSI disk in a system. All of these SCSI disks use the same device drivers but represent different instances of disks and have different minor numbers.

We will be discussing more about device files in Chapter 17. At the moment, however, it is useful to mention that the device directory contains many subdirectories depending on the types of devices. This is used to group device files in a more logical way. Files related to one type of device are kept in one subdirectory under /dev. Figure 8-2 shows some of these subdirectories.

As an example, the directory /dev/rdsk contains all of the device files that represent character-based or raw devices related to physical disks. The directory /dev/dsk contains block devices for these disks. Similarly, all volume groups have their own directories in /dev that contain device files for logical volumes. We will see more about logical volumes in Chapter 18. Files starting with tty in the /dev directory represent terminal types.

Almost all of the files in the /dev directory are special files, and if you take a listing with the ll command, you will find a special character in the

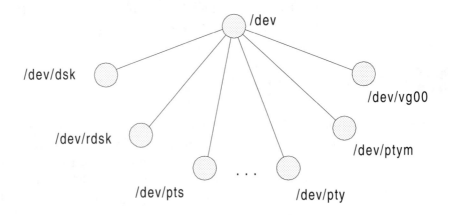

Figure 8–2 *The device directory (/dev) hierarchy.*

first column of the output showing whether a file represents a character-type device, block device, or something else. A listing of /dev/rdsk is presented as an example here.

```
$ ll /dev/rdsk
total 0
crw-r-----   1 bin   sys   188 0x003000 Nov 25  1998 c0t3d0
crw-r-----   1 bin   sys   188 0x004000 Nov 25  1998 c0t4d0
crw-r-----   1 bin   sys   188 0x005000 Nov 25  1998 c0t5d0
crw-r-----   1 bin   sys   188 0x006000 Oct  5 16:57 c0t6d0
crw-r-----   1 bin   sys   188 0x0a0000 Aug 31 13:40 c10t0d0
crw-r-----   1 bin   sys   188 0x0a0100 Aug 31 13:40 c10t0d1
crw-r-----   1 bin   sys   188 0x0a0200 Aug 31 13:40 c10t0d2
crw-r-----   1 bin   sys   188 0x0a0300 Aug 31 13:40 c10t0d3
crw-r-----   1 bin   sys   188 0x0a0400 Aug 31 13:40 c10t0d4
crw-r-----   1 bin   sys   188 0x0a0500 Aug 31 13:40 c10t0d5
crw-r-----   1 bin   sys   188 0x0a0600 Aug 31 13:40 c10t0d6
crw-r-----   1 bin   sys   188 0x0a0700 Aug 31 13:40 c10t0d7
crw-r-----   1 bin   sys   188 0x0a1000 Aug 31 13:40 c10t1d0
crw-r-----   1 bin   sys   188 0x0a1100 Sep 19 04:58 c10t1d1
$
```

As you can see, all of these are character-type devices.

8.4 The /etc Directory

The /etc directory is where a system administrator spends much of his or her time. All of the system configuration files are placed in this directory. The files here control system startup and shutdown procedures as well as the startup and shutdown of server and daemon processes. It also contains configuration files for applications installed on the HP-UX system. The /etc directory also contains subdirectories, as shown in Figure 8-3.

Files in the /etc/rc.config.d directory are configuration and control files for system startup and shutdown and other server and daemon processes.

Files in the /etc/opt directory contain configuration files for applications installed on the system.

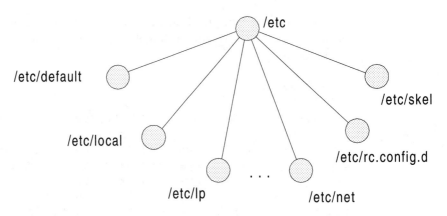

Figure 8–3   *The* /etc *directory hierarchy.*

8.5   The Home Directory (/home)

Traditionally, this directory contains the home directories of all system users. A home directory for user **linda** will be /home/linda. All users are owners of their respective directories and have full rights of files under these directories. The size of this directory usually depends on the number of users and varies widely as users add and delete files in their home directories.

Under the home directory of each user is located user-related configuration files. You have already used the $HOME/.profile and $HOME/.exrc files. There may be many other user configuration files. An example would be the file that controls how the X-Window system should start up for a particular user and what should be displayed on the user's desktop.

In a network where user information is shared, the home directories are kept on a central file server and are exported from that server to all other machines. A user can log into any one of the available systems, and he/she will find the same home directory everywhere. At this time, it must also be kept in mind that it is not mandatory to keep all home directories under the /home directory. The system administrator is free to make any choice for home directories. The name /home is just a convention. At the same time, some other directory names are mandatory. For example, a system administrator cannot place system configuration files in a directory other than /etc.

8.6   The System Binary Directory (/sbin)

This directory contains executable files needed at boot time. Under HP-UX, this directory also contains system scripts required at startup and shutdown

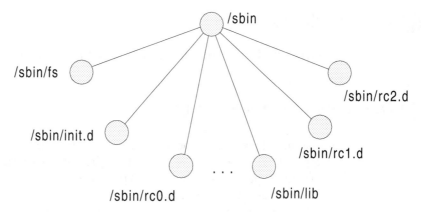

Figure 8–4 *The* /sbin *directory subtree.*

time. This directory also contains subdirectories. The most important script in the /sbin directory is the rc script that controls all of the system startup and shutdown processes. Another important program is init, which is used to control different system states like single-user mode, multiuser mode, etc. There is the /sbin/init.d directory that contains all scripts executed at system startup and shutdown or at the time when the system changes its state (e.g., from single-user to multiuser). A partial /sbin directory subtree is shown in Figure 8-4.

There are directories with names /sbin/rc0.d, /sbin/rc1.d, and so on. These control different runlevels or system states in conjunction with the /sbin/init program. You will find more information on runlevels in Chapter 11 where system startup and shutdown procedures are discussed. Most of the other daemon startup and shutdown scripts are also stored in this directory.

8.7 The /stand Directory

This is the directory where the HP-UX kernel is kept. The kernel configuration file is also present in this directory. The kernel file is /stand/vmunix and the configuration file is /stand/system. In addition, you can keep multiple kernel files in this directory so that if a new kernel fails to boot, you could use any old kernel file to recover such a situation. It also contains the /stand/build directory used to rebuild the new kernel.

8.8 The /net Directory

This is a reserved name for remote file system mount points.

8.9 The Application Directory (/opt)

The /opt directory is used for installing applications on an HP-UX system. Each application has a subdirectory in this directory. Starting from that sub-directory, each application may have its own directory tree containing binary files, manual pages, libraries, and so forth.

Putting applications in one directory solves many problems related to system administration. Not all vendors that supply software for HP-UX specify a particular directory for their application. This makes it easy to keep multiple versions of the same application on the system, as each version has its own directory structure, which is independent from the rest of the system or any other application. Also, it makes it easy to keep track of these applications when they are installed under one top directory, exactly like it is easy to maintain home directories of users when all of these exist under one main directory /home. You should keep in mind, however, that although application files are kept under this directory, some application files maintain configuration files in /etc/opt and log files in /var/opt directories. This scheme provides another advantage when application directories are shared among many systems on a network, since each sharing system can have its own separate configuration and log files depending on local system configuration.

A sample application directory tree is shown in Figure 8-5 showing the HP Ignite-UX application used for system recovery.

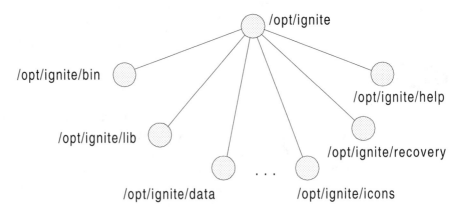

Figure 8–5 *A sample application directory tree for* ignite.

8.10   The Temporary File Directory (/tmp)

This directory has permissions for everybody to create or delete files. Most of the time, temporary files are placed in this directory and are deleted from time to time. Many system administrators prefer to empty this directory at boot time to avoid the piling up of unnecessary files. Anybody creating files in this directory must be aware of the public nature of this directory, and no important file should be placed here. It is a better idea to enable the sticky bit on this directory so that a user may not delete files in this directory created by other users.

Any applications that need to create temporary files should do so in the /var/tmp directory instead of /tmp.

8.11   The /usr Directory

This is an important directory, as most of the HP-UX system files are placed here. This directory contains a number of subdirectories that arrange different types of files. Figure 8-6 shows a partial structure of this directory. The most important file types are user-related commands, libraries, documentation and manual pages, contributed software, and X-Window system files.

/usr/bin

This directory contains user commands, applications, and utilities.

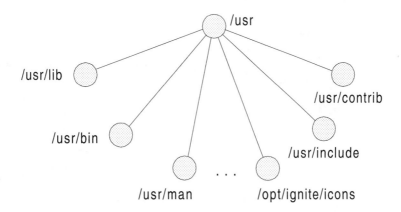

Figure 8–6   *Structure of the* /usr *directory.*

/usr/contrib

Contains contributed software from other sources.

/usr/include

Header and include files used for programming.

/usr/lib

Libraries for programming and machine-dependent database files. A user may need to look into this directory to check the existence of certain libraries in case there are compilation or run-time errors.

/usr/sbin

Many system administration commands are placed here.

/usr/share/man

Manual pages for HP-UX commands.

8.12 The Variable Files Directory (/var)

This directory contains basically three types of files: log files, spool files, and temporary files created by applications. The name of the directory comes from the fact that all of these file types are variable in nature. It means these files grow and shrink on a continual basis. A sample directory subtree is shown in Figure 8-7.

Log Files

Log files are arranged in many directories depending on the type of log. Some of these are explained here.

/var/adm   This directory is used for log files related to system administration programs. The software installation or removal files are in the /var/adm/sw directory. Log files for cron are placed in the /var/adm/cron directory. Log files generated by syslog are in the /var/adm/syslog directory. Crash dumps are kept in the /var/adm/crash directory.

/var/opt   Application run-time files and log files are placed in this directory.

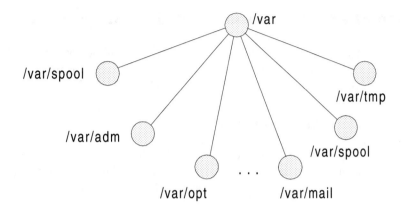

Figure 8–7 *Structure of the* /var *directory.*

Spool Files (/var/spool)

Spool files related to print services are kept in the /var/spool/lp directory. Spool files for electronic mail go into /var/mail. Other spool files are kept in a directory under /var/spool.

Temporary var files (/var/tmp)

Temporary files generated by some applications go into the /var/tmp directory. The mail system also keeps its temporary files in the /var/mail directory.

8.13 The lost+found Directory

These files are usually created by the fsck command, which is used to check file system integrity from time to time and at boot time. The files that have no valid links are copied to this directory. Each file system contains one lost+found directory.

Study Break

HP-UX Directory Tree

It is useful to have a look at your HP-UX system at this point. Log into HP-UX and try to construct a three-level directory tree. The first level is the root directory. All directories under the root directory are placed in the second level. In the third level, list all other directories found inside the directories at the second level.

8.14 Some Useful Commands Related to File System Hierarchy

If you understand file system hierarchy, it will not be difficult for you to find a file in UNIX. However, there are some useful commands to help you in your file search.

The which Command

If you want to find out in which directory an executable file or command is located, you can use the which command. For example, if you want to see in which directory the ls command is located, use the following procedure.

```
$ which ls
/usr/bin/ls
$
```

The which command finds all files that are located in your search path.

The whereis Command

Another command is whereis, which can search and locate source, binary, and manual pages. The following command shows two files that can be used as the cat command and the path to the manual page for the command.

```
$ whereis cat
cat: /sbin/cat /usr/bin/cat /usr/share/man/man1.Z/cat.1
$
```

More on the man Command

You can also use the man -k command to search all man pages related to a keyword. The command below searches man pages and shows all commands related to mkdir.

```
$ man -k mkdir
dosmkdir(1)              - make a DOS directory
mkdir(1)                - make a directory
mkdir(2)                - make a directory file
mkdirp(), rmdirp()(3G)  - create, remove directories in a
path nis_server, nis_mkdir, nis_rmdir, nis_servstate,
nis_stats, nis_getservlist, nis_freeservlist,
nis_freetags(3N) - miscellaneous NIS+ functions
nismkdir(1)             - create NIS+ directories
```

```
stmkdirs(1)              - Utility to build Scalable Type
fonts.dir and charsets.
dir files
$
```

Before you can use this command, you must create the `/usr/share/lib/whatis` file using the `catman` command. This file contains a list of all manual pages, with a short description of each command.

In the above listing generated by the `man -k mkdir` command, you can see that there is a number specified in parentheses after the name of a command. This number shows the section of the manual pages in which that entry is found. For example, you can see that both sections 1 and 2 contain a manual entry for `mkdir`. When you use the `man mkdir` command, the first manual page found by the `man` command is displayed. If you want to display a particular manual page, you need to specify the section as the argument to the `man` command. As an example, to display the manual page for `mkdir` in Section 2, you need to use the `man 2 mkdir` command instead of `man mkdir`.

■ Chapter Summary

In this chapter, you looked into the file system hierarchy of HP-UX. Now you know how different files and directories are arranged in the file system and which directories contain what types of files. Specifically, we studied the following concepts:

- Difference of static and dynamic parts of the file system. The static part contains those files and directories that don't change after installation of HP-UX. On the other hand, the dynamic part of the file system contains those files and directories that can change from time to time. The static directories are also called shared directories because these can be shared among many systems on a network.
- Arrangements of directories relative to root directories.
- Types of files contained in each directory.
- Directories that contain files related to HP-UX system administration.
- Directories where log files reside.
- Directories containing commands and other executable files.
- Place of installation of additional applications.
- Directory where the HP-UX kernel resides.
- Place of files and directories needed for system startup and shutdown.

In addition, you also use some commands to find particular types of files in HP-UX. You again used the man command and had an introduction to the sections of the manual pages.

I am of the strong opinion that if you understand the file system hierarchy well, half of the system administration task is done. This is the most important chapter in the first part of the book and you may need to have a look at it from time to time until you feel everything is at your fingertips.

▲ CHAPTER REVIEW QUESTIONS

1. Why are static directories also called shared directories?

2. If you install a new application on the system, where would you like to place its files? What is the recommended place for its configuration and log files?

3. What is the use of the /tmp directory?

4. What are spool files and where are they placed in the HP-UX file system hierarchy?

5. What are device files and how are they arranged?

6. What is the relation between physical disks and the directory structure of HP-UX?

7. What is the difference between the whereis and which commands?

▲ TEST YOUR KNOWLEDGE

1. *What can be determined about file name* /etc/named.boot?

    A. It is an executable program.

    B. It is a configuration file.

    C. It is a log file.

    D. It is a spool file.

2. *The HP-UX file system hierarchy is based on:*

    A. Berkley distribution (BSD).

    B. AT&T SVR4.

    C. a logical arrangement of files and directories, not based on BSD or AT&T SVR4.

    D. a random distribution of files and directories.

3. *Mail files are kept in which directory?*

    A. `/mail`

    B. `/var/spool/mail`

    C. `/home/mail`

    D. `/var/mail`

4. *What is true about the* `lost+found` *directory?*

    A. There is only one `lost+found` directory in a system.

    B. There are as many `lost+found` directories as the number of file systems.

    C. Common users create files in this directory if they find any file lost by another user.

    D. The system administrator creates files in it that announce the finding of lost files so that a user who lost a file can retrieve it from there.

5. *To find a command in the search path, we use the command:*

    A. `whatis`

    B. `which`

    C. `whois`

    D. `find`

6. *Which directory contains programs needed at boot time?*

    A. `/sbin`

    B. `/usr/sbin`

    C. `/startup`

    D. `/etc`

7. *The HP-UX kernel is located in:*

    A. `/kernel`

    B. `/var/kernel`

    C. `/usr`

    D. `/stand`

Working with the POSIX Shell and Job Control

The shell is an interactive program that gets user input, interprets it, and then takes necessary action accordingly. It acts like a command interpreter for the user. As soon as a command is received from a user, the shell looks for a matching intrinsic command and executes it. If it does not find an intrinsic command, it searches for a disk file corresponding to the command and executes it. During this process it substitutes any variables and other commands listed in the command line. It also handles I/O redirection and can execute batch files containing other UNIX commands and control structures.

You are already familiar with many of the shell features, such as environment variables, intrinsic and extrinsic commands, shell history, and shell configuration files. In this chapter, more features of the POSIX shell are presented. These include file name completion, setting terminal options, and job control. There is more information in this chapter on some of the features you are already

135

familiar with. These include shell history, command line editing, and substitution. We will start with a comparison of the capabilities of different UNIX shells and see what the subshells are. Then there is a brief introduction to the ulimit command that is used for limiting system resources. File name completion and shell history will be discussed next. Then you will find some more information on command line editing and substitution. In the substitution process, you will see how command substitution, variable substitution, and tilde substitution work. While working on different terminals, you may need to set some of the terminals' parameters, and you will learn the stty command that is used for this purpose. In the last part of the chapter, job control features of the POSIX shell are discussed.

9.1 POSIX Shell Capabilities

The POSIX shell is the default shell for HP-UX users. Other shells are also available on HP-UX. Important shells and their corresponding executable files are listed in Table 9-1.

Table 9–1 *Important UNIX Shells*

Name of Shell	Path to Shell File
POSIX shell	/usr/bin/sh
Bourne shell	/usr/old/bin/sh
Korn shell	/usr/bin/ksh
C shell	/usr/bin/csh

There are two other shells used in HP-UX. One of these is called the restricted shell (/usr/bin/rsh), which is used to provide restricted access to some users. The key shell (/usr/bin/keysh) is a context-sensitive shell that may be handy to use with HP terminals.

The capabilities of POSIX and other important shells available on HP-UX systems are presented in Table 9-2.

Table 9–2 *Features of Different UNIX Shells*

Feature	Description	POSIX	Bourne	Korn	C
History	Allows previous commands to be viewed and reused	Yes	No	Yes	Yes
Line editing	Allows a command line to be edited	Yes	No	Yes	No
File name completion	Enables the user to enter partial file names and complete these automatically by pressing certain keys	Yes	No	Yes	Yes
Command aliases	Allows creating aliases for standard commands	Yes	No	Yes	Yes
Job control	Allows for running jobs in background and moving jobs from background to foreground and vice versa	Yes	No	Yes	Yes

In the rest of this chapter, you will learn more about some of the capabilities of the POSIX shell.

Shell and Subshell

A subshell can be invoked inside a shell at any time by using the shell path as the command line. A subshell inherits all environment variables from the parent shell but doesn't inherit any shell variables. Sometimes a user may need to invoke a subshell to have a particular shell environment. The current shell also invokes subshells if required by a command. Shell scripts are usually executed in subshells. You can exit from a subshell using the `exit` command at any time.

Controlling Resources (ulimit)

The `ulimit` command is an intrinsic command of the POSIX shell and is used to limit user resources. If you specify the `-a` switch with this command, it lists current resource limits. A typical output of the command is as follows.

```
$ ulimit -a
time(seconds)           unlimited
file(blocks)            unlimited
data(kbytes)            135168
stack(kbytes)           8192
memory(kbytes)          unlimited
```

```
coredump(blocks)       4194303
nofiles(descriptors)  256
$
```

This command is very useful if you want to specify a limit for resources. For example, if you don't want the shell to create a core file larger than 1024 blocks, you can use following command.

```
$ ulimit -c 1024
$ ulimit -a
time(seconds)          unlimited
file(blocks)           unlimited
data(kbytes)           135168
stack(kbytes)          8192
memory(kbytes)         unlimited
coredump(blocks)       1024
nofiles(descriptors)  256
$
```

9.2   File Name Completion

File name completion is used when you are typing commands with long file names. Using this feature of the shell, you type in a few starting characters of the name of a file and then press the [Esc] key twice, and the shell completes the name of the file. Consider a directory that contains three files, and you want to see the contents of a file beta.

```
$ ls
alpha-334   alpha-434   beta
$ cat b Esc Esc
$ cat beta
```

As soon as you press the [Esc] key twice, the shell completes the file name as shown in the last line.

If there is more than one file that starts with the same characters you have typed, the shell completes the file name to the extent that all files have the same characters. After that you can press the [Esc] and [=] keys to list the available choices and then complete the file name by typing additional characters. Please see the next example where two files start with the letter a. By pressing the [Esc] key twice, the shell completes the file name up to alpha-. After that you can press the [Esc]-[=] keys to see the choices, and then complete the command using the usual command line editing method or by typing additional characters and again pressing the Esc key twice.

```
$ ls
alpha-334   alpha-434   beta
$ cat a Esc Esc
$ cat alpha- Esc  =
1) alpha-334
2) alpha-434
$
```

After displaying the matching files, you can type a few more characters on the command line to distinguish files and again press the Esc key twice to complete the file name.

The file name completion mechanism may be very useful when typing long commands with less keystrokes and without any error.

<h2>9.3 History and Reentering Commands</h2>

You have already seen that the shell keeps the history of the commands you type. The history command can be used to list previously used commands. You can use an option to list a particular number of previous commands. To list the three previous commands, you use:

```
$ history -3
457      cat /etc/profile
458      more /home/boota/.profile
459      ls -l /etc|more
$
```

To list a range of commands, you provide the starting and ending numbers of the commands in the history.

```
$ history 451 453
451      date
452      ls
453      mkdir tmp
```

To reexecute a previous command, you use the r command with the command number. The r command executes a numbered command from the history and prints the command as well as its result on stdout. In the next example, the command executed is the date command.

```
$ r 451
date
Wed Oct 13 22:33:17 EDT 1999
$
```

9.4   Command Line Editing

As you saw earlier, previous commands can be reused with the help of the history feature. But the history feature executes commands without any modification. If you want to execute a previous command with some modification, you can use the vi editing features for command editing. If you press the Esc-k keystroke combination, the last command appears on your command prompt. If you continue pressing k, you can go back as far as the history supports. To go to the next command, you can press the j key during this process. If you want to edit a particular command, first bring that command on your command prompt using this procedure and then use l to move right and h to move left. As you can see, all of these are vi commands. You can use other vi commands to insert or delete any text on the command line.

Use of vi commands with the command line editing feature is controlled by the EDITOR environment variable. The value of this variable must be set to vi to use vi commands.

Study Break

Practicing POSIX Shell Capabilities

Login with your name and go to directory /usr/bin. Type the partial command ll la and then press the Esc key twice. You will find that the shell does not complete the command. Now use the Esc-= keystroke combination and you will see a list similar to that shown here.

1) landiag
2) last
3) lastb
4) lastcomm

The shell did not complete the command when you pressed the Esc key twice because there are four files that start with the combination la. Now add three more characters to your command, making it ll lastc, and then press Esc twice. This time the shell completes the command.

Use the history command to list the last 10 commands in the history. Try to run the fifth-to-last command using the r command. Press the Esc-k keystroke combination to bring the last executed command to the command prompt and edit it to run the second-to-last command.

9.5 Substitution

There are three types of substitutions used in the POSIX shell. These will be explained next.

Variable Substitution

In a variable substitution, a variable name is used with the $ sign in the command line. The value of the variable is then substituted in the command line before it is executed. For example, the echo command prints whatever it receives on the command line.

```
$ echo HOME
HOME
$ echo $HOME
/home/boota
$
```

In the first case, the echo command printed what you typed at the command line. In the second case, echo substituted the variable $HOME and printed the value of the HOME variable.

Command Substitution

The result of another command can also be substituted in a command at the command line. Here I have used the same example of the echo command.

```
$ echo date
date
$ echo $(date)
Wed Oct 13 22:53:19 EDT 1999
$ echo `date`
Wed Oct 13 22:53:29 EDT 1999
$
```

In the first case, the echo command prints the word "date." In the second and third cases, the date command is executed and its result is substituted in the echo command.

Tilde Substitution

Tilde substitution is governed by the following rules.

- A ~/ is replaced by the HOME variable.

- A ~+ is replaced by the PWD variable.
- A ~- is replace by the OLDPWD variable.

Where HOME points to your home directory, PWD has the value of the current directory and OLDPWD has the value of the previous working directory. A good use of tilde substitution is to go to your home directory from any other directory. See the following where you move from the /etc directory to your home directory (/home/boota) using tilde substitution.

```
$ pwd
/etc
$ cd ~/
$ pwd
/home/boota
$
```

9.6 Setting Terminal Parameters

A variety of terminals having different capabilities are used with HP-UX systems. Many of these terminals have different keyboards and key mappings. As an example, different keys may be used for the delete and backspace characters on different types of terminals. HP-UX provides the facility to change and modify control key mappings with the *Set Terminal Type* (stty) command. This command can be used to map a certain control character to a key sequence. The stty command with no arguments shows current control commands and their respective key mappings. It also shows current baud rate, start/stop bits, parity, flow control, and other information when invoked with the -a option.

```
$ stty -a
speed 9600 baud; line = 0;
rows = 24; columns = 132
min = 4; time = 0;
intr = ^C; quit = ^\; erase = ^H; kill = ^U
eof = ^D; eol = ^@; eol2 = <undef>; swtch = <undef>
stop = ^S; start = ^Q; susp = <undef>; dsusp = <undef>
werase = <undef>; lnext = <undef>
parenb -parodd cs7 -cstopb hupcl -cread -clocal -loblk -
crts
-ignbrk brkint ignpar -parmrk -inpck istrip -inlcr -igncr
icrnl -iuclc
ixon -ixany ixoff -imaxbel -rtsxoff -ctsxon -ienqak
isig icanon -iexten -xcase echo echoe echok -echonl -noflsh
```

```
-echoctl -echoprt -echoke -flusho -pendin
opost -olcuc onlcr -ocrnl -onocr -onlret -ofill -ofdel -
tostop
$
```

If you want to set the underscore character (_) as the backspace key, you can use the following command. After that, you can use the underscore key to work as the backspace key.

```
$ stty erase _
$ stty -a
speed 9600 baud; line = 0;
rows = 24; columns = 132
min = 4; time = 0;
intr = ^C; quit = ^\; erase = _; kill = ^U
eof = ^D; eol = ^@; eol2 = <undef>; swtch = <undef>
stop = ^S; start = ^Q; susp = <undef>; dsusp = <undef>
werase = <undef>; lnext = <undef>
parenb -parodd cs7 -cstopb hupcl -cread -clocal -loblk -
crts
-ignbrk brkint ignpar -parmrk -inpck istrip -inlcr -igncr
icrnl -iuclc
ixon -ixany ixoff -imaxbel -rtsxoff -ctsxon -ienqak
isig icanon -iexten -xcase echo echoe echok -echonl -noflsh
-echoctl -echoprt -echoke -flusho -pendin
opost -olcuc onlcr -ocrnl -onocr -onlret -ofill -ofdel -
tostop
$
```

As you can see in the fourth line of the output, the new setting shown by the stty command, the value of *erase* is changed. Usually, people establish such settings in the startup files. If a setting is needed for all system users, the system administrator sets it as /etc/profile.

9.7 Job Control

A job is a running process in memory. Job control is a shell feature that moves jobs from the foreground to background, suspends running jobs, and restarts suspended jobs. You can also put a job into a wait state, where it waits for another job to finish and then restarts. The shell provides a mechanism to carry out these tasks with the help of some intrinsic shell commands. The process of job control is explained next.

Foreground and Background Jobs

Whenever a user starts a program or command, in UNIX terminology a job is initiated. To start another job, you have to wait for the job to finish and get the shell command prompt again. All these jobs are *foreground* jobs, as the user can interact with the running program. The user can't issue another command until the job is finished and the command prompt is back. This simply means that when a job is running in the foreground, no other job can be started. If you want to start more than one job simultaneously, you need to start them in the background. A *background* job is one that gives you back the shell command prompt after it starts running. For example, a big number-crunching program may need hours to finish and you just don't want to wait for it to finish. Instead, you would like do some other tasks. Background jobs are run by the shell but at the same time the shell lets you submit other jobs.

To start a job in the background you can put the & symbol at the end of your command prompt. Usually, the jobs that don't need any interactive input are started in the background. You may also run programs in the background that need input by redirecting stdin to some file on the disk. If a background job sends its output to stdout, it is displayed on your terminal screen unless you have redirected it. Redirection and pipes can be used with background jobs. Next is a typical output of a job started in the background.

```
$ ll /usr >mylist &
[1]     11633
$
```

Once a job is started in the background, the shell prints the job ID and *process ID* (PID) numbers of the command that started the job on the terminal display. You can then use this job ID to bring a job into the foreground at any time. You can also list background-running jobs with the jobs command.

```
$ jobs
[1] + Stopped                     vi myfile
[2] - Running                     vi file2
$
```

The jobs command lists all background jobs, job IDs, and whether these jobs are running or stopped. A plus symbol (+) in the output of this command shows that this is the current job; a minus sign (-) shows which job is scheduled to be run next after the current job. A -1 switch with the jobs command shows the PID of all jobs.

Jobs may be in a running or stopped state. A job may be stopped if it needs input that is not available or is suspended by the user. When a job is completed, it goes into the *Done* state. If you run a job in the background and it tries to read something from stdin, it is automatically stopped by the shell until brought into the foreground by the user.

Suspending a Foreground Job

Many times you start a job in the foreground and then you want to do something else without abandoning the program running in the foreground. For example, you may have started the vi editor and you need to copy files without abandoning the editor. The POSIX shell provides a mechanism to suspend a current job temporarily. To suspend a running job, you can use the key sequence represented by the susp value in the stty -a output, often defined as CTRL-z. Pressing that key sequence suspends the current job and gives you the command prompt. The job is *suspended*, and if you use the jobs command, you will see the job is stopped. You will also see a plus (+) symbol showing that this is the current job.

```
$ jobs
[1] + Stopped                    vi myfile
[2] - Stopped                    vi file2
$
```

To find the value of the susp sequence, use the stty -a command. If this value is not set, you can use the stty command to set its value as follows.

```
$ stty susp ^z
$
```

The (^) symbol shows the control key. After this command, you can use the CTRL-z key sequence to suspend a job.

Resuming Suspended Jobs and
Bringing Background Jobs to the Foreground

All suspended jobs can be resumed with the *foreground* (fg) command. The same command is used to bring background jobs to the foreground. To bring a job to the foreground, you need to know the job id with the jobs command. If you don't specify any job ID, the current job is brought into the foreground. For example, when you suspend the vi editor to do some other work, the fg command will bring the vi screen back, and you can use it again in the normal way.

```
$ jobs
[1] + Stopped                          vi myfile
[2] - Stopped                          vi file2
$ fg %2
```

Job numbers are used with the percent (%) symbol with the fg command. You can also use the command name with the fg command, which is sometimes more convenient when writing shell scripts.

Study Break

Job Control

Use the stty command to set the value of susp equal to CTRL–z. Start vi editor to edit a file file1. Suspend this vi session using the CTRL–z combination. Use the jobs command to list background jobs. Start another vi session with file file2. Also suspend this session. Bring the first vi session to the foreground using the fg command. Close the editor and then bring the second vi session to the foreground and close it.

Moving Jobs to the Background

As soon as you suspend a foreground job, it goes into a *stopped* state. You can start the job, keeping it in background with the bg (background) command. To send a foreground job into the background, first suspend it and then use the bg command. If there is more than one suspended job, you need to provide a job ID to the bg command to bring a particular job into running state from stopped state. The following sequence of commands lists background jobs and then changes the state of job number 2 to running.

```
$ jobs
[1] + Stopped                          vi myfile
[2] - Stopped                          vi file2
$ bg %2
[1] + Stopped                          vi myfile
[2] - Running                          vi file2
$
```

Stopping a Running Job

There is no direct way to stop a running job. We can, however, adopt an alternate method to stop a running job. We can bring a background job into the foreground and then suspend it. You may need to stop a running job temporarily when it is taking a lot of system resources and you want to run a more important job.

Waiting for Background Jobs to Finish

At any point, if you want to wait for background jobs to be finished, just use the `wait` command. This command stops the command prompt until all background jobs are finished. If you want to stop the `wait` command, just press the $\boxed{\texttt{Enter}}$ key on your keyboard. We can also wait for a particular job to finish by specifying the job number as an argument to the `wait` command.

```
$ wait %2
```

■ Chapter Summary

In this chapter, you learned more features of the POSIX shell. The chapter started with a brief comparison of capabilities of widely used shells in UNIX. A brief note on the subshell was the next topic. You used the `ulimit` command to limit use of system resources. The POSIX shell feature of file name completion was presented next. Here you learned how you can use the $\boxed{\texttt{Esc}}$ and $\boxed{\texttt{=}}$ keys to complete partially typed file names. You used the `history` and `r` commands to list and execute previous commands. You also used command line editing features and learned that the `EDITOR` environment variable controls which editor commands will be used for command line editing. Another POSIX shell feature is substitution, where you found some examples of variable, command, and tilde substitution. After learning how to set terminal parameters, you moved to job control. Here you created foreground jobs, suspended them, and moved them to the background. You also learned how to bring background jobs to the foreground. The commands used here are the intrinsic shell commands. You used the `jobs` command to list current jobs, `fg` to bring a job to the foreground, `bg` to send a job to the background, and `wait` to wait for the completion of a particular job.

In the next two chapters, you will be learning shell programming, where you will write shell scripts and use flow control structure and shell loops to control the flow of your scripts.

▲ CHAPTER REVIEW QUESTIONS

1. List two features that are present in the POSIX shell but not in the Bourne shell.

2. What types of substitutions are used in the POSIX shell? What are their advantages?

3. What is meant by job control?

4. What are the differences between foreground and background jobs?

▲ TEST YOUR KNOWLEDGE

1. *The default HP-UX shell is:*
   A. Bourne Shell
   B. Korn Shell
   C. POSIX Shell
   D. C Shell

2. *You are in a directory having three files,* `file1`, `file2`, *and* `afile`. *You type a command* `ls f` *and then press the* Esc *key followed by the* = *key. What happens?*
   A. The shell completes the command.
   B. The typed command is erased.
   C. You get a list of files in the directory.
   D. You get a list of files in the directory starting with f.

3. *You use the* `date` *command to see the current system time. Just after that, you press the* Esc *key followed by the* j *key. What happens?*
   A. The previous command is displayed on the command prompt.
   B. The `date` command is executed.
   C. The current shell is suspended.
   D. Nothing happens.

4. *What does the command* `r 3` *do?*
   A. It reads three lines of user input and then displays them on the screen.
   B. It repeats the last three commands.
   C. It returns three steps back in the command history.
   D. It executes command number 3 in the command history.

5. *For what purpose is the* stty *command used?*

    A. setting baud rate

    B. setting terminal control characters

    C. setting flow control

    D. all of the above

6. *Your home directory is* /home/boota. *You moved from your home directory to the* /etc *directory. How can you go back to your home directory?*

    A. using the cd HOME command

    B. using the cd ~/ command

    C. using the cd OLDPWD command

    D. all of the above

7. *A job running in the foreground can be suspended by:*

    A. the bg command

    B. the fg command

    C. using the susp control character

    D. using the suspend command

8. *Background jobs are always in:*

    A. a suspended state

    B. a stopped state

    C. a running state

    D. none of the above

Introduction to Shell Programming

Shell programs or *shell scripts* are files containing HP-UX commands, comments, and control structures. These are like batch processes where commands are interpreted and executed by the shell line-by-line. Any command that can be executed at the shell prompt can be included in a shell program. Comments begin with a pound character (#) and are not executed by the shell. The POSIX shell allows use of control structures that can be utilized for branching and looping within the shell program. These control structures use test conditions for conditional branching and looping.

The shell provides very powerful features for writing shell programs. Many of the shell programs are used at startup and shutdown time and will be discussed in Chapter 13. These programs are shipped with HP-UX and provide control over many critical tasks related to system administration.

Shell programs are also used by system administrators to automate routine jobs. Files containing the shell commands are executed at specified times using the HP-UX cron facility. Mostly shell programs help in controlling the size of log files, cleaning temporary files, and reporting errors to the system administrator through email.

In this chapter, you will start with simple programs and analyze the parts of a typical shell program. Then you will learn how variables can be used to pass information to a shell program. Command line parameters can be passed to a program and utilized within it. The command line parameters may be useful for passing data or control information that is used during execution. Many times you may need to interact with your shell programs during the execution. You may also need to enter some values at run time. Interactive programs are very helpful for such applications, and you will learn how to read user input during their execution. When a program finishes execution, it returns a result code to the shell that is used to determine if the program terminated successfully. You will learn the use of *exit codes*, which are used to report any errors that occurred during the execution.

Variables are used to store values temporarily within the programs. In Section 10.2, you will learn how to utilize these variables inside shell programs. Before you can use some control structures, you need to test a condition. The result of this test allows you to make a decision. In the last part of the chapter, you will see how to use the `test` command and make decisions depending on its result.

This chapter includes the basic features of shell programming. The terms shell program and shell script are used interchangeably in this and the next chapter. In the next chapter, you will find some more-complicated shell programs containing loop structures.

10.1 Anatomy of a Shell Program

Let us go directly to our first program and analyze it. I have used the file name `script-00` for this program. Contents of this file are shown below using the `cat` command.

```
$ cat script-00
#!/usr/bin/sh
# This is to show what a script looks like.
echo "Our first script"
echo "----------------"
echo   # This inserts an empty line in output.
echo "We are currently in the following directory"
pwd
echo
echo "This directory contains the following files"
ls
$
```

Before looking into the program and explaining what each line does, let us see what happens if we execute it. We execute it from the current directory with the command line:

```
$ ./script-00
Our first script
----------------

We are currently in the following directory
/home/boota

This directory contains the following files
PHCO_18132.depot   myfile              phco_18132.txt
PHCO_18132.text    phco_18131.txt      script-00
$
```

The program prints some messages on your terminal screen and then shows the current directory and lists files in this directory.

Let us have a closer look at it. Basically, any shell program has three parts.

1. the full path of the subshell that will be used to execute the program
2. some comment lines
3. commands and control structures

I will explain these one-by-one.

Which Subshell Will Execute It?

The current shell executes all programs unless otherwise specified. In case you need to execute a program in a specific shell (Bourne, C, or POSIX), you can specify it in your program. In that case, a subshell is created as soon as a program starts execution. The first program line shows which HP-UX shell will be used to execute commands found in the program. This line always starts with the "#!" character combination and shows the full path of the executable program that will be used as shell. All HP-UX extrinsic commands have the same syntax no matter which shell is used to execute them. The difference is in the execution of intrinsic commands. For example, the method of setting a shell variable in the C shell is different from the one used in the POSIX shell. So you need to execute your program in the proper shell. Depending on the information provided, your current shell will spawn the appropriate subshell to execute the program. As an example, you can't use the setenv command in a program that is expected to be run in a POSIX or Bourne shell because this command is specific to the C shell only.

In the example used here, the subshell that will be used to execute the program is /usr/bin/sh, which is the POSIX shell. You can use other shells, such as C, by changing this to /usr/bin/csh. It is a good habit to provide the shell name in the program so that if somebody else is using it in a different shell, the correct subshell is created and the program runs without any error.

Comments in a Shell Program

The second line in our example program contains a comment. A comment is that part of a program that is not executed. It is used for providing reference information about the program.

All comments start with a pound sign (#) except for the special combination used in the first line for specifying the subshell. A comment can be placed anywhere in the file. If a line starts with the "#" sign, all of the line is treated as a comment. If the "#" sign is placed somewhere else in a line, anything after that sign is considered a comment. In the example program script-00, comments are used in the second and fifth lines. The second line starts with the "#" sign, so all of the line is a comment, and nothing in this line is executed. The fifth line contains a command echo and after that a comment string. The command is executed but the comment is ignored.

Commands and Control Structures

This is the most important part of the program, where you put actual commands that are executed. The commands may be simple ones that the shell executes one-by-one, in the order they are placed in the program file. In the example program, we have used the commands pwd, echo, and ls. All of these commands are executed in order and their result is displayed on your terminal screen as you have already seen. The echo command without any argument just prints a blank line.

The control structures are used for branching and looping. The decision of branching or looping is made depending on the result of a test performed on some variables or constants. We will discuss branching at the end of this chapter and looping in the next chapter.

Steps for Creating a Shell Program

A shell program is created in two basic steps. In the first step, a file is created that contains commands and control structures. This file is saved on the disk. Usually this file is not executable. In the second step, you need to modify file permissions to make it executable. If you are not sharing the program with others, you can use the chmod u+x command to make it executable. If you are sharing your program with other users, you need to set the appropriate permissions for this purpose.

You can also execute a shell program without the execute bit set if you use the program name as an argument to sh as shown below.

```
$ sh script-00
```

After setting appropriate execute permissions, you can execute a program. Care must be taken while naming shell programs such that the names do not match with any existing HP-UX commands.

If the current directory is not included in the PATH variable, you will not be able to execute the program by simply typing its name on the command line. For that purpose you need to specify the full path of the file. You can give the full path on the command line in either the absolute or relative form. The better way is the relative form, where you use ". /" (dot slash) to refer to the current directory.

Note

Many times new script writers wonder why the script is not being executed, even though they have placed the correct commands and have the execution bit set. The reason is the directory in which they are placing the program is not included in the **PATH** variable, and they are not specifying the path to the file explicitly. Sometimes it may happen that your current directory is included in the **PATH** variable at the end. When you execute your program without specifying the full path to the file, you get unexpected results. This is the case when you use a file name for a program that already exists on your system. What happens is the shell starts searching the file name from the first directory specified in your **PATH** variable. It gets the *other* file before it reaches the current directory and executes it. So it is always recommended to use ". /" when you are testing your program for the first time to make sure that the shell is indeed executing the correct file.

Debugging Shell Programs

Debugging shell programs is a tricky business. There are many simple to complex procedures that can be applied for this purpose. Here is the simplest and basic method. You replace the first line of the program `#!/usr/bin/sh` with `#!/usr/bin/sh -x`. After that, when you execute the program, it displays each line on your terminal screen before executing it. The actual line present in the program is shown with a plus (+) sign in the start of the line. After that, its output is displayed. This method can be used to identify which program line is causing a problem. Below is the output of our example program `script-00` after this modification. Note that comments are not displayed.

```
$ ./script-00
+ echo Our first script
Our first script
+ echo ----------------
----------------
+ echo

+ echo We are currently in the following directory
We are currently in the following directory
+ pwd
/home/operator
+ echo

+ echo This directory contains the following files
This directory contains the following files
+ ls
PHCO_18132.depot   myfile           phco_18132.txt
PHCO_18132.text    phco_18131.txt   script-00
$
```

Study Break

Writing a Shell Program

If you are new to shell programming, this is the time to write your first shell program. Use the `vi` editor to create a new file named `myscript`. Use only one command (`who`) to list users currently logged into the system. Save the file and set its execution bit using the command `chmod u+x myscript`. Try to execute it and see if it is doing what you intend it to do.

10.2 Using Variables

Variables can be set and used in the same way you have used them on the command line. Any variable that is set during the execution of a shell program is not visible after the execution is finished. Shell programs can read environment variables and can also modify their values for the duration of the execution of the program. Variables are also a useful way of passing data to shell programs. Let us see another program named script-01 where we have set two variables TAB and FUR. These variables are then displayed using the echo command. The program is shown below.

```
$ cat script-01
#!/usr/bin/sh
echo "Use of Variables"
echo "----------------"
echo
TAB=table
FUR=furniture
echo "The $TAB is an example of $FUR"
$
```

When this program is executed, the results are:

```
$ ./script-01
Use of Variables
----------------

The table is an example of furniture
$
```

Note that these two variables are not available after the execution of the program is finished. If you try to display the values of any of these variables from the command line after executing the shell program, you will get the following message.

```
$ echo $TAB
sh: TAB: Parameter not set.
$
```

Now let us try to change the value of the TAB variable within the program from "table" to "chair" using the following program example (script-02).

```
$ cat script-02
#!/usr/bin/sh
echo "Use of Variables"
echo "----------------"
echo
TAB=table
FUR=furniture
echo "The $TAB is an example of $FUR"
TAB=chair
Echo "After change"
echo "The $TAB is an example of $FUR"
$
```

When this program is executed, the results are as follows. Note that the line used for printing the text is the same; only the variable value is changed.

```
$ ./script-01
Use of Variables
----------------

The table is an example of furniture
After change
The chair is an example of furniture
$
```

Passing Data Through Environment Variables

Shell programs can access environment variables. The example below is script-03, which prints the values of the PATH and TERM environment variables.

```
$ cat script-03
#!/usr/bin/sh
echo "The TERM variable is"
echo $TERM
echo "The current PATH setting is"
echo $PATH
$
```

The result after execution is:

```
$ ./script-03
The TERM variable is
ansi
The current PATH setting is
```

```
/baan/bse/bin:/usr/bin:/usr/ccs/bin:/usr/contrib/bin:/opt/
nettladm/bin:/opt/fc/bin:/opt/fcms/bin:/opt/upgrade/bin:/
opt/pd/bin:/usr/contrib/bin/X11:/usr/bin/X11:/opt/hparray/
bin:/opt/perf/bin:/opt/ignite/bin:/usr/sbin:/sbin:.
$
```

We can pass data to a program by using environment variables. As you already know, we can change the value of an environment variable in a program, but that change gets lost as soon as the program terminates. In script-04, we get an environment variable COLOR having value red and then change it to green. After execution of the program, when we check the value of the COLOR variable, it is still red. Let us first see the contents of script-04 and then execute it.

```
$ cat script-04
#!/usr/bin/sh
echo "The current COLOR variable is"
echo $COLOR
COLOR=green
echo "The new COLOR variable is"
echo $COLOR
$
```

Before executing this program, you need to set and export the COLOR variable. You can verify the exported value of the variable by using the echo command. After you execute the program, it changes the value and prints the new value green. When the program finishes, you use the echo command again to check the variable value, and you find out that it is the same as it was before executing the program.

```
$ COLOR=red
$ export COLOR
$ echo $COLOR
red
$ ./script-04
The current COLOR variable is
red
The new COLOR variable is
green
$
$echo $COLOR
red
$
```

10.3 Command Line Arguments

You can pass information to a shell program using command line arguments, the same as any other HP-UX command. These command line arguments can be used within the shell program. They are stored in variables, accessible within the program.

Using Command Line Arguments, or Positional Parameters

The command line arguments are stored in variables that show the position of the argument in the command line. That is why these are also called positional parameters. The variables that store command line arguments have names from $0 to $9. Beginning with the tenth command line argument, the argument number is enclosed in braces. The variable names are shown in Table 10-1.

Table 10–1 *Variables for Storing Command Line Arguments*

Variable Name	Description
$0	Shows value of the command itself (program name)
$1	First command line argument
$2	Second command line argument
.	.
.	.
.	.
$9	Ninth command line argument
${10}	Tenth command line argument
$#	Total number of command line arguments
$*	A space-separated list of command line arguments

Let's see script-05, which shows how many command line arguments are provided, a list of all arguments, and the value of the first argument. This program is now shown using the cat command.

```
$ cat script-05
#!/usr/bin/sh
echo "Total number of command line arguments is: $#"
echo "These arguments are: $*"
echo "The first argument is: $1"
$
```

When you execute the program with three arguments red, green, and blue, the result is as shown below.

```
$ ./script-05 red green blue
Total number of command line arguments is: 3
These arguments are: red green blue
The first argument is: red
$
```

The shift Command

The shift command is used to move the command line arguments one position left. The first argument is lost when you use the shift command. Shifting command line arguments is useful when you perform a similar action to all arguments, one-by-one, without changing the variable name. The shift command throws away the left-most variable (argument number 1) and reassigns values to the remaining variables. The value in $2 moves to $1, the value in $3 moves to $2, and so on. Let's modify script-05 into script-06 as shown below using the cat command.

```
$ cat script-06
#!/usr/bin/sh
echo "Total number of command line arguments is: $#"
echo "These arguments are: $*"
echo "The first argument is: $1"
shift
echo "New first argument after shift: $1"
shift
echo "First argument after another shift: $1"
$
```

Now let's execute script-06 with the same three arguments we used with script-05. You can see from the next result that after every shift, a new value is assigned to $1. This value is the variable that is just on the right side of $1 (i.e., $2).

```
$ ./script-06 red green blue
Total number of command line arguments is: 3
These arguments are: red green blue
The first argument is: red
New first argument after shift: green
First argument after another shift: blue
$
```

During the first shift operation, $1 value is lost forever and can't be recovered by the program. The shift command can also do multiple shift operations in one step. For this you need to supply an argument to the shift command. For example, shift 2 will shift two arguments in one step, such that the old values of $1 and $2 will be lost, the value of $3 will be assigned to $1, the value of $4 will be assigned to $2, and so on.

Study Break

Use of Variables in Shell Programs

Variables play an important role in shell programs. To have some practice with the shell variables, modify script-06 so that before using the shift command, you store the value contained in $1 in another variable. Use the shift 2 command in the program and then try to print the $1 variable. Print the old value of the $1 variable using the echo command.

10.4 Interactive Shell Programs

Interactive shell programs can read user input at run time with the help of the read command. Most of the time you will use the echo command to display a message before the read command is executed. This message informs the user of what the program is expecting. These programs are used in situations where a program first checks some system parameter and then requires user input to perform an operation on it. As an example, if you want to talk to another user on the system, you may first want to see who is logged into the system. After getting a list of users, you may initiate conversation with a particular user using the talk command.

The read Command

The read command takes one line of input from the user and assigns it to a variable. The variable name is provided as an argument to the read command. After entering some text, the user presses the ⌈Enter⌋ key. Below is script-07, which lists all users currently logged into the system and then waits for you to enter a user name. After getting the user name, it initiates conversation with that user using the talk command.

```
$ cat script-07
#!/usr/bin/sh
echo "Currently logged in users are:"
```

```
who
echo
echo
echo "Enter the name of the user to whom you want to talk"
read NAME
echo "initiating talk with $NAME"
talk $NAME
$
```

After you select a user, the program rings the other party and displays a message asking the other user to respond to your talk request. If that user accepts your request, a talk window appears. Before the talk window appears, the program executes as shown below. Here you initiate a talk session with a user **linda**.

```
$ ./script-07
Currently logged in users are:
boota        pts/t0        Oct 18 17:53
linda        pts/0         Oct 18 22:13


Enter the name of the user to whom you want to talk
linda

<The talk window appears which covers the full screen>
```

The echo Command

You have already used the echo command to display text on your screen. This command uses escape characters that can be used to format the displayed text to enhance its readability. The escape characters used with the echo command are listed in Table 10-2.

Table 10-2 *Escape Characters Used with the echo Command*

Character	Effect
\a	Alert character (beep)
\b	Backspace
\c	Suppress new line at the end of displayed text
\f	Form feed
\n	Insert a new line character
\r	Carriage return
\t	Insert a tab character
\\	Backslash
\nnn	Character having ASCII value nnn in the octal format. The first n is 0.

In the example of `script-07`, the cursor goes to the next line after the message, "Enter the name of the user to whom you want to talk". If you want the cursor to stay in the same line until you enter the user name, you need to suppress the new line character by using \c in the `echo` command as follows.

```
echo "Enter user name to whom you want to talk \c"
```

You can also use \a to add a beep to your program as soon as this command is executed.

10.5 Exit Codes

When a program terminates its execution, it returns a result code to the shell that shows the termination or *exit* status of the program. In the case of termination after successful execution, this code is zero. If the program terminates abnormally, the exit code is *not* equal to zero. The exit code of the last executed program can be checked by displaying the value of a special variable `$?`. See the following examples to get an idea of how the exit code works.

```
$ ls
PHCO_18132.depot    phco_18132.txt       script-02
PHCO_18132.text     scr                  script-03
phco_18131.txt      script-01            script-05
$ echo $?
0
$
$ mv
Usage: mv [-f] [-i] [-e warn|force|ignore] f1 f2
       mv [-f] [-i] [-e warn|force|ignore] f1 ... fn d1
       mv [-f] [-i] [-e warn|force|ignore] d1 d2
$ echo $?
1
$
```

The first command is the `ls` command, which executed successfully. After that, you used the `echo $?` command, and it showed you an exit code zero. The second command was `mv`. You did not provide any argument to this command, which is a must, so the command terminated abnormally and returned a value of 1.

You can use `exit` codes in your program to check the execution status of any commands used within the program. If a command used in the program did not execute successfully, you can make corrective measures.

You can also terminate your shell program at any point by using the `exit` command. The `exit` command can be supplied with an argument that will show the exit status of your program and can be used for debugging purposes. As an example, if you are writing a program and it needs at least one command line argument, you can terminate its execution if no argument is supplied.

10.6 The test Command

Branching decisions are made depending on the result of a `test` command. The `test` command can perform tests on numeric and string data as well as on files. The `test` command returns a true or false value. The true value is always zero, while false is a number other than zero. Usually this number is one. You can check the result code of the `test` command to make a branching decision. The `test` command can be used in *explicit* or *implicit* modes. In the explicit mode, the `test` command is used as follows.

```
$ test "ABC" = "abc"
```

In the implicit mode, the word "`test`" is not there; square brackets are used instead.

```
$ [ "ABC" = "abc" ]
```

The command does not print anything on the terminal screen. The result code can be checked using the `$?` variable as explained earlier in the chapter.

Testing Numeric Values

Tests can be performed to compare two or more integers. The relations that can be used with numeric data are shown in Table 10-3.

Table 10–3 *Numeric Tests*

Relation	Description
-eq	Equality check
-ne	Not equal
-lt	Less than
-gt	Greater than
-le	Less than or equal to
-ge	Greater than or equal to

Numeric testing will be used in shell programs later in this chapter.

Testing String Values

The string values can be checked for equality and nonequality. Other than that, a single string can be tested if it has a zero length or not. The string operations are shown in Table 10-4.

Table 10–4 *String Tests*

Operation	Description
string1 = *string2*	True if *string1* and *string2* are equal
string1 != *string2*	True if *string1* is not equal to *string2*
-z *string*	True if *string* length is zero
-n *string*	True if *string* length is nonzero
string	True if *string* length is nonzero

Testing Files

Testing on files can be performed in many ways. Some of these are shown in Table 10-5. A list of other supported file tests can be found using the man sh-posix command.

Table 10–5 *File Tests*

Operation	Description
-d *file*	True if the *file* is a directory
-f *file*	True if the *file* exists and is a normal file (not a directory)
-s *file*	True if the *file* is more than zero bytes in length
-r *file*	True if the *file* is readable
-w *file*	True if the *file* is writable
-e *file*	True if the *file* exists
-L *file*	True if the *file* is a symbolic link
file1 −nt *file2*	True if *file1* is newer than *file2*
file1 −ot *file2*	True if *file1* is older than *file2*
-x file	True if the *file* is executable

For example, if file file1 exists, and you use the following command to check its existence, you will get an exit code of zero (true).

```
$ [ -f file1 ]
$
$ echo $?
0
$
```

Testing with Logical Operators

Logical operations can be performed on two expressions with one of the logical operators shown in Table 10-6.

Table 10–6 *Logical Operators*

Operation	Description
expr1 −o *expr2*	Logical OR, true if either *expr1* or *expr2* is true
expr1 −a *expr2*	Logical AND, true if both *expr1* and *expr2* are true
! *expr*	Logical NOT, true if *expr* is false

The following code segment tests files represented by the first two command line arguments and prints a message if both files exist.

```
#!/usr/bin/sh
if [ -f $1 -a -f $2 ]
then
    echo "Test successful"
fi
```

10.7 Branching

Two types of branching are used in shell programming. One of these is represented by the *if* structure and the other one by the *case* structure. In this section, you will learn how to use both of these branches. You will also find some useful examples of shell programs.

The if-then-fi Structure

The `if-then-fi` structure is used to check a condition with the help of a `test` command. If the `test` returns a true value, then an action is performed. If the `test` returns a false value (not true), the action part of the program is not executed. The general syntax of this structure is as follows.

```
if expr
then
    action
fi
```

where *expr* is a test performed on some variables or constants. The action is a set of one or more commands that are executed if the test returned a true value. This is shown in Figure 10-1 using a flow diagram.

Previously you have seen how to check the number of arguments on the command line. You can write a shell program to check the number of arguments and print an error message if there is no argument on the command line. The program script-08 does the same thing and is listed here using the cat command.

```
$ cat script-08
#!/usr/bin/sh
if [ "$#" -lt 1 ]
then
    echo "Error: No arguments provided on command line"
    exit 3
fi
echo "Program terminated normally"
$
```

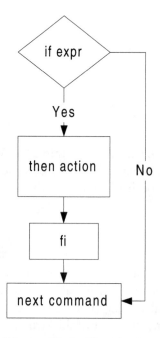

Figure 10–1 *The* if-then-fi *structure.*

When you execute this program without any command line argument, you will see the following message on your screen.

```
Error: No arguments provided on command line
```

If you check the return code using the `echo $?` command, a value of 3 will appear. On the other hand, if you provide at least one argument on the command line, the return code will be zero and the message on your screen will be:

```
Program terminated normally
```

This is a useful way of checking the number of command line arguments if your program expects a fixed number of arguments. For example, the `cp` command requires two command line arguments showing the source and destination paths of the file being copied. If you don't provide two arguments, the command prints an error message.

The if-then-else-fi Structure

This structure is used when you want to perform one of two actions, depending on the result of a test. The general syntax of the structure is:

```
if expr
then
    action1
else
    action2
fi
```

If the result of *expr* is true, *action1* is performed. In the other case, *action2* is performed. Each of *action1* and *action2* may be a set of one or more commands. The flow chart of this structure is shown in Figure 10-2. You can modify `script-08` so that it accepts two file names as argument and copies the first file to the second file. If there are not exactly two arguments, it tells you that you did not provide two arguments. It then displays all of the arguments it received from the command line. The modified form is `script-09`.

```
#!/usr/bin/sh
if [ "$#" -eq 2 ]
then
    cp $1 $2
else
    echo "You did not provide two arguments."
    echo "The arguments provided are $*"
fi
echo "Program terminated"
```

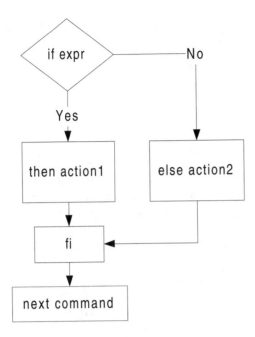

Figure 10–2 *The* `if-then-else-fi` *structure.*

This program works fine, but it does not incorporate any facility for dealing with a problem. The next program, `script-10`, is a more sophisticated shell program that performs a number of checks before copying one file to another. It first checks the number of arguments, and if you have not provided two arguments, it terminates at that point. Then it checks if the source and destination files are the same. If they are, it terminates at this point. The next check is to verify that the source file exists and that it is not a special file. After that, it checks if the source file exists and is readable. If both of the conditions are true, it checks the destination file. If the destination file already exists, it asks if you want to overwrite it. If you say "yes," it copies the source file to the destination; otherwise it terminates. If the destination file does not exist, it copies the source to the destination without interacting with you.

```
#!/usr/bin/sh
if [ "$#" -ne 2 ]
then
    echo "You have not provided exactly two arguments."
    exit 1
fi
if [ "$1" = "$2" ]
```

```
then
   echo "Source and destination names are the same."
   exit 1
fi
if [ ! -f "$1" ]
then
   echo "File $1 does not exist or not a regular file."
   exit 2
fi
if [ ! -r "$1" ]
then
   echo "File $1 is not readable."
   exit 3
fi
if [ -f $2 ]
then
   echo "File $2 already exists. Do you want"
   echo "to  overwrite (yes/no): \c"
   read ANSWER
   if [ "$ANSWER" = "yes" ]
   then
      cp $1 $2
      echo "File copied"
      exit 0
   else
      echo "File not copied"
      exit 4
   fi
fi
cp $1 $2
echo "File copied"
```

The exit status is different at every point so that you may come to know at what stage the program terminated by checking the exit code. You can use this program in place of the standard cp command as it is safer and does not overwrite existing files without notification.

The case Structure

The case structure is used where you want to branch to multiple program segments depending on the value of a variable. The general syntax of the case structure is:

```
case var in
   pattern1)
       commands
       ;;
   pattern2)
       commands
       ;;
   ...
   patternn)
       commands
       ;;
   *)
       commands
       ;;
esac
```

The value of *var* is checked. If this is equal to `pattern1`, the commands in the first block are executed. The first block ends at the `;;` pattern. If the value of *var* matches `pattern2`, the commands in the second block are executed. If *var* matches none of the pattern values, the commands in the last block after "`*)`" are executed. This last part is optional and can be omitted. The `case` statement is shown in the flow diagram of Figure 10-3.

Program `script-11` is used as an example here. It provides you with a few choices. If you select one of these, appropriate action is taken.

```
#!/usr/bin/sh
echo "Press w to list users"
echo "Press d to see date and time"
echo "Press p to see current directory"
echo
echo "Enter your choice: \c"
read VAR
case $VAR in
   w|W) who
        ;;
   d|D) date
        ;;
   p|P) pwd
        ;;
   *)   echo "You have not pressed a valid key"
esac
echo "The case structure finished"
```

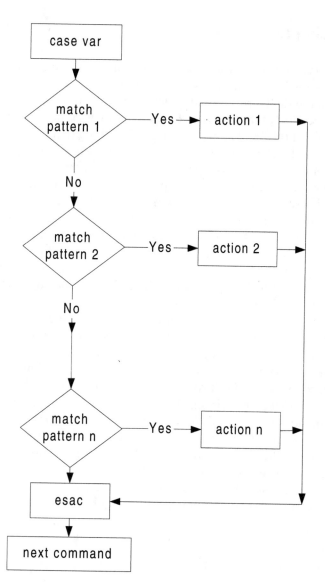

Figure 10-3 *The* case *structure.*

For example, if you press "w" or "W", the list of users currently logged into the system is displayed. Note that the "|" character is used for the logical OR operation in the case structure. If you make a choice that is not valid, the last part of the case structure is executed, which shows that you need to make a valid choice. Wildcard and range characters (*, ?, [ ]) can also be used in patterns to be matched.

■ Chapter Summary

This was an introductory chapter on shell programming, where you studied what a shell program looks like and how to write shell programs. The first line of the shell script is used to determine which subshell will be invoked for the execution of the program. Comments are used in the shell programs with the help of the "#" character, such that anything that follows this character is considered a comment. Then you learned how to debug a program using the -x option. Next was the use of variables in shell programs. Environment variables can be read in a shell program. Any change to environment variables is lost as soon as the program finishes its execution.

Command line arguments are stored in special variables whose names range from $0 to $9. Above $9, use braces to enclose the argument number. For example, ${12} would be the twelfth command line argument. The $0 variable shows the name of the program itself, and the rest keep values of other command line parameters. These command line parameters can be shifted left with the use of the shift command.

Interactive programs can be written with the help of the read command. This command takes input from the user at run time and stores it in a variable. The echo command is used to print something on the user terminal. It uses escape characters to format the printed data. You learned about the exit command and exit codes that show termination status of a program.

To make a conditional branch, you need to test a condition. The test command is used for this purpose, and you learned implicit and explicit use of this command. In the last part of the chapter, three branch structures were presented. The first one was the if-then-fi structure, the second was the if-then-else-fi structure, and the third one was the case structure. The if-then-fi structure is used for executing a block of commands if the result of a test is true. Its syntax is as shown here.

```
if expr
then
    action
fi
```

The if-then-else-fi structure is used to make either one or the other choice of the two available options. Its syntax is:

```
if expr
then
    action1
else
    action2
fi
```

The case structure is used to select one of many options available. The general format of the case structure is:

```
case var in
    pattern 1)
        commands
        ;;
    pattern 2)
        commands
        ;;
    ...
    pattern n)
        commands
        ;;
    *)
        commands
        ;;
esac
```

In the next chapter, you will learn about use of loops and some more features of shell programming.

▲ CHAPTER REVIEW QUESTIONS

1. What problem may arise if you don't provide the shell name inside a program?

2. Is it necessary to make a file containing a shell program executable?

3. Create a shell program that reads three command line arguments and then prints these in reverse order.

4. What is the importance of exit codes?

5. Write a shell program that uses the test command in explicit mode to check if the first and second command line arguments have the same value.

6. What is the major difference between the if and case structures?

▲ TEST YOUR KNOWLEDGE

1. *You create a shell program and save it into a file with name "*more*". Your current directory name is included in the PATH variable at the end. When you run this program by typing "*more*", nothing happens and the cursor just stops at the next line. What may be the problem?*

   A. You have written some commands in the program that the shell does not understand.

   B. The shell program file is not executable.

   C. You have used a program name that matches a standard HP-UX command.

   D. There is a problem with your terminal and you need to reset it.

2. *What is true about variables used in shell programs?*

   A. Variables starting with letters can be used in programs.

   B. Values of variables can be changed in the programs.

   C. The shell can read and modify environment variables for its own use.

   D. All of the above.

3. *You use the* echo $? *command. The result is* 2. *What do you conclude from this?*

   A. The echo command printed the number of characters in its first argument.

   B. The last command terminated abnormally.

   C. The "?" symbol has an ASCII value equal to 2.

   D. None of the above.

4. *You used* shift 3 *in your shell program. What will be its effect?*

   A. It will shift the first three command line arguments to the left.

   B. It will shift the last three command line arguments to the left.

   C. It will shift all command line arguments by three places toward the left.

   D. It will shift all command line arguments by three places toward the right.

5. *What does the* echo "\a" *command do?*

   A. It prints the character a.

   B. It prints the character \a.

   C. It prints a hexadecimal character "a" that represents decimal 10.

   D. It gives a beep sound.

6. *What is wrong with the command ["ABC" -eq "ABC"]?*
    A. You are comparing strings with a numeric operator.
    B. The same string is used on both sides of the operator.
    C. The quotation marks are not needed here.
    D. Parentheses should be used instead of square brackets.

7. *A shell script with the name* myscript *does not have the execution bit set. How can you execute it?*
    A. exec myscript
    B. sh myscript
    C. run myscript
    D. No shell script can be executed until its execution bit is set.

8. *How can you list all command line arguments?*
    A. using $*
    B. using $#
    C. using the shift command
    D. using the list command

9. *The true return value of the* test *command is:*
    A. 1
    B. 0
    C. any positive number
    D. any number not equal to zero

10. *You have a shell script as shown here. What will be the result when it is executed?*
    ```
    #!/usr/bin/sh
    ABC=aac
    case $ABC in
      a)        echo "First"
                ;;
    [aa]c)      echo "Second"
                ;;
    a*)         echo "Third"
                ;;
    *)          echo "Last"
                ;;
    esac
    ```
    A. First
    B. Second
    C. Third
    D. Last

Advanced Shell Programming

Loops are used to perform an operation repeatedly until a condition becomes true or false. The test or let command is used to check the condition every time a repetition is made. All loop structures used in shell programming start with a keyword. The block of commands that is executed repeatedly is enclosed by the do-done keywords.

There are three basic types of loops. The first one is the for-do-done loop, which is used to execute a block of commands for a fixed number of times. The while-do-done loop checks for a condition and goes on executing a block of commands until that condition becomes false. The until-do-done loop repeats the execution of a block of commands until a condition becomes true. As soon as the condition becomes true, the loop terminates.

All of these loops are controlled by a variable known as the *control variable*. This variable gets a new value on every repetition of the loop. The let command is also used to make arithmetic, logic,

179

and assignment operations inside the loops and to change the value of the control variable.

In this chapter, we will start with arithmetic and logic operations performed with the `let` command. The three loops will be discussed one-by-one. You will find the general syntax of each loop as well as a flow diagram. In the end, you will find some text processing examples and their use in loops.

11.1 Arithmetic and Logic Operations

The `let` command performs both arithmetic and logic operations. The use of the `let` command is important because all loops depend on the control variable. The value of this control must be changed during the execution of the loop. Usually this value is incremented or decremented with the help of the `let` command. The loop structures also need logic operations, used for the testing value of the control variable. This is the second use of the `let` command. Like the `test` command, the `let` command also has explicit and implicit modes.

Explicit Mode let Command

In the explicit mode, the word `let` is used in the command line. Consider the following example of the use of the command.

```
$ A=5
$ B=3
$ let "C=A+B"
$ echo $C
8
$
```

You created two new shell variables A and B and assigned these variables numeric values. Then you used the `let` command to sum these two values and assign the result to a third variable C. To display the value of this variable, you used the `echo` command. Like this arithmetic operation, you can also perform logic operations with the `let` command as shown in the following example.

```
$ var1=5
$ var2=3
```

```
$ let "var1<var2"
$ echo $?
1
$ let "var1>var2"
$ echo $?
0
$
```

In this example, you compared two variables. The first comparison was not true, so the result code returned is 1. The second comparison is true and the result code is zero.

Implicit Mode let Command

You can replace the word let with double parentheses on each side of the expression. The above example, where you added two variables, can also be accomplished as follows.

```
$ A=5
$ B=3
$ ((C=A+B))
$ echo $C
8
$
```

The let command can also perform complex operations like the one shown here.

```
((A=A+(3*B)/(A-1)))
```

While evaluating the result of an expression, the usual arithmetic rules are applied. Parentheses can be used to alter the order of evaluation.

Table 11-1 lists the operators that can be used with the let command.

The first two operators are unary operators that need only one operand. All other operators are binary operators and need two operands. You will find many examples of the use of the let command in this chapter.

Table 11-1 *Operators Used with the* `let` *Command*

Operator	Description
-	Unary minus
!	Unary negation (same value but with a negative sign)
=	Assignment
+	Addition
-	Subtraction
*	Multiplication
/	Integer division
%	Remainder
<	Less than
>	Greater than
<=	Less than or equal to
>=	Greater than or equal to
==	Comparison for equality
!=	Comparison for nonequality

11.2   The while-do-done Loop

The `while-do-done` loop is used to test a condition before the execution of the block of commands contained inside the loop. The command block is executed if the test is successful and returns a true value. It may happen that the command block never executes if the test fails the very first time. The loop continues to execute as long as the condition remains true. The general syntax of the while-do-done loop is shown here.

```
while condition
do
    command block
done
```

The condition is usually an expression containing a `test` or `let` command. Both of these commands are usually used in implicit mode. The `while-do-done` loop can be represented as a flow diagram as shown in Figure 11-1.

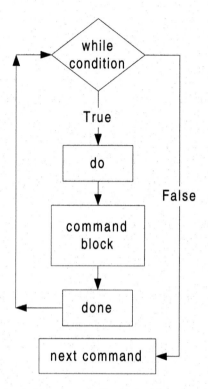

Figure 11–1   *The* while-do-done *loop.*

Let us see an example of the loop. We start with assigning the value 1 to a variable VAR1. Every time the loop executes, we double the value of the variable. The loop continues as long as the value of the variable is less than 100. As soon as the variable value reaches this limit, the loop execution terminates, and the next command after the done keyword is executed. The shell program script-20 follows.

```
#!/usr/bin/sh
echo "The while loop example"
echo
VAR1=1
while ((VAR1 < 100))
do
   echo "Value of the variable is : $VAR1"
   ((VAR1 = VAR1 * 2))
done
echo
echo "The loop execution is finished"
```

You can also use the `test` command instead of the `let` command in the comparison made in the `while` condition. In that case, this line will be:

```
while [ VAR1 -lt 100 ]
```

When you execute this program, you will see the output shown here.

```
$ ./script-20
The while loop example

Value of the variable is : 1
Value of the variable is : 2
Value of the variable is : 4
Value of the variable is : 8
Value of the variable is : 16
Value of the variable is : 32
Value of the variable is : 64

The loop execution is finished
$
```

A `while` loop may become an infinite loop if you make a mistake while making a `test` decision. For example, consider the following program where you start with a value of VAR1 equal to 1. You add 2 to the value of VAR1 at each step. You compare the value of the variable with 10. This condition is never fulfilled because the value of the variable never becomes 10. It goes from 9 to 11, skipping the value to which the comparison is made. By changing "!=" to "<=", you can solve the problem. The program `script-21` is shown here.

```
#!/usr/bin/sh
echo "The while loop example"
echo
VAR1=1
while ((VAR1 != 10))
do
    echo "Value of the variable is : $VAR1"
    ((VAR1 = VAR1 + 2))
done
echo
echo "The loop execution is finished"
```

Another example of an infinite loop is when you forget to modify the control variable inside the loop, such as in the code segment that follows.

```
VAR1=1
while ((VAR1 != 10))
do
    echo "Value of the variable is : $VAR1"
done
```

Here the value of VAR1 is always 1, and the condition remains true, resulting in an infinite loop.

11.3 The until-do-done Loop

The until-do-done loop is like the while-do-done loop. The only difference is that it tests the condition and goes on executing as long as the condition remains false. It terminates execution as soon as the condition becomes true. The general syntax of this loop is:

```
until condition
do
    command block
done
```

The flow diagram of the until-do-done loop is shown in Figure 11-2.
As you may have noticed, the only difference between Figure 11-1 and Figure 11-2 is that the "True" and "False" positions have been interchanged. Here is script-22, which has the same result as script-20 but was implemented using an until-do-done loop.

```
#!/usr/bin/sh
echo "The until loop example"
echo
VAR1=1
until (( VAR1 > 100 ))
do
    echo "Value of the variable is : $VAR1"
    ((VAR1 = VAR1 * 2))
done
echo
echo "The loop execution is finished"
```

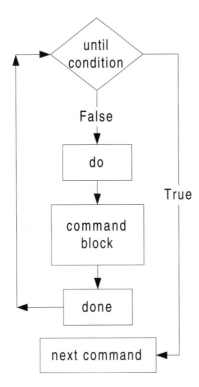

Figure 11–2 *The* until-do-done *loop.*

11.4 The for-do-done Loop

The for-do-done loop is executed on a list of elements. The list of elements is assigned to a variable one-by-one. The value of this variable is processed inside the loop. The loop continues to execute until all of the list elements are processed and there are no more elements in the list. The general syntax of the for-do-done loop is:

```
for var in list
do
    command block
done
```

The for-do-done loop flow diagram is shown in Figure 11-3.

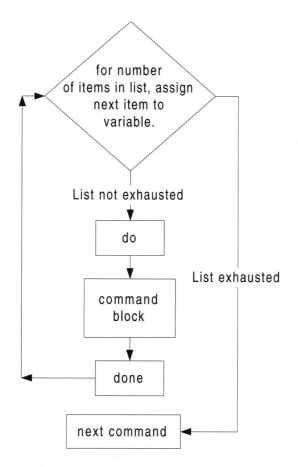

Figure 11–3 *The* `for-do-done` *loop.*

As an example of the use of this loop, if you want to list all executable files in your home directory, you can use the following program (`script-23`) for this purpose.

```
#!/usr/bin/sh
echo "List of all executable files in home directory"
cd $HOME
for F in *
do
    if [ -x $F ]
    then
        ll $F
    fi
done
```

The asterisk character represents all files in this directory. When you run this program, the result is shown as follows. You may have a different result on your system. There may be other uses of this program. You can utilize this script to find all files that have the SUID bit set or some other type of file with slight modifications.

```
$ ./script-23
List of all executable files in home directory
-rwxr-xr-x 1 boota    users   267 Oct 18 19:23 script-00
-rwxr-xr-x 1 boota    users   131 Oct 18 19:53 script-01
-rwxr-xr-x 1 boota    users   198 Oct 18 20:01 script-02
-rwxr-xr-x 1 boota    users   100 Oct 18 20:07 script-03
-rwxr-xr-x 1 boota    users   121 Oct 18 20:16 script-04
-rwxr-xr-x 1 boota    users   132 Oct 18 21:25 script-05
-rwxr-xr-x 1 boota    users   232 Oct 18 23:11 script-06
-rwxr-xr-x 1 boota    users   177 Oct 18 22:04 script-07
-rwxr-xr-x 1 boota    users   142 Oct 19 17:43 script-08
-rwxr-xr-x 1 boota    users   170 Oct 19 18:04 script-09
-rwxr-xr-x 1 boota    users   638 Oct 19 18:30 script-10
-rwxr-xr-x 1 boota    users   313 Oct 19 19:31 script-11
-rwxr-xr-x 1 boota    users   195 Oct 20 23:16 script-20
-rwxr-xr-x 1 boota    users   193 Oct 20 23:00 script-21
-rwxr-xr-x 1 boota    users   195 Oct 21 17:04 script-22
-rwxr-xr-x 1 boota    users   140 Oct 21 17:07 script-23
$
```

The script-24 is another example of the for-do-done loop, where a list is provided to the for command. This list contains the names of weekdays, which the program reads one-by-one and prints them on your terminal screen.

```
#!/usr/bin/sh
for DAY in Sunday Monday Tuesday Wednesday Thursday Friday
Saturday
do
    echo "The day is : $DAY"
done
```

The result of this program is:

```
$ ./script-24
The day is : Sunday
The day is : Monday
The day is : Tuesday
The day is : Wednesday
```

```
The day is : Thursday
The day is : Friday
The day is : Saturday
$
```

Changing File Access Date and Time

Let's suppose you want to change the access time of all files in your current directory to the current time. You can use the `touch` command with a small shell script as shown here.

```
for FILE in *
do
    touch $FILE
done
```

Accessing Command Line Parameters

To process all command line parameters one-by-one using a `for-do-done` loop, the following code segment may be used.

```
for ARG in $*
do
    echo $ARG
done
```

You can replace the `echo` command with any command or a block of commands to get a desired result.

Study Break

Use of Shell Loops

All of the three shell loops have their own applications. However, the `while-do-done` and `until-do-done` loops can be used interchangeably in many cases. Let's have some practice with these loops. Using a `while-do-done` loop, write a shell program that takes a number as input and then prints its table from 1 to 10. Now change the `while-do-done` loop to an `until-do-done` loop to get the same functionality. Use the `for-do-done` loop and pass a list of numbers from 1 to 10 to the `for` statement. Again print the table with this arrangement.

11.5 Breaking a Loop

There may be situations when you want to break or discontinue the execution of commands inside the command block of a loop. This is done when a particular condition is met and you don't want any further execution of commands in the command block. You may also need to check an error condition and discontinue execution of the program depending on that error condition.

The shell provides three mechanisms for breaking the normal execution of loops. These are break, continue, and exit.

The break Command

The break command discontinues the execution of loop immediately and transfers control to the command following the done keyword. You can pass a number *n* as an argument to the break command. In that case, the break command jumps to the command after *n*th occurrence of the done keyword. Consider script-25 shown here. It asks you to enter a file name. If the file is a regular file, it uses the cat command and displays its contents. If the file is not a regular file, it displays a message and then quits execution after displaying the message "Good bye." The program uses an infinite loop and will not terminate until you enter a nonregular file name, such as a directory name.

```
#!/usr/bin/sh
while true
do
    echo "Enter name of file to be displayed: \c"
    read FILE
    if [ ! -f $FILE ]
    then
       echo "This is not a regular file"
       break
    fi
    cat $FILE
done
echo "Good bye"
```

Let us execute and enter a nonregular file such as /etc.

```
$ ./script-25
Enter name of file to be displayed: /etc
This is not a regular file
Good bye
$
```

The continue Command

The continue command is slightly different from the break command. When encountered, it skips the remaining part of the loop and transfers the control to the start of the loop for the next iteration. The script-26 does the same job as script-25 but with the use of the continue command. In this script, we have changed the test condition, and the loop goes on executing until you enter a file name that is not a regular file. At this point, the loop breaks and the command after the loop is executed.

```
#!/usr/bin/sh
while true
do
    echo "Enter name of file to be displayed: \c"
    read FILE
    if [ -f $FILE ]
    then
        cat $FILE
        continue
    fi
    echo "This is not a regular file"
    break
done
echo "Good bye"
```

The exit Command

The exit command completely terminates the program. It returns an *exit code* that is optionally provided as its argument in the program. If the exit command doesn't have any arguments, it returns the exit code of the command executed just before it. This command is used when a critical error is encountered, and further execution of the program may cause faulty results. For example, dividing a number by zero is illegal, so you want to check this condition before a command is executed that divides a number by zero. Program script-27 reads a number entered by the user and then divides 100 by this number. It then displays the quotient and the remainder. If you try to divide by zero, the program displays an error message and terminates immediately.

```
#!/usr/bin/sh
NUM=100
while true
do
    echo "Enter a divisor for integer 100 : \c"
    read DIV
```

```
        if [ $DIV -eq 0 ]
        then
            echo "Divide by zero is not permitted"
            exit 1
        fi
        (( QUO = NUM / DIV ))
        (( REM = NUM % DIV ))
        echo "The quotient is   : $QUO"
        echo "The remainder is : $REM"
done
```

11.6 Text Processing

You have used the grep command as a filter to extract or delete lines containing a particular text pattern. Here you will learn two more commands that are useful for text processing. The sed command is a stream editor that takes text from stdin and sends it to stdout after editing it. The cut command is used to extract a desired part of text from a line. It also takes its input from stdin and sends its output to stdout.

Using sed

The stream editor is a useful tool to edit large amounts of text at one time. For example, you may need to search for a word in a large file and replace it with another word. Let's try to replace the word "echo" with "ECHO" in script-27. The sed command will do the job as follows.

```
$ sed s/echo/ECHO/g script-27
#!/usr/bin/sh
NUM=100
while true
do
    ECHO "Enter a divisor for integer 100 : \c"
    read DIV
    if [ $DIV -eq 0 ]
    then
        ECHO "Divide by zero is not permitted"
        exit 1
    fi
    (( QUO = NUM / DIV ))
    (( REM = NUM % DIV ))
    ECHO "The quotient is   : $QUO"
    ECHO "The remainder is : $REM"
done
```

If you want to do an operation on all files, you can write a shell program to accomplish the job. Program `script-28` shown here replaces "echo" with "ECHO" in all files of the current directory.

```
#!/usr/bin/sh
for FILE in *
do
    cat $FILE |sed s/echo/ECHO/g >tempfile
    cp tempfile $FILE
done
rm tempfile
```

As you can see, this is a very useful tool to make changes to a large number of files that could take a long time otherwise. Consider you are writing a book and want to change "figure" to "Fig" in all chapters. If you don't know how to do it in an efficient way, you may start editing all files manually, spending hours on a job that need take only a few minutes.

There are many ways to use sed that make it a very useful tool. For additional information, consult the sed manual pages.

Using cut

The cut command is used to extract a particular part of data from a line of text. If the data are in the form of fields, you can extract particular fields. For example, if you want to list all user names on your system, you can use the cut command on the /etc/passwd file as follows:

```
cut -f 1 -d : /etc/passwd
```

or

```
cat /etc/passwd | cut -f 1 -d :
```

Here the -f 1 option tells the command that you want to extract field number 1. The -d : option shows that the fields in the data are separated by a delimiter colon ":". Since user names are in the start of each line in /etc/passwd and they are followed by a colon, the command extracts all user names from the file.

You may also use the cut command to extract a particular number of characters from a file. To extract the first eight characters from every line in the /etc/passwd file, you may use the following command.

```
cat /etc/passwd | cut -c 1-8
```

Here you specified a range of characters using the `-c 1-8` option. See the manual pages for more information on the `cut` command.

Let us use the `cut` command in a shell program `script-29`. This script is used to send an email message to all users on a system. The message contents are stored in a file `mailfile`. You use the `mailx` command to send the message.

```
#!/usr/bin/sh
for USER in $(cut -f 1 -d : /etc/passwd)
do
    mailx -s "Test mail" $USER <mailfile
done
```

You have used the `cut` command to create a list of user names and then send a mail message to each name in the list.

The sleep Command

The `sleep` command is used to suspend execution for a certain amount of time. You provide the number of seconds as the argument to the `sleep` command. The following code segment lists all files in the current directory with a pause of five seconds between every file.

```
for FILE in *
do
    ll $FILE
    sleep 5
done
```

■ Chapter Summary

This was the second and last chapter on the topic of shell programming. Shell loops are discussed in this chapter. You started learning arithmetic and logic operations with the help of the `let` command. Explicit and implicit modes of the `let` command were discussed. Table 11-1 listed operators that can be used with the `let` command. Then you studied the `while-do-done` loop. The syntax of this loop is:

```
while condition
do
    command block
done
```

The `while-do-done` loop repeats itself until the condition becomes false. The `until-do-done` loop is similar to the `while-do-done` loop; the only difference is that it repeats until the condition becomes true. The syntax of this loop is:

```
until condition
do
    command block
done
```

Next you studied the `for-do-done` loop, which is used to process a list of elements provided as the argument to the `for` command. The syntax of the `for-do-done` loop is:

```
for var in list
do
    command block
done
```

The `for-do-done` loop continues to execute until it has processed all elements in the list. You also found flow diagrams of all these loops in this chapter.

When you need to break a loop, you can use the `break`, `continue`, or `exit` commands. The `break` command transfers program control to the command just after the next `done` keyword. The `continue` command skips all remaining commands in the loop and transfers control to the start of the loop. The `exit` command permanently terminates the program and returns an exit code. The `exit` command is used in situations where a critical error is encountered and it is dangerous to continue program execution.

In the last part of the chapter, you learned some text processing commands. The stream editor (`sed`) is used to edit data received at stdin. The edited data is sent to stdout. With the help of shell programs, you can perform some complex editing tasks using `sed`. The `cut` command is used to extract data coming from stdin. This command is especially useful when the data are in the form of fields separated by a delimiter. You can extract any field with the help of the `cut` command by specifying a field number. A small shell program was presented to send mail to all system users with the help of the `cut` command. The `sleep` command is used to suspend program execution for a certain amount of time.

This is the last chapter of the first part of the book. The next part contains chapters related to HP-UX system administration. The material presented in the next chapters is specific to HP-UX and may not be used on other UNIX systems.

▲ CHAPTER REVIEW QUESTIONS

1. What is the difference between the `test` and `let` commands?

2. Explain the unary and binary negative signs.

3. Consider the following program. What may be the possible problem?

```
VAR=1
(($VAR=$VAR+1))
while [ $VAR -lt 10 ]
do
    echo $VAR
done
```

4. Write a program that provides three options. The first option asks the user to enter a number. It then adds the number to 100 and displays the result. The second option subtracts the number from 100 and displays the result. The third option terminates the program.

5. Write a program that accepts a list of user names on the command line and then displays a message if any of these users is logged in.

6. Previously all users were using the Bourne shell. The administration has changed the policy and now everyone is asked to use the POSIX shell. Write a program that changes the shell of all users from `/usr/bin/old/sh` to `/usr/bin/sh`.

▲ TEST YOUR KNOWLEDGE

1. *Which command will you use to add the values of two variables* VAR1 *and* VAR2, *and store the result in* VAR3?
    A. `[ $VAR3 = $VAR1 + $VAR2 ]`
    B. `$VAR3 = [ $VAR1 + $VAR2 ]`
    C. `$VAR3 = (( VAR1 + VAR2 ))`
    D. `(( $VAR3 = VAR1 + VAR2 ))`

2. *You want to wait for 10 seconds at the end of the loop in each loop cycle. Which command will you use?*
    A. `sleep`
    B. `pause`
    C. `wait`
    D. Any of the three commands can be used.

3. *Consider the following code segment. How many times does the loop execute?*

```
A=1
until [ $A < 10 ]
do
    echo $A
    (( $A=$A+1))
done
```

    A. zero

    B. one

    C. nine

    D. ten

4. *What will be the output of the program shown here?*

```
#!/usr/bin/sh
A=1
while [ $A -lt 10 ]
do
    B=1
    while [ $B -lt 10 ]
    do
        break 2
        echo "Inner loop"
    done
    echo "Outer Loop"
done
```

    A. "Inner Loop" will be printed 10 times.

    B. "Outer Loop" will be printed 10 times.

    C. "Outer Loop" will be printed 9 times.

    D. Nothing will be printed.

5. *While writing a program, you meet a situation where you want to break the normal execution and shift control to the beginning of the loop, skipping the remaining commands in the loop. Which command will you use?*

    A. break

    B. continue

    C. exit

    D. shift

HP-UX
System
Administration

The System Administration Manager

The System Administration Manager (SAM) is a tool that simplifies routine HP-UX system administration. It is available both in text and GUI modes. If you are running X-Windows, SAM automatically detects the presence of your GUI terminals and starts in *graphical mode*. In case you are using a text terminal, SAM starts in text or *terminal mode*. In the graphical mode, you can use your mouse to click on different icons related to a desired system administration tasks. In the text mode, SAM provides menus that can be used by pressing the Tab and arrow keys to activate a particular option.

SAM is a very useful tool for day-to-day system administration jobs. At the same time, it can't do *every* job for a system administrator. Sometimes you will need to use commands manually for troubleshooting and specialized tasks. In this chapter, you will learn to use SAM in both text and graphical modes. You will learn how to start and stop SAM and how it looks when used in text

201

or graphical mode. You will go through a sample session of creating a new user, where you will learn how to use SAM menus and navigate your system. Everything done in SAM is logged into a log file, and you will see some parts of this file. SAM is also useful to distribute system administration tasks among many people. At the end of the chapter, you will see how you can grant restricted access to non-`root` users who have a need to use SAM.

This is an introductory chapter about SAM. In the coming chapters, you will learn how different tasks are done with the help of this tool.

12.1   Why Use SAM?

SAM is designed to help system administrators perform routine tasks. With SAM, tasks that require a number of steps can be performed in a single step. It is the responsibility of SAM to execute actual commands for you. Briefly, the advantages of using SAM are as follows.

1. You get menus and icons. They are easy to use and less laborious than typing long commands manually.
2. SAM provides you with comprehensive details of your system. For example, you can see a list of installed printers and their properties. Similarly, by just clicking an icon, you are able to see all disks attached to your system. Another icon will show you network adapters and network configuration related to each adapter. It is very useful to know the existing system configuration before adding a new piece of hardware.
3. You don't need to remember complex commands used for routine tasks.
4. It provides a uniform interface on all HP-9000 series servers and workstations.
5. It gives you centralized control for your network, as you can run it remotely on any machine and view the result on your local GUI.
6. You can assign limited root access to users if you want to distribute system administration tasks. For example, if you want to assign printer management to one person and network management to another, SAM provides you with the facility to define restricted areas for users. A user can only go into that area of SAM assigned to him or her.

At the same time, it must be remembered that true system administration is a complex job—you need to know what is going on behind the scenes.

Although SAM can add new users for you, you need to know how to add a user manually. An essential part of system administration is troubleshooting. SAM is not designed for this purpose, as there are no hard and fast rules used for the purpose of troubleshooting. As a system administrator, it is your experience and depth of knowledge about HP-UX that will help you in the troubleshooting process.

12.2 Starting and Stopping SAM

When you start SAM, it checks what type of terminal you are using. If you are using a text-type terminal and the DISPLAY variable is not set, SAM starts in text mode and displays the menu-based text interface. If you are using a graphical terminal or console, SAM starts in graphical mode. You can start SAM on a remote system and view the GUI at your local graphical terminal by correctly setting the DISPLAY variable.

Starting and Stopping SAM in Text Mode

To start SAM, you use the sam command. As already mentioned, if you are using a text-type terminal, SAM will start in text mode. In the first screen, it will show you some instructions on how to use menus and help. The first screen that appears after starting SAM is shown in Figure 12-1.

```
 Window  Edit  Options                                              Help

 Starting the terminal version of sam...

 To move around in sam:

 - use the "Tab" key to move between screen elements
 - use the arrow keys to move within screen elements
 - use "Ctrl-F" for context-sensitive help anywhere in sam

 On screens with a menubar at the top like this:

      ------------------------------------------------------------
      |File View Options Actions                         Help|
      |----- ---- ------- -------                        ---|

 - use "Tab" to move from the list to the menubar
 - use the arrow keys to move around
 - use "Return" to pull down a menu or select a menu item
 - use "Tab" to move from the menubar to the list without selecting a menu item
 - use the spacebar to select an item in the list

 On any screen, press "CTRL-K" for more information on how to use the keyboard.

 Press "Return" to continue...
```

Figure 12–1 *SAM starting page in text mode.*

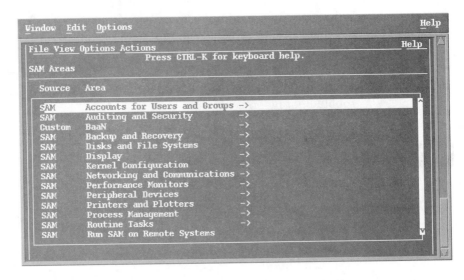

Figure 12–2 *SAM menus in text mode.*

Figure 12-1 shows basic instruction of how to use the `Tab`, `Enter`, and arrow keys. You can get more help by pressing `CTRL`-`k` whenever this message is displayed. If you press the `Enter` key, the next screen is displayed that shows actual SAM menus. This is shown in Figure 12-2.

In the top of the screen is the menu area where you can see the `File`, `View`, `Options`, `Actions`, and `Help` menus. You can activate a menu area by pressing the `Tab` key. When you press the `Tab` key, the `File` menu is activated. Then, by pressing the `Enter` key, you can see the list of actions that can be performed using this menu. You can use arrow keys or the `Tab` key to move forward in the menus. The `Shift`-`Tab` key combination is used for movement in the backward direction.

The remainder of the window shows the SAM functional areas and is divided into two columns. The first column is the *Source* column, which shows whether the area is a standard SAM component or one customized by the system administrator. The second column is a short description of the functionality provided by the component. SAM is organized in a tree structure such that minor functional groups are contained inside major groups. For example, `Account for Users and Groups` is a major area. Under this area, you can find options for separately managing users and groups. In this figure, a right arrow symbol at the end of a group shows that it contains other functional entities if you go inside it. It means that selecting this item will not perform any action but will lead to other items that may be used to perform an action.

SAM functional areas show the tasks that can be performed with the help of SAM. The built-in SAM areas are listed below.

- Auditing and Security
- Kernel and Device Configuration
- Networks and Communications
- Peripheral Device Management
- Printer and Plotter Management
- Process Management
- Remote System Administration
- Routine Tasks
- User and Group Account Management
- Backup and Recovery
- Disk and File System Management
- Display Management
- Performance Monitoring
- Software Management
- Time Server Management

In addition, you can build your own functional areas by customizing SAM. SAM also provides context-sensitive help that can be utilized at any time by pressing the `CTRL`-`k` key combination. More help can be obtained using the Help menu. To stop SAM, you go to the `File` menu and use the `Exit` option.

Starting and Stopping SAM in GUI

If you are using a monitor capable of using the X-Window system and the `DISPLAY` variable is correctly set, SAM will start in graphical mode. Figure 12-3 shows part of a typical GUI window that is displayed just after starting SAM.

You have the same menus in GUI as you have in the text mode. The functional area now contains icons. You can use your mouse to activate any menu by clicking the left mouse button on it. If you double-click on an icon in the functional area that represents an action, the action corresponding to that icon starts. If you double-click on an icon that represents a functional group, it will open the subgroups and action icons contained in that functional group.

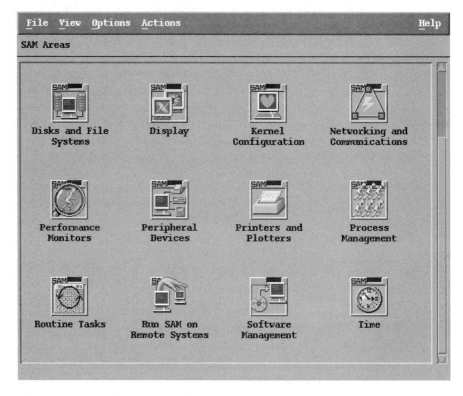

Figure 12–3   *SAM in GUI mode.*

12.3   A Sample SAM Session

Let's use SAM to create a new user on the system. To perform a certain job, you need to go to the proper SAM area. To manage users and groups, you need to go to the `Accounts for Users and Groups` area by double-clicking the left mouse button on this icon.

Creating a New User

Let's perform the job step-by-step. First of all, start SAM using the `sam` command. For this example, I assume that you are using SAM in GUI. You will see a window like the one shown in Figure 12-3. It may happen that all of the icons are not visible in the window. You can scroll up and down to navigate the icons by using the scroll bars.

Search for the `Accounts for Users and Groups` icon in the window. This is the SAM area used for user and group management. Double-click the left mouse button on this icon; you will see that the window is changed, and the two icons shown in Figure 12-4 appear in the window. The `Groups` icon is used for tasks related to the management of groups on your system, while the `Users` icon is for user management. The third icon, `.. (go up)`, is used to go back to the previous screen.

Double-click the left mouse button on the `Users` icon. You will see that a new window appears as shown in Fig. 12-5. This window lists all existing user accounts on your system. The window takes its information from the `/etc/passwd` and `/etc/groups` files. Here you can see login name, login IDs, group membership, and other information about each user. You can also modify an existing user by selecting that user with a single left-button mouse click and starting the proper action from the `Actions` menu.

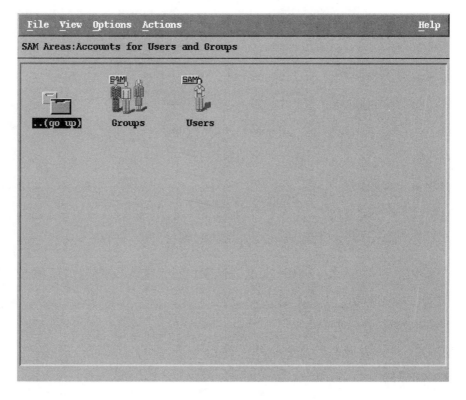

Figure 12–4 *SAM* `Accounts for Users and Groups` *functional area.*

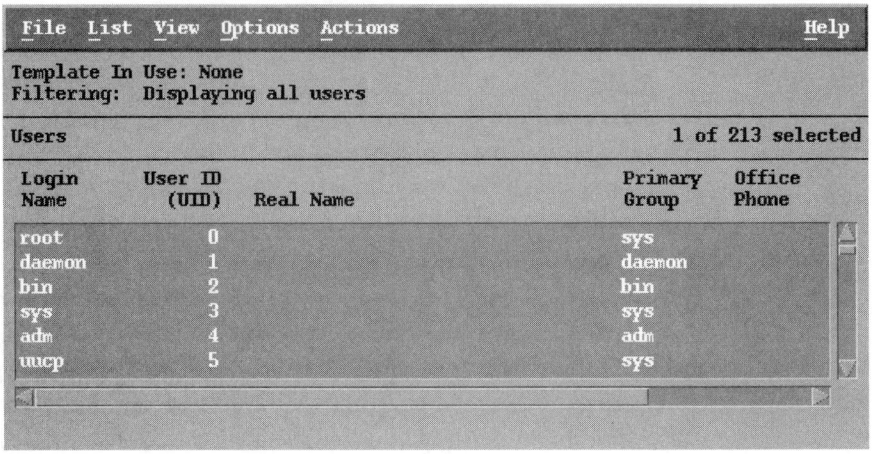

Figure 12–5 *SAM* Users *area.*

Now click on the Actions menu without selecting any user and choose Add from this menu. When you click the left mouse button on this menu, the pull-down menu appears as shown in Figure 12-6.

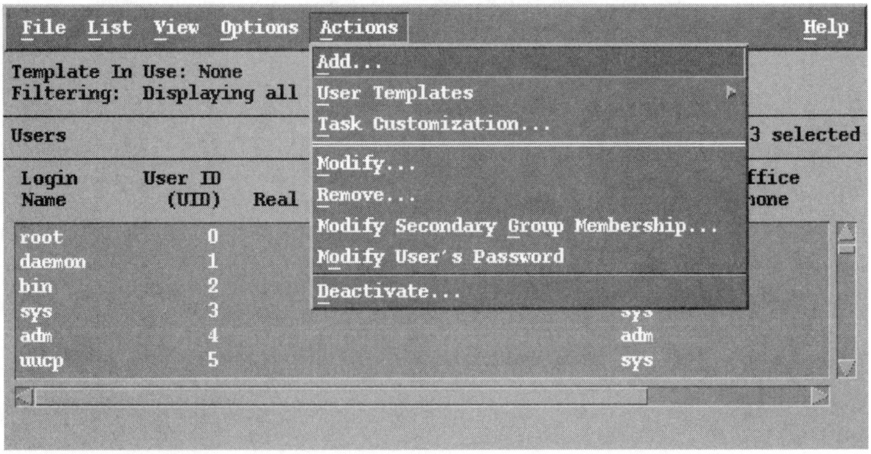

Figure 12–6 *SAM activating the* Action *menu.*

As you can see from the figure, you can take actions to modify, deactivate, or remove an existing user. You can also change a user's group membership and modify his or her password. To add a new user, select the Add option and a new window appears. This is a form that you need to complete with information related to the new user. This window is shown in Figure 12-7.

The first field is the login name. SAM will automatically select an available user ID and display it in the UID field of the form. However, you can change the user ID manually. Then you fill in the other information on the form. If the Create Home Directory box is checked, SAM will create a home directory for the user. The default shell is the POSIX shell, and you can change it to a shell desired for the user. The boxes that are marked Optional may be left blank. After filling out the form, you press the Apply button or

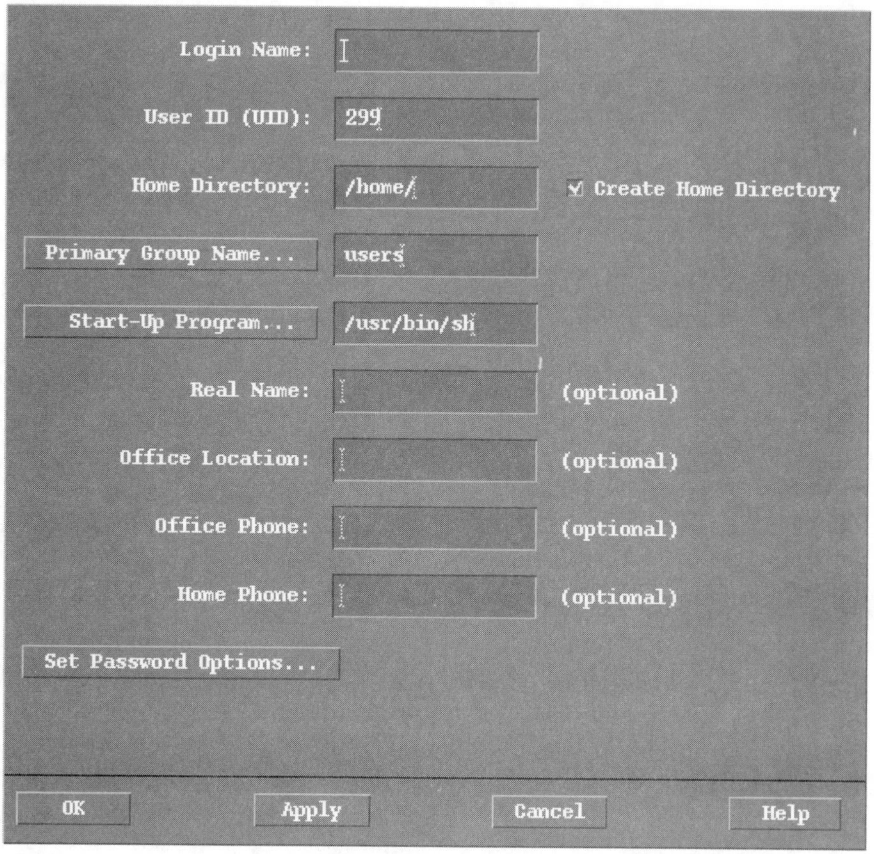

Figure 12-7 *SAM form for adding a user.*

Figure 12-8 *Entering a password for the newly created user.*

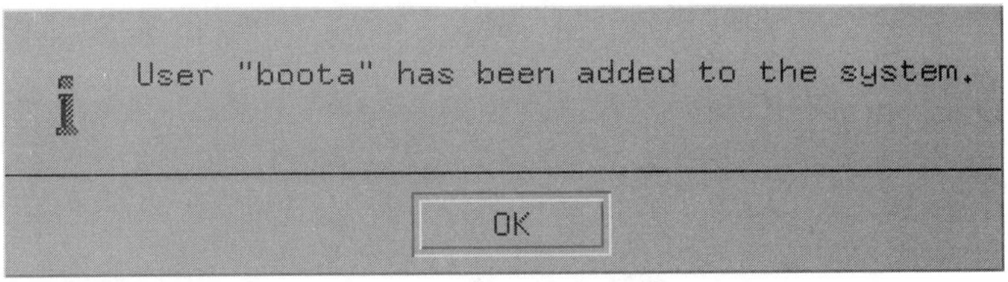

Figure 12-9 *Process of user creation is complete.*

the OK button. You will see a new window as shown, in Figure 12-8, where you have to enter a password twice for the new user. After you have entered the password, another window will appear showing that the user creation process is complete. This window is shown in Figure 12-9.

When you press the OK button in this window, the new user is listed in the user list, as shown in Figure 12-5. After that, you can quit using SAM using the Exit option from the File menu.

12.4 SAM Log Files

SAM keeps a record of all of its actions in a log file (SAMLOG). You can find the commands that SAM executed perform an operation in the /var/sam/log/samlog file. It contains entries as in the following.

```
Executing the following command:\C/usr/sbin/swlist -l
  fileset -a state AdvJou
@!@4@940265683@0
Command completed with exit status 0.
```

```
@!@8@940265683@0
Exiting Task Manager with task com_execute_swlist_command.
@!@8@940265683@0
Exiting Task Manager with task COM_IS_FILESET_LOADED.
@!@8@940265683@0
Entering Task Manager with task KC_GET_DRIVERS.
@!@4@940265683@0
Getting the kernel drivers/modules
@!@4@940265683@0
Getting the state of one or more kernel device driver/
  pseudo drivers that mat
ch "vxadv".
@!@4@940265683@0
Succeeded in getting the state of driver "vxadv".
@!@8@940265683@0
Exiting Task Manager with task KC_GET_DRIVERS.
@!@8@940265684@0
Entering Task Manager with task NNC_GET_INSTALL_STATUS.
@!@8@940265684@0
Exiting Task Manager with task NNC_GET_INSTALL_STATUS.
@!@8@940265684@0
Entering Task Manager with task nfs_check_remote_mounts.
@!@2@940265684@0
Performing task "Checks if any remote file systems are
  mounted.".
@!@2@940265684@0
Executing the following command:\C/usr/sbin/mount|/usr/bin/
  sed -n 's,^[^ ]* o
n \([^ :]*\):\([^ ]*\).*,\1 \2,p'\C
@!@2@940265684@0
Command completed with exit status 0.
@!@2@940265684@0
```

The raw data from SAMLOG is very difficult to read. More commonly, one would go into SAM and click Options, and then click View SAM Log to see a nicely formatted, easy-to-read SAMLOG. Figure 12-10 shows a typical window when the log file is viewed in this way. For a selective view, you can specify a time range or user name in this window.

The log file grows as you continue using SAM. After a certain limit, SAM copies it to the samlog.old file and creates a new samlog file.

SAM comes with a utility, /usr/sam/bin/samlog_viewer, which can be used to view the log file in an efficient way. You can apply filters to data displayed by this utility. You can also specify a range of dates and times for displaying activity during that period. It is also possible to view the log of

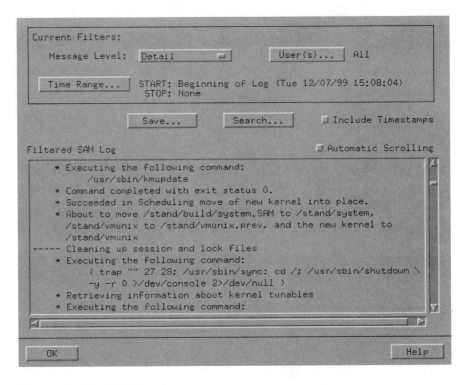

Figure 12–10 *SAM log view.*

SAM usage by a particular user. For more information, consult the manual pages of `samlog_viewer`.

12.5 Restricted Use of SAM by Non-Root Users

By default, only **root** is allowed to use SAM. However, SAM can be configured to provide a subset of its functionality to some users or groups other than **root**. For this purpose, you need to log in as **root** and start SAM in the *Restricted SAM Builder* mode using the -r option. In the builder system, you can assign some of the SAM functions to a user. You can use the -f option with SAM to verify that this assignment is operational. For example, you can assign printer management to a particular user. When that user starts SAM in the usual way, he or she will see only those icons that are related to printer management. This is a very useful tool to give restricted **root** access to some system users for system management in a complex and large computing environment.

■ Chapter Summary

The System Administration Manager or SAM is a comprehensive and useful tool to carry out routine system administration tasks. This chapter started with an introduction to SAM and the advantages of using it. You learned that SAM can be used in both text and graphical modes. If you are using a text-type terminal, SAM automatically detects it and starts in text mode. On X-Window terminals, it starts in GUI mode. Then you found out how to start and stop it in both of these modes and what the important areas of the SAM window are. You also learned how to use menus. In the text mode, a menu can be invoked by pressing the [Tab] key, and menus can be navigated using the [Tab] and arrow keys. In GUI, you used the mouse to perform actions.

You used SAM to create a new user in GUI. SAM records all of its commands in a log file, /var/sam/samlog. From SAM, you can click Options and then click View SAM Log to get information from this log file.

The restricted SAM builder is invoked by using the -r option and is used to grant restricted root access to some system users. This helps in distributing system administration tasks among many users in a complex computing environment.

▲ CHAPTER REVIEW QUESTIONS

1. List three advantages of using SAM.

2. What are the major parts of the SAM window?

3. Explain why SAM can't be used for system troubleshooting.

▲ TEST YOUR KNOWLEDGE

1. *SAM can't be used for:*
   A. HP-UX routine system administration
   B. HP-UX troubleshooting
   C. HP-UX network administration
   D. HP-UX kernel reconfiguration

2. *The SAM builder is used to:*
   A. compile SAM files
   B. build the SAM database
   C. grant restricted access to non-**root** users
   D. build SAM menus and icons

3. *The SAM log file is:*
   A. `/var/adm/samlog`
   B. `/var/sam/log`
   C. `/var/sam/log/samlog`
   D. `/var/sam/samlog`

4. *The utility for viewing the SAM log file is:*
   A. `samlog_viewer`
   B. `log_viewer`
   C. `viewlog_sam`
   D. `view_samlog`

Installing
HP-UX

The installation process starts by interrupting the normal boot process of an HP system. In the normal boot process, a server or workstation tries to boot from the primary boot path. By interrupting this boot process, you can specify a different boot path containing HP-UX Install and *Core OS* installation media. For a successful system installation process, you need to determine the type of your hardware and check its compatibility with the HP-UX version you are installing. If the HP-UX version is supported on your system, you can use Core OS Media (usually a CD-ROM) to install HP-UX. Once you start the installation process, you can select *guided installation*, *advanced installation*, or an installation with default values. Installation with default values requires minimum user interaction. During the installation process, you configure system parameters such as the HP-UX environment, system disk, swap space, and *Logical Volume Manager* (LVM) file systems. You can also select the system language and the num-

215

ber of user licenses. These parameters are common to both guided and advanced installations. However, when you use the advanced installation method, you can also make network settings and changes to logical volume sizes. An example of creating logical volumes on a 4-GByte disk space will be presented during the advanced installation process (Section 13.4).

After the installation process is complete, HP-UX restarts the computer, and you can log into HP-UX as user **root** and carry out postinstallation tasks. These tasks include installation of additional patches and applications. You may also have to install software drivers if a device driver is not already built into the kernel. An important task is to tune kernel parameters depending on the applications being installed. The kernel configuration process is discussed in Chapter 16.

This chapter starts with a brief introduction to HP servers and workstations. Then we will walk through an installation process on a server, where guided installation and advanced installation methods will be discussed.

13.1 Introduction to HP Workstations and Servers

On older machines, HP used 700-series numbering on workstations and 800-series numbering on servers. This convention has been changed, and all of these systems are now called 9000-series servers and workstations. The most common types of HP servers for entry-level solutions are the L-series, A-series, and R-series. For midrange use, K-Series and N-Series servers are recommended. The V-series servers are the most powerful machines from HP. These are considered best for performance, availability, and scalability. HP-UX workstations have the high performance and graphical capabilities required for personal or office use.

HP-UX has both 32-bit and 64-bit capabilities. Not all HP servers and workstations can run 64-bit HP-UX. Before installation, you need to know which CPU you have and whether it supports the 64-bit version of operating system.

Processor Dependent Code (PDC) is used to check and verify hardware configuration at boot time. It detects and shows what hardware devices are available to the system. From an installation point of view, you use PDC to determine the disks and CD-ROM drives attached to the system so that you may specify the installation device and boot options. There are minor differences in PDC commands for different servers and workstations. After checking the attached devices, the PDC tries to boot a machine from the *primary boot device*. You can interrupt the automatic boot process to check what commands are available on your system or boot from a device other than the primary boot device. There are other installation differences between servers and workstations, but in general the procedure applies to both. If you have installed HP-UX on one machine, you are able to install it on the other.

13.2 Installing HP-UX

When you turn on an HP machine, the PDC starts execution and checks system memory and peripherals. Before starting the automatic boot-up from the primary boot device, it stops for ten seconds to allow the user to interrupt the boot process. It displays a message like the following on the screen.

```
Processor is starting autoboot
To discontinue press a key within 10 seconds.
```

When you see this message, press the `Enter` key. You will see a menu of commands such as this.

```
--------------------- Main Menu --------------------------
Command                          Description
-------                          -----------
BOot [PRI|ALT|<path>]            Boot from specified path
PAth [PRI|ALT|<path>]            Display or modify a path
SEArch [Display|IPL] [<path>]    Search for boot device
COnfiguration menu               Displays or sets boot values
INformation menu                 Displays hardware information
SERvice menu                     Displays service commands
Help [<menu>|<command>]          Displays help for menu or cmd
RESET                            Restart the system
----------
Main Menu: Enter command or menu >
```

Commands can be abbreviated using uppercase letters as shown. For example, the `search` command can be abbreviated as `sea`. From this menu, you can use the `boot` command to boot the system from a CD-ROM containing the Core Operating System. But before that, you need to know the device name for the CD-ROM drive attached to your system. The `search` command is used to list all bootable devices attached to the system. This includes disk drives, tape drives, and CD-ROM drives. The search command will show you an output like the following.

```
Main Menu: Enter command or menu > search
Searching for potential boot device(s)
This may take several minutes.
To discontinue search, press any key
(termination may not be immediate)

Path Number   Device Path (dec)   Device Type
-----------   -----------------   -----------
P0            10/0/6              Random Access Media
P1            10/0/5              Random Access Media
P2            10/0/4              Random Access Media
P3            10/0/3              Random Access Media
P4            10/0/2              Random Access Media
P5            10/0/1              Random Access Media
P6            10/4/4.2            Toshiba CD-ROM Device
P7            10/4/4.1            Sequential Access Media
Main Menu: Enter command or menu >
```

On some systems, the output for the search command may be different. This command shows the path number, device path, and type of device. Path numbers are used to refer to a particular device when using commands that operate on devices. Device paths show the physical path associated with the device. The physical path of the device represents a system slot to which the device is attached. Random Access Media shows disks and CD-ROM drives. The Sequential Access Media type is usually used for tape drives.

Once you get this information and figure out which path number represents your CD-ROM drive, you can use the boot command to boot the system from the CD-ROM. If your CD-ROM is represented by P6, the boot command will be as follows:

```
Main Menu: Enter command or menu > Boot P6
```

You can also use device paths to boot the system instead of device numbers. After you issue the boot command, the system will ask you if you want to interact with the *Initial System Loader* (ISL). You have to answer no (N) at this point. This message is like the following.

```
Main Menu: Enter command or menu > Boot P6
Interact with IPL (Y or N) ?> N
```

Your *Install and Core OS* CD-ROM must be present in the drive at this moment. The system starts loading software from the CD and automatically goes into installation mode. A message appears on your screen similar to the following.

```
Booting . . .
Boot IO Dependent Code (IODC) revision 152

Hard Boot

ISL Revision A.00.38 Oct 26, 1994
ISL booting hpux (;0);INSTALL
```

You will see some other messages scrolling down when the system detects installed hardware. After these messages, the HP-UX installation/recovery window appears as shown in Figure 13-1. Here, basic instructions for cursor movement and menu selection are provided. A summary of detected hardware is also present. In the bottom section, three options are listed. These are:

Install HP-UX	This is used to start the HP-UX installation process.
Run a Recovery Shell	This is used to provide access to a recovery system used to recover a damaged system.
Advanced Options	Here you can select different advanced options. I would recommend going to this area and disabling DHCP. This is useful for first-time installation when you want to concentrate on the installation of the operating system without going into any network-related activity.

At this point, you can use the `Tab` key to navigate different parts of the screen and the `Enter` key to select an option. I would recommend going to `Advanced Options` and disabling DHCP (Dynamic Host Configuration Protocol, used to assign IP addresses to hosts automatically) first. Pressing the spacebar key toggles the `Enable` and `Disable` options. It is better to disable DHCP during the installation phase. By doing so, you can avoid any problems during booting if the DHCP server is not available at boot time or if you come across a network problem during the installation. You can enable it again after the installation process is complete. A screen similar to the one shown in Figure 13-2 appears when you go to `Advanced Options`.

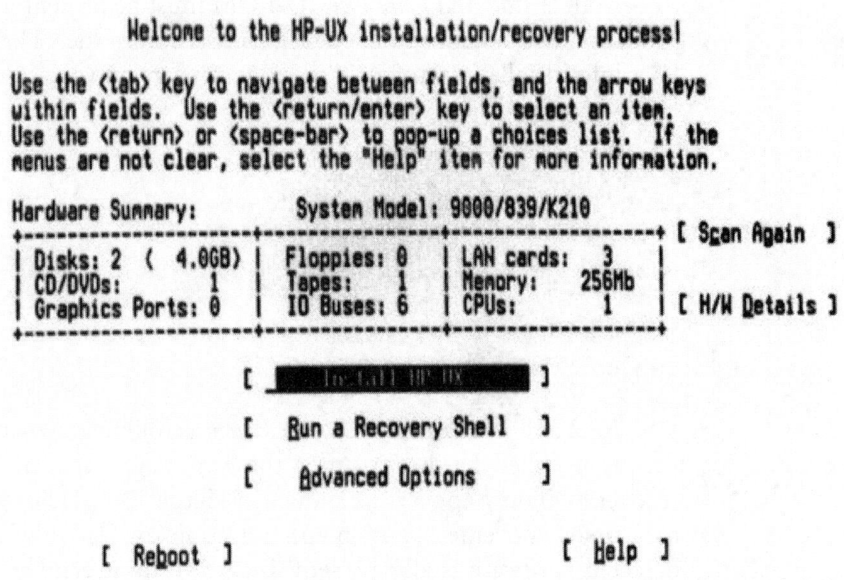

```
                  Welcome to the HP-UX installation/recovery process!

         Use the <tab> key to navigate between fields, and the arrow keys
         within fields.  Use the <return/enter> key to select an item.
         Use the <return> or <space-bar> to pop-up a choices list. If the
         menus are not clear, select the "Help" item for more information.

         Hardware Summary:          System Model: 9000/839/K210
         +-----------------------+----------------------+-----------------+ [ Scan Again ]
         | Disks: 2  ( 4.0GB) | Floppies: 0 | LAN cards:   3 |
         | CD/DVDs:          1 | Tapes:    1 | Memory:   256Mb |
         | Graphics Ports: 0 | IO Buses: 6 | CPUs:        1 | [ H/W Details ]
         +-----------------------+----------------------+-----------------+

                          [        Install HP-UX        ]

                          [   Run a Recovery Shell   ]

                          [     Advanced Options      ]


              [ Reboot ]                                [ Help ]
```

Figure 13–1 *The HP-UX installation process.*

```
                              Advanced Options

         The options in this menu are useful mainly for debugging
         customized installation setups and are not normally useful
         during the typical installation.


                      [       Show System Info      ]

                      [   Edit (vi) config file    ]

                      [  Edit (vi) environment vars  ]

                      [ * ] Enable use of DHCP for network defaults

                      [ ^H ] Erase Character

                      [ 0 ] Debug Level




         [  OK  ]                                          [ Help ]
```

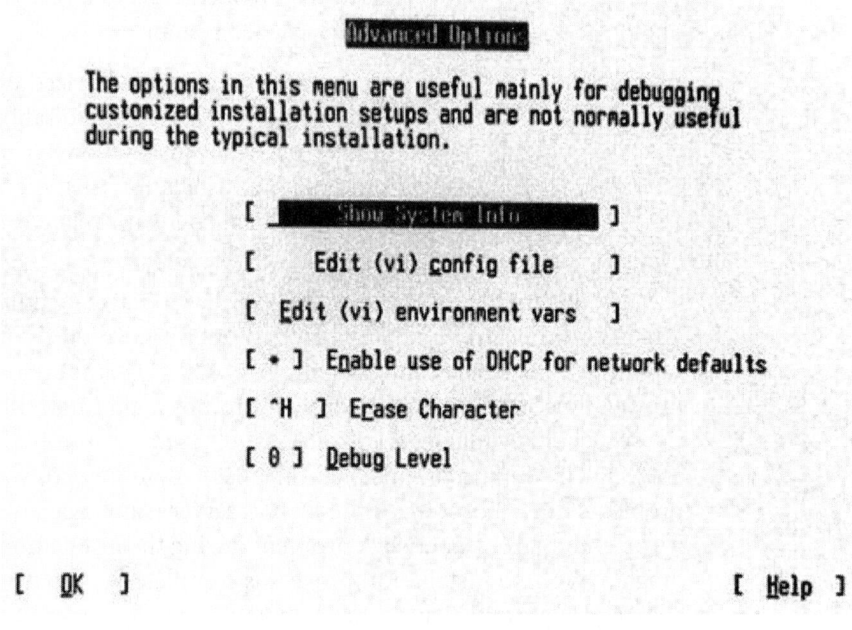

Figure 13–2 Advanced Options *of the HP-UX installation process.*

The asterisk character shows that use of DHCP is enabled by default. Pressing the spacebar key on this option disables it. After disabling DHCP, use the `Tab` key to go to the OK button and then press the `Enter` key to return to the screen shown in Figure 13-1. Now you will go to the `Install HP-UX` option and press the `Enter` key. The next screen appears, shown in Figure 13-3, where you can select user interface and media options.

There are three media selection options as follows.

Media only installation	This option is used to install HP-UX completely from Core OS media supplied by HP, for example, a CD-ROM.
Media with Network enabled	This option is used to install software from another machine on the network that is configured as Software Server. A software server machine contains software depots known as SD depots. Software depots are discussed in Chapter 15.
Ignite-UX server based	This type of installation is used for Ignite-UX.

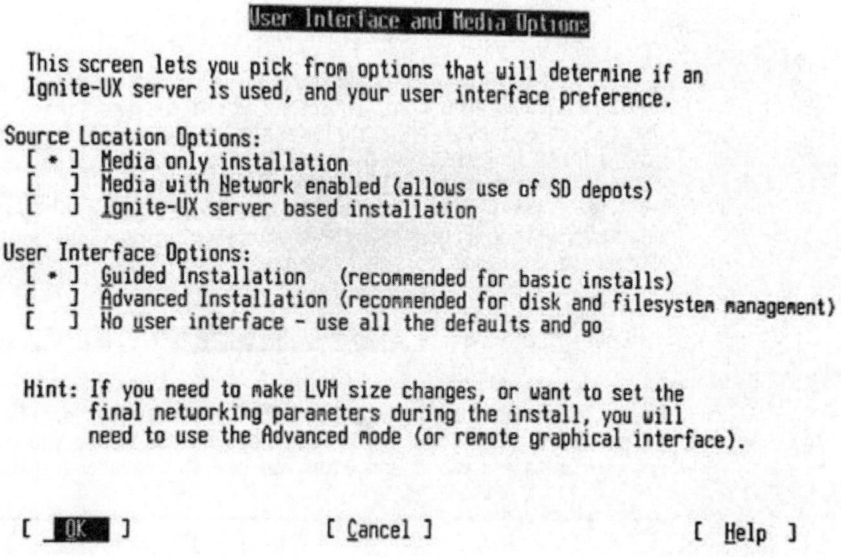

```
User Interface and Media Options

This screen lets you pick from options that will determine if an
Ignite-UX server is used, and your user interface preference.

Source Location Options:
   [ * ] Media only installation
   [   ] Media with Network enabled (allows use of SD depots)
   [   ] Ignite-UX server based installation

User Interface Options:
   [ * ] Guided Installation   (recommended for basic installs)
   [   ] Advanced Installation (recommended for disk and filesystem management)
   [   ] No user interface - use all the defaults and go

   Hint: If you need to make LVM size changes, or want to set the
         final networking parameters during the install, you will
         need to use the Advanced mode (or remote graphical interface).


   [  OK  ]               [ Cancel ]                 [ Help ]
```

Figure 13–3 *Selection of* User Interface and Media Options.

User interface selection options are shown below. We will discuss *Guided Installation* and *Advanced Installation* in more detail in this chapter.

Guided
Installation

This is recommended for basic installations.

Advanced
Installation

If you want to make LVM and file-system size changes during the installation process, you should use *Advanced Installation*. Networking parameters can also be set during the *Advanced Installation* process.

No User
Interface

This is the minimum user interaction mode of installation. It takes default values for the installation.

13.3 Guided Installation

The *Guided Installation* process performs the basic HP-UX installation. When you select this method of installation, you go through a number of steps. At every step, you have to configure one system parameter. After selecting `Guided Installation`, the first screen looks like the one shown in Figure 13-4.

Figure 13-4 is the first step toward guided installation. In this step you chose the overall system configuration. The default selection is `HP-UX`

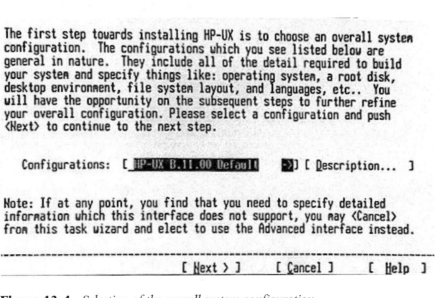

```
The first step towards installing HP-UX is to choose an overall system
configuration. The configurations which you see listed below are
general in nature. They include all of the detail required to build
your system and specify things like: operating system, a root disk,
desktop environment, file system layout, and languages, etc.. You
will have the opportunity on the subsequent steps to further refine
your overall configuration. Please select a configuration and push
<Next> to continue to the next step.


    Configurations:  [ HP-UX B.11.00 Default     ->] [ Description... ]


Note: If at any point, you find that you need to specify detailed
information which this interface does not support, you may <Cancel>
from this task wizard and elect to use the Advanced interface instead.
-------------------------------------------------------------------
                           [ Next > ]      [ Cancel ]      [ Help ]
```

Figure 13–4 *Selection of the overall system configuration.*

`B.11.00 Default`. Choose `Next` to go to the next step. You can also press the `N` key to select `next`. At each following step, you will see similar screens, where you can go to the previous screen by selecting `Back` instead of `Next` (not shown in Figure 13-4 as this is the first step in `Guided Installation` and no previous step is available). The `Guided Installation` steps are as follows.

1. Selection of overall system configuration as shown in Figure 13-4.
2. Environment selection. Here you can select a particular environment depending on the type of your hardware. For example, you can select 32-bit HP-UX with or without CDE support (CDE is the Common Desktop Environment used as the GUI on UNIX systems).
3. Root disk selection. A default selection is automatically made for you and you will see the disk model, its size, and its hardware path. This is the disk on which the operating system is going to be installed. The default selection is actually the primary boot device. You can make another selection if you understand how to change the primary boot device in PDC.
4. Selection of root swap area. A recommended value of swap space in megabytes is shown at this step. The amount of physical memory installed in your system is also listed. Depending on your requirements, you can change the swap area. More detail on the swap space can be found in Chapter 22.
5. Select the file system. Here you will find options for a particular type of file system. The options are:
   - Logical Volume Manager (LVM) with VxFS
   - Logical Volume Manager (LVM) with HFS
   - whole disk (not LVM) with HFS

   HFS and VxFS are types of file systems. You can find detailed information about these and the LVM in Chapter 18.
6. If you are using the LVM approach, you can put more than one disk in a volume group. During the installation process, the **root** volume group *vg00* is configured, and you can decide how many disks should be included in this volume group. However, if your system has many disks, HP recommends that a maximum of four disks be included in the **root** volume group. You can also select disk stripping if more than one disk is included in the **root** volume group. Disk stripping distributes data on all disks and hence increases performance.
7. Select a language. The default language is English.
8. User license selection. The default selection is the 2-User license.
9. Select additional software to be installed with the base HP-UX. Available software categories and products are listed with a short description.

Selected software products are marked with Yes, while others are marked No. Make sure that general patches are marked for installation.

10. Preinstall disk information. The installation process will analyze disks used for installation. Any errors or warning messages will be displayed. If a disk already contains the HP-UX file system, you will see a warning message showing that all data on the disk will be erased.

After the above step, select Go, and the actual installation process will start, where file systems will be created on disk(s) and the HP-UX system files will be copied from installation media. This is a long process and may take quite some time depending on the type of your system.

13.4   Advanced Installation

If you select Advanced Installation (Figure 13-3), you will see a screen as shown in Figure 13-5. Here you can select all of the options used in your guided installation. Additionally, you can set the network configuration and make changes to file system sizes in the LVM.

Here you can use the Tab key to move around. When the cursor is over a particular item, you can press the Enter key to change options. The topmost line lists five categories. By selecting a particular category, options

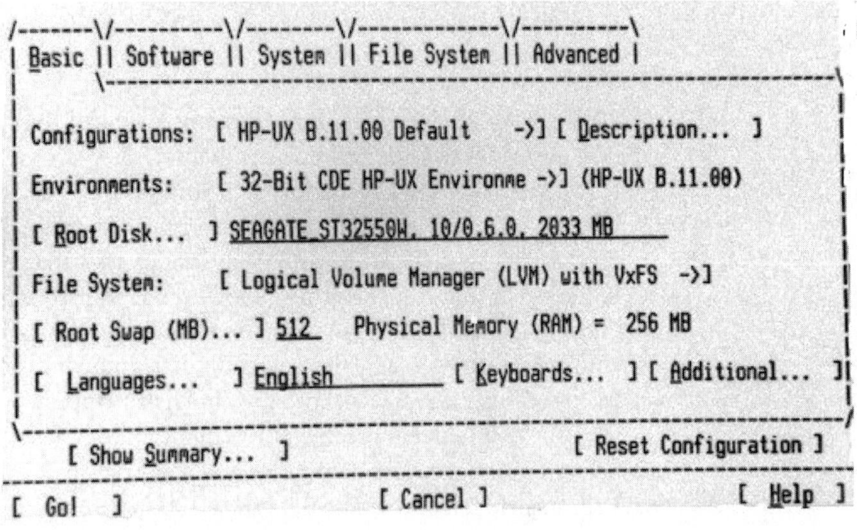

```
/-------\/----------\/---------\/------------\/----------\
| Basic || Software || System || File System || Advanced |
|       \-----------------------------------------------------------\
|                                                                    |
| Configurations:  [ HP-UX B.11.00 Default    ->] [ Description... ] |
|                                                                    |
| Environments:    [ 32-Bit CDE HP-UX Environme ->] (HP-UX B.11.00)  |
|                                                                    |
| [ Root Disk... ] SEAGATE ST32550W, 10/0.6.0, 2033 MB              |
|                                                                    |
| File System:     [ Logical Volume Manager (LVM) with VxFS  ->]    |
|                                                                    |
| [ Root Swap (MB)... ] 512   Physical Memory (RAM) = 256 MB        |
|                                                                    |
| [ Languages... ] English         [ Keyboards... ] [ Additional... ]|
|                                                                    |
\--------------------------------------------------------------------/
     [ Show Summary... ]                      [ Reset Configuration ]
------------------------------------------------------------------------
[ Go! ]                       [ Cancel ]                     [ Help ]
```

Figure 13–5   *Advanced HP-UX installation.*

related to that category are listed in the lower part of the screen. In Figure 13-5, you can see the basic configuration options with their default values. You can make changes to any of these. The basic reason for using the `Advanced Installation` is to make changes to the LVM file systems during the installation process or to make a network setup. Network setup can be performed in the `System` category of Figure 13-5. Changes to the LVM are made using the `File System` category. Figure 13-6 shows a screen shot of the `File System` category for adjusting file system sizes.

I have selected LVM with VxFS during this process. Default file systems present in this group are listed in this screen. You can scroll the list of file systems using the arrow keys. The following information about each file system is displayed in this screen.

1. Mount directory (`Mount Dir`) for the file system. Mount directories are automatically created during the installation process.
2. File system usage (`Usage`) shows the type of file system. All file systems are marked `VxFS` except the swap area and the file system having `/ stand` as its mount point. The `/stand` file system is used for the HP-UX kernel, and it is mandatory that it be of HFS type.
3. Size of the file system (`Size (MB)`) is shown in megabytes.
4. Percentage used (`% Used`) shows the percentage of the file system that will be used after the installation process is complete.

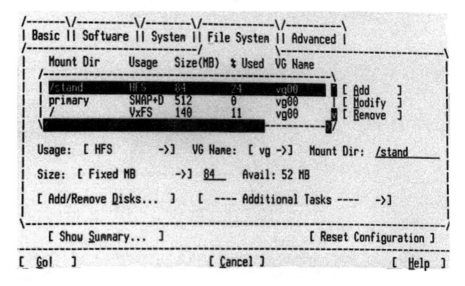

Figure 13–6 *Adjusting file system sizes during advanced HP-UX installation.*

5. Volume group name (VG Name). The root volume group name is vg00.

You can use the Tab key to move around this screen and make any desired changes to a particular file system. For this, you have to follow these three steps.

1. Select a file system using the Tab and arrow keys.
2. Make a desired change using the Tab, arrow, and Enter keys.
3. Go to the Modify option using the Tab key and press the Enter key. You can also press M for this purpose.

By default, HP-UX creates a volume group with the name vg00 and creates eight logical volumes in it. You need to adjust these sizes according to your requirements. For example, if you are installing a number of applications, the size of the /opt partition must be larger. On the other hand, if you expect that many users will be creating large files in their home directories, you will increase the size of the /home partition. Assign a reasonable amount of disk space to the /tmp directory, as some applications may create a large number of temporary files in this directory. Swap space is an important issue, and you should leave enough space for this on your disk. On a 4-GByte disk, I create partitions in the sizes shown in Table 13-1.

Table 13–1 *Size of Partitions on a 4-GByte Disk*

Partition	Size (MBytes)
/	100
/stand	100
Swap	512
/home	200
/opt	800
/tmp	700
/usr	800
/var	800

In addition to adjusting existing logical volume sizes, you can also create new logical volumes and add or remove physical volumes in the volume group.

When you are satisfied with the configuration, press the Enter key on the Go option. The installation process will analyze disks and show any warning or error messages. When you acknowledge these messages, file systems are created, software is copied and the configure process starts, which may take a long time.

13.5 Initial System Configuration

Assuming that the Set System Parameters at First Boot option was chosen from the System tab, at the end of the installation process, the HP-UX kernel is rebuilt and the system reboots. The system will start the initial configuration process after reboot. This process includes a number of steps, and these are carried out by the set_parms command invoked when HP-UX boots for the first time. You will be asked to provide the system name, time zone, **root** password, and IP configuration data. A typical session of initial configuration is shown here, where boldface letters show user input.

```
                    Welcome to HP-UX!

Before using your system, you will need to answer a few questions.
The first question is whether you plan to use this system on a network.
Answer "yes" if you have connected the system to a network and are
   ready to link with a network.
Answer "no" if you:
        * Plan to set up this system as a standalone (no networking).
        * Want to use the system now as a standalone and connect to a
          network later.
```

```
Are you ready to link this system to a network?

Press [y] for yes or [n] for no, then press [Return] y
```

```
   Before you begin using this system, you need to obtain the
   following information from your local network administrator:

        * Your system name (host name).
        * Your Internet Protocol (IP) address.
        * Your time zone.

   If you do not have this information, you may stop now and
restart your system once you have it.
```

```
Do you wish to continue?

Press [y] for yes or [n] for no, then press [Return] y
```

For the system to operate correctly, you must assign it a unique
system name or "hostname". The hostname can be a simple name
(example: widget) or an Internet fully-qualified domain name
(example: widget.redrock-cvl.hp.com).

A simple name, or each dot (.) separated component of a domain name,
  must:

  * Start with a letter.

  * Contain no more than 64 characters.

  * Contain only letters, numbers, underscore (_), or dash (-).
    Uppercase letters are not recommended.

NOTE: The first or only component of a hostname should contain 8
      characters or less for compatibility with HP-UX `uname'.

The current hostname is myhp.

Enter the system name, then press [Return] or simply press [Return]
to retain the current host name (myhp): **myhp**

You have chosen myhp as the name for this system.
Is this correct?

Press [y] for yes or [n] for no, then press [Return] **y**

   Working...

The following procedure enables you to set the time zone.

Select your location from the following list:

  1) North America or Hawaii

  2) Central America

  3) South America

```
4) Europe

5) Africa

6) Asia

7) Australia, New Zealand
```

Enter the number for your location (1-7) then press [Return] **1**

```
Select your time zone from the following list:

1) Newfoundland Standard/Daylight  |   8) Pacific Standard/Daylight
                                   |
2) Atlantic Standard/Daylight      |   9) Yukon Standard/Daylight
                                   |
3) Eastern Standard/Daylight       |  10) Aleutian Standard/Daylight
                                   |
4) Eastern Standard Only           |  11) Hawaii Standard
   (US: Most of Indiana)           |
                                   |  12) Unlisted time zone
5) Central Standard/Daylight       |
                                   |  13) Previous menu
6) Mountain Standard/Daylight      |
                                   |
7) Mountain Standard Only (Arizona)|
```

Enter the number for your time zone (1 - 13), then press [Return] **3**

```
You have selected:

    Eastern Standard/Daylight (EST5EDT).
```

Is this correct?

Press [y] for yes or [n] for no, then press [Return] **y**

This section enables you to set the system clock.

The current system time is Tue Dec 21 11:59:16 EST 1999

Is this correct?

Press [y] for yes or [n] for no, then press [Return] **y**

This section enables you to set the "root" password for the system.

The "root" account is used for system administration tasks.   To insure
the security of the system, the root account should have a password.

Do you want to set the root password at this time?

Press [y] for yes or [n] for no, then press [Return] **y**
New password:
Re-enter new password:

If you wish networking to operate correctly, you must assign the
system a unique Internet Protocol (IP) address.   The IP address must:

   * Contain 4 numeric components.

   * Have a period (.) separating each numeric component.

   * Contain numbers between 0 and 255.

   For example: 134.32.3.10

 Your current address is 192.168.3.23.   To retain this address,
 just press [Return].

Enter your IP address, then press [Return] or press [Return] to select
the current address (192.168.3.23): **192.168.3.23**

You have chosen 192.168.3.23 as the IP address for this system.
Is this correct?

Press [y] for yes, [n] for no or [c] to cancel then press [Return] **y**

Working...

You may configure some additional network parameters at this time:

* Subnetwork Mask and Default Gateway

* Domain Name System (DNS)

* Network Information Service (NIS)

Your local network administrator can tell you which if any of these
parameters should be configured for your system, and provide you the
appropriate values.

If you do not have these values now, you can configure them later.

Do you want to configure these additional network parameters?

Press [y] for yes or [n] for no, then press [Return] **n**
 .
 .
 .
To fully utilize the capabilities of your system, you may have to
perform some additional system configuration tasks using the HP-UX
"sam" (System Administration Manager) command. Consult your local
administrator or the "HP-UX System Administration Tasks" manual for
more information.

The system will now complete its boot process, and allow you to login
as '"'root'."

> Your minimum installation process is complete at this stage, and the
> system starts booting. It will show you the starting process of different ser-
> vices and system components as shown below.

```
HP-UX Start-up in progress
_____

Configure system crash dumps ............................ OK
Mount file systems ...................................... OK
Update kernel and loadable modules ...................... N/A
Initialize loadable modules ............................. N/A
Setting hostname ........................................ OK
```

Finally you will see a login prompt. At this point, you can log in as user **root**. Your system has the core software installed, and you can start the installation of additional software applications and patches.

When installing HP-UX, you can leave undone many of the steps in the initial system configuration. These steps can be completed later, after logging in as **root** and restarting the initial configuration process. To restart this process, use the set_parms command. If you use this command without any arguments, it will show you the following message.

```
Usage: set_parms <argument>
    Where <argument> can be:
hostname
timezone
date_time
root_passwd
ip_address
addl_netwrk
        or initial (for entire initial boot-time dialog sequence)
```

Using one of these listed options, you can repeat a partial configuration or reconfigure your system for all options. If you want to configure only one parameter, use the proper argument with the set_parms command. For example, to set the time zone only, use the command set_parms timezone. If you want to set all parameters, use the set_parms initial command and it will go through all steps. Depending on the type of terminal you are using, the set_parms command will start either in text-based or GUI mode. The options in both of the modes are the same. Let's start the set_parms initial command in GUI mode.

Just after starting the command, you will see a window as shown in Figure 13-7.

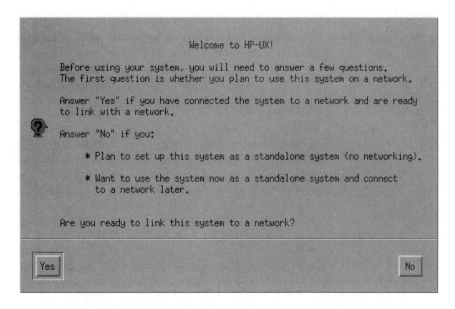

Figure 13–7 *The first window after starting the* set_parms *command.*

This window shows you initial information. If you want to connect the system to the network at this point, select Yes; otherwise select No. In this example, I selected Yes. After the selection is made, the next window appears and is shown in Figure 13-8.

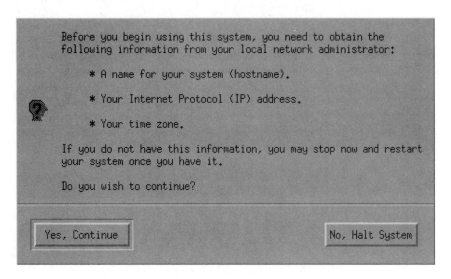

Figure 13–8 *Basic information needed for system setup.*

Figure 13-8 shows the basic information you need to set up the system. The information is the system name, the IP address for the system, and the time zone. After pressing the `Yes, Continue` button, you move to the next window, shown in Figure 13-9.

At this point, you enter a name for your system. Rules for the system name are mentioned in this figure. You can type the name in the box provided for this purpose. If you are on a network, you must have a naming convention to avoid any duplicate names. A name must start with a letter, although it can contain any number of numeric characters. A host name must not be longer than 64 characters. Once you enter the host name and press the `OK` button, another window will appear that will ask you to confirm the host name you have typed in.

After pressing the `Yes` button, you will move to the window shown in Figure 13-10, where you will select your location. The window shown in Figure 13-11 is used for time zone selection. First you select your location and then the actual time zone.

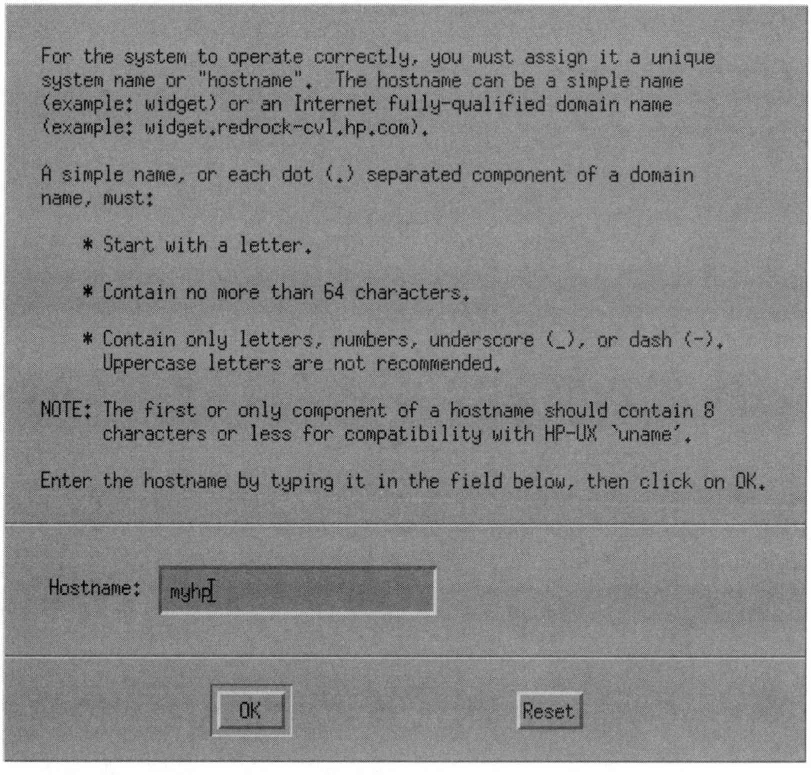

Figure 13–9 *Selecting the system name.*

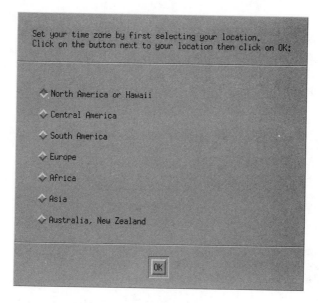

Figure 13–10 *Selecting the location.*

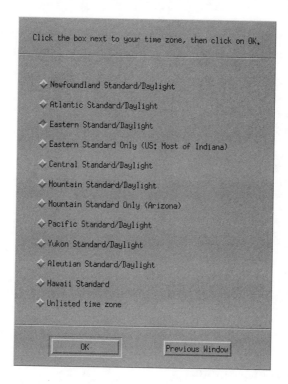

Figure 13–11 *Selecting the time zone.*

When you have made the selection for the time zone, HP-UX will show you the selection you have made. You will be asked to confirm the selection as shown in Figure 13-12. As you can see, the selection made is U.S. Eastern Standard time with daylight savings. This time is a 5-hour difference from Greenwich Mean Time, or GMT (EST5EDT).

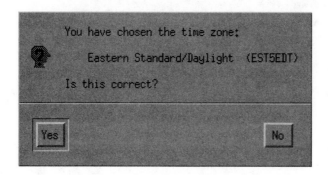

Figure 13–12 *Confirmation for the time zone selection.*

The next window will show the current time on your system clock, and you need to confirm it. If the time is not correct, you may answer No in Figure 13-13 and then select the correct time.

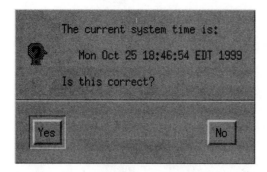

Figure 13–13 *Selecting the system time.*

After this, you will select the **root** password. Information about the **root** password is provided in Figure 13-14, while Figure 13-15 is used for selecting the **root** password.

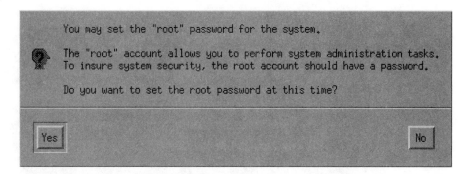

Figure 13–14 *Information about the root password.*

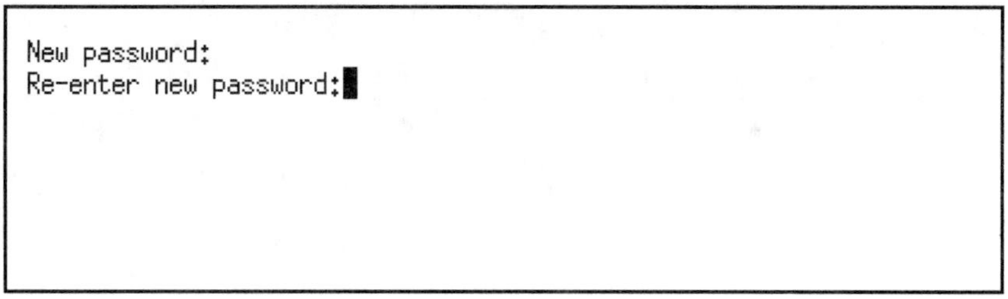

Figure 13–15 *Selection of the **root** password.*

You have to type the **root** password twice to confirm the password, as shown in Figure 13-15. If you provide the same password both times, a confirmation window appears as shown in Figure 13-16.

Figure 13–16 *Password confirmation window.*

Now you move to the IP address part of the configuration process. Figure 13-17 shows the window for entering the IP address of your machine.

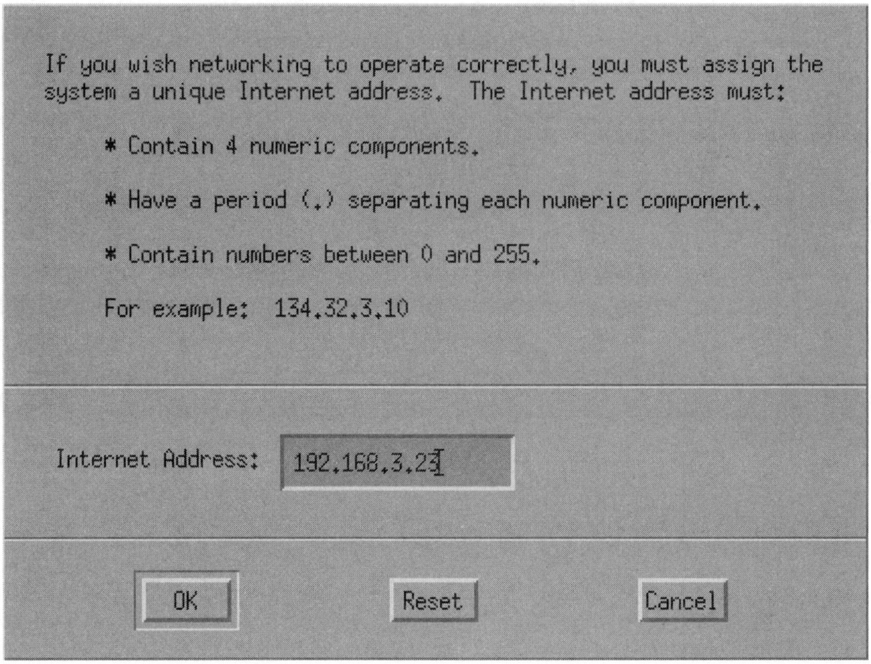

If you wish networking to operate correctly, you must assign the
system a unique Internet address. The Internet address must:

   * Contain 4 numeric components.

   * Have a period (.) separating each numeric component.

   * Contain numbers between 0 and 255.

   For example: 134.32.3.10

Internet Address: 192.168.3.23

[OK]   [Reset]   [Cancel]

Figure 13–17   *Selecting the IP address.*

After this, you may need to enter some other information such as the
Subnetwork Mask, Default Gateway address, and Domain Name System
name, as shown in Figure 13-18. This is the last part of the set_parms command session. Pressing the No button will terminate the command (I did the
same), while pressing the Yes button will show you additional windows for
these network configuration tasks.

Postinstallation Tasks

If your system has some hardware that needs additional software drivers not
already built into the kernel, you may need to install these drivers after completing the installation process. For example, if there are 100-Base-T Ethernet
or gigabit Ethernet adapters installed, you may need to install the drivers using
CDs provided by HP. The process of installing any additional software involves
the HP Software Distributor (SD-UX) which is discussed in Chapter 15.

After installing any drivers that necessitate rebuilding a new kernel, the
SD-UX will automatically rebuild the kernel and reboot the system for you.
For configuring these additional interfaces, use SAM (Chapter 12).

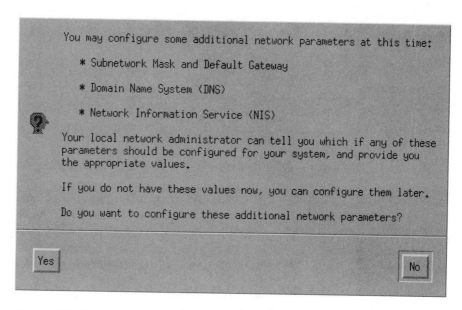

You may configure some additional network parameters at this time:

* Subnetwork Mask and Default Gateway

* Domain Name System (DNS)

* Network Information Service (NIS)

Your local network administrator can tell you which if any of these
parameters should be configured for your system, and provide you
the appropriate values.

If you do not have these values now, you can configure them later.

Do you want to configure these additional network parameters?

Yes   No

Figure 13–18   *Selecting additional network parameters.*

■ Chapter Summary

This chapter is included to give you a brief overview of the HP-UX installation process. In the start of the chapter, there was an introduction to HP 9000 servers and workstations. The Processor Dependent Code (PDC) controls initial bootup tasks, such as memory and CPU tests and the detection of attached peripherals. It determines the primary boot device and tries to boot HP-UX from the device. You can interrupt this process and use the search command in PDC to look for additional bootable devices. You can then boot from a device containing the HP-UX installation media.

Once the system boots from the HP-UX Install and Core OS installation media (usually a CD-ROM), you are prompted to either install HP-UX or run a recovery shell. When you select Install HP-UX, you have to select the source location and user interface. You can choose any of the three user-interface options.

1. Guided Installation is used for a basic install.
2. Advanced Installation is used for configuration of LVM file system sizes and network setup.
3. No User Interface is used to install HP-UX with all default values and minimum user interaction.

In the first two options, you can specify a number of options for installation parameters. After the installation process is complete, the system rebuilds the kernel and reboots itself. After the first boot, you can configure the system and connect it to the network. You can modify the initial configuration at any time using the set_parms command.

If your system contains additional devices for which drivers are not included in the standard HP-UX distribution, you need to install the drivers using SD-UX. After that, you can configure these devices with the help of SAM.

In the next chapter, you will learn about the HP-UX startup and shutdown processes.

▲ CHAPTER REVIEW QUESTIONS

1. The 64-bit HP-UX version can be installed on all HP-9000 servers and workstations (Yes/No).

2. Which media can be used for HP-UX installation?

3. How would you configure a 4-GByte disk for a fresh HP-UX installation?

4. What restrictions apply to the hostname for HP-UX?

5. What is the basic information you need for initial configuration of HP-UX?

6. What is the use of PDC?

▲ TEST YOUR KNOWLEDGE

1. *The length of the HP-UX host name may be:*
   A. 8 characters maximum
   B. 15 characters maximum
   C. 16 characters maximum
   D. 64 characters maximum

2. *The HP-UX host name may contain:*
   A. Letters only.
   B. Letters and numbers only.
   C. Letters, numbers, dash, and underscore characters.
   D. Letters, numbers, dash, underscore, and dot characters.

3.   Which command is used for initial configuration of the system?

>   A. the `sysconfig` command
>
>   B. the `set_parms` command
>
>   C. the `configure` command
>
>   D. the `setup` command

4.   Which statement is true?

>   A. At the boot time, HP-UX starts installation if the installation CD is inside the drive.
>
>   B. You need to interrupt the normal boot process and manually boot from a different boot device containing the installation media. After that, the install/recovery process starts, which can be used for a fresh installation.
>
>   C. You need to interrupt the normal boot process and manually boot from the installation media. After that, you need to start the installation using the `setup` command.
>
>   D. You need to interrupt the normal boot process and manually boot from the installation media. After that, you need to start the installation using the `set_parms` command.

5.   How can you change the primary boot path?

>   A. use PDC
>
>   B. use the `mkboot` command
>
>   C. with the help of ISL
>
>   D. use the `set_parms` command

6.   Which command do you use in PDC to find the device name for a CD-ROM drive?

>   A. `find`
>
>   B. `cdrom`
>
>   C. `search`
>
>   D. `list`

7.   You use the `search` command, and a list of devices is displayed as shown below. Which command will you use to boot from the CD-ROM?

```
Path Number   Device Path (dec)   Device Type
-----------   -----------------   -----------
P0            10/0/6              Random Access Media
P1            10/0/5              Random Access Media
P2            10/0/4              Random Access Media
P3            10/0/3              Random Access Media
```

```
P4          10/0/2          Random Access Media
P5          10/0/1          Random Access Media
P6          10/4/4.2        Toshiba CD-ROM Device
P7          10/4/4.1        Sequential Access Media
```

    A. Boot P6

    B. Boot 10/4/4.2

    C. BO 10/4/4.2

    D. all of the above

System Startup and Shutdown

Understanding of the system startup and shutdown processes is very important both for routine system administration and troubleshooting. Every HP-9000 server or workstation is supplied with boot code that resides on ROM. As soon as you power on the system, this code executes and performs self-tests and some initialization tasks. It then loads the HP-UX kernel and hands control over to it. The kernel does a number of system initialization tasks before you get a login prompt on your console or terminal. This chapter covers in detail all of the processes that take place from system power on to the display of the login prompt.

In the beginning, you will see an overview of the boot process. The boot process starts from *processor dependent code* (PDC) that resides on ROM in your system. You will learn how to work with PDC and use its commands by interrupting the boot process. During the boot process, the PDC checks for boot area on the primary boot disk. You will learn the structure of the boot area to

243

build an understanding of this part of the boot disk. The *initial system loader* (ISL) is used to load the kernel into memory. Its knowledge is important if you need to boot your machine in single-user mode. You have to rebuild the HP-UX kernel many times, and ISL helps you boot from an old kernel if your new kernel is misconfigured and fails to boot. You will also see how the autoboot works and how to enable or disable it.

Once the HP-UX kernel is loaded into memory, it initializes other processes. The init process is the most important of all of these. It is responsible for most of the system initialization. When you study the section containing information about the init process, you will see the structure of its configuration file and how it performs automatic initialization of other processes at different stages of the boot process.

Runlevels show the system state at a particular instant, and these are also controlled by the init process. You will see which runlevels are supported on HP-UX and what the function is of each. Changing system states by changing runlevels is also explained at this stage.

Many times you need to perform a task right after the system boots up. You may also need to run a program at the boot time. You will find a complete example of how programs are started and stopped during the system startup and shutdown processes. In the last part of this chapter, the shutdown process will be presented. You will see the difference between the shutdown and reboot commands.

After going through this chapter, you will understand the startup and shutdown processes and the different stages that involve these processes. In addition, you will have knowledge of commands and utilities that are used for this purpose. Having a good understanding of this process, you will be able to troubleshoot any HP-UX startup or shutdown problem.

14.1 Introduction to the Boot Process

The boot process of an HP-9000 server or workstation starts when you power it on or when you reboot a running system. It can be divided into two main parts.

- boot ROM startup
- HP-UX startup

In the first stage, the boot ROM startup process is carried out. At its completion, it initiates the HP-UX startup process, which is completed in a number of steps. On an abstract level, the boot sequence can be divided into the following steps.

1. Power on or reboot.
2. The processor dependent code (PDC) executes and performs self-tests. These tests include memory and CPU tests. The PDC also detects any peripherals attached to the system.
3. PDC initializes the console to display messages. It looks for the primary boot path for booting the system. The boot path is the hardware path to the disk used as the boot device.
4. PDC loads and executes the *initial system loader* (ISL) from the boot path and executes it. At this stage in the startup process, the role of the boot ROM ends.
5. ISL loads the secondary system loader known as `hpux`, which resides on the boot area of the disk.
6. The `hpux` loads the HP-UX kernel `/stand/vmunix` into memory and hands control over to the kernel.
7. The kernel starts the `swapper` process and then the `init` process.
8. The `init` process reads its initialization file, `/etc/inittab`, and initializes most of the operating system daemons and processes. It brings the system into an appropriate state and makes it usable for users.

As soon as the `init` process has completed its tasks, you see a login prompt at the console or at any terminal attached to the system. Part of a sample boot process is shown here.

```
Primary boot path   = 0/2/0.6.0
Alternate boot path = 7/2/0.6.0
Console path        = 15/1
Keyboard path       = 15/1
[*** Manufacturing (or Debug) Permissions ON ***]
System is HP9000/800/V2500 series
Processor is starting the autoboot process.
```

```
To discontinue, press any key within 10 seconds.

Device        : 0/2/0.6.0
File          : hpux
Arguments     : hpux
Loading       : hpux .......... 163808 bytes loaded.
102368  + 61440  + 864504   start 0xd01cc0

Boot
: disc(0/2/0.6.0;0)/stand/vmunix
6848512 + 1181408 + 6521760 start 0x3a168
5/2/0.8.0.255.1.2.0 sctl
Probing epic6
Probe of epic6 complete
6 saga
6/0/0 btlan6
6/1/0 fcT1
6/1/0.5 fcT1_cntl
6/1/0.8 fcp

System Console is on SPP DUART0 Interface
WARNING: max message size > 65535, adjusting.
WARNING: max bytes on msg q > 65535, adjusting.
Logical volume 64, 0x3 configured as ROOT
Logical volume 64, 0x2 configured as SWAP
Logical volume 64, 0x2 configured as DUMP
     Swap device table:  (start & size given in 512-byte blocks)
         entry 0 - major is 64, minor is 0x2; start = 0, size = 2097152
Starting the STREAMS daemons-phase 1
Checking root file system.
file system is clean - log replay is not required
Root check done.
Create STCP device files
Memory Information:
     physical page size = 4096 bytes, logical page size = 4096 bytes
     Physical: 16773120 Kbytes, lockable: 12203164 Kbytes, available:
     14014856 Kbytes

/sbin/ioinitrc:
Starting /sbin/ioscan -f 1> /dev/null
Starting /sbin/insf -e -C disk 1> /dev/null
        Done ioscan & insf
/sbin/bcheckrc:
Checking for LVM volume groups and Activating (if any exist)
Volume group "/dev/vg00" has been successfully changed.
Resynchronized volume group /dev/vg00
```

```
vxfs fsck: sanity check: root file system OK (mounted read/write)
```

```
/sbin/auto_parms: DHCP access is disabled (see /etc/auto_parms.log)

HP-UX Start-up in progress
      _____

      Configure system crash dumps ............................ OK
      Mount file systems ...................................... OK
      Update kernel and loadable modules ..................... N/A
      Initialize loadable modules ............................ N/A
      Setting hostname ........................................ OK
      Set privilege group .................................... N/A
      Display date ........................................... N/A
      Save system crash dump if needed ....................... N/A
```

```
Enable auxiliary swap space ............................... OK
Start syncer daemon ....................................... OK
Configure HP Fibre Channel interfaces ..................... OK
          ......................................... OK
Configure Loopback interfaces (lo0) ....................... OK
Start Software Distributor agent daemon ................... OK
Configuring all unconfigured software filesets ............ OK
Recover editor crash files ................................ OK
Clean UUCP ................................................ OK
List and/or clear temporary files ......................... OK
Clean up old log files .................................... OK
Start system message logging daemon ....................... OK
Start pty allocator daemon ................................ OK
Start network tracing and logging daemon .................. OK
Configure HP Ethernet interfaces .......................... OK
Configure HP 100BT interfaces ............................. OK
Configure HP SPP 100BT interfaces ......................... OK
Configure LAN interfaces .................................. OK
Start name server daemon .................................. N/A
Start NFS core subsystem .................................. OK
Start NIS+ server subsystem ............................... OK
Start NIS+ client subsystem ............................... OK
Start NIS server subsystem ................................ OK
Start NIS client subsystem ................................ OK
Start NFS client subsystem ................................ OK
Start the Trusted Mode with Nis+ subsystem ................ N/A
Configure pseudo devices for MAC/LLA access ............... OK
Start multicast routing daemon ............................ N/A
Start Internet services daemon ............................ OK
Start dynamic routing daemon .............................. N/A
Start router discover protocol daemon ..................... N/A
Configuring PPP Interface ................................. OK
Start RARP protocol daemon ................................ N/A
Start remote system status daemon ......................... N/A
Configuring man pages for Internet Services ............... OK
Starting mail daemon ...................................... OK
Starting outbound connection daemons for DDFA software .... N/A
Start SNMP Master Network Management daemon ............... OK
Start OSPF MIB Network Management subAgent ................ N/A
Start SNMP HP-UNIX Network Management subAgent ............ OK
Start SNMP MIB-2 Network Management subAgent .............. OK
Start SNMP Trap Dest Network Management subAgent .......... OK
Start DCE daemons ......................................... N/A
Start RPC daemon if needed ................................ OK
Start the Isogon License Server daemon .................... N/A
Start remote boot daemon .................................. OK
```

```
Starting X Font Server at TCP port 7000 ................... N/A
Start vt daemon ........................................... OK
Start time synchronization ................................ OK
Start accounting .......................................... OK
Starting the password/group assist subsystem ............. OK
Starting disk array monitor daemons. ...................... OK
Start print spooler .'..................................... OK
Starting HP Distributed Print Service ..................... OK
Start clock daemon ........................................ OK
Support Tools Informational Fileset ....................... OK
Start diagnostic subsystem ................................ OK
Starting hardware predictive .............................. OK
Start environment monitoring daemon ....................... OK
Start auditing subsystem .................................. N/A
Start audio server daemon ................................. N/A
SAM System administration configuration ................... OK
MeasureWare performance software is being started. ........ OK
Reinitialize Software Distributor agent daemon ............ OK
Starting Event Monitoring Service ......................... OK
Start EMS SNMP subagent ................................... OK
Start NFS server subsystem ................................ OK
Start X print server(s) ................................... N/A
Start CDE login server .................................... OK

The system is ready.

GenericSysName [HP Release B.11.00] (see /etc/issue)
Console Login:
```

In the next sections, you will learn more details on how these tasks are performed.

14.2 Processor Dependent Code

The boot procedure for all HP-9000 systems is controlled by program code, PDC, that resides on the ROM installed inside the system. The PDC is different for different computers (that is why its name is processor dependent). PDC is executed after the system is reset or turned on. It performs self-tests and then tests hardware attached to the system. After thoroughly scanning the memory, it initializes the console and copies the console path to the memory. It copies the boot path and autoboot flag into memory. If the autoboot is disabled, it displays a menu of commands. If the autoboot is enabled, it displays a message showing that the system is going to start the autoboot process and gives you the option to interrupt this process by pressing a key within 10 seconds. If you press a key within 10 seconds, you get the PDC menu; otherwise, the system starts booting from the primary boot path.

PDC is an important part, where you perform system administration tasks to specify primary and alternate boot devices. You can display hardware paths and search boot devices attached to the system. You can also use PDC to boot the system from a device other than primary or secondary boot devices. On V-Class machines, PDC can also be used to boot into single-user mode.

PDC Menus

You get PDC menus by interrupting the boot process by pressing a key when a message like the following is displayed.

```
Processor is starting the autoboot process.

To discontinue, press any key within 10 seconds.
```

PDC menus may differ on servers and workstations slightly, but most of the commands are the same on all systems. A typical PDC menu looks likes the following.

```
-------------------- Main Menu --------------------------
Command                          Description
-------                          -----------
BOot [PRI|ALT|<path>]            Boot from specified path
PAth [PRI|ALT|<path>]            Display or modify a path
SEArch [Display|IPL] [<path>]    Search for boot device
COnfiguration menu               Displays or sets boot values
INformation menu                 Displays hardware information
SERvice menu                     Displays service commands
Help [<menu>|<command>]          Displays help for menu or cmd
RESET                            Restart the system
----------
Main Menu: Enter command or menu >
```

You can use any of these commands; most of the arguments are optional. For example, using the boot command without any arguments will start the autoboot process. If you want to boot from the alternate boot device, you can use the boot alt command. In case you need to boot the system from a device that is neither a primary nor an alternate boot device (such as booting from CD-ROM when installing HP-UX), you can specify the device name as an argument to the boot command.

All of these commands can be abbreviated. The capital letters in the start of each command show the command abbreviation. For example, you can use "bo" instead of boot and "sea" instead of the search command. Help on commands is also available with the Help command.

Searching Boot Devices

You need to search for boot devices if you don't know the exact name of a device for boot purposes. This is often required when installing a new system. The search command shows all disk drives, CD-ROM devices, and tape drives attached to the system. Output of the search command is like the one given here.

```
Main Menu: Enter command or menu > search
Searching for potential boot device(s)
This may take several minutes.
To discontinue search, press any key
(termination may not be immediate)

Path Number   Device Path (dec)   Device Type
-----------   -----------------   -----------
P0            10/0/6              Random Access Media
P1            10/0/5              Random Access Media
P2            10/0/4              Random Access Media
P3            10/0/3              Random Access Media
P4            10/0/2              Random Access Media
P5            10/0/1              Random Access Media
P6            10/4/4.2            Toshiba CD-ROM Device
P7            10/4/4.1            Sequential Access Media
```

Random Access Media shows disks attached to the system, and Sequential Access Media is for tape drives. You can also see a line for a CD-ROM drive. Sometimes you will see Random Access Media in place of the CD-ROM drive. In that case, you have to make a guess which device shows the CD-ROM if you are not familiar with your HP system hardware configuration.

To boot from a particular device, you can use its path number or device path. For example, to boot from a CD-ROM, you can use any of the boot P6 or boot 10/4/4.2 commands.

Booting from an Alternate Disk

Many people use mirrored disks in servers for redundancy and reliability. In a mirror disk configuration, two disks have exactly the same data. Boot devices can also be mirrored so that in case one disk fails to boot the system, it may use the alternate one for the boot process.

To configure an alternate boot device, you can use the `configure` command. To manually boot from the alternate disk device, use the `boot alt` command.

Stable Storage

Stable storage is nonvolatile memory where your system stores information about the following.

* primary boot path
* alternate boot path
* console
* autoboot
* autosearch

This information is used by PDC. You can change this information using the `configure` command. Autoboot and autosearch are either on or off.

Booting in Single-User Mode

On V-Class machines, you can use PDC to boot the system in single-user mode for maintenance purposes. The PDC command used for this purpose is:

```
Main Menu: Enter command or menu > boot pri -is
```

On other machines, you can stop the boot process and use ISL to boot into single-user mode as shown here.

```
Main Menu: Enter command or menu > boot pri
Interact with ISL (Y or N)?> Y
```

When you get the ISL prompt, use the following command to boot into single-user mode.

```
ISL> hpux -is
```

14.3 Boot Area on the System Disk

The system disk from which HP-UX boots has a boot area and a root partition. It may also have swap space and other file systems. The boot area contains a bootstrap loader and necessary information that is used at boot time. ISL is also a part of the boot area. The files in this area are in *logical interchange format* (LIF). Important parts of the boot area are:

- an LIF volume header that identifies the LIF volume
- a file containing an HP-UX volume name
- a directory that contains a list of files contained in this area
- ISL
- secondary loader utility (hpux)
- a file with name AUTO

After PDC has finished its job, the ISL is loaded into memory from the boot device selected by PDC. Now the ISL takes control of the boot process and accesses the AUTO file. The AUTO file contains the hpux utility name and any arguments to be passed to the hpux utility. The ISL loads hpux into memory and provides all arguments to hpux. After starting execution, the hpux utility uses these arguments to find the location and file name for the HP-UX kernel. By default, the kernel is present in the /stand directory and has the name vmunix. The hpux loads the kernel into memory and hands control over to the kernel.

Commands Related to the LIF Area

HP-UX has some commands to display the LIF area contents. The lifls command takes a character disk device file as its argument and lists the files in its LIF area. The lifcp command can be used to show the contents of the AUTO file. The following command lists the LIF area in long format on disk c0t6d0.

```
# lifls -l /dev/dsk/c0t6d0
volume ISL10 data size 7984 directory size 8 99/04/22 03:47:46
filename   type     start   size      implement  created
=============================================================
HPUX       -12928   584     800       0          99/04/22 03:47:47
ISL        -12800   1384    240       0          97/11/06 02:10:13
AUTO       -12289   1624    1         0          97/11/06 02:10:13
PAD        -12290   1632    1700      0          97/11/06 02:10:14
LABEL      BIN      3336    8         0          99/11/24 15:36:41
#
```

The `mkboot` and `rmboot` commands are used to install, modify, or delete files in the LIF area.

14.4 Initial System Loader

If autoboot is on and you don't interrupt the boot process, ISL performs its intended tasks automatically. You can interact with the ISL by interrupting PDC. After interruption, when you use the `boot` command from the PDC menu, it gives you an option to interact with the ISL. At the ISL prompt you can use the commands shown in Table 14-1 to change the parameters in stable storage.

Table 14–1 *The ISL Commands*

Command	Description
display	Displays existing values
conspath	Modifies console path
primpath	Modifies primary boot path
altpath	Modifies alternate boot path
autoboot	Turns autoboot on or off
autosearch	Turns autosearch sequence parameters on or off

You can also use the `setboot` command on a running system to view or change these parameters. A typical output of the `setboot` command is shown next. You can use the `setboot` options to modify the parameters shown here.

```
# setboot
Primary bootpath : 0/2/0.6.0
Alternate bootpath : 7/2/0.6.0

Autoboot is ON (enabled)
Autosearch is OFF (disabled)
#
```

Secondary Loader

As mentioned earlier, the boot block of the disk contains the LIF area where the secondary loader `hpux` is located. By default, the ISL reads the AUTO file in the LIF area to supply arguments to `hpux`. However, it is possible to run hpux at the ISL prompt and to provide different arguments to the command manually. If hpux is run without any argument, it loads /stand/vmunix from the primary boot devices. Let's see some important uses of hpux from a system administration point of view.

BOOTING ANOTHER KERNEL

You can have multiple HP-UX kernels on your system. If a new kernel does not work, use an alternate kernel for booting. For example, if you have an old kernel with name vmunix.old in the /stand directory, you can boot the system from that kernel with the following command at the ISL prompt.

```
ISL> hpux /stand/vmunix.old
```

BOOTING IN SINGLE-USER MODE

To boot the system in single-user mode for system administration purposes, use:

```
ISL> hpux -is
```

You may need to boot the system in single-user mode with a previous kernel if the new kernel does not work and you need to restore the old kernel. For this, you can use following command.

```
ISL> hpux -is /stand/vmunix.old
```

The hpux command can also be used to list files in the /stand directory if you forget the name of the old kernel for booting purposes. You can also list files in the LIF area using hpux. Use of the hpux utility is summarized in Table 14-2.

Table 14–2 *Use of the* hpux *Command*

Command	Result
hpux	Loads /stand/vmunix from the primary boot path
hpux -is	Loads /stand/vmunix and boots in single-user mode from the primary boot path
hpux ll /stand	Lists files in the /stand directory
hpux show autofile	Displays the contents of the AUTO file
hpux set autofile <filename>	Sets new AUTO file with the contents of *filename*
hpux -v	Displays the version number of the hpux utility

14.5 | Loading the HP-UX Kernel

The default HP-UX kernel is /stand/vmunix, which is loaded into memory by the secondary loader hpux. After loading the kernel into memory, the control is transferred to it. The kernel then loads the device drivers and starts the swapper process. It then initiates a shell process to execute commands from /sbin/pre_init_rc. After executing these commands, the first process, /sbin/init, is started and control is transferred to this process.

Swapper Process

The swapper process has a process ID equal to 0. It manages memory for swapping in and out.

/sbin/pre_init_rc File

The most important command found in this file is fsck, which checks and repairs the root file system before any user starts using it.

14.6 | The init Process

This is the most important process in the boot sequence. It is always started with a process ID of 1. After startup, it reads its configuration file, /etc/inittab, and looks for an entry, initdefault in the action field. This tells init the default runlevel of the system. Runlevel is a state of the system, and at all times HP-UX is in one of the defined runlevels. If the initdefault entry is not present, init prompts for a default runlevel to enter. It then spawns ioinit, bcheckrc, rc, and getty processes depending on the default runlevel chosen.

The main actions taken by the init process are:

- Read the initdefault parameter from the /etc/inittab file
- Initialize the kernel data structures using /sbin/ioinitrc
- Run /sbin/bcheckrc
- Run /sbin/rc and bring the system to the default runlevel

/etc/inittab File

The /etc/inittab file is a configuration file read by the init process. This file contains entries in the following general format.

```
id:rstate:action:process
```

Each entry consists of one line in the file. However, an entry can be continued on the next line by ending the line with a backslash character. The fields in the inittab file are explained here.

id   It is a unique ID for each entry and can be 1 to 4 characters long.

rstate   This is the runlevel in which the entry is processed. Multiple runlevels can be specified in this field. If no runlevel is given, the process is assumed to run in all runlevels.

action   This is a keyword that tells init how to treat the process specified in the next field. A keyword "boot" in this field shows that the process is started at boot time but to not wait for its termination. The init process does not restart the process after it terminates. The keyword "bootwait" tells init to start the process at boot time and to wait for its termination; init does not restart the process after it terminates. The "initdefault" keyword tells init to which runlevel the system goes after the boot process is completed. It shows the default runlevel of the system. The "respawn" keyword tells the system that if this process does not exist or terminates due to some reason, restart it. A "sysinit" keyword in this file shows that this entry is processed before the init process accesses the console. This is usually for the initialization of devices. The keyword "wait" tells init to start the process and to wait for its termination.

process   This is the actual process or command line that is executed.

Initialization of I/O Devices with ioinit

After reading the initdefault entry in the file, the init process starts executing commands or scripts that have sysinit. Most important of these is /sbin/ioinitrc. The ioinitrc file uses information from /etc/ioconfig and invokes the ioinit command to check and maintain consistency between /etc/ioconfig and the kernel data structure. This command assigns instance numbers to all new devices found in the system and invokes the insf command to create special device files for all of these devices.

The /sbin/bcheckrc Script

This script does things that are necessary before mounting the file systems. It activates LVM if it is being used on your system. It also checks and cleans file systems using `fsck` before these are mounted. It also loads appropriate key maps depending on the keyboard used with the system. If your workstation is also equipped with a EISA backplane, it runs `eisa_config` in automatic mode to configure and initialize it.

The /sbin/rc Script

The `/sbin/rc` script is run whenever a new runlevel is created or when the system moves from a lower runlevel to a higher one or vice versa. When moving from a lower to a higher runlevel, the `rc` script starts daemons and server processes for that runlevel. When moving from a higher to a lower runlevel, the `rc` script stops all servers and daemons not needed in the lower runlevel. The `rc` script halts the system when moving to runlevel 0.

Sample /etc/inittab

This sample `inittab` file is taken from a 9000-series server.

```
init:3:initdefault:
ioin::sysinit:/sbin/ioinitrc >/dev/console 2>&1
tape::sysinit:/sbin/mtinit > /dev/console 2>&1
muxi::sysinit:/sbin/dasetup     </dev/console >/dev/console 2>&1 # mux init
stty::sysinit:/sbin/stty 9600 clocal icanon echo opost onlcr \
          ixon icrnl ignpar /dev/systty
pwr::bootwait:/etc/powerstartup </dev/console >/dev/console 2>&1 # PowerPath
brc1::bootwait:/sbin/bcheckrc </dev/console >/dev/console 2>&1 # fsck, etc.
link::wait:/sbin/sh -c "/sbin/rm -f /dev/syscon; \
          /sbin/ln /dev/systty /dev/syscon" >/dev/console 2>&1
cprt::bootwait:/sbin/cat /etc/copyright >/dev/syscon         # legal req
sqnc::wait:/sbin/rc </dev/console >/dev/console 2>&1         # system init
#powf::powerwait:/sbin/powerfail >/dev/console 2>&1          # powerfail
cons:123456:respawn:/usr/sbin/getty console console         # system console
#ttp1:234:respawn:/usr/sbin/getty -h tty0p1 9600
#ttp2:234:respawn:/usr/sbin/getty -h tty0p2 9600
#ttp3:234:respawn:/usr/sbin/getty -h tty0p3 9600
#ttp4:234:respawn:/usr/sbin/getty -h tty0p4 9600
#ttp5:234:respawn:/usr/sbin/getty -h tty0p5 9600
#ups::respawn:rtprio 0 /usr/lbin/ups_mond -f /etc/ups_conf
ems1::bootwait:/sbin/cat </dev/null >/etc/opt/resmon/persistence/reboot_flag
ems2::bootwait:/sbin/rm -f /etc/opt/resmon/persistence/runlevel4_flag
ems3:3:once:touch /etc/opt/resmon/persistence/runlevel4_flag
ems4:3456:respawn:/etc/opt/resmon/lbin/p_client
```

14.7 Runlevels

A runlevel is a state of the system showing which daemons and services are available at a particular time. HP-UX is in one of the eight runlevels at all times. These runlevels are 0 to 6, s, and S. The system default runlevel is determined by the `initdefault` entry in the `/etc/inittab` file. These runlevels are described in Table 14-3.

Table 14–3 *HP-UX Runlevels*

Runlevel	Description
0	Reserved for shutdown. When the system goes to this runlevel, it stops all processes and brings the system to a halted state.
s	This is a single-user runlevel and is used for system-administration-related tasks. Only one physical system console can be used. For this reason, it is called a single-user runlevel. The daemons available in this runlevel are those started by `init` having the `sysinit` keyword in the `/etc/inittab` file and any other daemon directly started by the HP-UX kernel.
S	This is similar to the single-user runlevel, the only difference being that the terminal you are logged into acts as the system console.
1	This starts some essential system processes and mounts the file system but still in single-user mode. This runlevel is also used for system administration tasks.
2	This is a multiuser runlevel; most of the system daemons and services are started at this runlevel.
3	Network services are started and NFS file systems are exported. This also starts the CDE graphical environment (for those users using it).
4	Activates the graphical user interface (GUI) for those users using the older HP VUE graphical environment.
5	Available for any user-defined services.
6	Available for any user-defined services.

Changing Runlevel

The runlevel of the system can be changed using the `init` command. The first argument to the command determines the new runlevel. If you are working in single-user mode for some maintenance work and want to bring the system into multiuser mode, you can use the following `init` command to bring the system to runlevel 3.

```
init 3
```

However, you should not use `init s` from a higher runlevel to go into single-user mode. This does not terminate other system activities and does not bring the system into single-user mode.

The `shutdown` command can also be used to bring the system into single-user mode. The `reboot` command changes the runlevel to 0 and reboots the system.

Determine Current Runlevel

You have already used the `who` command to determine who is currently logged into the system. Using `who` with the `-r` option determines the current system runlevel.

```
# who -r
.          run-level 3  Sep 26 03:51    3    0    S
#
```

The last three fields show the current system state, the number of times the system has been in this state, and the last runlevel state. These fields change each time you change the runlevel of the system.

14.8 Adding a Program to Run at Boot Time

To add a program to your system so that it executes at a particular runlevel involves a few steps. First, an execution script for starting and stopping a program is installed in the `/sbin/init.d` directory. This directory contain scripts for all daemons and services. The execution script contains the four major parts that are passed as command line arguments to these scripts.

`start_msg`	Displayed on the console when starting the script.
`stop_msq`	Displayed on the console at stop time of the script.
`start`	Command to start the program.
`stop`	Command to stop the program.

These scripts have configuration files in the `/etc/rc.config.d` directory that are used for setting the appropriate variables and options for these scripts. You must place a configuration file for the execution script in this directory. An execution script for the `cron` daemon (used for scheduling jobs) is `/sbin/init.d/cron` and is shown here.

```
#!/sbin/sh
# Start cron
case $1 in
'start_msg')
        echo "Start clock daemon"
        ;;
'stop_msg')
        echo "Stop clock daemon"
        ;;
'start')
        if [ -f /etc/rc.config.d/cron ] ; then
             . /etc/rc.config.d/cron
        fi
        if [ $CRON -eq 1 ] ; then
             /usr/sbin/cron
        fi
        ;;
'stop')
        PID=`ps -el | grep cron|cut -c 10-14`
        Kill $PID
;;
*)
        echo "usage: $0 {start|stop}"
        ;;
esac
exit
```

Once the script is installed, you need to decide at which runlevel it should be activated. HP-UX has directories with names /sbin/rcn.d, where *n* represents a runlevel. These directories are called *sequencer directories*. You place a link to your script in these directories. If you want to start your script at runlevel 3, you will place a link in the /sbin/rc3.d directory. You have to put one link for starting the script and another one for stopping it.

Sequencer Directories

A sequencer directory represents a particular runlevel. For example, /sbin/rc2.d contains links to scripts that need to be started or stopped when the system moves to runlevel 2. Every link starts with the S or K character. The files starting with S show that the scripts will be started when the system enters in this runlevel, while those scripts starting with K show that it will be stopped (killed). After the S or K character, there is a number that shows the sequence in which the script will be started or stopped. A typical link for starting the cron daemon is:

```
/sbin/rc2.d/S730cron
```

This shows that `cron` will be started in runlevel 2. The number 730 is the sequence number.

HP-UX executes scripts in the sequencer directories in the order of the sequence number. A script having a sequence of less than 730 will be executed earlier than the `cron`.

A typical sequencer script to stop the `cron` daemon is as follows.

```
/sbin/rc1.d/K270cron
```

It is located in the `rc1.d` directory showing that it will be executed when the system goes to runlevel 1. It starts with K, representing that it is a stop (kill) script. As you can see, the start and stop sequence numbers need not be the same. The "kill" links should be one runlevel behind the corresponding "start" link.

Configuration Files

Script configuration files are placed in the `/etc/rc.config.d` directory. These files are used by the sequencer scripts to check configuration for a particular daemon and usually have the same name as their corresponding script in the `/sbin/init.d` directory. The configuration file for the `cron` daemon is:

```
#!/sbin/sh
# @(#) $Revision: 72.3 $
# Cron configuration.   See cron(1m)
#
# CRON:          Set to 1 to start cron daemon
#
CRON=1
```

When this file is sourced by its execution script, it assigns the value 1 to the CRON variable, showing that the `cron` daemon is enabled. Assigning a value 0 means that the daemon is disabled. If you make a change to a configuration file and later want to restore it, you can copy the original file from the `/usr/newconfig/etc/rc.config.d` directory.

14.9 System Shutdown

System shutdown is needed when you want to carry out maintenance work, such as adding or replacing some devices or upgrading memory. You also need to shut down and restart your system when you build a new kernel. The shutdown command is used for this purpose. Important options with the shutdown command are:

-r   Reboot the system after shutdown

-h   Halt the system after shutdown

-y   Does not require any interactive response

You can supply time in seconds as an argument to the command to delay the shutdown process for a specified number of seconds. You must change to the / directory before using this command. A broadcast message is sent to all logged-in users notifying them that the system is going down.

To shut down and halt your system after two minutes, use the following command.

```
# shutdown -h -y 0
```

You will see shutdown messages like the following, appear on your screen.

```
SHUTDOWN PROGRAM
07/17/99 13:28:50 EDT
Broadcast Message from root (console) Sat Jul 17 13:28:51...
SYSTEM BEING BROUGHT DOWN NOW ! ! !

/sbin/auto_parms: DHCP access is disabled (see /etc/auto_parms.log)

    System shutdown in progress
    _____

    Stop CDE login server ....................................... OK
    Stop X print server(s) ...................................... N/A
    Stop NFS server subsystem ................................... OK
    Stopping Event Monitoring Service ........................... OK
    Stopping Netscape FastTrack Server .......................... OK
    Shutting down Measureware performance software ............. OK
    Stopping audio server daemon ................................ OK
    Stop auditing subsystem ..................................... N/A
    Stop environment monitoring daemon ......................... OK
    Stopping hardware predictive ................................ OK
    Stop diagnostic subsystem ................................... OK
    Stop clock daemon ........................................... OK
    Stopping HP Distributed Print Service ...................... OK
```

```
Stop print spooler ........................................ OK
Stopping disk array monitor daemons. ...................... OK
Stop accounting ........................................... OK
Stopping time synchronization ............................. FAIL *
Stop vt daemon ............................................ OK
Terminating X Font Server ................................. OK
Stop remote boot daemon ................................... OK
Stop the Isogon License Server daemon ..................... OK
Stop RPC daemon ........................................... OK
Stop DCE daemons .......................................... OK
Stop HA cluster SNMP subagent ............................. OK
Stopping OSPF MIB Network Management subAgent ............. N/A
Stopping SNMP HP-UNIX Network Management subAgent ......... OK
Stopping SNMP MIB-2 Network Management subAgent ........... OK
Stopping SNMP Trap Dest Network Management subAgent ....... OK
Stopping SNMP Master Network Management daemon ............ OK
Stopping outbound connection daemons for DDFA software .... N/A
Stopping mail daemon ...................................... OK
Stopping remote system status daemon ...................... N/A
Stopping RARP protocol daemon ............................. N/A
Stop PPP configuration .................................... OK
Stopping router discover protocol daemon .................. N/A
Stopping dynamic routing daemon ........................... N/A
Stopping Internet services daemon ......................... OK
Stopping multicast routing daemon ......................... N/A
Stop the Trusted Mode with Nis+ subsystem ................. OK
Stopping Internet Services ................................ OK
Stop NFS client subsystem ................................. OK
Stop NIS client subsystem ................................. OK
Stop NIS server subsystem ................................. OK
Stop NIS+ client subsystem ................................ OK
Stop NIS+ server subsystem ................................ OK
Stop NFS core subsystem ................................... OK
Stopping name server daemon ............................... N/A
Unconfigure LAN interfaces ................................ OK
Stop network tracing and logging daemon ................... OK
Stop pty allocator daemon ................................. OK
Stop system message logging daemon ........................ OK
Stop Software Distributor agent daemon .................... OK
Unconfigure Loopback interfaces (lo0) ..................... OK
Stop syncer daemon ........................................ OK
Killing user processes .................................... OK
Unload loadable modules ................................... N/A
Update kernel and loadable modules ........................ N/A
Unmount file systems ...................................... OK
```

```
Transition to run-level 0 is complete.
Executing "/sbin/reboot -h          ".
Shutdown at 13:30 (in 0 minutes)

        *** FINAL System shutdown message from root@myhp ***

System going down IMMEDIATELY

System shutdown time has arrived
reboot:  CAUTION: some process(es) wouldn't die
Timeout waiting for other processors to acknowledge reboot.

sync'ing disks (0 buffers to flush):
0 buffers not flushed
0 buffers still dirty
```

The shutdown command invokes /sbin/rc scripts which in turn use sequencer scripts to shut down all daemons before halting the system. The /etc/shutdown.log file keeps a log of shutdown or reboot of the system. Some log entries in this file are shown here.

```
15:24  Thu Sep 18, 1997.  Reboot:
06:58  Fri Sep 19, 1997.  Reboot:
08:10  Fri Sep 19, 1997.  Halt:  (by myhp!root)
12:16  Fri Sep 19, 1997.  Reboot:  (by myhp!root)
13:17  Fri Sep 19, 1997.  Reboot after panic: Data page fault
07:43  Mon Sep 22, 1997.  Reboot:  (by myhp!root)
08:20  Mon Sep 22, 1997.  Reboot:  (by myhp!root)
08:41  Mon Sep 22, 1997.  Reboot:
09:04  Mon Sep 22, 1997.  Reboot:  (by myhp!root)
10:18  Mon Sep 22, 1997.  Reboot:  (by myhp!root)
```

Shutdown and Reboot Commands

The reboot command kills all processes instead of gracefully terminating them. Therefore, this speeds up the shutdown process but may cause data loss if other users are working on the system at the time of the reboot. If you are working in single-user mode, then it is safe to use the reboot command. Otherwise, always use the shutdown command.

The shutdown.allow File

This file is used to allow some system users to execute the shutdown command. Each line contains a system name followed by user names. Any user listed in this file has the privilege to shut down the system. An asterisk in the system name allows a user of given name from any system to execute the shutdown command. Some sample entries in this file are:

```
myhp root
myhp operator
* boota
```

■ Chapter Summary

HP-UX startup and shutdown processes are explained in this chapter. We started with an introduction to the startup process and listed the steps involved. The startup process can be divided into two major parts. The first part consists of steps that are performed by code that resides in ROM. This code is called processor dependent code (PDC) and is different for each model of server and workstation. The second part consists of processes that are performed by the operating system. This part starts with the Initial System Loader (ISL). The ISL loads the hpux utility, which in turn loads the HP-UX kernel, /stand/vmunix, into the memory. The kernel starts the swapper process, ioinitrc, and then the init process. The init process starts the server daemons and brings the system into the appropriate runlevel state. At shutdown time, the init process changes the runlevel to 0 and halts the system.

In brief, the following items are discussed in the chapter.

- Processor dependent code (PDC) does a self-test and probes the hardware attached to the system.
- PDC menus can be used to search devices attached to the system and to specify primary and secondary boot devices.
- PDC can be used to boot from a particular device.
- PDC can be used to boot HP-UX in single-user mode.
- PDC uses the Stable Storage Area to keep configuration information.
- The boot area of the disk is in LIF format and it contains the ISL and some utility programs.
- The swapper process has process ID 0 and manages memory swapping.
- The init process reads the /etc/inittab file for its configuration.
- Runlevel is a state of the system that shows what services are available at a particular time. HP-UX is in one of eight runlevels at all times.
- To add a program to be run at boot time, you place an execution script in the /sbin/init.d directory and its configuration file in the /etc/rc.config.d directory. You place links to the script in the sequencer

directories. The sequencer directories have names like /sbin/rcn.d where *n* represents a runlevel.

- The shutdown command gets help from the execution scripts called by their respective links in the sequencer directories to stop server daemons and halt the system. The reboot command kills these daemons and reboots the system. The /etc/shutdown.allow files show which users are allowed to execute the shutdown command.

▲ CHAPTER REVIEW QUESTIONS

1. Why is understanding the startup and shutdown processes important for system administration?

2. Where does PDC store its configuration information? What potential problem may arise if this information is stored on the disk?

3. List the steps performed by PDC during the startup process.

4. What are runlevels and what is their utility?

5. List three tasks performed by the init process.

6. What are sequencer directories?

▲ TEST YOUR KNOWLEDGE

1. *All HP-9000 systems have processor dependent code (PDC). What is true about it?*

    A. It is used to add processors that are dependent on each other.

    B. PDC on all HP systems is the same.

    C. It is a programming language for HP processors.

    D. It is used to initialize and boot HP systems.

2. *The autoboot information is stored in:*

    A. the AUTO file in the LIF area

    B. the ISL

    C. PDC

    D. stable storage

3. *What can be used to boot HP-UX in single-user mode?*
   A. PDC
   B. the hpux utility when properly called from the ISL
   C. both of the above
   D. none of the above

4. *What is the function of the secondary loader?*
   A. It loads the HP-UX kernel if the primary loader fails.
   B. It is a utility that loads the HP-UX kernel during boot time.
   C. It loads the ISL in the second phase of the boot process.
   D. It is a configuration file for the kernel.

5. *The boot area of the primary system disk contains:*
   A. LIF
   B. the hpux utility
   C. the AUTO file
   D. all of the above

6. *The* search *command in PDC is used to:*
   A. search primary boot disks
   B. search all boot devices
   C. search all network interfaces
   D. search lost console devices

7. *What is the order of execution of scripts* bcheckrc, ioinitrc, *and* rc?
   A. bcheckrc, ioinitrc, rc
   B. ioinitrc, bcheckrc, rc
   C. rc, ioinitrc, bcheckrc
   D. rc, bcheckrc, ioinitrc

8. *What information is present in stable storage?*
   A. primary boot path
   B. alternate boot path
   C. information if autoboot is enabled or disabled
   D. all of the above

9. *What is true about the* `lifls` *command?*

   A. It is a standard HP-UX command to list files in the LIF area.

   B. It is an LIF command to list files in the LIF area.

   C. It is a PDC command to list files in the LIF area.

   D. It is an LIF command used to list files in an HP-UX partition.

10. *The ID field in* `/etc/inittab` *file shows:*

    A. the processor ID number

    B. the process ID number for the program in the action area

    C. an arbitrary string to represent an entry in the file

    D. runlevel in which the process is started

11. *What happens if the runlevel for a program is not specified in the* `/etc/inittab` *file?*

    A. The program is never started.

    B. The program is started in all runlevels.

    C. The program is started at the boot time.

    D. The program is started only in runlevel 0.

12. *Which runlevel can be used for multiuser operation?*

    A. 0

    B. 1

    C. s

    D. 3

13. *What command is used to check the current runlevel?*

    A. `runlevel`

    B. `who -r`

    C. `showrun`

    D. `init`

Software and Patch Management

Software on HP-UX systems is managed using Hewlett-Packard's Software Distributor, commonly known as SD-UX. This is not only a set of commands and utilities, but a system that defines how software should be packaged, bundled, copied, installed, and removed. SD-UX is based on the IEEE software distribution standard. It provides many commands that are used to install, remove, list, and verify software. SD-UX is used for managing and distributing operating systems, applications, and HP-UX patches. In a network environment, SD-UX can be used to set up a central software server from which any system on the network can install software as needed.

The main functions of SD-UX are to:

- install software
- remove software
- list installed software
- verify installed software
- copy and package software
- configure software

271

SD-UX can be used in either *graphical user interface* (GUI) or in a *text user interface* (TUI). The commands can also be used without any interface by using command line arguments.

SD-UX is used to manipulate all types of software, including HP-UX patches. The patches are additional software components that are released by Hewlett-Packard from time to time. These are used to add new functionality to existing system and application software, fixing bugs, or adding support of new hardware.

In this chapter, you will learn how the software is packaged and what the components of a software package are. You will use commands to list installed software, install new software, and remove installed software. Sometimes you need to verify the integrity of the installed software. SD-UX provides commands to verify installed software. Software depots are placeholders for software. You will see how to manage software depots with the help of SD-UX. An introduction to patches will be presented. You will learn how you can obtain patches for your software or hardware and how to install these. At the end of the chapter, a summary of commands used with SD-UX will be presented.

15.1 Software Packaging Structure

Software in SD-UX is organized in a hierarchy of components or objects. These components are *filesets*, *subproducts*, *products*, and *bundles*. The place where these components are stored is called a *software depot*. This provides a logical way to manage software. These components are explained below.

Filesets

A fileset is a collection of files and some control scripts. It is the basic entity in the SD-UX software packaging hierarchy. One fileset can belong to only one product, but it can be included in a number of subproducts and bundles. Some examples of filesets are shown here.

```
Ignite-UX.BOOT-KERNEL    A.1.45  Installation Boot Kernel
   for S700/S800 clients
Ignite-UX.BOOT-SERVICES A.1.45 Network Boot Services for
   System Installations
```

```
Ignite-UX.FILE-SRV-10-20    A.1.45 File Archives Used By
   Clients During HP-UX Install
Ignite-UX.IGNITE      A.1.45  Graphical Ignite User
   Interface for Installations
Keyshell.KEYS-ENG-A-MAN    B.10.20
Keyshell.KEYSHELL-RUN      B.10.20
LAN100-FRMAT-COM.LAN100-FORMAT  B.10.20.02     100Mb LAN/
   9000 formatter library
```

Subproducts

If a product contains several filesets, it is better to combine logically related filesets into subproducts. However, a fileset may be a member of many subproducts. Examples of subproducts are:

```
X11.Manuals              X11 man pages
X11.MessagesByLang       X11 Localized Messages
X11.MinimumRuntime       X11 minimum runtime subproduct
X11.Runtime              X11 full runtime subproduct
```

Products

A product is a superset of filesets and/or subproducts. By default, the SD-UX commands deal with products. An application, for example, is one product. A product may have many versions. Some of the products are:

```
UUCP          B.10.20          Unix to Unix Copy
Upgrade       B.10.20          Upgrade
X11           B.10.20          HP-UX X Window Software
Xserver       B.10.20          HP-UX X Server
Y2KDocs       B.10.20.B0315    Y2K Bundle Content file
```

Bundles

Bundles are usually packaged by HP-UX for the distribution of software. The bundles contain filesets that may belong to different products. A product may not necessarily be in one bundle, as bundles can have parts of different products. Operations related to software manipulation can be performed on bundles as one entity. Some examples of bundles are shown here.

```
J2760AA_APZ   B.10.20.02       HP-PB 100Base-T/9000
OnlineDiag    B.10.20.06       HPUX 10.0 Support Tools Bundle
Y2K-1020S800  B.10.20.B0315    Core OS Year 2000 Patch Bundle
```

Software Depots

Software depots are places where filesets, products, and bundles are stored. A software depot may a directory on your disk, a CD-ROM, or a tape (DDS, DAT) used for distributing software. By default, the software depot directory is /var/spool/sw, but you can use any directory as a software depot. Using SD-UX commands, software components can be added to or removed from a depot. For example, you can add new software patches to your local depot.

It is possible to create many software depots on one server for different applications. Software depots can be maintained on a central server in a network. Any machine on the network can install software from that central server. This is efficient, as installation of software from the network takes less time compared with installation from a CD-ROM or tape drive.

15.2   Listing Installed Software

The installed software can be listed using the swlist command. By default, the swlist command lists all software bundles and all products that are not part of a bundle. A typical output of the command is:

```
# Initializing...
# Contacting target "myhp"...
#
# Target:  myhp:/
#
#
# Bundle(s):
#
82491BA                      B.11.00            MirrorDisk/UX
B3693AA                      C.02.15.000        HP GlancePlus/UX for s800
   11.00
B3701AA                      B.11.00.41         HP GlancePlus/UX Pak for
   s800 11.00
B3835BA                      B.11.02            HP Process Resource
   Manager
B3901BA                      B.11.01.06         HP C/ANSI C Developer's
   Bundle for HP-UX 11.00 (S800)
B3919EA_AGL                  B.11.00            HP-UX 8-User License
B3929BA                      B.11.00            HP OnLineJFS (Advanced
   VxFS)
B4967AA                      C.02.15.000        HP MeasureWare Server
   Agent for s800 11.00
```

```
B5725AA                          B.1.51          HP-UX Installation
   Utilities (Ignite-UX)
HPUXEng64RT                      B.11.00         English HP-UX 64-bit
   Runtime Environment
Ignite-UX-11-00                  B.1.51          HP-UX Installation
   Utilities for Installing 11.00 Systems
J1642AA                          B.11.00.03      HP PCI/HSC Gigabit
   Ethernet Driver
XSWGR1100                        B.11.00.43      HP-UX Extension Pack,
   December 1998
#
# Product(s) not contained in a Bundle:
#
PHCO_14084                       1.0             csh(1) patch
PHCO_14257                       1.0             pwgrd consumes CPU when
   time set backwards
PHCO_14786                       1.0             Locales Y2K patch
PHCO_14859                       1.0             cumulative 10.20 libc
   compatibility support
PHCO_14887                       1.0             cumulative SAM/ObAM patch
PHCO_15217                       1.0             Cumulative SCCS(1)
   including Year 2000 Fix
```

You can use the options shown in Table 15-1 with this command to get a list of the installed software.

Table 15–1 *Options Used with* swlist *Command*

Option	Meaning
-l bundle	List bundles only
-l products	List products
-l fileset	List filesets
-d @ /var/spool/sw	List software in depot /var/spool/sw
-l file X11	List all files that are part of the X11 product
-d @ hp1:/mydepot	List software in depot named mydepot on host hp1

Partial output of the swlist -l product command is as follows.

```
# Initializing...
# Contacting target "myhp"...
Package-Manager    A.11.04       HP Package-Manager
PatchText                        Patch Documentation Files
PrinterMgmt        B.11.00       PrinterMgmt
Proc-Resrc-Mgr     B.11.02       HP Process Resource Manager
```

```
ProgSupport            B.11.00        ProgSupport
SCSI-Passthru          B.11.00        HP SCSI-Passthru Driver
SOE                    B.11.00        SOE
SUPPORT-TOOLS          B.11.00        HP SUPPORT TOOLS
SW-DIST                B.11.00        HP-UX Software Distributor
SecurityMon            B.11.00        SecurityMon
ServiceGuard           A.11.04        Service Guard
SourceControl          B.11.00        SourceControl
Spelling               B.11.00        Spelling
Streams                B.11.00        HP-UX_10.0_Streams_Product
Streams-TIO            B.11.00        HP-UX_10.0_Streams-TIO_Product
SystemAdmin            B.11.00        HP-UX System Administration Tools
SystemComm             B.11.00        System Communication utilities -
   ct,cu,ptydaemon,vt,kermit
TechPrintServ          B.11.00        HP-UX Technical Image Printing
   Service
TerminalMngr           B.11.00        TerminalMngr
TextEditors            B.11.00        TextEditors
TextFormatters         B.11.00        TextFormatters
UUCP                   B.11.00        Unix to Unix CoPy
Upgrade                B.11.00        Upgrade
UserLicense            B.11.00        HP-UX User License
WDB                    B.11.01.06     HP Wildebeest (HP WDB) Debugger
X11                    B.11.00        HP-UX X Window Software
X11MotifDevKit         B.11.00.01     HP-UX Developer's Toolkit - X11,
   Motif, and Imake
Xserver                B.11.00        HP-UX X Server
```

The swlist command can also be used to list software attributes such as size, revision, and vendor information.

15.3 Installing New Software

The swinstall command is used for software installation. Depending on the type of terminal you are using, the command starts in either text or graphic interface. If you are using a text-based terminal, you will see a message on your screen as shown in Figure 15-1. It is similar to the message screen you have seen while using SAM in Chapter 12.

After this message, the TUI appears as shown in Figure 15-2.

First of all, a subwindow appears that shows some basic information. The Source Depot Type is Local CD-ROM, showing that software is going to be installed from a CD-ROM device. Source Host Name shows the name of the host that is being used as the source of the software depot. If you are on

```
 Window  Edit  Options                                          Help

 root on      hp0  /home/root => swinstall
 Starting the terminal version of swinstall...

 To move around in swinstall:

 - use the "Tab" key to move between screen elements
 - use the arrow keys to move within screen elements
 - use "Ctrl-F" for context-sensitive help anywhere in swinstall

 On screens with a menubar at the top like this:

       --------------------------------------------------------
       |File View Options Actions                        Help|
       | ---- ---- ------- ------------------------------ ---|

 - use "Tab" to move from the list to the menubar
 - use the arrow keys to move around
 - use "Return" to pull down a menu or select a menu item
 - use "Tab" to move from the menubar to the list without selecting a menu item
 - use the spacebar to select an item in the list

 On any screen, press "CTRL-K" for more information on how to use the keyboard.

 Press "Return" to continue...
```

Figure 15–1   *Startup message of the* swinstall *command.*

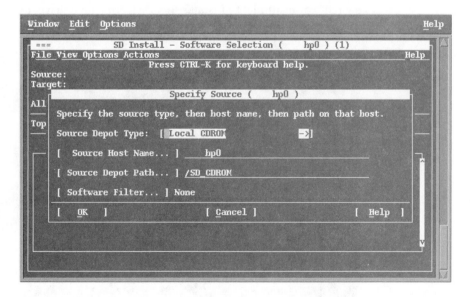

Figure 15–2   *The subwindow of the* swinstall *command.*

a network, you can change this source. Source Depot Path shows the path of the directory where the software depot resides. In this case, it is the directory where the CD-ROM is mounted. By default, the CD-ROM mount directory is /SD_CDROM, where the swinstall command looks for a software depot. With HP-UX version 10.20 and earlier, the system administrator needs to manually create a mount point and then manually mount the CD-ROM before using the swinstall command. With HP-UX 11.00 and later, SD-UX will automatically mount the CD-ROM via the swinstall command.

You can use the [Tab] key to change any of these options. After pressing the [OK] button, the subwindow disappears and you see a window like the one shown in Figure 15-3, which lists the software packages present on the CD-ROM.

Only the software listed is compatible with your system.

If you are using GUI, Figure 15-2 will look like Figure 15-4, and Figure 15-3 will be replaced by Figure 15-5. From a functionality standpoint, these are the same windows.

If you want to install from a particular software depot, you can also mention the software source at the command line with the help of the -s switch. For example, to install software from a tape drive, use this command.

```
swinstall -s /dev/rmt/0m
```

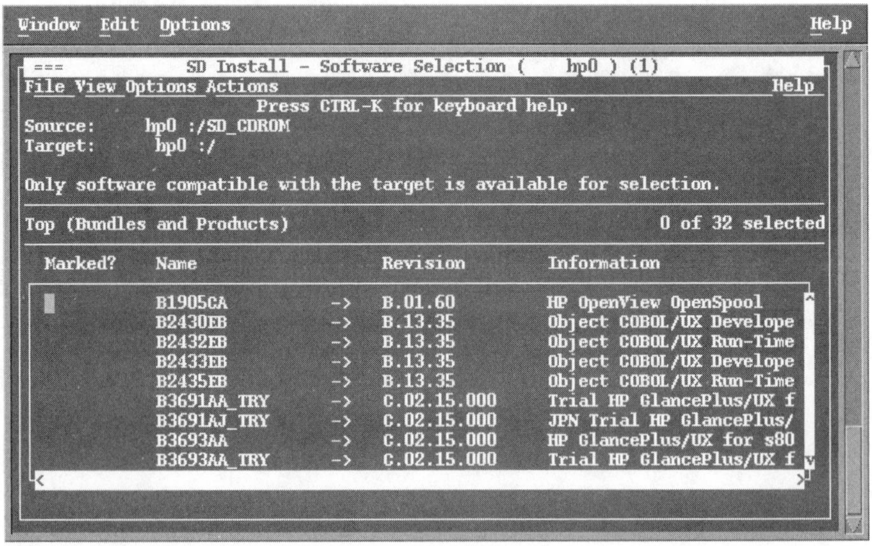

Figure 15–3 *The software list on the CD-ROM.*

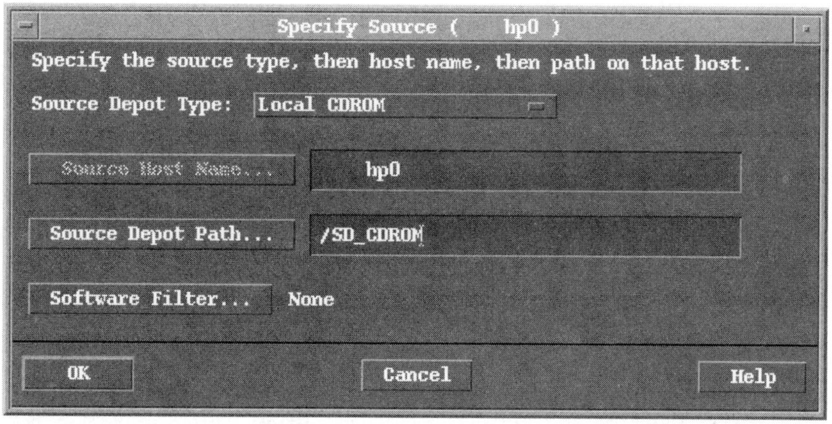

Figure 15–4   *The subwindow of the* swinstall *command as viewed in GUI.*

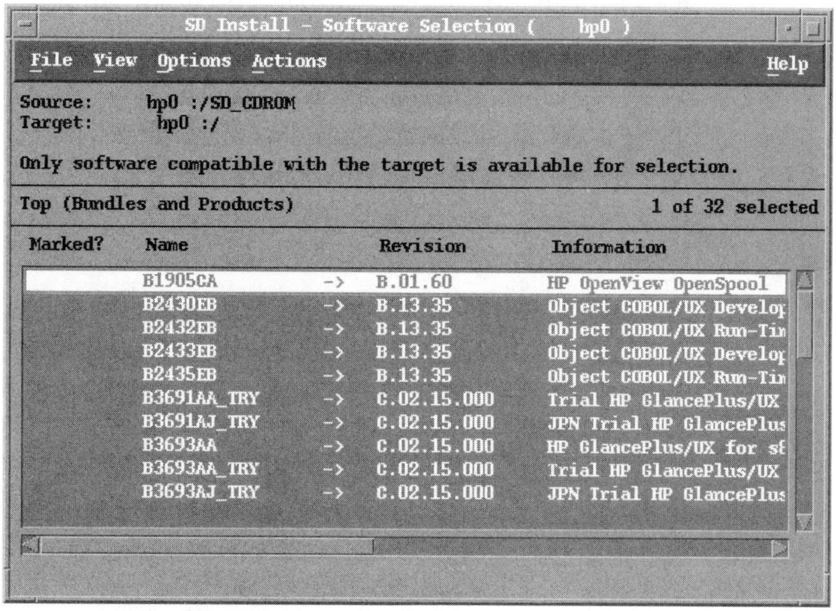

Figure 15–5   *The software list on the CD-ROM as viewed in GUI.*

To install software from a CD-ROM, with HP-UX 10.20 and earlier, mount the CD-ROM on /SD_CDROM with the help of the mount command and then use the following command. (For HP-UX 11.00, you don't need to use the mount command.)

```
swinstall -s /SD_CDROM
```

Phases of Software Installation

The software installation process is completed in only a few steps. In the first step, you initiate the swinstall command and select the software source depot. Once you get the list of software in that depot, you mark the software you want to install. To mark the software, first you need to highlight the software using the Tab and spacebar keys. After highlighting, you can go to the Actions menu and select Mark for Install. If you just want to upgrade the existing software, you can go to the Actions menu and select the option Match What Target Has, and the selection will be made for you automatically.

Once all of the software is marked, go to the Actions menu and select the Install (Analysis)... option. When you select this option, the second phase of software installation starts the analysis phase. During this phase, all software dependencies and disk space requirements are checked. If the analysis phase succeeds, you will see a dialog box where you can see the results of the analysis. In case of any error, you can modify your software selection. If there are no errors, you can go to the actual installation phase where files are copied to the disk.

During the installation phase, all files from the selected software are copied to the disk. If a fileset is already installed, it is not reinstalled. However, to forcibly reinstall already installed software, you can go to the Options menu and select Change Options to force the reinstallation of already-installed files.

The last part of the software installation is the configuration and cleanup, where configuration scripts are run and temporary files are deleted. Temporary files are created during the installation process.

Install/Update Log File

All activities of the swinstall command are logged in the /var/adm/sw/swinstall.log file. A sample of entries in this log file is shown here.

```
=======  06/23/99 12:25:57 EDT  BEGIN swinstall SESSION (interactive)

NOTE:   The interactive UI was invoked, since no software was
   specified.

Session started for user "root@myhp".
agent_auto_exit                 false
agent_timeout_minutes           10000
allow_downdate                  false
```

```
allow_incompatible              false
allow_multiple_versions         false
autoreboot                      false
autorecover_product             false
autoremove_job                  false
autoselect_dependencies         true
autoselect_reference_bundles    true
compress_files                  false
control_lang                    C
create_target_path              true
defer_configure                 false
enforce_dependencies            true
enforce_dsa                     true
enforce_kernbld_failure         true
enforce_scripts                 true
follow_controller               false
job_polling_interval            30
log_msgid                       0
logdetail                       false
logdetail                       false
loglevel                        1
match_target                    false
mount_all_filesystems           true
polling_interval                2
register_new_root               true
reinstall                       false
reinstall_files                 true
reinstall_files_use_cksum       true
retry_rpc                       1
rpc_binding_info                ncacn_ip_tcp:[2121] ncadg_ip_udp:[2121]
rpc_timeout                     5
select_local                    true
software_view                   all_bundles
source_cdrom                    /SD_CDROM
source_type                     directory
source_directory                hp1:/var/spool/sw
use_alternate_source            false
verbose                         1
write_remote_files              false
 * Source:                      myhp:/var/spool/sw
 * Targets:                     myhp:/
* Software selections:
* Software selections:
PHCO_16964.PHCO_16964,r=B.10.00.00.AA,a=HP-HX_B.10.20_700/800,v=HP
PHCO_17075.PHCO_17075,r=B.10.00.00.AA,a=HP-UX_B.10.20_700/800,v=HP
PHCO_17240.PHCO_17240,r=B.10.00.00.AA,a=HP-UX_B.10.01_700/800,v=HP
```

```
PHCO_17552.PHCO_17552,r=B.10.00.00.AA,a=HP-UX_B.10.20_700/800,v=HP
PHCO_17630.PHCO_17630,r=B.10.00.00.AA,a=HP-UX_B.10.20_700/800,v=HP
PHNE_16692.PHNE_16692,r=B.10.00.00.AA,a=HP-UX_B.10.20_700/800,v=HP
PatchText.Y2K-1020S800,r=B.10.20.B0315,a=HP-UX_B.10.20_800,v=HP
Y2KDocs.Y2K-1020S800,r=B.10.20.B0315,a=HP-UX_B.10.20_800,v=HP
* A "+" indicates an automatic selection due to dependency or the
  automatic selection of a reference bundle.
* Beginning Analysis
* The analysis phase succeeded for "myhp:/".
* Ending Analysis
* Beginning Task Execution
* Proceeding with Task Execution on the following targets:
* myhp:/
```

You can use this log file to view any complications occurring during the software installation process.

This log file contains some labels, which are explained next.

========	Indicates start or end of a task.
ERROR	Indicates a serious problem so that installation is not possible.
WARNING	Shows that although the installation is performed, there may be a problem. Read the warning message to see what action you need to take for this problem.
NOTE	Any information is placed under this label. It may or may not require action. Most of the time you may ignore these messages.

Installing Protected Software Using Codewords

If you receive protected software from HP, you will also receive your customer ID and codeword. A codeword is generated using the part number of the medium on which the software is shipped, your customer ID, and the product ID. Codewords are confidential, and it is your responsibility to protect them.

When you start software installation from a CD-ROM that contains protected software, the swinstall command will show you a message that the CD-ROM contains protected software. In that case, you need to go to the Actions menu and select Add New Codeword. You will see a window like the one shown in Figure 15-6, where you enter your customer ID and codeword.

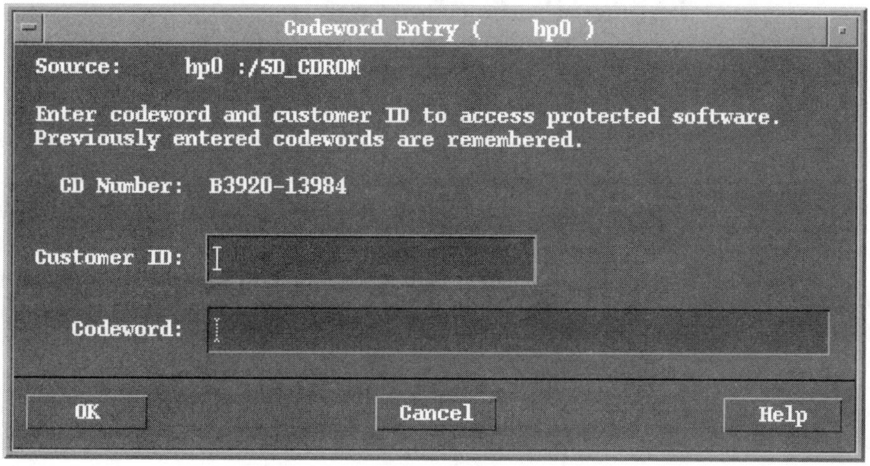

Figure 15–6 *The window to enter customer ID and codeword.*

You need to enter a codeword only once on your machine. It is then stored in the /var/adm/sw/.codewords file for future use.

Usually one codeword is used for one CD-ROM. Every time you purchase new software, you will receive a new codeword with it.

SD-UX Daemon and Agent

The software installation process is controlled by the daemon swagentd. If this daemon is not running, you can't start the software installation process. When you give the swinstall command, it connects to the swagentd daemon. The daemon starts the software agent named swagent whenever required. If the software depot is located on another machine on the network, the swagentd daemon connects to the daemon running on that host and initiates communication between the two hosts.

The SD-UX agent swagent is responsible for software management tasks. It is started by the swagentd daemon and terminates after the task is completed.

The SD-UX daemon is started at runlevel 2. So if you are in single-user mode, you can't install software. However, you can start the daemon manually in single-user mode using the following command.

```
/sbin/init.d/swagentd start
```

It can be stopped by the command:

```
/sbin/init.d/swagentd stop
```

Installed Product Database

HP-UX maintains a database of all installed software, the *installed product database* (IPD). During the analysis phase, the swinstall command uses this database to check the software already installed. The swlist command queries this database to list the installed software. Similarly, when the software is removed using the swremove command, this database is updated to reflect the removed software.

The SD-UX commands are responsible to maintain this database, which is stored in the /var/adm/sw/products directory structure.

15.4 Removing Software

The swremove command is used to remove software from the HP-UX system. It has a similar interface to the swinstall command. When you start the command, it will list in a window all installed software. You can mark the software that you want to remove from the system, after which you will go to the Actions menu and select Remove (Analysis) from it.

Once the software removal starts, the SD-UX checks the software dependencies and removes all files in the selected software that are not used by any other product or bundle. It then updates the IPD by removing software from it.

It is important to note that software is not removed only by deleting the directory in which the software was installed. In fact, manually deleting directories may cause problems because the software entries still exist in the IPD. Although you have deleted the files, your system *thinks* that they are still there. This may affect any other software installation or removal process when SD-UX checks software dependencies.

The software removal process is logged in the /var/adm/sw/ swremove.log file. It is similar to the log file used for the swinstall command and contains information showing whether the software removal process was successful.

Finding and Removing Unused Filesets

The freedisk command is used to list and remove software that has not been used for a long time. Filesets that have not been used since installation, but which have dependencies with other filesets that are in use, are treated as being in-use. After analyzing the filesets, the command activates the swremove command to remove packages interactively. At this point, you can select packages that can be removed from the system.

15.5 Verifying Installed Software

The `swverify` command is used to verify software installed on a system or in a depot. When used to verify installed software, it checks file existence and integrity and file dependencies in a software package. It also executes any scripts supplied with the software to verify the software's integrity. The command can be used to verify software on multiple hosts. It also checks file attributes and reports missing files. When used with the -d option, it operates on a depot instead of on installed software. It returns an exit code equal to zero if all software verification is successful. The log of the command is recorded in `/var/adm/sw/swverify.log`, which can be checked for any error messages. For example, to verify Laser ROM on a local host, you can use this command.

```
swverify LROM
```

15.6 Managing Software Depots

Managing a software depot is an important task for routine system administration. You need to create your own software depot for larger networks to avoid installing the installation media on every machine.

A depot can be created in any directory on disk. The default software depot location is `/var/spool/sw`. After selecting a directory for the software depot, software components can be added or removed from the depot.

A tape depot can be created using the `swpackage` command. Only one command can access a tape depot at a time.

Adding Packages to a Depot

A package can be added to a depot using the `swcopy` command. This command copies into a depot the software that can be installed using the `swinstall` command at a later stage. The following command copies all products from a tape drive to the default software depot.

```
swcopy -s /dev/rmt/0m @ /var/spool/sw
```

Removing Packages from a Depot

Software can be removed from a depot using the `swremove` command. The following command removes all software from the default depot `/var/spool/sw`.

```
swremove -d * @ /var/spool/sw
```

Listing Packages in a Depot

Software in a depot can be listed using the `swlist` command. The following command list contents of the local tape, `/dev/rmt/0m`.

```
swlist -d @ /dev/rmt/0m
```

Study Break

Software Management

You have now studied most of the software management concepts and SD-UX commands. Log into your system and use the `swlist` command to list the software already installed on your system. Put the HP-UX additional software CD-ROM in the drive and mount it on directory `/SD_CDROM`. If your CD drive device is `/dev/dsk/c2t5d0`, the `mount` command will be:

```
mount /dev/dsk/c2t5d0 /SD_CDROM
```

On HP-UX version 10.20 and earlier, the system administrator needs to manually create a mount point and then manually mount the CD-ROM before using the `swinstall` command. On HP-UX 11.00 and later, SD-UX will automatically mount the CD-ROM via the `swinstall` command. The mount point will be `/SD_CDROM`.

Now use the `swinstall` command to see the software components on the CD-ROM. Mark one of the products for installation and install it using options in the `Actions` menu. After installation is complete, use the `swlist` command again to make sure that the software is installed. Now use the `swremove` command to remove this software.

15.7   HP-UX Patches

HP-UX patches are software components that are released by Hewlett-Packard. These are used for one of the following purposes.

- to add new functionality to the HP-UX operating system or products
- to add support for new hardware; for example, support may be added for new types of adapters
- to fix bugs in the operating system and applications

Patch management is an ongoing system administration task in HP-UX, as many patches are released from time to time.

Patch Sources

Patches can be obtained using your Web browser through WWW or FTP. The WWW site address is:

```
http://ITResourceCenter.hp.com
```

The FTP site address is:

```
ftp://us-ffs.external.hp.com/hp-ux_patches
```

You can also order a patch CD-ROM from Hewlett-Packard to obtain a collection of all patches.

CUSTOM PATCH MANAGER

This tool is available on the Hewlett-Packard Web site. It can be used to take inventory of existing software installed on your system and suggest needed patches. To use the custom patch manager, your system needs to be connected to the Internet and you must have a Personalized System Support Agreement with Hewlett-Packard.

Types of Patches

All patch names start with PH. The next two characters show the type of patch. Following that, there is an underscore character and a four- or five-digit patch number. At the end of the patch name, there may be some other words to show the specific use of the patch. Depending on the characters in the type field, there are four types of patches as listed here.

- Command patches. The type field for these is CO.
- Kernel patches. The type field for these is KL.
- Network patches. The type field for these is NE.
- Subsystem patches. The type field for these is SS. These patches include all other types of patches.

Some example patch names are:

- PHSS_16473
- PHSS_14158
- PHCO_15623
- PHKL_16189

Usually you need to reboot the system after installing a kernel patch.

Listing Installed Patches

The procedure for listing patches is different for HP-UX versions. If you are using HP-UX 10.x, you can use following command.

```
swlist -l product PH*
```

On HP-UX 11.00, use:

```
swlist -l patch '*.*,c=patch'
```

or

```
swlist -l patch
```

15.8   Installing and Removing Patches

The process of patch management is not very different from general software management. The same SD-UX utilities are used for installing, removing, and listing patches as are used for general software.

Obtaining Patches

HP-UX patches are distributed as shar files. When you download a patch from the Hewlett-Packard FTP or Web site, use the sh command to unshar it. For example, to download the patch, PHCO_15220, you can use the following FTP process from the command line.

```
# ftp us-ffs.external.hp.com
Connected to hpcc933.external.hp.com.
220-
220-Welcome to the HP Electronic Support Center ftp server
220----------------------------------------------------------
220-
220-You are user 53, and there is a limit of 200 simultaneous accesses.
220-
220-Log in as user "anonymous" (using your e-mail address as your
  password)
220-to retrieve available patches for HP-UX, MPE/iX, and other
  platforms.
220-
220-If you are a user of other HP ESC services, log in with your
220-HP ESC User ID and password to deposit or retrieve your files.
```

```
220-
220-If you have questions, send email to:
220-
220-    support_feedback@us-ffs.external.hp.com
220-
220 hpcc933 FTP server (Version wu-2.4, HP ASL, w/CNS fixes (277) Wed
    Jun 24 18:
02:04 PDT 1998) ready.
Name (us-ffs.external.hp.com:boota): anonymous
331 Guest login ok, send your complete e-mail address as password.
Password:
230 Guest login ok, access restrictions apply.
Remote system type is UNIX.
Using binary mode to transfer files.
ftp> cd hp-ux_patches
250 CWD command successful.
ftp> cd s700_800
250 CWD command successful.
ftp> cd 11.X
250 CWD command successful.
ftp> get PHCO_15220
200 PORT command successful.
150 Opening BINARY mode data connection for PHCO_15220 (46784 bytes).
226 Transfer complete.
46784 bytes received in 1.04 seconds (44.02 Kbytes/s)
ftp> quit
221 Goodbye.
#
```

After downloading, use the following command to unshar the patch.

```
$ sh PHCO_15220
x - PHCO_15220.text
x - PHCO_15220.depot [compressed]
$
```

As you can see from the output of this command, two files are extracted from the package file. These files are always *Patch_Name*.text and *Patch_Name*.depot. The .text file is the patch description file and the .depot file is the actual patch in SD-UX depot format. The .text file contains the following information.

- Patch name
- Patch description
- Creation date: shows the date the patch was created
- Post date: shows the date when the patch was made public for general use

- Hardware platforms—OS releases
- Products
- Filesets
- Automatic reboot: shows whether the system will be rebooted after the installation of patch
- Status: shows whether it is a general release or a special release
- Critical: shows if the patch fixes a critical problem. A critical problem is one that causes system failure, crash, hang, panic, application failure, data loss, or corruption
- Category tags
- Path name: shows the file path on the FTP site
- Symptoms
- Defect description
- SR: service request number, which is assigned to a formal request about the problem from a customer
- Patch files
- `what(1)` output: shows output of the `what` command for each file
- `cksum(1)` output: used to detect any errors in the file
- Patch conflicts
- Patch dependencies
- Hardware dependencies
- Other dependencies
- Supersedes
- Equivalent patches
- Installation instructions

Before installing a patch, you must read this information to find out its exact purpose.

Creating a Patch Depot

After you have unshared a patch, you can install it directly from the `.depot` file or you can add the `.depot` file to a patch depot on your system. I prefer the second option. To add the patch to the `/var/spool/sw` depot, use this command.

```
swcopy -s PHCO_15220.depot PHCO_15220 @ /var/spool/sw
```

Installing Patches

Patches can be installed with the help of the `swinstall` command. If you are using individual patches with the above-mentioned procedure, you can use the following command to get a list of software and patches from your default depot.

```
swinstall -s /var/spool/sw
```

When you use this command and the patches are present in this depot, you will see a list of all patches in the `swinstall` window. After making a selection in the usual way, you can install the desired patches.

If you have the patch CD-ROM from Hewlett-Packard and are not sure which patches to install, adopt the following process.

- Insert the CD-ROM in the drive.
- For HP-UX 10.20 and earlier, mount the CD-ROM on the `/SD_CDROM` directory using the `mount` command. Remember that, with HP-UX 11.00 and later, the CD-ROM is automatically mounted by `swinstall`.
- Start `swinstall`.
- Go to the `Actions` menu and select `Match what target has` on HP-UX 10.x or `Manage patch selection` on HP-UX 11.00.
- Go to the `Actions` menu and select `Install (analyze). . .` to start the installation.

Removing Patches

Package removal is similar to general software removal. It is done with the help of the `swremove` command.

15.9   SD-UX Commands

Common SD-UX commands are presented in Table 15-2.

Table 15–2 *Common SD-UX Commands*

Command	Description
swinstall	Install software
swremove	Remove installed software; also remove software from a depot
swlist	List installed software or software in a depot
swcopy	Copy software components to a software depot
swpackage	Package software in a depot
swreg	Make a software depot visible to other systems on the network

Command	Description
swverify	Verify integrity of installed software
swagentd	SD-UX daemon
swagent	SD-UX agent
swacl	Control access to software
swconfig	Configure installed software

■ Chapter Summary

You have used HP Software Distributor (SD-UX) in this chapter. You began with learning the structure of HP software packages. Filesets are combination of files. Subproducts are used to logically combine filesets of the same type. Products contain subproducts and filesets. Packages are used to distribute software and can contain full or partial products. The software is stored in software depots. A software depot may be a CD-ROM, a tape, or a directory on a server.

Software is installed with the help of the swinstall command, which can be started in text or graphical interfaces. For listing installed software or the contents of a software depot, you use the swlist command. The swremove command is used for removing software from a software depot or from the system. The swverify command checks the integrity of the installed software. To manage a software depot, you can use the swcopy, swremove, swlist, and swpackage commands. The *installed product database* (IPD) is used to keep a record of installed or removed software. If new software is installed, it is added to this database. If you remove software using the swremove command, it is removed from the database. To use SD-UX, you need to run the SD-UX daemon named swagentd. This daemon invokes the SD-UX agent, swagent, whenever required. The freedisk command can be used to list and remove any unused software from the system.

Hewlett-Packard releases software updates from time to time. These updates are called patches. Patches are used to add new functionality, remove bugs, or add support for new hardware. The patches can be downloaded from the Hewlett-Packard Web site or the FTP site. Patches are managed in a way similar to general software management.

▲ CHAPTER REVIEW QUESTIONS

1. What tasks are carried out using SD-UX?

2. What is a software depot? What is the difference between the `swinstall` and `swcopy` commands?

3. A depot is a superset of products (True/False).

4. What is included in the output of the `swlist` command if you use it without any arguments or options?

5. Software is installed in separate directories under the `/opt` directory. Is it possible to remove software by deleting the directory used for a particular software? Why?

6. Describe the purposes of patches.

▲ TEST YOUR KNOWLEDGE

1. *What is* not *true about a fileset?*
   A. A fileset is a collection of files.
   B. One fileset can belong to only one product.
   C. One fileset can belong to many products.
   D. Filesets may have dependencies with one another.

2. *What is the default location of software on your disk?*
   A. `/var/spool/sw`
   B. `/etc/default/sw`
   C. `/var/sd-ux/sw`
   D. none of the above

3. *When the* `swlist` *command is used without any arguments, it lists:*
   A. all bundles
   B. all products
   C. all bundles and all products
   D. all bundles and only those products that are not included in a bundle

4. When using the `swinstall` command in the text menu, you can activate the menus using the:
    A. `Tab` key
    B. `Alt` key
    C. `F1` function key
    D. Spacebar

5. In which runlevel is the SD-UX software daemon started?
    A. 1
    B. 2
    C. 3
    D. 4

6. What is the use of the `freedisk` command?
    A. to check the amount of free space on a disk
    B. to check for unused software on a disk
    C. to check a disk that is completely free
    D. to wipe out all software from a disk to make it free

7. Which SD-UX command is used to install software?
    A. `swinstall`
    B. `swcopy`
    C. `swconfig`
    D. all of the above

8. For what purpose are patches not used?
    A. add new functionality
    B. fix bugs in applications
    C. fix bugs in hardware
    D. add support for new hardware

9. Every patch is a `shar` file when you download it from the Hewlett-Packard Internet site. How many files are created when you `unshar` it?
    A. 2
    B. 3
    C. 7
    D. 10

Reconfiguring the HP-UX Kernel

The default HP-UX kernel is stored in the /stand directory with the name vmunix. Kernel configuration is a process of rebuilding the kernel after adding or removing drivers or subsystems. You also need to rebuild the kernel if you change kernel parameters, such as the maximum number of processes in memory. HP-UX is shipped with all supported device drivers and subsystems present in the /usr/conf directory. Support of new devices is provided through kernel patches. The kernel is also rebuilt after installing any kernel patches.

The kernel rebuilding process can be divided into three major steps. In the first step, the kernel configuration file /stand/system is created and/or modified to incorporate the required changes. In the second step, the kernel is regenerated. Then, in the third step, you install the newly generated kernel and reboot your system. If all goes well, the new kernel is loaded at reboot time. After that you

295

can verify whether the required changes were made or you need to repeat the process.

In this chapter, first you will see in which circumstances you need to build a new kernel and what the kernel configuration process is. Then you will look at the kernel configuration file and how to change parameters in it. Sometimes you are not able to boot your system with the new kernel due to a problem in the regeneration process or a misconfigured kernel parameter. In that case, you need to boot your system from the old kernel. You will learn how to do so in the event that you are caught in such a situation. In the last part of the chapter, you will find information about some common kernel tunable parameters and how to use SAM for kernel configuration.

After reading the chapter, you will be able to reconfigure the HP-UX kernel to incorporate new subsystems, drivers, and system parameters. You will also learn commands to list existing drivers known to the kernel and the value of system parameters.

16.1 Why Reconfigure the Kernel?

Many times, SD-UX reconfigures your kernel automatically after installing software or a patch that requires modification to the kernel. In such a situation, SD-UX informs you before installing the software that a new kernel will be needed for the software. This is also done after installing patches related to kernel configuration. You also need to reconfigure your kernel if you perform one of the following tasks.

Adding or Removing Device Drivers

HP-UX communicates with all devices by using device drivers. Many of these device drivers are already built into the kernel. If you add a new device whose device driver is not present in the kernel, you need to rebuild the kernel to add the device driver for that device. Once the device driver is built into the kernel, you need to reboot your system so that the new kernel gets loaded into memory.

All device drivers occupy some space in memory as well as increase the size of your kernel. If you are not using some devices on your systems and their device drivers are present in the kernel, they are wasting memory. In systems where memory is constrained, this may become a performance-degrading issue. In such a case, it is better to remove all unwanted device drivers from the kernel to reduce its size and memory utilization. Once you remove any device driver from the kernel, you build a new kernel and install it. You always need to reboot the system after installing a new kernel.

Adding or Removing a Subsystem

HP-UX is divided into subsystems. A subsystem is a major part of HP-UX. An example of this is the network subsystem and the *Logical Volume Manager* (LVM) subsystem. In a standalone workstation, you don't need the network subsystem in the kernel. If this is built into your kernel, it is taking up memory without any utilization. You need to remove any unwanted subsystems from the kernel.

Similarly, if you are moving a standalone HP-UX system to a network, you need to have the network subsystem installed and built into your kernel. Any time you install or remove a subsystem, you reconfigure your kernel.

Changing Swap or Dump Devices

The primary swap location may be specified in the kernel configuration, although it is not necessary in the case where you use LVM or a whole-disk approach. A dump device is the place that is used to create a memory dump in case of problems with your system. These memory dumps can be used for troubleshooting later on. The dump location is usually the primary swap space. It may happen that your primary swap space is less than the amount of memory installed in your system, and you need to specify a separate dump space. In such a case, you will tell the kernel that you are using additional or alternate dump space and rebuild it.

Modifying System Parameters

The kernel contains system-specific information, which is represented by kernel parameters. Kernel parameters show how many users can access the system simultaneously, what the maximum number of open files and processes is, and other information particular to a specific installation of HP-UX. You may wish to change the values of these parameters depending on your local requirements. For example, if you have many users on the system who are accessing a lot of files, you may need to increase the number of files that can be opened simultaneously. Similarly, if many applications are installed and they create a lot of processes in memory, it may happen that the system process table becomes full. In this case, you will be required to increase the size of your process table by increasing the number of simultaneous processes.

Many vendors specify special kernel parameter value that they need to make sure their product functions properly. But if you have many applications, this will not be of much help and you will have to decide what the appropriate value for a system parameter will be.

16.2 The Reconfiguration Process

The HP-UX kernel may be configured using the command line method or SAM. First, you will see how to do it using the command line. The SAM method will be presented at the end of the chapter. The kernel reconfiguration process may be divided into the following phases.

Preparing a New System Configuration File

The kernel configuration file is /stand/system. Whenever you need to build a new kernel, you need to prepare a new configuration file. The best way is to build a configuration file from the running kernel using the system_prep command and then make changes to it. See the examples of system_prep on the following pages. Before starting the kernel build process, you should look at the existing kernel parameters. The sysdef command analyzes the running system and shows its tunable parameters. A typical output of the command follows.

```
# sysdef
NAME                  VALUE      BOOT      MIN-MAX     UNITS     FLAGS
acctresume              4          -        -100-100               -
acctsuspend             2          -        -100-100               -
allocate_fs_swapmap 0              -           -                   -
bufpages            26214          -          0-         Pages     -
create_fastlinks      0            -           -                   -
dbc_max_pct          10            -           -                   -
dbc_min_pct          10            -           -                   -
default_disk_ir       0            -           -                   -
dskless_node          0            -          0-1                  -
eisa_io_estimate    768            -           -                   -
eqmemsize            19            -           -                   -
file_pad             10            -          0-                   -
fs_async              0            -          0-1                  -
hpux_aes_override     0            -           -                   -
```

maxdsiz	16384	-	0-655360	Pages	-
maxfiles	1024	-	30-2048		-
maxfiles_lim	2048	-	30-2048		-
maxssiz	2048	-	0-655360	Pages	-
maxswapchunks	2111	-	1-16384		-
maxtsiz	16384	-	0-655360	Pages	-
maxuprc	1000	-	3-		-
maxvgs	20	-	-		-
msgmap	67043328	-	3-		-
nbuf	26780	-	0-		-
ncallout	7016	-	6-		-
ncdnode	150	-	-		-
ndilbuffers	30	-	1-		-
netisr_priority	-1	-	-1-127		-
netmemmax	0	-	-		-
nfile	12690	-	14-		-
nflocks	200	-	2-		-
ninode	11464	-	14-		-
no_lvm_disks	0	-	-		-
nproc	7000	-	10-		-
npty	300	-	1-		-
nstrpty	300	-	-		-
nswapdev	10	-	1-25		-
nswapfs	10	-	1-25		-
public_shlibs	1	-	-		-
remote_nfs_swap	0	-	-		-
rtsched_numpri	32	-	-		-
sema	0	-	0-1		-
semmap	314507264	-	4-		-
shmem	0	-	0-1		-
shmmni	1024	-	3-1024		-
streampipes	0	-	0-		-
swapmem_on	1	-	-		-
swchunk	2048	-	2048-16384	kBytes	-
timeslice	10	-	-1-2147483648	Ticks	-
unlockable_mem	14200	-	0-	Pages	-

From the sysdef output you find out what the values of tunable kernel parameters on your system are. After finding these values, you are in a better position to decide what changes are needed. In addition, you may want to see a list of hardware attached to your system before adding or deleting any device drivers. For this purpose you use the ioscan command. A part of the output from the ioscan command is shown below.

```
# ioscan -f
Class       I   H/W Path    Driver      S/W State   H/W Type    Description
===========================================================================
bc          0               root        CLAIMED     BUS_NEXUS
bc          1   8           ccio        CLAIMED     BUS_NEXUS   I/O Adapter
ba          0   8/0         GSCtoPCI    CLAIMED     BUS_NEXUS   PCI Bus Bridge
lan         5   8/0/1/0     gelan       CLAIMED     INTERFACE   HP 1000Base-SX
ba          1   8/4         GSCtoPCI    CLAIMED     BUS_NEXUS   PCI Bus Bridge
lan         6   8/4/1/0     gelan       CLAIMED     INTERFACE   HP 1000Base-SX
ba          2   8/8         GSCtoPCI    CLAIMED     BUS_NEXUS   PCI Bus Bridge
lan         0   8/8/1/0     btlan4      CLAIMED     INTERFACE   PCI(10110009)
lan         1   8/8/2/0     btlan4      CLAIMED     INTERFACE   PCI(10110009)
ba          3   8/12        GSCtoPCI    CLAIMED     BUS_NEXUS   PCI Bus Bridge
lan         2   8/12/1/0    btlan4      CLAIMED     INTERFACE   PCI(10110009)
lan         3   8/12/2/0    btlan4      CLAIMED     INTERFACE   PCI(10110009)
bc          2   10          ccio        CLAIMED     BUS_NEXUS   I/O Adapter
ext_bus     0   10/0        c720        CLAIMED     INTERFACE   GSC Wide SCSI
target      0   10/0.1      tgt         CLAIMED     DEVICE
disk        0   10/0.1.0    sdisk       CLAIMED     DEVICE      SEAGATE ST34572
target      1   10/0.2      tgt         CLAIMED     DEVICE
disk        1   10/0.2.0    sdisk       CLAIMED     DEVICE      SEAGATE ST34572
target      2   10/0.3      tgt         CLAIMED     DEVICE
disk        2   10/0.3.0    sdisk       CLAIMED     DEVICE      SEAGATE ST34572
target      3   10/0.4      tgt         CLAIMED     DEVICE
disk        3   10/0.4.0    sdisk       CLAIMED     DEVICE      SEAGATE ST34572
target      4   10/0.5      tgt         CLAIMED     DEVICE
disk        4   10/0.5.0    sdisk       CLAIMED     DEVICE      Quantum XP34361
target      5   10/0.6      tgt         CLAIMED     DEVICE
disk        5   10/0.6.0    sdisk       CLAIMED     DEVICE      SEAGATE ST15150
target      6   10/0.7      tgt         CLAIMED     DEVICE
ctl         0   10/0.7.0    sctl        CLAIMED     DEVICE      Initiator
bc          3   10/4        bc          CLAIMED     BUS_NEXUS   Bus Converter
tty         0   10/4/0      mux2        CLAIMED     INTERFACE   MUX
ext_bus     1   10/8        c720        CLAIMED     INTERFACE   GSC SCSI
target      7   10/8.7      tgt         CLAIMED     DEVICE
ctl         1   10/8.7.0    sctl        CLAIMED     DEVICE      Initiator
ba          4   10/12       bus_adapter CLAIMED     BUS_NEXUS   Core I/O Adapte
ext_bus     3   10/12/0     CentIf      CLAIMED     INTERFACE   Parallel Interf
ext_bus     2   10/12/5     c720        CLAIMED     INTERFACE   Built-in SCSI
target      8   10/12/5.0   tgt         CLAIMED     DEVICE
tape        0   10/12/5.0.0 stape       CLAIMED     DEVICE      HP      C1537A
target      9   10/12/5.2   tgt         CLAIMED     DEVICE
disk        6   10/12/5.2.0 sdisk       CLAIMED     DEVICE      TOSHIBA CD-ROM
target      10  10/12/5.7   tgt         CLAIMED     DEVICE
ctl         2   10/12/5.7.0 sctl        CLAIMED     DEVICE      Initiator
lan         4   10/12/6     lan2        CLAIMED     INTERFACE   Built-in LAN
ps2         0   10/12/7     ps2         CLAIMED     INTERFACE   Keyboard/Mouse
bc          4   10/16       bc          CLAIMED     BUS_NEXUS   Bus Converter
bc          5   12          ccio        CLAIMED     BUS_NEXUS   I/O Adapter
bc          6   14          ccio        CLAIMED     BUS_NEXUS   I/O Adapter
```

```
ext_bus      4   14/8         c720       CLAIMED   INTERFACE   GSC add-on
target      11   14/8.0       tgt        CLAIMED   DEVICE
disk         7   14/8.0.0     sdisk      CLAIMED   DEVICE      SEAGATE ST34572
target      12   14/8.1       tgt        CLAIMED   DEVICE
disk         8   14/8.1.0     sdisk      CLAIMED   DEVICE      SEAGATE ST34572
target      13   14/8.2       tgt        CLAIMED   DEVICE
disk        23   14/8.2.0     sdisk      CLAIMED   DEVICE      SEAGATE ST34572
target      14   14/8.3       tgt        CLAIMED   DEVICE
disk        24   14/8.3.0     sdisk      CLAIMED   DEVICE      SEAGATE ST34572
target      15   14/8.7       tgt        CLAIMED   DEVICE
ctl          3   14/8.7.0     sctl       CLAIMED   DEVICE      Initiator
target      16   14/8.11      tgt        CLAIMED   DEVICE
disk        25   14/8.11.0    sdisk      CLAIMED   DEVICE      SEAGATE ST34572
disk        26   14/8.11.1    sdisk      CLAIMED   DEVICE      SEAGATE ST34572
disk        27   14/8.11.2    sdisk      CLAIMED   DEVICE      SEAGATE ST34572
disk        28   14/8.11.3    sdisk      CLAIMED   DEVICE      SEAGATE ST34572
disk        29   14/8.11.4    sdisk      CLAIMED   DEVICE      SEAGATE ST34572
disk        30   14/8.11.5    sdisk      CLAIMED   DEVICE      SEAGATE ST34572
disk        31   14/8.11.6    sdisk      CLAIMED   DEVICE      SEAGATE ST34572
disk        32   14/8.11.7    sdisk      CLAIMED   DEVICE      SEAGATE ST34572
target      17   14/8.12      tgt        CLAIMED   DEVICE
disk        33   14/8.12.0    sdisk      CLAIMED   DEVICE      SEAGATE ST34572
disk        34   14/8.12.1    sdisk      CLAIMED   DEVICE      SEAGATE ST34572
disk        35   14/8.12.2    sdisk      CLAIMED   DEVICE      SEAGATE ST34572
disk        36   14/8.12.3    sdisk      CLAIMED   DEVICE      SEAGATE ST34572
disk        37   14/8.12.4    sdisk      CLAIMED   DEVICE      SEAGATE ST34572
disk        38   14/8.12.5    sdisk      CLAIMED   DEVICE      SEAGATE ST34572
disk        39   14/8.12.6    sdisk      CLAIMED   DEVICE      SEAGATE ST34572
disk        40   14/8.12.7    sdisk      CLAIMED   DEVICE      SEAGATE ST34572

processor    0   32           processor  CLAIMED   PROCESSOR   Processor
processor    1   34           processor  CLAIMED   PROCESSOR   Processor
processor    2   36           processor  CLAIMED   PROCESSOR   Processor
processor    3   38           processor  CLAIMED   PROCESSOR   Processor
memory       0   49           memory     CLAIMED   MEMORY      Memory
```

Similarly, you can use the `lanscan` command to view the network interfaces installed in your computer. You can also use the `-C` option with the `ioscan` command to find information about a particular class of devices. For example, you can type: `ioscan -fC disk` to obtain an ioscan of only the disk devices. After getting this information, create a new configuration file with the following two steps.

1. Go to the directory `/stand/build` using the `cd` command.

   ```
   cd /stand/build
   ```

2. Use the `system_prep` command to create a new system file from the running system.

   ```
   /usr/lbin/sysadm/system_prem -s system
   ```

Once this system file is created in the `/stand/build` directory, edit it to make the appropriate changes. A typical system file is as follows.

```
* Drivers and Subsystems

CentIf
CharDrv
DlkmDrv
GSCtoPCI
arp
asp
autofsc
beep
btlan4
c720
ccio
cdfs
clone
core
diag0
diag2
dlkm
dlpi
dmem
echo
fc
fcT1
fcT1_fcp
fc_arp
fcgsc
fcgsc_lan
fcms
fcp
fcp_cdio
fcparray
fcpdev
ffs
gelan
hp_apa
hpstreams
inet
ip
kload
klog
lan2
lasi
```

```
ldterm
lv
lvm
mux2
netdiag1
netqa
nfs_client
nfs_core
nfs_server
nfsm
nms
nuls
pa
pci
pckt
pipedev
pipemod
prm
ps2
ptem
ptm
pts
rawip
sad
sc
sctl
sdisk
sio
stape
stcpmap
strlog
strpty_included
strtelnet_included
tcp
telm
tels
timod
tirdwr
tlclts
tlcots
tlcotsod
token_arp
tun
udp
ufs
uipc
```

```
vxadv
vxbase
wsio


* Kernel Device info

dump lvol


* Tunable parameters

STRMSGSZ          65535
dbc_max_pct       10
dbc_min_pct       10
maxfiles          256
maxswapchunks     2113
maxuprc           500
maxusers          64
msgmap            258
msgmax            65536
msgmnb            65536
msgmni            200
msgseg            8192
msgtql            256
nfile             11500
ninode            11500
nproc             7000
npty              300
nstrpty           300
semmni            600
semmns            600
semmnu            600
semume            600
```

The first part shows the drivers and subsystems included in the kernel. Remove any drivers you don't need. You can make a decision while referring to the output of the `ioscan` command. Also remove any subsystem that is not required. The second part is the dump device information. The third part is the kernel tunable parameters. You may want to change any value here. After you are done with the changes, save the system file and move on to the next step of compiling the kernel.

Compiling the Kernel

To build a new kernel, you use the mk_kernel command.

```
/usr/sbin/mk_kernel -s ./system
```

The mk_kernel command uses master and library files from the /usr/conf directory. Files for any additional modules are expected to be in the /stand/system.d directory. If the kernel rebuild process is successful, the newly built kernel executable file is created in the /stand/build directory with the name vmunix_test.

Installing New Kernel and Configuration Files

As you already know, the default HP-UX kernel and system files are in the /stand directory with the names vmunix and system, respectively. You need to copy the new kernel and the system files into their default locations. But before that, you must create a backup copy of the existing working kernel. This is required so you can boot from the previous kernel if the new kernel fails to boot the system. You can back up the previous kernel and install the new kernel using the following sequence of commands.

```
mv /stand/system /stand/system.old
mv /stand/vmunix /stand/vmunix.old
mv /stand/build/system /stand
mv /stand/build/vmunix_test /stand/vmunix
```

Now the previous kernel is saved with name vmunix.old and can be used in case of emergency.

Rebooting the System

After building and installing the new kernel, you can reboot the system. This is necessary because the new kernel does not load until you reboot. If all goes well, your system will reboot with the new kernel. Use sysdef to make sure that the changes have taken place.

16.3 Kernel Rebuilding in a Nutshell

The kernel rebuilding process is accomplished using the following steps.

1. Change the directory to /stand/build.

   cd /stand/build

2. Create the kernel parameter system file from the running system.

   /usr/lbin/sysadm/system_prep -s system

3. Edit the system file to make necessary changes.

   vi system

4. Build the new kernel using the mk_kernel command.

   /usr/sbin/mk_kernel -s ./system

5. Back up the old kernel and system files.

   mv /stand/system /stand/system.old
   mv /stand/vmunix /stand/vmunix.old

6. Install the new kernel.

   cp /stand/build/system /stand
   cp /stand/build/vmunix_test /stand/vmunix

7. Reboot the system.

   shutdown -r 0

8. Verify the changed parameters and additional devices using the following commands.

   sysdef
   ioscan

You will see the presence of additional configured devices and any changes in the system parameters.

16.4 Booting from the Old Kernel

Sometimes you are not able to boot the system with the newly created kernel. In that case, you need to interact with the *initial system loader* (ISL). ISL calls a utility called hpux, which is used to load the HP-UX kernel. By default, it loads the /stand/vmunix kernel unless otherwise specified.

In case of a bad kernel, restart the system and wait for the following message.

```
Processor is starting the autoboot process.
To discontinue press a key within 10 seconds.
```

As soon as this message appears, press a key to enter the *processor dependent code* (PDC) menu. At the PDC command prompt, enter the boot command to start the boot process from the primary boot device. Your system will ask you if you want to interact with the ISL. Answer "yes" and you will get the ISL prompt. This process looks like the following.

```
--------------------- Main Menu -------------------------
Command                          Description
-------                          -----------

BOot [PRI|ALT|<path>]            Boot from specified path
PAth [PRI|ALT|<path>]            Display or modify a path
SEArch [Display|IPL] [<path>]    Search for boot device
COnfiguration menu               Displays or sets boot values
INformation menu                 Displays hardware information
SERvice menu                     Displays service commands
Help [<menu>|<command>]          Displays help for menu or cmd
RESET                            Restart the system
----------
Main Menu: Enter command or menu > boot pri
Interact with ISL (Y or N) ?> Y
ISL>
```

Now, at the ISL prompt use the hpux command to boot from the old kernel.

```
ISL> hpux /stand/vmunix.old
```

The system will boot with vmunix.old instead of vmunix. After reboot, you can restore the old kernel or make changes to correct the problems with the new kernel.

16.5 Common Kernel Tunable Parameters

As you have seen in the kernel system file, there are many kernel tunable parameters. Values of these parameters greatly affect system performance. Some of these parameters are explained in Table 16-1.

Table 16–1 *Important Kernel Tunable Parameters*

Name	Function
shmmax	Maximum amount of shared memory in bytes
shmseg	Maximum number of shared memory segments that can be attached to a process
maxvgs	The value of the highest numbered volume group
bufpages	Static buffer cache pages
maxfiles	Soft limit to the number of files a process can open
maxfiles_lim	Hard limit to the number of files a process can open; no more open files allowed
nfile	Maximum number of open files on the system at any time
nflocks	Maximum number of file or record locks
fs_async	Enable/disable synchronous disk write
maxuprc	Maximum number of processes per user
nproc	Maximum number of processes that can exist simultaneously on a system
timeslice	Allocation of time slice among competing processes
maxusers	Maximum size of system table
npty	Number of pseudoterminals
maxswapchunks	Maximum amount of swap space that can exist on the system
nswapdev	Maximum number of devices that can be used as device swap
remote_nfs_swap	Enable or disable swap to remote NFS access

Before changing any of these parameters, be sure that you know what is its effect on the system performance.

16.6   Using SAM to Reconfigure the Kernel

SAM can be used to reconfigure the kernel. When you go to the `Kernel Configuration` area of SAM, you will see a window like the one shown in Figure 16-1.

Figure 16-2 shows the window for configuring kernel drivers. It shows the names of the drivers and their current state. The `In` state shows that the driver is currently included in the kernel, while `Out` shows that the driver is not built into the kernel. The `Pending State` shows what will happen to the driver when you rebuild the kernel. When you add or remove a driver during the process of kernel building, the pending state changes. You can use the `Actions` menu to add or remove a driver.

Figure 16-3 shows the kernel configurable parameters. The current and pending values have the same meaning as discussed in the case of drivers. You can change the value of a parameter by using the `Actions` menu. As soon as you change a parameter value, the `Pending  Value` will change. Once again, make sure that you understand what you are doing here.

Figure 16-4 is the subsystem window and is used to add or remove subsystems from the kernel.

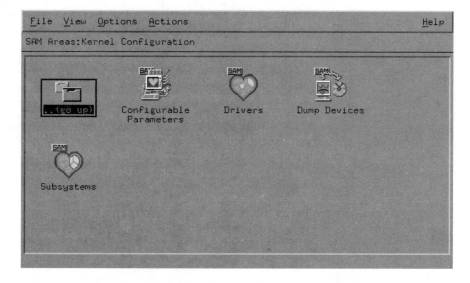

Figure 16–1   *The* `Kernel  Configuration` *area of SAM.*

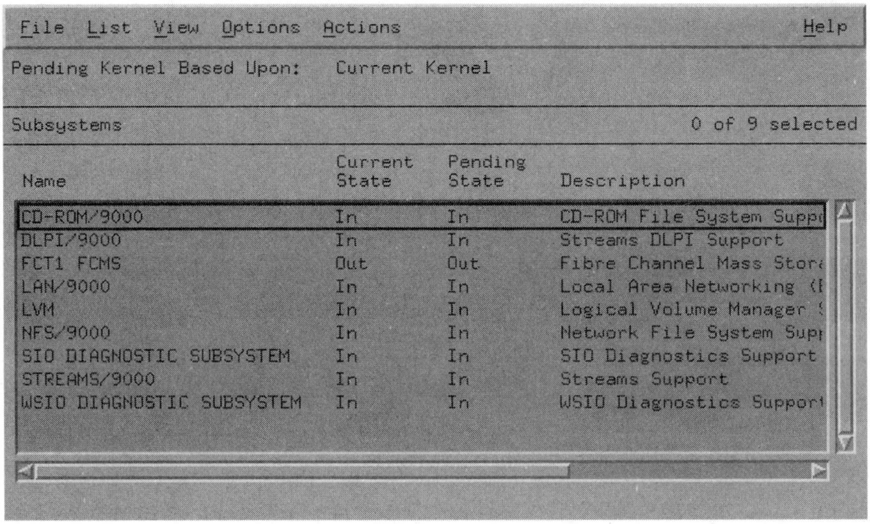

```
 File  List  View  Options  Actions                                    Help

 Pending Kernel Based Upon:    Current Kernel

 Subsystems                                              0 of 9 selected

                          Current    Pending
         Name             State      State      Description
         CD-ROM/9000      In         In         CD-ROM File System Supp
         DLPI/9000        In         In         Streams DLPI Support
         FCT1 FCMS        Out        Out        Fibre Channel Mass Stor
         LAN/9000         In         In         Local Area Networking (
         LVM              In         In         Logical Volume Manager
         NFS/9000         In         In         Network File System Sup
         SIO DIAGNOSTIC SUBSYSTEM   In    In    SIO Diagnostics Support
         STREAMS/9000     In         In         Streams Support
         WSIO DIAGNOSTIC SUBSYSTEM  In    In    WSIO Diagnostics Suppor
```

Figure 16–2 *Drivers window of* Kernel Configuration.

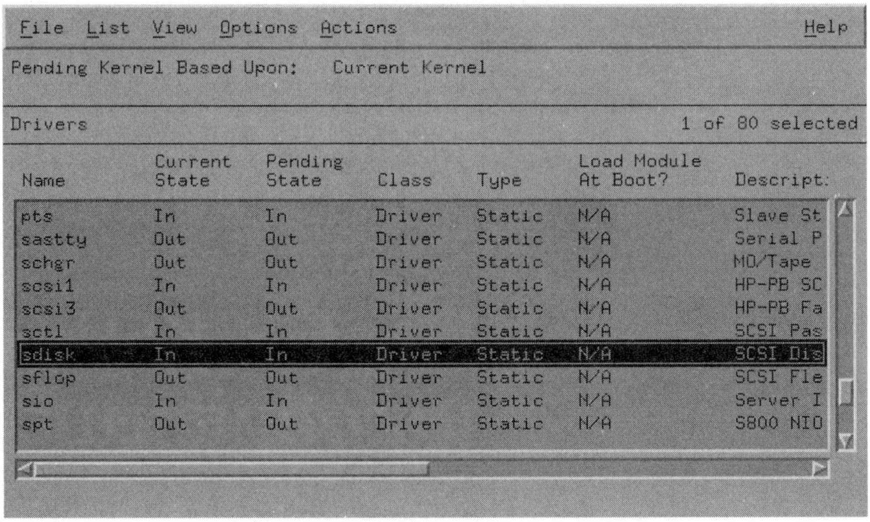

```
 File  List  View  Options  Actions                                    Help

 Pending Kernel Based Upon:    Current Kernel

 Drivers                                                 1 of 80 selected

                   Current   Pending                       Load Module
         Name      State     State     Class    Type       At Boot?    Descript:
         pts       In        In        Driver   Static     N/A         Slave St
         sastty    Out       Out       Driver   Static     N/A         Serial P
         schgr     Out       Out       Driver   Static     N/A         MO/Tape
         scsi1     In        In        Driver   Static     N/A         HP-PB SC
         scsi3     Out       Out       Driver   Static     N/A         HP-PB Fa
         sctl      In        In        Driver   Static     N/A         SCSI Pas
         sdisk     In        In        Driver   Static     N/A         SCSI Dis
         sflop     Out       Out       Driver   Static     N/A         SCSI Fle
         sio       In        In        Driver   Static     N/A         Server I
         spt       Out       Out       Driver   Static     N/A         S800 NIO
```

Figure 16–3 *Kernel* Configurable Parameters.

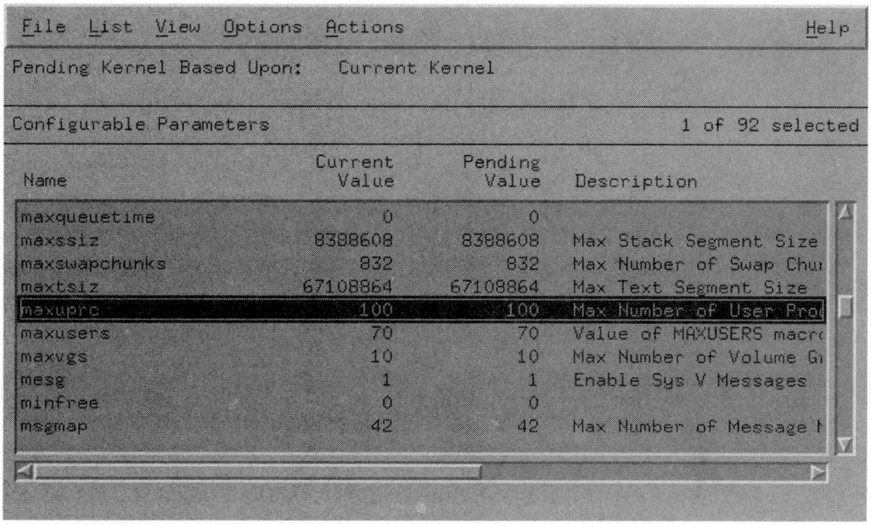

Figure 16–4 *Kernel Subsystems window.*

After making changes in any of the three windows shown earlier, it is time to rebuild the kernel. For this, you select the Create a New Kernel option from the Actions menu as shown in Figure 16-5.

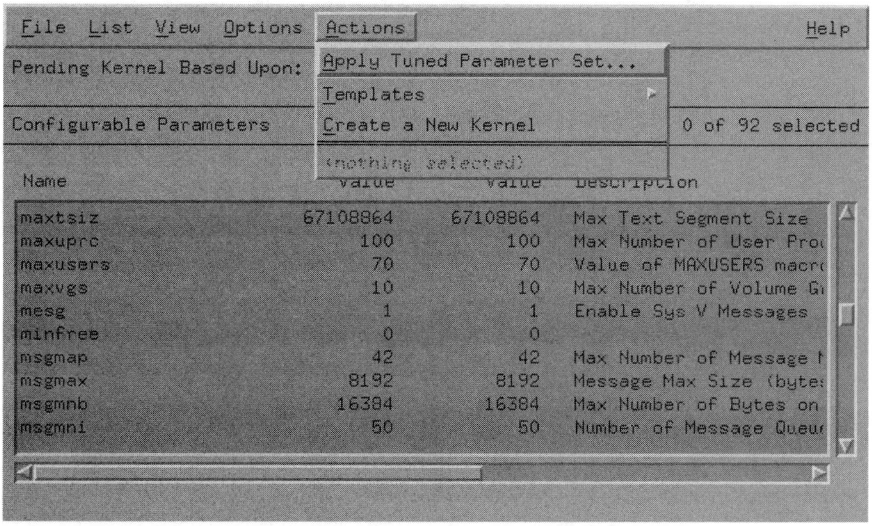

Figure 16–5 *Kernel compilation using the Actions menu.*

When you select this option, a new window appears with a warning message, as shown in Figure 16-6. When you press the Yes button in this window, you move to the window shown in Figure 16-7.

Pressing the OK button in Figure 16-7 moves the newly created kernel file into the /stand directory.

In addition to moving the kernel to its default place in the /stand directory, the newly created system is also copied into this directory, as shown in Figure 16-8. When you press the OK button in this window, the system is rebooted with the new kernel after moving the files into their respective directories.

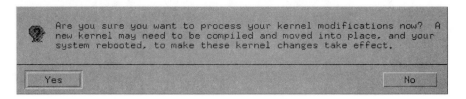

Figure 16–6 *Warning window showing that a new kernel will be built and the system rebooted.*

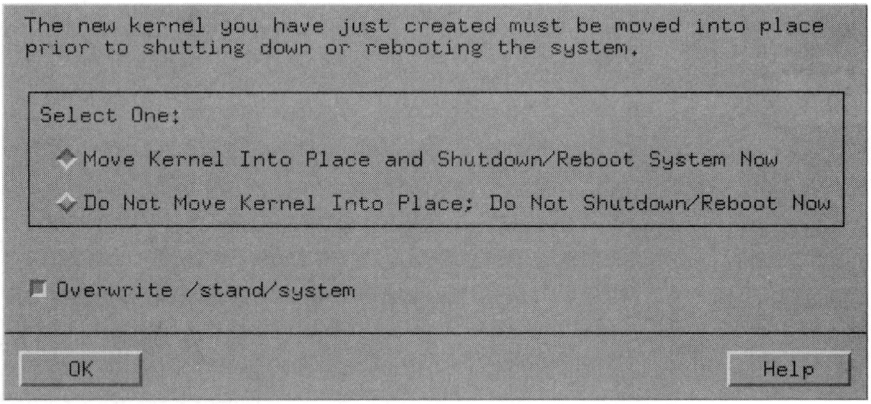

The new kernel you have just created must be moved into place prior to shutting down or rebooting the system.

Select One:

◆ Move Kernel Into Place and Shutdown/Reboot System Now

◇ Do Not Move Kernel Into Place; Do Not Shutdown/Reboot Now

☐ Overwrite /stand/system

OK   Help

Figure 16–7 *Move the new kernel into place and reboot the system.*

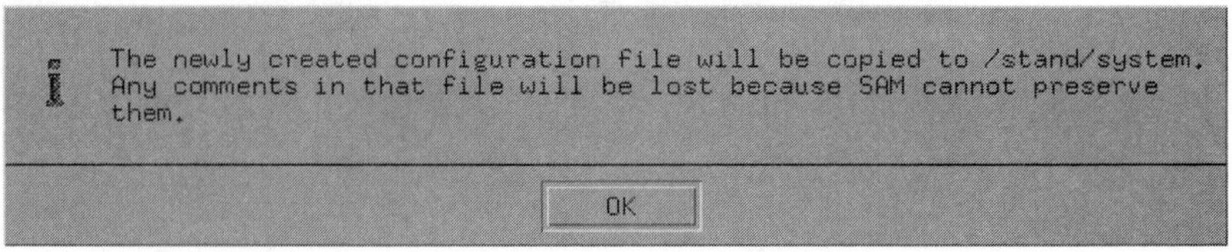

The newly created configuration file will be copied to /stand/system. Any comments in that file will be lost because SAM cannot preserve them.

OK

Figure 16–8 *Move the new system file into place.*

This completes the task of kernel reconfiguration with the help of SAM.

■ Chapter Summary

Kernel rebuilding is needed whenever you add or remove a device from your system, add or remove a subsystem, make changes to a swap or dump device, or change the value of a kernel tunable parameter. In the kernel rebuild process, you first create a new `system` file from the running system configuration using the `system_prep` command. After that, you need to edit this file to carry out the desired changes. For this you use the `ioscan` and `sysdef` commands to check existing device drivers and system parameters. Once you are satisfied with your system file, you create the new kernel using the `mk_kernel` command. In the next step, you back up the old kernel, install the new kernel, and reboot the system. You can also use SAM to rebuild the kernel.

In this chapter, you have seen all of this process in a step-by-step approach. You learned how to boot from an old kernel with the help of the ISL and the `hpux` command if the new kernel goes bad. A list of important kernel tunable parameters was presented in Table 16-1.

After going through this chapter, you have the knowledge of how to rebuild and install the HP-UX kernel, how to recover from a bad kernel, and what the important kernel parameters are.

▲ CHAPTER REVIEW QUESTIONS

1. List at least three situations in which you would need to rebuild the HP-UX kernel.

2. Why is it important to keep your old kernel?

3. How can you find existing kernel configurable parameters?

4. What is the name of the newly created kernel?

5. Why is it necessary to reboot the system after building the kernel? Is it possible to load a new kernel on a running system?

▲ TEST YOUR KNOWLEDGE

1. *The default HP-UX kernel is:*
    A. `/stand/hpux`
    B. `/hpux/kernel`
    C. `/stand/vmunix`
    D. `/stand/hpux/kernel`

2. *The HP-UX kernel is:*
    A. an executable file
    B. a text file
    C. a system image file that is loaded into memory at boot time
    D. a nonexecutable binary file

3. *If you don't back up the old kernel:*
    A. The new kernel never boots because it checks for the existence of the old kernel.
    B. You can't recover if the new kernel does not boot properly.
    C. The new kernel refuses to install if there is no backup copy, a safety feature enabled by Hewlett-Packard.
    D. None of the above.

4. *A new kernel is rebuilt whenever you:*
    A. install a new application
    B. change a kernel configurable parameter
    C. install a patch related to HP-UX commands
    D. don't shut down the system properly

5. *For a proper memory dump, the size of the swap space must be larger than:*
    A. the kernel size
    B. physical memory size
    C. any application size
    D. primary boot disk size

6. *What does the* `sysdef` *command show?*
    A. the system definition
    B. kernel tunable parameters
    C. kernel subsystems
    D. device drivers configured into the kernel

7. *The* `maxswapchunks` *kernel parameter shows the value of maximum swap space:*

   A. that can exist on the system

   B. used by each user

   C. per disk

   D. that can be used by a single application

Peripheral Devices

HP-UX communicates with all devices through device files placed in the /dev directory. Logically, there is no difference between I/O to these files and to ordinary disk files. But these files are not like ordinary disk files in that they don't occupy any space on the disk. As soon as data are written to any of the device files, they are sent to the device represented by that file. For example, if you output some data to a printer device file, they go to an attached printer for the printing process. Any data read request from a device file is also redirected to the actual device. A read request from the modem file reads incoming data from the modem.

Most of the device files are created automatically by HP-UX. During the boot process, HP-UX probes all devices and executes /sbin/ioinit.rc scripts that create new device files if needed. If any device file is not created automatically, HP-UX provides commands to create the device files manually. These files follow a particular naming con-

317

vention that indicates the hardware path a device is connected to and the type of the device. There are two major types of devices: character-type devices and block-type devices. These files also contain two special fields, listed with the `ll` command. These are major and minor device numbers. These numbers indicate the device driver and the encoded hardware address of that device.

In this chapter, you will be introduced to hardware paths and device files. You will see how device files in the `/dev` directory are arranged. You will find information about major and minor numbers, character- and block-type devices, the naming conventions used for device files, and some examples of device names. Then you will move on to how to list devices installed in your system and how to determine which devices are usable. Device drivers will be the next topic, and after that you will find information about how to install and configure new devices in your system. Finally, you will find information on modems and terminals, the device files related to them, and how they are configured.

After going through this chapter, you will be able to install and remove devices from HP-UX systems, and to diagnose and correct problems related to devices.

17.1　Devices and Physical Paths

All HP-9000 series servers and workstations use PA-RISC processors that are connected to several types of device adapters by using buses. All devices are connected to these device adapters. HP systems use many different types of buses, so you need to specify what type of expansion card you need. The buses that are used in HP systems are:

- Extended Industry Standard Architecture (EISA)
- General System Connect (GSC)
- Hewlett-Packard Precision Bus (HP-PB)
- High Speed System Connect (HSC)
- PCI

Each bus has its own characteristics, such as clock speed, data throughput, and signaling. The type of adapter is also different for each bus. For example, you will find different Ethernet adapters for PCI and GSC buses.

Common Types of Device Adapters

Some of the device adapters commonly used in HP-9000 systems are listed here. This list does not include all types of adapters; there are many others.

SCSI adapters   Small Computer System Interface (SCSI) adapters are used to connect disk drives, tape drives, and CD-ROM drives to the system. Many devices can be connected to one adapter. There are different standards for SCSI adapters used today. The Fast/Wide SCSI adapter is the fastest of all types and has the capability of transferring data at the speed of 20 Mbytes per second. It can support up to 15 devices on a single adapter. Standard SCSI adapters support seven devices and can have a throughput of 5 Mbytes per second. Fast/Narrow or differential SCSI can support up to seven devices and have a throughput of 10 Mbytes per second. You need to purchase a particular type of adapter after verifying the type of bus present in your system.

      All devices attached to SCSI adapters have a number that determines the priority of the device. The SCSI controller itself uses address 7. On SCSI adapters to which you can attach seven devices, device number 6 has the highest priority and device number 0 has the lowest priority. If you are using a Fast/Wide SCSI adapters the additional addresses have lower priorities than 0. Number 15 has a lower priority than number 0 and number 8 has the least priority level. The priority ordering for a Fast/Wide SCSI is: 7,6,5,4,3,2,1,0,15,14,13,12,11,10,9,8.

      Care must be taken while powering up and down the SCSI devices. All SCSI devices must be powered up before starting the system and powered off after the system is shut down. No device should be attached or detached to a running system.

Multiplexer   A multiplexer or MUX is used to connect serial devices to the system. Typically, this is used for connecting modems, terminals, and any serial plotter or printer. A variety of MUXs is available from Hewlett-Packard.

LAN card   LAN/9000 supports Ethernet and IEEE 802.3 networks and is used to connect your machine to a local area network. Hewlett-Packard manufactures LAN cards for different buses, topologies, and speeds.

You can add a new device adapter any time you want. For example, to have a network-efficient server, you may add Gigabit Ethernet to your system. Similarly, you can add SCSI adapters to increase the number of disk drives in the system.

Hardware Paths

A *hardware path* indicates the location of a device in your system. Typically, a hardware path is a string of numbers separated by the slash (/) and dot (.) symbols. Starting from the left, the first part of the device path is usually a bus number. This is followed by a slash (/) and then a bus converter number (if any). Then there are some other numbers separated by dots. These numbers show the path to the device in a systematic way.

Let us analyze a device path name. A hardware path of 8/12.5.0 represents a SCSI disk connected to the system. The number 8 represents a bus in the system. The number 12 is the address of the SCSI adapter on the bus. The disk is connected to that SCSI adapter at address 5, having a logical unit number 0. Similarly, hardware address 8/5/0 represents a fiber channel adapter connected to bus 8, bus converter number 5, and adapter number 0. On the backside of an HP-9000 server, you can see expansion slots, and some of these numbers may be present there. To list the devices in your system, you can use the ioscan command, which shows the hardware paths of all devices connected to your system. A typical output of this command is as follows.

```
# ioscan -f
Class       I   H/W Path    Driver    S/W State H/W Type  Description
==========================================================================
bc          0               root      CLAIMED   BUS_NEXUS
bc          1   8           ccio      CLAIMED   BUS_NEXUS I/O Adapter
ext_bus     0   8/0         c720      CLAIMED   INTERFACE GSC add-on
                                                Fast/Wide SCSI Interface
target      0   8/0.7       tgt       CLAIMED   DEVICE
ctl         0   8/0.7.0     sctl      CLAIMED   DEVICE    Initiator
ext_bus     1   8/4         c720      CLAIMED   INTERFACE GSC add-on
                                                Fast/Wide SCSI Interface
bc          2   10          ccio      CLAIMED   BUS_NEXUS I/O Adapter
ext_bus     2   10/0        c720      CLAIMED   INTERFACE GSC built-in
                                                Fast/Wide SCSI Interface
target      13  10/0.1      tgt       CLAIMED   DEVICE
disk        16  10/0.1.0    sdisk     CLAIMED   DEVICE    SEAGATE ST34371W
target      14  10/0.2      tgt       CLAIMED   DEVICE
disk        17  10/0.2.0    sdisk     CLAIMED   DEVICE    SEAGATEST34572WC
target      15  10/0.3      tgt       CLAIMED   DEVICE
disk        18  10/0.3.0    sdisk     CLAIMED   DEVICE    SEAGATE ST34371W
target      16  10/0.4      tgt       CLAIMED   DEVICE
```

```
disk       19  10/0.4.0     sdisk        CLAIMED  DEVICE     SEAGATE ST34371W
target     17  10/0.5       tgt          CLAIMED  DEVICE
disk       20  10/0.5.0     sdisk        CLAIMED  DEVICE     SEAGATE ST15150W
target     18  10/0.6       tgt          CLAIMED  DEVICE
disk       21  10/0.6.0     sdisk        CLAIMED  DEVICE     SEAGATE ST15150W
target     19  10/0.7       tgt          CLAIMED  DEVICE
ctl         2  10/0.7.0     sctl         CLAIMED  DEVICE     Initiator
bc          3  10/4         bc           CLAIMED  BUS_NEXUS  Bus Converter
tty         0  10/4/0       mux2         CLAIMED  INTERFACE  MUX
lan         0  10/4/4       btlan1       CLAIMED  INTERFACE  HP HP-PB 100 Base TX
 card
lan         1  10/4/8       btlan1       CLAIMED  INTERFACE  HP HP-PB 100 Base TX
 card
ba          0  10/12        bus_adapter  CLAIMED  BUS_NEXUS  Core I/O Adapter
ext_bus     3  10/12/5      c720         CLAIMED  INTERFACE  Built-in SCSI
target     20  10/12/5.0    tgt          CLAIMED  DEVICE
tape        0  10/12/5.0.0  stape        CLAIMED  DEVICE     HP      C1537A
target     21  10/12/5.2    tgt          CLAIMED  DEVICE
disk       22  10/12/5.2.0  sdisk        CLAIMED  DEVICE     TOSHIBA CD-ROM
target     22  10/12/5.7    tgt          CLAIMED  DEVICE
ctl         3  10/12/5.7.0  sctl         CLAIMED  DEVICE     Initiator
lan         4  10/12/6      lan2         CLAIMED  INTERFACE  Built-in LAN
ps2         0  10/12/7      ps2          CLAIMED  INTERFACE  Built-in
                                                            Keyboard/Mouse
processor   0  32           processor    CLAIMED  PROCESSOR  Processor
processor   1  34           processor    CLAIMED  PROCESSOR  Processor
memory      0  49           memory       CLAIMED  MEMORY     Memory
#
```

A short description of the fields in the `ioscan` command output is presented here.

Class	Shows the category of the device.
I	Instance: When multiple devices or adapters of the same category are present, they are distinguished from one another by instance numbers. Usually instance numbers are assigned at installation time.
H/W Path	This is the hardware path as already discussed in this chapter.
Driver	Name of the driver that controls the device. The device drivers are built into the HP-UX kernel. When adding a device that needs a new device driver, the kernel needs to be reconfigured.
S/W State	CLAIMED means the device driver is loaded in the kernel and is bound to the device. UNCLAIMED means the device driver is not available in the kernel for that device.
H/W Type	Shows what type of device it is.
Description	A short description of the device.

The `ioscan` command can be used, with the help of command line switches, to list devices of a specific type only or devices connected to a particular adapter.

17.2 Device Files

Every device in HP-UX has a corresponding device file in the `/dev` directory. This file describes the hardware path of the device and is used to communicate with the device. As you have seen in the `ioscan` listing, all devices (keyboard, mouse, disks, etc.) have device drivers associated with them.

The device files don't contain any data; instead, these are special files used for input or output purposes related to that device. These device files are created by HP-UX; however, you need to know which device file represents a particular device. You can use the `ioscan` command to list devices and device files simultaneously. For example, if you want to list devices and device files of category `disk`, use the following command.

```
# ioscan -funC disk
Class   I   H/W Path   Driver S/W State H/W Type   Description
==============================================================
disk   16   10/0.1.0   sdisk  CLAIMED    DEVICE     SEAGATE
   ST34371W                /dev/dsk/c2t1d0   /dev/rdsk/c2t1d0
disk   17   10/0.2.0   sdisk  CLAIMED    DEVICE     SEAGATE
   ST34572WC               /dev/dsk/c2t2d0   /dev/rdsk/c2t2d0
disk   18   10/0.3.0   sdisk  CLAIMED    DEVICE     SEAGATE
   ST34371W                /dev/dsk/c2t3d0   /dev/rdsk/c2t3d0
disk   19   10/0.4.0   sdisk  CLAIMED    DEVICE     SEAGATE
   ST34371W                /dev/dsk/c2t4d0   /dev/rdsk/c2t4d0
disk   20   10/0.5.0   sdisk  CLAIMED    DEVICE     SEAGATE
   ST15150W                /dev/dsk/c2t5d0   /dev/rdsk/c2t5d0
disk   21   10/0.6.0   sdisk  CLAIMED    DEVICE     SEAGATE
   ST15150W                /dev/dsk/c2t6d0   /dev/rdsk/c2t6d0
disk   22   10/5.2.0   sdisk  CLAIMED    DEVICE     TOSHIBA CD-
   ROM XM-5401TA           /dev/dsk/c3t2d0   /dev/rdsk/c3t2d0
```

Here you can see that device files related to all disk type devices are listed. Each disk has two device files, one that represents a character-type device and the other that represents a block-type device. To list an individual device file, you can use the `ll` command with a result as shown.

```
brw-r-----   1 root    sys   31 0x010500 Jun 10  1996 c2t5d0
```

Output of the `ll` command for a device file is different from a normal file and it contains additional fields such as major and minor numbers. These fields will be explained shortly.

Devices Directory Hierarchy

Usually the device files are present in the /dev directory. However, some device files are also grouped in a subdirectory under the /dev directory. For example, all block-type device files for disk drives are located in the /dev/dsk directory. Table 17-1 lists some other directories used for grouping device files.

Table 17–1 *Directories Used for Grouping Device Files*

Directory	Type of Files Present
/dev/dsk	Block device files for disk drives and CD-ROM
/dev/rdsk	Raw or character device files for disk drives and CD-ROM
/dev/vg00	Device for volume group vg00; every volume group has its own directory
/dev/rmt	Device files for tape drives
/dev/pts	Stream-based pseudoterminal device files
/dev/pty	Pseudoterminal slave device files
/dev/ptym	Pseudoterminal master device files

Major and Minor Numbers

Let's look at a list of files. This list is an output of the `ll` command, and it does not show file sizes. Instead, there is some other information in fields 5 and 6. Field 5 shows the *major device number* and field 6 shows the *minor device number.*

```
brw-r-----   1 root    sys   31 0x010500 Jun 10   1996 c1t0d5
brw-r-----   1 root    sys   31 0x010600 Jun 10   1996 c1t0d6
brw-r-----   1 root    sys   31 0x010700 Jun 10   1996 c1t0d7
brw-r-----   1 root    sys   31 0x011000 Jun 10   1996 c1t1d0
brw-r-----   1 root    sys   31 0x011100 Jun 10   1996 c1t1d1
```

Major device numbers represent the kernel driver used for the device. The kernel driver is a software component that is invoked when an I/O request is made for the device. All devices of the same type have the same major number, because the same driver is used for all of them. For example, the list shown is for disk drives of the same type, so these have the same major device number of 31.

Minor device numbers show the physical location of a device. It is a six-digit hexadecimal number. It may also be considered to distinguish among devices that have the same major number. The minor number is also used for device specific options. Consider this list of tape devices.

```
$ ll /dev/rmt/0m*
crw-rw-rw-  2 bin bin   212 0x030000 Oct 28 1997 /dev/rmt/0m
crw-rw-rw-  2 bin bin   212 0x030080 Sep 29 1997 /dev/rmt/0mb
crw-rw-rw-  2 bin bin   212 0x030040 Sep 29 1997 /dev/rmt/0mn
crw-rw-rw-  2 bin bin   212 0x0300c0 Sep 29 1997 /dev/rmt/0mnb
$
```

All of these device files represent the same tape drive but they have different minor numbers. These numbers represent a specific type of tape cartridge or format used when accessing the drive.

Character Devices

Character devices are also called raw devices. I/O to these devices is performed one character at one time. These devices are used for serial data transfer. The types of character devices are terminals, modems, serial printers, and tape drives. Disk drives also have character devices that are used for low-level functions on a disk.

When you use the ll command to list device files, the first character of every line in the output is "c" for these device files.

Block Devices

Block devices are used for transferring a block of data to and from a device. The data are exchanged through a buffer space in memory. An actual write to the device is performed only when the buffer is full. Similarly, when a read operation is performed, a block of data is read and put into the buffer. All disk drives and CD-ROM drives are examples of block-type devices.

When you use the ll command to list device files, the first character of every output line is "b" in block-type device files.

Device Files and Hardware Paths

> Go to the /dev directory and write down all subdirectories in this directory. Use the ioscan command to list all disk devices. Also write down the hardware paths for all disk drives. Are all of the disks attached to one SCSI interface? How many interfaces are installed in the system? You can find out by looking into the hardware path of the disk drives. From the output of the ll command you can also find out if all disk drives are using the same driver. Note the major device number associated with the disk device files. If the major number is the same, all disks use the same device driver.

17.3 SCSI Device File Naming Convention

SCSI device files in HP-UX follow a common naming convention, although it is possible to assign other names to these files. The general format of device file naming is shown in Figure 17-1.

The first letter of the device file name is "c" followed by a digit that represents an instance number. This part shows the interface card and the instance number assigned to that card. Instance numbers are automatically assigned by the kernel and can be listed using the ioscan command as explained earlier in this chapter.

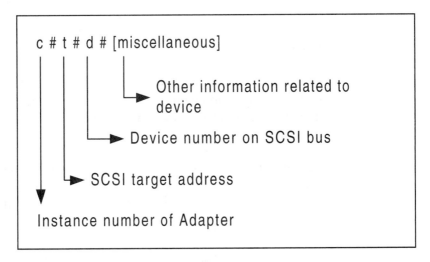

Figure 17–1 *Device file naming convention.*

The character "t" is followed by the SCSI target address. The target address shows the device number on the SCSI bus. These target addresses may be from 0 to 6 for single-ended or differential SCSI adapters, and from 0 to 15 (excluding 7) for Fast/Wide SCSI adapters. Usually target addresses are set through dipswitches or jumpers on the devices. For example, you can set a particular address for a disk by selecting a jumper setting before it is connected to the SCSI adapter. All target addresses for a particular SCSI adapter must be unique.

The device number or logical unit number (LUN) is represented by "d#". It is usually the number 0.

After that, there may be other optional device-dependent information. This part may or may not be present in the device name depending on the type of the device.

As an example, we consider a device name c0t1d0. It shows that the SCSI adapter to which the device is attached has an instance number of 0. The device target ID is 1, and it has a logical unit number 0.

Disk Naming

Every disk drive has two device files attached to it. The character-type device file is stored in the /dev/rdsk directory and is also called the raw device file. The block-type device file is stored in the /dev/dsk directory.

For example, if a disk is attached to an SCSI adapter having instance number 2 and a target ID of 4, the character device file for the disk will be /dev/rdsk/c2t4d0 and the block device file will be /dev/dsk/c2t4d0.

Tape Devices

The tape devices also follow the same naming convention as used for disk devices. However, depending on the type of tape cartridge and its format, a number of other optional features are also included in the device name. Consider the output of ioscan -funC tape command.

```
Class I  H/W Path Driver  S/W State H/W Type  Description
=========================================================
tape  1  10/8.1.0 stape   CLAIMED   DEVICE    QUANTUM DLT
         /dev/rmt/1m                 /dev/rmt/c4t1d0BEST
         /dev/rmt/1mb                /dev/rmt/c4t1d0BESTb
         /dev/rmt/1mn                /dev/rmt/c4t1d0BESTn
         /dev/rmt/1mnb               /dev/rmt/c4t1d0BESTnb
```

This list shows the device names for a tape device. The name /dev/ rmt/c4t1d0BESTnb shows that the tape device is attached to an adapter having instance number 4. The device target number is 1 and the logical unit number is 0. The word "BEST" indicates that with this device file, the highest possible capacity format will be used. This will also include data compression if it is supported by the device. The character "n" shows that the tape will not be rewound at the end of the operation. The "b" character shows that the tape drive will follow the Berkley style instead of AT&T.

Prior to HP-UX version 10.x, a different naming convention was used for tape devices. The tape device names were, for example, /dev/rmt/0m, /dev/ rmt/1m, and so on. In this scheme, an arbitrary number (such as 0 and 1) followed by the letter "m" was used for tape devices. This number was followed by additional characters showing the properties of the device. For example, /dev/ rmt/c4t1d0BEST was represented by /dev/rmt/1m, and /dev/rmt/ c4t1d0BESTn was represented by /dev/rmt/1mn. This naming convention is still used for backward compatibility. The output of the ioscan -funC tape command shows both types of devices.

Options used with tape drive devices are listed in Table 17-2.

Table 17–2 *Tape Drive Device File Options*

Option	Description
Density	Use one of the four: BEST, NOMOD, DDS, or D. The BEST option uses the highest capacity, including compression. The NOMOD option can be used on DDS and 8-mm devices only, and it maintains the density of previously written data. DDS shows the number of the DDS standard used, i.e., DDS2 or DDS3. The D option followed by a number defines the density of the tape as a numeric value.
C	Compress. The optional number following C shows the compression algorithm.
n	No rewind at the end of the operation.
b	Berkley-style tape behavior.
w	Wait for the physical completion of the operation before returning the status.

17.4 Listing Installed Devices

The device files associated with the installed devices can be listed using one of the ll, ioscan, or lssf commands. Each of these commands lists particular characteristics of device files.

Using the ll Command

Consider this list of files displayed by the ll command.

```
$ ll /dev/rmt/0m*
crw-rw-rw- 2 bin bin  212 0x030000 Oct 28 1997 /dev/rmt/0m
crw-rw-rw- 2 bin bin  212 0x030080 Sep 29 1997 /dev/rmt/0mb
crw-rw-rw- 2 bin bin  212 0x030040 Sep 29 1997 /dev/rmt/0mn
crw-rw-rw- 2 bin bin  212 0x0300c0 Sep 29 1997 /dev/rmt/0mnb
$
```

The ll command lists the following features of a device file.

- Type of the file. If the first character of an output line is "c", it is a character or raw device file. If the first character is "b", it is a block-type file.
- The major number of the device file in field 5, which is 212 in this listing.
- The minor number of the file in field 6.

Using the ioscan Command

The ioscan command has an advantage over the ll command in that it shows which device is attached to which file. It can also be used to list device files related to a particular class of devices. Output of the ioscan -funC disk command is shown here, which displays a list of all device files linked to class disk.

```
# ioscan -funC disk
Class  I H/W Path  Driver S/W State H/W Type  Description
=================================================================
disk  16  10/0.1.0  sdisk  CLAIMED   DEVICE     SEAGATE
   ST34371W          /dev/dsk/c2t1d0   /dev/rdsk/c2t1d0
disk  17  10/0.2.0  sdisk  CLAIMED   DEVICE     SEAGATE
   ST34572WC         /dev/dsk/c2t2d0   /dev/rdsk/c2t2d0
disk  18  10/0.3.0  sdisk  CLAIMED   DEVICE     SEAGATE
   ST34371W          /dev/dsk/c2t3d0   /dev/rdsk/c2t3d0
disk  19  10/0.4.0  sdisk  CLAIMED   DEVICE     SEAGATE
   ST34371W          /dev/dsk/c2t4d0   /dev/rdsk/c2t4d0
disk  20  10/0.5.0  sdisk  CLAIMED   DEVICE     SEAGATE
   ST15150W          /dev/dsk/c2t5d0   /dev/rdsk/c2t5d0
disk  21  10/0.6.0  sdisk  CLAIMED   DEVICE     SEAGATE
   ST15150W          /dev/dsk/c2t6d0   /dev/rdsk/c2t6d0
disk  22  10/5.2.0  sdisk  CLAIMED   DEVICE     TOSHIBA CD-
   ROM XM-5401TA     /dev/dsk/c3t2d0   /dev/rdsk/c3t2d0
```

Note that CD-ROM is also included in the "disk" class of devices. Similarly, to list all tape devices, you can use the `ioscan -funC tape` command. The `ioscan` command lists the following device file characteristics.

- Device class. If you use `ioscan` without any class option, it lists all devices attached to the system. From the first column of the output, you can find which device is related to which class.
- Instance number of the device.
- Hardware path of the device.
- Kernel driver used for the device.
- S/W state that shows whether the device driver is attached to the device.
- Description field that shows what type of device it is.

Using the lssf Command

You have seen that more than one file is attached to a tape device. The `lssf` command shows the characteristics of each device file. Consider the output of the following command.

```
$ lssf /dev/rmt/c4t1d0BESTn
stape card instance 4 SCSI target 1 SCSI LUN 0 at&t no
  rewind best density available at address 10/8.1.0 /dev/
  rmt/c4t1d0BESTn
$
```

This output shows additional information that `ioscan` does not provide. Specifically it shows that:

- The tape device file uses AT&T-style tape behavior.
- It will not rewind automatically.
- It will use the best density available for writing data.

Usable Devices

The `ioscan` command with the `-u` option shows only usable devices. The usable devices have the software driver bound to the device.

Listing and Naming Device Files

You have seen that a particular naming convention is used with devices attached to an SCSI interface. Use the command `ioscan -funC lan` to list all network interfaces attached to the system and see if there is any particular naming convention. The `lssf` command shows additional features of a device file. Go to the `/dev/rmt` directory where tape device files are stored. Use the `lssf` command on all of these files and see what characteristics each file has. Consult Table 17-2 to compare these characteristics with the device name.

17.5 Creating Device Files

The device files are automatically created when you install HP-UX on your system. After that, every time you boot your system, HP-UX scans all attached devices and creates device files if the device is *autoconfigurable*. However, you may need to create device files yourself for devices that are not autoconfigurable. One of the following methods is used for creating device files.

Autoconfiguration

At boot time, the kernel probes all hardware devices. It builds a list of the devices and initiates the `init` process during the boot process. The `init` process in turn starts the `/etc/ioinitrc` script. This script executes the `ioinit` command. This command checks the list of devices in the `/etc/ioconfig` file and compares it with the list of devices probed by the kernel. If new devices are found, `ioinit` executes the `insf` command, which creates device files for the new devices. This process is called *autoconfiguration*.

Using the insf Command

The `insf` command creates device files for new devices. It is automatically executed during the boot process; however, you can also use it later to create additional devices. For example, to create device files for tape drives, you can use the following command.

```
insf -C tape
```

This command does not create device files for existing devices. If you delete device files accidentally, `insf` will not recreate the device files at boot time. For creating device files for existing devices, you need to use the command line option -e. For example, if you accidentally delete the device file for your CD-ROM, which is attached to hardware path 0.1.0, use the following command to recreate it.

```
insf -H 0.1.0 -e
```

The options used with this command are listed in Table 17-3.

Table 17–3 *Options Used with the* insf *Command*

Option	Description
-d	Select device by driver name
-C	Select device by class name, such as "disk" and "tape" classes
-H	Create device files for a given hardware path
-I	Create device for card instance
-e	Reinstall files for existing devices

Using the mksf Command

This command is used to create device files if the system already knows the devices. An existing device is one that already has been assigned an instance number by the system. The mksf command can also create a directory if needed for the device file. It has some built-in options and file naming conventions; however, you can override these options using the command line. Table 17-4 shows command line options that can be used with this command.

Table 17–4 *Options Used with the* mksf *Command*

Option	Description
-d	Select device by driver name
-C	Select device by class name, such as "disk" and "tape"
-H	Create device files for a given hardware path
-I	Create device for card instance
-m	Create file with minor number

There are some other options that can be used with this command. For example, if you want to create a character-type (raw) device file for a disk attached at hardware address 2.4.0, the command will be:

```
mksf -H 2.4.0 -r
```

Using the mknod Command

The `mknod` command can be used to create character device files, block device files, or files representing named pipes. To create character or block device files, you have to specify major and minor numbers at the command line. To create a character device file for a tape drive with major number 212 and minor number 0x030080, you will use this command.

```
mknod /dev/rmt/0m c 212 0x030080
```

To create a block device file, replace "c" with "b" on the command line.

Using SAM

You can use the SAM `Peripheral Devices` area to install device files. This area looks like the window shown in Figure 17-2.

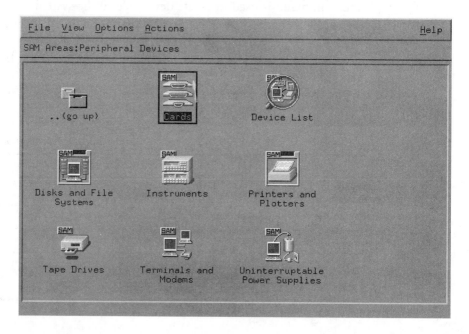

Figure 17–2 *SAM* Peripheral Devices *area for creating new device files.*

```
 File  View  Options  Actions                                    Help

 I/O Cards                                            1 of 10 selected

    Hardware
    Path          Driver    Description

    8/0           c720      GSC add-on Fast/Wide SCSI Interface
    8/4           c720      GSC add-on Fast/Wide SCSI Interface
    10/0          c720      GSC built-in Fast/Wide SCSI Interface
    10/4/0        mux2      MUX (3 ports)
    10/4/12       scsi1     HP 28655A - SE SCSI ID=7
    10/8          c720      GSC add-on Fast/Wide SCSI Interface
    10/12/0       CentIf    Built-in Parallel Interface
    10/12/5       c720      Built-in SCSI
    10/12/6       lan2      Built-in LAN
    10/12/7       ps2       Built-in Keyboard/Mouse
```

Figure 17–3 *List of adapters installed in the system.*

From here you can select a particular type of device by clicking on one of the icons displayed in the window. You can also list the I/O adapters installed in the system by selecting Device List. When you select this area, a window like the one shown in Figure 17-3 will appear. Here you can see the hardware path of each I/O card and its corresponding driver name. The Description column shows a short description of the adapter.

To create a new device file, go to the corresponding area and select Add from the Actions menu.

17.6 Installing a New Device

Adding a new device is quite a simple task. A step-by-step procedure for installing a new device is as follows:

1. If the device driver for the device is already built into the kernel, skip to the next step. If the device driver is not built into the kernel, reconfigure the kernel to include the device driver.
2. Shut down the system, turn off the power and install the device.
3. Reboot the system.
4. The HP-UX kernel will probe the new device and install device files during the startup procedure.

5. After the system is ready, login as **root** and use the `ioscan` command to verify that the device is detected and the device files are installed. If the files are not installed, use one of the commands you have studied to install the device files.

17.7 Terminals and Modems

Terminals and modems are serial devices and are connected to a serial port or an MUX. The device files for these are placed directly under the `/dev` directory (not in a subdirectory). Each terminal device file starts with `tty` followed by an MUX number. The next letter is "p" followed by a port number on the MUX. For example, a device file `/dev/tty0p3` represents a terminal on port 3 of the first MUX.

Pseudoterminal device files are used by applications that use terminal emulation and network services. These device files are found in pairs of master and slave files. The master files are found in `/dev/ptym` with a name starting with `pty`. These are linked to files with the same name in the `/dev` directory. The slave files are found in the `/dev/pty` directory, and their names start with `tty`. These are also linked to files in the `/dev` directory with the same name. The stream-based pseudoterminal files are present in the `/dev/pts` directory.

By default, 60 pseudoterminal device files are present. You can increase the number of pseudoterminals using the `insf` command. The following command creates 90 pseudoterminal device files.

```
insf -e -n 90 -d ptym
```

A modem is represented by three device files. Files for a modem attached to port number 4 of the first MUX are:

```
/dev/cua0p4
/dev/cul0p4
/dev/ttyd0p0
```

■ Chapter Summary

All devices in an HP-UX system are represented by one or more device files. I/O operations on these devices are carried out using these files. The device files are present under the `/dev` directory. Every device file is linked to a device with a particular hardware path. Hardware paths show the physical location of the device inside the system. A hardware path starts with a bus number and contains a bus converter number and the instance number of the interface card. A major device number shows the device driver, and a minor device number identifies the device's hardware address and, optionally, other device characteristics. Character or raw devices are used for transferring one character of data at one time, while block devices are used for transferring a block of data at one time. All SCSI device files follow a general naming convention c#t#d#, where the first # sign shows the instance number of an interface card, the second is for the SCSI target address, and the third is for LUN. Tape device files have additional characters that show the characteristics of the tape drive. Device files can be listed with the help of the ls, ioscan, and lssf commands. New device files are created with one of the following methods.

- autoconfiguration
- using the insf command
- using the mksf command
- using the mknod command
- using SAM

Terminal device files are in the /dev directory and show to which MUX port a terminal is connected. Pseudoterminal device files are used for making network connections. Each modem is represented by three device files.

▲ CHAPTER REVIEW QUESTIONS

1. What is the difference between major and minor device numbers?

2. Write two commands to list device files.

3. Describe the autoconfiguration process.

▲ TEST YOUR KNOWLEDGE

1. *What is the usual or default target address of an SCSI controller card?*

    A. 0

    B. 1

    C. 7

    D. may be assigned any address

2. *What is the interface card instance number of disk* 8/6.5.0?

    A. 8

    B. 6

    C. 5

    D. 0

3. *What is the device file name for disk* `7/3.4.0` *attached to a card having instance number 1?*

    A. `/dev/dsk/c1t3d4`

    B. `/dev/dsk/c1t4d0`

    C. `/dev/disk/c1t3d0`

    D. `/dev/c3t4d0`

4. *Which command can't be used for creating a device file?*

    A. `insf`

    B. `lssf`

    C. `mksf`

    D. `mknod`

5. *The device class* `disk` *includes:*

    A. disk drives only

    B. disk drives and CD-ROM

    C. disk drives and tape drives

    D. disk drives, tape drives, and CD-ROM

6. *A terminal is represented by how many files in the* `/dev` *directory?*

    A. 1

    B. 2

    C. 3

    D. none of the above

7. *What information is necessary for the* `mknod` *command on the command line?*

    A. major device file number

    B. minor device file number

    C. device type (character or block)

    D. all of the above

8. *Which command is executed automatically for new devices at boot time?*

    A. `mksf`

    B. `lssf`

    C. `insf`

    D. `mknod`

HP-UX File Systems and Logical Volume Manager

Disk and file system management is one of the important system administration tasks. It includes adding and removing disks, configuring these disks, creating file systems within these configurations, managing file systems, and repairing any disk problems. A disk may contain one or more file system. HP-UX offers the whole-disk and the Logical Volume Manager (LVM) approaches for disk management. While both of these approaches have their own advantages and disadvantages, it is possible to use both on a system simultaneously.

Whenever you run short of disk space, you add one or more disk drives to the system. The process of making these new disks usable for the system involves a number of steps. In this chapter, you will start with an introduction to disk devices and configuration schemes. Before creating logical volumes, you need to create physical volumes and volume groups. Once you have created the logical volumes, you can move to the file system creation process. You will find an introduction to the

337

High-Performance File System (HFS) and the Journaled File System (JFS) and how to create a new file system and mount it automatically at startup time. The `/etc/fstab` file is a file system table used for file system mounting at the system startup time with user-defined options. Occasionally you may need to extend or reduce the sizes of different file systems, and you will learn some commands to carry out such operations.

If you don't shut down your system properly or in the case of a system crash, the file system may go bad. In such a case, you have to repair it. The `fsck` command is used for this purpose, and you will learn how to use it.

After going through this chapter, you will be able to handle system administration tasks related to disks and logical volumes and to troubleshoot disk drives and file system problems.

18.1 Disk Devices and Their Configuration

Every physical disk has two device files associated with it. These device files are used for disk I/O activities. One of these is the raw device file and the other is the block device file. Each disk must be configured before it can be used with HP-UX. A disk may be subdivided and each of these subdivisions used for a specific purpose. A disk may be subdivided in such a way that a subdivision contains all the available space on the disk or only a part of it. The boot area is a special subdivision that contains utilities and files used at boot time, as you have seen in Chapter 14. Other than that, a subdivision may be utilized for one of the following.

- A file system that contains an area for storing files. Examples of this type of area are /usr, /var, and /home. Each of these is used for storing a particular type of file.
- A swap area used for swap space. Swap space is used in place of physical memory when the system needs more memory than what is installed in the system. It is also used for crash dumps. The size of swap space must be larger than the physical memory for a successful dump creation.
- A storage location for raw data, such as might be used by Sybase, Informix, Oracle, or other database products.

Other than these two types of areas, databases also use raw data areas that can be directly accessed by a database.

18.2 Introduction to Logical Volume Manager

You can configure a disk either by using the whole-disk approach or with the help of *Logical Volume Manager* (LVM). SAM can be used to implement either of these approaches.

The Whole-Disk Approach

If you are using a whole-disk approach, a disk can be used for only one purpose. For example, a disk can be used as a file system, a swap area, or a raw data area. However, there are two exceptions as follows.

- The swap area can coexist with a file system disk. For example, you can allocate 2 GBytes to the swap area and 4 GBytes to the file system in a 6-GByte disk.
- The boot area can also coexist with a file system disk. The boot area of the disk is where utilities related to the boot process are stored. This area is in LIF format and occupies 2 MBytes of disk space.

It may also be noted that the swap and boot areas can be created on a file system disk. The whole-disk approach is easy to implement, but it has some serious limitations. Some of these are as follows.

- Only one file system can exist on the disk. This means that you can't create a file system larger than the disk size.
- If you run short of space at a later stage, it is not possible to extend the file system. In another case, if you have allocated more space to a file system than is really needed, that space goes to waste, as there is no way to take it back. It may happen that you still have plenty of space on some of the file systems but you need some space on another file system that is full. If you are using the whole-disk approach, you can't use this space for the file system that needs more space.

These limitations are removed if you use LVM as explained next.

The Logical Volume Manager Approach

To better understand LVM, let's define three basic terms: *physical volume, volume group*, and *logical volume*.

PHYSICAL VOLUME

Physical volume is the actual physical disk drive. To use a disk with LVM (and hence to mark it as a physical volume), some data structures are created on the disk. The physical volumes use the same device file names as are used with the disk drives.

VOLUME GROUP

You can combine many physical volumes to form a volume group. A volume group is used to combine all space as one entity on the included physical volumes. For example, if you have four physical disks installed in your system, each with a 10-GByte capacity, a volume group can be created having a 40-GByte capacity. On an abstract level, HP-UX treats a volume group as a single storage space of 40 GBytes. This space can then be configured into desired smaller sizes. For example, you can create an area of 26 GBytes, which was not possible if you were using the whole disk approach.

The default volume group name is vg00, which is created when you first install HP-UX on your system. This is called the *root volume group*. It contains the boot disk and most of the operating system utilities and commands. You can create additional volume groups with names of your choice at any later stage.

Each volume group has a subdirectory the same name under the /dev directory. The subdirectory for the root volume group vg00 is /dev/vg00.

LOGICAL VOLUME

Considering a volume group as a single storage space of large capacity, you can divide it in logical volumes. A logical volume may be considered as an area on the disk in which you can create a file system. You can also use a logical volume as a swap or raw data area. Also, you can resize a logical volume at any time without losing any data on it. Other properties of a logical volume are as follows.

You can create a logical volume that occupies space only on one physical volume. You can also distribute space occupied by a logical volume to multiple physical volumes if you wish to do so.

Each logical volume has a device file inside the volume group directory. These device files have the names lvol1, lvol2, lvol3, and so on. However, this naming convention can be changed. A list of logical volumes in the root volume group /dev/vg00 is shown here.

```
crw-r-----   1 root    sys    64 0x000000 Jul  7 20:32 group
brw-r-----   1 root    sys    64 0x000001 Oct 29 20:40 lvol1
brw-r-----   1 root    sys    64 0x000002 Jul  7 20:32 lvol2
brw-r-----   1 root    sys    64 0x000003 Jul  7 20:32 lvol3
brw-r-----   1 root    sys    64 0x000004 Aug 26 15:44 lvol4
brw-r-----   1 root    sys    64 0x000005 Aug 26 15:44 lvol5
brw-r-----   1 root    sys    64 0x000006 Aug 26 15:44 lvol6
brw-r-----   1 root    sys    64 0x000007 Aug 26 15:44 lvol7
brw-r-----   1 root    sys    64 0x000008 Aug 26 15:44 lvol8
```

```
crw-r-----   1 root    sys   64 0x000001 Jul  7 20:32 rlvol1
crw-r-----   1 root    sys   64 0x000002 Jul  7 20:32 rlvol2
crw-r-----   1 root    sys   64 0x000003 Jul  7 20:32 rlvol3
crw-r-----   1 root    sys   64 0x000004 Jul  7 20:32 rlvol4
crw-r-----   1 root    sys   64 0x000005 Jul  7 20:32 rlvol5
crw-r-----   1 root    sys   64 0x000006 Jul  7 20:32 rlvol6
crw-r-----   1 root    sys   64 0x000007 Jul  7 20:32 rlvol7
crw-r-----   1 root    sys   64 0x000008 Jul  7 20:32 rlvol8
```

As you can see, the first file in the list is named group. This is the volume group device file. Every logical volume has two device files, like disk drives. One of these files is the block device file, and the other one is the character or raw device file. The name of the raw device file starts with "r".

Like other device files, each of these files has a major and a minor device number. The major device number for all LVM device files is 64. The minor number shows the logical volume name and its volume group membership. The first two digits from the left side show the group membership. In this listing, these are "00", showing that the file is related to the vg00 group. The last two digits (first two digits from the right side) show the file name. A pattern "04" shows a file name lvol04. The middle two digits are not used, and should be "00".

When you create a volume group, the volume device file is created using the mknod command. At a later stage, if you add a new logical volume to a volume group, new device files will be created automatically in the volume group directory.

18.3 Listing and Creating Logical Volumes

Information about LVM can be listed using a number of commands. You can display information about physical volumes, volume groups, and logical volumes. All physical and logical volumes are divided into smaller data units known as *LVM extents*. A physical volume consists of physical extents.

A physical extent (PE) is the smallest amount of disk space that can be allocated to a logical volume. By default, a physical extent occupies 4 MByte of disk space. It means that a logical volume can have disk space that is a multiple of 4 Mbyte.

A logical extent is similar to a physical extent. It is a pointer in kernel memory to a physical extent on a physical volume. A logical volume may have some logical extents that point to one disk and some to another disk. Thus, a logical volume can span multiple physical disk drives.

Physical extent size is fixed at the time of the creation of a volume group and it is constant throughout the group. All physical disks in a volume group have physical extents of the same size.

Listing Physical Volumes

The pvdisplay command is used to list physical volumes. The command expects a block-type device file for the disk drive as its argument. Let's see the output of the command shown here.

```
$ pvdisplay /dev/dsk/c2t5d0
--- Physical volumes ---
PV Name                  /dev/dsk/c2t5d0
VG Name                  /dev/vg00
PV Status                available
Allocatable              yes
VGDA                     2
Cur LV                   2
PE Size (Mbytes)         4
Total PE                 1023
Free PE                  868
Allocated PE             155
Stale PE                 0
IO Timeout (Seconds)     default
$
```

From this output, you get the following information about a physical volume.

- The volume group name to which this disk is related is vg00.
- Currently it has space allocated to two logical volumes.
- The physical extent size is 4 Mbytes.
- The total number of PEs on this disk is 1023.
- Out of 1023 PEs, 155 are allocated to volume groups, and 868 are free. The free PEs can be allocated to a logical volume when its size is extended or to create a new logical volume.

Let's take a more-detailed listing of the physical volume by using the -v option with the pvdisplay command as follows.

```
$ pvdisplay -v /dev/dsk/c2t5d0
--- Physical volumes ---
PV Name                  /dev/dsk/c2t5d0
VG Name                  /dev/vg00
PV Status                available
Allocatable              yes
```

```
VGDA                        2
Cur LV                      2
PE Size (Mbytes)            4
Total PE                    1023
Free PE                     868
Allocated PE                155
Stale PE                    0
IO Timeout (Seconds)        default

   --- Distribution of physical volume ---
   LV Name                 LE of LV  PE for LV
   /dev/vg00/lvol4         75        75
   /dev/vg00/lvol8         80        80

   --- Physical extents ---
   PE    Status   LV                   LE
   0000  current  /dev/vg00/lvol8      0170
   0001  current  /dev/vg00/lvol8      0171
   0002  current  /dev/vg00/lvol8      0172
   0003  current  /dev/vg00/lvol8      0173
   0004  current  /dev/vg00/lvol8      0174
   0005  current  /dev/vg00/lvol8      0175
   0006  current  /dev/vg00/lvol8      0176
   0007  current  /dev/vg00/lvol8      0177
   <some output deleted from here>
   0078  current  /dev/vg00/lvol8      0248
   0079  current  /dev/vg00/lvol8      0249
   0080  current  /dev/vg00/lvol4      0025
   0081  current  /dev/vg00/lvol4      0026
   0082  current  /dev/vg00/lvol4      0027
   0083  current  /dev/vg00/lvol4      0028
   <some output deleted from here>
   0150  current  /dev/vg00/lvol4      0095
   0151  current  /dev/vg00/lvol4      0096
   0152  current  /dev/vg00/lvol4      0097
   0153  current  /dev/vg00/lvol4      0098
   0154  current  /dev/vg00/lvol4      0099
   0155  free                          0000
   0156  free                          0000
   0157  free                          0000
   0158  free                          0000
   0159  free                          0000
   0160  free                          0000
   0161  free                          0000
   <some output deleted from here>
   1023  free                          0000
   $
```

This listing shows more useful information. First of all, it shows that the space on this disk is allocated to the logical volumes lvol4 and lvol8. Out of a total of 155 allocated PEs, 75 PEs are allocated to lvol4 and 80 PEs are allocated to lvol8. It also lists all PEs and the logical volumes to which these are attached. From the detailed list it can be verified that PEs 0–79 are allocated to lvol8 and PEs 80–154 are allocated to lvol4. The remaining PEs are free.

Listing Volume Groups

The vgdisplay command shows information about a volume group. I have used the following command to get information about volume group vg00.

```
$ vgdisplay /dev/vg00
--- Volume groups ---
VG Name                     /dev/vg00
VG Write Access             read/write
VG Status                   available
Max LV                      255
Cur LV                      8
Open LV                     8
Max PV                      16
Cur PV                      2
Act PV                      2
Max PE per PV               2500
VGDA                        4
PE Size (Mbytes)            4
Total PE                    2046
Alloc PE                    1178
Free PE                     868
Total PVG                   0
Total Spare PVs             0
Total Spare PVs in use      0
$
```

You can find the following information from the output of this command.

- The maximum number of logical volumes that can be created in this volume group. This value is 255 for vg00.
- There are currently eight logical volumes in the group.
- There can be 16 maximum physical volumes (disks) in the volume group.

- Currently there are two physical volumes in the volume group, which means you can add 14 more physical disks to this volume group.
- Every physical volume can have 2500 physical extents of 4 MBytes each. It means that you can add disks of up to 10 GBytes to this volume group.
- Currently there are 2046 physical extents. Of these, 1178 are allocated and 868 are free. This is important information that enables you to extend the size of any logical volume or create a new logical volume, as there are plenty of unallocated PEs in the volume group.

A detailed list can be obtained using the -v option with the vgdisplay command as follows. This list shows all logical and physical volumes in the volume group and their size in terms of logical or physical extents.

```
$ vgdisplay -v vg00
--- Volume groups ---
VG Name                    /dev/vg00
VG Write Access            read/write
VG Status                  available
Max LV                     255
Cur LV                     8
Open LV                    8
Max PV                     16
Cur PV                     2
Act PV                     2
Max PE per PV              2500
VGDA                       4
PE Size (Mbytes)           4
Total PE                   2046
Alloc PE                   1178
Free PE                    868
Total PVG                  0
Total Spare PVs            0
Total Spare PVs in use     0

   --- Logical volumes ---
   LV Name                 /dev/vg00/lvol1
   LV Status               available/syncd
   LV Size (Mbytes)        100
   Current LE              25
   Allocated PE            25
   Used PV                 1

   LV Name                 /dev/vg00/lvol2
   LV Status               available/syncd
```

```
LV Size (Mbytes)              512
Current LE                    128
Allocated PE                  128
Used PV                       1

LV Name                       /dev/vg00/lvol3
LV Status                     available/syncd
LV Size (Mbytes)              200
Current LE                    50
Allocated PE                  50
Used PV                       1

LV Name                       /dev/vg00/lvol4
LV Status                     available/syncd
LV Size (Mbytes)              400
Current LE                    100
Allocated PE                  100
Used PV                       2

LV Name                       /dev/vg00/lvol5
LV Status                     available/syncd
LV Size (Mbytes)              1000
Current LE                    250
Allocated PE                  250
Used PV                       1

LV Name                       /dev/vg00/lvol6
LV Status                     available/syncd
LV Size (Mbytes)              500
Current LE                    125
Allocated PE                  125
Used PV                       1

LV Name                       /dev/vg00/lvol7
LV Status                     available/syncd
LV Size (Mbytes)              1000
Current LE                    250
Allocated PE                  250
Used PV                       1

LV Name                       /dev/vg00/lvol8
LV Status                     available/syncd
LV Size (Mbytes)              1000
Current LE                    250
Allocated PE                  250
Used PV                       2
```

```
--- Physical volumes ---
PV Name                     /dev/dsk/c2t6d0
PV Status                   available
Total PE                    1023
Free PE                     0

PV Name                     /dev/dsk/c2t5d0
PV Status                   available
Total PE                    1023
Free PE                     868
```

Listing Logical Volumes

As with the physical volumes and volume groups, information about individual logical volumes can also be displayed. You use the lvdisplay command for this purpose, providing the logical volume block device file as the argument.

```
$ lvdisplay /dev/vg00/lvol4
--- Logical volumes ---
LV Name                     /dev/vg00/lvol4
VG Name                     /dev/vg00
LV Permission               read/write
LV Status                   available/syncd
Mirror copies               0
Consistency Recovery        MWC
Schedule                    parallel
LV Size (Mbytes)            400
Current LE                  100
Allocated PE                100
Stripes                     0
Stripe Size (Kbytes)        0
Bad block                   on
Allocation                  strict
IO Timeout (Seconds)        default
$
```

A more-detailed list can be generated with the help of the -v option with this command. It shows each logical extent and the disk to which it points. The output of the following lvdisplay command is truncated at the end.

```
$ lvdisplay -v /dev/vg00/lvol4
--- Logical volumes ---
LV Name                       /dev/vg00/lvol4
VG Name                       /dev/vg00
LV Permission                 read/write
LV Status                     available/syncd
Mirror copies                 0
Consistency Recovery          MWC
Schedule                      parallel
LV Size (Mbytes)              400
Current LE                    100
Allocated PE                  100
Stripes                       0
Stripe Size (Kbytes)          0
Bad block                     on
Allocation                    strict
IO Timeout (Seconds)          default

   --- Distribution of logical volume ---
   PV Name            LE on PV   PE on PV
   /dev/dsk/c2t6d0      25          25
   /dev/dsk/c2t5d0      75          75

   --- Logical extents ---
   LE    PV1                  PE1   Status 1
   0000 /dev/dsk/c2t6d0       0203  current
   0001 /dev/dsk/c2t6d0       0204  current
   0002 /dev/dsk/c2t6d0       0205  current
   0003 /dev/dsk/c2t6d0       0206  current
   0004 /dev/dsk/c2t6d0       0207  current
   0005 /dev/dsk/c2t6d0       0208  current
   0006 /dev/dsk/c2t6d0       0209  current
   <Some output deleted from here>
```

At this point, you know what type of information is associated with physical and logical volumes and volume groups. Let's see how we can create a logical volume by first creating physical volumes and volume groups.

Creating Physical Volumes

The creation of physical volumes is the first step for using a disk with LVM. To find out the device file name associated with a disk, you can use the `ios-can` command. You may wish to format and analyze the integrity of a disk with the help of the `mediainit` command before creating a physical volume on it as follows.

```
mediainit /dev/rdsk/c2t5d0
```

Since disk formatting and analysis is a low-level task, you need to use a raw device file with the `mediainit` command.

The `mediainit` command performs read and write operations on all parts of the disk. It may take an excessively long time depending on the type and capacity of the disk. Most of the disk drives are already initialized, and you don't need to run this command before using them with LVM. Use this command only if you have some doubt about the integrity of a disk.

To create a physical volume, use the `pvcreate` command as shown below.

```
pvcreate /dev/rdsk/c2t5d0
```

If the disk on which a physical volume is being created was part of a volume group earlier, the physical volume will not be created. If you are sure that you are creating a physical volume on the right disk, use the `-f` option with the `pvcreate` command to *force* the creation of a physical volume. However, one should be very careful when using this option. Using `pvcreate` on the wrong disk may have catastrophic results.

Creating Volume Groups

After creating physical volumes on all disks you want to add to a volume group, you can move to the process of volume group creation. Creation of a volume group involves a number of steps as follows.

1. Create a directory in `/dev` with the group name. For example, if the volume group name is `vg03`, the directory will be `/dev/vg03`.
2. Create the group special file in this directory. The name of this control file is always `group`, and it has a major number of 64. The minor number shows the group number. For example, if the group number is 03 (`vg03`), the minor number is 0x030000. The last four digits of the minor number are always 0000. To create a group special file for group `vg03`, use the command:

```
mknod /dev/vg03/group c 64 0x030000
```

3. Create a volume group using the `vgcreate` command. Provide physical volume names as command-line arguments to the `vgcreate` command. To create volume group `vg03` containing a single physical volume `c2t5d0`, the command is:

```
vgcreate /dev/vg03 /dev/dsk/c2t5d0
```

The `vgcreate` command accepts the command-line options listed in Table 18-1.

Table 18–1 *Options Used with the* `vgcreate` *Command*

Option	Description
`-l`	Maximum number of logical volumes in the volume group
`-p`	Maximum number of physical volumes in the volume group
`-e`	Maximum number of physical extents in the volume group
`-s`	Size of physical extents in the volume group

After creating a volume group, you can use the `vgdisplay` command to verify its characteristics.

Creating Logical Volumes

Logical volumes are created using the `lvcreate` command. When you create a new logical volume, its raw and block device files are created in the volume group directory. To create a logical volume of 800 MBytes with the name `myvolume` in volume group `vg03`, you can use following command.

```
lvcreate -L 800 -n myvolume vg03
```

Command-line options that can be used with the `lvcreate` command are shown in Table 18-2.

Table 18–2 *Options Used with the* `lvcreate` *Command*

Option	Description
`-L`	Size of logical volume in megabytes
`-l`	Size of logical volumes in number of logical extents
`-n`	Name of logical volume; if not specified, default names are used (`lvol1`, `lvol2`, etc.)
`-C`	Use contiguous space to create the logical volume
`-i`	Set the number of disks to be included in the logical volume; may be set to the total number of physical volumes in the volume group
`-I`	Set the size of stripe across each physical volume when more than one disk are used in a logical volume; options `-i` and `-I` must be used together

LVM Data Structure

LVM data structures are created on every disk included in a volume group. These data structures include the following.

1. *Physical volume reserved area* (PVRA): created by the `pvcreate` command and contains information about the physical volume.
2. *Volume group reserved area* (VGRA): created by the `vgcreate` command and contains the volume group status area (VGSA) and volume group descriptor area (VGDA), which contains device driver information used for the volume group.
3. *Bad block relocation area* (BBRA): an area at the bottom of the disk used by LVM whenever a physical defect is seen on the physical volume. This area is created by the `pvcreate` command.

The LVM boot disk also contains additional information used for system bootup.

Study Break

Logical Volume Manager

> You have gone through an introduction to LVM and how to display and create LVM components. To have some practice with LVM, log into your system and use the `vgdisplay -v vg00` command to list the root volume group. How many physical volumes are in this volume group? Note how many physical extents are present in the volume group and how many of these are free. If you find some free physical extents, use the `lvcreate` command to create a new logical volume with the name `myvol`. Use the `vgdisplay` command again to list the presence of the new logical volume.

18.4 Introduction to File Systems

A file system is a structure in which files and directories are stored. A file system determines how disk space will be allocated to different files on the disk. The file system also keeps records of allocated and free space on a disk. The file system maintains a directory tree for listing files and directories existing on the file system. It keeps owner and group information and user access permissions for files and directories.

HP-UX creates multiple file systems. If you are using LVM, each logical volume contains one file system. Thus, the number file systems created is eight by default. Multiple file systems are used for a number of reasons. A file system can be managed and repaired while other file systems are in use. You can also extend or reduce individual volumes so that disk space may be utilized in a more efficient way.

The area allocated to a file system is divided into two major parts, the user area and the *metadata* area. The user area contains actual user data (the data that you store in files). The metadata area contains file system structural information partitioned as follows.

- The *Superblock* contains information about the file system type, size, and pointers to other metadata structures. HP-UX keeps multiple copies of the superblock.
- *Inodes* keep records of file attributes, such as the owner and group of the file, file permissions, type of file, number of hard links associated with the file, time and date stamps, and file size. It also has pointers to the file data area. Every file is associated with an inode. Inodes are referenced by numbers. Inode 02 always represents the root directory.
- The directory area keeps records of file names and related inode numbers.

When you use the `cat` command to display the contents of a file, HP-UX goes to the directory area to find the inode number associated with the file. It then locates the inode and from it gets a pointer to the data area of the file. After that, it displays the contents of that area on your terminal screen.

File System Types

HP-UX supports many types of file systems. *High Performance File System* (HFS) is used for the `/stand` mount point where the HP-UX kernel is stored. *Journaled File System* (JFS) is used for other volumes in LVM. *Network File System* (NFS) is used for mounting file systems over the network from a file server. *CD-ROM File System* (CDFS) is used for storing files on CD-ROM.

Every file system has its own characteristics and methods of storing information. From the user point of view, all file systems are the same, as the same commands are used for file manipulation in all file systems.

One system can simultaneously have all supported types of file systems. You can use the `fstyp` command to determine what type of file system is on a particular device.

More on Hard and Soft Links

File links are created using the `ln` command and are used to access a single file with multiple file names. By default, the `ln` command creates a hard link.

For example, to link the file `/home/boota/myfile` with `/home/boota/linkfile`, you can use following command.

```
ln /home/boota/myfile /home/boota/linkfile
```

After using this command, `linkfile` will be created and will contain the same data as `myfile`. On the file system level, a directory entry with the name `linkfile` is created, which points to the same inode used by `myfile`. Hard links can be created only within a file system; you cannot link directories with hard links.

To create a soft link, you use the `-s` option with the `ln` command. When creating a soft link, HP-UX creates a file entry with its own inode number in the directory area. This inode number then points to a data block that contains the file name to which the link is established. Soft links can link directories and can be used between file systems.

If you delete a file that has soft links, the links are not actually deleted, as they have their own inodes. But when you try to access a linked file for which the original file has been deleted, an error message will be shown.

18.5 The High-Performance File System

HFS is the legacy file system used with HP-UX. Although JFS is used in the newer versions of HP-UX, HFS is still in use for the `/stand` file system and is supported on all HP-UX releases.

The first 8 Kbytes of all HFS file systems contain the HFS superblock, which contains general information and pointers to the metadata area as already discussed. HFS contains more than one copy of the superblock, and the locations of these redundant copies are recorded in the `/var/adm/sbtab` file. If the main superblock is damaged, it can be recovered from one of the backup copies. If you use the `cat` command, this file looks like the following.

```
/dev/vg00/rlvol1: super-block backups (for fsck -b#) at:
    16,    2504,    4992,    7480,    9968,   12456,   14944,   17432,
 19728,   22216,   24704,   27192,   29680,   32168,   34656,   37144,
 39440,   41928,   44416,   46904,   49392,   51880,   54368,   56856,
 59152,   61640,   64128,   66616,   69104,   71592,   74080,   76568,
 78864,   81352,   83840,   86328,   88816,   91304,   93792,   96280,
 98576,  101064
```

The remaining HFS area is divided into one or more *cylinder groups*. Each cylinder group contains a data area as well as inodes. You can specify the number of inodes when you create the file system. The disadvantage is that if you create too few inodes, you can run short. It may happen that the data area space is still vacant, but you can't create new files as no free inode is available. There is no way to increase the number of inodes without allocating more disk space to the file system or recreating the file system, damaging all of the data stored on it.

HFS is easy to manage. However, you can't reduce its size. Another disadvantage is that you must unmount the file system if you want to increase its size.

HFS Blocks

The HFS block is the minimum data that are read in one read request. The default HFS block size is 8 Kbytes. You can use block sizes of 4, 8, 16, 32, or 64 Kbytes when you create a file system. So, in case you are using a 64-Kbyte block size, a request for reading even 512 bytes will need 64 Kbytes to be read; a large block size for small files may be inefficient to use. Similarly, if you are using large files on a file system and the block size is small, the system may have to make many read requests when reading a large amount of data. And if these blocks are scattered across the disk, it may take a longer time for the read head to locate the data. You must be careful when selecting the block size, keeping in mind the size of the files that will be stored on the file system.

The block size cannot be changed once a file system is created.

HFS Fragments

A fragment is the smallest unit of data that can be allocated to a file. HFS blocks are divided into fragments. A block may contain one, two, four or eight fragments. The number of fragments and the fragment size are also set at the time of file system creation and cannot be changed later. A block may contain fragments related to different files.

18.6 The Journaled File System

JFS is the HP-UX version of the Veritas journaled File System (VxFS). This file system exhibits fast recovery features. HP OnLineJFS (Advanced JFS) is an extension to the base JFS and can be managed online (without unmounting). For example, you can extend or shrink the file system without unmounting it. Advanced JFS can also be defragmented and reorganized while it is in use. HP OnlineJFS is not included with the standard HP-UX distribution and must be purchased separately. A disadvantage of JFS is that the HP-UX kernel can't reside on it.

Like HFS, JFS also maintains multiple copies of the superblock, but these are not stored in any file. JFS keeps a record of these copies automatically. JFS keeps a record of all transactions to the file system metadata area in an *intent log*. The intent log is used for system recovery in case of a system crash. If a file system update is completed successfully, a "done record" is written to the intent log showing that this update request was successful. In case of a system crash, the intent log is consulted and the file system brought to the stable state by removing all unsuccessful transactions with the help of the intent log.

Another big advantage of JFS over HFS is that it creates inodes dynamically. So if the inode table is full but there is still space on the file system, JFS can create new inodes automatically.

Like HFS, JFS also divides the file system in JFS blocks. By default, the size of each block is 1 KByte. JFS allocates a group of blocks when you create a new file. This group of blocks is called an *extent*. If the file size grows, JFS tries to allocate contiguous blocks to the file, thus increasing the size of the file extent. However, if the contiguous blocks are not available, JFS creates a new extent and allocates it to the file.

18.7 Creating a New File System

You may create a new file system if you want to separate a particular type of file from the rest of the system or to separately allocate some disk space for a set of users. A file system can be created on a logical volume or by using the whole-disk approach using command-line utilities. You can also use SAM for this purpose.

File System Creation Process

Making a file system usable involves four basic steps.

1. Create the new file system using the `newfs` command.
2. Create a mount point for the file system using the `mkdir` command. A mount point is a directory on which the file system is mounted.
3. Mount the new file system on the mount point using the `mount` command.
4. Create an entry in the `/etc/fstab` file for the file system so that it is automatically mounted every time you boot up your system.

Creating a File System with the newfs Command

The newfs command is used to create a new file system. If you are using LVM, this command can be used after you have carried out the following three steps.

1. Physical volumes have been created.
2. One or more volume group has been created using these physical volumes.
3. Logical volumes have been created.

After these steps, you can use the newfs command to create a file system on a logical volume. To create a JFS file system on /dev/vg03/lvol4, you can use following command.

```
newfs -F vxfs /dev/vgo3/rlvol4
```

Other options that can be used with the newfs command are listed in Table 18-3.

Table 18–3 *Options Used with the* newfs *Command*

Option	Description
-F	Type of file system. You can use "hfs" for an HFS file system and "vxfs" for JFS. You can use the newfs_hfs command to create the HFS file system only and the newfs_vxfs command to create a JFS file system.
-s	Size of the file system in blocks. If you don't specify this option, newfs will use all available space on a logical volume.
-v	Verbose mode to display what is going on during the execution of the command.
-o largfiles	Used for support of large files. By default, the maximum file size is 2 GBytes. Using this option, you can create files up to 128 GBytes.
-b	Block size in bytes (HFS only).
-i	Space per inode in bytes (HFS only).
-f	Fragment size in bytes (HFS only).
-R	Reserves swap space in megabytes at the end of the file system. This option can't be used with -s option.
-m	Minimum amount of free space allowed. If the file system is full to this amount, no user can use the file system except the **root** user. The default amount is 10% of the total file system space. If you are using a large file system, you may wish to reduce this space (HFS only).

Let's see some examples of the use of the `newfs` command. To create a file system with largefile support on `/dev/vg03/lvol5`, use:

```
newfs -F vxfs -o largefiles /dev/vg03/rlvol5
```

To create an HFS with a block size of 2 Kbytes, use the following.

```
newfs -F hfs -b 2048 /dev/vg03/rlvol5
```

To create a JFS file system using the whole-disk approach on disk `c2t5d0` and leaving 100 MBytes of space for swap, use this command.

```
newfs -F vxfs -R 100 /dev/rdsk/c2t5d0
```

18.8 Mounting and Unmounting a File System

A file system needs to be mounted on a directory before it can be used. The root file system is mounted on the / directory. Other file systems are mounted on a directory created on the root file system or on a directory in another mounted file system. The directory on which a file system is mounted is called a *mount point*. The `mount` command is used for this purpose. To mount a JFS file system `/dev/vg03/lvol4` on the `/mnt` directory, you can use the `mount` command as follows.

```
mount -F vxfs /dev/vg03/lvol04 /mnt
```

When a file system is mounted, it is recorded in the mount table. Now, when you access the directory that is used as a mount point, you are actually accessing the file system that is mounted on that directory. If the directory contains some files before mounting the file system, these will not be visible. Instead, when you list the directory, files on the mounted file system will be listed. You can't use a directory as a mount point if some of the files in that directory are in use at the time. All mounted file systems can be displayed using the `mount -v` command as shown below.

```
$ mount -v
/dev/vg00/lvol3 on / type vxfs log on Tue Oct 19 15:15:04 1999
/dev/vg00/lvol1 on /stand type hfs on Tue Oct 19 15:15:05 1999
/dev/vg00/lvol8 on /var type vxfs on Tue Oct 19 15:15:30 1999
/dev/vg00/lvol7 on /usr type vxfs on Tue Oct 19 15:15:30 1999
/dev/vg00/lvol6 on /tmp type vxfs on Tue Oct 19 15:15:31 1999
/dev/vg00/lvol5 on /opt type vxfs on Tue Oct 19 15:15:31 1999
/dev/vg00/lvol4 on /home type vxfs on Tue Oct 19 15:15:31 1999
$
```

You can also use the `bdf` command to list mounted volumes. To unmount a mounted file system, you use the `umount` command. The file system mounted on `/home` can be unmounted using the following command.

```
umount /home
```

A file system can't be unmounted if it is currently in use. To see if a file system is in use, you can use the `fuser` command. To see if `/home` is used by some users, use:

```
fuser /home
```

To terminate processes that are using file system `/home`, use the following command.

```
fuser -ku -c /home
```

After this, you can unmount the file system. You can use the `-a` option with the `umount` command to unmount all file systems currently mounted. The `-F` option can be used to unmount file systems of a specific type. For example, the following command will unmount all JFS file systems.

```
umount -aF vxfs
```

Automatic Mounting at Startup

To automatically mount a file system at boot time, you need to put an entry for the file system in the `/etc/fstab` file. This file devotes one data line to each file system's information. This line contains the file system name, its mount point, the file system type, and other options related to the file system. A typical entry for a file system may be as follows.

```
/dev/vg00/lvol4  /home  vxfs  delaylog 0 2
```

The first column in the file is the block device file used for the file system. The second column represents the mount point that is `/home` in this example. The third column is used for the type of file system. A file system type may be one of the types supported by HP-UX. The supported file system types are shown in Table 18-4.

Table 18–4 *Supported File System Types in HP-UX*

Type	Explanation
cdfs	File system used for CD-ROM
hfs	High-Performance File System
vxfs	Journaled File System
swap	Device swap file system
swapfs	File system directory used as swap
lofs	Loopback file system

The options are listed in the fourth column and may be used to enable/disable read and write permissions and the quota. The defaults keyword shows that the file system is mounted in read/write mode, SUID is allowed, and no quota restrictions are imposed. The fifth column is reserved for future use, and the sixth column shows the order that the fsck command will use when checking the file systems.

During the boot process, the /sbin/init.d/localmount script is executed, which executes the mount -a command to mount all file systems listed in the /etc/fstab file.

Sample /etc/fstab File

```
/dev/vg00/lvol3   /  vxfs  delaylog 0 1
/dev/vg00/lvol1   /stand  hfs defaults 0 1
/dev/vg00/lvol4   /home  vxfs delaylog 0 2
/dev/vg00/lvol5   /opt  vxfs delaylog 0 2
/dev/vg00/lvol6   /tmp  vxfs delaylog 0 2
/dev/vg00/lvol7   /usr  vxfs delaylog 0 2
/dev/vg00/lvol8   /var  vxfs delaylog 0 2
```

Study Break

Creating and Mounting New File Systems

Create a JFS file system on the newly created logical volume in the previous study break using the newfs command. Create a new directory /extra with the help of the mkdir command. Create some files in this directory and list these files using the ll command. Now mount the new file system on this directory. Again list the directory. The files you created earlier are no longer visible. Create more files and then unmount the files system using the umount command. Now the old files are visible but those files created after mounting the file system are not. This is because the files you created in the `/extra` directory after mounting the file system are not created in this directory. These are actually on the new file system. Now create another directory, `/test`, and mount the file system on this directory. When you list the `/test` directory after mounting the file system, these files will be visible. We conclude that the files created on a file system are visible under the mount point on which the file system is mounted.

Add the file system to the `/etc/fstab` file to mount it automatically every time the system boots. Reboot the system using the `bdf` or `mount` commands to make sure that your new file system is mounted on the `/extra` directory.

18.9 Managing a File System

Data are read and written to a file system using block device files. These device files employ a data buffer in memory. Data are actually written to a disk when the buffer is full and the system needs the buffer for writing more data or for some other purpose. The buffer is also flushed when the file system is unmounted or the machine is shut down. You can force the data buffer to be written to the disk with the use of the `sync` command. A daemon called `syncer` executes the `sync` command on a regular basis. This daemon is started at boot time. The `sync` command is used to update file systems at any time and make them current.

One of the file system management tasks is to monitor the disk space used by the file system so that you may change file system size before it is 100% utilized. You may also need to use commands to extend or shrink a file system from time to time.

Monitoring Disk Usage

Disk space utilization can be viewed with the help of the `bdf` command, which lists all mounted file systems and shows the following information about each file system.

- file system name
- total capacity in kilobytes
- used capacity in kilobytes
- available capacity in kilobytes
- percentage of utilization
- mount point

Output of this command is shown here.

```
$ bdf
Filesystem            kbytes     used    avail %used Mounted on
/dev/vg00/lvol3       204800    21074   172272   11% /
/dev/vg00/lvol1        99669    29579    60123   33% /stand
/dev/vg00/lvol8      1024000   190842   782071   20% /var
/dev/vg00/lvol7      1024000   340190   641121   35% /usr
/dev/vg00/lvol6       512000     9707   472770    2% /tmp
/dev/vg00/lvol5      1024000   307544   672235   31% /opt
/dev/vg00/lvol4       409600    83081   306150   21% /home
```

Extending Volume Groups

Changing the size of a file system involves three steps. If there is no unallocated space left on a volume group, you first need to extend the volume group. The volume group can be extended by adding a new disk to it. You use the pvcreate command to create a physical volume on the disk. After that you use the vgextend command to add the new disk to the volume group. For example, to add a disk c0t3d0 to volume group vg03, you will use following two commands.

```
pvcreate /dev/rdsk/c0t3d0

vgextend vg03 /dev/dsk/c0t3d0
```

After using these two commands, you can use the vgdisplay -v vg03 command to verify that the volume group is indeed extended.

Extending Logical Volumes

After extending the volume group, you have extra space for extending a logical volume using the lvextend command. If logical volume /dev/vg03/lvol4 had 400 Mbytes of space and you want it to be extended to 800 Mbytes, you can use the following command.

```
lvextend -L 800 /dev/vg03/lvol4
```

If you want the extra space to be allocated from a particular disk, you can also provide a disk device file as an argument to the lvextend command as shown here.

```
lvextend -L 800 /dev/vg03/lvol4 /dev/dsk/c0t3d0
```

After extending a logical volume, you may use the lvdisplay command to verify its new size.

Extending File Systems

Extending the size of a logical volume does not automatically extend the size of a file system. You need to use the `extendfs` command to add new space to a file system. To extend a file system, you must first unmount it. For example, if you want to extend a JFS file system on `/dev/vg03/lvol4`, use the following command.

```
extendfs -F vxfs /dev/vg03/lvol4
```

To extend an HFS file system, replace `vxfs` with `hfs` in the above command. After execution of this command, all space on this logical volume will be allocated to the file system. Now you need to mount the extended file system and use the `bdf` command to verify that the extra space has been allocated to the file system.

```
$ bdf
Filesystem          kbytes     used    avail %used Mounted on
/dev/vg00/lvol3     204800    21074   172272   11% /
/dev/vg00/lvol1      99669    29579    60123   33% /stand
/dev/vg00/lvol8    1024000   190842   782071   20% /var
/dev/vg00/lvol7    1024000   340190   641121   35% /usr
/dev/vg00/lvol6     512000     9707   472770    2% /tmp
/dev/vg00/lvol5    1024000   307544   672235   31% /opt
/dev/vg00/lvol4     409600    83081   306150   21% /home
/dev/vg03/lvol4     819200     9200   810000   99% /extra
```

If you are using HP OnlineJFS, you don't need to unmount the file system to extend it. Instead, you can use the `fsadm` command to extend a JFS file system. This command takes the new file system size in number of blocks. By default, each JFS block is of 1 KByte. The following command will extend the size of the file system to 800 Mbytes, where `819200` represents 800 MBytes converted to kilobytes.

```
fsadm -F vxfs -b 819200 /extra
```

Using SAM for LVM Administration

SAM can be used to manage LVM. Go to the `Disk and File Systems` SAM area, and you will see a window like Figure 18-1.

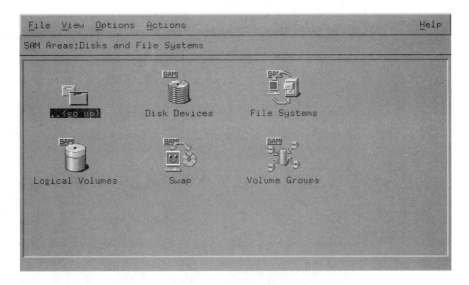

Figure 18–1 *SAM* Disk and File Systems *area.*

You can use icons displayed here to carry out a required task. To view a list of disk devices and the volume group to which these are related, use the Disk Devices icon. A list of disk devices will be listed as shown in Figure 18-2.

File List View Options Actions					Help
Disk Devices					0 of 227 selected
Hardware Path	Number of Paths	Use	Volume Group	Total Mbytes	Description
10/0.5.0	1	LVM	vg00	4095	SEAGATE ST34371W
10/0.6.0	1	LVM	vg00	4095	SEAGATE ST34371W
10/12/5.2.0	1	Unused	--	0	Toshiba CD-ROM SC!
8/0.0.0	1	Unused	--	4154	SEAGATE ST34371W
8/0.0.1	1	Unused	--	4154	SEAGATE ST34371W
8/0.0.2	1	Unused	--	4154	SEAGATE ST34371W
8/0.0.3	1	Unused	--	4154	SEAGATE ST34371W
8/0.1.0	1	Unused	--	4154	SEAGATE ST34371W
8/0.1.1	1	Unused	--	4154	SEAGATE ST34371W
8/0.1.2	1	Unused	--	4154	SEAGATE ST34371W

Figure 18–2 *The* Disk Devices *area in SAM.*

The third column shows whether a disk is used in a volume group. You can add a disk to a particular volume group using the `Actions` menu.

The volume groups can be listed using the `Volume Groups` icon as shown in Figure 18-3.

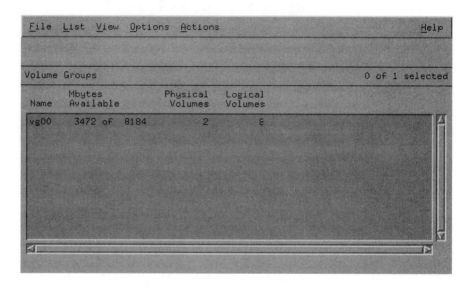

Figure 18–3   *List of* `Volume Groups`.

Figure 18-3 lists the names of the volume groups and the total capacity and number of physical and logical volumes in each group. You can go to the `Actions` menu and select the `View more information...` option to display more information about a particular volume group. Figures 18-4 and 18-5 show more information about volume group `vg00`.

Figure 18-4 shows the maximum capacity that the volume group can handle and its current capacity; how much space is utilized and how much is free; the maximum number of logical volumes that can be created in this volume group; and the current number of logical volumes.

Figure 18-5 lists disk information of the disk drives that are part of this volume group. Currently, there are two disks, and you can see the hardware path and the capacity of each. In the bottom part of the figure, you see a list of logical volumes, the space used by each one, and the file system type on each one.

When you click on the `Logical Volumes` icon in Figure 18-1, a window like the one shown in Figure 18-6 will appear.

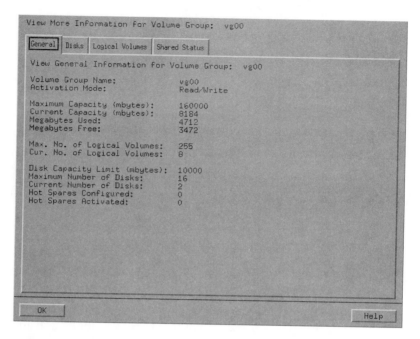

Figure 18–4 *General information about a volume group.*

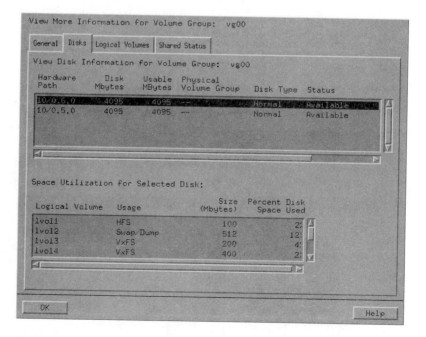

Figure 18–5 Disk Information *in a logical volume.*

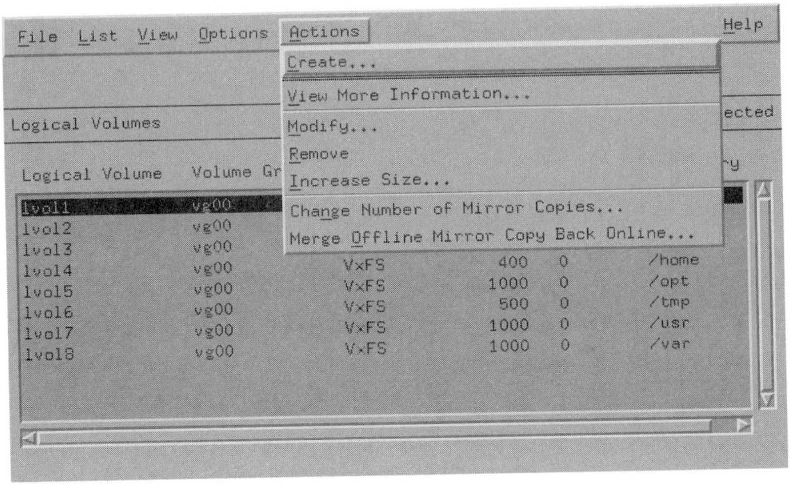

Figure 18–6 Logical Volumes *window in SAM.*

Here, all logical volumes are listed. Using the Actions menu, you can perform operations on one of these logical volumes and add new ones to the volume group.

Figure 18-7 is the File Systems window where all file systems and their mount points are listed. Here, you can perform actions on these file systems as shown in the Actions menu in the figure.

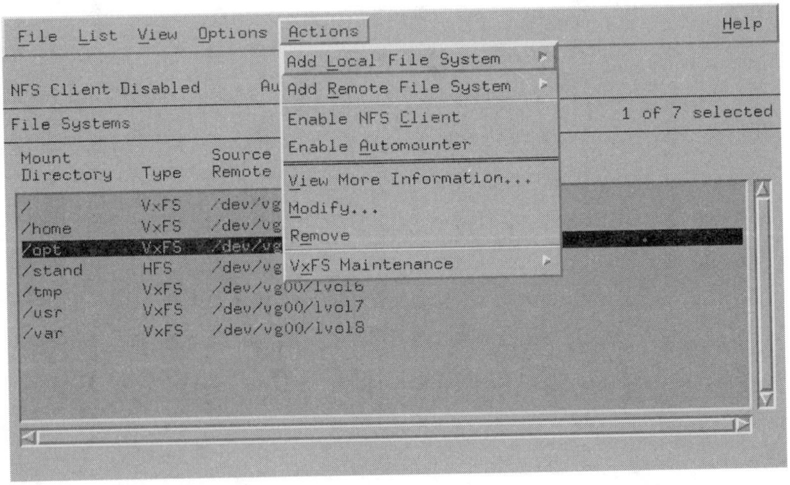

Figure 18–7 File Systems *window in SAM.*

18.10 File System Repair

A system crash or improper shutdown may cause errors to the file system metadata. You need to repair a file system in such a case. The fsck command is used to check and repair file systems.

Repairing a File System Using the fsck Command

The fsck command is used to repair a file system. It is run automatically if your system crashes or has improperly shut down, and it can be run manually at any time if necessary. It checks the file system metadata integrity and repairs it if needed.

Before running fsck manually, you must unmount a file system. If fsck is run on JFS, it checks the intent log and commits any pending changes in the intent log. If run on HFS, it goes through a number of passes and reports any problems it encountered. It also suggests a solution for each problem and asks if you want to use that solution. You may answer "yes" or "no" for these questions depending on whether you want to implement a change.

If there are inconsistencies in the metadata area, the fsck command deletes some of the files. Some files may be put in the lost+found directory if they are not completely recognized by fsck. These files are also called *orphan files*. After running the fsck command, you should check the contents of the lost+found directory to note the files created by the fsck command. The names of these files may be different from the original files. You may use the file or strings command to find out information about these files. After fsck finishes its job, you need to restore the damaged files from a previous backup.

To check the JFS on the /dev/vg03/lvol4 file system, use the following fsck command. The file system must first be mounted using the umount command.

```
fsck -F vxfs /dev/vg03/rlvol4
```

There are some options that can be used with the fsck command. Some of these options are special to a particular type of file system and are listed in Table 18-5.

Table 18–5 *Options Used with the* fsck *Command*

Option	Description
-F	Type of file system. Use vxfs for the JFS and hfs for the HFS file systems. You may also use the fsck_vxfs command for the JFS file system and fsck_hfs for the HFS file system.
-n	Assumes a "no" answer for fsck questions.
-y	Assumes a "yes" answer for fsck questions.
-b	Tells fsck to use an alternate superblock. The alternate superblocks are listed in the /var/adm/sbtab file. If this file is not accessible, use number 16, which is always the first alternate superblock (HFS only).
-f	Forces fsck to run on a mounted file system (HFS only).
-o full	Forces fsck to make a full check of the metadata instead of just replaying the intent log (JFS only).
-o nolog	Prevents intent log replay (JFS only).

18.11 Important LVM Commands

Table 18-6 lists important LVM commands with a small description of each.

Table 18–6 *Important LVM Commands*

Command	Description
extendfs	Extends a file system.
lvchange	Changes the characteristics of a logical volume
lvcreate	Creates a logical volume
lvdisplay	Displays information about a logical volume
lvextend	Extends a logical volume
lvlnboot	Makes a logical volume usable as root, dump, or swap
lvreduce	Decreases the size of a volume
lvremove	Removes the logical volume(s) from a volume group
lvrmboot	Makes a volume unusable for a root, swap, or dump volume previously enabled for use in one of these capacities
pvchange	Changes the characteristics of a physical volume
pvcreate	Creates a physical volume

Command	Description
`pvdisplay`	Displays information about a physical volume
`pvmove`	Moves physical extents from one volume to another
`vgcfgbackup`	Backs up an LVM configuration
`vgcfgrestore`	Restores a backed-up LVM configuration
`vgchange`	Changes the characteristics of a volume group
`vgcreate`	Creates a volume group
`vgdisplay`	Displays information about a volume group
`vgextend`	Extends a volume group
`vgexport`	Exports a volume group from a system
`vgimport`	Imports a volume group to a system
`vgreduce`	Reduces the size of a volume group by removing the physical volume(s)
`vgremove`	Removes a volume group(s)

■ Chapter Summary

The Logical Volume Manager (LVM) approach is used to add flexibility to disk management tasks. In this chapter, you learned about disk devices and the ways of using disks for file systems. The whole-disk approach assigns the whole disk to a file system. The LVM approach introduces concepts of physical volumes, volume groups, and logical volumes. Physical volumes represent actual physical disks. Physical volumes are combined to create a volume group. Different logical volumes can then be created in a volume group. Information about LVM can be displayed with the help of the `pvdisplay`, `vgdisplay`, and `lvdisplay` commands. These commands show physical and logical extents that represent the smallest amount of disk space that can be allocated on a physical and logical volume.

The `pvcreate` command is used to create a physical volume. You may want to use the `mediainit` command to initialize physical media. After creating a physical volume, you can create volume groups and logical volumes with the help of the `vgcreate` and `lvcreate` commands. During the volume group creation process, the volume group directory and control file are created using the `mkdir` and `mknod` commands.

A file system is a structure for creating and storing files and directories. HP-UX supports many types of file systems. The most important of these are the High-Performance File system (HFS) and the Journaled File System (JFS). HFS is the traditional HP-UX file system and is mandatory for storing kernel files. JFS is a new and more-flexible file system. HP OnlineJFS (Advanced JFS) provides additional advantages over the base JFS file system as it can be maintained without unmounting. HFS is divided into blocks and fragments. A block is the minimum amount of data that is read in one cycle. A fragment is the minimum space that can be allocated to a file. JFS is an extent-based file system.

A new file system can be created using the `newfs` command. After creating a new file system, you need to mount it on a directory. This directory is called the mount point for that file system. File systems can be mounted automatically at boot time by putting them in the `/etc/fstab` file.

Space utilization on a file system is monitored using the `bdf` command. If you are running short of space on a file system, you can extend volume groups, logical volumes, and file systems with the help of the `vgextend`, `lvextend`, and `extendfs` commands, respectively. Before extending a file system, you need to unmount it. A file system can't be unmounted if some of its files are being used by running processes. The `fuser` command is used to terminate processes that are using files on a file system.

You can also use SAM to carry out all these operations on disks and file systems. A damaged file system can be repaired with the help of the `fsck` command.

▲ CHAPTER REVIEW QUESTIONS

1. What are the differences between the whole-disk and LVM approaches?

2. Explain how physical volumes, volume groups, and logical volumes are arranged in LVM.

3. What are physical and logical extents?

4. What steps must be completed before creating logical volumes when creating a new volume group?

5. What are the differences between the HFS and the JFS file systems?

6. How are hard and soft links different from each other?

7. What is a mount point?

8. Can you extend a file system without extending a volume group?

9. For what purpose is the `lost+found` directory used?

▲ Test Your Knowledge

1. *What is the name used for the root volume group?*

   A. vg00

   B. root

   C. rootvg

   D. vgroot

2. *Which statement is not true?*

   A. Each logical volume has a character and block device file.

   B. The major device number for all logical volume device files is 64.

   C. The minor device number of a logical volume device file shows the logical volume number.

   D. Names of logical volume device files always start with lvol followed by a number.

3. *The default physical extent size is:*

   A. 4 MBytes

   B. 8 MBytes

   C. 4 KBytes

   D. 8 KBytes

4. *The* pvdisplay *command uses:*

   A. a block device file as its argument

   B. a raw device file as its argument

   C. either a block or raw device file as its argument

   D. a logical volume device file as its argument

5. *What is true about space allocation to a logical volume?*

   A. Space from multiple physical disks can't be allocated to a logical volume.

   B. Space from multiple physical disks can be allocated to a logical volume.

   C. The amount of space allocated to a logical volume can't be changed.

   D. The space from multiple volume groups can be allocated to a logical volume.

6. *By default, how many logical volumes can be created in a volume group?*

   A. 16

   B. 127

   C. 255

   D. 1023

7. *Which command can be used to create a physical volume?*

   A. `pvcreate /dev/rdsk/c2t5d0`

   B. `pvcreate /dev/dsk/c2t5d0`

   C. `pvcreate /dev/vg00/c2t5d0`

   D. `pvcreate /dev/vg00/lvol3`

8. *Which command would you use to create a logical volume of 200-MByte size with the name* `myvol` *in volume group* `vg02`?

   A. `lvcreate 200 -n myvol vg02`

   B. `lvcreate -L 200 myvol vg02`

   C. `lvcreate -L 200 -n myvol vg02`

   D. `lvcreate -L 200 -n vg02 myvol`

9. *Which statement is true?*

   A. An HFS file system block size can be changed at any time.

   B. The minimum amount of data read at one time is equal to an HFS fragment.

   C. The minimum amount of data allocated to a file is equal to an HFS fragment.

   D. An HFS segment contains one or more HFS blocks.

10. *What is not true about the JFS file system?*

    A. It is an extent-based file system.

    B. The default size of each block is 1 KByte.

    C. "Base JFS" file systems can be resized without unmounting.

    D. It can create new inodes automatically.

11. *You use the* `pvcreate`, `vgextend`, `lvextend`, *and* `extendfs` *commands to increase the size of a file system. In which sequence would you use these?*

    A. `vgextend, pvcreate, lvextend, extendfs`

    B. `pvcreate, vgextend, extendfs, lvextend`

    C. `pvcreate, vgextend, lvextend, extendfs`

    D. `pvcreate, lvextend, vgextend, extendfs`

12. *Which command can you use to list the mounted file systems?*

    A. the `bdf` command

    B. the `mount` command

    C. both of the above

    D. none of the above

User and Group Management

A user must log into a system before starting to use it. The system administrator creates user accounts and assigns a login name and password to every user. Each user is a member of one or more groups. A group is a set of users that has something common among them. For example, people working in an accounts department may be in one group and those working in a support department may be in another group. The scheme of grouping is used for security purposes as discussed in Chapter 7.

User and group management is an ongoing system administration task, and this chapters covers procedures for creating and managing users and groups. They can be created either by using command-line utilities or with the help of SAM. Both of these methods will be discussed in this chapter. A number of operations are performed on user accounts, like enabling and disabling accounts, setting password expiration policy, managing group memberships, and so on. All user accounts and passwords are recorded in the `/etc/passwd` file. You will learn about the format of this file. The group information is present in the `/etc/group` file, and the format of this file will also be discussed. As these files are very important, you need to make sure that they are error free. You will learn some commands to check the consistency of these files. At the end of the chapter you will use SAM for user and group management.

After going through this chapter, you will be able to create new user and group accounts and manage the existing ones with the help of command-line utilities as well as with SAM.

19.1 Managing Users

A user login name is a combination of letters and numbers. Every user account has a user ID related to it. The user ID is a number that is used internally by HP-UX to record ownership and permissions. If two or more users have the same user ID, they will have the same permissions in the file system although they log in with different login names. A user password may be six to eight characters long and contain letters, digits, and special characters. You can choose a password longer than eight characters but only the first eight characters are significant.

In the user management process, you have to add and delete users and perform operations on user accounts. Let's see how it is done.

Creating Users

A user can be created using the `useradd` command. You have to specify the user (login) name at the command line to create a new user. For example, the following command creates a new user **boota** and creates the home directory for the user as `/home/boota`. It also copies startup files from the `/etc/skel` directory to the home directory.

```
useradd -m boota
```

The -m option is used to create the home directory and copy startup files into this directory. The contents of the home directory `/home/boota` at its creation are as follows.

```
# ll /home/boota
total 8
-r--r--r--    1 boota    users       814 Nov  9 19:09 .cshrc
-r--r--r--    1 boota    users       347 Nov  9 19:09 .exrc
-r--r--r--    1 boota    users       341 Nov  9 19:09 .login
-r--r--r--    1 boota    users       446 Nov  9 19:09 .profile
#
```

When you create a new user, an entry in the /etc/passwd file is created for the user, which looks like the following.

```
boota:*:1225:20::/home/boota:/sbin/sh
```

The asterisk character (*) after the first colon shows that the user password is not enabled. A user is not able to log into the system until you assign him or her a password. A password to the newly created user **boota** is assigned by the passwd command as follows.

```
# passwd boota
Changing password for boota
New password:
Re-enter new password:
Passwd successfully changed
#
```

When you type a new password for the user, it is not displayed on your terminal screen. After assigning a password, the user entry in the /etc/ passwd file changes as shown below and the login is permitted.

```
boota:OV81GT8LCiRO.:1225:20::/home/boota:/sbin/sh
```

As you can see, the asterisk character (*) is replaced by some other mysterious combination of characters. These characters show the encrypted user password.

You can provide many options with the useradd command to customize the new user creation process. For example, the following command creates a new user **gama** with a home directory of /home/gama. The user's primary group is accounts and he is member of two other groups, staff and support. The shell assigned to the user is /usr/bin/sh.

```
useradd -m -s /usr/bin/sh -g accounts -G staff,support gama
```

If you don't specify an option with the command, it assumes the default options. You can list the default options as shown below with the useradd command.

```
# useradd -D
GROUPID  20
BASEDIR  /home
SKEL     /etc/skel
SHELL    /sbin/sh
INACTIVE -1
EXPIRE
#
```

The command shows that by default the user will be assigned to Group 20 (users). The home directory of the user will be created under the /home directory. Files from /etc/skel will be copied to this home directory, and the user will be assigned shell /sbin/sh. The files in the /etc/skel directory will be discussed in Section 19.5. There will be no inactivity check on the user account to disable it and it will not expire.

You are also able to change a default option. For example, to change the location of the base directory, use the following command.

```
useradd -D -b /extra/home
```

After using this command, if you create a new user, the new user's home directory will be created in /extra/home instead of /home.

By default, a user is assigned the next available user ID. The user ID assigned to user **boota** is 1225, but you can assign a user ID of your own choice with the help of the -u option.

The syntax of the useradd command is as shown here.

```
useradd [-u uid [-o] ] [-g group] [-G group [, group...]]
        [-d dir] [-s shell]  [-c comment]  [-m [-k skel_dir]]
        [-f inactive] [-e expire]   login
```

Deleting Users

A user can be deleted by using the userdel command and providing the name of the user as an argument. To delete user **boota**, use the following command.

```
userdel -r boota
```

The -r option also deletes the user's home directory. If you don't use this option, the user entry from the /etc/passwd file will be removed, but the home directory is not deleted. You may want to retain a user's home directory if it contains some files that you want to keep.

Modifying a User

User attributes can be modified with the help of the `usermod` command. For example, you can modify the user ID, group membership, command shell, and login name. General syntax of the `usermod` command follows.

```
usermod [-u uid [-o] ] [-g group] [-G group [, group...]]
        [-d dir [-m] ] [-s shell] [-c comment] [-f inactive]
        [-l new_logname] [-e expire]  login
```

To modify the command shell of user **boota** from /sbin/sh to /usr/bin/sh, use the following command.

```
usermod -s /usr/bin/sh boota
```

User Inactivity and Expiration

If a user does not log into the system for some time, this is considered an inactivity period. You can put a limit on this period after which the user account is considered invalid. The inactivity period of a user is defined using the -f option with the `useradd` and `usermod` commands. This period is counted in number of days, and normal values are represented by positive integers. If you assign a value of -1 as the inactivity period, this option is turned off and the user remains active regardless of how long the inactivity period is.

Other than the inactivity period, an expiration limit may also be imposed on a user. The expiration of an account occurs on a specific date. After expiration, the user is not able to log into the system. Expiration is used with temporary accounts. To close the account of user **boota** on the 9th of July 1999, use the following command.

```
usermod -e 9/7/99 boota
```

The expiration can be turned off if you use an empty string with the -e option.

19.2 Managing Groups

As mentioned earlier, every user belongs to one or more groups. A group contains users who are related to each other in one way or another. Information about groups is kept in the /etc/group file. There is one entry for each group in this file. Every group has a group name and a group ID. The file also contains a list of users who are members of more than one group (users who are members of a single group are not listed in this file). Like users, groups can also be added or deleted using command-line utilities as well as SAM.

Standard Groups

There are many standard groups on HP-UX. Some of these are:

- `bin`
- `sys`
- `adm`
- `daemon`
- `mail`
- `lp`
- `users`

Each of these groups is used for a special purpose. For example, files and processes related to printing fall under the `lp` group. The default group for general users is `users`, mail files belong to the `mail` group, and so on.

Creating, Deleting and Modifying Groups

A group can be created using the `groupadd` command. To create a group for accounts, use a command like the following.

```
groupadd accounts
```

You can also specify a *group ID* (GID) on the command line using the `-g` option. If you don't specify a group ID, the next available one is used for the new group.

A group can be deleted with the help of the `groupdel` command. A group name is provided as the argument to the command as follows.

```
groupdel accounts
```

The `groupmod` command is used to modify a group name or group ID. To change the name of the `accounts` group to `acct` use this command.

```
groupmod -n acct accounts
```

Multiple Group Membership

A user can be a member of multiple groups. The group ID of the primary group is stored in the `/etc/passwd` file with the user's record. For all secondary groups, the user name is listed in the `/etc/group` file in the respective group line. A user can use the `id` or `groups` command to list the current group membership. Watch the output of the `id` command used by the **root** user.

```
# id
uid=0(root), gid=3(sys)
groups=0(root),1(other),2(bin),4(adm),5(daemon),6(mail),
7(lp),20(users)
#
```

This command shows user and group IDs for the **root** user. The user ID is 0 and the default or primary group ID is 3. The primary group name is sys. The user **root** is a member of other groups as listed after the `groups` keyword. Each group is listed as a pair of group ID and group name.

The `groups` command lists the names of the groups the user is a member of. Output of this command for the **root** user is shown here.

```
# groups
sys root other bin adm daemon mail lp users
#
```

When you create a new file, its group membership is that of your current group. To change your group membership temporarily, use the `newgrp` command. To change the group of **root** user temporarily to bin, use the following command.

```
newgrp bin
```

After that, when you use the `id` command, the output will be as follows.

```
# id
uid=0(root), gid=2(bin)
groups=0(root),1(other),3(sys),4(adm),5(daemon),6(mail),
7(lp),20(users)
#
```

19.3 The Password File (/etc/passwd)

The `/etc/passwd` file contains seven fields. Each of these fields is separated by a colon (`:`) character. The general format of each line in the file is shown in Figure 19-1.

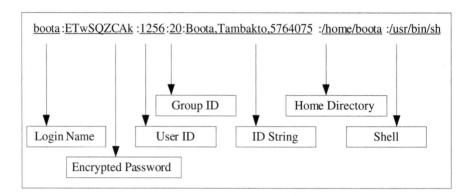

Figure 19–1   *Format of the* /etc/passwd *file.*

The passwords of all users are stored in encrypted form. The fifth field is the *ID String*. This field is optional, and you can put any information about the user here. This information may be the user's full name, address, telephone number, or any other important information. It is used by the `finger` command to utilize the network to retrieve user information. Other fields are self-explanatory.

Some sample entries from this file are shown here.

```
root:8JgNSmFv806dA:0:3:,,,:/home/root:/sbin/sh
daemon:*:1:5::/:/sbin/sh
bin:*:2:2::/usr/bin:/sbin/sh
sys:*:3:3::/:
adm:*:4:4::/var/adm:/sbin/sh
boota:ETwSQZCAk:1256:20:Boota,Tambakto,5764075:/home/
   boota:/usr/bin/sh
```

19.4 The Group File (/etc/group)

Like the /etc/passwd file, the /etc/group file also contains fields separated by a colon character (:). Figure 19-2 shows the format of this file.

The second field is the Group Password field and is usually empty. Group List contains a list of users who are members of this group. A sample /etc/passwd file follows.

```
root::0:root
other::1:root,boota
bin::2:root,bin
```

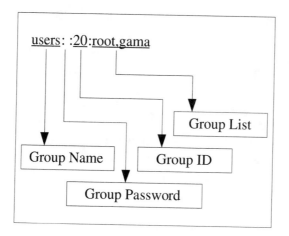

Figure 19–2 *Format of the* /etc/group *file.*

```
sys::3:root,uucp
adm::4:root,adm
daemon::5:root,daemon
mail::6:root
lp::7:root,lp
tty::10:
nuucp::11:nuucp
users::20:root
nogroup:*:-2:
```

Restricted User Access

Restricted user access is made possible with the help of a special command shell known as the *restricted shell* (rsh). It provides the same functionality as a normal POSIX shell except the following restrictions.

1. A user can't change directories.
2. A user can't set or change the environment variables SHELL, PATH, or ENV.
3. A command cannot be issued that starts with /.
4. I/O redirection is disabled.

Verifying Consistency of Password and Group Files

To check the consistency of the /etc/passwd and /etc/group files, you can use the pwck and grpck commands, respectively. The pwck command checks consistency of the password files and reports incorrect or incomplete entries. It also reports if you have used group IDs that don't exist in the /etc/group file. It will also show if it does not find any home directory for a user. The grpck command checks the /etc/group file and lists anything wrong in it. It also verifies that the user names used in the group membership are present in the /etc/passwd file. It lists any missing users on your terminal screen.

To manually edit the /etc/passwd file, use the vipw editor instead of vi or another editor. The vipw is a special editor that puts a lock on the file so that users may not change their passwords during the time that **root** is in the editing process. If you use some other editor, inconsistencies may occur if someone else also makes changes to the file during that time.

19.5 The Skeleton Directory (/etc/skel)

This directory contains default configuration files for new users. These files are copied to the newly created home directory of a user when the useradd command is executed with the -m option. You can configure these files with default settings. The .exrc file is used as the startup configuration file for the vi editor. If the user is assigned to the C shell, the .cshrc and .login files are used at the time of login. If a user has POSIX or Bourne shell as the default shell, the .profile file is used at login. Environment settings like the PATH variable, default printer, and user prompt may be configured in these files. A listing of this directory is as follows.

```
$ ll -a /etc/skel
total 20
drwxrwxr-x   2 root   sys        96 Nov  9  1997 .
dr-xr-xr-x  27 bin    bin      6144 Nov  9 20:20 ..
-r--r--r--   1 bin    bin       814 Nov  7  1997 .cshrc
-r--r--r--   1 bin    bin       347 Oct 27  1997 .exrc
-r--r--r--   1 bin    bin       341 Nov  7  1997 .login
-r--r--r--   1 bin    bin       446 Nov  7  1997 .profile
$
```

19.6 Using SAM for User and Group Management

SAM can also be used for user and group management and provides the same functionality as do the command line utilities. For user and group management, you go to the Accounts for Users and Groups area, where a window appears similar to the one shown in Figure 19-3.

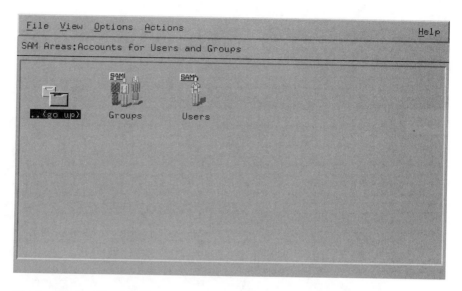

Figure 19–3 *The SAM* Accounts for Users and Groups *area.*

To add or modify users, you click the Users icon and for group management you use the Groups icon. When you double-click the Users icon, a window appears like the one shown in Figure 19-4.

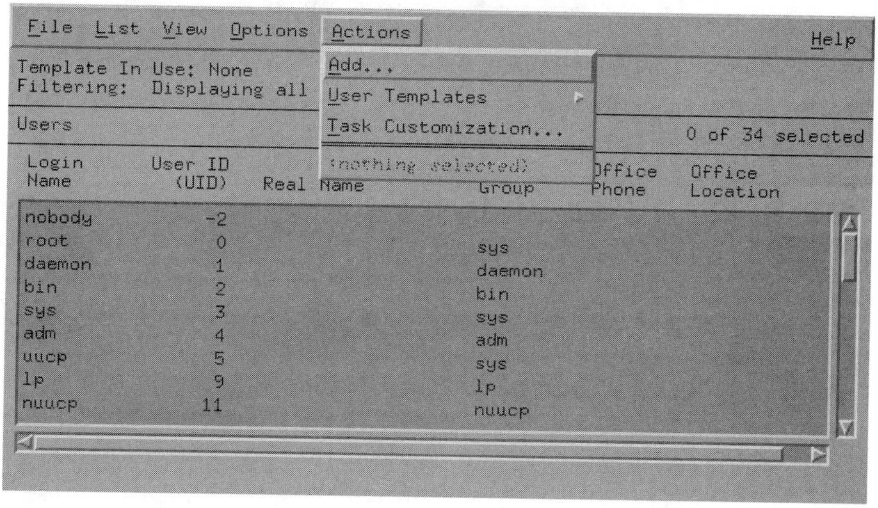

Figure 19–4 *The SAM user management window.*

You can select the Add option from the Actions menu to add a new user. The window for adding a new user is shown in Figure 19-5.

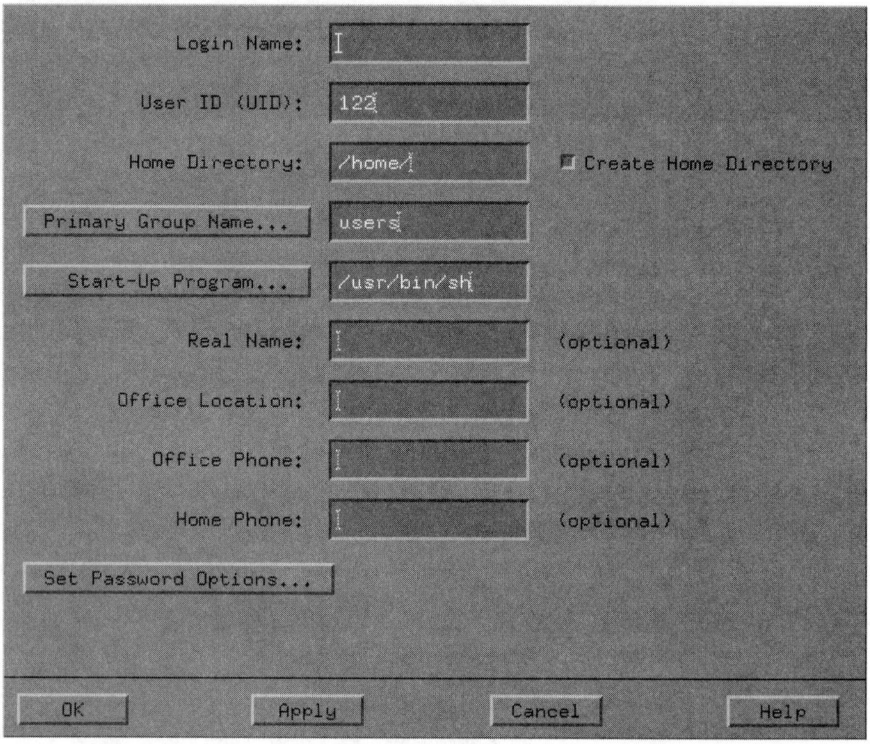

Figure 19–5 *Adding a user with SAM.*

Here you can fill in all the data for a new user; SAM automatically selects an available user ID. However, it can be changed. The optional items in Figure 19-5 are placed in the *ID String* section of the /etc/passwd file. If you click on Set Password Options..., a window such as the one shown in Figure 19-6 is displayed, where you can select different options. If you Force Password Change at the next login, the user will be asked to change the password as soon as he or she logs into the system the next time. You can set Password Aging such that a user needs to change the password after a specified period of time.

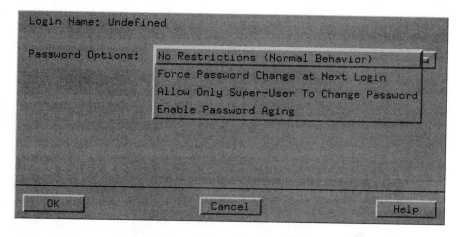

Figure 19–6 Password Options *for a user in SAM.*

User Templates

If you are creating many users with a similar configuration, you can create a user template in SAM. A template contains information about users that is common to all users. After creating a template, you can use it to create a particular type of user. To create a new template, go to the Actions menu and select User Templates as shown in Figure 19-4. When creating a new template, you will find a window as shown in Figure 19-7.

In a user template, you can specify general options used for new user accounts. These options are group membership of users, location of home directories, command shells, and password specifications. You can create one template for each group on your system.

■ Chapter Summary

Every user on a system has a login name and password and is a member of one or more groups. A new user is created using the useradd command, and the password for the newly created user is assigned with the help of the passwd command. The useradd command uses default options for new users that can be listed and modified using the useradd -D command. For deleting a user, you use the userdel command. User properties or attributes can be modified with the help of the usermod command. Inactivity and expiration limits can also be imposed on users after which a user account is disabled.

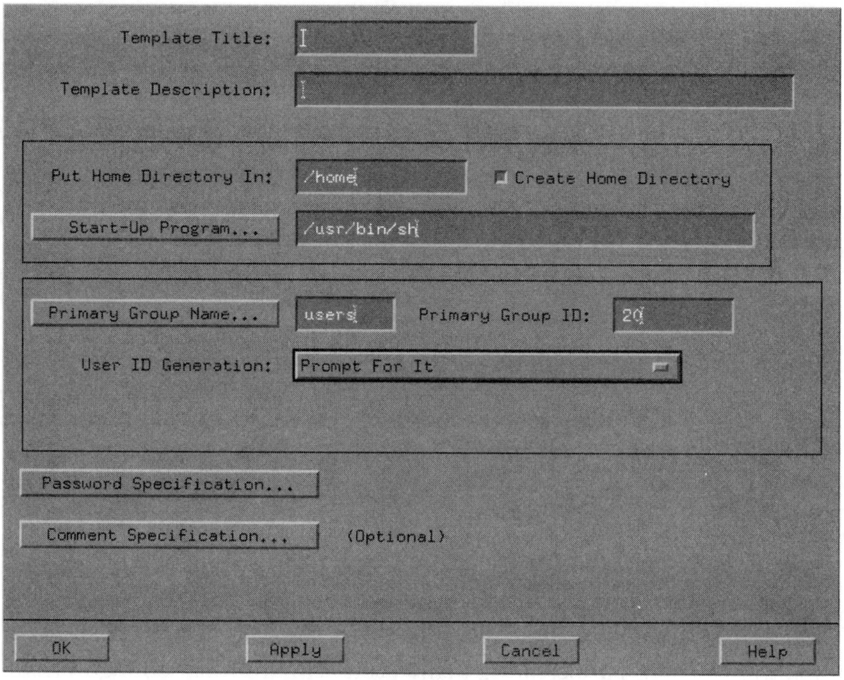

Figure 19–7 *Creating a new user template in SAM.*

Like users, groups can be added, deleted, and modified using the grou-
padd, groupdel, and groupmod commands, respectively. A user can be a
member of more than one group, and the id and groups commands can be
used to list a user's group membership.

Both the /etc/passwd and /etc/group files follow a defined file syntax where every field of a line is separated by a colon character. Consistency
of these files can be checked using the pwck and grpck commands. The vipw
editor is used to manually edit the /etc/passwd file. When a new user is
created, default configuration files are copied into the user's home directory.
These files are stored in the /etc/skel directory. SAM can also be used to
create and manage users and groups and define user templates.

▲ CHAPTER REVIEW QUESTIONS

1. Can you create a new user with the help of an editor (without using any
   specific commands for this purpose or SAM)? How?

2. What are a user's inactivity and expiration periods?

3. Explain the syntax of the /etc/passwd file.

▲ TEST YOUR KNOWLEDGE

1. *To change a group ID temporarily, which command is used?*
   A. chgrp
   B. newgrp
   C. tmpgrp
   D. any chgrp or newgrp command

2. *What information is a must when you use the* useradd *command?*
   A. the login name of the new user
   B. the login name and path of home directory
   C. the login name and user ID of the new user
   D. the login name, group ID, and user ID of the new user

3. *How many fields are present in the* /etc/passwd *file?*
   A. 5
   B. 6
   C. 7
   D. 10

4. *In which directory are stored the default configuration files for a user?*
   A. /etc/default
   B. /etc/skel
   C. /etc/skeleton
   D. /usr/default

5. *What is wrong with the following* /etc/passwd *entry?*
   boota:OV81GT8LCiRO.:1225:20::/home/boota:/sbin/sh:

   A. A field at the end of the line is missing.
   B. There is an extra colon character at the end of the line.
   C. There are two consecutive colons in the line and information between these two is missing.
   D. The locations of the home directory and the shell are interchanged.

6. *Which command would you use to change a user ID?*
   A. id
   B. chmod
   C. usermod
   D. The ID of a user can't be changed.

7. *For what purpose is a restricted shell used?*

    A. to stop a user from changing a directory

    B. to stop a user from setting the environment variables SHELL, PATH, and ENV

    C. to disable I/O redirection for a user

    D. all of the above

TWENTY

Dealing with HP-UX Processes

Every time you start a command or a program, a process is created in memory. A *process* is an instance of a running program. On an abstract level, it contains text, data, and stack parts. Text is the code that is being executed and the data are acted on by the code. A process is either in a user or kernel state. In either of these two states, a process uses temporary space for storing data. This temporary space in memory is called the *stack*. If a process is in user mode, it is using the *user stack*, and if it is in kernel mode, it uses the *kernel stack*. A process is in kernel mode when it is accessing system calls. The HP-UX kernel maintains a data structure known as the *process table*. As soon as a process starts, its entry is created in the process table. It remains in the process table until it finishes its execution and is terminated. The process table keeps a record of process attributes, for example, the owner and group of the process, its start time, and priority. However, the actual process table data structure is quite complex. The total number of processes that can be stored in the process table is determined by the `nproc` variable value used in the kernel reconfiguration process, as discussed in Chapter 16. Every process is assigned a unique identification number called the *process ID* (`PID`). A process that creates another process is the parent of that process. The process ID associated with the parent process is the *parent process ID* (`PPID`). If a parent process dies while any of its children are still active, the `init` process becomes its parent process. The `init` process is started at boot time and has the PID of 1.

A process is in one of many states at every moment. It may be running, waiting to run, stopped, waiting for some other process or resource, or in the zombie state. Every process has a priority number associated with it. The kernel uses this priority number when scheduling processes.

Processes run in the foreground or the background. All foreground and background processes may be listed at any time. A user can also send different signals to processes that affect their execution progress. A signal is like an interrupt that communicates some information.

In this chapter, you will learn how to list the process table and the state of processes. You will be able to send signals to running processes. You will also see what process nice values are and how these can be changed.

20.1 Process Table

The process table is a kernel data structure that keeps records of all processes in memory. Each process has information associated with it that resides in the process table. You can use the `ps` command to list process attributes in tabular form containing different fields. Some of the fields in the process are shown in Table 20-1.

Table 20–1 *Process Attributes in the Process Table*

Field	Description
PID	Process ID
PPID	Process ID of the parent
STAT	Current process state
UID	User who created the process
GID	Group ID of the owner
C or CPU	Processor utilization
PRI	Priority of the process
NI	Nice value used in the priority calculation
ADDR	The memory address of the process
SZ	Size in physical pages of the process image
WCHAN	Event for which the process is waiting
STIME	Starting time of the process
TTY	Controlling terminal of the process
TIME	Cumulative execution time of the process
COMM	The command that started the process
MAX	Maximum number of open files allowed

At system startup, the swapper process is created that has a process ID of 0. The swapper process initiates the `init` process that has a PID of 1. The `init` process is then responsible for creating other processes using the `fork` system call.

The kernel has a scheduling mechanism used to determine which process will be executed during a given time slice. The state of a process is represented by a process context that contains information about process data and register values. When a time slice for a process is finished, its context is saved, and the next process is started.

20.2 Process States

A process is always in one of the many states. A *state* shows the current activity of a process. In a multitasking system, although to a user it appears that all processes are running simultaneously, strictly speaking only one process is active on one CPU at a time. The kernel schedules the processes such that every process gets a time slice for its execution. During the life cycle of a process, it changes its state many times.

Running

A process is in a running state when its text (code) is being executed. The kernel schedules processes such that each process has its time slice during which the kernel executes its code. A process may go to another state from the running state depending on several factors.

Sleeping

A process may have to wait for a resource or event that is currently not available. It makes a sleep system call that puts the process on a queue of sleeping processes. This system call also changes the state of the process. When the resource becomes available, the kernel wakes up the process.

Ready to Run Process

When the kernel wakes up a sleeping process, its state changes and becomes runnable. It means that the process becomes ready to run and waits for its scheduled time slice.

Stopped

The stop signal puts a process in the stopped or suspended state. A stop signal changes the state of the process immediately. The process remains stopped until its gets a continue signal. After getting this signal, the stopped process goes into a runnable (or ready to run) state. If a process receives a stop signal when it is sleeping, it goes back to a sleep state after receiving a continue signal.

Zombie

When a process terminates, it sends an `exit` system call. At this time, the kernel releases resources used by the process. The process becomes a zombie and remains in the zombie state until its parent process gives it permission to die. If the parent process is not responding, the process may be left in a zombie state indefinitely.

20.3   Listing Processes

Processes are listed using the ps command. The ps command listed without
arguments will display all processes owned by the user who issued the command. A typical output of the command is shown next.

```
$ ps
  PID TTY           TIME CMD
17838 pts/ta       00:00 -sh
21828 pts/ta       00:00 ps
17817 pts/ta       00:00 telnetd
$
```

To list all processes, you can use the -ef option with the ps command.

```
# ps -ef
UID       PID  PPID  C  STIME    TTY    TIME  CMD
root        0     0  0  Nov  9   ?      00:11 swapper
root        1     0  0  Nov  9   ?      00:01 init
root        2     0  0  Nov  9   ?      00:00 vhand
root        3     0  1  Nov  9   ?      00:42 statdaemon
root        4     0  0  Nov  9   ?      00:01 unhashdaemon
root        8     0  0  Nov  9   ?      00:00 supsched
root        9     0  0  Nov  9   ?      00:00 strmem
root       10     0  0  Nov  9   ?      00:00 strweld
root       11     0  0  Nov  9   ?      00:00 strfreebd
root       12     0  0  Nov  9   ?      00:00 ttisr
root       18     0  0  Nov  9   ?      00:00 lvmkd
root       19     0  0  Nov  9   ?      00:00 lvmkd
root       20     0  0  Nov  9   ?      00:00 lvmkd
root       21     0  0  Nov  9   ?      00:00 lvmkd
root       22     0  0  Nov  9   ?      00:00 lvmkd
root       23     0  0  Nov  9   ?      00:00 lvmkd
root       24     0  0  Nov  9   ?      00:00 smpsched
root       25     0  0  Nov  9   ?      00:00 smpsched
root       26     0  0  Nov  9   ?      00:00 smpsched
root       27     0  0  Nov  9   ?      00:00 smpsched
root       28     0  0  Nov  9   ?      00:00 smpsched
root     2007     1  0  Oct 19   ?      0:00 /usr/sbin/rpcbind
root     2949     1  0  Oct 19   ?      0:00 /usr/sbin/nfsd 4
root       28     0  0  Oct 19   ?      8:04 vxfsd
root      488     1  0  Oct 19   ?      0:00 /usr/sbin/ptydaemon
root     2683     1  0  Oct 19   ?      0:00 /usr/sbin/cron
root     2456     1  0  Oct 19   ?      0:00 /usr/sbin/snmpdm
root     2110     1  0  Oct 19   ?      0:00 /usr/sbin/inetd
```

```
root    2907    1  0  Oct 19  ?    5:50 /usr/sbin/swagentd
root    2760    1  0  Oct 19  ?    0:00 /opt/perf/bin/ttd
root    2502    1  0  Oct 19  ?    9:01 /usr/sbin/mib2agt
```

This list of processes has been truncated. Depending on the applications used on your system, this process list may be quite long.

Description of Fields in the Process Table

A brief description of the different fields used in the output of the ps command are as follows.

UID	User ID of the owner of the process.
PID	Process ID, a number used to represent a process in the process table.
PPID	Process ID of the parent process. Your shell is the parent process of all processes created by the commands you use.
C	Processor utilization for scheduling.
STIME	Starting time of the process. If the difference between the starting time and the current time is more than 24 hours, the starting date is specified.
TTY	Controlling terminal of the process, usually the terminal device file used by a terminal. A question mark may be present if there is no controlling terminal; most of the processes started at boot time do not have one.
TIME	Cumulative execution time for the process.
CMD	Command name that initiated the process.

If you use the -l option with the ps command, other fields are displayed. Some of the important fields are listed here.

NI	Nice priority value of the process. This is a number ranging from 0 to 39, used for priority calculation by the kernel for process scheduling. (This will be discussed later in this chapter.)
F	Flag field that shows a number of things, including if the process is swapped out of or into the main memory. This also shows if the process is a system process.
ADDR	Memory address of the process.

%CPU	Percentage of CPU time used by the process.
S	State of the process (running, sleeping, stopped, etc.).
SZ	Size of the core of the process image in number of pages.
WCHAN	Event for which the process is waiting. If the process is not sleeping or waiting for any event, a hyphen is placed in this column.

20.4 Sending Signals to Processes

Signals are used to send some information to a process or to handle an exception. Signals are sent to processes using the `kill` command explicitly. Some signals are bound to keyboard key combinations and are sent to the processes that are currently attached to the terminal. Every signal has a signal name and a number associated with it. All signals have default responses. Some signals are ignored by default. A list of signals and their default responses is shown in Table 20-2.

Table 20–2 *Signals*

Signal Name	Signal Number	Description
SIGNULL	0	Check access to PID
SIGHUP	1	Hangup
SIGINT	2	Interrupt
SIGQUIT	3	Quit
SIGILL	4	Illegal instruction (not reset when caught)
SIGTRAP	5	Trace trap (not reset when caught)
SIGABRT	6	Process abort signal
SIGIOT	SIGABRT	IOT instruction
SIGEMT	7	EMT instruction
SIGFPE	8	Floating point exception
SIGKILL	9	Kill (cannot be caught or ignored)
SIGBUS	10	Bus error
SIGSEGV	11	Segmentation violation
SIGSYS	12	Bad argument to system call

Signal Name	Signal Number	Description
SIGPIPE	13	Write on a pipe with no one to read it
SIGALRM	14	Alarm clock
SIGTERM	15	Software termination signal from the kill; the default signal sent when using the `kill` command
SIGUSR1	16	User-defined signal 1
SIGUSR2	17	User-defined signal 2
SIGCHLD	18	Child process terminated or stopped
SIGCLD	SIGCHLD	Death of a child
SIGPWR	19	Power state indication
SIGVTALRM	20	Virtual timer alarm
SIGPROF	21	Profiling timer alarm
SIGIO	22	Asynchronous I/O
SIGPOLL	SIGIO	For HP-UX `hpstreams` signal
SIGWINCH	23	Window size change signal
SIGWINDOW	SIGWINCH	Added for compatibility reasons
SIGSTOP	24	Stop signal (cannot be caught or ignored)
SIGTSTP	25	Interactive stop signal
SIGCONT	26	Continue if stopped
SIGTTIN	27	Read from the control terminal attempted by a member of a background process group
SIGTTOU	28	Write to the control terminal attempted by a member of a background process group
SIGURG	29	Urgent condition on the I/O channel
SIGLOST	30	Remote lock lost (NFS)
SIGRESERVE	31	Save for future use
SIGDIL	32	DIL signal
SIGXCPU	33	CPU time limit exceeded (`setrlimit`)
SIGXFSZ	34	CPU file size limit exceeded (`setrlimit`)
SIGCANCEL	35	Used for `pthread` cancelation
SIGGFAULT	36	Graphics framebuffer fault
SIGRTMIN	37	First (highest priority) realtime signal
SIGRTMAX	44	Last (lowest priority) realtime signal

The `kill` command is used to send a signal to a process. If no signal is specified on the command line, it sends SIGTERM (signal 15) to the process specified. The general syntax of the `kill` command is:

```
kill [-signal] process
```

To send a SIGTERM signal to a process having process an ID of 1556, use one of the following commands; all of these are equivalent.

```
kill -SIGTERM 1556
kill -15 1556
kill 1556
kill -s SIGTERM 1556
kill -s 15 1556
```

The SIGTERM signal is used to terminate a process gracefully if it doesn't have a disabled signal. If a process ignores this signal, you can send a SIGKILL (signal 9) signal to terminate it. This signal can't be ignored and it forces a process to terminate. The following command terminates a process having a process ID of 1556.

```
kill -9 1556
```

However, it must be noted that a signal is not received by a process that hangs in an I/O operation and it therefore never gets scheduled after that. So it may happen that you are sending a SIGKILL to a process and it does not terminate. The `kill -l` command lists available signals and their respective numbers as shown here.

```
# kill -l
 1) HUP           23) WINCH
 2) INT           24) STOP
 3) QUIT          25) TSTP
 4) ILL           26) CONT
 5) TRAP          27) TTIN
 6) ABRT          28) TTOU
 7) EMT           29) URG
 8) FPE           30) LOST
 9) KILL          31) RESERVED
10) BUS           32) DIL
11) SEGV          33) XCPU
12) SYS           34) XFSZ
13) PIPE          35) The specified trap
                      syntax is not correct.
14) ALRM          36) The specified trap
                      syntax is not correct.
```

15)	TERM	37)	RTMIN
16)	USR1	38)	RTMIN+1
17)	USR2	39)	RTMIN+2
18)	CHLD	40)	RTMIN+3
19)	PWR	41)	RTMAX-3
20)	VTALRM	42)	RTMAX-2
21)	PROF	43)	RTMAX-1
22)	IO	44)	RTMAX

The nohup Command

The nohup command executes another command with the hangup and quit signals ignored. Usually a process is attached to a terminal (TTY) or a pseudoterminal (pty). If the user logs out from that terminal, the process also terminates. The nohup command stops process termination in such a case. Unless the screen output is redirected, the screen output of the executing program is stored in the nohup.out file. If a program takes a long time, such as a batch program, you may start it using the nohup command and then log out. The following command line runs a shell program myprog with the help of the nohup command.

```
nohup myprog &
```

The nohup command applies to all lines in the shell script. If you are using more than one command with nohup on the command line, these can be grouped as follows.

```
nohup (prog1 ; prog2)
```

Signals can also be sent to a processes using the SAM Process Control area as shown in Figure 20-1. Just select a process and use the Actions menu to kill it or change its priority, as discussed in the next section.

20.5 Process Nice Values

The "nice value" or "nice number" is one of several factors that allow the system to compute the process priority number for every process. Every system process runs at a nice level between 0 and 39, inclusive. A nice value of 0 is the highest priority and 39 is the lowest. When the system starts, the init process runs with a nice value of 20. Every process that is initiated by another process inherits its nice value from its parent. Thus processes started by the init process have a nice value of 20. At the time a user logs in, a shell pro-

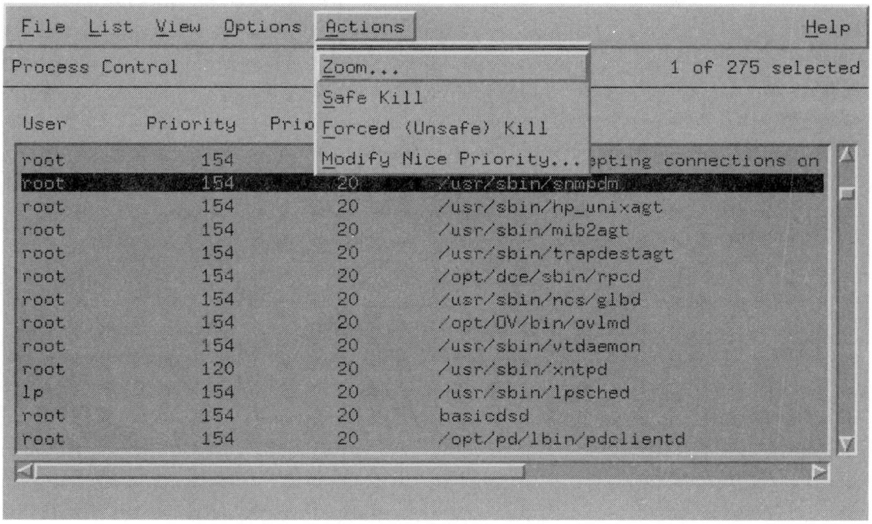

Figure 20–1   *Managing processes using SAM.*

gram is started. Every user command is a child process of the shell so it has the same nice value the shell has. However, the shell provides a mechanism to increase or decrease process nice values with the help of the `nice` command. Any user can lower the nice value by increasing the nice number. However, to increase priority, you need more privileges. The `nice` command is used to change the nice value of a new process, while the `renice` command is used to change the nice value of a running process.

The nice value scheme provides a facility where you can run lengthy jobs at a lower priority while processes that are required to be completed in a short time are run at a higher priority level.

Listing Nice Priorities

If you use the `ps` command with the `-l` option, it lists the nice number under the `NI` column. Most processes have a default nice value as shown next. I have used the `cut` command to get rid of unwanted information in the output.

```
$ ps -efl|cut -c 1-37,85-110
    F S        UID   PID  PPID  C PRI NI COMD
    3 S       root     0     0  0 128 20 swapper
  141 S       root     1     0  0 168 20 init
    3 S       root     2     0  0 128 20 vhand
    3 S       root     3     0  0 128 20 statdaemon
    3 S       root     4     0  0 128 20 unhashdaemon
```

```
 3 S    root      7    0  0 -32 20 ttisr
 3 S    root     22    0  0 100 20 supsched
 3 S    root     23    0  0 100 20 smpsched
 3 S    root     24    0  0 100 20 sblksched
 3 S    root     25    0  0 100 20 sblksched
 3 S    root     26    0  0 100 20 strmem
 3 S    root     27    0  0 100 20 strweld
 1 S    root  29582    1  0 156 20 /usr/sbin/getty console
 1 S    root   2052    1  0 154 20 /opt/hpnp/bin/hpnpd
 1 S    root   1849    1  0 154 20 /usr/sbin/cron
41 S    root   1527    1  0 120 20 /usr/sbin/xntpd
 1 S      lp   1562    1  0 154 20 /usr/sbin/lpsched
 1 S    root    407    1  0 154 20 /usr/sbin/syncer
 1 S    root    461    1  0 154 20 /usr/sbin/swagentd
 1 S    root    795    1  0 154 20 /usr/sbin/portmap
 1 S    root    537    1  0 154 20 /usr/sbin/syslogd -D
 1 S    root    546    1  0 155 20 /usr/sbin/ptydaemon
 1 S    root    565    1  0 127 20 /usr/lbin/nktl_daemon 0
 1 S    root   1295    1  0 154 20 /opt/dce/sbin/rpcd
 1 S    root    982    1  0 154 20 /usr/sbin/snmpdm
 1 S    root    827    1  0 154 20 /usr/sbin/biod 4
 1 S    root    828    1  0 154 20 /usr/sbin/biod 4
<Some output truncated here>
```

As you can see, all of the processes have a nice value equal to 20. If you want to run a process with a nice value other than the default, you use the `nice` command when starting the process. The `nice` command accepts a nice change value that shows the difference between the default nice value and the new nice value. To run a program `myprog` with a nice value of 25 (lower than the default value of 20), use the following command.

```
nice -5 myprog
```

To run a program at a higher nice level of 15, use the following command.

```
nice --5 myprog
```

Note that you need to provide two negative symbols to raise the priority of a program. If you are running a program in the background with the "&" symbol at the command line, it is run with a `nice -4` value by default. It means that the program will run at a nice level of 24 instead of 20. The default nice value of the following program is 29.

```
nice -5 myprog &
```

If the nice change value is not specified with the command, a default value of 10 is used. For example, the following command runs the `vi` editor at a nice level of 30 instead of 20.

```
nice vi
```

You can create a subshell of the current shell that is running at a lower level as shown here.

```
nice -5 sh
```

Now the new shell is running at a nice level of 25. Any command that you create after that will have a default nice level of 25. Now the command, `nice vi`, will result in running the `vi` editor at the nice level of 35. To go back to the previous shell, use the `exit` command.

Changing the Nice Values of Running Processes

Nice values of running process can be changed using the `renice` command. This command accepts a change value, like the `nice` command does, which is relative to the current nice level of the process. The `renice` command takes the PID of the running process as its argument. Let's take the example of the process created when running a shell program named `myprog` in the background. Since it was running in the background, its nice value was 24. To change the nice value of `myprog` running in background from 24 to 25, use the following command, where `5116` is the process ID of the process created by `myprog`.

```
renice -n 5 5116
```

Note that the nice value is changed from 24 to 25 (not from 24 to 29). This is because the new nice value is determined with respect to the default nice value.

The `renice` command can be used to alter the nice values of a group of processes by using one of the following options.

`-g`   Use the group ID instead of process ID with this option. It will change the nice values of all processes that fall into that group.

`-u`   Use the user ID with this option. It will change the nice values of all processes owned by that user.

20.6 Some Useful Commands

Two commands are very useful when dealing with processes and signals. These are the `timex` and `trap` commands. The `timex` command tells you about the amount of time used by a process or a group of processes, and the `trap` command is used to capture signals on your system.

The timex Command

The `timex` command is used to report process and system activity. This command can be used to calculate the time used by a command or set of commands. For example, to check user and system time used during the execution of the `ll /etc` command, use the following command.

```
timex ll /etc
```

At the end of the normal output of the `ll` command, you will find additional lines showing the time used by the process created by the `ll` command in user and system modes and its total (real) execution time. This output is shown here.

```
real        0.13
user        0.04
sys         0.05
```

You can use this command with your shell programs or with any other code to check their efficiency and how they load the system.

The trap Command

The `trap` command captures signals and takes an action if a particular signal is received. If the command is used without arguments, it lists current traps. Output of this command may look like the following.

```
$ trap
trap -- 'echo '\''logout'\' EXIT
$
```

This line shows that a `trap` for the `EXIT` signal is set and the `echo logout` command will be executed when you exit from the shell.

If you use the following command, it will not show you any output and will set a trap on the `INT` signal.

```
trap 'ls /etc' INT
```

After using this command, use the `trap` command without arguments to verify that a trap for the `INT` signal is set. You will see an output like the following.

```
$ trap
trap -- 'ls /etc' INT
trap -- 'echo '\''logout'\' EXIT
$
```

Now send an `INT` signal by pressing the CTRL-C key combination. You will see that the `ls /etc` command is executed and a list of all files in the `/etc` directory is displayed. In this way, you can set any response with a signal. The `DEBUG` signal can be used to do something after every command. For example, the following command will cause the current directory to be displayed after every command.

```
trap pwd DEBUG
```

All traps that are set once remain effective for the life cycle of your shell. Traps can be changed by setting a new trap value. For example, the trap for the `DEBUG` signal will be changed with the following command.

```
trap date DEBUG
```

Now the date and time will be displayed after every command. A trap value can be deleted if you use a null string with the `trap` command. The following command will stop displaying anything after every command.

```
trap "" DEBUG
```

Traps are very useful if you want to capture an event in your system. Setting a trap on a particular signal, for example, can inform you about a system event via email.

■ Chapter Summary

A process in an instance of a running program. In a multitasking system like HP-UX, many processes are running simultaneously. A record of these processes is kept in a kernel data structure known as a process table. The HP-UX kernel implements a scheduling policy to run these processes by allocating time slices to them. Every process in the process table is identified by a process ID number and carries other attributes that show process statistics. The size of the process table is limited by the `nproc` kernel parameter.

When the HP-UX kernel is loaded into memory, it starts the `init` process, which has a PID of 1. The `init` process then creates other processes that are its children processes. During its life cycle, a process changes its state many times. Processes in the process table can be listed using the `ps` command. This command shows a number of process attributes, such as the PID, owner and group, parent process ID or PPID, and time used by the process.

Signals can be sent to a process using the `kill` command or keyboard shortcuts. Every signal has a signal name and a numeric value associated with it. If no signal is specified with the `kill` command, it sends SIGTERM to a specified process by default. A process may ignore some signals such as SIGTERM. However, there are some signals that can't be ignored by a process. SIGKILL is one of these signals and is used to kill a process that is not responding to any other signal.

When you start a process, it is usually attached to your terminal. If you log out while a process is still running, it loses the connection with its controlling terminal and is terminated. The `nohup` command is used to disable hangup and quit signals so that the process continues to run even if you log out. This command is used for those processes that take a long time to complete, where you don't want to keep a terminal busy.

Every process has a nice level that is used by the kernel for scheduling purposes. The default nice value is 20. The `nice` and `renice` commands are used to change this value for new and running processes, respectively. The `timex` command is used to calculate the time utilization by a process. The `trap` command in used to capture a signal and carry out a task when a particular signal is received.

▲ CHAPTER REVIEW QUESTIONS

1. What information do you get from the `ps` command?

2. Why does a process go into a sleeping state?

3. What are signals and how can they be sent to a process?

4. For what purpose is the `nohup` command used?

5. How can you execute both the `pwd` and `date` commands when a DEBUG signal is received?

6. A sleeping process can go to a running state directly. (True/False)

▲ TEST YOUR KNOWLEDGE

1. *Which kernel tunable parameter determines the maximum size of a process table?*

    A. maxssiz

    B. nproc

    C. maxuprc

    D. maxusers

2. *Which signal is sent by the* kill *command by default?*

    A. SIGHUP

    B. SIGKILL

    C. SIGTERM

    D. SIGNULL

3. *The default nice level is 20. You start a new process in the background using the "&" symbol. What will be its nice level?*

    A. 20

    B. 25

    C. 24

    D. 16

4. *A process is in a sleep state while waiting for a resource that is currently busy. It receives a stop signal (*SIGSTOP*) and goes into a stopped state. After some time it receives a continue signal (*SIGCONT*). To which state will it go?*

    A. running

    B. sleeping

    C. ready to run

    D. zombie

5. *You are logged in as user* **boota** *and want to change the nice level of the* init *process to 15. Which of the following commands will you use? Remember the PID for the* init *process is 1.*

    A. nice -n -5 1

    B. renice -n -5 1

    C. renice --n 5 1

    D. You don't have privileges that permit you to change the nice value of the init process.

Printing on HP-UX

In multiuser systems, many printers may be used for a large number of users. When many users are accessing shared printers, it becomes important to carefully manage these printers so that the print requests are serviced properly. Some of these requests may be of excessive length but of less priority, like weekly or monthly reports. On the other hand, some requests may be of immediate need and require high priority. Users may also be divided into a number of groups depending on their printing needs. Different printers may be assigned to these groups. In such an environment, printer management becomes an important task that needs careful planning.

A printer may be connected locally to a system or connected to another system on the network. Some printers have network interface adapters installed inside them that can be directly connected to network cables. Management of these printers is done through a print server that runs HP JetAdmin software. Every printer is attached to one or more print queues. These print queues are managed using the HP-UX printer spooling system.

In this chapter, we will start with an introduction to the printing system and how it can be used for sending, altering, or canceling print requests. Types of printers will be discussed next. You will see how the print spooling system works and how it manages print queues. You will also learn about setting priorities and managing print queues. SAM will be used to add and manage printers. It is an easy and preferable way to configure and manage printers compared with command-line utilities. In the last part of the chapter, you will learn how to troubleshoot a printing system.

21.1   Introduction to the Printing System

A printing system in HP-UX is collectively called the *LP spooler*. It is a collection of programs and utilities that are used to manage print requests and to make sure that each print request is printed separately. It is also responsible for ensuring that any printed matter be identifiable with whoever sent the print request.

A functional printing system offers the following capabilities to its users.

1. submitting a print request
2. checking the status of a print request
3. making changes to a print request
4. canceling a print request

An administrator of the printing system can accomplish the following tasks.

1. add a new printer
2. remove an existing printer
3. enable and disable printers
4. add printer classes
5. change priorities of print jobs
6. set fence priorities that don't allow a print request to go to a printer having a priority less than a defined value
7. define a system default destination
8. check the status of printers and print jobs
9. move print jobs from one printer to another

A printer system is controlled by a scheduler daemon (lpsched). This daemon is started at boot time and manages print requests, scheduling them according to priority.

Sending a Print Request

A print request is sent using the lp command. You can use the -d option with the lp command to specify a destination printer name. If the destination is an individual printer, the print request goes directly to that printer. However, you can also send a print request to a class of printers. A class is a collective name for printers of the same type. For example, all HP laser jet printers of the same type may be included in one class. When you send a print request to a class of printers, the first available printer in the class prints it. Usually printers of one class are physically located close to each other so that a user may find output at one location, no matter which printer is used to print it. To print the .profile file in your home directory on a printer named LJ4, you can use the following command.

```
$ lp -dLJ4 ~/.profile
Request ID is LJ4-345 (1 file)
$
```

When you submit a print request, the lp command will return a request ID that will be used later on for tracking your print job. This number will be of type LJ4-345, where the first part (LJ4) is the printer name and the second part (345) is a sequence number.

If you don't use a destination with the lp command, the spooler system checks for a LPDEST environment variable. This variable defines your destination printer name or class for the print job. In case this variable is not present, the default queue is checked. If there is no default queue and the LPDEST variable is not defined, an error message is printed.

Other options that can be used with the lp command are shown in Table 21-1.

Table 21–1 *Option Used with the* lp *Command*

Option	Description
-c	Copy the file being printed to the spool directory. If this option is not defined, the file is not copied to the spool directory. Instead, the file is read when the printing starts. It may happen that you submit a job and there is a large amount of print requests already queued. If your print job's turn comes after one hour and you have made changes to the file by that time, the new file will be printed instead of the one that was present at the time of sending the print request. So it is better to use this option as soon as you submit the print request so that the file is copied to the print queue.
-d	Defines the destination printer name or printer class.
-m	Sends a mail message to the user when the job is printed.
-n	Sets the number of copies to be printed. By default, one copy is printed.
-p	Sets the job priority: 0 is the lowest priority and 7 is the highest. The default priority is set by SAM or the lpadmin command.
-t	Print a title on the banner page. A banner page is the first page of the printed output. You can use a title of your own choice. By default, the user login name is printed.
-w	Write a message on the user's terminal screen when the job is finished. If the user is not logged in, a mail message is sent.

Canceling a Print Request

You can cancel a print request using the cancel command. The cancel command needs a request ID as its argument. To cancel the print job LJ4-345, you can use the following command.

```
cancel LJ4-345
```

The cancel command can also be used to cancel print requests of a particular user, requests on a local printer only, or requests on a specified printer only. See the manual pages for more detail on the cancel command. If you cancel a print request that is currently being printed, the remaining part of the request is canceled and the printer starts the next print job.

Modifying a Print Request

You may need to modify a print request. The modification is made using the lpalt command. This command takes a print request ID as its argument. You can use the same options used with the lp command to alter a print request. For example, the following command sets the number of copies to three for the print job LJ4-345.

```
lpalt LJ4345 -n3
```

You can also use this command to change the priority of a job if your job is urgent and is currently at the end of a long queue.

21.2   Types of Printers

Printers connected to HP-UX systems may be classified into three categories. This division depends on how a printer is attached to a system. These three types of printers are shown in Figure 21-1.

The method of setting up and managing each of these types of printers is different. You also need different utilities to manage print jobs. A brief explanation of the three types is presented next.

Local Printers

A local printer is directly attached to the machine a user is logged in on. Printers attached to standalone systems are always called local printers. In Figure 21-1, the local printer is attached to the rightmost system, and the user is logged in on the same system. A local printer is attached to the system with a parallel printer port or a serial port, depending on the type of the printer.

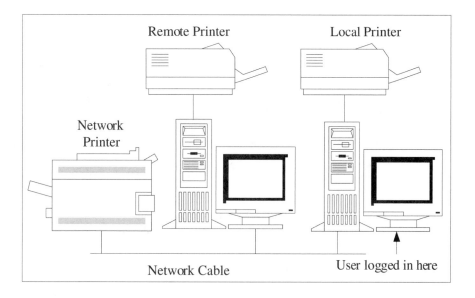

Figure 21–1   *Types of printers used in HP-UX.*

Remote Printers

A remote printer is configured on a machine other than the one the user is logged in on. The user machine and the machine where the printer is configured are connected through a network. A remote printer is first defined on some other system, then it is made accessible for other systems on the network. The system on which the printer is configured must be running the rlpdaemon program in order to accept remote print requests.

Network Printers

A network printer has its own network interface adapter and is directly connected to the network cable as shown in Figure 21-1. Usually a network printer has a JetDirect card and behaves like any other network device. This printer can be accessed directly by any system on the network. It is also possible to use one system as the print server, and users access all network printers through that print server. In such a case, the print server keeps track of all print queues attached to the network printers.

21.3 Directory Hierarchy of the Printing System

The directory hierarchy of a print spooler system is shown in Figure 21-2. Due to the complexity of the directory tree, some of the directories are missing from this figure. What follows is a short description of some of these directories and the type of files they contain.

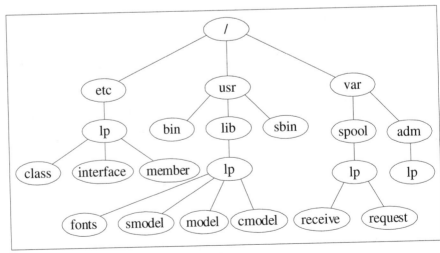

Figure 21–2 *Directory hierarchy of an HP-UX print spooler system.*

`/etc/lp/classes`	This directory contains files that define which printer is related to which class. A class is a set of printers of similar capabilities. When a user sends a print request to a printer class, the first available printer prints it. For example, all laser jet printers may be in one "laser" class. When a user sends a print request using the `lp` command and specifies the destination as "laser," the request goes to the first available laser printer. Printers of the same class should be located at one place physically.
`/etc/lp/inter-faces`	This directory contains programs that are used to format printed data for a particular type of printer. A system administrator can modify an interface of a printer.
`/etc/lp/member`	This directory contains files that show configured printers on a system. Each printer has one file with the printer name and the device file name of the attached printer.
`/usr/bin`	Contains utilities such as `lp`, `cancel`, `lpalt`, and `lpstat`. These utilities are for use by a general user.
`/usr/sbin`	Contains utilities for printer administration. These utilities are for the system administrator.
`/usr/lib/lp/model`	This directory contains interface programs for all supported models on HP-UX. When you add a printer, the appropriate program is copied from this directory to the `/etc/lp/interfaces` directory. While copying, this program is renamed to match the printer name. The interface programs contain information about the banners and fonts used with a printer.
`/usr/lib/lp/fonts`	This directory contains fonts for laser jet printers.
`/usr/lib/lp/cmodel`	This directory contains scripts to cancel requests on a remote system.
`/usr/lib/lp/smodel`	This directory contains scripts to check the status of a print job on a remote system.

`/var/spool/lp/ request`	This is the place for print queues. This directory contains other subdirectories, each of which represents one print queue. The actual print requests are spooled in this directory.
`/var/adm/lp`	This directory contains log files for the print spooler system.

There is an important file in the `/var/spool/lp` directory. This is the SCHEDLOCK file, which is created when you start the print scheduler (`lpsched`). It is used to ensure that only one copy of the scheduler is running at a given time. When you shut down the print scheduler, this file is automatically removed. If the scheduler gets terminated abnormally, you need to remove this file manually before restarting the scheduler.

21.4 Adding a Printer

A printer can be added using the `lpadmin` command or SAM. The `lpadmin` command accepts a number of command-line arguments that can be used to create and modify a printer. Adding a printer using the command line is laborious compared with SAM. You get a comprehensive window while you add a printer with SAM. Let's first see the command-line method.

Adding a Printer

The `lpadmin` command can be used to add a printer with the name `laser` as shown in the following command.

```
lpadmin -plaser –mhplj4 -v/dev/lp
```

This command adds a printer named `laser` on device file `/dev/lp`. The interface program used for this printer is `hplj4`.

Setting a Printer as Default Destination

A printer may be established as a default destination for users of a system by using the `lpadmin` command. The following command sets a printer named `laserjet` as the default destination.

```
lpadmin -dlaserjet
```

Deleting a Printer

Deleting a printer with the lpadmin command is shown next, where printer laserjet has been deleted.

```
lpadmin -xlaserjet
```

Adding Printers Using SAM

Adding a printer is done using the SAM Printers and Plotters area. Figure 21-3 shows a list of printers in SAM where you can see a printer named laserjet and its type is remote. It also shows that the print spooler is running on the system. The Actions menu is used for printer administration. Using this menu, you can add local, remote, and network printers. You can also start and stop the print scheduler using this menu. When you add a local printer using SAM, you can select how the printer is physically connected to the system. Most of the common printers are connected using a parallel port.

   When adding a parallel port printer, SAM looks for the parallel ports installed in your system. After scanning the hardware, you will see a window like the one shown in Figure 21-4, where all parallel ports are listed.

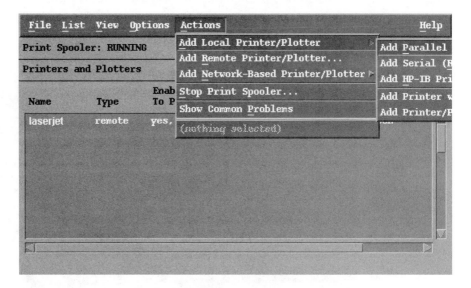

Figure 21–3 *The* Printers and Plotters *area in SAM.*

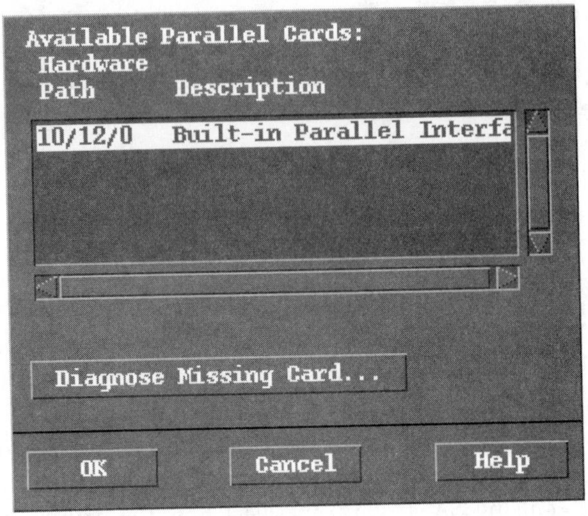

Figure 21–4 *List of parallel ports installed in the system.*

From this list, you can select one of the ports to attach the printer. A parallel port is represented as a Hardware Path in this window. This Hardware Path is represented as a parallel port device in the /dev directory. When adding a printer, the parallel port device is used.

After selecting a parallel port, you press the OK button and enter the Printer Name and its properties as shown in Figure 21-5.

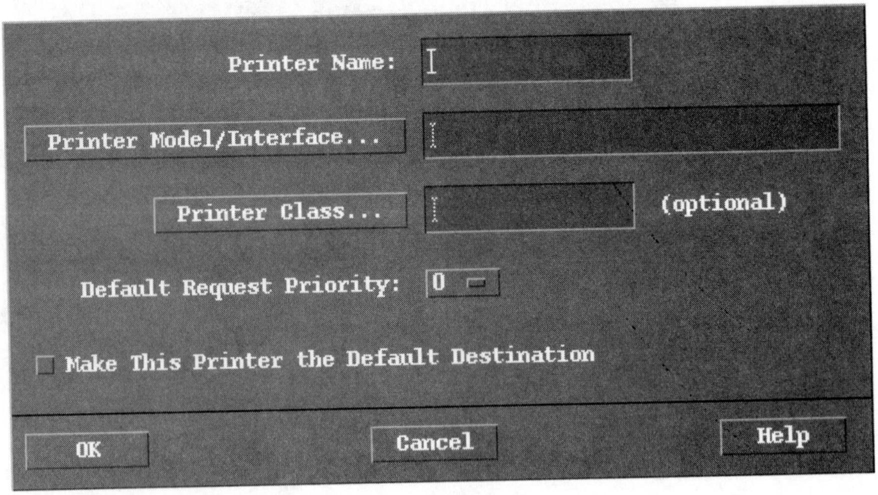

Figure 21–5 *Adding a local printer.*

A `Printer Name` is any name of your choice. The printer will be known with this name on your system. For example, you can select a name `laserjet` here. This is the same name that you used with the `lpadmin` command using the `-p` option. When you use the `lp` command to print a document, you use this name with the `-d` option.

The `Printer Model/Interface` is the name of the interface program that will be used with the printer. The model or interface names are present in the `/usr/lib/lp/model` directory. If there is no interface program for your printer, you can use a "dumb" model, but in this case, you will not be able to use all of the printer capabilities.

`Printer Class` is an optional parameter. You use `Printer Class` if you are using more than one printer of the same type and want to share print requests among them. You may not need to use a class if you are using only one printer.

The `Default Request Priority` setting is used if no priority is explicitly mentioned using the `-p` option of the `lp` command. Priorities are numbered from 0 to 7, 0 being the lowest priority. You can also use the `-g` option with the `lpadmin` command to set the default priority for a printer.

In this window, you can also set a printer as the default printer for the entire system. If no destination is mentioned with the `lp` command, the print request is sent to the default printer. However, it should be noted that the default printer location is changed if the `LPDEST` variable is set in the user shell. The `lp` command uses the printer name set with the `LPDEST` variable. If this variable is not set, only then the default printer is used for printing purposes.

If the `LPDEST` variable is set but contains an invalid value, the result of the `lp` command is unpredictable.

Adding a printer causes the print spooling system to be stopped and restarted. All jobs currently being printed are also restarted. A printer should be added when there are no jobs in progress.

If you are adding a remote printer, the window shown in Figure 21-6 appears. Here you need to fill out a number of parameters for use with a remote printer.

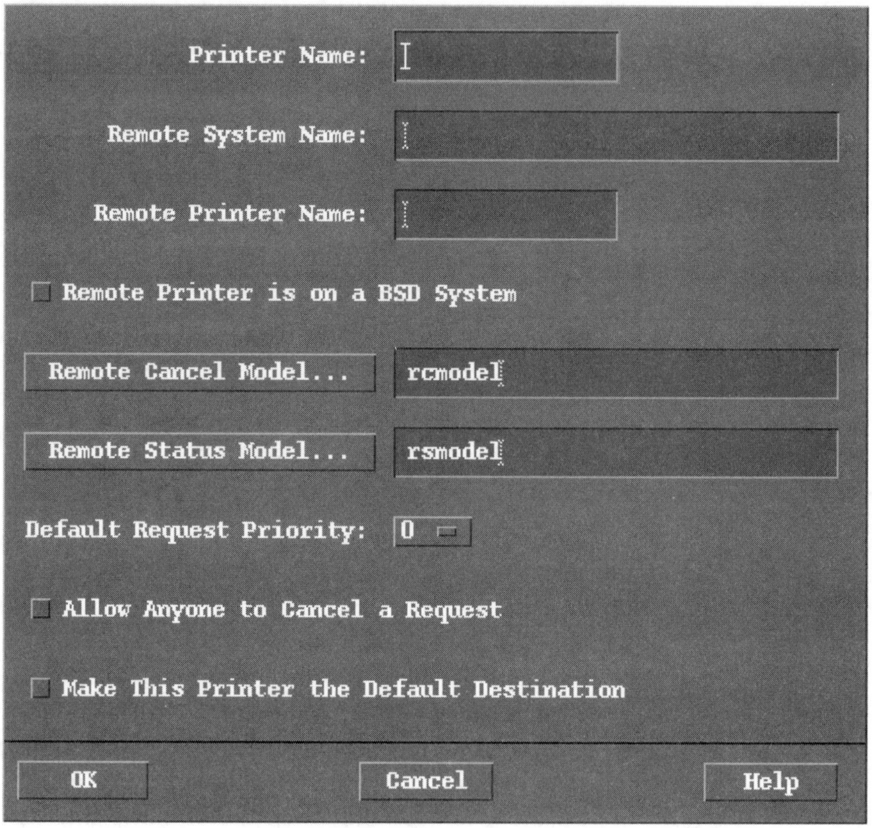

Figure 21–6   *Adding a remote printer using SAM.*

In addition to the local printer name, you also need to know the system to which the remote printer is attached and the name used for the printer on that system. The `Remote System Name` must be known to your system. For this you need to enter the `Remote System Name` in the `/etc/hosts` file. Users of your system will use the `Printer Name` you define yourself (not the `Remote Printer Name`).

If the remote system is using Berkley Software Distribution (BSD) print services, you must check the box for that purpose.

SAM already fills the `Remote Cancel Model` and `Remote Status Model` name boxes for you. The remote cancel script is used to cancel print jobs on the remote printer. The remote status script is used to check the status of a print job on a remote printer.

`Default Request Priority` can be specified, as in the case of adding a local printer. Its value is from 0 to 7, 0 being the lowest priority.

You can allow anyone to cancel a print job on a remote printer. If you don't do this, only the owner of the job can cancel it. The last option can be used to set this printer as a default printer for the local system. You don't specify any printer interface model script as you did in the case of a local printer. For a remote printer, the `rmodel` script is used by default, which uses the `rlp` command to send print jobs to a remote printer.

On the remote system, you must edit the `/etc/services` file and remove any comments in the `printer` line. You must also edit the `/etc/inetd.conf` file to enable `rlpdaemon` and restart the `inetd` daemon. The `/etc/hosts` file on the remote system must contain the name and address of the local system.

21.5 Managing Print Queues

Print queues are controlled by the `lpsched` process that runs as a daemon on your system. It is typically invoked by the `/sbin/rc` script at boot time. If the `-v` and `-a` options are used with this daemon, it writes its log data in the `/var/adm/lp` directory.

A print queue is a printer name or a class name, which either accepts print jobs at a particular time or not. Print queues may be enabled or disabled.

Starting and Stopping the Print Scheduler

To stop the print scheduler, use the following command.

```
/usr/sbin/lpshut
```

To restart the scheduler, use this method.

```
/usr/sbin/lpsched
```

Moving Print Jobs

Print jobs can be moved from one printer to another using the `lpmove` command. To move a print job `LJ4-345` to a printer `laser3`, you can use the following command.

```
lpmove LJ4-345 laser3
```

You can also use this command to move all print jobs from one printer to another. For example, to move all print jobs from printer `laser1` to printer `laser3`, use the following command.

```
lpmove laser1 laser3
```

This command can only be used when `lpsched` is not running. After using the command, printer `laser1` stops accepting new print jobs.

Deleting Print Jobs

Print jobs can be deleted using the `cancel` command, which accepts a print job ID as its argument and cancels that print job. If, instead of a print job ID, you provide the name of a print queue, all requests on that print queue are canceled.

Enabling and Disabling Printers

To enable a printer, use the `enable` command. If the designated printer is a member of a class print queue, it starts printing jobs sent to that queue. If you disable a printer that is member of a class print queue, the requests are printed on another printer in the class. To enable and disable printer `laserjet3`, you can use following commands.

```
enable laserjet3
```

```
disable laserjet3
```

If you use the `-c` option with the `disable` command, it will cancel all requests being printed on the designated printer. You can also use the `-r` option with a reason string with the `disable` command. This reason is reported with the `lpstat` command when checking the status of the printing system.

Accepting and Rejecting Print Requests

The `lp` command can send a request to a queue that is accepting print requests. For example, to temporarily disconnect a printer for maintenance, you may stop accepting requests for that printer. The `reject` command is used for this purpose. You can also specify a message that is displayed on a user screen if the user attempts to send a print job to a printer that is not accepting print requests. The command to reject requests for printer `laserjet3` is as follows.

```
reject -r "laserjet3 is temporarily out of order" laserjet3
```

To start accepting print requests again, use the following command.

```
accept laserjet3
```

The `enable` and `disable` commands determine whether a printer will print requests sent to a queue, while the `accept` and `reject` commands determine whether a user can send a request to a printer.

Current Printer Status

The current status of the printing system may be checked using the `lpstat` command. If you use the `lpstat` command without any argument or option, it prints the status of all print jobs requested by the user. You can use the options shown in Table 21-2 with this command.

Table 21–2 *Options Used with* `lpstat` *Command*

Option	Description
-a	List the acceptance status of all printer queues
-c	Write the class names and their members
-d	Show the default system destination
-o	Write the status of output requests
-p	Write the status of printers
-r	Write the status of the print scheduler
-t	Write all status information
-u	Write the status of a particular user

Study Break

Checking the Current Printer Status

Use the `lpstat` command to check the status of all printers configured on your system. Now use the `reject -r` command with a rejection response message for a particular printer. Try sending a print request to that printer. You should see the rejection message on your terminal screen.

21.6 Print Job Priorities

Every print job has a priority associated with it. The value of this priority is a number between 0 and 7, inclusive. The number 0 shows lowest priority and the number 7 is used for the highest priority. Print jobs are placed in a print queue depending on the priority associated with these jobs. If you want to print something urgently, you can specify a high priority number for that job when starting it with the lp command. Job priorities can be changed later by using the lpalt command.

A default print priority for a printer is assigned with the help of SAM or the lpadmin command with the -g option.

Fence Priority

The fence level determines the minimum priority that a print job must carry to be printed on a printer. The fence priority of a printer is set using SAM or the lpfence command. For example, to set a fence priority of 5 with printer laserjet3, use the following command.

```
lpfence laserjet3 5
```

After making this change, any job sent to the printer that has a priority lower than 5 will sit in the print queue and will never be printed. You can print such jobs by either lowering the fence priority or by raising the job priority using the lpalt command.

21.7 Troubleshooting

A print spooler performance can be checked using the lpana command. You can use the -d option and a printer name with this command to check the performance of a particular printer. While troubleshooting a printer, check its physical connections and cables. You can check the physical connections by sending a file directly to the printer device port. For example, if the printer is using the /dev/lp0 device file, the following command must print the /etc/profile file on the printer if the physical connections are correct.

```
cat /etc/profile >/dev/lp0
```

To check the physical connections of a network printer, use the ping command.

If the print scheduler `lpsched` terminates abnormally, it does not delete the `/var/spool/lp/SCHEDLOCK` file. Existence of this file ensures that only a single scheduler is running. If you try to restart the scheduler, it will check for the existence of this file and think that the scheduler is already running. After this check, it will terminate. You have to remove this file manually using the `rm` command and then restart the scheduler using the `/usr/sbin/lpsched` command.

If there are any problems in the printing process, you will want to disable the printer, enable it again, and then restart a job from the beginning.

■ Chapter Summary

Depending on how a printer is physically attached to a system, it may be a local, remote, or network printer. A local printer is attached directly to the system where a user is logged in. A remote printer is a printer configured on another system on a network. Network printers are directly connected to network media and have a network interface card installed inside.

A printer may be member of a printer class. The `lp` command is used to send print requests to a particular printer or a printer class. A submitted print job may be canceled or altered using the `cancel` and `lpalt` commands, respectively. The printing system has a large directory hierarchy where different subdirectories hold specific types of files. A printer can be added or modified using the `lpadmin` command or SAM. To add a remote printer, you should know the remote host name and printer name defined on that host. The `rlpdaemon` must also be running on the host to which the printer is attached. The `/etc/hosts`, `/etc/inetd.conf`, and `/etc/services` files must also be configured properly.

Every print request has a priority associated with it. This priority is used by the `lp` scheduler process (`lpsched`) to queue print jobs. If no priority is specified when a print request is sent, a default priority is used. A priority may be a number from 0 to 7 where 0 shows the lowest priority and 7 shows the highest priority.

The `lpshut` command is used to shut down the print spooler daemon. The scheduler can be started again using the `lpsched` command. Print jobs can be moved from one printer to another using the `lpmove` command. The `enable` and `disable` commands are used to enable or disable the printer itself, while the `accept` and `reject` commands are used to allow or deny new print requests. The `lpstat` command is used to check printer status at any time.

▲ CHAPTER REVIEW QUESTIONS

1. Depending on how a printer is physically connected, what are the different types of printers in an HP-UX system?

2. What are print priorities and how are these used to allow only selective requests to be serviced by a printer (using a fence priority)?

3. What is the role of the interface program in the printing system?

4. A printer is not printing anything sent to it. What steps will you follow to troubleshoot this problem?

5. A network printer is physically connected to a system on the network. (True/False)

▲ TEST YOUR KNOWLEDGE

1. *What is the result of the* `lp -dLJ4 /etc/profile` *command?*
   A. It deletes a print request to print file `/etc/profile`.
   B. It deletes a print request to print file `/etc/profile`, if it is sent to printer `LJ4`.
   C. It sends a print request to printer `LJ4` to print file `/etc/profile`.
   D. It sends a print request to printer `LJ4` to print file `/etc/profile`, while all other jobs on the printer are deleted due to the `-d` option.

2. *How are local print jobs scheduled?*
   A. using the kernel process scheduling mechanism
   B. using the LP scheduling daemon `lpsched`
   C. using the LP daemon `rlpdaemon`
   D. using the `lpadmin` command

3. *How can the print priority of a job be increased when this job is waiting in the print queue?*
   A. using the `lpadmin` command
   B. with the help of the `lpalt` command
   C. using the `lp` command with the `-p` option
   D. There is no way to change the priority of a submitted job. However, you can cancel a job and resubmit it with a higher priority.

4. *What do you need to do to set up a remote printer, assuming DNS or NIS is not used?*

    A. Add an entry for the remote host in the `/etc/hosts` file on the local system.

    B. Add an entry for the local host in the `/etc/hosts` file on the remote system.

    C. Enable `rlpdaemon` on the remote system.

    D. All of the above.

5. *What happens after you issue the following command?*

    ```
    disable -r "Printer disabled" laserjet3
    ```

    A. No print job can be submitted to printer `laserjet3`.

    B. No print job can be printed to printer `laserjet3`.

    C. When a user sends a print job, a message `Printer disabled` appears on the terminal screen.

    D. Printer `laserjet3` disables any error messages.

6. *What is the result of the following command?*

    ```
    lpfence laserjet3 5
    ```

    A. Jobs of priorities less than 5 are not printed on printer `laserjet3`.

    B. Jobs of priorities less than 5 can't be submitted to printer `laserjet3`.

    C. Any queued job having a priority of less than 5 is deleted from the queue.

    D. All of the above.

Memory and Swap Space Management

Every system has some physical memory installed in it. The physical memory is used to hold programs and data loaded from disk drives and to perform operations on the data by using the loaded programs. The CPU can execute only those programs that are loaded into the physical memory. In a multitasking system, usually many programs are running simultaneously. There may also be many users logged in at one time and performing data operations. In a typical system, the amount of physical memory installed is not sufficient to hold all programs and data. This is where the concept of *virtual memory* comes in, where a systems uses space on secondary storage media (usually disk) to hold some of the programs and data being used by the CPU.

The part of the disk used for temporary data storage is called *swap space*. Although there are many processes running on a system in a given time slice, strictly speaking only one process is being executed by a CPU. In case the physical

427

memory is constrained, the system may *swap out* some of the programs loaded into the physical memory to the swap area, creating space for the running process. When the time slice for this process expires, the code and data related to this process may be swapped out, and another process may start using the same physical memory.

HP-UX uses a sophisticated memory management system that takes care of the memory requirements of all processes. Depending on certain criteria, it decides which process should stay in the main memory and which should be swapped out. This system always ensures that some space is available in the main memory to create new processes. The amount of swap space needed may be different for different installations depending on how much physical memory is installed and what types of applications are running. The `swapper` and `vhand` daemons are used for swap space management. The swap space may be of different types depending on which disk device is used for it and whether it is available at boot time. A swap area that is available at the boot time is a *primary swap area*, and it is usually present on the disk being used as the boot device. You may also use one or more secondary swap areas depending on your needs.

Management of swap areas can be done through the use of command-line utilities as well as using SAM. Both of these methods are quite simple. To activate swap areas at the system startup, entries of the swap space are put in the `/etc/fstab` file.

Use of swap space is based on a priority system. Every swap space is assigned a priority that is a number from 0 to 10. The number 0 is the highest priority swap space. If two swap areas have the same priority, these are used in a round robin fashion, thus dividing the load among different disk drives.

The application vendor usually specifies the amount of swap space needed for different applications. However, you should monitor the swap space usage from time to time to check its actual usage and increase it if necessary.

22.1 System Memory and Swap Space

The system memory is the actual physical memory installed in a system. When you boot a system, it probes all installed memory and displays information about the total memory. You can also use the dmesg command later to list the memory installed. If you extract information about the total memory by using the dmesg command, it looks like the following.

```
Memory Information:
physical page size = 4096 bytes, logical page size = 4096
  bytes
Physical: 16773120 Kbytes, lockable: 12179356 Kbytes,
  available: 13986844 Kbytes
```

As you can see, the command has listed three types of memory. The physical memory is the actual amount of memory installed in the system. When you boot your system, some amount of this memory is used by the kernel code and data structures. The remaining memory is the available memory. If you have a large kernel, with all subsystem and device drivers, it will consume more space compared with a carefully tuned kernel. Similarly, kernel parameters also affect how much memory will be used for kernel data structures. That is why it is important to fine-tune your kernel so that it consumes minimum memory when loaded.

User and system processes are loaded into the available memory. Processes and data in the lockable area are not eligible for swapping (paging).

A *page* is the minimum amount of memory that is considered one unit, used when data is transferred to and from the main memory to a swap area on the disk. A typical page size is 4 Kbytes. HP-UX keeps a record of free and occupied memory pages in a data structure known as a *page table*. When the kernel needs a page of data that is swapped out to the swap area, a *page fault* occurs and that data is brought back to the main memory from the swap area. If there are too many page faults, the system performance is degraded, as it is always busy moving data between main memory and the swap area.

Daemons Used with the Swap System

As soon as your system boots up and the kernel is loaded into memory, two daemons are started. These are the swapper and the vhand daemons and both perform separate jobs.

As has already been mentioned, the physical storage area is divided into pages and a record of these pages is kept in a page table. There is no swap activity as long as the number of these free pages remains larger than a pre-defined minimum limit. This threshold limit is known as *lotsfree*. As soon as this threshold limit is crossed and more memory is demanded by some of the processes, the vhand daemon is activated and starts using swap space. The vhand daemon implements a replacement policy for pages, one of which is the *least recently used* (LRU) policy, where pages that have been least used in the recent past are shifted to the swap area. There may be other policies such as the *least frequently used* (LFU) policy. Depending on the policy used, the daemon copies some of the pages that are not currently in use in the physical memory to the swap area. After copying these pages, it marks these pages as free in the page table area so that these may be used by some other processes.

If a page is referenced by a process that is currently on the swap area, a page fault occurs and the vhand daemon brings back that page to the main memory. To do so, it has to free other pages by copying them to the swap area. If the system has a small amount of physical memory installed, it may happen that the vhand daemon is overloaded with moving data to and from the swap space. This is the situation where the disk is continuously in use and vhand is taking most of the system time. No useful work is done in such a situation, and the system seems to have stopped swapping data. This situation is known as system *thrashing*.

Thrashing can be avoided if we are able to decrease the number of running processes. Some may be deactivated temporarily and swapped out of memory. Now the physical memory contains only that number of processes that can run smoothly. When some running processes are finished, the processes that were previously deactivated can be brought back to memory. The swapper daemon is used for this purpose. It checks the memory threshold known as *desfree*: When the memory falls below the value defined by desfree, it assumes that thrashing has started. It then deactivates some processes and puts them on hold. The memory pages allocated to these processes are swapped out of memory and are marked free in the page table. The swapper daemon reactivates these processes when conditions favorable to run these processes have returned.

To avoid running out of swap area, the system allocates swap space to a process as soon as the process is created. If all of the swap space is allocated, the system does not allow the creation of new processes. It may be noted that a swap space reserved for a process may never be used if not required by the system. Some processes may need additional memory at run time. This will also increase the demand for swap space for such processes. The system will terminate a process that is demanding more swap space than it has available.

22.2 Types of Swap Space

Depending on the physical location of the swap space and how it is used with the rest of the file system, there are two major categories of the swap. The first one is the device swap and the second one is the file system swap. These two categories are briefly explained next.

Device Swap Space

If you are using an entire disk exclusively for the swap space, or an entire file system in the LVM, it is called *device swap*. In the whole disk approach of the file system, you can leave space for the device swap area at the end of a disk by using the newfs command. Device swap may be used in the following ways.

1. If you are using a swap area of 200 Mbytes at the end of disk device c2t5d0 and rest of it for a file system, the newfs command can reserve this space as follows.

    ```
    newfs -R 200 /dev/rdsk/c2t5d0
    ```

2. In case you use a complete disk for the device area, you can enable that disk for use with swap using the swapon command directly.
3. If you are using LVM, you can use an entire logical volume as device swap. After creating logical volumes, use the swapon command on the designated logical volume.

    Device swap is more efficient than file system swap, and it should be created on a disk that has better throughput than the others.

File System Swap Space

The file system swap area can coexist with other files on a file system. It can be configured dynamically and is usually used when device swap space is full. Usually, a low priority level is attached with file system swap. You can use a directory in a file system that is used for file system swap. Also, you can put an upper limit on the file system swap if you don't want it to grow beyond a certain limit.

Primary Swap Space

The primary swap is the swap area that is available at boot time; at least one primary swap area must be available. It is usually located on the same disk used as the primary boot device for the system. If you are using LVM, you can designate a logical volume as the primary device swap.

Secondary Swap Space

A file system swap is always a secondary swap area. You can also use other device swap areas as secondary swap space. However, it is always a better idea to keep additional swap areas on different physical disk drives.

22.3   Creating Swap Space

After you have decided how much space you want to use for swap area and where it will be located, you can use the swapon command to actually create it. The swap space can also be created using SAM.

Creating Swap Space Using the Command Line

To create swap space on logical volume lvol3 in volume group vg03, use the following swapon command.

```
swapon /dev/vg03/lvol3
```

After you use the swapon command, the swap area is created, and it becomes immediately usable to the system. If the logical volume already contains a file system, you need to use the -f option with the swapon command to force the creation of the swap area.

If you are using the whole-disk approach and want to use the c2t5d0 disk for swap space only, use the following command.

```
swapon /dev/dsk/c2t5d0
```

If you are using the whole-disk approach and you have created a file system on disk c2t5d0, leaving some space at the end of the disk for swap space, use the following command.

```
swapon -e /dev/dsk/c2t5d0
```

Keep in mind that the -e and -f options are mutually exclusive and can't be used simultaneously while creating swap space.

If you want to create swap on c2t5d0 with a priority of 3, use this command.

```
swapon -p 3 /dev/dsk/c2t5d0
```

To create file system swap, you need to provide the mount point for the file system on which the swap space will be created. The swap space is created in a directory called `paging` on that file system. For example, the following command creates a file system swap on a file system mounted on the `/myswap` directory. The command puts a maximum limit of 200 Mbytes on the swap area. The actual directory that will be used for the swap space is `/myswap/paging`.

```
swapon -l 200M /myswap
```

When you create a file system swap, it can't be deleted while the system is using its swap space.

Creating Swap Space Using SAM

You can manage swap space using the `Disk and File Systems` area in SAM. You will use the `Swap` icon in this area and move a window similar to the one shown in Figure 22-1.

This figure shows the current swap space used on your system and its type. It also shows the amount of swap space, how much of this space is used, and how much is free. The `Enabled` column shows whether this swap area is currently enabled. It also shows if it will be enabled when you reboot the system. It also shows how much space on the swap area is currently reserved by the running processes and how much is free. You can use the `Actions` menu to add a device swap area or file system swap area as shown in the figure.

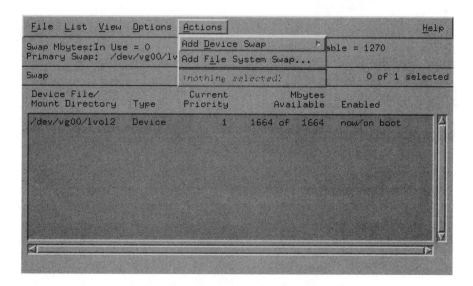

Figure 22–1   *Using SAM to manage swap space.*

Enabling Swap Space at System Startup

To activate swap area at boot time, you must put its information in the /etc/ fstab file. All swap system entries in this file can be activated using the following command at any time.

```
swapon -a
```

When you reboot your system, the /sbin/init.d/swap_start script gets executed in run level 1. This script executes the above command to turn on the swap.

A device swap using LVM logical volume lvol3 in volume group vg03 has an entry in /etc/fstab as shown here.

```
/dev/vg03/lvol3    .    swap    defaults    0    0
```

Note that there is no mount point specified with this line. Instead, a dot is put in the mount point column. The file system type is swap.

If you are using a whole disk, c2t5d0, as the swap space in the /etc/ fstab file, you will use an entry like the following.

```
/dev/dsk/c2t5d0    .    swap    defaults    0    0
```

In case of a file system swap, you don't mention the block device file. Instead, a dot is placed for it. However, you specify the mount point for the file system being used as swap space and use options with it, as you have used on the command line.

```
.    /myswap    swapfs    lim=200M    0    0
```

22.4 Monitoring Swap Space

The swapinfo command shows statistics about device swap as well as file system swap. A typical output of the command follows.

```
# swapinfo
          Kb      Kb      Kb       PCT    START/      Kb
TYPE    AVAIL  USED  FREE      USED    LIMIT  RESERVE   PRI   NAME
dev  1048576      0  1048576     0%        0        -     1   /dev/vg03/lvol2
dev  8888320      0  8888320     0%        0        -     1   /dev/vg03/lvol8
dev  8888320      0  8888320     0%        0        -     1   /dev/vg03/lvol9
reserve           -  317916  -317916
memory  12204752  972444  11232308       8%
#
```

This listing shows that the system has three device swap areas located on lvol2, lvol8, and lvol9 in volume group vg03. The kb AVAIL column shows total swap space on each of these areas; kb USED and kb FREE show the amount of swap space used and the amount of swap space free, respectively. The PCT USED shows the percentage of used swap space. The START/LIMIT column is usually zero except for the file system swap, where it shows the limit imposed on the swap space. The kb PRESERVE column is used for the file system swap area, where it shows the amount of space reserved for ordinary files on the file system. The PRI column shows the swap area priority. The NAME column shows the block device name for the device swap area and the mount point for the file system swap area.

You can use options with the swapinfo command as shown in Table 22-1.

Table 22–1 *Options Used with the* swapinfo *Command*

Option	Description
-d	Show device swap areas only
-f	Show file system swap areas only
-m	Display sizes in megabytes instead of kilobytes
-t	Add a total line at the end of the output, which shows the total amount of physical memory and swap area

22.5 Swap Space Priorities and Performance

Every swap area has a priority level, which is a number from 0 to 10. Number 0 is used for the highest priority. If there is more than one swap area in a system, the swap space having the highest priority is used first. When this swap space is full, the next in the row is used, and so on.

In case you have disks of different capabilities installed in your system, it is a good idea to keep the highest priority swap space on the best performing disk.

If two or more swap areas have the same priority, these are used in a round robin fashion. The round robin mechanism is better when all of the disks that contain swap space are of a similar type. In this way, you can distribute data read and write operations among disks used for the swap. This process is called swap interleaving.

If two file system swap areas have the same priority, they are used in round robin fashion as well. However, if a file system swap area and a device swap area have the same priority, preference goes to the device swap area.

As a general guideline, you should use the disks with better data throughput for the swap space. Also, you should try to distribute swap space among a number of disks so that any bottleneck caused by the physical movement of the disk head may be minimized. You should avoid using multiple swap spaces of the same priority on the same disk. In this case, the system will use the swap space in a round robin fashion and there will be a lot of disk head movement. Also, you should avoid using swap space on file systems that are already too busy.

■ Chapter Summary

Swap space is a disk area that is used to temporarily store memory pages if the demand for physical memory on the system increases beyond what is installed. Out of the total installed physical memory, some is used by kernel code and data structures. The remaining memory is available for other processes. If a process demands more memory, some of the pages that are not currently in use are swapped out to the disk swap area. Two daemons known as swapper and vhand are used for memory management. If you use a complete disk or logical volume for the swap area, it is called a device swap. If you are using some of a file system for the swap and the rest of it for ordinary files, it is called file system swap. Device swap is faster, whereas file system swap is more flexible. At least one primary swap area must be available to the system during the startup process. Usually some space on the boot disk is used for the primary swap.

Swap space may be created using the swapon command or SAM. The swapon command accepts options used to set the priority of the swap space. To activate swap space at boot time, place swap space entries in the /etc/fstab file. Swap performance can be greatly affected depending on the priorities used with different swap devices.

▲ CHAPTER REVIEW QUESTIONS

1. What are the different types of swap?

2. How is the swapper process used to handle thrashing?

3. What is the advantage of file system swap over device swap?

4. How do swap priorities affect system performance?

▲ TEST YOUR KNOWLEDGE

1. *Which swap area must be available at system bootup time?*

    A. primary swap

    B. file system swap

    C. disk swap

    D. secondary swap

2. *Where can you create a device swap?*

    A. a logical volume

    B. a whole disk used entirely for swap area

    C. free area at the end of a disk used in the whole-disk approach

    D. all of the above

3. *You have three identical disk drives. How would you like to use these for swap and file systems for the best swap performance?*

    A. Create file systems on two disks and use the third one as device swap.

    A. Create device swap areas on all three disks and assign them the same priority.

    A. Create device swap areas on all three disks and assign them different priorities.

    A. Use file system swap with the same priority on all three disks.

4. *You have three different swap areas in LVM. These are:*

    ```
    /dev/vg03/lvol2
    /dev/vg03/lvol8
    /dev/vg03/lvol9
    ```

    You want to stop using /dev/vg03/lvol2 *as swap space. How can you do it?*

    A. Use the swapoff command with /dev/vg03/lvol2 as an argument.

    B. Use the -d option with the swapon command and /dev/vg03/lvol2 as its argument.

    C. Delete the /dev/vg03/lvol2 entry in the /etc/fstab file and reboot the system.

    D. Create a new file system on this swap area using the newfs command.

5.   *What information is* not *displayed by the* swapinfo *command by default?*
   A. type of swap area
   B. total physical memory installed
   C. percentage of swap space used
   D. percentage of swap space free

System Backup and Recovery

Like any other machine, your HP-UX system can develop a fault at any time. As a system administrator, it is your responsibility to protect users' data and restore it as soon as possible. Individual users are concerned about their data, as they may consist of years of hard work. Business data are more critical, as most of the time the entire business depends on the safety of its data.

Data may be lost in a variety of circumstances, such as a system crash, hardware failure, natural disaster, or accidental file damage. The system backup process ensures that you will be able to recover data with minimum loss. While planning a system backup procedure, a number of data safety measures are kept in mind. The backed-up data are stored at a different location from that of the system. This is to avoid damage caused by fire or any natural disasters. Keeping multiple copies of backed-up data is useful so that in case you lose one copy, you will have another one.

439

It is also important to decide which system components should be backed up. You may decide to back up the entire system once per month, but it is not practicable to do it on a daily basis. If you decide to back up only partial data on a daily basis, you may decide to back up one or more components of the following.

- users' home directories
- important configuration information files; most of these files are kept in the /etc directory
- mailboxes
- databases

Even if you decide to back up the entire system, it is not wise to include /tmp or CD-ROM in it. The method of keeping a partial backup is called *incremental backup*, where multiple levels of backup are used. Each backup level is represented by a number. A lower backup level (higher number) saves only those files and directories that are created or modified after taking a backup at a higher level. While restoring data backed up using incremental backup, data backed up at the topmost level (least number) is restored first. After, that the next lower level data is restored and finally the most recent lowest level backup is restored. The incremental backup method saves time and amount of backup media.

In this chapter, you will learn types of backup and different methods used for taking a backup. Two of the these methods will be presented in detail. You will also use SAM to back up and restore data and schedule backups. Usually the backed up data can't be recovered until you have a running system. A tape created using Ignite-UX is used to boot and install a base system, in case your boot disk is damaged. The Ignite-UX backup and recovery method will also be discussed in this chapter.

23.1   Types of Backup

While creating a backup, you may not need to create a full system backup every day. This is because much of the data on your system are static in nature and do not change often. Examples of static data are system binary files and applications installed on your system. However, it is better to keep one full backup of your system just after the installation. You may also want to prepare a full backup every month. However, on a weekly basis, you can back up only those files that have been changed since the last monthly backup. Similarly, daily backups may contain only those files that have been changed since the last weekly backup.

The method of taking a partial backup is called an incremental backup. In an incremental backup scheme, different backup levels are defined. Backup level 0 is a full backup. If you perform a backup at level 1 after taking a full backup at backup level 0, only those files are backed up that were changed or created after taking the full backup. Similarly, if you perform a backup at level 2 after you have performed a backup at level 1, those files are backed up that have changed since backup level 1. However, keep in mind that all these backup levels are relative to each other. For example, if you have never performed a backup at level 0 or 1, a backup taken at backup level 2 will be a full backup. Every backup that is not a full backup is an incremental backup. A complete backup plan is usually a combination of a full backup and one or more incremental backups.

Full Backup

When you perform a backup using a backup level, its information is stored in a file that keeps a record of the date and time along with the backup level. This information is used when the next backup is taken to check whether a backup at a higher level has already been taken. For example, if you are using the fbackup command to back up a system, the information is stored in the /var/adm/fbackupfiles/dates file. A full backup is always taken if there is no record of any backup at a higher backup level. However, since the topmost backup level is 0, a backup taken at level 0 is always a full backup. It is, therefore, a general convention that a full backup is always taken at backup level 0.

A full backup can take a considerably long time depending on how much disk space is used with your system. You should design a backup schedule such that the full backup is performed when there are few or no users logged into the system. It is better to bring the system to single-user mode before starting a backup. If you are taking a full backup every month, the first weekend of the month may be a good time to prepare a full backup.

Incremental Backup

An incremental backup is a partial system backup where only those files are backed up that have been modified or created since the last backup at a higher level. If you are using level 0 for a full backup, you can use backup level 1 for a weekly backup to be carried out on a Friday night. For a daily backup, you may use backup level 2, which will back up only those files that have been changed since last Friday.

Incremental backup is useful for weekly and daily routines. Incremental backup takes much less time as only a part of the system is backed up. It also consumes less backup media. For example, you may need only one tape cartridge for an incremental backup, whereas a number of tape cartridges may be required for a full backup depending on how much disk capacity you are using with your system.

Recovering from an Incremental Backup

The method of recovery using an incremental backup involves more than one step, depending on how many backup levels you are using for your system. Let's suppose that you are using three backup levels as shown here.

Backup level 0   Used for taking a full backup on the first weekend of every month.

Backup level 1   Used for a weekly backup on Friday night.

Backup level 2   Used for a daily backup every night at 11 P.M.

If your system goes down on Thursday, you will perform three steps to fully restore the data. These three steps are:

1. Restore the monthly backup first. This will bring your system to the state it was at the first weekend of the month.
2. Restore the weekly backup taken on the previous Friday night. This will bring your system back to the state it was in last Friday.
3. Restore the daily backup taken yesterday (Wednesday), and it will bring your system back to the state at which it was at the end of yesterday. The only data you lose are the data entered today.

23.2 Methods of Backup and Restore

On HP-UX, you can use a number of methods for creating a backup and restoring data. However, data backed up with one method can't be restored with another method. Each of these methods has its own merits and demerits. On all types of UNIX systems, tar is the most widely used backup and restore method. However, HP-UX has a more-flexible mechanism that uses the `fbackup` and `frecover` commands. The common methods used for backup and restore are listed here.

- `fbackup/frecover`
- `cpio`
- `tar`
- `dump/restore`
- `vxdump/vxrestore`
- `pax`

While making a decision about which method should be used for a particular situation, consider the following criteria.

- Is this method supported on other UNIX platforms?
- Can it be used over a network?
- Does the method support incremental backup?
- How efficient is the method with tape utilization?
- How easy is it to make file selections from many directories while creating the backup?

Depending on your environment, one or more of these criteria may be of more importance than others. For example, if you want to copy some files from HP-UX to some other UNIX system, you can't use `fbackup`. Similarly, if you want to create a backup of files larger than 2 GBytes, `tar` can't be used.

Comparison of Backup Methods

Table 23-1 shows a comparison of the two most widely used methods on HP-UX. These are the `fbackup/frecover` and `tar` methods. In the `fbackup/frecover` method, the `fbackup` command is used for backup, and the `frecover` command is used for restore. In the case of `tar`, the same command is used both for backup and restore using command line options.

Table 23–1 *Comparison of Backup and Restore Methods*

Feature	`fbackup/frecover`	`tar`
Supported on other UNIX platforms	No	Yes
Across the network use	Yes	Yes
Incremental backup supported	Yes	Can add new files at the end of an archive but is not a true multilevel backup method
Tape utilization	Medium	High

Feature	`fbackup/frecover`	`tar`
Backup of files larger than 2 GBytes	Supported	Not supported
Multiple backups on a single tape	Not supported	Supported
Verify backup	Supported	Not supported
Find a file on tape	Possible, takes relatively less time	Possible, takes relatively more time as all of the tape is searched
Across the file system backup	Possible	Possible
Ease of selecting files from different directories	Relatively easy using graph files	Possible but relatively difficult
Use of extended file attributes	Possible	Not possible

Using dd

The dd command is not a general-purpose backup method in the true sense. It is used to copy raw data from one place to another. For example, you can use the dd command to make an exact copy of a disk as it reads and copies data bit by bit. It may be useful to make a copy of a bootable disk.

23.3 Using fbackup and frecover

The first thing to keep in mind about the fbackup and frecover commands is that they are specific to HP-UX. In case you want to transfer data to a non–HP-UX system, don't use fbackup. However, if you want to back up data for disaster recovery, use of these commands may be more flexible and convenient compared with tar. The fbackup command is used to create a backup and frecover is used to restore data. You can use 10 backup levels with fbackup ranging from 0 to 9. Zero is the topmost backup level and is used for a full backup. If the fbackup command is used without a backup level, level 0 is assumed as the default level, and a full backup is performed. Backup levels 1–9 are used for incremental backup. As in the three-level backup scheme mentioned earlier, use backup level 0 for a full backup, backup level 1 for a weekly backup, and backup level 2 for a daily backup. However, you can use any level between 2 and 9 for a daily backup.

Creating a Backup

The fbackup command requires some command line options to perform a backup. You should specify the media on which the backed-up data is going to be stored and the files to be included in the backup process. A typical fbackup command to backup the /etc directory and its output is as shown here.

```
# fbackup -v -f /dev/rmt/0m -i /etc
fbackup(1004): session begins on Wed Nov 24 10:25:17 1999
fbackup(3203): volume 1 has been used 1 time(s)
fbackup(3024): writing volume 1 to the output file /dev/rmt/0m
    1: / 2
    2: /etc 12
    3: /etc/#hosts 4040
    4: /etc/.pwd.lock 0
    5: /etc/.supported_bits 3
    6: /etc/MANPATH 1
    7: /etc/PATH 1
    8: /etc/SHLIB_PATH 1
    9: /etc/SnmpAgent.d 1
   10: /etc/SnmpAgent.d/snmpd.conf 14
   11: /etc/SnmpAgent.d/snmpinfo.dat 111
   12: /etc/TIMEZONE 1
<Output truncated from here>
  538: /etc/wall
  539: /etc/whodo
  540: /etc/wtmp
  541: /etc/xtab 0
  542: /etc/yp
  543: /etc/ypbind
  544: /etc/zoneinfo
fbackup(1005): run time: 21 seconds
fbackup(3055): total file blocks read for backup: 7674
fbackup(3056): total blocks written to output file /dev/rmt/0m:
  10158
```

This command backs up the /etc directory on tape drive /dev/rmt/0m. The output of the command is truncated from the middle to keep it short. At the start of execution, the fbackup command shows the start time of the backup. At the end of the backup process, the commands shows the total time used for the backup and the number of blocks written to the output media. The start and end times are used when you perform incremental backup to determine which files have already been backed up. The -i option is used to include files or directories in the backup. If you don't want to include a complete directory tree in the backup, you can use the -e option to exclude some of its subdirectories. For example, the following command includes every file under the /etc directory tree except the /etc/lp subdirectory.

```
fbackup -v -f /dev/rmt/0m -i /etc -e /etc/lp
```

Using Graph Files

For a routine backup process where only selective directories are included in the backup process, you need not specify all included directories and subdirectories on the command line. Instead, you can create a graph file that contains a list of all included and excluded directories. The following is an example of a typical graph file.

```
# cat gfile
i /etc
i /home
i /var/spool/cron
i /var/mail
e /etc/lp
#
```

The lines starting with the character i show directories that are included in the backup. The lines starting with the character e show excluded directories. An fbackup command that uses this graph file is like the following.

```
fbackup -v -g gfile -f /dev/rmt/0m
```

The fbackup command checks every line in the graph file and backs up all the directories included in the backup, excluding the others. You can create multiple graph files for routine backup tasks.

Creating an Incremental Backup

When you use the fbackup command with the -u option, it updates the /var/adm/fbackupfiles/dates file that keeps a record of fbackup activity. Don't forget that the dates file will be created or appended ONLY if the subdirectory /var/adm/fbackupfiles already exists. This is a simple text file and the information included in the file is as follows.

- date, start time, and end time of the backup
- backup level
- graph file used with the fbackup command

This information is used when creating a backup in the future. At the next backup, the fbackup command checks if the graph file was used with an earlier backup at a higher backup level (lower number) and the time of that backup. If the graph file is used with such a backup at an earlier time, only those files are backed up that have a time stamp newer than that time. To create a backup using the gfile at level 2, the following command is used. The first few lines are also shown where you can see additional information about the history of the previous backup. Since this is the first backup with the -u option, no history below level 2 is available.

```
# fbackup -v -g gfile -u -2 -f /dev/rmt/0m
fbackup(1421): no history is available for graph file gfile
   (below level 2)
fbackup(1004): session begins on Wed Nov 24 20:39:54 1999
fbackup(3203): volume 1 has been used 1 time(s)
fbackup(3024): writing volume 1 to the output file /dev/rmt/0m
   1: / 2
   2: /etc 12
```

Because no history of any backup above level 2 is available, this will be a full backup. Now information of this backup is stored in the /var/adm/ fbackupfiles/dates file, which will be used at the next backup time. Let's perform a backup at level 3 with the same graph file.

```
# fbackup -v -g gfile -u -3 -f /dev/rmt/0m
fbackup(1418): the last level 2 session for graph gfile was
         started  : Wed Nov 24 20:41:16 1999
         finished : Wed Nov 24 20:41:36 1999
fbackup(1004): session begins on Wed Nov 24 20:42:41 1999
fbackup(1019): warning: none of the specified files needed
   to be backed up
fbackup(1005): run time: 1 seconds
fbackup(3055): total file blocks read for backup: 0
fbackup(3056): total blocks written to output file : 0
```

No file is backed up as expected because a backup was performed at level 2 and none of the included files were changed after the completion of that backup. As you can see, the command also lists the start and finish times of the last backup.

It should be noted that incremental backup can only be performed using a graph file by using the -g option along with the -u option. If you include or exclude directories on the command line, the -u option can't be used with fbackup.

Other common options used with the fbackup command are shown in Table 23-2.

Table 23–2 *Options Used with the* fbackup *Command*

Option	Meaning
-f	Device used for backup media
-0 to -9	Backup level
-u	Update the /var/adm/fbackupfiles/dates file
-v	Verbose mode; display the activity of the command
-i	Include the path in the backup
-e	Exclude the path from the backup
-g	Graph file used with fbackup
-I	Create an index file showing a list of files backed up

Recovering Backed-up Data

The frecover command is used to restore a backup. While restoring, it compares files that already exist on the system and restores only those files that are needed. A typical frecover command to restore data from a tape drive is as follows.

```
frecover -x -v -f /dev/rmt/0m -g gfile
```

If you use this command and no file needs to be restored, it shows nothing, as all the files already exist. However, if you remove one file or directory from your system, it will restore it. Let's remove /home/lost+found and then use the same command again.

```
# rm -r /home/lost+found
# frecover -x -v -f /dev/rmt/0m -g gfile
drwxr-xr-x      root      root      /home/lost+found
#
```

Now only the removed directory is restored. If you want to recover everything, use the -r option with the frecover command. The frecover defaults to the /dev/rmt/0m tape drive, and the above command can also be used as:

```
frecover -x -v -g gfile
```

Options used with the frecover command are listed in Table 23-3.

Table 23–3 *Options Used with the* `frecover` *Command*

Option	Meaning
`-r`	Recover everything
`-g`	Use the graph file for the selection of recovered files
`-v`	Verbose mode; display the command activity
`-o`	Force the command to overwrite a new file with an older file
`-x`	Restore the selected files specified by the graph file or selected with the `-i` and `-e` options
`-i`	Include the files in the restore process
`-e`	Exclude the files in the restore process
`-f`	Use the device from which to restore data

23.4 Using tar

The `tar` method is the traditional UNIX backup and restore method. Its major benefit is that it can be used across many manufacturers' UNIX computers. The same command is used both for backup and restore purposes. The backup created using `tar` makes efficient use of the media.

Creating a Backup with tar

To create a backup of the `/etc` and `/home` directories using the `tar` command on a tape device, the command is as follows. The `tar` command uses `/dev/rmt/0m` as the default tape drive, so you can omit this on the command line.

```
# tar -cvf /dev/rmt/0m /etc /home
a /etc/MANPATH 1 blocks
a /etc/PATH 1 blocks
a /etc/SHLIB_PATH 1 blocks
a /etc/SnmpAgent.d/snmpinfo.dat 111 blocks
a /etc/SnmpAgent.d/snmpd.conf 14 blocks
a /etc/TIMEZONE 1 blocks
a /etc/X11/X0screens 35 blocks
a /etc/X11/X0devices 16 blocks
a /etc/X11/X0pointerkeys 25 blocks
a /etc/X11/rgb.txt 43 blocks
a /etc/X11/XHPKeymaps 553 blocks
a /etc/X11/fs/config 3 blocks
a /etc/X11/rgb.dir 8 blocks
a /etc/X11/rgb.pag 58 blocks
a /etc/X11/C/print/attributes/document 2 blocks
<Some part of the output is truncated here>
```

The `-c` option is used when creating a backup. You can also create a `tar` backup file on another file system instead of on a tape device. For this purpose, use a file name with the `-f` option instead of the device name. To create a tar backup of the `/home` directory in a file, `/extra/home.tar`, use the following command.

```
tar -cvf /extra/home.tar /home
```

To list the contents of a `tar` backup, use the `-t` option with the `tar` command. The following command lists the contents of a tape device.

```
tar -tvf /dev/rmt/0m
```

You can also use the command as follows, as `/dev/rmt/0m` is the default tape drive used by the `tar` command.

```
tar  -tv
```

Restoring Data Using tar

To restore data from a `tar` backup, use the `-x` option with the `tar` command. The following command restores data from a tape backup device.

```
# tar -xvf /dev/rmt/0m
x MANPATH, 279 bytes, 1 tape blocks
x PATH, 163 bytes, 1 tape blocks
x SHLIB_PATH, 9 bytes, 1 tape blocks
x SnmpAgent.d/snmpinfo.dat, 56769 bytes, 111 tape blocks
x SnmpAgent.d/snmpd.conf, 6959 bytes, 14 tape blocks
x TIMEZONE, 21 bytes, 1 tape blocks
<Some output of the command is truncated here>
```

Study Break

Creating Incremental Backup

After learning backup and recover methods, let's create an incremental backup using the `fbackup` command. First, create a graph file to include directories `/sbin`, `/home` and `/etc`. Use this file to create a backup at backup level 0 without the `-u` option. Now create a backup with the same graph file at level 1. You will see that this is again a full backup instead of an incremental one. This is because the `fbackup` log file was not updated during the last backup, as you did not use the `-u` option. Remember to also use the `-g` option whenever you use the `-u` option. Now create a backup at level 0 with the `-u` option. After that, another backup at level 1 will be an incremental backup.

23.5 Using SAM to Back Up and Restore Data

SAM can be used to create automated or interactive backup. When you go to the SAM Backup and Recovery area, a window like the one shown in Figure 23-1 appears.

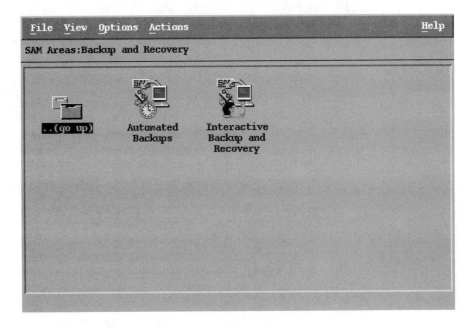

Figure 23-1 *SAM* Backup and Recovery *area.*

Click on the Automated Backups icon, and the window shown in Figure 23-2 will appear. Here an empty screen shows that there is no automated backup scheduled. To schedule a backup, first you need to add a device on which the backup will be created. This is done using the Actions menu as shown in the figure.

When you move to the window shown in Figure 23-3, you will put in the information for the backup device, backup scope, and backup time.

When you click on the Specify Backup Device button, SAM will search for valid devices and will show you a list of the devices, as shown in Figure 23-4.

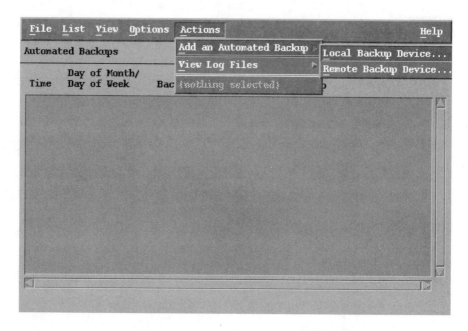

Figure 23–2 *Adding a device for* Automated Backup.

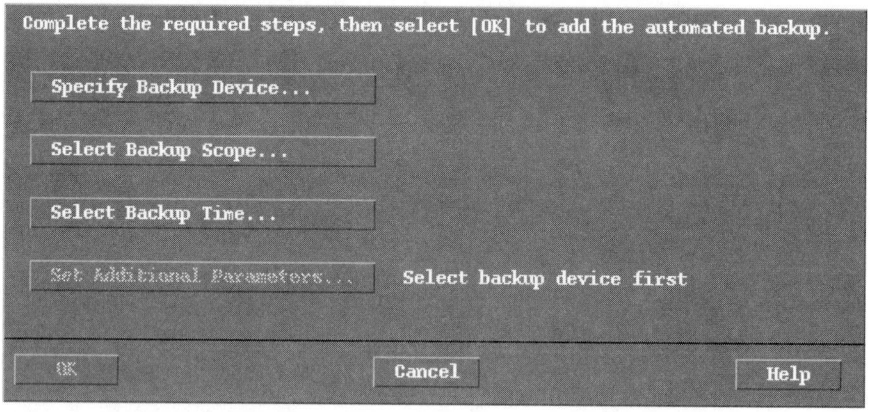

Figure 23–3 *Option selection for* Automated Backup.

Valid Backup Devices on the System:
Hardware Path Description
10/12/5.0.0 C1533A 4 GB DDS Data Compression Tape Dr
OK
Cancel
Help

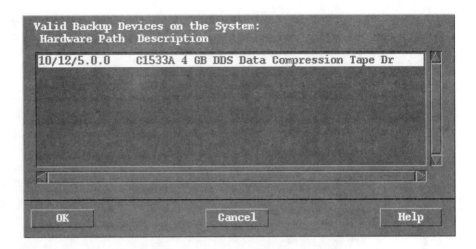

Figure 23-4 *List of detected backup devices.*

You have to select one of the displayed devices in Figure 23-4 and press the `OK` button. Since the device shown here is a tape backup device and you can use different tape characteristics, the window shown in Figure 23-5 will appear, where you can select a tape device for a particular set of characteristics. Let's select the `0m` device for the tape drive.

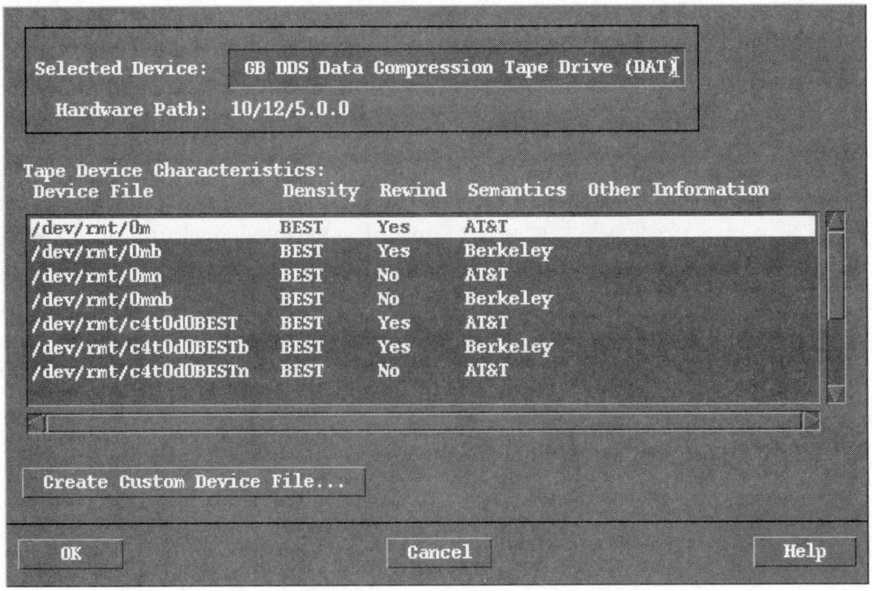

Selected Device: GB DDS Data Compression Tape Drive (DAT)
Hardware Path: 10/12/5.0.0
Tape Device Characteristics:
Device File Density Rewind Semantics Other Information
/dev/rmt/0m BEST Yes AT&T
/dev/rmt/0mb BEST Yes Berkeley
/dev/rmt/0mn BEST No AT&T
/dev/rmt/0mnb BEST No Berkeley
/dev/rmt/c4t0d0BEST BEST Yes AT&T
/dev/rmt/c4t0d0BESTb BEST Yes Berkeley
/dev/rmt/c4t0d0BESTn BEST No AT&T
Create Custom Device File...
OK
Cancel
Help

Figure 23-5 *Selecting tape device characteristics.*

Now you will select `Backup Scope`. Here you select directories to be included or excluded from the backup as shown in Figure 23-6. This will help in creating a graph file for the backup.

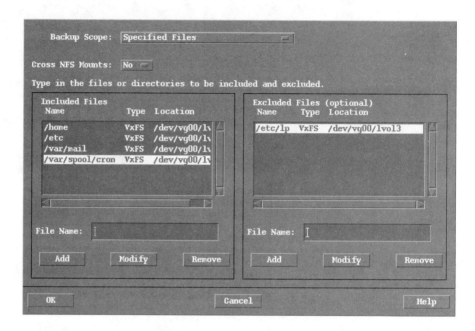

Figure 23–6 *Selection of directories to be included or excluded from the backup.*

In the last step, you have to select the backup time, as shown in Figure 23-7.

After making these selections, you go back to the window shown in Figure 23-2, but now a list of scheduled backups appear in the window, as shown in Figure 23-8. The first line shows that a full backup will be performed on the first day of the month at 1 A.M. The second line shows that an incremental backup will be done on the days from Monday to Friday at 2 A.M.

During the scheduled backup time, a tape cartridge must be present in the tape drive. You can replace the tape cartridge during the daytime, and the backup may be unattended in the night.

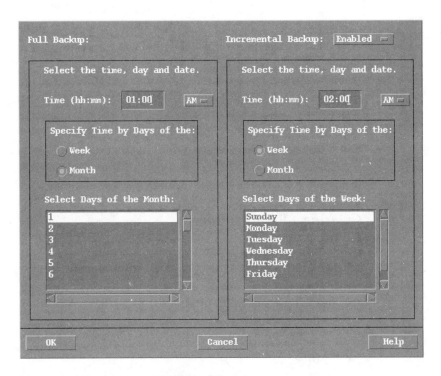

Figure 23–7 *Selection of the backup time.*

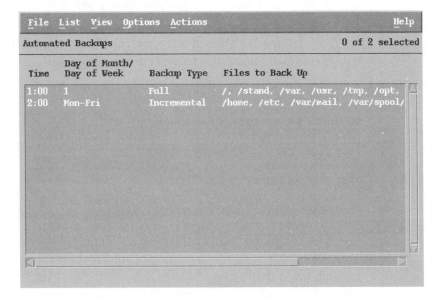

Figure 23–8 *List of scheduled backups.*

23.6 Using Ignite-UX

Ignite-UX is an additional software package that is used to recover a system from a damaged boot disk. No data can be restored if you are not able to boot a system, as commands for restoring data can be executed only on a running system. The Ignite-UX package contains commands to create a bootable tape. The bootable tape contains all critical system and configuration files so that a minimal system can be rebuilt using this tape. The necessary components of a recovery tape are the image of the boot area of the system boot disk, root volume group (`vg00`), and critical system files.

Creating a Recovery Tape

If you have installed the Ignite-UX package on your system, you can use the `/opt/ignite/bin/make_recovery` command to create a recovery tape. Other than the boot area of the system disk, the following four directories are completely backed up by default.

- the `/stand` directory containing the HP-UX kernel
- the `/sbin` directory containing commands and scripts used at boot time
- the `/dev` directory containing device files including those for the root volume group
- the /etc directory containing configuration information

Some selected files from other partitions are also backed up. To create a full recovery tape of all files in `vg00`, use the `-A` option with the command. A typical command to create a recovery disk is shown here.

```
/opt/ignite/bin/make_recovery -A -C -v -d /dev/rmt/0m
```

or, since `/dev/rmt/0m` is the default, just use:

```
/opt/ignite/bin/make_recovery   -A   -C   -v
```

or even more simply

```
/opt/ignite/bin/make_recovery   -ACv
```

This command creates a full recovery on the tape device. The `-c` option is used to create a log file consisting of information about backed-up files. This log file is used when updating a recovery tape. The log file name is `/var/opt/ignite/recovery/makerec.last`.

Updating a Recovery Tape

You can use the `check_recovery` command at any time to check if a new Ignite-UX recovery tape is needed. This command compares system files with the information contained in the Ignite-UX log file. Before using this command, there must be a previous recovery tape created using the `-c` option. If the command reports that some system files have been changed, you can create a recovery tape again. The `check_recovery` command should be run from time to time.

■ Chapter Summary

Backup and restore are important system administration tasks that ensure data safety. You can take a full backup or an incremental backup depending on the frequency and time needed for the backup process. HP-UX provides a number of utilities for backup and restore. The `fbackup/frecover` and `tar` utilities are the most important of these. In addition to these command line tools, you can also use SAM for scheduling backups. All of these methods have their own pros and cons. A particular method is used depending upon requirements.

It is recommended that regardless of the backup type, when using `fbackup`, backup levels should always be used. Backup level 0 is always a full backup. If a backup is carried out at another level after a full backup, it backs up only those files that have been created or modified after the full backup. Backups created with the `fbackup` command should routinely use a graph file that contains a list of directories included or excluded from the backup. The `fbackup/frecover` combination is more flexible but can't be used across different UNIX platforms. The `tar` command can be used to transfer data from one UNIX system to another and makes better use of the backup media. However, it is not as flexible as `fbackup/frecover`.

A backup can be restored only on a working system. If the boot disk is damaged, you can recover it with an Ignite-UX recovery tape. After that, you can restore the backed-up data from a full or incremental backup. The `make_recovery` command is used for creating the Ignite-UX recovery tape and the `check_recovery` command is used to verify that the recovery tape is up-to-date.

▲ CHAPTER REVIEW QUESTIONS

1. What is difference between a full backup and an incremental backup?

2. What is the advantage of `tar` over `fbackup`?

3. What is the role of the graph file in a backup?

4. Why do you use an Ignite-UX recovery tape? Isn't it sufficient to make a full backup of a system?

▲ TEST YOUR KNOWLEDGE

1. *You are using incremental backup in two levels. The levels used are 1 and 5. When restoring data, in what order will you restore the backup?*

   A. first level 1 and then level 5

   B. first level 5 and then level 1

   C. The order doesn't matter; you can restore in any order.

   D. You need a level 0 backup in addition to these two backups to recover the system.

2. *You used the* `tar` *command to back up your system. Which command will you use to restore it?*

   A. `tar`

   B. `restore`

   C. `untar`

   D. `recover`

3. *You are using files larger than 2 GBytes on your system. Which utility will you prefer to use to back up the system?*

   A. `fbackup`

   B. `tar`

   C. `cpio`

   D. `dump`

4. *While creating incremental backup at level 2, you used the following command.*

   ```
   fbackup -v -g gfile -2 -f /dev/rmt/0m
   ```

   The next day you performed backup at level 3 using the following command.

   ```
   fbackup -v -g gfile -u -3 -f /dev/rmt/0m
   ```

Which files will be backed up?

A. all files listed in graph file `gfile`

B. files that have been modified or created after the first backup

C. only files newly created after the first backup

D. only those files that have been modified after the first backup

5. *Which backup level is always a full backup, no matter how the previous backup has been performed?*

A. level 0

B. level 1

C. level 9

D. a backup created with the `level=full` option on the command line

6. *Which* `tar` *command is used to restore data?*

A. `tar -xvf /dev/rmt/0m`

B. `tar -cvf /dev/rmt/0m`

C. `tar -tvf /dev/rmt/0m`

D. `tar -tf /dev/rmt/0m`

7. *Why is a recovery tape made with the* `make_recovery` *command important?*

A. Without creating a recovery tape, you can't use the `tar` command for backup.

B. Without creating a recovery tape, you can't use the `fbackup` command for backup.

C. Without creating a recovery tape, you can't recover from a damaged boot disk by booting off your recovery tape.

D. The recovery tape is used with the `frecover` command.

8. *Which statement is true?*

A. SAM can be used to create a full backup only.

B. SAM can be used to create both full and incremental backups.

C. A time schedule for backups can't be specified in SAM.

D. It is not possible to use SAM for interactive backup and restore.

9. *What information is present in* Backup Scope *when using SAM?*
    A. the time at which the backup will be performed
    B. the directories included in the backup
    C. the device on which the data will be backed up
    D. all of the above

Automating Jobs

Routine system administration tasks should be done on a regular basis. For example, you must clean out temporary files and trim system log files; otherwise, file systems will become full. Similarly, system backup is an important task that is done on a regular basis, as you have studied in Chapter 23. Some of these tasks may take a long time, and it is not practical to carry out these tasks manually. You can also schedule a task that is to be done on a regular basis. An example of this may be the preparation of weekly or monthly reports. Other than these routine tasks that are carried out repeatedly, sometimes you may also need to run commands only once at a specified time. For example, you may need to run a command at 2 A.M., but you may not like to be awakened for this purpose at that time.

Tasks can be scheduled using cron. You can specify a time at which a task must be carried out. At system startup, cron runs as a daemon and is started at run level 2. It reads its configuration files and schedules jobs listed in these files. The `cron` writes its activities to a log file. The system administrator can configure `cron` to allow or deny job scheduling for common system users. Selected system users may be granted `cron` access. Each user who is granted `cron` access can create his or her own configuration file containing tasks to be scheduled and the time needed for these tasks. HP-UX provides commands that can be used to create, edit, list, or delete the configuration files.

There are two types of jobs that are scheduled using `cron`: jobs that are executed only once and jobs that are executed repeatedly. If you want to execute a job repeatedly after a specified interval of time, you use the `crontab` command. If you want to execute a job only once, you use the `at` command. This chapter will start with an introduction to the `cron` daemon that schedules all jobs. Then you will learn how to use `crontab` files to execute jobs repeatedly. Finally, you will use the `at` command to execute a job only once at a specified time.

24.1   Introduction to cron

Jobs may be scheduled to run at a specified time using `cron`. It serves two types of jobs, submitted either by the `crontab` or the `at` command. The `crontab` command creates a file that is read and executed according to the schedule contained within the file. Programs listed in these files are executed on a regular basis. On the other hand, the `at` command creates files that are removed after the execution of the program. Thus, any program scheduled using the `at` command is executed only once. The `cron` daemon is started at boot time at run level 2. It reads `crontab` and `at` files created in the `/var/spool/cron` directory at startup and schedules the programs for a given time.

The cron Daemon

The `cron` daemon is started at run level 2 and stopped at run level 1. A variable named `CRON` in the `/etc/rc.config.d/cron` file controls whether the daemon will be started at boot time. If this variable value is 1, the daemon is started at boot time, and if the value is zero (0), the daemon is not started. The startup script for the `cron` daemon is `/sbin/init.d/cron` and is normally executed at boot time. To start the daemon manually, you can use the following command.

```
/sbin/init.d/cron start
```

To stop the cron daemon at any time, use the following command.

```
/sbin/init.d/cron stop
```

Start and stop link files for this script are /sbin/rc2.d/S730cron and /sbin/rc1.d/K270cron. At startup, the daemon reads its configuration files and schedules its tasks. Other than crontab files, the cron daemon also schedules programs timed with the at command.

If you make a change to any of the configuration files manually, you may stop and restart the cron script so that it reads its configuration files again. However, if you use the crontab command to modify a configuration file, the command automatically updates cron schedules and you don't need to restart the daemon.

Granting Access to Users

Two files are used to allow/deny access to the cron daemon for ordinary system users. These files are /var/adm/cron/cron.allow and /var/adm/cron/cron.deny. If neither of these files is present, only the **root** user can access cron. If both of these files are present, the precedence goes to the cron.allow file, and all users who are listed in this file are allowed to use cron. If cron.allow exists but is empty, only the **root** user can use cron. If only the cron.deny file exists, all users except those listed in this file are allowed to use cron. Table 24-1 shows the use of these two files in allowing or denying cron access.

Table 24–1 *Role of* cron *Files to Allow/Deny Use of* cron.

cron.allow	cron.deny	Effect on User
Not exists	Not exists	Only the **root** user can use cron.
Not exists	Exists	All users except those listed in cron.deny can use cron.
Not exists	Exists (empty)	All users can use cron.
Exists	Not exists	Only those users listed in the cron.allow file can use cron.
Exists	Exists	Only those users listed in the cron.allow file can use cron.
Exists (empty)	Not exists	Only the **root** user can use cron.
Exists (empty)	Exists	Only the **root** user can use cron.

> **Warning**
>
> You must be careful of the case where `cron.allow` does not exist and `cron.deny` exists but is empty. In this case, all users of the system are granted `cron` access.

When a user tries to create a schedule, these two files are checked for access rights. Only those users who are granted `cron` access are allowed to create schedules.

Log Files

The `cron` daemon creates its log files in the `/var/adm/cron` directory. The `/var/adm/cron/log` file is used to log all `cron` activity. Contents of the file look like the following.

```
!*** cron started *** pid = 1961 Sun Nov 11 14:41:11 EST 1999
>  CMD:  /home/root/trimlog >> /home/root/trimlog.log
>  root 2316 c Sun Nov 14 14:42:00 EST 1999
<  root 2316 c Sun Nov 14 14:42:02 EST 1999
>  CMD:  /home/root/cleandisk  >> /home/root/cleandisk.log
>  root 2459 c Sun Nov 14 14:43:00 EST 1999
<  root 2459 c Sun Nov 14 14:52:00 EST 1999
>  CMD: /usr/sbin/lpsched -v
>  root 2672 c Sun Nov 14 14:45:00 EST 1999
<  root 2672 c Sun Nov 14 14:45:06 EST 1999
```

As you can see from the file, the first line shows the start time of the `cron` daemon and its PID. This time is logged whenever `cron` starts. Lines containing `CMD` show a command that is executed. Lines that start with the greater-than symbol (`>`) show the start time of the job with an ID number. Lines starting with the less-than symbol (`<`) show the completion time of the job.

24.2 Automating Jobs Using the crontab Command

All users who are allowed to use `cron` can create a file in their home directory using an editor and then submit it for execution using the `crontab` command. If you are logged in as user **boota** and have created a file `mycrontab` in your home directory, the following command will create a file with name `boota` in the `/var/spool/cron/crontabs` directory having the same contents as `mycrontab`.

```
crontab mycrontab
```

The file contains scheduled programs during which user commands will be executed.

Format of crontab Files

The `crontab` file for each user is stored in the `/var/spool/cron/crontabs` directory with the file name being the same as the person's user name. A `crontab` file for user **boota** has the name `/var/spool/cron/crontabs/boota`. A line in the file that starts with a hash symbol (#) is considered a comment. An entry for a scheduled program in the file contains six fields. The first five fields are used to specify the time and the last field shows the command that is to be executed at that time. A typical entry in the file is shown in Figure 24-1.

The first field in a line shows the minute of the hour at which the command will be executed. The value of this field may be from 0 to 59. In this figure, the value is 30. The next field shows the hour of the day. Its value may range from 0 to 23. The third field shows the date of the month and its range is 1–31. The fourth field is the month, and its value can range from 1 to 12. The fifth field shows the day of the week, and its value ranges from 0 to 6, where 0 = Sunday, 1 = Monday, etc.

If multiple values are to be used in a field, these are separated by commas. An entry 1,16 in the date field shows that the command will be executed on the first and sixteenth days of a month. An asterisk shows all values. For example, an asterisk in the month field shows that the command will be executed every month. The command shown in Figure 24-1 copies the `/etc/passwd` file to `/etc/passwd.bak` on the first and sixteenth days of every month.

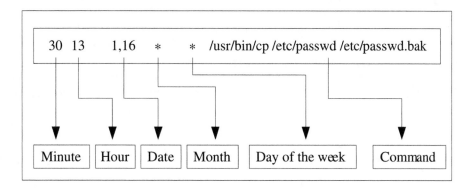

Figure 24–1 *A typical entry in a* `crontab` *file.*

Editing crontab Files

The files used for scheduling cron tasks are edited using the crontab command. With no option, it takes input from stdin and saves it in the user crontab file, overwriting the older file. If you provide a file name on the command line, this file will be copied as your crontab file. For example, the following command will copy a file named mycrontab to /var/spool/cron/crontabs/boota, if you are logged in as user **boota**.

```
crontab mycrontab
```

It is a good practice to create a file using the vi editor in your home directory and then submit it for execution using the above command. You can also use this command to list or delete crontab files. Other options that can be used with the crontab command are as follows.

-l   Lists the contents of the current crontab file for the user

-e   Edits the crontab file for the user

-r   Removes the crontab file for a user

Sample crontab File for a Root User

A sample crontab file is shown here that contains three tasks. The first task (/dailybackup) is a shell script that is executed once every day at 11:30 P.M. for daily backup. The second one is used to remove core files every hour. The third task is also a shell script that is used to trim log files, and it runs at 11:00 P.M. twice a month on the first and the sixteenth days.

```
# crontab file for root
# format:
# min hour day month dow command
30    23    *    *    *    /dailybackup
# remove core every hour
0    *    *    *    *    find / -name core -exec rm {} \;
# Trim log files 1st. and 16th. Of every month at 11 PM.
0    23    1,16    *    *    /trimlog
#
```

Study Break

Submitting a Job Using the crontab Command

Log in as **root** and use the `crontab -l` command to list what schedules are already created. Copy the `/var/spool/cron/crontab/root` file to your home directory as `root.bak`. Use the `crontab -r` command to remove the schedules. Now if you again list the contents of the files, you will see an error message showing that the system is not able to open your file. Create a new file using the `crontab -e` command and schedule a command `ll` to be executed every 5 minutes, and redirect its output to a temporary file in your home directory. Wait for some time and you will find output of the command in the file to which you redirected the output. Remove the newly created file and install the old file using the `crontab root.bak` command. Again list this file to make sure that it is indeed installed.

24.3 Automating Jobs Using the at Command

The at command is used to execute a job at a particular time only once compared with `crontab`, where jobs are executed repeatedly. The `cron` daemon is responsible for executing at jobs at the required time. A record of spooled at jobs is created in the `/var/spool/cron/atjobs` directory, where a separate file is created for each job. This file contains commands to be executed and the values of environment variables.

Submitting a Job

To submit a job, you start the at command on the command line by specifying the time at which the job is to be scheduled. After that, you type in the commands that are to be executed at that time. When you have finished entering the commands, use the CTRL-D key combination to end the command entering process. A sample session used with the at command is as follows.

```
# at -t 12081210
/home/root/trimlog
CTRL-D
job 945018720.a at Sun Dec 08 12:10:00 1999
#
```

Here you have used the at command to execute a job on December 8, 1999 at 12:10 A.M. After you start the command on the command line with the time, you go to the next line, which is blank. Here you type the command that is to be executed at the specified time. You can enter multiple commands or program names by pressing the [Enter] key and going to the next line. When you have finished entering the command names, pressing the [CTRL]-[D] key combination will end the at session, and you will get back the command prompt.

When you press the [CTRL]-[D] combination to end entering command names, the at command displays a line showing you that a job has been scheduled. It shows the job ID and the time at which the job will be executed.

You can specify time with the at command in a number of ways, as shown in the following examples.

```
at 1210 Dec 08
at 12:10 Dec 08
at 12:10am tomorrow
at now + 1 day
at now + 10 minutes
```

The first and second examples have the same time setting as you have already used. In the third example, the job will be executed at 12:10 A.M. the next day. In the fourth example, the job will be executed at the current time tomorrow. In the last example, the job will be executed after 10 minutes.

You can also list commands or jobs to be executed in a file and then specify that file name on the command line with the at command. In the following example, a file named myfile contains commands to be executed after one hour.

```
at -f myfile now + 1 hour
```

Listing and Deleting at Jobs

To list the current jobs, you can use the at -l command as shown here.

```
# at -l
945018720.a     Sun Dec 08 12:10:00 1999
#
```

This command lists job IDs and the time at which these jobs will be executed. To remove the above job, use the following command containing the job ID.

```
at -r 945018720.a
```

When you submit a job, a spool file is created in the /var/spool/cron/atjobs directory. This file has the same name as the job ID and contains commands to create environment variable values that were present at the time of submitting the job in addition to a list of commands that will be executed. The file created by the above job is shown here.

```
# cat /var/spool/cron/atjobs/945018720.a
: at job
export _; _=/usr/bin/at
export MANPATH; MANPATH=/usr/share/man/%L:/usr/share/man:/
    usr/contrib/man/%L:/usr/contrib/man:/usr/local/man/%L:/
    usr/local/man:/optn
export PATH; PATH=/usr/bin:/usr/ccs/bin:/usr/contrib/bin:/
    opt/nettladm/bin:/opt/pd/bin:/usr/bin/X11:/usr/contrib/
    bin/X11:/opt/upgra.
export EDITOR; EDITOR=vi
export LOGNAME; LOGNAME=root
export MAIL; MAIL=/var/mail/root
export ERASE; ERASE=\^H
export SHELL; SHELL=/usr/bin/sh
export HOME; HOME=/home/root
export TERM; TERM=vt320
export PWD; PWD=/home/root
export TZ; TZ=EST5EDT
export LINES; LINES=24
# @(#) Revision: 27.1
cd /home/root
ulimit 4194304
umask 22
/home/root/trimlog
#
```

The variables are saved to create the same environment as the user is using at the time of submitting the job. When cron runs the job, it creates a shell and executes the commands in this file to create the environment and then executes the actual job. Note that the programs or command names submitted with the at command are present in the last line of the output.

Allowing/Denying User Access

Like crontab, use of the at command can also be restricted using the /var/adm/cron/at.allow and /var/adm/cron/at.deny files. The effect of these two files is identical to the one used with the cron.allow/cron.deny files and is listed in Table 24-2.

Table 24–2 *Roles of the at Files to Allow/Deny Use of the* at *Command*

at.allow	at.deny	Effect on User
Not exists	Not exists	Only the **root** user can use at.
Not exists	Exists	All users except those listed in at.deny can use at.
Not exists	Exists (empty)	All users can use at.
Exists	Not exists	Only those users listed in the at.allow can use at.
Exists	Exists	Only those users listed in the at.allow can use at.
Exists (empty)	Not exists	Only the **root** user can use at.
Exists (empty)	Exists	Only the **root** user can use at.

Warning

You must be careful of the case where at.allow does not exist and at.deny exists but is empty. In this case, all users of the system are granted at access.

■ Chapter Summary

The crontab utility is used to schedule jobs to be run at specified times. Jobs are run by the cron daemon, which is started at boot time. The cron daemon stores a log of its activity in the /var/adm/cron/log file. If you want to execute a job only once, you use the at command. In case a job is to be run repeatedly, such as daily system backup, crontab files are used. Jobs in the crontab files are listed in a specified format. Each user has his or her own crontab file in the /var/spool/cron/crontabs directory. Access to the crontab files is restricted by using cron.allow and cron.deny files in the /var/adm/cron directory. Access to the at command is restricted using the at.allow and at.deny files in the same directory. To create, edit, list, and delete crontab files, you use the crontab command. To time a job for one-time execution, you use the at command. Job files created by the at command are stored in the /var/spool/cron/atjobs directory and contain all environment variable settings in addition to the command itself.

▲ CHAPTER REVIEW QUESTIONS

1. What is the difference between jobs submitted using the `crontab` and those using the `at` commands?

2. Write a `crontab` file entry that executes the `ll` command every minute.

3. Schedule a daily backup at 2 A.M. using a graph file that creates a backup of the `/home` directory.

▲ TEST YOUR KNOWLEDGE

1. *At what run level is the* cron *daemon started?*
    A. 1
    B. 2
    C. S
    D. 4

2. *On your system, file* cron.allow *exists and is empty. File* cron.deny *is also present and contains the login name of user* **boota**. *Who is allowed to use* cron?
    A. all users
    B. all users except user **boota**
    C. only the **root** user
    D. Nobody is allowed to use cron.

3. *A* crontab *entry is shown below. At what time will the* trimlog *command be executed?*

    ```
    0   *   1,6   1    *    /home/root/trimlog
    ```

    A. At 1 A.M. and 6 A.M. of the first day of every month.
    B. At 1 A.M. and 6 A.M. of every day of January.
    C. At every hour of the first and sixth days of January.
    D. At every hour of the first and sixth days of the first week.

4. *It is exactly 12:00 noon. You want to execute a command at the same time the next day. Which of the following commands will you use?*
    A. at now + 1 day
    B. at now + 24 hour
    C. at 12 pm tomorrow
    D. All of the above.

System Performance Monitoring

Monitoring system activity provides information to diagnose a problem. Performance of individual system components plays a vital role in overall system response. HP-UX provides many tools that are used to monitor different system activities. Using these tools enables you to find any bottlenecks causing degradation in system performance. A slow system response may not always be due to a slow CPU. It may be caused by a slow disk, less memory installed in the system, a congested network, or some other slow responding system component. To diagnose the actual problem of a slow system, these tools are very helpful.

Some of the tools are bundled with HP-UX, while others may be purchased separately. One of the most important additional tools is GlancePlus/UX, which is a comprehensive monitoring system. It generates reports for a number of system components and activities.

In this chapter, we will start with a list of available tools. We will discuss some of these tools in more detail as we move along in this chapter. Command-line tools will be used to monitor the CPU, disk, virtual memory, and process activity. System Activity Reporter (sar) will be used to check a number of parameters. Another tool, top, will be used to list processes that heavily use CPU resources. In the last part of the chapter, we will go through GlancePlus and use it in both text and graphic modes.

The study of these tools is important for effective system administration. When upgrading a slow system, if you are not able to diagnose the actual cause of a slow performance of a system, you may make a wrong decision.

25.1   Tools Used for Performance Monitoring

HP-UX has a number of tools that are bundled with the operating system. Additional sophisticated tools can be purchased separately. The bundled tools usually work in text mode. Some of these utilities are listed here.

- The iostat command is used to monitor I/O activity for disk drives.
- The vmstat command is used to monitor activity of virtual memory.
- The netstat and lanadmin commands are used to monitor network activity such as incoming and outgoing network traffic, use of protocols, IP addresses assigned to interface adapters, etc.
- The top utility is used to monitor processes that are utilizing more CPU time. Processes are listed in a sorted form. Percentage of CPU idle time is also displayed. This utility also shows some information about real and virtual memory.
- The System Activity Reporter (sar) shows a number of kernel parameters and CPU utilization.

Other than these utilities, you may also use GlancePlus, which is an additional software application. It has both text and graphic interfaces. This tool provides comprehensive system information. It can be used to collect information including the following.

- list of processes
- CPU utilization
- memory utilization
- network utilization

- disk utilization
- swap space utilization

GlancePlus plots graphical representation of the data collected in real time so that you may have an overview of the running system. It will be discussed in more detail later in this chapter.

Monitoring Memory Performance

Virtual memory statistics are displayed using the vmstat command. It displays information about processes, page faults, memory, and CPU as shown here. (The output is formatted to fit onto the page.)

```
# vmstat -n
VM
   memory                        page
 avm     free    re    at    pi    po    fr    de    sr
2275   44047     2     0     0     0     1     0     0
       faults
 in      sy    cs
106      88    33


CPU
     cpu            procs
 us sy id    r      b     w
  0  0 99    0      0     0
#
```

The -n option is used with the command to improve the format of the output.

The virtual memory (VM) part of the output is divided into three parts: memory, page, and faults. The explanation of fields under the memory subheading is as follows.

avm   Active virtual memory. These are the pages that have been assigned to some processes.

free   Free pages.

A number of columns are present under the page subheading.

re   Page reclaims. A large number shows a memory shortage.

at   Address translation faults.

pi   Pages paged in.

po   Pages paged out.

fr   Pages freed per second.

de   Anticipated short term memory shortfall.

sr   Pages scanned by clock algorithm, per second.

The `faults` subheading shows trap and interrupt rate averages per second over the last 5 seconds.

in   Device interrupts per second.

sy   System calls per second.

cs   CPU context switch rate.

The CPU part of the output has been divided into two subparts, `cpu` and `procs`. The columns under the `cpu` subheading show CPU utilization.

us   User time for normal and low-priority processes.

sy   System time.

id   CPU idle time.

An explanation of the different fields under the `procs` subheading is as given here.

r   The process is in run queue.

b   Number of processes blocked for some resource.

w   It shows runable but swapped out from the main memory.

More-detailed information can be displayed using this command using different options at the command line. See the manual pages for more details.

Monitoring Disk Performance

Performance of disk I/O is monitored using the `iostat` command. This command formats the data of each disk in four columns as shown next.

```
# iostat
  device     bps      sps     msps
  c0t6d0     105     10.8      1.0
  c0t5d0       0      0.0      1.0
#
```

An explanation of these columns is given here.

device   Shows the actual disk device for which the report is given.

bps   Shows kilobytes transferred per second to/from the device.

sps   Lists the number of seeks per second.

msps   The time in milliseconds per average seek.

If you have a number of disks installed, the command is very useful to determine if one of these disks is heavily used. In such a case, you may redistribute data on different disks such that every disk is sharing the system load. A number of factors may cause heavy utilization of only one disk. For example, you may have configured high-priority swap space on the same disk which is already loaded with a database.

By default, the iostat command displays its output once and then exits. If you want to display the disk statistics after every four seconds for five times, you can use the following command.

```
# iostat 4 5

  device     bps      sps     msps
  c0t6d0     105     10.8      1.0
  c0t5d0       0      0.0      1.0

  c0t6d0      21      3.0      1.0
  c0t5d0       0      0.0      1.0

  c0t6d0      31      5.8      1.0
  c0t5d0       0      0.0      1.0

  c0t6d0      12      2.0      1.0
  c0t5d0       0      0.0      1.0

  c0t6d0       8      3.0      1.0
  c0t5d0       0      0.0      1.0
#
```

The first parameter shows the delay in seconds between executions, and the second parameter shows the number of times the statistics will be calculated. The above output shows that most of the load is on disk c0t6d0.

Using top

The most widely used tool for system performance monitoring is top and it is available on almost all UNIX systems. It shows the top CPU utilization processes. When you start top, it displays a screen of information after every five seconds. A typical screen shown by top is like the one shown in Figure 25-1. In each screen, the topmost line shows the system name and the time at which the information was collected and displayed. Output of the top command is divided into three major parts. These three parts are CPU, memory, and processes. The CPU part shows the following information.

1. Load average in preceding 5 and 15 minutes. This information is useful to check any abrupt changes in the system load.
2. Number of processes currently active on the system.
3. Processes in each state. Figure 25-1 shows that out of 67 processes, 65 are in sleep state, and two are in running state.
4. Percentage of CPU time used in each CPU state. If your system has multiple CPUs, one line for every CPU will be present here. In Figure 25-1, 99.2% of CPU time is idle, showing that most of the time, the CPU is sitting idle. Any performance problem with this system is definitely not a CPU problem.

Next is the memory area, which shows the following information.

1. total physical memory installed
2. active physical memory
3. virtual memory
4. free virtual memory
5. total free memory

The process data consists of a number of columns. These columns are sorted depending on the CPU utilization in descending order. The process that is utilizing the CPU the most is listed at the top (the reason the command is named top).

```
Window  Edit  Options                                                    Help

System: hp0                                          Wed Nov 24  1:02:37 1999
Load averages: 0.02, 0.14, 0.18
67 processes: 65 sleeping, 2 running
Cpu states:
 LOAD   USER   NICE    SYS    IDLE  BLOCK  SWAIT    INTR   SSYS
 0.02   0.0%   0.4%    0.4%  99.2%   0.0%   0.0%    0.0%   0.0%

Memory: 19408K (4148K) real, 15124K (2256K) virtual, 160828K free  Page# 1/5

 TTY      PID USERNAME PRI NI   SIZE    RES STATE   TIME %WCPU   %CPU COMMAND
pts/ta  5002 root      154 24   392K   972K sleep   0:00  0.39   0.39 dtterm
  ?       28 root      152 20     0K     0K run     0:06  0.38   0.38 vxfsd
pts/0   5005 root      168 24   420K   316K run     0:00  0.28   0.27 top
  ?       12 root      -32 20     0K     0K sleep   0:17  0.16   0.16 ttisr
  ?        3 root      128 20     0K     0K sleep   0:11  0.13   0.13 statdaemon
  ?     2197 root      154 20   196K   292K sleep   0:04  0.06   0.06 pwgrd
  ?     1280 root      127 20   120K   384K sleep   0:02  0.05   0.05 netfmt
pts/ta  5000 root      154 24   328K   392K sleep   0:00  0.05   0.04 xterm
  ?      319 root      154 20    32K    80K sleep   0:04  0.04   0.04 syncer
  ?        0 root      128 20     0K     0K sleep   0:18  0.02   0.02 swapper
  ?        1 root      168 20   380K   152K sleep   0:00  0.02   0.02 init
  ?        2 root      128 20     0K     0K sleep   0:00  0.02   0.02 vhand
  ?        4 root      128 20     0K     0K sleep   0:00  0.02   0.02 unhashdaemo
  ?        8 root      100 20     0K     0K sleep   0:00  0.02   0.02 supsched
```

Figure 25–1   *Using* top.

A brief explanation of the columns in the process area is given below.

CPU	This is the first column, which is not shown in Figure 25-1. It is present on systems with multiple CPUs. This represents a CPU number on which the process is being executed.
TTY	The terminal used by the process.
PID	Process ID.
USERNAME	Name of the owner of the process.
PRI	Process priority.
NI	Nice value.
SIZE	Total size of the process in memory.
RES	Resident size of the process. This is an approximation.
STATE	Current state of the process.
TIME	CPU time consumed by the process.
%WCPU	Weighted CPU percentage utilization by the process.
%CPU	Raw CPU percentage utilization by the process.
COMMAND	Name of the command that started the process.

To display information after a specified time, use the -s option. The following command displays top information after every 7 seconds.

```
top -s7
```

To quit using top, press the [q] key. You can also use the -d option with a number and top will exit after showing that many number of screens.

Using System Activity Reporter (sar)

This utility can be used to monitor system activity over a period of time. For example, to monitor system activity for 24 hours, you can start this command, and it can log the activity in a disk file. This disk file can be analyzed later at a convenient time. The following command stores system activity data in a file /home/root/sar.data 360 times, once every 10 seconds (total time one hour).

```
sar -o /home/root/sar.data 10 360
```

This file can be analyzed later by using the following command.

```
sar -f /home/root/sar.data
```

A number of system parameters can be monitored using sar. Some of these are shown next.

MONITORING CPU ACTIVITY WITH THE **sar** COMMAND

The -u option of the sar command shows CPU statistics. The output shows a division of CPU time as user, system, waiting for I/O, and idle states. The following command shows CPU statistics five times, once each second.

```
# sar -u 1 5
HP-UX hp0 B.11.00 A 9000/839    11/29/99
12:27:53    %usr     %sys     %wio     %idle
12:27:54      1        1        0        98
12:27:55      0        0        0       100
12:27:56      0        0        0       100
12:27:57      0        0        0       100
12:27:58      0        0        0       100

Average       0        0        0       100
#
```

MONITORING BUFFER CACHE ACTIVITY
WITH THE **sar** COMMAND

Checking buffer cache activity is useful for database applications. Using the -b option with sar can do this.

```
# sar -b 1 5

HP-UX hp0 B.11.00 A 9000/839     11/29/99

12:28:52 bread/s lread/s %rcache bwrit/s lwrit/s %wcache pread/s pwrit/s
12:28:53       0      61     100       0       1     100       0       0
12:28:54       0     113     100       0       1     100       0       0
12:28:55       0       0       0       0       0       0       0       0
12:28:56       0       0       0       0       0       0       0       0
12:28:57       0       2     100       0       0       0       0       0

Average        0      35     100       0       0     100       0       0
#
```

The different fields in the output of the command are explained here.

bread/s	Number of read operations per second from disk to buffer cache.
lread/s	Number of read operations per second from buffer cache.
%rcache	Buffer cache hit ratio for read requests.
bwrit/s	Number of write operation per seconds from buffer cache to disk.
lwrit/s	Number of write operations per second to the buffer cache.
%wcache	Buffer cache hit ratio for write requests.
pread/s	Number of read operations per second from raw device.
pwrit/s	Number of write operations per second to raw device.

The sar utility can be used for other tasks as well. Options that can be used with sar are listed in Table 25-1.

Table 25–1 *Options Used with* sar

Option	Meaning
-b	Monitor buffer cache
-d	Monitor disk activity
-q	Monitor queue length
-u	Monitor CPU activity
-w	Monitor swap space activity
-o	Save data into a file
-f	Read previously saved data from a file

25.2 Using GlancePlus

GlancePlus is an additional package that is used for system monitoring. It can be used either in text or graphic mode. GlancePlus shows statistics about a number of system components. Some of these components are system memory, virtual memory, CPU, processes, and disk and I/O utilization. You can start GlancePlus using the `glance` command in text mode. You will see a screen similar to that shown in Figure 25-2 when you start `glance`.

In this figure, the first line shows information about GlancePlus itself and the system on which it is running. The next lines show information about CPU, disk, memory, and swap utilization.

CPU Utilization

The line that shows CPU utilization starts with a bar of different shades. It is divided into parts that show CPU utilization for different purposes. Each part of the bar starts and ends with a character that shows one of four types of information.

- The s part indicates the percentage of CPU time utilized for system activities.

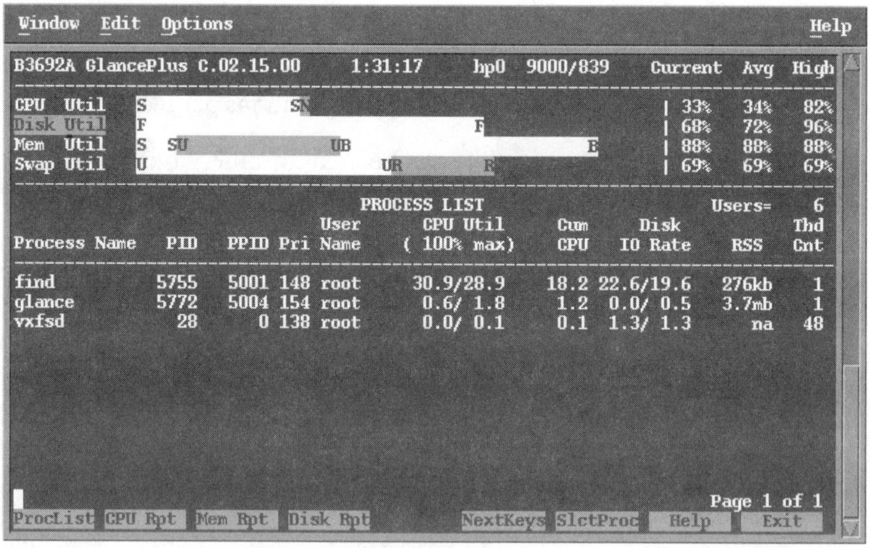

Figure 25–2 *GlancePlus in text mode.*

- The N part shows the percentage of CPU time utilized for *niced* processes. These are the processes that are running at a lower priority level.
- The U part shows the percentage of time spent in running user processes.
- The R part shows the percentage of time utilized for real time processes.

The rightmost part of the line shows the current, average, and highest percentage of CPU utilization since the start of GlancePlus.

Disk Utilization

The disk utilization bar has two parts. Like the CPU utilization bar, these parts show the percentage of disk utilization for different activities.

- The F part shows file system activity. This is the utilization of disk I/O for file read or write operations.
- The V part shows virtual memory activity. If this part is constantly large, it shows insufficient physical memory in your system.

In the rightmost part of the line, the current, average, and highest percentage of disk utilization is displayed.

Memory Utilization

Below the disk utilization bar is the memory utilization bar. It is divided into three parts.

- The S part shows memory used by system processes.
- The U part shows memory used by user programs.
- The B part indicates memory used by buffer cache.

The rightmost part of the line shows the current, average, and highest utilization, which has the same meaning as in the case of CPU and disk utilization.

Swap Utilization

The next line contains a bar for swap space utilization.

- The U part shows the swap space in use.
- The R part indicates the reserved part of swap space. An area in the swap is reserved as soon as a process is created. A reserved area may not be in use.

Processor List

The bottom part of the screen is the process list. This list is similar to that created by the ps and top commands. By default, all processes are not listed here. Only those processes that are using system resources are present in the list. Columns in this part are:

Process Name	Name of the command that created the process.
PID	Process ID.
PPID	Process ID of the parent process.
PRI	Priority of the process. This is a number between 0 and 255. The higher the number, the lower the priority.
User Name	Name of the user who started the process.
CPU Util	The first number is the percentage of CPU used during the last interval. The second number is the percentage of CPU utilization since the start of GlancePlus. By default, GlancePlus updates this list every five seconds.
Cum CPU	Cumulative CPU usage by a process.
Disk IO Rate	The first number is the average disk I/O rate during the last interval. The second number is the average disk I/O rate since GlancePlus started.
RSS	Amount of RAM used by a process.
Thd Cnt	Thread Count.

If you start GlancePlus in GUI mode by using the gpm command, a window is displayed as shown in Figure 25-3. The process list window can be opened using the Reports menu and is shown in Figure 25-4.

The topmost line in Figure 25-3 shows the system name, how many times the graph has been updated (Graph Points), and the elapsed time following the update. The second line shows the start time and the time of the last update. The duration of the current session is 19 seconds, as shown in the last part of the second line. The question mark button can be pressed at any time to get help. The major part of the window contains four graphs, showing CPU, memory, disk, and network statistics. Clicking on the button displayed under the respective graph may further expand any of these parts. For example, if you want to get more information about network activity, clicking the network button will show you a window like the one displayed in Figure 25-5.

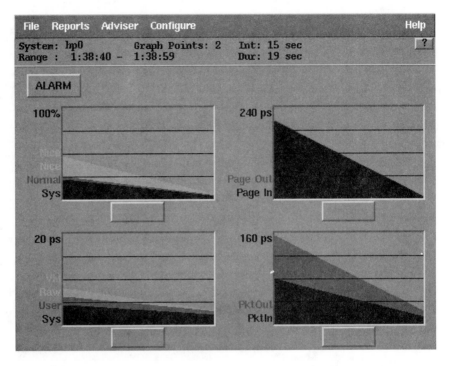

Figure 25–3 *GlancePlus in GUI.*

Process Name	PID	CPU %	Phys IO Rt	Stop Reason	Pri	User Name	App Name
gpm	5832	0.5	0.0	SLEEP	154	root	other_user_root
dtterm	5002	0.4	0.0	SLEEP	154	root	xwindows
ttisr	12	0.1	0.0	SLEEP	-32	root	network
vxfsd	28	0.1	1.4	CACHE	138	root	other_user_root
midaemon	5837	0.1	0.0	SYSTM	50	root	other_user_root
statdaemon	3	0.1	0.0	SLEEP	128	root	other_user_root
dtsession	2870	0.0	0.0	SLEEP	154	root	xwindows
inetd	1687	0.0	0.0	SLEEP	154	root	network
trapdestagt	2096	0.0	0.0	OTHER	154	root	network
nfsd	2355	0.0	0.0	OTHER	154	root	network
sendmail:	2002	0.0	0.0	SLEEP	154	root	other_user_root
mib2agt	2082	0.0	0.0	OTHER	154	root	network
biod	1609	0.0	0.0	OTHER	154	root	network
automount	1637	0.0	0.0	SLEEP	154	root	network
dtrc	2408	0.0	0.0	OTHER	158	root	xwindows
biod	1611	0.0	0.0	OTHER	154	root	network
nfsd	2353	0.0	0.0	OTHER	154	root	network
rpc.lockd	1626	0.0	0.0	OTHER	154	root	network
snmpdm	2036	0.0	0.0	OTHER	154	root	network

Figure 25–4 *GlancePlus process list.*

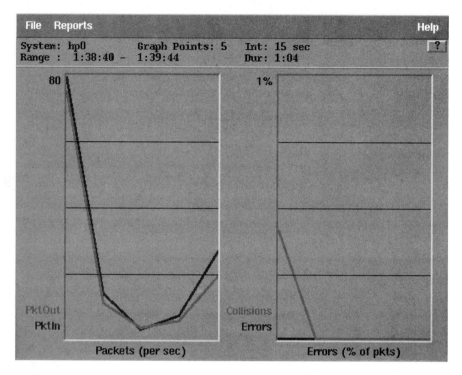

Figure 25–5   *Network activity.*

There are many reports that can be generated using the Reports menu in the GlancePlus window. Figure 25-6 shows I/O activity taking place on logical volumes. A detailed discussion of GlancePlus is beyond the scope of this book.

■ Chapter Summary

System monitoring is important for performance tuning and discovering bottlenecks. HP-UX provides command-line utilities that can be used to get information about different system components. The iostat command is used for monitoring disk activity. To monitor swap space, you can use the vmstat command. Network activity can be monitored using the netstat and lanadmin commands. There are two full-screen-based tools called top and sar. These provide a handful of information about different system components.

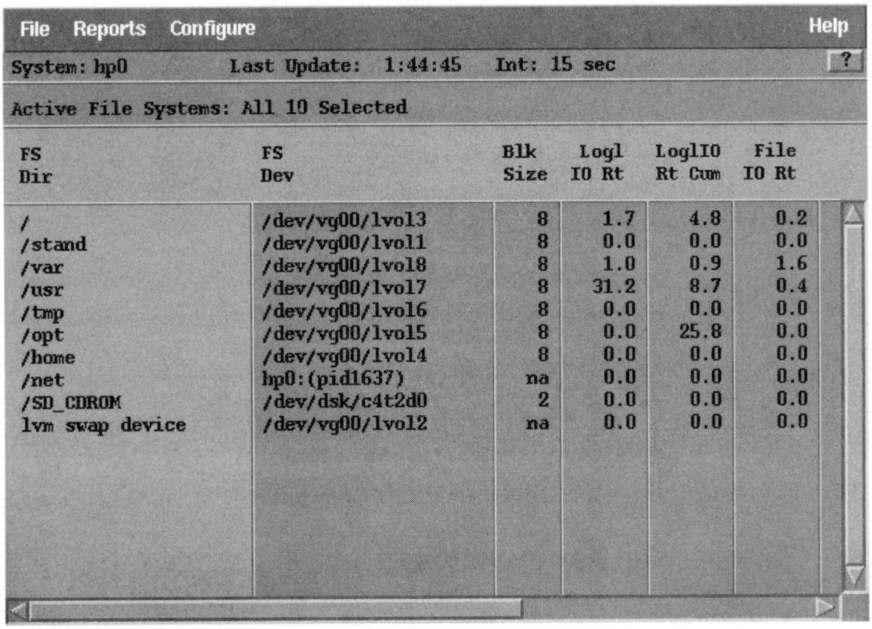

FS Dir	FS Dev	Blk Size	Logl IO Rt	LoglIO Rt Cum	File IO Rt
/	/dev/vg00/lvol3	8	1.7	4.8	0.2
/stand	/dev/vg00/lvol1	8	0.0	0.0	0.0
/var	/dev/vg00/lvol8	8	1.0	0.9	1.6
/usr	/dev/vg00/lvol7	8	31.2	8.7	0.4
/tmp	/dev/vg00/lvol6	8	0.0	0.0	0.0
/opt	/dev/vg00/lvol5	8	0.0	25.8	0.0
/home	/dev/vg00/lvol4	8	0.0	0.0	0.0
/net	hp0:(pid1637)	na	0.0	0.0	0.0
/SD_CDROM	/dev/dsk/c4t2d0	2	0.0	0.0	0.0
lvm swap device	/dev/vg00/lvol2	na	0.0	0.0	0.0

Figure 25–6 *I/O by logical volumes.*

GlancePlus can be installed separately and provides text as well as graphic interfaces that show system activity. It provides detailed reports about activities taking place on the system. Of all the tools mentioned in this chapter, GlancePlus is the most comprehensive.

HP-UX
Network
Administration

Basic Network Concepts

This is an era of global connectivity, and it is hard to imagine any computer system not being connected to a network. All types of corporate and business communications are carried out using some type of network. A network is a set of computers connected to each other using some communication medium. Computers on a network communicate with each other using a set of rules and regulations commonly known as a *network protocol*. It is not necessary for the computers connected to a network to be running a common operating system; however, they must use a common network protocol to talk to each other. Depending on the geographical span of a computer network, it is either a *Local Area Network* (LAN) or a *Wide Area Network* (WAN). LANs are usually confined to a small area such as one building and owned by one organization. WANs, on the other hand, may span any geographical area and may even spread through other countries. Many business organizations have corporate networks

491

that fall into the WAN category. LANs operate at a higher speed than WANs do. A WAN usually interconnects multiple LANs.

Networks are used for resource sharing and fast communication. A resource may be data files, applications, printers, or computing facilities. They increase productivity and decrease the overall cost of information management.

This chapter is an introduction to network terminology and a reference network model proposed by the International Standard Organization (ISO) called *Open Systems Interconnects* (OSI). This model is commonly known as ISO-OSI. This is a layered model, where the functions of a network are divided into seven layers. Each layer in a network is responsible to carry a specific type of function and communicate to its adjacent layers in the network model. The functions of all seven OSI layers will be discussed in this chapter. Although ISO-OSI is not implemented in its original form in any current network protocol, it provides guidelines for designing network protocols. The most commonly used network model is TCP/IP, which is a five-layer network model, and it will be discussed in Chapter 28.

The last part of this chapter contains an introduction to how data transfer takes place between two computers connected through a network.

26.1 Network Terminology

The area of computer networking and communications is full of terminology. This chapter is focused on some basic terms that are commonly used in daily life.

Local and Wide Area Networks

All networks fall into one of the two main categories. A LAN is a network that spans over a limited distance within a single site. The communication links used in LANs are of relatively high speed, from 10 Mbits for older Ethernet LANs to gigabit speeds for the newer Ethernet LANs. LANs are usually privately owned and used to transfer large amounts of data. Usually a

LAN uses a broadcast mechanism for data transfer and is connected by a continuous media.

WANs cover large geographical distances and usually connect LANs to each other. Communication speed is slow compared with LANs. Different types of communication mediums are used in WANs, such as telephone links, satellite, wireless, and fiber optic cables. Typical examples of WANs are the Internet and ATM machine networks used by banks and financial institutions.

Due to different types of communication media, equipment used in LANs and WANs may be of different types. A LAN may require only a cable connection and a network interface adapter for a computer to be connected to a network. On the other hand, a WAN needs sophisticated equipment such as routers for interconnection.

Protocol

A *protocol* is a set of rules and regulations that govern communication between two computers attached to a network. It may be thought of as a human language where two persons can talk to each other once they know a common language.

Host

A *host* or *node* is a computer attached to a network. A host may be an HP-UX system, a PC, or a network device such as a router.

Physical Medium

Physical medium is the communication medium that connects devices in a network. In the simplest form, it is coaxial or twisted pair cable used in LANs. Other media are fiber optic cables, satellite links, and microwaves in wireless LANs.

Network Interface Adapter

A *network interface adapter* is installed inside a computer. It is used to connect a computer to a physical medium.

Bandwidth

This is the data transfer capacity of the physical medium used to connect hosts in a network. The greater the bandwidth, the faster the data transfer rate.

Client and Server

A *client* is a system or a user program that requests a service from a host on the network. A *server* is a host or a software program that responds to a request from a client. Most of the communications on a network take place between a client and a server, and the applications are known as working in *client-server mode*.

Route

A *route* is a data communication path between a source and destination host on a network. A route is used to transfer data within two nodes and may be either statically defined or calculated depending on network conditions.

26.2 The OSI Model

The ISO has proposed a network model to provide guidelines for developing network protocols. This model is called *Open Systems Interconnects*, commonly known as OSI. This is a layered model where the functions of a network protocol are divided into seven layers. The OSI layered structure can be divided into two main parts. The lower four layers are related to data transfer functions taking place among participating hosts. Functions performed in these layers are error detection and correction, determination of route from source to destination, and utilization of underlying physical topology to transfer data in the form of electrical signals. The top three layers are related to the application-related matters such as data formats, opening/closing communication sessions, and user interaction.

OSI Layers

The OSI network model contains seven layers. The combination of these layers is known as the *OSI protocol stack* and is shown in Figure 26-1. In some literature, it is also known as OSI protocol suite. These layers are numbered from 1 to 7. The topmost layer (layer 7) is the application layer where most of the user interaction takes place. The bottommost layer is the physical layer where actual data transfer takes place from one point to another in the form of electrical signals.

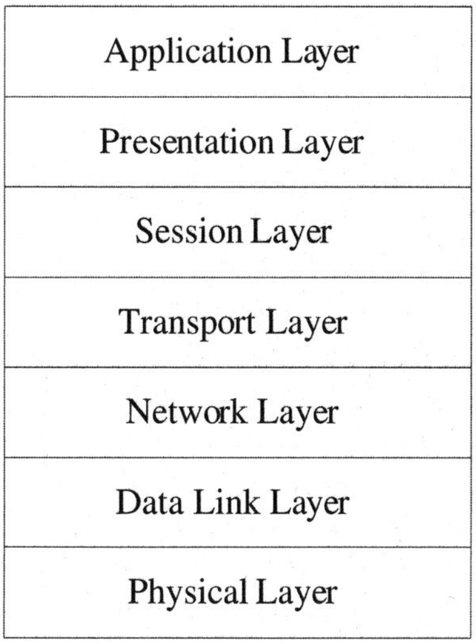

| Application Layer |
| Presentation Layer |
| Session Layer |
| Transport Layer |
| Network Layer |
| Data Link Layer |
| Physical Layer |

Figure 26–1   *The ISO-OSI protocol stack.*

Each layer in the OSI protocol suite is responsible for certain operations. During the data transfer process, a layer interacts with its immediate upper layer and with the lower layers.

APPLICATION LAYER

The application layer provides user interface to the network. This layer consists of applications that initiate network communication. For example, you use the `ftp` command to transfer files from one host to another and the `telnet` or `rlogin` commands to log in to a remote system. These programs fall into the application layer and provide an interface where input from a user is taken and a network operation is performed according to that input.

Applications in the topmost layer usually act as a client or a server. A program started by a user is a client, and it interacts with a server application on the destination host. The destination host may be the same host or another host on the network. For example, when you start the `ftp` command, it interacts with the FTP server on a destination host.

PRESENTATION LAYER

Different computers on a network may use different data formats. For example, one machine may use the ASCII format while another may use EBCDIC. There may be some other machine-specific data formats. The presentation layer is responsible to format data according to a specific data format understandable to a machine.

SESSION LAYER

The session layer establishes, manages, and terminates a communication session. Applications use virtual connection points for communication between two systems on a network. These connection points are called network ports. By using these ports, it is possible to run multiple client and server applications simultaneously using one physical machine. During the session establishment process, the session layer opens a *socket* (which is a combination of a network port and the network address of a host) on the client side and connects it to the socket opened by the server application on a predefined port. The session layer then synchronizes and sequences the data transfer process during the data communication period. At the end of the data transfer process, the session layer closes the opened sockets on both sides, thus closing the session. On HP-UX, the defined ports for different applications can be found in the `/etc/services` file. For example, the port number of the *telnet* application is 23, while for *FTP* the port number is 21. If you are using your own application, you can use a port number that is not already in use by some other application.

TRANSPORT LAYER

The transport layer is used for reliable data transfer between a source and a destination. It provides end-to-end error detection and correction. If data are lost or contain errors, the transport layer on the receiving side requests the sending side to retransmit the data.

The data communication takes place in the form of data packets over the network. The transport layer also keeps a record of the sequence of these data packets. Sometimes, the data packets are received out of sequence. The transport layer is responsible for the correct sequencing of data packets before the data are transferred to the upper layer. The transport layer also drops duplicate packets in case more than one copy of the same data packet is received. Large amounts of data at the transport layer are divided into smaller data packets, which are reassembled at the receiving side.

NETWORK LAYER

The network layer is where unique logical network addresses, used to distinguish among hosts on a network, are assigned to hosts. It also provides routing information to transfer data within a LAN and across WANs. A *route* is a path from a source system to a destination system. The network layer is responsible for determining the best route between a source and destination. The network layer keeps the routing information updated, and a different route may be used during the same data transfer session if it becomes available. Determination of a route depends on many factors, such as the capacity of a communication path, traffic conditions along a path, number of intermediate points between the source and destination (hops), and so on.

A route falls into one of two categories. It is either a *static route* or a *dynamic route*. Static routes are predefined by a network administrator and are not dependent on network conditions. Dynamic routes, on the other hand, are calculated on the fly and change as network conditions change. The choice of a static or dynamic route depends on the availability, type, and number of interconnection paths. HP-UX supports both static and dynamic routing.

If the source and destination are not directly connected, the communication takes place with the help of intermediate machines known as *routers*. In this case, the data transfer process is completed in a number of *hops*, depending on the number of intermediate points. The network layer is responsible for point-to-point error detection and correction in such a case. Data packets at the network layer are called *datagrams*.

DATA LINK LAYER

The data link layer (DLL) is responsible for error-free data transfer over a physical medium (also known as hardware error correction). It is divided into two sublayers known as *Logical Link Control* (LLC) and *Medium Access Control* (MAC). LLC is used for communication with the network layer while MAC is used to access and control the physical medium. A physical addressing scheme is used at the MAC sublayer. These physical addresses are also called *MAC addresses*. Physical addresses are permanent addresses burnt into a network interface adapter. Data are divided into *frames* at the DLL and transferred from one system to another using the physical addresses. Special protocols are used to map physical (MAC) addresses to logical (network) addresses in a network.

PHYSICAL LAYER

The physical layer receives data frames from the DLL and converts these into electrical signals of 0s and 1s. It uses actual cable connections and signaling to transfer these data streams of 0s and 1s from source to destination.

Table 26-1 shows a listing of ISO-OSI network model layers and their responsibilities.

Table 26–1 *The OSI Layers and Their Functionality*

Layer Number	Layer Name	Description
7	Application	Top-level applications that serve as user interfaces to the network. Data are generated in this layer on the sending side and received on the receiving side.
6	Presentation	Serves as data format converter if hosts participating in a network are using different data formats.
5	Session	Establishes and manages a communication session between two hosts. It terminates the session when the data transfer is complete. It uses port numbers, which are logical addresses used to establish data communication between client and server applications.
4	Transport	Used for reliable end-to-end data transfer, packet sequencing, retransmission, and acknowledgment of transmitted data. Data are divided into packets at this layer.
3	Network	Used for network addressing, routing, and point-to-point data error detection and recovery. Data packets are called *datagrams* at this layer.
2	Data link	Serves as an interface between the network layer and the physical layer. Physical or hardware (MAC) addresses are implemented at this layer. It controls access to the physical medium. Data packets at this layer are called *frames*.
1	Physical	Converts data frames received from the DLL to electrical signals and transmits these on the physical medium.

How Data Transfer Takes Place Among Layers

Data transfer starts when an application in the top layer initiates a network data transfer request. The data transfer process starts from the application layer, and the data to be transferred are handed over to the presentation layer. The presentation layer performs code conversion tasks, converts the data received from the application layer into the appropriate format and appends a presentation layer header to the data. This header contains information about changes made by the presentation layer and is used by the presentation layer on the receiving side to recover data. The presentation layer then hands over the data to the session layer. The session layer establishes a communication session with the destination host. It appends its header information to the data received from the presentation layer and hands it over to the transport layer. Each layer in this top-to-bottom approach adds its own header to the data and sends to its lower layer. These headers contain protocol information for the same layer (also called the peer layer) on the receiving side. When the data reach the physical layer, they are converted into a stream of 0s and 1s and transferred to the destination host.

On the receiving side, the physical layer receives data and sends them to the data link layer. Each layer on the receiving side takes off the header attached by the peer layer on the sending side and sends data to its upper layer. This process continues until the data reach an application in the application layer. This process is shown in Figure 26-2.

PEER PROTOCOLS

Communication between peer layers, which are layers having the same layer number on both the source and destination hosts in the OSI protocol stack, is governed by certain rules and regulations called *peer protocols*. For example, the transport layers on the sending and receiving side of data are responsible for end-to-end data error detection and recovery process. Both layers follow certain rules to accomplish this job and to talk to each other in an orderly fashion. During the data transfer process, these two layers communicate with each other to acknowledge the accurate transfer of data (or otherwise) using a peer protocol.

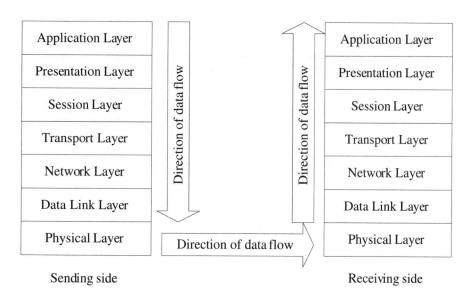

Figure 26–2 *Data flow between two hosts in the OSI protocol stack.*

INTERFACES

Each layer in the OSI model communicates only with the layer immediately above or below it. The rules and regulations that govern data transfer between two adjacent layers in the OSI model are called *interfaces*.

Layered Network Model

The layered network model is designed to divide the complex task of network communication into different stages. User applications run in the topmost application layer. This is the layer where data originate for sending. A data transfer process starts at the application layer. On the sending side, each layer in a layered model communicates with the next lower level layer until the data reach the physical layer. Different operations take place during the data transfer from one layer to another. At the physical layer, the data are converted to electrical signals and are transferred to the destination process. On the receiving host, the data travel from the physical layer toward the topmost application layer, and reverse operations take place. Finally, the data are received by the application running on the destination host.

Peer protocols are used to convey information to peer layers between the source and destination hosts. The protocol information is transferred using layer headers appended to data at each layer. Thus, the amount of data transferred on the network is always larger than the actual data is. The additional data transfer the protocol information and may be called *protocol overhead*. The process of adding layer headers is shown in Figure 26-3. You can see that the physical layer data contain header information from all upper layers.

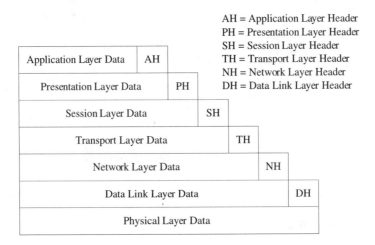

AH = Application Layer Header
PH = Presentation Layer Header
SH = Session Layer Header
TH = Transport Layer Header
NH = Network Layer Header
DH = Data Link Layer Header

Figure 26–3 *Addition of header information at each layer of OSI model.*

■ Chapter Summary

Rules and regulations known as network protocols control communication among systems connected on a network. The International Standards Organization has developed guidelines for the development of network protocols and has proposed a network model known as Open Systems Interconnect or OSI. This is a seven-layer network model. Layer names and their corresponding numbers are:

1. physical layer
2. data link layer (DLL)
3. network layer
4. transport layer
5. session layer
6. presentation layer
7. application layer

Each layer in the layered model performs a specific operation during the data transfer process. The data transfer process originates in the application layer. The presentation layer is responsible for the conversion of data formats. The session layer establishes, manages, and terminates a communication session between two systems on a network. The transport layer is responsible for end-to-end data integrity, error detection, and correction. It fragments data received from the transport layer into packets and transfers these packets using lower level layers. The network layer is used for addressing and routing. The data link layer controls medium access and transmits data in the form of frames by using the physical layer.

During the data transfer process, an application starts the data transfer process and data travel down the layers of the protocol stack until they reach the physical layer where they are sent over to the receiving node. The reverse process takes place on the receiving node where data travel from the physical layer toward the application layer.

Layers having the same level on the sending and the receiving hosts are called *peer layers*. Data communication between peer layers is controlled by peer protocols. Each layer conveys its protocol information to its peer layer on the destination host. This information is called the *layer header*. Layer headers are added to data on the sending side and are stripped off on the receiving side.

▲ CHAPTER REVIEW QUESTIONS

1. What is a protocol?

2. What is the advantage of a layered network model?

3. What are peer protocols?

4. What is the function of the network layer?

▲ TEST YOUR KNOWLEDGE

1. *The order of the top four OSI layers from top to bottom is:*
    A. transport, presentation, application, session
    B. application, presentation, session, transport
    C. application, session, presentation, transport
    D. presentation, session, transport, application

2. *What is the function of the network layer?*
    A. host addressing and routing
    B. starting a communication session
    C. end-to-end error detection
    D. end-to-end error correction

3. *Peer protocols are used between:*
    A. two adjacent layers in the OSI protocol suite
    B. any two layers in the OSI protocol suite
    C. the same layers of the OSI protocol suite on two hosts communicating with each other
    D. different layers of the OSI protocol suite on two hosts communicating with each other

4. *Which OSI layer is divided into Logical Link Control (LLC) and Medium Access Control (MAC)?*
    A. the network layer
    B. the transport layer
    C. the physical layer
    D. the data link layer

5. *What is* not *true about the OSI model?*

    A. It is a seven-layer protocol.

    B. Support of exchanging data formats is provided in the presentation layer.

    C. Routing takes place at the session layer.

    D. Data packets at the data link layer are called frames.

Network Components and Topologies

A network is a set of servers and workstations connected to each other through some communication medium. Network components are used for the interconnection purpose. Network interface adapters are installed in computer systems to connect to a cable that serves as the communication medium. Different types of cables are used depending on particular requirements. Cable connectors and terminators are used to connect cables to network interface adapters. A layout of the cables connecting different systems is called a network topology. Different network topologies are used depending on the network requirements such as the length of a network, cost, and speed of data transmission. Other network components are also used depending on the complexity of a network. Some of these components are repeaters, bridges, and routers. All network components fall into one or more layers as defined by the OSI model. Common examples of physical layer network components are network cables, connectors,

505

cable terminators, and repeaters. Examples of data link layer network components are bridges and switches. Routers are used in the network layer of the OSI model.

The transmission media in the physical layer of the OSI network model is accessed by the data link layer using an access method. Different types of access methods are available, such as CSMA/CD and token passing. An access method also depends on the underlying network topology.

This chapter starts with an introduction to network topologies. In the next section, network components are covered, where you will find a brief introduction to the commonly used network devices. Physical or MAC addresses are used at the data link layer level, and you will find an introduction to the structure of MAC addresses. CSMA/CD and token passing access methods are discussed next. In the last part of the chapter, an introduction to Ethernet, token ring, and FDDI is presented.

27.1 Network Topologies

A network topology is the physical layout of a network. The physical communication media (e.g., cables) are used to connect network components depending on the selection of a network topology. Common network topologies are bus, star, and ring. Selection of a particular network topology depends on network cost, reliability, and performance.

Bus Topology

In a bus topology, all hosts are connected to a common bus, usually a cable. This is shown in Figure 27-1. A bus is terminated at both ends with cable terminators. The cable terminators absorb all signals reaching the cable ends and stop signal reflection. The bus topology is a low-cost networking method. The disadvantage is that if the cable fails at any point, the entire network breaks down, and no data communication can take place.

Star Topology

In a star topology, all hosts are connected to a central place. This central place is a network device known as a hub. The advantage of this topology is that in

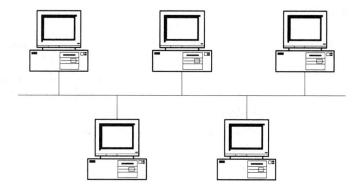

Figure 27–1 *The bus interconnection topology.*

case of a single cable fault, only the host connected to that cable is affected. All other hosts continue to function normally. The disadvantage is that if the hub fails, the entire network fails. Thus the hub is the single point of failure in this topology. The star topology is shown in Figure 27-2.

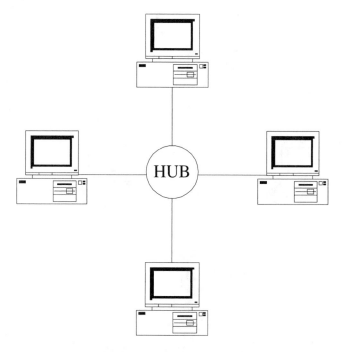

Figure 27–2 *The star interconnection topology.*

Ring Topology

In a ring topology, hosts are connected in a ring structure. Data are transferred from one host to another host in the order defined in the ring. Each host in the path receives data frames, compares the destination MAC (physical) address with its own address and captures data if the two addresses match. If the two addresses don't match, the data are relayed to the next host on the ring. Figure 27-3 shows a ring-connected network. MAC addresses are explained later in this chapter.

Hybrid Networks

Practical networks may be combinations of different topologies. For example, a network based on Ethernet may be a combination of a star topology and bus topology as shown in Figure 27-4.

In most of the medium-to-large LANs, computers are connected to multiple hubs or switches located at convenient places. Computers connected to each hub form a star network. All of these hubs and switches are then connected to each other using a backbone cable that acts as a bus.

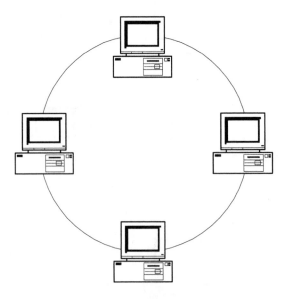

Figure 27-3 *The ring interconnection topology.*

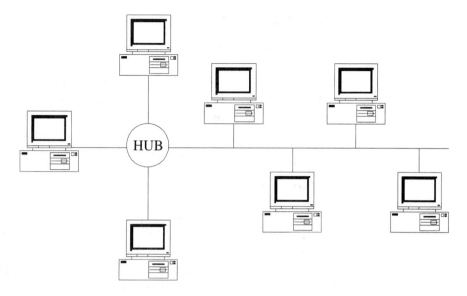

Figure 27–4 *A hybrid network consisting of star and bus topologies.*

27.2 Network Hardware Components

Besides servers and workstations, other hardware components take part as building blocks of a network. Some network components are explained here.

Network Cables

Different types of cables and connectors are used in the physical layer of a network. The selection of a cable determines the data transmission speed and the length of a single cable segment.

COAXIAL CABLE

Coaxial cable consists of a center wire and a cladding that surrounds the center wire. A dielectric material is placed between the two that acts as an insulator. Plastic is used to cover and insulate the cable. Coaxial cables are end terminated. BNC connectors are used to connect coaxial cables to each other and to network interface adapters. BNC connectors will be discussed in more detail later in this chapter. Coaxial cables support data transfer speeds of up to 10 Mbits per second.

TWISTED PAIR CABLE

Twisted pair cable is used in many Ethernet and token ring networks with RJ-45 or 9-pin d-type connectors. Twisted pair cable is either shielded or unshielded. Different cable categories are used with different standards of twisted pair cable, where each category is capable of handling a specific bandwidth. The most commonly used twisted pair cables are category 3 and category 5. Category 3 twisted pair cable is used for data transfer speed of 10 Mbits per second, and category 5 cable is used for speeds of 100 Mbits per second.

FIBER OPTIC CABLE

Fiber optic cable is made of glass, and data transmission takes place using light instead of electrical signals. Fiber optic cable is capable of very high bandwidths and is used for high-speed networks. Typically, this cable is used in FDDI and gigabit Ethernet networks. Data transmission speed of up to 1 Gbit per second is used in a gigabit LAN. Fiber cable is expensive and difficult to install. It provides excellent reliability for data transfer.

Selection of a specific type of cable depends on factors like cost, ease of installation, transmission speed, and reliability of data transfer. The cost of selecting a specific type of cable is reflected in other network components, such as hubs and switches. For example, if you use fiber optic cable, you have to use more expensive network interface adapters and switches.

Network Interface Adapter

A network interface adapter is installed inside a server or workstation. It is the connection point for a network cable to the host. HP provides different LAN adapter products, such as LAN/9000, Token Ring/9000, and FDDI/9000.

Cable Connectors

Cable connectors are used to connect cables to network interface adapters. Some of the cable connectors available with HP networking products are as follows.

BNC CONNECTORS

BNC connectors are used with coaxial cables. A BNC connector is built into the network interface adapter.

LAN-TP CONNECTORS

This type of connector is used with twisted pair cable. The socket is built into the network interface adapter. This is used to connect a network adapter to a hub or switch by using an RJ-45 connector.

AUI CONNECTORS

An *attachment unit interface* (AUI) is a 15-pin connector used to connect a network interface adapter to a thin or thick coaxial cable, twisted pair cable, or fiber optic cable with the help of a transceiver. A different type of transceiver is used for each type of cable.

Transceiver

A transceiver acts as a *medium attachment unit* (MUI) and its function is to connect a network interface adapter with a particular type of cable. It takes data from the network interface adapter and converts them into electrical signals suitable for the cable. A transceiver can be used to connect a network interface adapter to a coaxial cable, twisted pair cable, or fiber optic cable.

Repeaters

A repeater is a physical layer device used to regenerate electrical signals. In the case of long cables, the signal gets distorted due to noise as it travels a long distance over the cable. The repeater filters out the noise and regenerates the signal. Repeaters are used to increase the length of a cable segment. Figure 27-5 shows how a repeater reshapes the signal.

Hubs

A hub is also a physical layer device. It is used to connect a number of hosts in the star topology. A hub provides many sockets or ports where network cables may be plugged in. Typical hubs contain 8, 16, 24, or 32 ports. Some

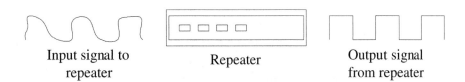

| Input signal to repeater | Repeater | Output signal from repeater |

Figure 27–5 *The signal regeneration process using a repeater.*

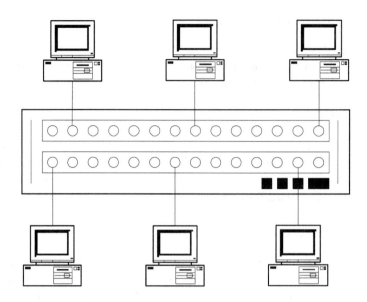

Figure 27–6 *Cable connection using a hub.*

manufacturers also provide hubs that can be stacked. A hub is shown in Figure 27-6, where hosts are connected to ports. Most modern hubs also provide network management features.

   If you are using a hub, an incoming data frame is replicated to all ports of the hub. Thus, every host connected to a hub listens to all data being sent on the network transmission media. A hub also functions as a repeater and is known in some literature as a multiport repeater.

Bridges

Bridges are devices that cover the physical and data link layers. They are used to connect LAN segments. A bridge can filter traffic depending on the MAC addresses of the source and destination hosts. Bridges help improve utilization of bandwidth available to a network by creating additional collision domains. A network without a bridge is a single collision domain. It means that only a single data packet can be transmitted over the network media at any time. In case two or more hosts try to transmit data frames, a collision occurs. The network shown in Figure 27-7 provides two collision domains because two hosts, one on each side of the bridge, can transmit data frames at the same time.

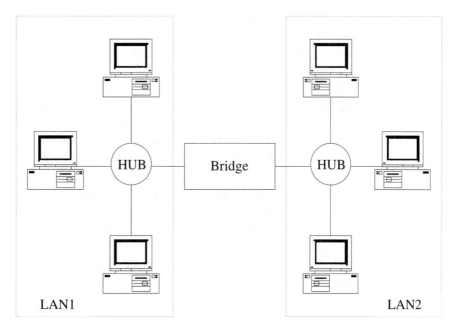

Figure 27–7 *Bridge connecting two LAN segments shown as LAN1 and LAN2.*

A bridge listens to the data frames on both sides and forwards a data frame to the other side only if it contains source and destination MAC addresses not on the same side of the bridge. Another advantage of the bridge is that it stops any error or collision to pass from one segment to another. It utilizes the store-and-forward method for this purpose.

Little or no configuration is required for a bridge. It automatically learns MAC addresses on each segment and builds its own table of MAC addresses to filter data traffic. Bridges work in the data link layer of the OSI model, and up to eight bridges can be used in a LAN in addition to repeaters.

Switches

Like a bridge, a switch operates in the data link layer and filters and forwards frames based on MAC addresses. Like a bridge, which is used to connect LAN segments, a switch is also used for this purpose and provides traffic filtering facility. In addition, if used in place of a hub, a switch may provide many parallel paths for data transfer, enabling many hosts to communicate simultaneously. A host is connected to one port of a switch. After receiving a data frame, a switch forwards it to only that port that connects to a host having a destination address equal to the MAC address of the host.

Any incoming data frame is not replicated on all ports of the switch (unless it is a broadcast). Instead, it is sent on a particular port depending on the destination MAC address in that data frame. A switch also works in the data link layer of the OSI model.

Routers

Routers operate at the network layer of the OSI model and are used to connect LANs and WANs. A router may filter and route traffic depending on network addresses (not MAC addresses). A router may use static or dynamic routing to send a data packet to a required destination.

In the lower three layers of the OSI model, routers are able to connect networks having different technologies. For example, a router can be used to connect an Ethernet network to an X.25 network. Routers use complex configuration tasks that require setting up traffic routing and filtering methods. A router can perform all tasks of a bridge and a switch.

Gateway

A gateway is capable of connecting completely dissimilar networks. It covers all layers of the OSI model. As an example, if you want to connect a Novell Netware LAN running on IPX/SPX protocol to a TCP/IP network, you need a gateway.

Table 27-1 lists network devices and the OSI layers covered by each device.

Table 27–1 *OSI Layers Covered with Network Devices*

Network Device	OSI Layers Covered with the Device
Cable	Physical layer
Cable connector	Physical layer
Network interface adapter	Physical layer
Transceiver	Physical layer
Repeater	Physical layer
Hub	Physical and data link layers
Bridge	Physical and data link layers
Switch	Physical and data link layers
Router	Physical, data link, and network layers
Gateway	All layers of the OSI model

27.3 MAC Addresses

A MAC address is a unique address assigned to each network interface adapter. It is a 48-bit address and is represented as a 12-digit hexadecimal number. This is also called a *physical address, station address, Ethernet address,* or *hardware address.* Data frames that are sent on the physical layer contain source and destination MAC addresses. Usually every host on a LAN listens to all incoming data. If a received data frame contains a destination address that matches the MAC address of the host, the frame is transferred to the network layer; otherwise, it is dropped.

Every network interface adapter installed in a system has its own unique MAC address. Thus, a host has as many MAC addresses as the number of network adapters installed. HP-UX provides commands to check the MAC addresses of installed network adapters. The most common command is the `lanscan` command. Output of this command is like the following.

```
# lanscan
Hardware Station          Crd Hdw   Net-Interface  NM  MAC      HP-DLPI DLPI
Path     Address          In# State NamePPA         ID  Type     Support Mjr#
10/4/16  0x080009D41DBB   1   UP    lan1 snap1      1   ETHER    Yes     119
10/4/8   0x080009D481F6   0   UP    lan0 snap0      2   ETHER    Yes     119
10/12/6  0x080009F02610   2   UP    lan2 snap2      3   ETHER    Yes     119
#
```

The second field of the output under the `Station Address` column heading is the MAC address of installed network adapters. It starts with `0x` showing that it is a hexadecimal number.

27.4 Access Methods

An access method is used to access physical transmission medium and send data over it. Computers connected to a network don't start sending data over network transmission media of their own volition. Before a host on the network starts sending data, it must obey some rules to access the transmission media. This is to ensure that the transmission media are used by all hosts in an orderly fashion.

Different types of access methods are used. CSMA/CD and token ring are discussed here.

CSMA/CD

The *Carrier Sense Multiple Access with Collision Detection* (CSMA/CD) method is used to check the medium before starting the transmission. When a host wants to send data on the network, it first senses if another host is already sending data at that time. In case another host is sending data, it waits. If no host is sending data, it starts sending data on the network transmission medium.

Sometimes it may happen that two or more hosts listen to the transmission medium and find that no one is transmitting data. They then start sending their own data simultaneously. A *collision* occurs in such a case. To resolve such a condition, each host that sends data also listens simultaneously to detect if any collision occurred. In case of a collision, all hosts wait for a random time and retry data transfer.

The CSMA/CD method is a broadcast method and is useful for connecting large numbers of hosts. It is the standard access method for Ethernet and IEEE 802.3 networks.

Token Passing

The token passing method uses a data frame as the token. This token is passed from one host to another in a network in an orderly fashion. When a host needs to transmit data, it waits for the token. When a host gets the token, it can transmit its data. If a host has no data to transmit, it passes the token to the next host.

The token passing method guarantees network access to every host. It can be used to transmit data at a higher rate. Priorities can also be used in token passing networks. IEEE 802.5 networks use the token passing access method. It can also be used in a bus topology, known as a token bus network.

27.5 Ethernet and IEEE 802.3

With some minor differences, IEEE 802.3 and the Ethernet are the same network standards. Both of these use the same type of frames with a difference of type and frame length field. The Ethernet uses a 2-byte-long field containing the *type* of frame, while the same field in an IEEE 802.3 frame contains the frame *length*. Both of the standards can coexist on the same network. Both of these standards are commonly called Ethernet.

Ethernet uses CSMA/CD as the access method. Different types of cables can be used with Ethernet. Depending on the type of cable used and the transmission speed, this type of network falls into one of the following standards.

10BASE-2 Ethernet

Ethernet standard names show information about the standard itself. The 10BASE-2 Ethernet is based on baseband signaling, where a single frequency is used as carrier to transmit data. The data transmission rate is 10 Mbits per second. The maximum length of a single cable segment in this network is 185 meters. However, up to four repeaters (maximum five segments) can be used to extend the length of 10BASE-2 networks. A 50-ohm thin coaxial cable is used, which is terminated at both ends with 50-ohm end terminators. The terminators are used to stop reflection of signals from cable ends. This is also called thin Ethernet.

10BASE-5 Ethernet

The maximum length of a single cable segment in 10BASE-5 networks is 500 meters with a thick 50-ohm cable. This type of network is called thick Ethernet. It is also based on the baseband 10 Mbits per second CSMA/CD access method. 10BASE-2 and 10BASE-5 networks are based on bus topology.

10BASE-T Ethernet

This is again a baseband Ethernet network specification. Twisted pair cable is used for interconnection. Maximum segment length is 100 meters, and the data transmission speed is 10 Mbits per second.

100BASE-T Fast Ethernet

This is similar to 10BASE-T networks. The data transmission speed is 100 Mbits per second and the maximum cable segment length is 100 meters.

100VG-AnyLAN Local Area Network

This is a 100 Mbits per second specification that supports both Ethernet and token ring frames.

27.6 Token Ring and IEEE 802.5

IBM developed token ring and it provides a base for IEEE 802.5 token ring specification. The transmission media is twisted pair cable most of the time. Typical token ring networks support 4 Mbits per second and 16 Mbits per second data transfer speeds.

The HP Token Ring/9000 product provides IEEE 802.5 functionality and supports up to 255 stations on a token ring network. A 9-pin D-type connector or an RJ-45 connector is used to connect a host to the network. Physically, a token ring network is not really a ring topology network. It is more similar to a star network.

A data token is passed from one host to another in the network in a pre-defined sequence. If a host wants to transmit data, it waits for the token. When it receives the token, it attaches its data to the token and passes it to the next host in the sequence. Each host on the way checks if the attached data are for it. If the destination address does not match the host address, the token is passed to the next host until it reaches the destination host. The receiving host detaches the data, frees the token, and passes to the next host. One of the hosts on a token ring network monitors the token activity so that if a token is lost, it generates a new one. In case a destination host dies and nobody can receive data attached to the token, this host detaches the data and marks the token as free again.

27.7 FDDI

The FDDI networks use a dual ring topology with a token passing access method. One of these rings is the primary ring and the other one is the secondary. Two rings are used to provide redundancy so that the network does not fail in case of the failure of one ring. Fiber optic cable is used for interconnection. FDDI networks operate at 100 Mbits per second speed. An FDDI network may be visualized as shown in Figure 27-8.

Single and dual attachment stations (SAS and DAS) are used with an FDDI network. A single attachment station is attached to one ring, while a dual attachment station is attached to both rings. The dual attachment stations are also used to automatically reconfigure the ring in case of cable failure.

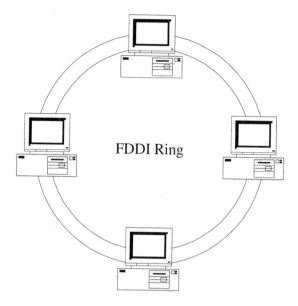

Figure 27–8 *An FDDI network.*

■ Chapter Summary

Hosts in a network are connected using a communication medium. In most of the cases, this communication medium is a cable. The physical layout of this cable shows network topology. Commonly used network topologies are bus, star, and ring. Networks of medium-to-large size use multiple topologies. The selection of a network topology depends on many factors, including cost and reliability of the network.

Network devices serve different purposes. Other than network cables and connectors, transceivers, repeaters, and hubs are used at the physical layer. A transceiver connects the AUI port on the network interface adapter to a network cable. The repeater is used to extend the length of a network cable by regenerating and reshaping electrical signals. The hub is a central part in a star-connected network. These also serve as a multiport repeater. On the data link layer level, bridges and switches are used. A bridge connects network segments and creates additional collision domains. It filters traffic and stops errors, including collisions, to pass through to other network segments. A switch provides multiple parallel paths for data transfer at the data link layer. Routers operate at the network layer of the OSI model and are used to connect multiple networks. A router can also connect networks with different protocols at the first three layers of the OSI model. Gateways can be used to connect networks using different protocols at all network layers.

A MAC address or station address is the physical address of a host. It is a permanent address assigned by the manufacturer of a network interface adapter. It is a 48-bit long number and must be unique for all hosts on a LAN. The `lanscan` command can be used to display the MAC addresses of all network interface adapters installed in a system.

An access method is used to access network cables and transfer data. Carrier Sense Multiple Access with Collision Detection (CSMA/CD) is used in Ethernet networks, while the token passing method is used in token ring and token bus networks. CSMA/CD employs a technique whereby each network station checks the network cable for any existing network traffic before sending its own data. If the cable is free, the host starts sending its data. If two hosts start sending data at the same time, a collision occurs and is detected by all sending hosts. In case of collision, all hosts wait for a random time and retry data transfer. In token passing networks, a data token is passed in an orderly fashion from one host to another in the network. If a host wants to transfer some data, it waits for the token.

Multiple standards of Ethernet networks are in use. The most common are 10BASE-2, 10BASE-5, 10BASE-T, and 100BASE-T. Each of these standards employs a particular type of cable and spans a defined cable length. The data transfer speeds are also defined for each standard. FDDI networks operate at 100 Mbits per second and use a dual ring of fiber optic cable.

▲ CHAPTER REVIEW QUESTIONS

1. What is an access method? Explain how CSMA/CD works.

2. What is the difference between a hub and a switch?

3. Write one characteristic of each of the following network topologies.

   A. bus

   B. ring

   C. star

4. What is the function of a repeater?

▲ TEST YOUR KNOWLEDGE

1. *Which cable is used in 100BASE-T networks?*

    A. thin coaxial cable

    B. thick coaxial cable

    C. category 3 twisted pair cable

    D. category 5 twisted pair cable

2. *What is* not *true about a bridge?*

    A. It filters data frames depending on MAC addresses.

    B. It filters data packets depending on IP addresses.

    C. It connects LAN segments.

    D. It provides multiple collision domains.

3. *Which of the following is* not *a physical layer device?*

    A. hub

    B. repeater

    C. transceiver

    D. switch

4. *Terminators are used in:*

    A. coaxial cable to stop the reflection of a signal from cable ends

    B. category 5 cable to stop the reflection of a signal from cable ends

    C. coaxial cable to stop collisions

    D. FDDI networks to terminate a broken cable

5. *CSMA/CD is* not *used in:*

    A. 10BASE-T networks

    B. 10BASE-5 networks

    C. Ethernet networks

    D. token ring networks

6. *The maximum length of a 10BASE-2 cable segment is:*

    A. 100 meters

    B. 200 meters

    C. 185 meters

    D. 500 meters

7. *What is the maximum number of repeaters that can be used in an Ethernet network?*

    A. 2

    B. 4

    C. 5

    D. 10

8. *Which statement is true?*

    A. The token passing access method can be used on ring networks only.

    B. In CSMA/CD, multiple hosts can transmit data at the same time without a collision.

    C. Ethernet and IEEE 802.3 can coexist on a network segment.

    D. In case of a collision in CSMA/CD, only one transmitting station detects that a collision has occurred.

Introduction to the TCP/IP Protocol

Transmission Control Protocol/Internet Protocol (TCP/IP) is the most widely used protocol in computer networks in the world. All modern network operating systems support TCP/IP. It is a five-layer protocol where the lower four layers have the same functionality as the lower four layers of the OSI model. The fifth layer in the TCP/IP protocol is the application layer, which covers the upper three layers of the OSI model. All hosts in a TCP/IP network are assigned a unique address called an IP address. It is a 32-bit long number divided into four parts of 8 bits each. Each of these parts is called an *octet*. An octet is written as a decimal number ranging from 0 to 255. An IP address is written as a combination of the four octets separated by dot characters. IP addresses are divided into two parts for routing purposes. One of these parts is called the network part, which is common to all hosts on a network, and the other one is the host part. IP networks are classified depending on the length of the network part into A, B, and C

523

classes. Class A addresses are used for very large networks, class B addresses are used for medium-size networks, and class C is reserved for small networks.

TCP and User Datagram Protocol (UDP) are used in the transport layer of the protocol stack. The TCP protocol provides connection-oriented and reliable data delivery. The UDP protocol, on the other hand, is an unreliable protocol used for connection-less data transfer. The UDP protocol has less communication overhead compared with TCP and is used for faster but noncritical data transfer, where loss of some data can be tolerated. Examples of the use of the UDP protocol are voice and video communication over IP networks.

In this chapter, we will start with an introduction to the TCP/IP protocol stack and will discuss IP address classes. When building an IP network, you have to assign IP addresses to participating hosts in an orderly fashion, and you will learn how to obtain IP addresses and how to assign these to hosts in a network. *Netmasks* will be used for different network classes to divide larger networks into smaller ones and for routing purposes. You will find a brief introduction to the Address Resolution Protocol (ARP) and the Reverse Address Resolution Protocol (RARP). A short comparison of TCP and UDP protocols will be presented. In the last part of the chapter, you will find an introduction to sockets and ports.

28.1 Introduction to TCP/IP

The *Transmission Control Protocol/Internet Protocol* (TCP/IP) is the most widely used network protocol in the world. This is a five-layer protocol where the lower four layers of the protocol stack resemble the OSI model. The application layer in the TCP/IP model provides the same functionality as do the upper three layers in the OSI model. The Internet Protocol (IP) is used in the network layer of this model for host addressing. Each host on a TCP/IP network is known by its IP address, which is a 32-bit number divided into four parts. TCP/IP provides connection-oriented and connection-less data transfer with the help of two protocols (TCP and UDP) in the fourth layer, which will be discussed shortly.

TCP/IP Layers

The physical layer and the data link layer of the TCP/IP model are like any other network protocol stack. These two layers consist of cabling, network interface adapters, and software drivers for these adapters. A comparison of the TCP/IP and OSI models is shown in Figure 28-1.

IP Address

Addresses assigned to each host in the IP layer are called *IP addresses*. Each IP address is a 32-bit number divided into four parts of 8 bits each. Each part consisting of 4 bits is called an octet. Octets in the IP address are separated by dot symbols. Since an octet consists of 8 bits, its value can range from 0 to 255. A typical IP address looks like 192.168.3.45. All nodes on a network must have unique IP addresses.

IP addresses are not assigned randomly, but in an orderly fashion. If you want to connect your local network to the Internet, you have to get *legal* IP addresses from your network provider to avoid duplication of IP addresses and maintain of proper routing. However, if your network is an isolated one, you can use your own IP address assignment scheme.

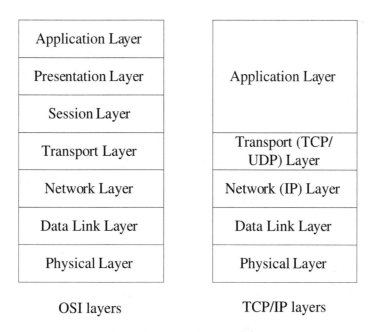

OSI layers   TCP/IP layers

Figure 28–1 *Comparison of TCP/IP and OSI models.*

It should be clarified at this point that IP addresses are not like MAC addresses that are used at the data link layer. MAC addresses are hardware addresses that are fixed for network interface adapters. IP addresses are logical addresses and are assigned by a network administrator during the configuration process of a network. Another difference is that MAC addresses are 48 bits long whereas IP addresses are 32 bits long.

Network Address

An IP address consists of two parts, a network part and a host part. The network part of the IP address is called a *network address*. It is common to all hosts on a network, whereas the host part is unique for every system connected to a network. For example, 24 bits starting from the left can be used as the network address, and the remaining 8 bits can be used for host addresses.

 Note   Network addresses in an IP-based network are logical addresses. More than one IP network can exist on a single physical network. HP-UX also supports virtual adapters for assigning multiple IP addresses to a single physical network interface adapter.

IP Address Classes

Depending on the number of bits used for the network part of an IP address, IP addresses are divided into classes, each of which is intended for a specific purpose.

- Class A is used for very large networks having more than 65,000 nodes.
- Class B is used for medium-size networks where the number of nodes is less than 65,000 but more than 254.
- Class C is used for small networks with less than 255 nodes.
- Class D is a special class of IP addresses intended for multicast networks.
- Class E is reserved for future use.

CLASS A NETWORKS

Class A networks use the leftmost octet as the network address and the other three octets as the host or node address. All IP addresses that start with a first bit of 0 fall into this category. This is the range of IP addresses with a first octet value ranging from 1 to 127. The maximum number of hosts in a class

A network is $2^{24} - 2$. Figure 28-2 shows the division of class A IP address bits into network and host parts.

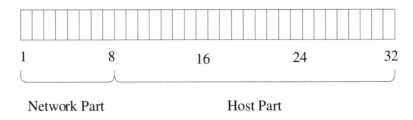

| 1 | 8 | 16 | 24 | 32 |

Network Part   Host Part

Figure 28–2 *Division of network and host parts in a class A IP address.*

CLASS B NETWORKS

Two octets of an IP address from the left-hand side are used as the network part in class B networks. All IP addresses starting with bit pattern 10 are class B addresses. IP addresses with a first octet value from 128 to 191 fall into class B category. The maximum number of hosts in a class B network is $2^{16} - 2$. Figure 28-3 shows the division of class B IP address bits into network and host parts.

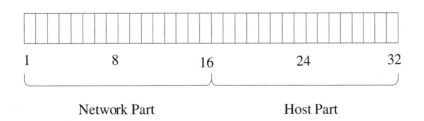

| 1 | 8 | 16 | 24 | 32 |

Network Part   Host Part

Figure 28–3 *Division of network and host parts in a class B IP address.*

CLASS C NETWORKS

Three octets from the left-hand side in an IP address are used for the network part while the rightmost octet is used for the host part. All IP addresses starting with bit pattern 110 are class C IP addresses. IP addresses with a first octet value from 192 to 223 fall into this category. At the most, 254 hosts can be placed in a class C network. Figure 28-4 shows division of class C IP address bits into network and host parts.

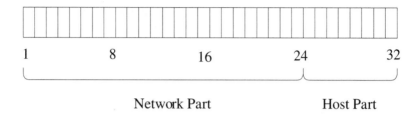

Figure 28–4 *Division of network and host parts in a class C IP address.*

Table 28-1 summarizes the properties of IP address classes, where the starting bit pattern and number of bits in the host and network parts for each class are shown.

Table 28–1 *Summary of IP Address Classes*

Class	Starting Bit Pattern	Network Bits	Host Bits
A	0	8	24
B	10	16	16
C	110	24	8

28.2 Building an IP Network

The first step toward building an IP-based network is to select a particular class of network addresses. For this you need to know or estimate how many hosts will be included in your network. When deciding on the number of hosts, you should also keep in mind future expansion of the network. Based on the number of hosts, you can decide which class of network addresses should be used.

If you don't plan to connect your network to any public network such as the Internet, you can select any network address for your network. If you want to connect the network to the Internet, you must get a range of IP addresses from your Internet service provider or from the address assignment organization for your geographic location. These organizations are listed below according to geographic region.

For North and South America
American Registry for Internet Numbers
ARIN
4506 Daly Drive, Suite 200
Chantilly, VA 20151
Phone Number: +1-703-227-0660
Fax Number: +1-703-227-0676
E-Mail: hostmaster@arin.net
WWW: http://www.arin.net

For Asia Pacific Region
Asia Pacific Network Information Center
APNIC
Level 1, 33 Park Road
P.O. Box 2131
Milton, QLD 4064
Australia
Phone Number: +61-7-3367-0490
Fax Number: +61-7-3367-0482
E-Mail: hostmaster@apnic.net
WWW: http://www.apnic.net

For Europe
Réseaux IP Européens
RIPE NCC
Singel 258
1016 AB Amsterdam
The Netherlands
Phone Number: +31-20-535-4444
Fax Number: +31-20-535-4445
E-Mail: hostmaster@ripe.net
WWW: http://www.ripe.net

Even if you don't want to connect your network with the Internet at the present time, it is better to get a network address from one of these organizations so that when you decide to have an Internet connection, you won't need to make any changes to the network.

Assigning IP Addresses

After selecting a network class and getting a network number, you can assign IP addresses to individual hosts. When assigning IP addresses, keep the following considerations in mind.

- The first IP address (the smallest IP address) in your network is the network number or network address. This is also called a *generic network address*. Don't assign this address to any host. For example, if you are using a class C network address 192.168.4, don't assign IP address 192.168.4.0 to any host.
- The last IP address in your network (the largest IP address in a network) is the *broadcast address*. This should not be assigned to any host. All hosts in the network receive any data packet sent to this IP address. In the above example, 192.168.4.255 is the broadcast address.
- You should reserve the first working IP address in your network for the router. This is not mandatory but it makes it easy to remember the router address and is a general convention. In the above example, 192.168.4.1 should be reserved for the router.
- You should also devise an IP address assignment scheme to ensure that no IP addresses are duplicated in your network.
- If a host has multiple network interface adapters, a unique IP address must be assigned to each one.
- Multiple IP addresses can be assigned to a single network interface adapter.
- IP address 127.0.0.1 is a special address known as the *loopback address*. It is used for test purposes. A data packet sent at this address is received by the host itself.

Netmasks and Subnetting

A *netmask* is used to separate the network and host parts of an IP address. It consists of a continuous sequence of 1s equal to the number of bits in the network part of an IP address. After that, a sequence of 0s equal to the number of bits in the host part is present. For example, class C networks consist of 24 bits in the network part and 8 bits in the host part. A netmask for class C networks consists of twenty-four 1s and eight 0s. Thus the netmask for all class C networks (if these are not subnetted) is always 255.255.255.0 (11111111111111111111111100000000). Similarly, the netmask for class B networks is 255.255.0.0, and the netmask for class A networks is 255.0.0.0. The netmask is the same for all hosts in a network.

A netmask plays an important role in subnetting. *Subnetting* is a process in which a network is broken into smaller networks. For example, if you have only one class C network address space and want to set up two networks of 20 hosts each, you can break the class C network into a number of smaller networks. A class C network consists of 256 IP addresses (including generic network and broadcast addresses) in total. This can be broken into four subnetworks of 64 IP addresses each with the help of netmasks. This is accomplished by using 26 bits in the network part of an IP address and 6 bits in the host part of an IP address. In this case, the netmask will contain twenty-six 1s and six 0s resulting in 255.255.255.192 (11111111111111111111111111000000). The generic network addresses and broadcast addresses are shown in Table 28-2. The class C network used in this example is 192.168.4.0.

Table 28–2 *Dividing a Class C Network into Four Networks*

Network Address	Netmask	Broadcast Address	Range of Host Addresses
192.168.4.0	255.255.255.192	192.168.4.63	192.168.4.1 – 192.168.4.62
192.168.4.64	255.255.255.192	192.168.4.127	192.168.4.65 – 192.168.4.126
192.168.4.128	255.255.255.192	192.168.4.191	192.168.4.129 – 192.168.4.190
192.168.4.192	255.255.255.192	192.168.4.255	192.168.4.193 – 192.168.4.254

Using the same subnetting technique, class A and class B networks can also be divided into smaller networks. Netmasks also play an important role in data routing.

IP Routes

When two or more IP networks are connected with the help of routers, IP routes are defined that are used to send data through a specific router when the source and destination hosts are not present on the same network. Figure 28-5 shows a scenario where three networks are attached to each other using three routers. A fourth router connects these three networks to the Internet.

Networks A and B are connected together with the help of router A. Networks B and C are connected together with the help of router B. Networks A and C are connected using router C. All of these three networks are connected to router D, which is also connected to the Internet.

Multiple routes are defined in each network. For example, hosts in network A have a route defined to network B that passes through router A. They also have a route defined to network C, that passes through router C. Similarly, the other two networks have their own route definitions.

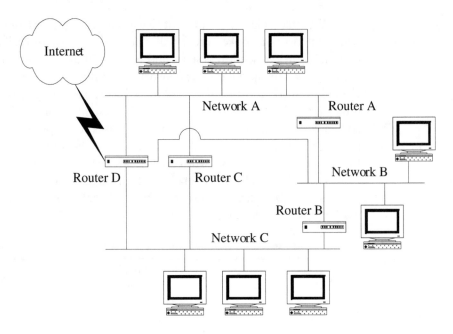

Figure 28–5   *Use of routers in IP networks.*

DEFAULT ROUTE

Router D in Figure 28-5 is connected to all three networks and the Internet. If the destination address does not lie in any of these three networks, the data packet is sent to router D, which acts as a default route. The default route is used as a last resort in the routing process to send a data packet. It is the responsibility of the default router to determine where a packet should go if the destination address is not present in any of the local network addresses. Router D is also responsible for distributing incoming data packets from the Internet among these three networks.

ROUTING PROCESS

When a host wants to send a data packet, the network layer checks the destination IP address for the routing information. If the destination host is in the same network as the sending host, the data packet is sent directly to the destination host without involvement of a router. In case the destination host is not on the local network, other defined routes are tried. If a route is found, the data packet is forwarded to a specific router depending on the destination address. The router then forwards the data packet to the destination host. In

case no defined route is found for the destination address, the packet is forwarded to the router acting as default gateway using the default route. It is then the responsibility of this router to deliver the data packet to the destination host with the help of its own routing method.

ROUTING PROTOCOLS

Static routes are defined by the network administrator and remain fixed. Dynamic routes are calculated in real time and keep changing depending on network conditions. Different routing protocols are used for calculating dynamic routes. HP-UX supports the most commonly used routing protocols.

- Routing Information Protocol (RIP)
- Open Shortest Path First Protocol (OSPF)
- Border Gateway Protocol (BGP)
- Exterior Gateway Protocol (EGP)

Address Resolution Protocol

IP addresses are used at the network layer. These are the logical addresses used for hosts connected to a network. At the network layer level, the data packets contain source and destination IP addresses. However, at the physical and data link layer level, hosts recognize each other with physical (MAC) addresses instead of IP addresses. When the data reach the data link layer on the sending host, the host must know the physical addresses of the receiving host in addition to the destination IP address. A special protocol known as *Address Resolution Protocol* (ARP) is used for this purpose. The address resolution protocol may be thought of as a function that takes the destination of the IP address as input and gives the destination MAC address as its output.

ARP uses a broadcast mechanism to determine the MAC address of the destination host. It sends a broadcast data packet on the network asking the identity (MAC address) of the host who is assigned the destination IP address. The request is like the following.

"Send me your MAC address if you have *this IP address*," where "this IP address" is the IP address of the destination host. Every host on the network listens to this request and only that host responds whose IP address matches the destination IP address.

The HP-UX kernel maintains a special data structure in memory known as the *ARP cache*, which contains a mapping of IP addresses to MAC addresses. When ARP successfully resolves an IP address, its entry is added into the ARP cache and remains in the table for 10 minutes.

HP-UX provides the `arp` command, which is used to display and manage the contents of the ARP cache. The following command displays the contents of the ARP cache.

```
# arp -a
192.168.3.45 (192.168.3.45) at 0:10:83:36:d1:dc ether
192.168.3.10 (192.168.3.10) at 0:60:b0:59:fe:99 ether
192.168.3.17 (192.168.3.17) at 0:60:83:2:50:20 ether
#
```

In addition to displaying ARP cache contents, the `arp` command can be used to add and delete ARP entries manually.

Study Break

Adding Entries to the ARP Cache

You can easily display the contents of the ARP cache using the `arp -a` command. If you had no network communication for more than 10 minutes, you will see only one ARP cache entry, showing your own IP address. To add additional ARP entries, you can use the `arp -s` command. However, if you use the `ping` command to send data packets to some other hosts on the network, ARP will be used to resolve the MAC addresses of these hosts, and new ARP entries will be created in the ARP cache. Try to `ping` at least three other hosts and then use the `arp -a` command again. You will find MAC addresses of these hosts along with their IP addresses in the ARP cache.

Reverse Address Resolution Protocol (RARP)

In some cases, you need the reverse process of the ARP. You already know the MAC address and want to find out the IP address corresponding to that MAC address. One example of this situation is a diskless client. A diskless client does know its MAC address at boot time, but due to nonavailability of disk files, it is unaware of its IP address. Just after the boot process, it contacts a BootP or DHCP server using the *Reverse Address Resolution Protocol* (RARP) and asks it to provide the IP address corresponding to its MAC address. A BootP or DHCP server provides the IP address to the client after receiving the request. An HP-UX machine can be configured as an RARP server.

Internet Control Message Protocol

The *Internet Control Message Protocol* (ICMP) is used for network monitoring and troubleshooting purposes. ICMP uses data packets to convey information about the status of the network, such as network congestion and network unreachable conditions. The common use of ICMP is the `ping` command. Using this command, you send a data packet to a host to check if the host is alive. When the receiving host receives this data packet, it returns it to the sending host. If you then receive the data packet, you know that the host is alive. In the other case, it is assumed that the host is dead or can't communicate on the network. The returned data packet also contains time information that shows the time taken by the data packet in the round trip. The simplest form of the `ping` command is shown here. To stop the command, use the CTRL-c key combination.

```
# ping 192.168.3.13
PING 192.168.3.13: 64 byte packets
64 bytes from 192.168.3.13: icmp_seq=0. time=2. ms
64 bytes from 192.168.3.13: icmp_seq=1. time=0. ms
64 bytes from 192.168.3.13: icmp_seq=2. time=0. ms
64 bytes from 192.168.3.13: icmp_seq=3. time=0. ms
64 bytes from 192.168.3.13: icmp_seq=4. time=0. ms
64 bytes from 192.168.3.13: icmp_seq=5. time=0. ms
64 bytes from 192.168.3.13: icmp_seq=6. time=0. ms
64 bytes from 192.168.3.13: icmp_seq=7. time=0. ms

----192.168.3.13 PING Statistics----
8 packets transmitted, 8 packets received, 0% packet loss
round-trip (ms)  min/avg/max = 0/0/2
#
```

By default, the data packet size of the ICMP packet used by the `ping` command is 64 bytes. You can change the data packet size to check delivery of large packets on the network. The following command uses a data packet size of 20,000 bytes. Note that the larger the data packet size, the more time it takes to process them.

```
# ping 192.168.3.13 20000
PING 192.168.3.13: 20000 byte packets
20000 bytes from 192.168.3.13: icmp_seq=0. time=10. ms
20000 bytes from 192.168.3.13: icmp_seq=1. time=9. ms
20000 bytes from 192.168.3.13: icmp_seq=2. time=9. ms
20000 bytes from 192.168.3.13: icmp_seq=3. time=9. ms
```

```
----192.168.3.13 PING Statistics----
4 packets transmitted, 4 packets received, 0% packet loss
round-trip (ms)  min/avg/max = 9/9/10
#
```

28.3 TCP and UDP Protocols

The *Transmission Control Protocol* (TCP) and the *User Datagram Protocol* (UDP) are used in the transport layer (fourth layer) of the TCP/IP protocol stack. Depending on particular requirements, different applications in the application layer of the TCP/IP protocol stack use one or both of these protocols for data communication. A short explanation of these two protocols is presented here.

TCP Protocol

TCP is designed for reliable data transfer. When this protocol is used, the sending side fragments data into smaller data packets. These data packets are then transferred to the destination host. Each data packet contains source and destination IP addresses, data, a sequence number, and checksum fields, in addition to other information. When these data packets reach their destination, the receiving host checks for errors and packet sequences. It then acknowledges the sending host that the packets were received. If a data packet contains an error or is lost along the way, the receiving host requests the sending host to retransmit the data packets. After successfully receiving all data packets, the receiving host reassembles the data packets according to their sequence numbers and regenerates the actual data.

TCP is a reliable data transmission method because the transport layer is responsible for recovering from lost or faulty data packets. TCP is also called a connection-oriented protocol because both sending and receiving hosts establish a connection before actual data transfer takes place. A TCP connection can be thought of as a phone call where you have to establish a connection before starting the conversation.

UDP Protocol

UDP is a connection-less protocol because no connection is established between sending and receiving hosts before starting the communication process. It is not a reliable protocol in that the receiving host does not send any acknowledgement to the sending host after receiving data packets. If a packet is lost along the way, the sending host never knows about it. A UDP data transfer can be thought of as a letter sent by mail. Before sending a letter, you don't establish a link with the recipient. And you don't get any acknowledgment from the post office whether the letter is delivered.

In the UDP protocol, the application layer has responsibility for the reliability of the data. Due to less communication overhead, UDP is used in applications where speed is more important and loss of some data can be tolerated. Examples of such communication are voice and video communications over IP networks. Comparison of TCP and UDP protocols is presented in Table 28-3.

Table 28–3 *Comparison of TCP and UDP Protocols*

TCP Protocol	UDP Protocol
It is a reliable protocol. Any errors or lost data is recovered with the acknowledgement mechanism.	UDP is not a reliable protocol. If data are lost, UDP remains ignorant about it and continues to send the remaining data.
It is a connection-oriented protocol. A connection is established between source and destination hosts before starting data transmission.	It is a connection-less protocol. The sending side starts transmitting data without establishing a connection with the receiving side.
TCP is a slow protocol because a considerable amount of the network traffic consists of acknowledgment packets. The transmitting side stops sending data when the TCP window (explained next) limit is reached, and no acknowledgement is received from the receiving side. This happens even if there is no error in the transmission.	UDP is a fast protocol because there are no acknowledgment packets. This reduces communication overhead.

TCP Window Size

During data transfer using TCP, a host can send multiple packets without receiving an acknowledgment from the receiving host. The amount of data that can be transmitted without being acknowledged is called the *TCP window size*. If an acknowledgment is not received during this time, the sending host stops sending data until it gets an acknowledgment from the receiving host.

TCP window size plays an important role in the efficiency of a network, especially wide area networks. Usually a larger window size is used on slower networks to improve efficiency of data transfer. Different window sizes can be used for sending and receiving data. The ndd command can be used to fine tune TCP window sizes.

Ports and Sockets

Usually many network applications are running on one system simultaneously. These applications may be communicating to many other hosts using underlying TCP and UDP protocols. The question arises: how does the transport layer come to know that a received data packet corresponds to a particular application? To solve this problem, applications use a *port number*. A port number is a unique identification number assigned to an application. These port numbers are used while sending data to a particular application on another host. Port numbers for standard applications are listed in the /etc/services file on HP-UX. As an example, Telnet uses port number 23, and Web browsers use port number 80.

Many clients may be using one server application on a host at the same time with the help of the same port number. For example, many clients may be accessing the same Web server simultaneously. Since the port number used is the same, the server needs to have additional information to process client requests separately and send data to a client depending on a particular request. In our example of a Web server, different clients (Web browsers) are requesting different files, so the server needs to know to which client a particular file goes. This additional information is provided through the use of sockets. A *socket* is a combination of an IP address and port number. For example, when a client starts communication with a server, the server opens a socket on its side. For this socket, the client uses an available port number. If the IP address of the client is 192.168.3.l7 and the first available port number is 1035, the socket address will be 192.168.3.17.1035. Using this socket address, the client sends a request to the Web server having IP address 192.168.3.20, who is listening to incoming requests at port number 80 (HTTP port). The socket address of the server is 192.168.3.20.80. If the server accepts the request, a socket connection is established between sockets 192.168.3.17.1035 and 192.168.3.20.80 and data communication starts. Each client has a different socket address, so the server can communicate with each client separately.

A list of opened ports and connected sockets can be displayed using the netstat -a command on HP-UX. This list may be quite long depending on the network traffic on a host.

■ **Chapter Summary**

TCP/IP is the most widely used and de facto protocol of the Internet. It is a five-layer protocol. The first four layers of the protocol provide the same functionality as defined by the OSI model. The fifth layer combines the upper three layers of the OSI model. TCP/IP layers are listed here.

1. physical layer
2. data link layer
3. network or IP layer
4. transport or TCP layer
5. application layer

Unique network addresses known as IP addresses are assigned in the IP layer of the protocol stack. An IP address is a 32-bits-long number consisting of four octets of 8 bits each. An octet is written as a decimal number from 0 to 255. While writing an IP address, the four octets are separated by dot symbols.

Each IP address has two parts, a network part and a host part. The network part is common to all hosts on a network. Netmasks are used to separate the network and host parts of an IP address. Depending on the length of the network part, IP networks are divided into different classes. In class A networks, the network part is 8 bits, and the remaining 24 bits are used for the host part. In class B networks, 16 bits are used for the network part, and in class C networks, 24 bits are used in the network part. IP addresses start in class A networks with a 0 bit, in class B networks with a 10-bit pattern, and in class C networks with a 110-bit pattern.

If you have an isolated network, you can select a network address of your own choice. However, if you want to connect your network to a public network like the Internet, you have to get IP addresses from the network registration body for your geographical location. When you connect two or more networks, routes are established for data transfer among these networks. A default route is defined to transfer data through a particular router for which no other route is available. A route may be a static route or a dynamic route. HP-UX supports static as well as a number of dynamic routing protocols.

Network communication on the physical media takes place using physical addresses instead of IP addresses. For this you have to map IP addresses to physical or MAC addresses. Address Resolution Protocol (ARP) is used for this purpose. The Reverse Address Resolution Protocol (RARP) does the reverse job. The mapping of IP addresses to MAC addresses is kept in the ARP cache, which is maintained in memory by the HP-UX kernel. The `arp` command can be used to display and manage the ARP cache. Another protocol, known as Internet Control Message Protocol (ICMP), is used to monitor and troubleshoot TCP/IP networks.

TCP and UDP protocols are transport layer protocols. TCP is used for reliable, connection-oriented data transfer, and UDP is used for unreliable, connection-less data transfer. TCP uses a window and acknowledgment mechanism to ensure that data are delivered without any error. Since UDP has no acknowledgment mechanism, it is faster than TCP. When multiple applications on the same host are communicating over the network, ports and sockets are used at the transport layer level to route data packets to different applications. A port is a number assigned to all applications. Standard port numbers are present in the /etc/services file. A socket is a combination of an IP address and a port number.

▲ CHAPTER REVIEW QUESTIONS

1. What is the use of a netmask?

2. What are the major differences between the TCP and UDP protocols?

3. What is the use of sockets?

4. Why is ARP necessary for network communication?

▲ TEST YOUR KNOWLEDGE

1. *The application layer of the OSI model covers which three layers?*
   A. network, transport, session
   B. application, session, presentation
   C. application, presentation, transport
   D. application, session, transport

2. *What is the starting bit pattern of a class C IP address?*
   A. 01
   B. 011
   C. 10
   D. 110

3. *The maximum number of hosts in a class C network are:*
   A. 128
   B. 256
   C. 254
   D. 1024

4. *A host on an IP network has an IP address 192.168.3.65 with a netmask 255.255.255.224. What is the broadcast address?*
   A. 192.168.3.255
   B. 192.168.3.128
   C. 192.168.3.96
   D. 192.168.3.64

5. *Given a netmask of 255.255.255.240, how many hosts can be placed in the network?*
   A. 14
   B. 16
   C. 240
   D. 256

6. *In an IP network, 18 bits are used in the network address. What is the value of the netmask?*
   A. 255.255.192.0
   B. 255.255.252.0
   C. 255.255.0.0
   D. 255.255.255.192

7. *Address resolution protocol is used to:*
   A. map IP addresses to MAC addresses
   B. map MAC addresses to IP addresses
   C. resolve host addresses
   D. resolve address conflicts

8. *Which statement is true with reference to an IP address and a socket address?*
   A. The IP address is longer than the socket address.
   B. The socket address is longer than the IP address.
   C. The IP address is used in the transport layer.
   D. The socket address is used in the network layer.

9. *Which file on HP-UX contains standard port numbers assigned to different applications?*
   A. /etc/ports
   B. /etc/services
   C. /etc/protocols
   D. /etc/inetd.conf

Configuring LAN Interface Adapters

Configuring a LAN adapter is the first step toward connecting any HP-UX system to a network. There may be one or more LAN adapters installed in a system. HP-UX recognizes an adapter with a name of the form `lanx` where *x* is an integer. Many device drivers for LAN adapters are built into the HP-UX kernel. However, you may have to install additional device drivers for some LAN adapters. HP-UX provides commands to list installed adapters in your system. After physical installation, the next step is to configure one or more of these adapters by assigning IP addresses. If network cables are connected, your system can communicate on the network after getting an IP address.

A network adapter may be configured using command-line utilities or SAM. If you are using command-line utilities, you should also configure the IP addresses to be assigned to adapters at boot time. If you use SAM, it automatically updates system files so that all configured network adapters get their address at boot time. After assigning

543

IP addresses to each adapter, you have to add routing entries. If your LAN consists of only one network, there is no need to add any additional routing. However, if there are multiple networks or the LAN is connected to the Internet, you need to add additional routing table entries. If you use a router, you can assign a *default* route to that router so that any packet with a destination address not on the local network is forwarded to the router. It is then the responsibility of the router to forward this packet to the destination address or another router.

In this chapter, we will start with the configuration of a LAN adapter. You will find information about the adapter-naming convention used for LAN adapters. Commands will be used to list installed network adapters. You will also learn some commands to view and set properties of these adapters. The next part is to assign IP addresses to the adapters. Here you will use command-line utilities. You will also learn how to configure IP addresses so that these are assigned to network adapters at system boot time. After configuration you will learn how to add and remove network routes. A default routing entry will be set that will point to the gateway machine used to connect the LAN to the outside world. SAM will also be used to configure network adapters. Sometimes things don't go smoothly and you may have to do some troubleshooting. The last part of the chapter is devoted to this. Here some commands will be presented that are useful for LAN troubleshooting.

29.1   Configuring LAN Adapters

The first step toward the configuration of a LAN adapter is to list the available adapters. Some of the adapters may not have their device drivers installed with the standard HP-UX installation. These adapters are not visible until you install related device drivers for them. The lsdev command can be used to list configured drivers for the LAN adapters as follows.

```
# lsdev -C lan
    Character      Block       Driver         Class
        52          -1         lan2           lan
       140          -1         fcgsc_lan      lan
       169          -1         btlan3         lan
```

```
        170          -1          btlan4          lan
        172          -1          fddi3           lan
        173          -1          btlan1          lan
        236          -1          maclan          lan
   #
```

The command shows the major number for the driver and the driver name. Each adapter has some parameters associated with it, such as data transfer speed and maximum transfer unit (MTU). You can modify some of these parameters using HP-UX commands.

LAN Adapter-Naming Convention

Names for LAN adapters follow a convention where the name of each adapter consists of two parts. The first part is the name and the second part is a number showing the physical point of attachment (PPA). The combination of these two is called the *NamePPA*. Usually this combination starts with lan or snap followed by a PPA number. Any operation on an adapter is performed through this name. Names starting with lan are used for Ethernet encapsulation, while those starting with snap are used for IEEE 802.3 encapsulation. Common device names are lan0, lan1, and so on.

Detecting LAN Adapters

You have already used the ioscan command to list disk and tape drives. All LAN adapters fall into the lan class of devices. The following command lists all installed devices of class lan.

```
# ioscan -funC lan
Class     I  H/W Path  Driver      S/W State H/W Type  Description
==================================================================
lan       0  10/4/8    btlan1      CLAIMED    INTERFACE HP HP-PB 100
   Base TX card
lan       1  10/4/16   btlan1      CLAIMED    INTERFACE HP HP-PB 100
   Base TX card
lan       2  10/12/6   lan2        CLAIMED    INTERFACE Built-in LAN
                       /dev/diag/lan2   /dev/ether2
   #
```

The command shows that there are three LAN adapters installed in the system. You can see the instance number, hardware path, and driver name for each of these adapters. A CLAIMED in the S/W State column shows that the software driver is successfully bound with the adapter. The INTERFACE in the

`H/W Type` column shows this type of hardware is an interface adapter. The last column shows a small description of the interface card. The last line shows device file names for `lan2`.

In addition to the `ioscan` command, a more-specific command named `lanscan` can be used to list LAN adapters. This command shows additional information about each adapter. Output of this command is shown here.

```
# lanscan
Hardware  Station         Crd Hdw   Net-Interface  NM   MAC    HP-DLPI  DLPI
Path      Address         In# State NamePPA         ID   Type   Support  Mjr#
10/4/16   0x080009D41DBB  1   UP    lan1 snap1      1    ETHER  Yes      119
10/4/8    0x080009D481F6  0   UP    lan0 snap0      2    ETHER  Yes      119
10/12/6   0x080009F02610  2   UP    lan2 snap2      3    ETHER  Yes      119
#
```

In the output of the `lanscan` command, columns that show additional information are as follows.

`Station Address`	This column shows a 48-bit Ethernet address. This is represented in hexadecimal notation. Each LAN adapter has a unique Ethernet address. This address is also called *MAC address* or *physical address*.
`NamePPA`	A single adapter can support more than one protocol. The combination of name and PPA is shown under this column. A name starting with `lan` is used for Ethernet encapsulation, while a name starting with `snap` is used for IEEE 802.3 encapsulation.
`NM ID`	Network Management ID. This is used with the `lanadmin` command for diagnosis and for changing network parameters.
`MAC Type`	Shows what type of MAC layer is used with this adapter.
`HP-DLPI Support`	Shows whether the device will work with an HP Data Link Provider Interface.

Use of the `-v` option with the command shows the extended station address and supported encapsulation methods as shown next. The `Extended Station Address` is used for interfaces that need more than 48 bits of physical address. The `LLC Encapsulation Methods` lists supported encapsulation methods on this interface adapter.

```
# lanscan -v
------------------------------------------------------------------------
Hardware Station          Crd Hdw   Net-Interface  NM  MAC      HP-DLPI DLPI
Path     Address          In# State NamePPA         ID  Type     Support Mjr#
10/4/16  0x080009D41DBB   1   UP    lan1 snap1      1   ETHER    Yes     119

Extended Station                    LLC Encapsulation
Address                             Methods
0x080009D41DBB                      IEEE HPEXTIEEE SNAP ETHER NOVELL

Driver Specific Information
btlan1
------------------------------------------------------------------------
Hardware Station          Crd Hdw   Net-Interface  NM  MAC      HP-DLPI DLPI
Path     Address          In# State NamePPA         ID  Type     Support Mjr#
10/4/8   0x080009D481F6   0   UP    lan0 snap0      2   ETHER    Yes     119

Extended Station                    LLC Encapsulation
Address                             Methods
0x080009D481F6                      IEEE HPEXTIEEE SNAP ETHER NOVELL

Driver Specific Information
btlan1
------------------------------------------------------------------------
Hardware Station          Crd Hdw   Net-Interface  NM  MAC      HP-DLPI DLPI
Path     Address          In# State NamePPA         ID  Type     Support Mjr#
10/12/6  0x080009F02610   2   UP    lan2 snap2      3   ETHER    Yes     119

Extended Station                    LLC Encapsulation
Address                             Methods
0x080009F02610                      IEEE HPEXTIEEE SNAP ETHER NOVELL

Driver Specific Information
lan2
------------------------------------------------------------------------
#
```

29.2 Configuring an IP Address to a LAN Adapter

To assign an IP address to a LAN adapter, the `ifconfig` command is used. This command is also used to display the IP address assigned to an adapter. For example, the following command shows an IP address assigned to `lan0`.

```
# ifconfig lan0
lan0: flags=843<UP,BROADCAST,RUNNING,MULTICAST>
inet 192.168.2.11 netmask ffffff00 broadcast 192.168.2.255
#
```

To configure interface `lan2` with IP address 192.168.3.1, use the following command.

```
ifconfig lan2 192.168.3.1 netmask 255.255.255.0 broadcast
192.168.3.255 up
```

The `netmask` keyword is used to specify a netmask with the IP address. Netmask is used for subnetting. A broadcast keyword is used to set the broadcast address for the interface. Now if you display the interface with the following command, it shows the configuration just assigned to it.

```
# ifconfig lan2
lan2: flags=843<UP,BROADCAST,RUNNING,MULTICAST>
inet 192.168.3.1 netmask ffffff00 broadcast 192.168.3.255
#
```

Enabling LAN Adapters at Boot Time Using the /etc/rc.config.d/netconf File

A configuration that was created using the `ifconfig` command will be finished if you reboot the system. It means you need to execute the `ifconfig` command at system startup time. This is done through the execution of the `/sbin/init.d/net` script at run level 2. This script reads configuration information from the `/etc/rc.config.d/netconf` file. This configuration file keeps information of IP addresses assigned to each network interface. At system boot time, this information is used to configure LAN adapters. Typical entries in the configuration file for the two configured interfaces are shown next. The first two lines show the IP address and netmask, while the third line contains the name of the interface to which this address is assigned. Square brackets in every line enclose the reference number used for all entries related to one LAN adapter. The number 0 is used for all lines related to `lan0`, and the number 2 is used for all lines related to `lan2`.

```
IP_ADDRESS[0]=192.168.2.11
SUBNET_MASK[0]=255.255.255.0
INTERFACE_NAME[0]=lan0
BROADCAST_ADDRESS[0]=192.168.2.255
```

```
INTERFACE_STATE[0]=up
ROUTE_GATEWAY[0]=192.168.2.1
ROUTE_COUNT[0]=1
ROUTE_DESTINATION[0]=default
DHCP_ENABLE[0]=0
IP_ADDRESS[2]=192.168.3.1
SUBNET_MASK[2]=255.255.255.0
INTERFACE_NAME[2]=lan2
BROADCAST_ADDRESS[2]=192.168.3.255
INTERFACE_STATE[2]=up
```

If you are not using SAM, you have to manually create these entries for every LAN adapter.

After assigning IP addresses with the `ifconfig` command, you can use the `netstat` command to verify that the network interfaces are up and correct addresses are assigned to them.

```
# netstat -in
Name   Mtu Network          Address          Ipkts     Opkts
lan2  1500 192.168.3.0      192.168.3.1          0         0
lan0  1500 192.168.2.0      192.168.2.11     31740     32864
lo0   4136 127.0.0.0        127.0.0.1          303       303
#
```

Assigning Multiple IP Addresses to a Single LAN Adapter

You can also assign multiple IP addresses to one physical network adapter. This may be needed if you want to run different services using unique IP addresses. To assign a second IP address, you add a logical instance number to a LAN adapter name. It is a number that is added to the NamePPA (e.g., `lan2`) after a colon. The following command adds a second IP address, 192.168.3.5, to `lan2`.

```
ifconfig lan2:1 192.168.3.5 netmask 255.255.255.0 broadcast
192.168.3.255 up
```

After assigning the second IP address, you can use the `netstat` command to verify it. To make the second address permanent, you have to add its configuration the `/etc/rc.config.d/netconf` file.

```
# netstat -in
Name     Mtu Network        Address          Ipkts     Opkts
lan2    1500 192.168.3.0     192.168.3.1          0         0
lan0    1500 192.168.2.0     192.168.2.11     31740     32864
lo0     4136 127.0.0.0       127.0.0.1          303       303
lan2:1  1500 192.168.3.0     192.168.3.5          0         0
#
```

Updating the /etc/hosts File

After assigning an IP address to a network adapter, you should add one or more aliases for that IP address in the /etc/hosts file. These aliases are arbitrary names used to refer to the adapter's IP address. In this case, the host name is myhp, which is linked to IP address 192.168.2.11. When we configure a second adapter, we can add an alias hp0 with it. The resulting /etc/hosts file looks like the following.

```
## Configured using SAM by root on Fri Dec  3 12:30:36 1999
# @(#)hosts $Revision: 1.9.14.1 $ $Date: 96/10/08 13:20:01 $
#
# The form for each entry is:
# <internet address>    <official hostname> <aliases>
#
# For example:
# 192.1.2.34    hpfcrm  loghost
#
# See the hosts(4) manual page for more information.
# Note: The entries cannot be preceded by a space.
# The format described in this file is the correct format.
# The original Berkeley manual page contains an error in
# the format description.
#

192.168.3.1 myhp hp0
192.168.2.11 myhp myhp
127.0.0.1       localhost       loopback
```

If you are using SAM, this file is automatically updated. More information about this file will be presented in Chapter 34 where name resolution is discussed.

29.3 Adding Routes

When two or more networks are connected, routes must be defined to send data traffic from one network to another. These routes may be static or dynamic in nature. Static routes are manually defined and are fixed until changes are made. Dynamic routes, on the other hand, are established on the fly, depending on network conditions and available network paths between the source and destination. In this chapter, we will discuss only static routes.

A static route may represent a host route or a network path. A host route represents a path to a single machine, while a network route represents a path to a complete network.

Networks are connected through routers. A router is called a gateway when defining routes. Static routes are defined using the `route` command in HP-UX. These routes are set up at system startup along with assignment of IP addresses to the LAN adapters. Static routes can also be configured in the `/etc/rc.config.d/netconf` file. A default route is used to send IP packets for which no other route is available. The default route entry is present in the `/etc/rc.config.d/netconf` file, for example:

```
ROUTE_GATEWAY[0]=192.168.2.1
ROUTE_COUNT[0]=1
ROUTE_DESTINATION[0]=default
```

These lines are used to set a default route to a router having IP address 192.168.2.1. All routes are present in a data structure known as a routing table. The `netstat` command is also used to display the current routing table. The following command lists all routes.

```
# netstat -rn
Routing tables
Dest/Netmask          Gateway             Flags  Refs    Use  Interface  Pmtu
127.0.0.1             127.0.0.1           UH     0       303  lo0        4136
192.168.3.1           192.168.3.1         UH     0       0    lan2       4136
192.168.2.11          192.168.2.11        UH     0       126  lan0       4136
192.168.2.0           192.168.2.11        U      2       0    lan0       1500
192.168.3.0           192.168.3.1         U      2       0    lan2       1500
127.0.0.0             127.0.0.1           U      0       0    lo0        4136
default               192.168.2.1         UG     0       0    lan0       1500
#
```

Different fields in the output of the `netstat -rn` command are:

Dest/Netmask   Route destination. This may be either a host or a network.

Gateway   The host IP address that will be used to send packets for this destination.

Flags   Shows type of route. A "U" is this field shows that the route is currently up. If only this character is present in this column, the route is for a network. The "H" character shows that this route is for a single host. The "G" character shows that the route is through a gateway.

Refs   Shows current use of the route.

Use   Shows the number of packets sent through the route.

Interface   LAN interface that is being used by the route.

Pmtu   Path MTU. Its minimum value is 68.

Creating a Route

Routes are created using the `route` command. You can add specific host or network routes with the help of this command. The following example creates a route for network 192.168.4.0 and its gateway is router 192.168.2.1.

```
route add net 192.168.4.0 netmask 255.255.255.0 192.168.2.1
```

After adding this route, any data packets going to the 192.168.4.0 network will be forwarded to gateway 192.168.2.1. To add a host specific route for 192.168.5.3 through the same gateway, use the following command.

```
route add host 192.168.5.3 netmask 255.255.255.255
192.168.2.1
```

Newly created routes can be displayed using the `netstat -rn` command.

Deleting a Route

A route is deleted using the `route` command. The following example deletes a network route through gateway 192.168.2.1.

```
# route delete net 192.168.4.0 192.168.2.1
delete net 192.168.4.0: gateway 192.168.2.1
#
```

An entire routing table may be flushed using the `route -f` command.

Default Routes

A default route through gateway 192.168.2.1 is added with the following command.

```
route add default 192.168.2.1 1
```

29.4 Using SAM to Configure a LAN Adapter

Like other configuration tasks, SAM can also be used to configure LAN adapters. To configure one or more LAN adapters, go to the `Networking and Communications` area of the main SAM window. Figure 29-1 shows the window that appears.

From this figure, select `Network Interface Cards` by double-clicking on this button. The window for the configuration of LAN adapters is shown in Figure 29-2.

This figure shows a list of installed LAN adapters and any previous configurations used with them. You can select one of the `Not Configured` adapters and use the `Actions` menu to make a new configuration. If you select a previously configured adapter, the `Actions` menu shows additional options to make changes to the previous configuration. Let's select `lan2` and configure it. When you select `Configure` from the `Actions` menu, a new window will appear, as shown in Figure 29-3.

This window is used to assign the `Internet Address` and `Subnet Mask` to the adapter. The `Add Host Name Aliases` button is used to add the name of this network interface in the `/etc/hosts` file. When you click on this button, the window shown in Figure 29-4 appears. Multiple aliases can be added for one adapter.

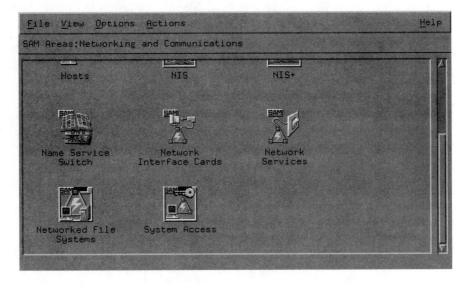

Figure 29–1 *SAM* `Networking and Communications` *area.*

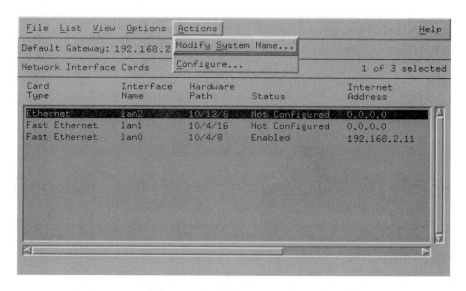

Figure 29–2   *Configuration window for network adapters.*

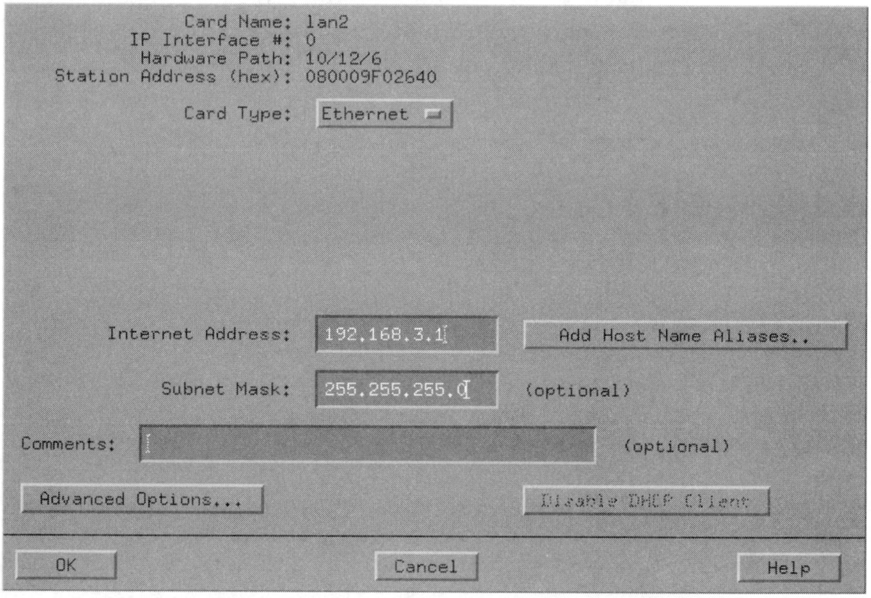

Figure 29–3   *Configuring a new LAN adapter.*

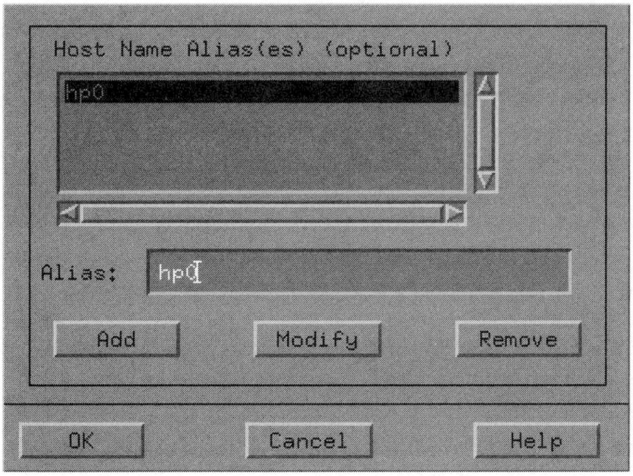

Figure 29–4 *Selecting host name aliases for a network adapter.*

You can also use this window to remove or modify a host name alias. You should create at least one alias name for each adapter. After adding an alias, press the OK button and you will go back to the window shown in Figure 29-3. Again press the OK button to complete the configuration task for the adapter. Now you will see the same screen as in Figure 29-1 but with updated information as shown in Figure 29-5.

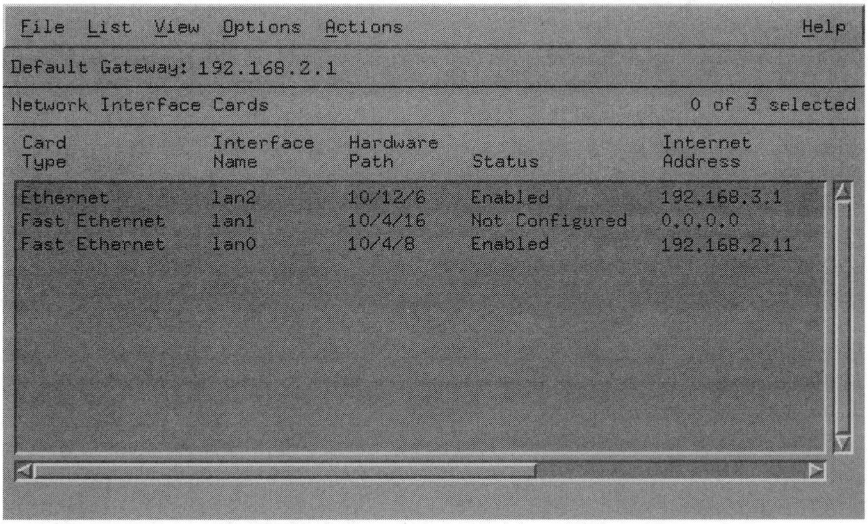

Figure 29–5 *SAM* Networking and Communications *area after configuring* lan2.

29.5   Troubleshooting LAN Connectivity

Common network problems are of two types: those related to physical connectivity and those due to configuration error. The physical problems are as follows.

- network adapter is not installed properly
- in case of coaxial cable, terminator is not connected
- a broken cable
- LAN segment is too long
- router machine is not working

The configuration problems are as follows.

- one IP address is assigned to more than one station
- wrong IP address is assigned to an adapter
- incorrect netmask
- incorrect routing entries

If you are facing any problem with LAN configuration, first try to use the ping command to send data packets to another machine on the network. This command sends ICMP packets to another system on the network that are echoed back. A typical response of the ping command, where you are trying to send ICMP packets to machine 192.168.2.34, is shown.

```
# ping 192.168.2.34
PING s124hp0a.ham.am.honda.com: 64 byte packets
64 bytes from 192.168.2.34: icmp_seq=0. time=2. ms
64 bytes from 192.168.2.34: icmp_seq=1. time=0. ms
64 bytes from 192.168.2.34: icmp_seq=2. time=0. ms
64 bytes from 192.168.2.34: icmp_seq=3. time=0. ms
64 bytes from 192.168.2.34: icmp_seq=4. time=0. ms
64 bytes from 192.168.2.34: icmp_seq=5. time=0. ms
CTRL - C
----192.168.2.34 PING Statistics----
6 packets transmitted, 6 packets received, 0% packet loss
round-trip (ms)  min/avg/max = 0/0/2
#
```

By default, this command continues to send ICMP packets until interrupted by the CTRL-C key combination. At this point, it shows how many packets are sent and how many of these returned from the system. If you don't receive any packets back, it indicates a problem.

Although there is no hard and fast rule for troubleshooting, I would suggest to check for physical problems if the `ping` fails. After that, you can use one of the following commands for specific checks.

- Use `lanscan` to list installed LAN adapters.
- Use the `netstat -in` command to list the assigned IP addresses of the installed software.
- Use the `netstat -rn` command to check routing entries.
- Before assigning a second IP address, use the `ping 255.255.255.255` command to check if the IP address is assigned to another live machine. This commands sends ICMP packets to all machines on your network, and you get responses from all live machines.

Some commands list detailed information about the network. These can be used for low-level troubleshooting and fine-tuning. The `netstat` and `lanadmin` commands are as follows.

Analyzing Protocol Statistics with netstat

The `netstat` command can also be used to get statistics of network activity of each protocol. The following command shows statistics of each protocol on the network.

```
# netstat -sv
tcp:
        20456 packets sent
                17910 data packets (4292600 bytes)
                90 data packets (117386 bytes) retransmitted
                2546 ack-only packets (1176 delayed)
                0 URG only packets
                0 window probe packets
                0 window update packets
                45 control packets
        19044 packets received
                12649 acks (for 4292621 bytes)
                428 duplicate acks
                0 acks for unsent data
                11364 packets (945474 bytes) received in-sequence
                1 completely duplicate packet (32 bytes)
                0 packets with some dup, data (0 bytes duped)
                1 out of order packet (32 bytes)
                0 packets (0 bytes) of data after window
                0 window probes
                5945 window update packets
                0 packets received after close
                0 segments discarded for bad checksum
```

```
        0 bad TCP segments dropped due to state change
20 connection requests
3 connection accepts
23 connections established (including accepts)
24 connections closed (including 1 drop)
1 embryonic connection dropped
12547 segments updated rtt (of 12547 attempts)
20 retransmit timeouts
        0 connections dropped by rexmit timeout
0 persist timeouts
11 keepalive timeouts
        0 keepalive probes sent
        0 connections dropped by keepalive
0 connect requests dropped due to full queue
1 connect request dropped due to no listener
```
udp:
```
21 incomplete headers
0 bad checksums
0 socket overflows
```
ip:
```
21134 total packets received
0 bad IP headers
0 fragments received
0 fragments dropped (dup or out of space)
0 fragments dropped after timeout
0 packets forwarded
0 packets not forwardable
```
icmp:
```
76 calls to generate an ICMP error message
0 ICMP messages dropped
Output histogram:
 echo reply: 76
 destination unreachable: 0
 source quench: 0
 routing redirect: 0
 echo: 0
 time exceeded: 0
 parameter problem: 0
 time stamp: 0
 time stamp reply: 0
 address mask request: 0
 address mask reply: 0
0 bad ICMP messages
Input histogram:
 echo reply: 571
 destination unreachable: 22
 source quench: 12
 routing redirect: 0
```

```
        echo: 76
        time exceeded: 0
        parameter problem: 0
        time stamp request: 0
        time stamp reply: 0
        address mask request: 0
        address mask reply: 0
       76 responses sent
igmp:
       0 messages received
       0 messages received with too few bytes
       0 messages received with bad checksum
       0 membership queries received
       0 membership queries received with incorrect fields(s)
       0 membership reports received
       0 membership reports received with incorrect field(s)
       0 membership reports received for groups to which this host belongs
       0 membership reports sent
#
```

Using the lanadmin Command

The lanadmin command is used for interface adapter administration. It can be used for a number of tasks, including the following.

- Display and change the physical address of a station.
- Display and change the *maximum transfer unit* (MTU). The MTU shows the maximum number of bytes that can be transferred in one packet.
- Display and change the speed setting. This can't be done on all adapters.
- Display and clear the LAN adapter statistics. The statistics include inbound and outbound bytes since the last statistics clearing, different types of errors, types of packets, and so on.
- Reset a network interface.

The command can be used with different options or in interactive mode. The following command displays the physical address of a LAN adapter having NM ID equal to 2 (lan2 in the output of the lanscan command).

```
# lanadmin -a 2
Station Address                 = 0x080009f02610
#
```

The next command shows current MTU size.

```
# lanadmin -m 2
MTU Size                            = 1000
#
```

To change the MTU size of an adapter with NM ID 2, you can use the following command. Here both old and new MTU values are displayed.

```
# lanadmin -M 1500 2
Old MTU Size                        = 1000
New MTU Size                        = 1500
#
```

The current speed setting of an adapter can be displayed using the following command.

```
# lanadmin -s 2
Speed                               = 10000000
#
```

As I mentioned earlier, the lanadmin command can also be used in interactive mode. When you don't provide any command-line options, the command starts in this mode. It displays a number of subcommands and then waits for user input. In the following lanadmin interactive session, the words in boldface show user input. This session is used to display and then clear network statistics of an interface adapter with NM ID equal to 2. Statistics are once again displayed after clearing.

```
# lanadmin


         LOCAL AREA NETWORK ONLINE ADMINISTRATION, Version 1.0
                 Wed, Dec 1,1999  12:01:38

             Copyright 1994 Hewlett Packard Company.
                   All rights are reserved.

Test Selection mode.

         lan      = LAN Interface Administration
         menu     = Display this menu
         quit     = Terminate the Administration
         terse    = Do not display command menu
         verbose  = Display command menu


Enter command: lan
```

```
LAN Interface test mode. LAN Interface PPA Number = 1

        clear    = Clear statistics registers
        display  = Display LAN Interface status and statistics registers
        end      = End LAN Interface Administration, return to Test Selection
        menu     = Display this menu
        ppa      = PPA Number of the LAN Interface
        quit     = Terminate the Administration, return to shell
        reset    = Reset LAN Interface to execute its selftest
        specific = Go to Driver specific menu

Enter command: ppa 2
Enter PPA Number.  Currently 1: 2

LAN Interface test mode. LAN Interface PPA Number = 2

        clear    = Clear statistics registers
        display  = Display LAN Interface status and statistics registers
        end      = End LAN Interface Administration, return to Test Selection
        menu     = Display this menu
        ppa      = PPA Number of the LAN Interface
        quit     = Terminate the Administration, return to shell
        reset    = Reset LAN Interface to execute its selftest
        specific = Go to Driver specific menu

Enter command: display

                     LAN INTERFACE STATUS DISPLAY
                     Wed, Dec 1,1999  12:01:52

PPA Number                        = 2
Description                       = lan2 Hewlett-Packard LAN Interface Hw Rev 0
Type (value)                      = ethernet-csmacd(6)
MTU Size                          = 1500
Speed                             = 10000000
Station Address                   = 0x80009f02640
Administration Status (value)     = up(1)
Operation Status (value)          = down(2)
Last Change                       = 100
Inbound Octets                    = 4312
Inbound Unicast Packets           = 0
Inbound Non-Unicast Packets       = 0
Inbound Discards                  = 0
Inbound Errors                    = 0
Inbound Unknown Protocols         = 0
Outbound Octets                   = 6468
Outbound Unicast Packets          = 33
Outbound Non-Unicast Packets      = 0
```

```
Outbound Discards            = 0
Outbound Errors              = 0
Outbound Queue Length        = 0
Specific                     = 655367


Ethernet-like Statistics Group

Index                        = 3
Alignment Errors             = 0
FCS Errors                   = 0
Single Collision Frames      = 0
Multiple Collision Frames    = 0
Deferred Transmissions       = 0
Late Collisions              = 0
Excessive Collisions         = 0
Internal MAC Transmit Errors = 0
Carrier Sense Errors         = 11
Frames Too Long              = 0
Internal MAC Receive Errors  = 0


LAN Interface test mode. LAN Interface PPA Number = 2

        clear   = Clear statistics registers
        display = Display LAN Interface status and statistics registers
        end     = End LAN Interface Administration, return to Test Selection
        menu    = Display this menu
        ppa     = PPA Number of the LAN Interface
        quit    = Terminate the Administration, return to shell
        reset   = Reset LAN Interface to execute its selftest
        specific = Go to Driver specific menu

Enter command: clear
Clearing LAN Interface statistics registers.

LAN Interface test mode. LAN Interface PPA Number = 2

        clear   = Clear statistics registers
        display = Display LAN Interface status and statistics registers
        end     = End LAN Interface Administration, return to Test Selection
        menu    = Display this menu
        ppa     = PPA Number of the LAN Interface
        quit    = Terminate the Administration, return to shell
        reset   = Reset LAN Interface to execute its selftest
        specific = Go to Driver specific menu

Enter command: display
```

```
                       LAN INTERFACE STATUS DISPLAY
                       Wed, Dec 1,1999  12:02:04

PPA Number                         = 2
Description                        = lan2 Hewlett-Packard LAN Interface Hw Rev 0
Type (value)                       = ethernet-csmacd(6)
MTU Size                           = 1500
Speed                              = 10000000
Station Address                    = 0x80009f02640
Administration Status (value)      = up(1)
Operation Status (value)           = down(2)
Last Change                        = 100
Inbound Octets                     = 0
Inbound Unicast Packets            = 0
Inbound Non-Unicast Packets        = 0
Inbound Discards                   = 0
Inbound Errors                     = 0
Inbound Unknown Protocols          = 0
Outbound Octets                    = 0
Outbound Unicast Packets           = 0
Outbound Non-Unicast Packets       = 0
Outbound Discards                  = 0
Outbound Errors                    = 0
Outbound Queue Length              = 0
Specific                           = 655367


Ethernet-like Statistics Group

Index                              = 3
Alignment Errors                   = 0
FCS Errors                         = 0
Single Collision Frames            = 0
Multiple Collision Frames          = 0
Deferred Transmissions             = 0
Late Collisions                    = 0
Excessive Collisions               = 0
Internal MAC Transmit Errors       = 0
Carrier Sense Errors               = 0
Frames Too Long                    = 0
Internal MAC Receive Errors        = 0


LAN Interface test mode. LAN Interface PPA Number = 2

        clear    = Clear statistics registers
        display  = Display LAN Interface status and statistics registers
```

```
    end       = End LAN Interface Administration, return to Test Selection
    menu      = Display this menu
    ppa       = PPA Number of the LAN Interface
    quit      = Terminate the Administration, return to shell
    reset     = Reset LAN Interface to execute its selftest
    specific  = Go to Driver specific menu

Enter command: quit
#
```

The `ppa 2` command is used to select an adapter with the name `lan2`. As you can see, the number of `Carrier Sense Errors` is 11 before clearing the interface. When you use the `display` command after the `clear` command, its value changes to 0. This command is useful when you want to see what is happening on the network media in real time. For example, if you wait for one minute after clearing an interface and then repeat the `display` command, you can find out what happened during the previous minute. The interactive session can be terminated using the `quit` command.

Using the ndd Command

The `ndd` command can be used to fine-tune TCP/IP protocol parameters. This command is used for in-depth troubleshooting and fine-tuning. The list of supported parameters is displayed using the following command.

```
# ndd -h supported

SUPPORTED ndd tunable parameters on HP-UX:

IP:
    ip_def_ttl               -  Controls the default TTL in the IP header
    ip_forward_directed_broadcasts -  Controls subnet broadcasts packets
    ip_forward_src_routed -  Controls forwarding of source routed packets
    ip_forwarding            -  Controls how IP hosts forward packets
    ip_fragment_timeout   -  Controls how long IP fragments are kept
    ip_icmp_return_data_bytes -  Maximum number of data bytes in ICMP
    ip_ill_status            -  Displays a report of all physical interfaces
    ip_ipif_status           -  Displays a report of all logical interfaces
    ip_ire_hash              -  Displays all routing table entries, in the order
                                searched when resolving an address
    ip_ire_status            -  Displays all routing table entries
    ip_ire_cleanup_interval  -  Timeout interval for purging routing entries
    ip_ire_flush_interval    -  Routing entries deleted after this interval
    ip_ire_gw_probe_interval -  Probe interval for Dead Gateway Detection
    ip_ire_pathmtu_interval  -  Controls the probe interval for PMTU
    ip_ire_redirect_interval -  Controls 'Redirect' routing table entries
```

```
    ip_pmtu_strategy        -  Controls the Path MTU Discovery strategy
    ip_reass_mem_limit      -  Maximum number of bytes for IP reassembly
    ip_send_redirects       -  Sends ICMP 'Redirect' packets
    ip_send_source_quench   -  Sends ICMP 'Source Quench' packets
    ip_strong_es_model      -  Controls support for 'Strong End-System Model'
    ip_udp_status           -  Reports IP level UDP fanout table

TCP:
    tcp_conn_request_max         -  Max number of outstanding connection request
    tcp_ignore_path_mtu          -  Disable setting MSS from ICMP 'Frag Needed'
    tcp_ip_abort_cinterval       -  R2 during connection establishment
    tcp_ip_abort_interval        -  R2 for established connection
    tcp_ip_notify_cinterval      -  R1 during connection establishment
    tcp_ip_notify_interval       -  R1 for established connection
    tcp_ip_ttl                   -  TTL value inserted into IP header
    tcp_keepalive_detached_interval - Send keepalive probes for detached TCP
    tcp_keepalive_interval       -  Interval for sending keepalive probes
    tcp_largest_anon_port        -  Largest anonymous port number to use
    tcp_recv_hiwater_def         -  Maximum receive window size
    tcp_recv_hiwater_lfp         -  Maximum receive window size for fast links
    tcp_recv_hiwater_lnp         -  Maximum receive window size for slow links
    tcp_rexmit_interval_initial  -  Initial value for round trip time-out
    tcp_rexmit_interval_initial_lnp - tcp_rexmit_interval_initial for LNP
    tcp_rexmit_interval_max      -  Upper limit for computed round trip timeout
    tcp_rexmit_interval_min      -  Lower limit for computed round trip timeout
    tcp_sth_rcv_hiwat            -  Sets the flow control high water mark
    tcp_sth_rcv_lowat            -  Sets the flow control low water mark
    tcp_syn_rcvd_max            -  Controls the SYN attack defense of TCP
    tcp_status                   -  Get netstat-like TCP instances information
    tcp_time_wait_interval       -  How long stream persists in TIME_WAIT
    tcp_xmit_hiwater_def         -  The amount of unsent data that triggers
                                       TCP flow control
    tcp_xmit_hiwater_lfp         -  The amount of unsent data that triggers
                                       TCP flow control for fast links
    tcp_xmit_hiwater_lnp         -  The amount of unsent data that triggers
                                       TCP flow control for slow links
    tcp_xmit_lowater_def         -  The amount of unsent data that relieves
                                       TCP flow control
    tcp_xmit_lowater_lfp         -  The amount of unsent data that relieves
                                       TCP flow control for fast links
    tcp_xmit_lowater_lnp         -  The amount of unsent data that relieves
                                       TCP flow control for slow links

UDP:
    udp_def_ttl             -  Default TTL inserted into IP header
    udp_largest_anon_port   -  Largest anonymous port number to use
    udp_status              -  Get UDP instances information.
```

```
RAWIP:
    rawip_def_ttl              -  Default TTL inserted into IP header

ARP:
    arp_cache_report           -  Displays the ARP cache
    arp_cleanup_interval       -  Controls how long ARP entries stay in the
                                     ARP cache
#
```

■ Chapter Summary

A LAN adapter is recognized by the HP-UX kernel when it is physically installed in the system and its driver is built into the kernel. To list network drivers built into the kernel, the `lsdev` command is used. The `lanscan` or `ioscan` commands are used to list installed adapters. After physically installing an adapter, either SAM or command-line utilities can be used to configure it.

IP addresses, `netmask`, and broadcast addresses are assigned with the help of the `ifconfig` command. Logical instance numbers can be used to assign multiple IP addresses to a single physical network adapter. Configuration made by `ifconfig` is lost whenever you reboot the system. To make a configuration permanent, the configuration information is stored in the `/etc/rc.config.d/netconf` file. This file is read by the `/sbin/init.d/net` script, and all adapters listed in this file are configured at boot time. If your network is connected to another LAN or to the Internet, the routing table must be created using the `route` command. The configured IP addresses and routing table can be displayed with the help of the `netstat` command. A default route is used to send data packets for which no route is available.

The SAM `Networking and Communications` area is used to configure network adapters. A list of available adapters is displayed when you go to this area. After selecting one of the listed adapters, you can use the `Actions` menu to configure it. During the configuration process, the IP address, netmask, and host name aliases are assigned to the network adapter.

If a network adapter is not working properly, it may be due to hardware or configuration problems. A broken cable or missing cable terminator are the most common physical problems. Common configuration problems are a bad netmask, duplicate or wrong IP address, and incorrect routing entry. A number of commands can be used for troubleshooting network problems, including `lanscan`, `ping`, `netstat`, and `lanadmin`. The `ndd` command can be used to configure TCP/IP protocol-related parameters.

▲ CHAPTER REVIEW QUESTIONS

1. List the steps involved to configure a network adapter.

2. What does NamePPA mean?

3. Is it always necessary to add a default route? Why or why not?

4. What steps can you take if a network adapter is not visible with the `lanscan` command?

5. Multiple IP addresses can be assigned to a network interface (True/False).

▲ TEST YOUR KNOWLEDGE

1. *Which command is used to list network drivers configured into the kernel?*
   A. `lanscan`
   B. `ioscan`
   C. `lanadmin`
   D. `lsdev`

2. *For what purpose is the `ifconfig` command used?*
   A. assigning the IP address to a network interface
   B. displaying the configured IP address of a network interface
   C. assigning the IP address to a virtual network interface
   D. all of the above

3. *The following statements are related to the assignment of IP addresses to network interfaces. Which of these is true?*
   A. Multiple netmask values can be assigned with a single IP address.
   B. More than one physical adapter can have IP addresses that fall into the same network address.
   C. A broadcast address is used to send a message to all computers on the Internet.
   D. The `ifconfig` command can be used to set the MAC address of a network interface.

4. *For what purpose is the* `/etc/rc.config.d/netconf` *file used?*

    A. It is a script used to configure network adapters.

    B. It is a text file that contains configuration information for network interfaces.

    C. It contains hardware addresses assigned to network interfaces.

    D. It contains dynamic routing information.

5. *Which command is used to display a routing table?*

    A. `route`

    B. `netstat`

    C. `ifconfig`

    D. all of the above

6. *When creating a default route, you see a* `network unreachable` *message. What may be the cause?*

    A. The router is down.

    B. The router address does not fall into any network address assigned to the host.

    C. The cable to the router is faulty.

    D. An end terminator for a coaxial cable is missing.

7. *Which command is used for listing installed network adapters?*

    A. `lanscan`

    B. `ioscan`

    C. both of the above

    D. none of the above

Configuring and Managing ARPA/Berkeley Services

ARPA and Berkeley services are the most widely used network applications on HP-UX networks or any other modern UNIX platform. The ARPA services are commonly used on the Internet and are also available on operating systems other than UNIX. Berkeley services, on the other hand, are mostly available only on UNIX systems, with few exceptions. Collectively, ARPA and Berkeley services are also called Internet services. Applications based on these services are used for file transfer, remote login, routing, electronic mail, and other network-related activities.

These Internet services are used in the client/server model. A server offers some of its resources to clients. The client and server communicate with each other on a network by using ports and sockets. Well-defined ports are used for standard services. A common user of HP-UX utilizes only clients for these services. The server services are configured by the system administrator and are started at system boot time. One HP-UX system may be running many server applications simultaneously. As an example, a single HP-UX system can act as a mail server, an FTP server, and a domain name server, all at the same time. A system may also act as client and server at the same time where server applications are running as background processes while a user is using a client application.

HP-UX includes utilities for both ARPA and Berkeley services. These server applications are configured to run a daemon or through `inetd`. When a service is started as a daemon, it starts listening to incoming client requests on its designated port. If a service is started using the `inetd` daemon, it listens to all ports for the services configured through it. When a client sends request for a particular service, the server process is initiated by `inetd`. The server and client then establish connection with the help of sockets. The network services have their own security features that can be used to selectively allow or deny hosts and users access to local resources.

In this chapter, we will start with a list of available services and how to configure and start these on HP-UX. We will then look into the formats of some of configuration files used with these services. We will also discuss some security issues of different services. SAM will also be used to configure some service daemons.

30.1 Introduction to Internet Services

Internet services work in the client-server model. The server programs are either started at the system startup time or are invoked by the `inetd` daemon when a new request arrives. One machine can act as a server for multiple services by using port numbers. A system may be acting as a server for one type of service and a client for another type. Internet services are used for many purposes, including remote login, remote file transfer, electronic mail, and host name resolution. Some of the widely used services are discussed in this chapter.

ARPA Services

ARPA services are commonly available on all network operating systems in common use today. These services are popular due to their use on the Internet. For example, you can use HP-UX, Windows PC, Linux, or any other modern operating system to transfer files from one place to another using FTP. Similarly, you can use the telnet client available on a Windows PC to log in to an HP-UX server connected to the Internet. Some of the common ARPA services are presented here.

REMOTE LOGIN USING TELNET

Telnet can be used to remotely log in to a UNIX system. The `telnet` command is used on the client side while the `telnetd` daemon runs as a server process on the HP-UX server. If you are currently logged into a system named `myhp` and want to log into another system named `hp0` using user name **boota**, the `telnet` session will be as follows.

```
$ telnet hp0
Trying...
Connected to hp0.
Escape character is '^]'.
Local flow control on
Telnet TERMINAL-SPEED option ON

HP-UX hp0 B.11.00 A 9000/839 (tb)

login: boota
Password:
Please wait...checking for disk quotas
(c)Copyright 1983-1997 Hewlett-Packard Co.,  All Rights Reserved.
(c)Copyright 1979, 1980, 1983, 1985-1993 The Regents of the Univ. of
  California
(c)Copyright 1980, 1984, 1986 Novell, Inc.
(c)Copyright 1986-1992 Sun Microsystems, Inc.
(c)Copyright 1985, 1986, 1988 Massachusetts Institute of Technology
(c)Copyright 1989-1993  The Open Software Foundation, Inc.
(c)Copyright 1986 Digital Equipment Corp.
(c)Copyright 1990 Motorola, Inc.
(c)Copyright 1990, 1991, 1992 Cornell University
(c)Copyright 1989-1991 The University of Maryland
(c)Copyright 1988 Carnegie Mellon University
(c)Copyright 1991-1997 Mentat, Inc.
(c)Copyright 1996 Morning Star Technologies, Inc.
(c)Copyright 1996 Progressive Systems, Inc.
(c)Copyright 1997 Isogon Corporation
```

After logging into the remote system, you can perform any task you want depending on user privileges on the system, just as on your local system. To terminate the `telnet` session established with the remote system, use the `exit` command. You will see a "connection closed" message similar to the one shown here.

```
$ exit
logout
Connection closed by foreign host.
$
```

Pseudoterminal devices are used to establish a `telnet` session. The default number of pseudoterminal devices is 60, which can be increased using the `npty` kernel configuration parameter (See Chapter 16, *Reconfiguring the HP-UX Kernel*).

FILE TRANSFER USING FTP

File transfer protocol (FTP) is used to transfer files from one system to another over a network. Files can be received from or sent to a system depending on the type of permissions you have. On the client side, you use the `ftp` command with the remote host name as the first command-line argument. The command then contacts the server process on the remote system. The server system requests a login name and password from the client to authenticate a user. If you supply a login name and password that are valid on the remote system, you are granted access. After that, you can perform different operations on files, such as listing, uploading, or downloading files. In the following FTP session, you are currently logged into system myhp as user **root** and download a file myfile from the home directory of user **boota** on system hp0.

```
# ftp hp0
Connected to hp0.
220 hp0 FTP server (Version 1.1.214.4 Mon Feb 15 08:48:46 GMT 1999) ready.
Name (myhp:root): boota
331 Password required for boota.
Password:
230 User boota logged in.
Remote system type is UNIX.
Using binary mode to transfer files.
ftp> get myfile
200 PORT command successful.
150 Opening BINARY mode data connection for myfile (655 bytes).
226 Transfer complete.
655 bytes received in 0.00 seconds (1071.44 Kbytes/s)
ftp> quit
221 Goodbye.
#
```

After establishing the FTP session, the ftp command displays its prompt, which is used to issue FTP commands. This command prompt is ftp>, as shown in the above FTP session. The words shown in boldface are FTP commands. The FTP get command is used to download a file while the FTP quit command is used to end an FTP session. A list of available commands can be displayed using the help command on an FTP prompt at any time as shown here. Help about a particular command can be found by using the command name as an argument to the help command.

```
ftp> help
Commands may be abbreviated.    Commands are:

!               debug           mget            put             size
$               dir             mkdir           pwd             status
account         disconnect      mls             quit            struct
append          form            mode            quote           system
ascii           get             modtime         recv            sunique
bell            glob            mput            reget           tenex
binary          hash            newer           rstatus         trace
bye             help            nmap            rhelp           type
case            idle            nlist           rename          user
cd              image           ntrans          reset           umask
cdup            lcd             open            restart         verbose
chmod           ls              prompt          rmdir           ?
close           macdef          proxy           runique
cr              mdelete         sendport        send
delete          mdir            passive         site
ftp>
```

Many systems on the Internet allow anonymous FTP, where any user can log into a system and download files with the help of user name `anonymous`. You can enter your email address as the password for this user. The anonymous FTP is usually limited to file download from files under a restricted directory tree.

NETWORK TIME PROTOCOL (NTP)

Network Time Protocol (NTP) is used to synchronize the system time of a machine with a standard time source. Many time servers are available on the Internet that can be used as standard sources of time. NTP uses the `xntpd` daemon on HP-UX, which is responsible for synchronization of time with one or more time sources. Time synchronization is necessary for applications that exchange time-critical data. More explanation of NTP is provided in Chapter 35.

DYNAMIC ROUTING USING GATED

You have already used static routes in the last chapter. Static routes are used in simple networks. If you have a complex network where multiple paths exist from a source to a destination, dynamic routes are more efficient. Dynamic routing tables change depending on the availability of paths and load conditions on these paths. The `gated` daemon is used on HP-UX to keep the dynamic routing table updated. It supports several routing protocols, such as RIP, BGP, and OSPF.

Berkeley Services

In many cases, Berkeley services provide the same functionality as the ARPA services. Traditionally, Berkeley services are those applications that are used with the Berkeley System distribution (BSD). Many of the commands used as client processes start with the letter `r` and sometimes may be more convenient in LANs, as you don't have to type login names and passwords when switching from one system to another. However, the commands starting with `r` are considered to be less secure compared with the ARPA commands.

REMOTE LOGIN USING RLOGIN

The command used for remote login is `rlogin`. Like the `telnet` command, it needs the remote system name as its first argument. The remote login daemon `rlogind` should be enabled on the server side. To log into a system `hp0`, you can use the following command:

```
rlogin hp0
```

REMOTE COPY USING RCP

The `rcp` command is used to copy files to and from a host on a network. Its syntax is similar to the UNIX `cp` command, where a remote system name followed by a colon character is added to the source or destination file name. The following command is used to copy file `/etc/passwd` from a remote system `hp0` to the current directory.

```
rcp hp0:/etc/profile .
```

Proper permissions are required for executing the `rcp` command on the remote system. The user and group ownership can't be copied with the `rcp` command.

REMOTE EXECUTION USING REMSH

A command can be executed remotely on another system on a network. The `remsh` command is used for this purpose. The result of the command is displayed on a local terminal screen. For example, the following command shows a listing of the `/etc` directory of remote system `hp0`.

```
remsh hp0 ll /etc
```

Again, a user with the same name as your login name must exist on the remote system, and you must be permitted to execute this command on that system.

BIND

Berkeley Internet Name Domain (BIND) is used for host name resolution. The system that is running the BIND service is also called *Domain Name Server* (DNS). It can resolve host names to IP addresses and vice versa. You don't need to run DNS in small isolated LANs. The configuration of DNS is discussed in detail in the next chapter.

SENDMAIL

Sendmail is used to transfer electronic mail within and across networks. Sendmail supports a number of mail transfer protocols including SMTP, which is the standard protocol for mail transfer on the Internet. Sendmail is the most widely used *Mail Transport Agent* (MTA) on the Internet. HP-UX includes a sendmail package in its standard distribution.

REMOTE PRINTING

You have already studied the use of the remote printer in Chapter 21. The `rlpdaemon` is responsible for managing remote print requests.

NETWORK INFORMATION

Different types of information about a network can be collected using HP-UX commands: You can get information about a user on any host on your network. To get information about another user on a remote system, you can use the `finger` command. Similarly, to get information about how long a remote server is up, you can use the `ruptime` command. A list of common client and server processes for Internet services is presented in Table 30-1.

Table 30–1 *Clients and Servers for Internet Services*

Service	Client	Server
Remote login	telnet	telnetd
Remote login	rlogin	rlogind
File transfer	ftp	ftpd
File transfer	rcp	remshd
Remote command execution	remsh	remshed
Remote command execution	rexec	rexecd
User information	finger	fingered
System information	rup, ruptime	rwhod

As mentioned earlier, all services use port numbers for establishing connections between a client and server. Table 30-2 shows well-known services and related port numbers.

Table 30–2 *Ports Used by the ARPA and Berkeley Services*

Service Name	Network Port
Telnet	23
FTP	21
SMTP Mail	25
NTP	123
rlogin	513
DNS	53
finger	79

Security of Commands Starting with "r"

Commands starting with the letter "r" (rlogin, rcp, remsh) can be used on a network if proper security is maintained. There are two ways to enable users of one system to remotely access another system using these commands. The first method is where all users of a system are allowed to access services on another system. This method is called *host equivalency*, and it is enabled by the system administrator on the server system. In the second method, individual users can allow users on other systems to access the system with their own login name. This method is called *user equivalency*.

HOST EQUIVALENCY

To allow all users of a remote system to access resources on the local system, the /etc/hosts.equiv file is used. The following conditions apply for host equivalency.

- If a remote host name is listed in the file, users of the remote host are allowed to access the local system if the local user name also matches the remote system user name.
- If the host name starts with a negative sign, access for all users on that system is denied. However, access for individual users can be granted using user equivalency.
- If a line contains a + symbol, it matches every host. For example, if the file consists of only one line with a + symbol in it, every host is granted access.

USER EQUIVALENCY

A user can set up his or her own permissions for the use of r-commands by overriding host equivalency. The remote user has the same privileges and restrictions as the local user. Each user can create a .rhosts file in the home directory. The syntax of this file is like the /etc/hosts.equiv file, the only difference being that user names that don't match the local user name can also be specified to grant access to the account. For example, the following line in the .rhosts file of user **boota** grants permission to a remote user **jeff** from any system to log in as user **boota** on the local system without a password.

```
+ jeff
```

The line below allows access to user **jeff** from host myhp only.

```
myhp jeff
```

The following rules apply to this file.

- This file can allow or deny access, overriding the `/etc/hosts.equiv` file.
- A line that contains only a host name allows a user with the similar name from that host.
- A line starting with the host name and containing a user name allows the user with that name from that host.
- If a + symbol is used in the host name, all hosts are granted access.
- If a host name or user name starts with a - symbol, the access for that host or user is denied.

These two files must be readable for everybody, but write permissions should be granted only to the owners of these files. To disable use of the `.rhosts` file by system users (and hence to increase system security), you can use the `-l` option when a daemon is invoked through `inetd` by using the `/etc/inetd.conf` file.

Study Break

Using Internet Services

Internet services are used in daily routine work. The most commonly used services are remote login and file transfer. Let's use the `ftp` command to download a file from a remote host. Establish an FTP session with a remote host using the `ftp` command. Log in using a user name and password when a login prompt appears. After the login process, you will see an `ftp>` prompt where you can use FTP commands. Download the `/etc/hosts` file from that server using the FTP `get` command. Use the FTP `help` command to list available commands for use with the FTP prompt. Now terminate the session using the FTP `quit` command. Once again establish the FTP session with the same remote host using the `anonymous` user name and your email address as password. Again try to download the `/etc/hosts` file. This time you are unable to download this file due to the anonymous FTP restrictions.

Create an `.rhosts` file in your home directory on the remote system and add your local system name in this file. Now try the `rcp` and `rlogin` commands for file copy and remote login.

30.2 Starting Internet Services

The network services can be started in one of two ways. In the first case, a service daemon is started at boot time with the help of `rc` scripts. These scripts are stored in the `/sbin/init.d` directory and are linked to startup and shutdown scripts in the `/sbin/rcn.d` directories where *n* shows a system run level. Configuration files for these scripts are present in the `/etc/rc.config.d` directory. Management of startup and shutdown scripts has already been discussed in Chapter 14.

The second method of starting a service is through the `inetd` daemon. It is also called a TCP wrapper and listens for a number of network ports, depending on network services enabled through it. When a connection request arrives at a particular port, it starts a server process, depending on its configuration file entry for that service.

Starting a Service as a Daemon

Server daemons are started with the help of the `/sbin/rc` script. This is executed during the system startup process. It scans the `/sbin/rcn.d` directories at each system run level, where *n* in the directory name represents a run level. Each of these directories contains link files associated with actual scripts in the `/sbin/init.d` directory. These link files start with either letter S or K. A link file name starting with S shows that the service is being started at this run level, while a link file name starting with K shows that the service is being stopped when the system moves into this run level. For example, file `S370named` in directory `/sbin/rc2.d` is linked to the `/sbin/init.d/named` file. It shows that script `/sbin/init.d/named` will be run when the system enters into run level 2. This script starts the domain name server daemon used to resolve host names.

When a daemon is started, it binds itself to its designated port and starts listening to incoming connection requests on that port. Any client on the network can then send a request at that port and start communication with the server process.

Starting a Service through inetd

The `inetd` daemon is started at run level 2. It listens to incoming connection requests for many services. When a request arrives at a certain port, it invokes the server process corresponding to that port and starts listening to the port again. At startup time, the `inetd` daemon reads its configuration file, `/etc/inetd.conf`, that contains a list of the services to be served by `inetd`. This file contains one line for each service. A line starting with the # character is considered a comment line. A typical entry for telnet service in this file is as follows.

```
telnet    stream tcp nowait root /usr/lbin/telnetd  telnetd
```

Each line contains seven fields as listed next. These fields show how the service will behave and what server process will be invoked.

Service Name
: This is the name of the service as mentioned in the `/etc/services` or `/etc/rpc` file. In the `telnetd` example above, the service name is `telnet`.

Socket Type
: This is either `stream` or `dgram`. This shows the type of socket used for the service. In the above-mentioned example, the socket type is `stream`. The `stream` type socket is used with the TCP protocol and the `dgram` type socket is used with the UDP protocol.

Protocol
: The list of protocols as present in `/etc/protocols`. This shows the protocol used for the service. The protocol used for telnet service is TCP.

Wait/nowait
: The `wait` applies for dgram sockets only. For stream-based sockets, `nowait` is used. This is used to configure a service as a single-threaded or multithreaded service. The `wait` keyword causes `inetd` to wait until any previously started server process finishes. When the previous instance finishes, then `inetd` starts listening to the port again, thus causing a service to be activated as single threaded. With a `nowait` keyword, `inetd` starts the server process for an incoming request and immediately starts listening to the port again. If a second request arrives while the first server instance is still running, another instance of the server process is started. Usually UDP-based services use `wait`, whereas TCP services use `nowait`.

User
: This is the name of the user who will be the owner of the server process.

Server Program
: The complete path to the server program file.

Arguments
: This last field contains a list of arguments to be passed to the server program. The first argument is the program name itself.

A sample `/etc/inetd.conf` file is shown next where you can find a list of services invoked with the help of the `inetd` daemon. An entry can be continued to the next line by using a backslash character at the end of a line. Lines starting with the # character are comments.

```
# @(#)inetd.conf $Revision: 1.24.214.3 $ $Date: 97/09/10 14:50:49 $
#
# See the inetd.conf(4) manual page for more information.
#
#       ARPA/Berkeley services
#
ftp          stream tcp nowait root /usr/lbin/ftpd       ftpd -l
telnet       stream tcp nowait root /usr/lbin/telnetd  telnetd

# Before uncommenting the "tftp" entry below, please make sure
# that you have a "tftp" user in /etc/passwd. If you don't
# have one, please consult the tftpd(1M) manual entry for
# information about setting up this service.
tftp         dgram  udp wait   root /usr/lbin/tftpd     tftpd\
        /opt/ignite\
        /var/opt/ignite
#bootps      dgram  udp wait   root /usr/lbin/bootpd    bootpd
#finger      stream tcp nowait bin  /usr/lbin/fingerd   fingerd
login        stream tcp nowait root /usr/lbin/rlogind   rlogind
shell        stream tcp nowait root /usr/lbin/remshd    remshd
exec         stream tcp nowait root /usr/lbin/rexecd    rexecd
#uucp        stream tcp nowait root /usr/sbin/uucpd     uucpd
ntalk        dgram  udp wait   root /usr/lbin/ntalkd    ntalkd
ident        stream tcp wait   bin  /usr/lbin/identd    identd
printer      stream tcp nowait root /usr/sbin/rlpdaemon rlpdaemon -i
daytime      stream tcp nowait root internal
daytime      dgram  udp nowait root internal
time         stream tcp nowait root internal
#time        dgram  udp nowait root internal
echo         stream tcp nowait root internal
echo         dgram  udp nowait root internal
discard      stream tcp nowait root internal
discard      dgram  udp nowait root internal
chargen      stream tcp nowait root internal
chargen      dgram  udp nowait root internal
##
#       rpc services, registered by inetd with portmap
#       Do not uncomment these unless your system is running portmap!
##
# WARNING: The rpc.mountd should now be started from a startup script.
#          Please enable the mountd startup script to start rpc.mountd.
##
#rpc  stream tcp  nowait  root  /usr/sbin/rpc.rexd      100017 1
  rpc.rexd
#rpc  dgram udp  wait    root  /usr/lib/netsvc/rstat/rpc.rstatd  100001
  2-4   rpc.rstatd
#rpc  dgram udp  wait    root  /usr/lib/netsvc/rusers/rpc.rusersd 100002
  1-2   rpc.rusersd
```

```
#rpc   dgram  udp   wait      root   /usr/lib/netsvc/rwall/rpc.rwalld      100008
   1   rpc.rwalld
#rpc   dgram  udp   wait      root   /usr/sbin/rpc.rquotad   100011   1
   rpc.rquotad
#rpc   dgram  udp   wait      root   /usr/lib/netsvc/spray/rpc.sprayd      100012
   1   rpc.sprayd

##
#
#  The standard remshd and rlogind do not include the Kerberized
#  code. You must install the InternetSvcSec/INETSVCS-SEC fileset and
#  configure Kerberos as described in the SIS(5) man page.
#
##
kshell stream tcp nowait root /usr/lbin/remshd remshd -K
klogin stream tcp nowait root /usr/lbin/rlogind rlogind -K
```

The /etc/services file maps service names to corresponding port numbers and protocols used for that port. The services mentioned in this file are well known. When the inetd daemon reads its configuration file, /etc/inetd.conf, and decides which services to start, it consults the /etc/services file to determine ports for each of these services. A sample file is shown next. Following the port number and protocol, an alias may be specified for the service.

```
# @(#)services $Revision: 1.32.214.7 $ $Date: 97/09/10 14:50:42 $
# The form for each entry is:
# <official service name>   <port number/protocol name>   <aliases>
tcpmux          1/tcp                       # TCP port multiplexer (RFC 1078)
echo            7/tcp                       # Echo
echo            7/udp                       #
discard         9/tcp    sink null          # Discard
discard         9/udp    sink null          #
systat          11/tcp   users              # Active Users
daytime         13/tcp                      # Daytime
daytime         13/udp                      #
qotd            17/tcp   quote              # Quote of the Day
chargen         19/tcp   ttytst source      # Character Generator
chargen         19/udp   ttytst source      #
ftp-data        20/tcp                      # File Transfer Protocol (Data)
ftp             21/tcp                      # File Transfer Protocol (Control)
telnet          23/tcp                      # Virtual Terminal Protocol
smtp            25/tcp                      # Simple Mail Transfer Protocol
time            37/tcp   timeserver         # Time
time            37/udp   timeserver         #
rlp             39/udp   resource           # Resource Location Protocol
whois           43/tcp   nicname            # Who Is
domain          53/tcp   nameserver         # Domain Name Service
```

```
domain          53/udp   nameserver       #
bootps          67/udp                    # Bootstrap Protocol Server
bootpc          68/udp                    # Bootstrap Protocol Client
tftp            69/udp                    # Trivial File Transfer Protocol
rje             77/tcp   netrjs           # private RJE Service
finger          79/tcp                    # Finger
http            80/tcp   www              # World Wide Web HTTP
http            80/udp   www              # World Wide Web HTTP
link            87/tcp   ttylink          # private terminal link
supdup          95/tcp                    #
hostnames      101/tcp   hostname         # NIC Host Name Server
tsap           102/tcp   iso_tsap iso-tsap # ISO TSAP (part of ISODE)
pop            109/tcp   postoffice pop2  # Post Office Protocol - Version 2
pop3           110/tcp   pop-3            # Post Office Protocol - Version 3
portmap        111/tcp   sunrpc           # SUN Remote Procedure Call
portmap        111/udp   sunrpc           #
ident          113/tcp   authentication   # RFC1413
sftp           115/tcp                    # Simple File Transfer Protocol
uucp-path      117/tcp                    # UUCP Path Service
nntp           119/tcp   readnews untp    # Network News Transfer Protocol
ntp            123/udp                    # Network Time Protocol
netbios_ns     137/tcp                    # NetBIOS Name Service
netbios_ns     137/udp                    #
netbios_dgm    138/tcp                    # NetBIOS Datagram Service
netbios_dgm    138/udp                    #
netbios_ssn    139/tcp                    # NetBIOS Session Service
netbios_ssn    139/udp                    #
bftp           152/tcp                    # Background File Transfer Protocol
snmp           161/udp   snmpd            # Simple Network Management Protocol Agent
snmp-trap      162/udp   trapd            # Simple Network Management Protocol Traps
bgp            179/tcp                    # Border Gateway Protocol
biff           512/udp   comsat           # mail notification
exec           512/tcp                    # remote execution, passwd required
login          513/tcp                    # remote login
who            513/udp   whod             # remote who and uptime
shell          514/tcp   cmd              # remote command, no passwd used
syslog         514/udp                    # remote system logging
printer        515/tcp   spooler          # remote print spooling
talk           517/udp                    # conversation
ntalk          518/udp                    # new talk, conversation
route          520/udp   router routed    # routing information protocol
efs            520/tcp                    # Extended file name server
timed          525/udp   timeserver       # remote clock synchronization
tempo          526/tcp   newdate          #
courier        530/tcp   rpc              #
conference     531/tcp   chat             #
netnews        532/tcp   readnews         #
netwall        533/udp                    # Emergency broadcasting
uucp           540/tcp   uucpd            # uucp daemon
```

< Some data deleted from here>

SECURING INETD

To add security to the `inetd` daemon, the `/var/adm/inetd.sec` file is used. This file provides an extra layer of security for services started with `inetd`. This is in addition to security implemented by a service itself. The `inetd` daemon can selectively allow or deny access to other hosts using the `/var/adm/inetd.sec` file. The following rules apply to this file.

- If this file does not exist, all hosts are granted access to start an `inetd` service.
- If this file exists but is empty, access to all `inetd` services is allowed.
- If the file exists and contains some of the service names in the specified format, only access to listed services is allowed.

Each line in the file starts with a service name followed by the `allow` or `deny` keyword. After that, a host specifier is present that may contain a host name or an IP address. Multiple host names can be separated by spaces. Wild cards can be used in IP addresses. Consider the following line in this file as an example.

```
ftp     allow   192.168.2.* hp0
```

This line grants FTP access for all hosts in network 192.168.2 and the host with the name hp0. A sample `/var/adm/inetd.sec` file is shown next.

```
login        allow   10.3-5 192.34.56.5 ahost anetwork
#
# The above entry allows the following hosts to attempt to access your system
# using rlogin:
#             hosts in subnets 3 through 5 in network 10,
#             the host with an Internet Address of 192.34.56.5,
#             the host by the name of "ahost",
#             all the hosts in the network "anetwork"
#
mountd       deny    192.23.4.3
#
# The mountd entry  denies host  192.23.4.3  access to the NFS  rpc.mountd
# server.
#
# Hosts and network names must be official names, not aliases.
# See the inetd.sec(4) manual page for more information.
```

Table 30-3 lists configuration and security files used for Internet services and a short description of each.

Table 30–3 *Configuration Files for ARPA/Berkeley Services*

File Name	Description
/etc/inetd.conf	Configuration file for the inetd daemon
/etc/services	Lists service names and ports/protocols used with these services
/var/adm/inetd.sec	Security file to add an extra layer of security for inetd
/etc/hosts.equiv	Host equivalency file used to allow or deny access for specific services
$HOME/.rhosts	User-defined file used to allow or deny incoming network requests

How a Connection Is Established

Before actual data communication starts, the client and server establish a communication session. If the server process is started as a daemon at boot time, it listens to its well-defined port for any incoming connection. If the server process is controlled by inetd, the inetd daemon reads its /etc/ inetd.conf file configuration, gets the port number for all services from the /etc/services file, and starts listening to all of these ports. As soon as a connection request is received on a port, the inetd daemon starts the corresponding service daemon.

On the client side, when you start a client, for example, telnet, it does not need to know the port name for the server process on the server host as it is already defined. It opens a socket on an available port number, usually larger than 1024 on the client side, and tries to connect to the server port (Port number 23 in the case of telnet). After accepting the incoming connection, a session is established between client and server and data communication starts, depending on the protocol used. A list of open network ports and established socket connections may be displayed using the netstat -a command.

30.3 Using SAM to Manage Network Services

Some of the network services can be started and stopped using SAM. You can find the Network Services icon in the Networking and Communications area of SAM. When you double-click on this icon, a list of services that can be started or stopped with SAM is displayed, as shown in Figure 30-1. You can see service names and their current status along with a short

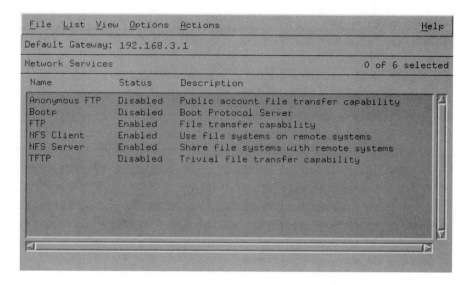

Figure 30–1 *Enabling/disabling network services using SAM.*

description. After selecting a service by clicking on it, you can use the `Actions` menu to change its status.

Some of the services that can be enabled or disabled using this screen area must be configured somewhere else in SAM. For example, the `NFS Client` must be configured in the `Network File Systems` area of SAM.

■ Chapter Summary

Network services are used as client/server applications on UNIX. Server applications are started as daemons or are invoked using `inetd`. Common server applications use well-defined ports for communication. System-wide security of commands starting with the letter `r` is controlled using the `/etc/hosts.equiv` file. Any user can also create a `$HOME/.rhosts` file in the home directory to allow or deny access to his or her account by other users over the network. Security of `inetd` is controlled using the `/var/adm/inetd.sec` file. By using this file, selective hosts can be allowed or denied access to services.

If a service is started as a daemon at system boot time, its control files are created in `/sbin/rcn.d` directories where *n* represents a system run level. If a service is started with the help of `inetd`, it is configured using the

`/etc/inetd.conf` file, where a complete path to the server process is defined. The `inetd` daemon uses the `/etc/services` file to get service names and corresponding port numbers for defined services.

Ports opened by server processes and established connections can be listed at any time using the `netstat  -a` command. SAM can be used to enable or disable selected services.

▲ CHAPTER REVIEW QUESTIONS

1. What are the advantages and disadvantages of activating a service using `inetd`?

2. List four Internet services used on HP-UX.

3. What rules apply to entries in the `/etc/hosts.equiv` file?

▲ TEST YOUR KNOWLEDGE

1. *What port number is used for telnet service?*
    A. 23
    B. 25
    C. 21
    D. 53

2. *The telnet service is invoked using* `inetd`. *The configuration entry for this service contains the keyword* `nowait`. *What does it mean?*
    A. The service will be used in multithreaded mode.
    B. The `inetd` process will not wait for any client to terminate before accepting a new connection.
    C. It is most likely that the service uses the TCP protocol.
    D. All of the above.

3. *What is the server process for the* `rcp` *command?*
    A. `remshd`
    B. `rcpd`
    C. `inetd`
    D. `in.rcpd`

4. *Which command is used to execute a program on a remote system?*

   A. rsh

   B. remsh

   C. rksh

   D. remexec

5. *Which of the following is not a network service?*

   A. rcp

   B. ftp

   C. rsh

   D. rlogin

6. *An HP-UX server contains a single character + (plus) in the /etc/ hosts.equiv file. Which hosts are allowed to use the network services?*

   A. all hosts

   B. all hosts on the local network only

   C. only those hosts that have an entry in the .rhosts file in the home directory or the **root** user

   D. No hosts can access network services, as the plus symbol is not followed by a host name.

7. *You want to allow a user* **jeff** *at host* myhp *to access your account using the* rlogin *command. What should be present in the* .rhosts *file in your home directory?*

   A. jeff@myhp

   B. jeff myhp

   C. myhp jeff

   D. - jeff

Host Name Resolution and Domain Name Server

A computer on a TCP/IP network is known by its IP address. Data communication among hosts on a network takes place through IP data packets, also known as IP datagrams, which contain source and destination IP addresses. Keeping in mind the complexity of large IP networks like the Internet, it is not possible for users to remember IP addresses of all servers. To solve this problem, convenient and easy-to-remember names are assigned to hosts in addition to IP addresses. When using the network services discussed in the last chapter, users usually use the host name of the server machine on the command line instead of the IP address. Before starting a communication session, this host name is mapped to its IP address. Host name resolution is a process used to map a host name to its corresponding IP address for communication purposes.

Different techniques are used for host name resolution. The simplest one is the use of the /etc/ hosts file. This is a text file that maps a host name

589

to its IP address. This technique is not practical as networks grow larger because this file has to be maintained on all systems on the network. Sun Microsystems has developed a name resolution system known as the *Network Information Service* (NIS). However, this service has limitations and can't be used on the Internet. The most widely used host name resolution system is the *Domain Name System*, commonly know as DNS. It can be used on a local network as well as on the Internet. One or more servers are used to keep a record of host name mapping. These servers are called domain name servers. DNS is a hierarchical approach to host name assignment and resolution where a domain name may be assigned to an entire organization and subdomain names can be used for different departments within the organization.

DNS is the default method used on the Internet for name resolution. Internet domains follow a well-defined hierarchy. Every domain name falls under one of the predefined top-level domain names. *Root name servers* on the Internet have information about a domain name or a pointer to another server that can be used to get that information. If a local domain name server is not able to resolve a host name, it contacts one of the root name servers to get information about another domain name server that can provide the desired information.

Three types of domain name servers are used. The *primary domain name server* is the main contact for host name resolution inside a domain. The *secondary domain name server* is used in case a primary name server goes down for any reason. The secondary name server(s) keep their data updated by polling primary servers from time to time. Secondary name servers are also used for load sharing on heavily loaded networks. A third type of domain name server is the *caching domain name server*, which is used to resolve host names but does not have its own data base files.

A DNS can be setup on HP-UX using command line utilities as well as SAM. The `named` daemon runs as a server process for a DNS and listens to TCP port 53 for incoming requests. At startup time, this daemon reads its configuration file, `/etc/named.boot`, where names of the domains and directory containing data files are specified. If the server is being used as a secondary name server, it reads configuration data from the primary DNS at boot time.

This chapter starts with an introduction to the host name resolution process and the methods used for this purpose. An introduction to the domain name system is presented. After that, you will learn how to configure primary, secondary, and caching domain name servers. In the next part you will learn about the configuration and testing of a DNS client. In the last part of the chapter, you will use SAM to configure a DNS server.

31.1 Host Name to IP Address Mapping

Hosts on an IP network are recognized by their IP addresses. On large-scale IP networks like the Internet, it is difficult for a user to remember IP addresses of different servers. The solution is to assign easy-to-remember host names to them. User applications use these host names for network communication. However, network traffic uses IP addresses instead of these host names. Before starting a network communication process, a computer must map a host name to an IP address. The process of mapping host names to IP addresses is called *name resolution*. Once a name is resolved to its IP address, communication can start in its usual way. The name resolution process works in two ways.

- Find an IP address when given a host name.
- Find a host name when given an IP address. This is also called reverse name resolution.

The first type of resolution is performed through the `gethostbyname()` function, while the second type of resolution is performed through the `gethostbyadd()` library function. These functions are used in application programs and are collectively called resolver library functions or simply *resolver*.

Multiple Host Names for a Single IP

Host name aliases or canonical names can be used such that a single IP address is known by multiple host names. This situation arises when multiple services are running on a single host, and you want to use a separate name for each service. For example, if a single machine is serving as FTP, Web, and mail server, you may want to access the Web server with the name www.mydomain.com, the FTP server using the name ftp.mydomain.com, and the mail server using mail.mydomain.com.

A single host may also serve multiple domain names. For example, the Web hosting services on the Internet use one server for hosting Web pages for many companies. A separate host name is used for each company. Theoretically, you can map one IP address to as many host names as you want.

Multiple IP Addresses for a Single Host

As a reverse of the above-mentioned process, sometimes it is required that multiple IP addresses are used for the same host name. This is done for load-sharing purposes. For example, if a Web server is heavily loaded, multiple hosts can be assigned the same name but different IP addresses. In such a case, the load is evenly distributed among these servers. This is true only when you are using DNS as the name resolution method.

31.2 Name Resolution Methods

There are multiple methods used to resolve a host name to its IP address. The simplest of these is using the /etc/hosts file. This method is used for networks having a small number of hosts. This file contains the host names and IP addresses of all hosts on the network. A copy of the file is maintained on each host on the network. When the network grows in size, it becomes practically impossible to maintain consistency of this file on each host. In such a case, you have to use some other name resolution service. More popular services are NIS, NIS+, and DNS. NIS is discussed in more detail in the next chapter. A brief introduction to /etc/hosts and DNS follows. NIS+ is beyond the scope of this book.

The /etc/hosts File

This file contains one line for each host to IP address mapping. A line starts with an IP address followed by the official host name. The host name part may be followed by one or more host name aliases. An entry in the /etc/hosts file is of the following format.

```
<IP address>    <Host name>    <aliases>
```

Any line starting with the # symbol is a comment line. No entry can start with a space character in this file. The file is consulted from top to bottom. If you specify more than one line for a host name, only the first line is used for the resolution purpose.

Warning

A common mistake while configuring the host file is that you add a new entry for a host name at the end of the file while another entry already exists for that host. During the host name resolution process, the first entry is always used, as it is matched first while traversing the file from top to bottom. While adding a new entry, always check if it already exists or add a new entry at the start of the file instead of at the end.

A sample /etc/hosts file is shown next. The first line contains an entry for a host name myhp.boota.com, while a host name with the alias myhp is also used. The second line is for another host, hp0. The third line shows a local host with a loopback address. The loopback address is the same for all systems and is used for testing purposes.

```
## Configured using SAM by root on Fri Dec  3 12:30:36 1998
# @(#)hosts $Revision: 1.9.214.1 $ $Date: 96/10/08 13:20:01 $
#
192.168.3.10    myhp.boota.com   myhp
192.168.3.12    hp0.boota.com    hp0
127.0.0.1       localhost        loopback
```

Network Information Service

Network Information System (NIS) is used in small LANs. It was developed by Sun Microsystems; a more advanced resolution service with the name NIS+ was introduced later. NIS keeps a central data base of hosts and users and uses a flat name space that uses a master NIS server. Slave NIS servers can also be used to share load and provide redundancy in case of failure of the master server.

Domain Name Server

DNS uses a hierarchical naming scheme for assigning host names. A domain name server is a machine on a network that keeps a record of local host names within its zone of authority. It is used for both local and remote host name resolution if the network is connected to a public network. The resolver forwards all host name resolution queries to the domain name server. The name server looks into its own data files for a match. If a match is found, the query is answered straight away. If no match is found, the name server contacts a root name server on the Internet. The root name server provides the address of another DNS that can resolve the host name. Your name server then contacts the name server address provided by the root name server. When it receives the IP address of the host, it relays the address back to the querying machine. Fig-

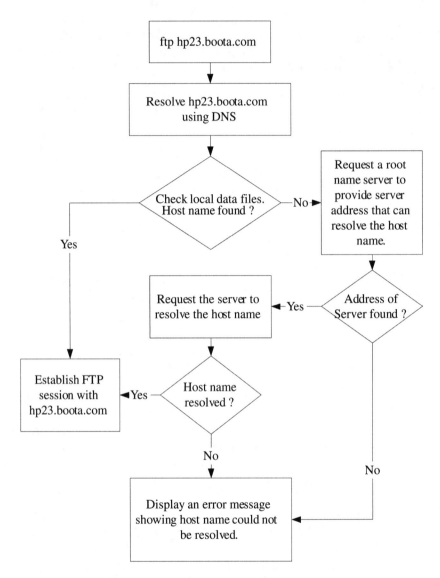

Figure 31–1 *Process of name resolution using DNS.*

ure 31-1 shows a sequence of steps before the command `ftp hp23.boota.com` initiates an FTP session with server `hp23.boota.com`.

Usually more than one domain name server are used in a network. One of these acts as a primary domain name server and the others are secondary name servers. The secondary name servers take data from the primary name server.

31.3 Introduction to the Domain Name System

A domain name system consists of three major parts that interact with each other in the name resolution process. These are as follows.

- A tree-like hierarchical name space is used when assigning names to hosts. A domain name is used as a common name for a set of hosts (not necessarily on the same network). A complete host name is a combination of host name and domain name. This is called a *fully qualified domain name* (FQDN). The different parts of an FQDN are separated by the dot character. For example, the FQDN for a host myhp in domain boota.com is myhp.boota.com.
- One or more name servers used to resolve a host name to its IP address and vice versa.
- Resolver library functions used by an application program to request host name resolution. These resolver functions determine which name resolution service is being used (/etc/hosts, NIS, or DNS) and then use this service to resolve a name. The gethostbyname() function is used to map a host name to an IP address, while the gethostbyaddr() function is used to map an IP address to a host name.

The name space and name server components of the domain name system are discussed in more detail in the following part of the chapter.

Name Space

A name space is a tree-like structure starting with top-level domain names as shown in Figure 31-2. The top-level domain names in this figure are edu, com, and org. The name of a domain is written from bottom to top. Each level of the tree is separated by a dot character while writing the domain name boota.com.

Many hosts are included in a domain name. In Figure 31-2, three hosts with names myhp, hp0, and hp23 are shown in domain boota.com. Each of these hosts has a fully qualified domain name where the domain name is appended to the host name using a dot character. The fully qualified domain name for host hp23 is hp23.boota.com.

If you are connecting your network to the Internet, you have to register your domain name with any of the domain name registrars on the Internet. A list of domain name registrars can be found at the http://www.internic.net Web site. If you don't want to connect your network to any public network, you can use a domain name of your own choice.

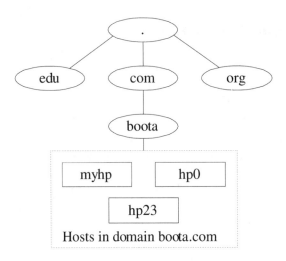

Figure 31–2 *Domain name system hierarchy.*

RELATIVE AND ABSOLUTE NAMES

Resolver keeps a record of the local domain names in the `/etc/resolv.conf` file. If you try to resolve a host name without specifying a domain name, the resolver automatically appends the local domain name to the host name before resolving it. For example, if you try to resolve host name `myhp` and this host lies in domain `boota.com`, the resolver will resolve `myhp.boota.com` when using DNS. This method is called relative host name resolution. However, if you put a dot at the end of the name, the resolver takes this name as an absolute name and does not append the domain name to it. It then tries to resolve it using DNS.

REVERSE NAME LOOKUP

The reverse name lookup is used when you have an IP address and want to map it to a host name. This is often required for authentication purposes on the server side. The incoming connection requests contain the IP address of a client. The server has to resolve this IP address to map it to a host name to verify whether the host is allowed to establish a connection. The `in-addr.arpa` name space is used for reverse host name resolution. Here, IP addresses are written in reverse order followed by keyword `in-addr.arpa`. You will see an example of this name space in the reverse name resolution configuration file later in this chapter.

Name Server

Three types of name servers are used on the Internet. Each of these name servers is used in a particular situation. Primary and secondary name servers have data base resources that are used to resolve local host names. The caching server doesn't have any record of local hosts and is used to resolve host names with the help of other name servers.

NAME SERVER ZONES

A *zone* is a part of a domain name. A primary domain name server has the authority of a domain. It can then divide the domain into zones and delegate authority of these zones to other name servers. This means that an administrator of a domain can add or remove hosts in the zone of its authority. A delegated name server has authority over the delegated zone and is able to add, remove, or modify hosts in the zone.

PRIMARY NAME SERVER

A primary name server maintains data about hosts in the domain and pointers to delegated servers responsible for zones inside the domain. It is the primary point of contact for resolving host names in its domain. A primary server can create subdomains delegated to other servers.

SECONDARY NAME SERVER

The secondary server is used as a backup server in case a primary server fails. It takes its data from the primary server and synchronizes them with the primary server after defined intervals of time.

CACHING NAME SERVER

It does not have local data files. It is used only to look up host names and distribute load in large networks where several clients are resolving host names.

31.4 Configuring the Primary DNS

A DNS server process is called `named`, which is started at system boot time when the system enters in run level 2. Automatic startup of the DNS server process is controlled by the `NAMED` variable in the `/etc/rc.config.d/namesvrs` file. If the value of this variable is 1, `named` is started at boot time.

The startup script for the domain name server is /sbin/init.d/named. The named process looks into its configuration file, /etc/named.boot, which contains a list of domain names served by the server. The basic DNS configuration process on HP-UX is not complicated and is completed using the hosts_to_named command-line utility provided with HP-UX. The process consists of the following steps.

1. Register your own domain name with one of the registrars on the Internet. Before that, you must have the IP addresses being used on your network. You have to provide two IP addresses of hosts that will be used as primary and secondary name servers for your domain.
2. Create a list of host names and corresponding IP addresses in the /etc/ hosts file on the system that will be used as the primary domain name server. You can add host name aliases in the file. This file should look like the following.

```
192.168.3.10    myhp.boota.com    myhp
192.168.3.12    hp0.boota.com     hp0
127.0.0.1       localhost         loopback
```

3. Create a directory /etc/named.data using the mkdir command.
4. Go to this directory using the cd command.
5. Create a file named param that will be used by hosts_to_named to create DNS data files. The file that I used when creating the examples in this chapter contains the following lines.

```
-d boota.com
-n 192.168.3
-z 192.168.3.10
-b /etc/named.boot
-s
```

The -d option shows the domain name. The -n option shows the network number used in this domain. The -z option creates the configuration file for the secondary name server. The IP address used with this option is for the primary name server. This IP address is used by the secondary server to download data files from the primary server. The -s option adds a name server (NS) resource record entry in the configuration file.

6. Run hosts_to_named to create server configuration and data files. You will see output of this command like that shown next.

```
# hosts_to_named -f param
Translating /etc/hosts to lower case ...
Collecting network data ...
        192.168.3
```

```
Creating list of multi-homed hosts ...
Creating "A" data (name to address mapping) for net
    192.168.3 ...
Creating "PTR" data (address to name mapping) for net
    192.168.3 ...
Creating "MX" (mail exchanger) data ...
Building default named.boot file ...
Building default db.cache file ...

WARNING: db.cache must be filled in with
         the name(s) and address(es) of the
         rootserver(s)

Building default boot.sec.save for secondary servers ...
Building default boot.sec for secondary servers ...
Building default boot.cacheonly for caching only servers ...
done
#
```

This command creates several files as shown in Table 31-1.

7. Download the db.cache file from the Internet and copy it into the /etc/named.data directory. This file contains addresses of root name servers present on the Internet. You can find it on several servers on the Internet.

8. Modify the /etc/rc.config.d/namesvrs file so that the named process starts every time you boot the system. Change the value of the NAMED variable to 1 in this configuration file.

9. Start the DNS server using the following command.

```
/sbin/init.d/named start
```

If everything goes well, the name server should be running fine at this point. Use the following command to verify that the named process is running.

```
ps -ef|grep named
```

Table 31-1 *Files Created by the* hosts_to_named *Command*

File Name	Description
/etc/named.data/boot.cacheonly	Boot file for a caching server. This should be copied as /etc/named.boot to a caching server, if one if being used.
/etc/named.data/boot.sec.save	Boot file for a secondary server that saves DNS data files on its disk. This file should be copied as /etc/named.boot on the secondary server.

Table 31–1 *Files Created by the* `hosts_to_named` *Command (continued)*

File Name	Description
`/etc/named.data/boot.sec`	Boot file for a secondary server that does not save data files on its disk. This file should be copied as `/etc/named.boot` on the secondary server.
`/etc/named.data/db.boota`	File contains host names to IP address mapping for all hosts in domain `boota.com`.
`/etc/named.data/db.192.168.3`	File contains reverse host name mapping (IP to host name) for hosts in network 192.168.3.
`/etc/named.data/db.127.0.0`	File contains mapping for the loopback address.
`/etc/named.boot`	Boot file used by the `named` process.

DNS Configuration Files

Let's have a closer look at the DNS configuration and data files. At startup time, `named` looks for the `/etc/named.boot` file. This file contains a list of domain names served by the DNS and their related data files. It also contains the name of the directory where these data files are located. Following is a sample `/etc/named.boot` file. Lines starting with a semicolon in these files are treated as comments.

```
;
; type          domain                      source file
;
directory       /etc/named.data ; running directory for named

primary         0.0.127.IN-ADDR.ARPA    db.127.0.0
primary         boota.com                   db.boota
primary         3.168.192.IN-ADDR.ARPA      db.192.168.3
cache           .                       db.cache
```

This file shows that the data files are stored in the `/etc/named.data` directory and that this is a primary server for domain `boota.com`. The host name data base is stored in file `db.boota` and the `db.192.168.3` file is used for reverse name lookup.

The loopback data file `db.127.0.0` is shown next. It contains a pointer to the local host only. Its structure is almost the same everywhere.

```
@       IN      SOA     myhp.boota.com. root.myhp.boota.com. (
                                1        ; Serial
                                10800    ; Refresh every 3 hours
                                3600     ; Retry every hour
                                604800   ; Expire after a week
                                86400 )  ; Minimum ttl of 1 day
        IN      NS      myhp.boota.com.

1       IN      PTR     localhost.
```

File db.192.168.3 is used for mapping host names to IP addresses. A sample file is shown here. It should contain all hosts in network 192.168.3.

```
@       IN      SOA     myhp.boota.com. root.myhp.boota.com. (
                                1        ; Serial
                                10800    ; Refresh every 3 hours
                                3600     ; Retry every hour
                                604800   ; Expire after a week
                                86400 )  ; Minimum ttl of 1 day
        IN      NS      myhp.boota.com.

10      IN      PTR     myhp.boota.com.
12      IN      PTR     hp0.boota.com.
```

File db.boota is used for mapping host names to IP addresses. It contains all hosts in domain boota.com. A sample file is shown here having two host names, myhp and hp0.

```
@         IN      SOA     myhp.boota.com. root.myhp.boota.com. (
                                  1        ; Serial
                                  10800    ; Refresh every 3 hours
                                  3600     ; Retry every hour
                                  604800   ; Expire after a week
                                  86400 )  ; Minimum ttl of 1 day
          IN      NS      myhp.boota.com.

localhost IN      A       127.0.0.1
myhp      IN      A       192.168.3.10
hp0       IN      A       192.168.3.12
myhp      IN      MX      10      myhp.boota.com.
hp0       IN      MX      10      hp0.boota.com.
```

File db.cache contains addresses of root name servers. It can be downloaded from several servers on the Internet. It is standard for all name servers and is shown next.

```
;
;    This file holds the information on root name servers needed to
;    initialize cache of Internet domain name servers
;    (e.g. reference this file in the "cache  .  <file>"
;    configuration file of BIND domain name servers).
;
;    This file is made available by InterNIC registration services
;    under anonymous FTP as
;        file                /domain/named.root
;        on server           FTP.RS.INTERNIC.NET
;    -OR- under Gopher at    RS.INTERNIC.NET
;        under menu          InterNIC Registration Services (NSI)
;            submenu         InterNIC Registration Archives
;        file                named.root
;    last update:   Oct 5, 1994
;    related version of root zone:   94100500
;
.                         99999999 IN  NS   NS.INTERNIC.NET.
NS.INTERNIC.NET.          99999999     A    198.41.0.4
.                         99999999     NS   NS1.ISI.EDU.
NS1.ISI.EDU.              99999999     A    128.9.0.107
.                         99999999     NS   C.PSI.NET.
C.PSI.NET.                99999999     A    192.33.4.12
.                         99999999     NS   TERP.UMD.EDU.
TERP.UMD.EDU.             99999999     A    128.8.10.90
.                         99999999     NS   NS.NASA.GOV.
NS.NASA.GOV.              99999999     A    128.102.16.10
                          99999999     A    192.52.195.10
.                         99999999     NS   NS.ISC.ORG.
NS.ISC.ORG.               99999999     A    192.5.5.241
.                         99999999     NS   NS.NIC.DDN.MIL.
NS.NIC.DDN.MIL.           99999999     A    192.112.36.4
.                         99999999     NS   AOS.ARL.ARMY.MIL.
AOS.ARL.ARMY.MIL.         99999999     A    128.63.4.82
                          99999999     A    192.5.25.82
                          99999999     NS   NIC.NORDU.NET.
NIC.NORDU.NET.            99999999     A    192.36.148.17
; End of File
```

These files are used for running the primary domain name server. The following files are generated on the primary domain name server but are copied to another machine to be used as a secondary or caching server. Next is the boot.cacheonly file that is copied to a server intended to be used as a caching server. The file is renamed as /etc/named.boot on that server.

```
;
; type           domain                      source file
;


directory        /etc/named.data ; running directory for named

primary          0.0.127.IN-ADDR.ARPA      db.127.0.0
cache            .                          db.cache
```

The boot.sec file is used for a secondary server. It is copied as /etc/named.boot on the secondary server. A secondary name server with this configuration file does not maintain its data base files on disk. It requires the primary server to be up at boot time. If the primary server is not up and running, the secondary server with this configuration does not start as it can't get its data base file. A sample boot.sec file is shown next. As you can see, this file contains the IP address of the primary name server (192.168.3.10).

```
;
; type           domain                      source file
;


directory        /etc/named.data ; running directory for named

primary          0.0.127.IN-ADDR.ARPA      db.127.0.0
secondary        boota.com          192.168.3.10
secondary        3.168.192.IN-ADDR.ARPA           192.168.3.10
cache            .                          db.cache
```

The boot.sec.save file is copied to a secondary name server as /etc/named.boot. A secondary server with this configuration maintains its own data base files on disk, which are copies of the files on the primary name server. The secondary name server updates these files automatically after defined intervals of time. A sample boot.sec.save file is shown here.

```
;
; type           domain                      source file
;


directory        /etc/named.data ; running directory for named

primary          0.0.127.IN-ADDR.ARPA      db.127.0.0
secondary        boota.com          192.168.3.10 db.boota
secondary        3.168.192.IN-ADDR.ARPA   192.168.3.10 db.192.168.3
cache            .                          db.cache
```

Resource Records

Entries in DNS data base files are called *resource records* (RR). Some common types of RRs are:

A   Address record. It is used for assigning an IP address to a host.

CNAME   Used for host name aliases or *canonical names*. It is used to assign additional names to a host. For example, if you want to use a host name as Web server and ftp server, you can use CNAME to assign the host different names for both services.

HINFO   Host information record. It shows host information such as operating system and CPU type. It is not commonly used.

MX   Mail resource record. It is used with sendmail to deliver email. Mail server priorities can be set using this record.

NS   Name server record. It shows the DNS server for a domain.

SOA   Start of authority resource record. It contains information for the domain for which the server is authority and information for the secondary server.

Updating Data Base Files on the Primary Server

A DNS server reads its data base files at boot time. Every time you update these files, you have to ask the server to reload its files or restart the server. Although DNS data base files can be edited manually, the preferred method is as follows.

1. Edit and update the /etc/hosts file used for the creation of data base files on the primary server.
2. Go to the directory /etc/named.data where the param file resides.
3. Run the hosts_to_named -f param command to regenerate DNS data files.
4. Reload these files using the sig_named restart command.

31.5   Configuring the Secondary DNS

The secondary name server provides backup to the primary DNS so that if the primary server fails, users can still resolve host names using the secondary name server. To configure the secondary name server, you don't need to run hosts_to_named. Simply follow these steps.

1. Create a `/etc/named.data` directory using the `mkdir` command.
2. Copy the `boot.sec` or `boot.sec.save` file as `/etc/named.boot` from the primary name server. If you copy `named.sec`, DNS data base files will not be created on the local disk. This is useful if you have limited disk space on the secondary server. The drawback is that the server will not be started at boot time if the primary server is not up and running. If you use `named.sec.save`, local DNS data base files will be created and the server will be able to start at boot time even if the primary server is down.
3. Copy `db.127.0.0` from the primary server to the `/etc/named.data` directory.
4. Copy `db.cache` from the primary server to the `/etc/named.data` directory.
5. If you want to create local disk data base files, download the remaining files from the `/etc/named.data` directory on the primary server to the local `/etc/named.data` directory.
6. Update the `/etc/rc.config.d/namesvrs` file to start `named` at boot time. The value of the NAMED variable in this file should be changed to 1.
7. Start `named` using the `/sbin/init.d/named start` command.

Updating Data Base Files on the Secondary Server

DNS data base files contain a part in the beginning like the one shown here.

```
@       IN      SOA     myhp.boota.com. root.myhp.boota.com. (
                                1        ; Serial
                                10800    ; Refresh every 3 hours
                                3600     ; Retry every hour
                                604800   ; Expire after a week
                                86400 )  ; Minimum ttl of 1 day
```

This part contains important information for the secondary name server. Fields in this part are explained next.

Serial
: This field shows the serial number of the data base file. When updating data base files on the primary server, this serial number should be incremented. The secondary server checks the serial number from time to time, and if it finds that the serial number is incremented on the primary server, it downloads the updated file automatically.

Refresh
: This is the time in seconds after which the secondary server checks any updated files on the primary server. The above entry uses a refresh time of 3 hours. This is the time when the secondary server checks the serial numbers of data files on the primary server to refresh its own files.

Retry   If the primary server can't be contacted at the refresh time, the secondary server retries after the retry interval. This is again a time in seconds.

Expire   All data are expired if the primary server can't be contacted within this time.

Minimum ttl   This is the minimum time for a file to be retained if no time is specified.

The secondary server keeps its data base updated automatically depending on this information. However, you can update the secondary server data base at any time using the `sig_named restart` command.

31.6   Configuring the Caching DNS

To configure a caching server is easy using the following steps.

1. Create a `/etc/named.data` directory using the `mkdir` command.
2. Copy the `named.cacheonly` file from the primary DNS as `/etc/named.boot`.
3. Copy `db.127.0.0` from the primary server to the `/etc/named.data` directory.
4. Copy `db.cache` from the primary server to the `/etc/named.data` directory.
5. Update the `/etc/rc.config.d/namesvrs` file to start `named` at boot time. The value of the NAMED variable in this file should be changed to 1.
6. Start `named` using the `/sbin/init.d/named start` command.

31.7   Configuring the DNS Client

The resolver library on client servers is configured to contact a specific type of service for host name resolution. This is controlled through the name service switch file the `/etc/nsswitch.conf`. This file lists the order in which different services are tried for resolution purposes. Usually `/etc/hosts` is used if DNS is not configured. If the DNS is configured, it is given preference over other methods. The names of DNS servers are listed in the `/etc/resolv.conf` file. Multiple DNS servers can be listed in this file, which are consulted in order.

Configuring the Name Service Switch

HP-UX uses a number of sources for information. For example, a host name may be resolved using the /etc/hosts file, DNS, or NIS server. The /etc/ nsswitch.conf file controls which service will be used for a particular type of information and in what order. The following line in this file shows that DNS will be tried first for host name resolution and then the /etc/hosts file will be used.

```
hosts:          dns files
```

Configuring /etc/resolv.conf

When the resolver wishes to try a DNS for name resolution, it first checks the /etc/resolv.conf file for a list of domain names and DNS servers. Two types of lists are present in /etc/resolv.conf. The first part of the file contains a list of domains used for relative host names. Each line in this list starts with the search keyword. If a domain name is present in this list, you don't need to fully specify qualified host names in your commands. The resolver itself adds a domain name to a short host name during the resolution process. For example, if domain name boota.com is present in this file and you use a command telnet hp0, the resolver will try to find host name hp0.boota.com. The second part of the file consists of a list of domain name servers. Each line in this part starts with the keyword nameserver followed by the IP address of the name server. A maximum of three name servers can be listed in this file. A sample /etc/resolv.conf file is shown next.

```
search boota.com
nameserver 192.168.3.10
nameserver 192.168.3.12
```

The domain name servers are consulted in the order they occur in this file. If the first name server is available, others are not tried. To distribute the load on all name servers, the order of name servers on different client machines should be changed.

The resolv.conf file should be set up on all machines in the domain, including the primary and secondary domain name servers.

Note The `nsswitch.conf` file should be modified to put DNS first in line starting with the word `hosts:` so that a DNS is consulted *before* trying any other host name resolution method.

Testing with nslookup

The `nslookup` command is used for testing and resolving a host name. The host name to be resolved is provided on the command line. The command first contacts the DNS server in the `/etc/resolv.conf` file and displays an IP address corresponding to the host. A typical output of the command is as follows.

```
# nslookup www.hp.com
Name Server:  myhp.boota.com
Address:  192.168.3.10

Trying DNS
Non-authoritative answer:
Name:    www.hp.com
Addresses:  192.151.11.32, 192.151.11.13, 192.151.52.13
            192.6.35.16, 192.151.52.10

#
```

This command can also be used in interactive mode when invoked without any arguments. In this case, the command displays the address of the name server, which will be used for name resolution, and waits for user input at its prompt, a greater-than sign >. At this command prompt, the user enters a host name. The command then resolves it and displays a message showing the IP address. If the name can't be resolved, an error message is displayed instead. A typical session for resolving host name www.hp.com is shown next.

```
# nslookup
Name Server:  myhp.boota.com
Address:  192.168.3.10

> www.hp.com
Name Server:  hamdns2.ham.am.honda.com
Address:  207.130.253.66

Trying DNS
```

```
Name:    www.hp.com
Addresses:  192.151.52.10, 192.151.11.32, 192.151.11.13,
   192.151.52.13
           192.6.35.16

> exit
#
```

The command can also be used for reverse name resolution. In that case, you can enter an IP address and the host name corresponding to that IP address as displayed.

```
# nslookup
Default Name Server:  myhp.boota.com
Address:  192.168.3.10

> 192.151.52.10
Name Server:  hamdns2.ham.am.honda.com
Address:  207.130.253.66

Trying DNS
Name:     i3107im4.external.hp.com
Address:  192.151.52.10

> exit
#
```

The default DNS server used by nslookup can be changed with the server sub-command. In the following session, the default server is changed to ns.uu.net before resolving host name www.hp.com.

```
# nslookup
Default Name Server:  myhp.boota.com
Address:  192.168.3.10

> server ns.uu.net
Default Name Server:  ns.uu.net
Address:  137.39.1.3

> www.hp.com
Name Server:  ns.uu.net
Address:  137.39.1.3

Trying DNS
Addresses:  192.151.52.10, 192.151.11.32, 192.151.11.13
           192.151.52.13, 192.6.35.16

>
```

31.8 Using SAM to Configure DNS

SAM can also be used to create a basic structure of DNS data base files. When you select the DNS (BIND) icon in the Networking and Communications area of SAM, a window like the one shown in Figure 31-3 appears.

From this window the DNS Local Name Server icon is used to configure DNS data base files and the DNS Resolver icon is used to configure the /etc/resolv.conf file. Click on the DNS Local Name Server icon to move to the window in Figure 31-4.

If a DNS is already running, you will find its data files listed here. If a DNS is not running, use the Actions menu to create files for a primary or secondary DNS as shown in Figure 31-4. When you select Add Primary/ Secondary Information from the Actions menu, you find a new window as shown in Figure 31-5.

Here you enter information for a primary or secondary server. The selection of a primary or secondary server is made using the Name Server Type button at the top part of the figure. When you click the OK button, a warning window appears as shown in Figure 31-6.

After selecting Yes in this window, you return to the window shown in Figure 31-3 but with the DNS data files now listed as shown in Figure 31-7.

You can modify any of these files using options in the Actions menu.

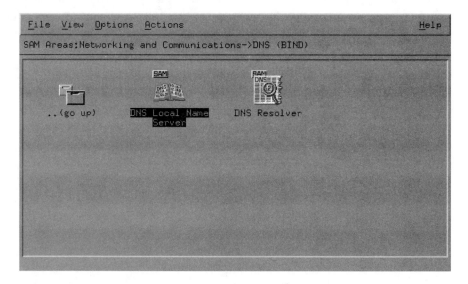

Figure 31–3 *DNS configuration window.*

File
List
View
Options
Actions
Help
DNS Server: Not Running
DNS Local Name Server
Name Server Type
Domain
Add Primary/Secondary Information...
Specify a Root/Parent Domain...
Configure Caching-Only Server
Start the DNS Name Server
(nothing selected)

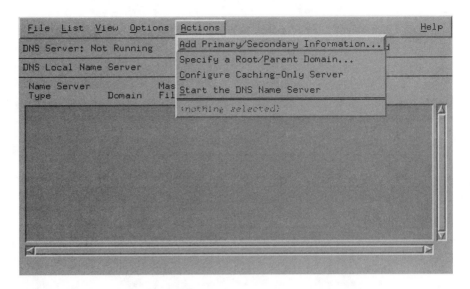

Figure 31–4 *Creating a primary name server.*

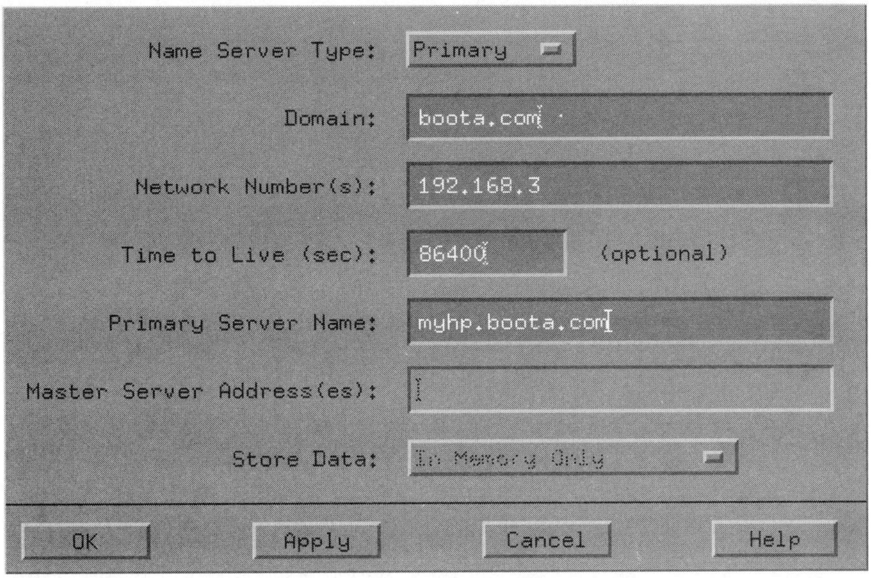

Name Server Type:
Primary
Domain:
boota.com
Network Number(s):
192.168.3
Time to Live (sec):
86400
(optional)
Primary Server Name:
myhp.boota.com
Master Server Address(es):
Store Data:
In Memory Only
OK
Apply
Cancel
Help

Figure 31–5 *Entering information for the primary DNS data files.*

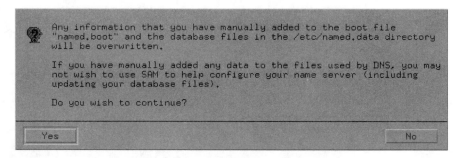

Figure 31–6 *Confirmation to create data files.*

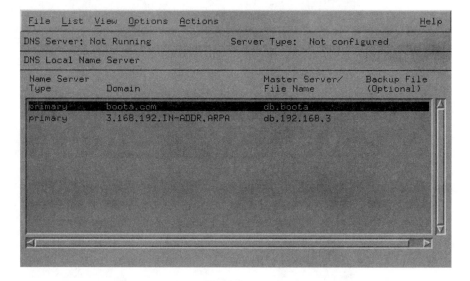

Figure 31–7 *List of newly created DNS data files.*

■ Chapter Summary

Host name resolution methods are used to map host names to IP addresses and vice versa. The most widely used method is the Domain Name System (DNS). Other than this method, the /etc/hosts file or simply *hosts* and NIS are also used in different circumstances. The hosts file contains a listing of IP addresses and host names. Aliases can also be used in the hosts file. It is scanned from top to bottom in the resolution process and the first matching entry is chosen.

A DNS consists of three parts: the *name space*, the *resolver*, and the *name server*. The name space is a hierarchical data structure used to assign host names. The resolver library routines are used to select a particular name resolution method. The name server keeps a record in its data files of all hosts in a domain and resolves a host name. Three types of name servers are used. The primary name server has authority over a domain name, while secondary name servers are used for backup to the primary name server. The caching server does not have any data files and is used for load sharing only.

Name server data files are created using the `hosts_to_named` command line utility. It reads the `/etc/hosts` file and generates the configuration and data files for primary, secondary, and caching servers. Configuration files for secondary and caching servers are then transferred to desired machines from the primary name server. A secondary name server keeps its files updated by consulting the primary server after defined intervals of time.

A DNS client has the `/etc/resolv.conf` file consisting of a list of local domain names and name servers. The `/etc/nsswitch.conf` file is used to set up the order in which host name resolution services are used. The `nslookup` command can be used to test and resolve host names using a DNS.

▲ CHAPTER REVIEW QUESTIONS

1. What are the three most common host name resolution methods?

2. Give a short description of the three types of domain name servers.

3. Why is the `db.cache` file used?

4. How are DNS data files updated on the secondary server?

▲ TEST YOUR KNOWLEDGE

1. *A system has the following* `/etc/hosts` *file.*
   ```
   192.168.2.1 hp01
   192.168.4.5 hp01
   ```
   You use the `ping hp01` *command to send an ICMP packet to host* `hp01`. *To which IP address will these packets be sent?*

   A. `192.168.2.1`

   B. `192.168.4.5`

   C. Alternate packets will be sent to each host starting with `192.168.2.1`.

   D. Alternate packets will be sent to each host starting with `192.168.4.5`.

2. *Which file determines the order in which different services try to resolve a host name?*

   A. `/etc/hosts`

   B. `/etc/resolv.conf`

   C. `/etc/nsswitch.conf`

   D. `/etc/named.boot`

3. *At which run level is* `named` *started?*

   A. 3

   B. 2

   C. s

   D. 4

4. *What is the DNS port number?*

   A. 21

   B. 23

   C. 25

   D. 53

5. *The* `hosts_to_named` *command is run on which server?*

   A. primary name server

   B. secondary name server

   C. caching name server

   D. all of above

6. *Which file on a client machine is used for listing available name servers?*

   A. `/etc/hosts`

   B. `/etc/resolv.conf`

   C. `/etc/nsswitch.conf`

   D. `/etc/rc.config.d/namesvrs`

7. *Which is the configuration file used by* `named` *at boot time?*

   A. `/etc/named.conf`

   B. `/etc/named.boot`

   C. `/etc/named.data/db.cache`

   D. `/etc/named.data/named.sec`

8. *You have your own domain name and want to create zones and delegate authority of these zones to a departmental name server. Which name server will delegate this authority?*

    A. root name server

    B. primary name server

    C. secondary name server

    D. All of these can delegate authority to departmental zones.

9. *For what purpose is the NS resource record used in DNS data files?*

    A. For a domain name server IP address

    B. For a Netscape server IP address

    C. For a domain name space

    D. For assigning IP addresses to all hosts

Configuring and Managing NIS

The administration of multiple UNIX hosts on a network requires lots of time and effort, particularly in cases of large networks. For example, it is hard to keep user names and passwords on all network systems consistent. Similarly, if you are not using a DNS, maintenance of host files is cumbersome when the number of hosts grows large. Different techniques are used to keep the maintenance and management work as centralized as possible. In the last chapter, you studied the Domain Name System, where a centralized data base of host names and IP addresses is maintained. The Network Information Service (NIS) is a method of maintaining centralized data bases of host and user information. This centralized management concept decreases system administration overhead and maintains consistent information across the network.

NIS is based on a domain concept. Every system using NIS is part of one domain. This domain name is not like the Internet domain names where a domain hierarchy is used. The name of this domain is valid only for private networks and both NIS and DNS can coexist. A master NIS server maintains the central NIS data base. One or more slave NIS servers can exist on a network. These slave servers collect a copy of the entire data base or a part of it from the master server. The master server can also "push" a copy of the data base to all slave servers at any time. NIS clients contact the master NIS server for any type of data required. If the master server is not available, a slave server may also be contacted. Both NIS servers and clients run daemon programs used for communicating among master, slave, and clients.

NIS was formerly known as Yellow Pages (yp), and most of the commands used in the NIS system start with "yp." NIS is bundled with the standard HP-UX distribution and is a part of the NFS product.

This chapter starts with an introduction to NIS, where NIS maps, NIS domains, and the role of different machines in an NIS domain will be discussed. The configuration part of NIS is divided into three parts.

• configuration of a master NIS server
• configuration of a slave NIS server
• configuration of an NIS client

All three types of hosts need one or more daemon processes and configuration files. During the process of configuration, these three parts will be discussed separately. After completing the configuration process, you will use some commands to verify the configuration.

You may be adding or removing some hosts from the network over a period of time. Similarly, users change passwords and configuration data may need to be updated. In the managing part of the chapter, you will learn how to update NIS maps on a master server and how to propagate these changes to slave servers. As another case, you may not want to allow all users present in NIS maps to have access to some machines on the network. For example, the master server may be made accessible only for the network administrator. Similarly, access to the data base server may be granted only to some users. Methods of providing selective access to NIS servers and clients will be discussed. In the last part of the chapter, SAM will be used to configure NIS.

32.1 NIS Concepts

The Network Information System is based on the domain concept. Each host on a network may be part of one domain only. Data files about hosts and users are maintained on the NIS master server. Text files are converted into dbm format with the help of the ypmake program and are commonly called NIS maps. Each map consists of two files ending with .pag and .dir. For example, when the /etc/passwd file is converted into an NIS map that is indexed on user names, it results in two files named passwd.byname.dir and passwd.byname.pag.

Any NIS-enabled host on a network may be an NIS master server, a slave server, or a client. The NIS server can also act as a client at the same time. Some of the terminology used with NIS is as follows.

NIS Domains

The NIS domain is a single word and is used to group a number of hosts on a network. Any host may be a member of only one domain although multiple NIS domains can exist on a single physical network. Domain names can be set in the /etc/rc.config.d/namesvrs file with the help of the NIS_DOMAIN variable or by using the domainname command at any time. There is no relation between an NIS domain and a DNS domain. In this book we will use testdom as the NIS domain name.

NIS Maps

An NIS map is a data base built from ASCII configuration files. Maps are indexed on some field in the data base. For example, the password data base is indexed on the user name or user ID. The map that uses the user name as the index field is known as passwd.byname, and the one indexed on the user ID is called passwd.byuid. Common NIS maps are listed in Table 32-1.

Table 32–1 *NIS Maps*

Map Name	Description
group.bygid	Group map based on /etc/group and indexed on the group ID.
group.byname	Group map based on /etc/group and indexed on the group name.
hosts.byaddr	Hosts map based on /etc/hosts and indexed on the host IP address.
hosts.byname	Hosts map based on /etc/hosts and indexed on the host name.
mail.aliases	Map showing mail aliases.
networks.byaddr	Based on /etc/networks and indexed on network addresses.
networks.byname	Based on /etc/networks and indexed on network names.
passwd.byname	Passwords map indexed on login names.
passwd.byuid	Passwords map indexed on user IDs.
protocols.byname	Map for supported protocols. It is indexed on protocol names and is based on the /etc/protocols file.
protocols.bynumber	Map for supported protocols. It is indexed on protocol numbers and is based on the /etc/protocols file.
services.byname	Based on /etc/services and indexed on service names.
ypservers	This map is automatically generated and does not depend on any file.

Every map has two files stored in a directory with the domain name under /var/yp. For example, if our domain name is testdom, the directory where the map files are stored is /var/yp/testdom. One of these files ends with .pag and the other one ends with .dir.

NIS Roles

Any host participating in an NIS domain falls into one of three categories. A brief explanation of these categories is given next.

MASTER NIS SERVER

The master NIS server keeps NIS maps. All of the text files on which these maps are based are present on the master server. Whenever any information on the master server changes, one or more map files are regenerated. These updated maps can be transferred to slave servers by either of two methods. Either the master server pushes the updated maps to slave servers, or the slave servers can pull the maps from the master server. Neither of these operations is automatic. You have to do it manually or use cron at regular time intervals.

SLAVE NIS SERVER

Slave servers depend on information provided by the NIS master server. Slave servers keep the same copy of NIS maps as the master server. They also update their maps from time to time using the ypxfr command. Usually, system administrators run this command through cron.

NIS CLIENT

An NIS client gets system and user information from one of the NIS servers. For example, during the login process, the client machine contacts an NIS server for user name and password verification.

32.2 Configuring NIS

The configuration process of NIS involves at least one NIS master server and one or more NIS clients. The NIS server is an NIS client at the same time. During this process, startup files used for NIS are edited and daemon processes are started. The first step toward configuration is setting up an NIS domain name.

Setting Up an NIS Domain Name

The domainname command is used to set up an NIS domain. For example, the following command sets up testdom as an NIS domain.

```
domainname testdom
```

If the command is used without an argument, the current domain name is displayed. To set an NIS domain name every time the system boots, the following line is included in the /etc/rc.config.d/namesvrs file.

```
NIS_DOMAIN=testdom
```

NIS Startup Files

Server NIS processes are started at run level 2 using the `/sbin/init.d/nis.server` script. The client processes are started using the `/sbin/init.d/nis.client` script. Both of these scripts use variables in the `/etc/rc.config.d/namesvrs` file for their operation. This file contains a number of variables related to NIS, some of which are shown in Table 32-2.

Table 32–2 *Configuration Variables for NIS*

Variable Name	Description
NIS_MASTER_SERVER	Value 1 is assigned to this variable if this node is the master NIS server, 0 if not.
NIS_SLAVE_SERVER	Value 1 is assigned to this variable if this node is a slave NIS server, 0 if not.
NIS_CLIENT	Value 1 is assigned to this variable if this node is an NIS client, 0 if not. Both NIS master and slave servers must also be NIS clients.
NISDOMAIN	This variable is used to set an NIS domain name (see the `domainname(1)` command).
MAX_NISCHECKS	This variable shows the maximum number of bind attempts the NIS client will make.
YPSERV_OPTIONS	Specifies command line options for `ypserv`.
YPBIND_OPTIONS	Specifies command line options for `ypbind`.
YPPASSWDD_OPTIONS	Specifies command line options for `yppasswdd`.
KEYSERV_OPTIONS	Specifies command line options for `keyserv`.
YPUPDATED_OPTIONS	Specifies command line options for `ypupdated`.
YPXFRD_OPTIONS	Specifies command line options for `ypxfrd`.

The `ypserv` process is the NIS server daemon and `ypbind` is the NIS client daemon. The above-mentioned files can be edited to automatically start NIS at boot time. It must be noted that a server may be either a master NIS server or a slave NIS server, but not both. To enable a server either in master or slave mode, one of the `NIS_MASTER_SERVER` or `NIS_SLAVE_SERVER` variables should be set to 1 while editing this file. If a host is configured as the master NIS server, it must also be an NIS client at the same time.

Typical entries for our `testdom` NIS server are shown next. Here we have set the host to run as master server and client for domain name `testdom`.

```
NIS_MASTER_SERVER=1
NIS_SLAVE_SERVER=0
NIS_CLIENT=1
NIS_DOMAIN="testdom"
MAX_NISCHECKS=2
YPPASSWDD_OPTIONS="/etc/passwd -m passwd PWFILE=/etc/passwd"
YPUPDATED_OPTIONS=""
YPXFRD_OPTIONS=""
```

NIS Daemons

NIS is an RPC-based service. If you are using HP-UX 10.20 or earlier, the `portmap` daemon must be running. For higher versions of HP-UX, `portmap` is replaced with the `rpcbind` daemon. These daemons are started during NFS startup, which is started before NIS starts. However, if the RPC daemon is not running, it is started during the NIS startup process. Other processes and daemons used for NIS are listed in Table 32-3. The files are found under the `/usr/lib/netsvc/yp` directory.

Table 32–3 *NIS Daemons and Their Roles*

Daemon Name	Role
`ypserv`	An NIS server process. It runs on both master and slave NIS servers. Its job is to listen to incoming requests and respond to them after consulting NIS maps.
`rpc.yppasswdd`	Runs only on NIS master servers. When a user runs the `yppasswd` or `passwd` command to change a password, this daemon updates the password file used for building NIS password maps. It then updates the maps and pushes these to all slave servers.
`ypxfrd`	Runs on master and slave NIS servers. Its function is to transfer maps between master and slave servers. It is placed in the `/usr/sbin` directory.
`rpc.updated`	Runs on master NIS servers. This daemon is part of secure RPC. It provides a secure mechanism to update NIS source files on the master NIS server.
`keyserv`	Runs on all machines. This is also a part of secure RPC and is used to keep encryption keys for all logged in users. It is found in the `/usr/sbin` directory.
`ypbind`	The client process. It runs on all hosts taking part in the NIS domain. Client applications use `ypbind` to communicate to the `ypserv` process on the server.

Configuring the NIS Master Server

The configuration process of the master NIS server is carried out using the following steps.

1. Create the NIS domain name. This is done through the `domainname` command as mentioned earlier in this chapter.
2. Update all ASCII configuration files (not map files). The ASCII configuration files are `/etc/passwd`, `/etc/group`, `/etc/services`, `/etc/hosts`, `/etc/protocols`, and others as mentioned in this chapter while listing NIS maps.
3. Add `/var/yp` to `PATH`.
4. Edit the `/etc/rc.config.d/namesvrs` file; it should contain at least the following lines.

   ```
   NIS_MASTER_SERVER=1
   NIS_CLIENT=1
   NIS_DOMAIN=testdom
   ```

   The last line shows your domain name and should be set accordingly.
5. Run the `ypinit -m` command to configure the server as the NIS master. A typical session for this command is as follows. This command creates a directory with the domain name in the `/var/yp` directory and creates NIS map files in it. It also asks you for a list of slave servers. If you are not using any slave server, just press the Enter key at this point.

```
# ypinit -m
You will be required to answer a few questions to install the Network
  Information Service.
All questions will be asked at the beginning of this procedure.
Do you want this procedure to quit on non-fatal errors? [y/n: n]   n
OK, but please remember to correct anything which fails.
If you don't, some part of the system (perhaps the NIS itself) won't work.

At this point, you must construct a list of the hosts which will be NIS
  servers for the "testdom" domain.
This machine, myhp, is in the list of Network Information Service servers.
Please provide the hostnames of the slave servers, one per line.
When you have no more names to add, enter a <ctrl-D> or a blank line.
        next host to add:  myhp
        next host to add:

The current list of NIS servers looks like this:

myhp
```

```
Is this correct?  [y/n: y]  y

There will be no further questions. The remainder of the procedure should
   take 5 to 10 minutes.

Building the ypservers database... ypservers build complete.

Running make in /var/yp:
updated passwd
updated group
updated hosts
updated networks
updated rpc
updated services
updated protocols
updated netgroup
WARNING: writable directory /var/yp/testdom
WARNING: writable directory /var/yp/testdom
WARNING: writable directory /var/yp/testdom
updated aliases
updated publickey
updated netid
updated auto.master

myhp has been set up as a master Network Information Service server without
   any errors.

If there are running slave NIS servers, run yppush(1M) now for any
   databases which have been changed.  If there are no running slaves, run
   ypinit on those hosts which are to be slave servers.
#
```

6. After finishing this process, you can either reboot your system or run the following two commands.

```
/sbin/init.d/nis.server start
/sbin/init.d/nis.client start
```

These two commands start server and slave processes on the master server.

Configuring an NIS Slave Server

The configuration process of a slave server is similar to the master server with few exceptions. The steps are as follows.

1. Create an NIS domain name using the `domainname` command.
2. Add `/var/yp` to `PATH`.
3. Edit the `/etc/rc.config.d/namesvrs` file; it should contain at least the following lines. Here you have to enable a slave server instead of the master server.

```
NIS_SLAVE_SERVER=1
NIS_CLIENT=1
NIS_DOMAIN=testdom
```

4. Run the `ypinit -s myhp` command to configure the slave server, where `myhp` is the name of the master server you have already configured.
5. After finishing this process, you can either reboot your system or run the following two commands.

```
/sbin/init.d/nis.server start
/sbin/init.d/nis.client start
```

Configuring an NIS Client

To configure an NIS client, follow these simple steps.

1. Use the `domainname` command to set an NIS domain name.
2. Edit the `/etc/rc.config.d/namesvrs` file such that it contains the following lines.

```
NIS_CLIENT=1
NIS_DOMAIN=testdom
```

3. After finishing this process, you can either reboot your system or run the following command.

```
/sbin/init.d/nis.client start
```

Name Service Switch

HP-UX uses a number of sources of information. For example, a host name may be resolved using the `/etc/hosts` file, DNS, or NIS server. The `/etc/nsswitch.conf` file controls which service will be used for a particular type of information and in which order. For example, when a user logs into a computer, the following entry in this file shows how the process of user name and password verification will be carried out.

```
passwd:        files nis
```

This line shows that for password verification, local files (/etc/passwd) will be used first. If this method fails, then NIS will be used. A similar method is used for other types of information. A typical /etc/nsswitch.conf file is shown next.

```
passwd:        files nis
group:         files nis
hosts:         files dns
networks:      nis [NOTFOUND=return] files
protocols:     nis [NOTFOUND=return] files
rpc:           nis [NOTFOUND=return] files
publickey:     nis [NOTFOUND=return] files
netgroup:      nis [NOTFOUND=return] files
automount:     files nis
aliases:       files nis
services:      nis [NOTFOUND=return] files
```

When multiple sources are contacted for particular information, it may be precisely defined what to do when one of the sources fails. When contacted, a source returns one of the codes listed in Table 32-4.

Table 32–4 *Return Codes*

Status Code	Meaning
SUCCESS	Shows that the requested data base entry was found.
UNAVAIL	Shows that the source is not responding or is corrupted. This may be due to a server down or network fault.
NOTFOUND	Shows that there is no such entry available on the source.
TRYAGAIN	Shows that the source is busy, and it may respond if you retry.

Depending on the status code, one of two decisions may be made. These two choices are as follows,

continue   Try the next source in the list.

return   Return and don't try the next source.

The following entry in the /etc/nsswitch.conf file tells the system not to try files if a request to resolve a network name returns the status code NOTFOUND from the NIS server.

```
networks:      nis [NOTFOUND=return] files
```

However, if a request to NIS returns the UNAVAIL status code, the local file (/etc/networks) will be tried to resolve the network address.

Testing NIS Configuration

After configuring an NIS server (which is also an NIS client), first check the domain name directory /var/yp/testdom to verify that map files are created in this directory. If the files are there, use the ypcat command to list a few of these maps. For example, the following command lists maps for user names and passwords.

```
# ypcat passwd.byname
root:BCRwpNgfFq3Zc:0:3::/:/sbin/sh
daemon:*:1:5::/:/sbin/sh
bin:*:2:2::/usr/bin:/sbin/sh
sys:*:3:3::/:
adm:*:4:4::/var/adm:/sbin/sh
uucp:*:5:3::/var/spool/uucppublic:/usr/lbin/uucp/uucico
lp:*:9:7::/var/spool/lp:/sbin/sh
nuucp:*:11:11::/var/spool/uucppublic:/usr/lbin/uucp/uucico
hpdb:*:27:1:ALLBASE:/:/sbin/sh
nobody:*:-2:-2::/:
www:*:30:1::/:
dba:D2aLVIizQMwI6:102:101:,,,:/home/dba:/usr/bin/sh
boota:VUj3GoygfBOvA:103:20:,,,:/home/boota:/usr/bin/sh
#
```

If you see an output like this, your client and server are correctly configured. Try the same command on some other client on the network.

Some utilities that can be used with NIS are listed in Table 32-5.

Table 32–5 *NIS Utilities*

Name	Function
ypcat	Displays NIS maps
ypinit	Builds and installs NIS map files
ypmake	Rebuilds NIS tables
ypmatch	Matches and lists particular values in NIS tables
ypset	Binds NIS clients to particular NIS servers
ypwhich	Shows host names of NIS servers

Study Break

Configuring an NIS Server and Client

You have now learned how to configure an NIS server and clients. You know that an NIS server is also used as an NIS client. Let's configure both an NIS server and client on an HP-UX machine. Use the `domainname` command to set `mynis` as the domain name. Use the `ypinit -m` command to configure an NIS server. Use the `cd` command to go to the `/var/yp` directory. You should find a subdirectory with the name `mynis`. List the files in this directory using the `ll` command and you will find a number of NIS map files. Use the following commands to start the NIS server.

```
/sbin/init.d/nis.server start
/sbin/init.d/nis.client start
```

Now list the running processes using the `ps` command. You should find NIS server daemons running. Start the NIS client using the following command.

```
/sbin/init.d/nis.client start
```

Use the following command to verify that both NIS client and server are working properly.

```
ypcat passwd.byname
```

32.3 Managing NIS

There are a number of day-to-day tasks in NIS management. Some of these tasks include updating NIS maps on master and slave servers, managing user accounts and passwords, and maintaining security. These tasks are discussed next.

Updating NIS Maps on the Master Server

NIS maps can be updated on the master server using the `/var/yp/ypmake` command. It reads ASCII files and regenerates the required NIS maps. For example, if you change the shell of a user in the `/etc/passwd` file, the following command updates the `passwd.byname` and `passwd.byuid` maps and pushes to slave NIS servers.

```
# /var/yp/ypmake

For NIS domain testdom:

Building the passwd map(s)... passwd build complete.
   Pushing the passwd map(s):  passwd.byname  passwd.byuid
The group map(s) are up-to-date.
The hosts map(s) are up-to-date.
The networks map(s) are up-to-date.
The rpc map(s) are up-to-date.
The services map(s) are up-to-date.
The protocols map(s) are up-to-date.
The netgroup map(s) are up-to-date.
The aliases map(s) are up-to-date.
The publickey map(s) are up-to-date.
Building the netid map(s)... netid build complete.
   Pushing the netid map(s):   netid.byname
The auto_master map(s) are up-to-date.

ypmake complete:  no errors encountered.

#
```

Updating NIS Maps on a Slave Server

NIS maps from the master server are transferred to the slave server at the time of configuring the slave server. These maps should be updated periodically using the ypxfr command on all slave servers or the yppush command on the master server. The yppush command initiates the ypxfr command on slave servers, which then uses the ypxfrd daemon to transfer updated maps from the master server. These commands should be invoked using cron on a regular basis. The following command copies the passwd.byname map from the master server.

```
ypxfr passwd.byname
```

In addition to these two commands, NIS comes with scripts in the /var/ yp directory that can be used with cron for the regular update of NIS maps on all clients. These scripts are preconfigured to update appropriate maps at regular time intervals.

ypxfr_1perhour	This script should be invoked every hour.
ypxfr_1perday	This should be invoked once per day.
ypxfr_2perday	This should be invoked twice every day.

Sample cron entries for these scripts are as shown here.

```
1   *    *   *   *    /var/vp/ypxfr_1perhour
1   1    *   *   *    /var/vp/ypxfr_1perday
1   2,14 *   *   *    /var/vp/ypxfr_2perday
```

The first script is executed at the first minute of every hour. The second script is executed at the first minute of 1 A.M. every day. The third script is executed at the first minute of 2 A.M. and 2 P.M. every day.

Changing a Password on a Client

You can change a password on a client host in the normal way using the passwd command. When you use this command, it contacts the rpc.yppasswdd daemon on an NIS server. This daemon verifies the old password and updates its ASCII password file as well as the NIS maps. The old way of changing a password on an NIS server is through the use of the yppasswd command. Its use is similar to the passwd command. The following session is used to change the password for user **boota** on an NIS server using the yppasswd command.

```
# yppasswd boota
Changing password for boota on NIS server
Old NIS password:
New password:
Re-enter new password:
NIS(YP) passwd/attributes changed on myhp, the master NIS server.
#
```

If the user is not being administered by NIS and his or her login name and password resides in the local /etc/passwd file on the local system, the NIS server is not contacted and the change is made locally. Commands for changing a password use the rpc.yppasswdd daemon and can be executed on any NIS client machine.

Using rpcinfo

The rpcinfo command is used for troubleshooting purposes. It can be used to verify that an NIS server is running and responding to client's requests. The following command lists RPC services registered on NIS server myhp.

```
# rpcinfo -s myhp
program version(s) netid(s)                               service     owner
100000  2,3,4      udp,tcp,ticlts,ticotsord,ticots        rpcbind     superuser
100024  1          tcp,udp                                status      superuser
100021  2,4,3,1    udp,tcp                                nlockmgr    superuser
100020  1          tcp,udp                                llockmgr    superuser
100068  5,4,3,2    udp                                    cmsd        superuser
100083  1          tcp                                    ttdbserver  superuser
100069  1          tcp,udp                                ypxfrd      superuser
100028  1          udp,tcp                                ypupdated   superuser
100029  2,1        ticots,ticotsord,ticlts                keyserv     superuser
100004  1,2        tcp,udp                                ypserv      superuser
100009  1          udp                                    yppasswdd   superuser
100007  1,2        udp,tcp                                ypbind      sys
#
```

Make sure that the NIS server processes are present in this list. To check the response of a particular service, you can send a request to it using the TCP or UDP protocol. The following command sends a UDP request to ypserv on host myhp.

```
# rpcinfo -u myhp ypserv
program 100004 version 1 ready and waiting
program 100004 version 2 ready and waiting
#
```

The output of the command shows that ypserv is running and accepting requests at program number 100004. More information about rpcinfo is presented in the next chapter.

32.4 Controlling Access

The order in which different services are consulted when searching for information are listed in the /etc/nsswitch.conf file. The following line in this file shows that the /etc/passwd file should be consulted first when searching for a user name, and if the search is not successful, then to go to the NIS server.

```
passwd:        files nis
```

When using this method, every user name in the NIS maps is tried. To restrict a user name search to the /etc/passwd file and only to selected users in the NIS database, change the above line to:

```
passwd:        compat
```

After that, you have to add escape entries in the /etc/passwd file for those NIS users to whom you want to grant access on a particular NIS client machine. The resulting /etc/passwd file that grants access to all locally defined users in addition to the two NIS users **boota** and **gamma** is shown here.

```
root:BCRwpNgfFq3Zc:0:3::/:/sbin/sh
daemon:*:1:5::/:/sbin/sh
bin:*:2:2::/usr/bin:/sbin/sh
sys:*:3:3::/:
adm:*:4:4::/var/adm:/sbin/sh
uucp:*:5:3::/var/spool/uucppublic:/usr/lbin/uucp/uucico
lp:*:9:7::/var/spool/lp:/sbin/sh
nuucp:*:11:11::/var/spool/uucppublic:/usr/lbin/uucp/uucico
hpdb:*:27:1:ALLBASE:/:/sbin/sh
nobody:*:-2:-2::/:
www:*:30:1::/:
+boota
+gamma
```

The plus (+) symbol shows that these are NIS users. You can add different user names on different NIS clients for granting selective access. Similar processes can be repeated with the /etc/group file.

To grant selected user access on an NIS server, additional steps are needed as compared to an NIS client. First of all, you should not use the /etc/passwd file for creating NIS maps. Create a separate password file for this purpose. For example, if you use the /etc/passwd.nis file for creating NIS maps, follow these two steps.

1. Change the YPPASSWDD_OPTIONS variable in the /etc/rc.config.d/ namesvrs file by replacing /etc/passwd with /etc/passwd.nis. This tells the rpc.yppasswdd daemon to make password changes to this file instead of to the /etc/passwd file when a user changes a password on an NIS client.
2. Edit the /var/yp/ypmake file and replace /etc/passwd with /etc/passwd.nis. This causes the /etc/passwd.nis file to be used when creating NIS maps instead of /etc/passwd.

After carrying out these two steps, you should regenerate the NIS maps and propagate them to slave servers. All other steps are the same as with NIS slave servers.

32.5 Using SAM to Configure NIS

NIS can be configured using the NIS button from the Networking and Communications area of SAM. When you go to the NIS configuration window for the first time, you will see a blank screen as shown in Figure 32-1. The NIS configuration process starts with setting an NIS domain name using the Actions menu.

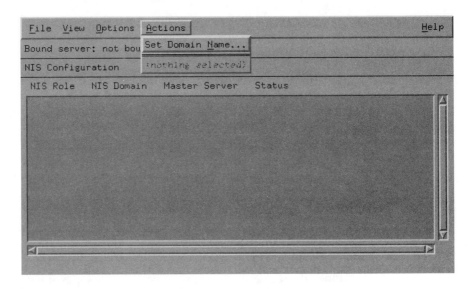

Figure 32–1 *NIS window in SAM.*

When you select Set Domain Name in the Actions menu, a small window shown in Figure 32-2, appears where you can enter a domain name. Here we have used testdom as the NIS domain name.

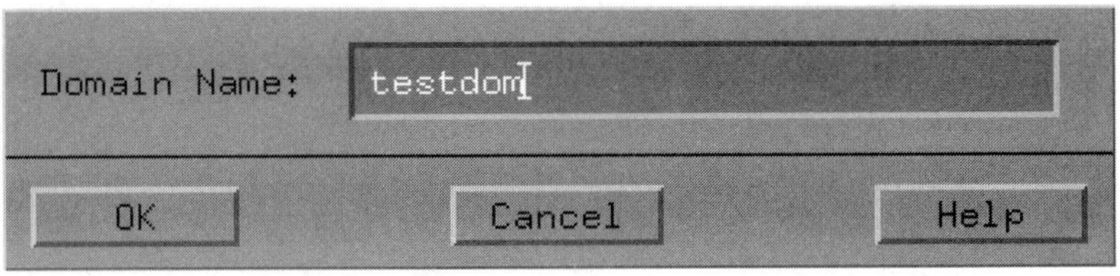

Figure 32–2 *Setting an NIS domain name using SAM.*

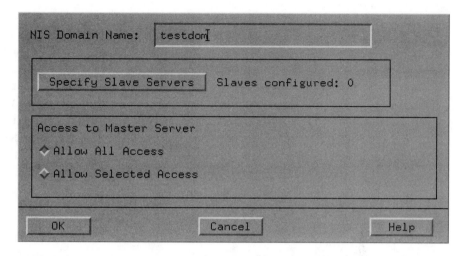

Figure 32–3 *Configuring the master NIS server.*

After you press the OK button in the window shown in Figure 32-2, you will return to the previous window shown in Figure 32-1. Now you will find a line showing the new domain name for the NIS client. The NIS client is disabled at this point. Again go to the Actions menu and select the Configure Master Server option, and you will find yourself in the window shown in Figure 32-3, where you will configure the master NIS server. After specifying information in this window, press the OK button to return to the previous window.

Go to the Actions menu once again and select the Enable Client option to enable the NIS client. On client-only machines, you will not configure any NIS server.

■ Chapter Summary

NIS provides a centralized host and user information. It is based on a flat name space called an NIS domain. A master NIS server in the domain keeps the central NIS information in dbm format, called NIS maps. One or more NIS slave servers can be used within an NIS domain. The slave servers take their information from the master server. NIS is also known as Yellow Pages, and most of the NIS command names start with yp. All NIS servers are also NIS clients at the same time.

NIS domain names can be set using the `domainname` command or the `NIS_DOMAIN` variable in the `/etc/rc.config.d/namesvrs` file, where a number of other variables are also defined. The `ypserv` daemon is started on the NIS server and the `ypbind` daemon is used on an NIS client. In addition to that, a number of other daemons are used to carry out different tasks. Both master and slave servers are configured using the `ypinit` command. However, different command-line switches are used for master and slave servers. NIS map files are kept in the `/var/yp` directory. The `/etc/nsswitch.conf` file is used to define the order in which different services are tried while searching for particular information. The `ypmake` command is used to regenerate NIS maps. Users can change their passwords using the `passwd` or `yppasswd` command.

▲ CHAPTER REVIEW QUESTIONS

1. What is the function of NIS?

2. For what purpose are escape entries used in the `/etc/passwd` file?

3. What is the difference between NIS and DNS?

▲ TEST YOUR KNOWLEDGE

1. *An NIS client can take part in how many NIS domains?*
    A. only one
    B. all domains existing on a single physical network
    C. all domains existing on one IP network
    D. There is no limit on the number of domain names in which a host can take part.

2. *What is true about an NIS domain name?*
    A. It consists of only one word.
    B. It is a combination of multiple words separated by a dot character.
    C. It is a combination of multiple words separated by a space character.
    D. It is a combination of multiple words separated by underscore characters.

3. *The* ypxfr *command is used on:*
    A. master NIS servers
    B. slave NIS servers
    C. NIS clients
    D. DNS servers

4. *Which daemon is used for an NIS password change?*
    A. passwd
    B. yppasswd
    C. yppasswdd
    D. rpc.yppasswdd

5. *What is true about NIS?*
    A. It provides a flat name space.
    B. It provides a hierarchical name space.
    C. An NIS domain name can be used on the Internet.
    D. An NIS domain name is always the same as a DNS domain name.

6. *Which of the following is* not *an NIS map?*
    A. group.byname
    B. host.byname
    C. mail.aliases
    D. mail.byname

7. *Which command is used to display the name of an NIS server bound to a host?*
    A. ypset
    B. ypmatch
    C. ypwhich
    D. ypserv

## THIRTY-THREE

Configuring and Managing the Network File System

The Network File System (NFS) is used to share files and directories over a network. It is an RPC-based system and works in the client-server model. The NFS server makes some of its file systems shareable with other systems on a network. The NFS client mounts shared file systems from the server to its local mount points. Users of the client machines can use NFS-mounted file systems just like the local file systems. NFS support is available on many platforms including personal computers. On UNIX systems, this has become a de facto standard and provides a transparent way for sharing files. When used in combination with NIS, it facilitates users' logging in from any machine on the network and finding the same environment, home directories, and mailboxes.

NFS is used to save disk space in a number of ways. All files that are static in nature can be shared on a network. These files include application directories under /opt and operating system files under the /usr directory. The files that are

639

shared by individual users are users' home directories and mail-boxes. The directories that contain configuration files or log files are usually not shared.

NFS version 2 is supported on HP-UX versions 10.20 and earlier. Version 3 is supported on HP-UX 10.30 and later. The new version provides some extra benefits, like larger file sizes and improved performance. NFS version 3 is used by default on HP-UX 10.30 and later.

This chapter begins with an introduction to NFS, where NFS concepts and terms are presented. After that you will move to the configuration of an NFS server. Here you will learn how to start NFS services and how to export file systems to be mounted remotely by NFS clients. In the NFS client configuration process, you will start NFS client services and mount file systems exported by a particular NFS server. In this process, the /etc/fstab file is updated. After that a list of NFS daemons with their specific responsibilities in the NFS system is presented. In the last part of the chapter, you will learn some utilities and commands that can be used to monitor and configure NFS activity. Using these utilities, you will be able to see what file systems are exported and what clients are accessing them.

33.1 NFS Concepts

When an NFS server makes one or more of its files and directories shareable, this process is called *exporting*. The exported files or directories are placed in the /etc/exports file. Only the exported files and directories can be accessed by an NFS client. The rules that govern communication between a client and server are as follows.

- A system can act as an NFS client and server at the same time.
- A server can export a file, a directory, or a complete file system.
- A server can export only local file systems. File systems mounted from other servers can't be re-exported.
- If a directory is exported, all of the directory tree under this directory are automatically exported.
- A client can mount the exported directories or a subdirectory in the directory tree under the exported directory.

- User and group IDs must match on the client and server machines for proper permissions.

Remote Mount Process

The process of mounting a remote file system is complete when the following steps are completed on the NFS server and client.

- The NFS server processes are started on the server machine. This is done by running the `/sbin/init.d/nfs.core` and `/sbin/init.d/nfs.server` scripts at boot time.
- The shared directories are located in the `/etc/exports` file and are exported using the `exportfs` command. This command is executed at boot time by the `nfs.server` script. However, if you make any change to the `/etc/exports` file, you must use this command to re-export shared directories.
- NFS client processes are running on the client machine. These are started with the help of the `/sbin/init.d/nfs.core` and `/sbin/init.d/nfs.client` scripts. Both of these scripts are invoked at run level 2.
- The remote file system names and mount points are present in the `/etc/fstab` file.

Remote file systems can also be mounted at any time using the `mount` command. However, to have a remote file system mount automatically each time you reboot the system, it must be present in the `/etc/fstab` file.

NFS and RPC

Remote Procedure Calls (RPCs) allow procedures on the server machine to be called by programs on a client machine. All NFS communication between client and server takes place through RPCs. Since RPC (and NFS) is supported on a number of operating systems and platforms, a common data format must be used between client and server for passing data to RPCs. RPCs are made through program numbers. These program numbers are listed in the `/etc/rpc` file, which is displayed here.

```
##
# pragma VERSIONID "@(#)rpc:    11R2-4"
#       file of rpc program name to number mappings
##
rpcbind         100000  portmap sunrpc rpcbind
rstatd          100001  rstat rup perfmeter
rusersd         100002  rusers
```

```
nfs              100003   nfsprog
ypserv           100004   ypprog
mountd           100005   mount showmount
ypbind           100007
walld            100008   rwall shutdown
yppasswdd        100009   yppasswd
etherstatd       100010   etherstat
rquotad          100011   rquotaprog quota rquota
sprayd           100012   spray
selection_svc    100015   selnsvc
#
pcnfsd           150001   pcnfs
#
# NEW SERVICES ADDED AT 6.5
#
rexd             100017   rex
llockmgr         100020
nlockmgr         100021
status           100024
#
# SUN SUPPORTS THE FOLLOWING THAT HP DOES NOT @ release 6.5
#
3270_mapper      100013
rje_mapper       100014
database_svc     100016
alis             100018
sched            100019
x25.inr          100022
statmon          100023
bootparam        100026
ypupdated        100028   ypupdate
keyserv          100029   keyserver
tfsd             100037
nsed             100038
nsemntd          100039
ypxfrd           100069
nisd             100300   rpc.nisd
nispasswd        100303   rpc.nispasswdd
nis_cachemgr     100301
nisd_resolv      100302   rpc.nisd_resolv
automountd       100099
ttdbserver       100083
cmsd             100068   dtcalendar
 #
```

Each line in this file starts with the RPC server name followed by a program number. Aliases can be listed after a program number. A line that starts with the # character is a comment.

The portmap and rpcbind Daemons

Contact between any RPC client and server starts with the help of the `portmap` or `rpcbind` daemon. Up to version 10.20, the `portmap` daemon was used, which was replaced by `rpcbind` in the later versions. The process of establishing a connection between client and server is carried out through the following steps. When an RPC server starts, it registers its program number with `portmap` and the TCP or UDP ports to which it is listening.

1. The client contacts `portmap` using port number 111 on the server machine requesting the port number used by the RPC server. The client sends the RPC program number of the server program as defined in the `/etc/rpc` file.
2. The `portmap` returns the port number used by a server using that program number.
3. The client connects to the server at the port number returned by `rpcbind`.

The `rpcbind` daemon facilitates dynamic binding of program numbers to ports.

NFS Versions

Starting with HP-UX version 10.30, NFS version 3 has been used by default. Advantages of version 3 over NFS version 2 are:

- NFS version 3 supports 64-bit file offset, whereas version 2 is limited to 32 bits. A file offset of 32 bits can address a maximum file size of 2 GBytes. NFS version 3 supports a maximum file size of 128 GBytes.
- Version 3 supports asynchronous I/O using kernel buffer cache management that provides data safety.
- File handle size up to 64 bits can be used.
- Cache management is improved.

A detailed discussion of the features supported by different NFS versions is beyond the scope of this book.

33.2 Configuring an NFS Server

The networking subsystem and NFS subsystem must be present in the kernel configuration to use NFS. The configuration process of an NFS server consists of multiple steps which will be discussed shortly. You may want to set up one or more NFS servers depending on the requirements and nature of the use of shared files and directories. For powerful NFS servers, the ratio of clients per server may be increased compared with a slow server. Similarly, you may consider changing this ratio depending on the type of applications used. For applications that are disk intensive, a lower ratio may be more efficient. Similarly, the network also plays an important role in the speed of data transfer. For high-volume data transfer, you may plan to have a high-capacity network or segment your network to divide network traffic.

After the planning process, you can follow the following steps to configure an NFS server. For proper access permissions to files shared through NFS, keep the UID and GID of all users the same on the NFS server and client machines. This can be done by copying the /etc/passwd and /etc/group files from the NFS server onto all client machines. If you are using NIS, all NFS server and client machines should be NIS clients in the same NIS domain.

Creating the /etc/exports File

This file consists of a list of file systems that are made available or *exported* to NFS clients. The following major rules apply to this file.

- Each line in the file starts with a file or directory name followed by a set of options related to that file or directory. See Table 33-1 for a list of options.
- Multiple options can be listed by using a comma to separate these options.
- The exported files and directories may have restricted access permissions. For example, some directories may be exported only to particular NFS clients. Similarly, if you don't want any modification to files in some directories, like manual pages, you can export these as read-only.
- All subdirectories are automatically exported when you export a parent directory.
- You can export an individual file or a directory.
- A file system mounted from another NFS server can't be exported.

- You should not export the root file system to all clients. This makes every file and directory visible to all NFS clients.
- If a file system is exported with the `root` option, clients will have **root** user access on that file system. This should be done very carefully. The **root** permission is not granted by default.

A sample `/etc/exports` file is shown next.

```
/home               -access=myhp:hp0
/usr/share/man      -ro
/opt/apps           -ro
```

The first line grants access to the `/home` directory to users on hosts `myhp` and `hp0`. The second and third lines grant read-only access to the `/usr/share/man` and `/opt/apps` directories to all hosts.

The options used in this file are listed in Table 33-1.

Table 33–1 *Options Used in the* `/etc/exports` *File*

Option	Description
`-ro`	Used to grant read-only access to clients.
`-rw`	Used to grant read-write access to clients.
`-access=client1[:client2]`	Used to grant access to one or more clients only. The list of clients is separated using a colon.
`-root=client1[:client2]`	Used to grant **root** access to one or more clients. The list of clients is separated using a colon.
`-anon=uid`	If a request comes from an unknown user, he or she is granted access using the UID specified here. Usually a UID of –2 is used that corresponds to a user **nobody** with minimum access rights.
`-anon=65534`	Access to unknown users is not granted.

You can also use SAM to export file systems using the `Network File System` button in the `Networking and Communications` area of SAM.

A file system does not become available automatically for clients until it is exported using the `exportfs` command. File systems in `/etc/exports` are exported at boot time with the help of the `exportfs` command. If you want to export these manually without rebooting after making a change, use the `exportfs -a` command. This command reads the `/etc/exports` file and copies these entries to the `/etc/xtab` file. Use the following command to export all file systems in the `/etc/exports` file.

```
exportfs -a
```

To unexport all exported file systems, use the following command.

```
exportfs -au
```

To unexport a particular file system, e.g., /usr/share/man, use this command.

```
exportfs -u /usr/share/man
```

Starting the Server Process at Boot Time

There are three startup scripts for the NFS system in the /sbin/init.d directory. The scripts are listed next.

1. The nfs.core script is executed at system run level 2 and is used for both NFS client and server machines. It starts portmap or rpcbind depending on the HP-UX version. The rpcbind daemon is used in HP-UX 10.30 and above, while the earlier versions use portmap.
2. The nfs.client script is executed at system run level 2 on an NFS client.
3. The nfs.server script is executed at system run level 3 on an NFS server. Among other tasks, it executes the exportfs command mentioned earlier.

These scripts use configuration parameters present in the /etc/rc.config.d/nfsconf file at startup time. The following values should be present for a system acting as an NFS server.

```
NFS_CLIENT=0
NFS_SERVER=1
NUM_NFSD=4
NUM_NFSIOD=4
PCNFS_SERVER=0
START_MOUNTD=1
```

Starting an NFS Server and Exporting Directories Manually

If you want to start an NFS server without rebooting the system, follow these steps.

1. Edit the /etc/exports file and add entries for exported file systems.
2. Use the exportfs -a command to export these file systems.
3. Edit the /etc/rc.config.d/nfsconf file and set proper values to different variables as mentioned earlier.

4. Execute the `/sbin/init.d/nfs.core` start command.
5. Execute the `/sbin/init.d/nfs.server` start command.

Viewing Exported and Mounted File Systems

Exported file systems can be listed using the `exportfs` command without any arguments. To list file systems remotely mounted by NFS clients, you can use the `showmount` command. The command can also be used to list exported file systems on a particular NFS server using the `-e` command-line option. If a client name is specified on the command line, it only lists file systems mounted by that client. The following command shows a list of hosts who have recently mounted local file systems.

```
# showmount
myhp
hp0
#
```

The following command lists file systems mounted by remote hosts in the `host:filesystem` format.

```
# showmount -a
hp0:/home
myhp:/usr/share/bin
#
```

Entries of all remotely mounted file systems and remote NFS clients are present in the `/etc/rmtab` file. It is a text file and can be viewed using the `cat` command.

33.3   Configuring an NFS Client

The NFS and LAN/9000 subsystems must be configured in the HP-UX kernel to configure a system as an NFS client. During the configuration process, you have to start some daemons and edit the `/etc/fstab` file to mount remote file systems at the system boot time. The client configuration process may be completed with the following steps.

1. Edit the `/etc/rc.config.d/nfsconf` file to enable an NFS client to be started at boot time.
2. Edit the `/etc/fstab` file to mount remote file systems at system boot time.

3. Create mount points for the remote file systems.

4. Ensure that the name of the NFS server is present in the `/etc/hosts` file if NIS or DNS are not being used.

5. Synchronize client and server clocks to ensure that time stamps are correct on modified files.

6. Either reboot the system or start the NFS client and mount remote file systems manually.

7. Verify mounted file systems using the `mount` command.

Let's discuss some of these steps in more detail.

Starting an NFS Client at Boot Time

The NFS client script `/sbin/init.d/nfs.client` is started at run level 2 during the boot process. Before this, `/sbin/init.d/nfs.core` scripts get executed. These scripts get configuration parameters from the `/etc/rc.config.d/nfsconf` file. The following line should be present in this file to start a system as an NFS client.

```
NFS_CLIENT=1
NFS_SERVER=0
NUM_NFSD=0
NUM_NFSIOD=4
PCNFS_SERVER=0
START_MOUNTD=0
```

These configuration parameters are used to start NFS daemons, which will be presented in the next section of this chapter.

Creating Mount Points and Configuring /etc/fstab

To mount any local or remote file system, you need a mount point. The mount point is a directory that is used as a reference to access a mounted file system. Create separate mount points for all remote file systems. Entries of all mount points and related file systems should be present in the `/etc/fstab` file so that remote file systems are mounted automatically at boot time. Sample NFS mount file system entries in the `/etc/fstab` file are:

```
myhp:/home              /home03         nfs   rw   0   0
myhp:/usr/share/man     /usr/share/man  nfs   ro   0   0
```

The syntax of these entries is the same as you studied in Chapter 18 except for the following two changes.

1. The first field in each line is changed from a file system to a combination of host name used for the NFS server followed by a colon followed by the pathname of the remote file system that exists on the NFS server.
2. The file system type is `nfs` for remotely mounted file systems.

We have used a read-write option in the first line of the `/etc/fstab` file above and a read-only option for the second line. Table 33-2 lists options that can be used with remote file systems.

Table 33–2 *Options Used for NFS File Systems in the* `/etc/fstab` *File*

Option	Description
`rw`	Grants read and write access to the file system
`ro`	Grants read-only access
`fg`	Retry the mount operation in the foreground
`suid`	SUID is allowed on this file system
`hard`	Retry mount request until the server responds
`intr`	Permits user interrupt during hard mount retry

Mounting Remote File Systems

The NFS client executes the `mount -aQF nfs` command during execution of the `nfs.client` script at startup. However, if you have recently configured an NFS client and don't want to reboot the system, use the following commands.

```
/sbin/init.d/nfs.core start
/sbin/init.d/nfs.client start
```

If the NIS client is already running and you have made a change in the `/etc/fstab` file, use the following command instead of the above two.

```
mount -aF nfs
```

Any file system that is not listed in the `/etc/fstab` file can be mounted using the `mount` command. The following command mounts a file system `/opt/apps` from an NFS server `myhp` on a local mount point `/apps`.

```
mount myhp:/opt/apps /apps
```

You can unmount an NFS file system in the usual way using the `umount` command. Entries of all mounted file systems are stored in the `/etc/mnttab` file.

Viewing Mounted File Systems

The `mount` command can be used to list all mounted file systems. To view mounted file systems, use this command without any command-line argument or option.

Viewing Exported File Systems by a Server

You can list file systems exported by a particular NFS server using the `showmount` command. The following command lists file systems exported by server `myhp`.

```
showmount -e myhp
```

Study Break

Study Break: Configuring an NFS Server and Client

A system can be configured as an NFS client and server simultaneously. An NFS server can also mount its own exported file systems. Let's configure a host `myhp` as both an NFS server and client. Create the `/etc/exports` file with a single line in it to export the `/home` file system. Edit the `/etc/rc.config.d/nfsconf` file and set variable values as discussed earlier. Now start the NFS client and server processes using scripts in the `/sbin/init.d` directory. These should be run in the following order.

```
nfs.core
nfs.client
nfs.server
```

Create a mount point to mount the exported directory (`/home`). Let's suppose you create directory `/kaka` as a mount point. Use the following command to mount the exported `/home` directory to this mount point.

```
mount myhp:/home /kaka
```

Use the `mount` command without any argument to verify that the directory is mounted.

33.4 NFS Daemons

NFS uses a number of daemon processes to provide reliable file system access over a network. A number of clients may be accessing shared files, and it is the responsibility of the NFS system to guarantee file system integrity. NFS is a stateless server, which means that it does not keep a record of the state of files and clients that are accessing them. To keep consistency of files, a file locking mechanism is used through NFS daemons to ensure that files are properly locked when accessed by a client. Table 33-3 shows a list of NFS daemons and their functions on the client and server.

Table 33–3 *NFS Daemons*

Name	NFS System	Description
portmap	Both client and server	RPC daemon used in HP-UX 10.20 and earlier versions.
rpcbind	Both client and server	RPC daemon used in HP-UX 10.30 and later versions.
rpc.statd	Both client and server	RPC daemon used with the rpc.lockd daemon to provide crash recovery functions.
rpc.lockd	Both client and server	Used for file locking on both NFS servers and clients. Both client and server rpc.lockd daemons interact with each other to provide file locking functions.
nfsd	Server	The NFS server daemon. A number of server daemon processes (by default, 4) are started at startup time. All of these processes register themselves with portmap or rpcbind. A heavily loaded NFS server may start more daemon processes.
rpc.pcnfsd	Server	Used with PCNFS. Not required if all clients are UNIX machines.
rpc.mountd	Server	Keeps a record of mounted and exported file systems. Replies to mount requests.
biod	Client	Used to handle buffer cache in asynchronous I/O on NFS clients.

33.5 Troubleshooting

In any network-related problem, first use the `ping` command to ensure that network is operational. Most NFS problems are related to either the configuration or NFS daemons. The `/etc/exports` file on an NFS server and the `/etc/fstab` file on a client are important to check for any configuration problem. You should also verify that all required daemons are running on the server and client. The order of starting NFS daemons also matters. For example, `rpcbind` or `portmap` should be started before starting the `nfsd` daemon. Similarly, the `inetd` daemon, which serves ARPA/Berkley and RPC services, must be started after NFS daemons have been started. HP-UX provides some commands for NFS troubleshooting. Some of these are discussed here.

The rpcinfo Command

This command verifies if a service is registered with `portmap` or `rpcbind` and is running. It contacts the `rpcbind` or `portmap` daemon and displays all registered services. A short listing of all the registered services can be displayed using the `-s` command-line switch as shown here.

```
# rpcinfo -s
program version(s) netid(s)                              service    owner
100000  2,3,4      udp,tcp,ticlts,ticotsord,ticots       rpcbind    superuser
100024  1          tcp,udp                               status     superuser
100021  2,4,3,1    udp,tcp                               nlockmgr   superuser
100020  1          tcp,udp                               llockmgr   superuser
100068  5,4,3,2    udp                                   cmsd       superuser
100083  1          tcp                                   ttdbserver superuser
100005  3,1        tcp,udp                               mountd     superuser
100003  3,2        udp                                   nfs        superuser
100069  1          tcp,udp                               ypxfrd     superuser
100028  1          udp,tcp                               ypupdated  superuser
100029  2,1        ticots,ticotsord,ticlts               keyserv    superuser
100004  1,2        tcp,udp                               ypserv     superuser
100009  1          udp                                   yppasswdd  superuser
100007  1,2        udp,tcp                               ypbind     sys
#
```

Here you should find `rpcbind`, `mountd`, and `nfs` registered under the `service` column of the output. You can also find a list of RPC registered services on a remote host using the remote host name as the command-line argument. The following command lists all registered RPC services on host `hp0`.

```
rpcinfo hp0
```

To verify that a service is listening to your requests and responding, make a UDP or TCP call to a particular service. The following command makes a UDP call to the nfs service on host myhp.

```
# rpcinfo -u myhp nfs
program 100003 version 2 ready and waiting
program 100003 version 3 ready and waiting
#
```

The output shows that the host is listening to NFS requests and accepting version 2 and version 3 requests. Other options used with the rpcinfo command are shown in Table 33-4. All of these options can be used with a host name on the command line to find information about a particular host on the network.

Table 33–4 *Options Used with the* rpcinfo *Command*

Option	Description
-d	Deletes the registration of a particular program
-m	Displays statistics of RPC operation
-p	Probes rpcbind using version 2 of rpcbind
-s	Displays a short list
-t	Makes an RPC call using TCP
-u	Makes an RPC call using UDP

Using the nfsstat Command

The nfsstat command displays NFS activity on a host. By default it displays information about the client, server and RPC. Different command-line options can be used to display information about the NFS client or server only. The following is the output of the command used without any option.

```
# nfsstat

Server rpc:
Connection oriented:
N/A
Connectionless oriented:
calls                   badcalls                nullrecv
55769                   0                       0
```

badlen	xdrcall	dupchecks
0	0	3397
dupreqs		
1		

Server nfs:

calls	badcalls	
55769	0	

Version 2: (0 calls)

null	getattr	setattr
0 0%	0 0%	0 0%
root	lookup	readlink
0 0%	0 0%	0 0%
read	wrcache	write
0 0%	0 0%	0 0%
create	remove	rename
0 0%	0 0%	0 0%
link	symlink	mkdir
0 0%	0 0%	0 0%
rmdir	readdir	statfs
0 0%	0 0%	0 0%

Version 3: (55769 calls)

null	getattr	setattr
1 0%	243 0%	2155 3%
lookup	access	readlink
48700 87%	1181 2%	0 0%
read	write	create
5 0%	883 1%	359 0%
mkdir	symlink	mknod
0 0%	0 0%	0 0%
remove	rmdir	rename
0 0%	0 0%	0 0%
link	readdir	readdir+
0 0%	0 0%	1389 2%
fsstat	fsinfo	pathconf
47 0%	1 0%	0 0%
commit		
805 1%		

Client rpc:
Connection oriented:
N/A
Connectionless oriented:

calls	badcalls	retrans
1529	0	0
badxids	timeouts	waits

```
0                       0                       0
newcreds                badverfs                timers
0                       0                       16
toobig                  nomem                   cantsend
0                       0                       0
bufulocks
0


Client nfs:
calls                   badcalls                clgets
1529                    0                       1529
cltoomany
0
Version 2: (503 calls)
null                    getattr                 setattr
0 0%                    3 0%                    0 0%
root                    lookup                  readlink
0 0%                    0 0%                    0 0%
read                    wrcache                 write
0 0%                    0 0%                    0 0%
create                  remove                  rename
0 0%                    0 0%                    0 0%
link                    symlink                 mkdir
0 0%                    0 0%                    0 0%
rmdir                   readdir                 statfs
0 0%                    0 0%                    500 99%
Version 3: (1026 calls)
null                    getattr                 setattr
0 0%                    12 1%                   0 0%
lookup                  access                  readlink
0 0%                    6 0%                    0 0%
read                    write                   create
0 0%                    0 0%                    0 0%
mkdir                   symlink                 mknod
0 0%                    0 0%                    0 0%
remove                  rmdir                   rename
0 0%                    0 0%                    0 0%
link                    readdir                 readdir+
0 0%                    0 0%                    0 0%
fsstat                  fsinfo                  pathconf
1006 98%                2 0%                    0 0%
commit
0 0%
#
```

Fields like `badcalls`, `nullrecv`, `badlen`, and `timeout` show errors. Pay special attention to these fields. Options used with this command are listed in Table 33-5.

Table 33–5 *Options Used with the* `nfsstat` *Command*

Option	Description
`-c`	Displays client information
`-s`	Displays server information
`-r`	Displays information about RPC
`-m`	Displays information about all mounted file systems
`-z`	Can be used by the superuser only; displays NFS information and then reinitializes it

■ Chapter Summary

The Network File System (NFS) is used to share file systems over a network. The system works in the client/server model and is based on RPC. An NFS server exports its shared file systems that can be mounted remotely by NFS clients on local mount points. A system may act as an NFS server and client at the same time. The `portmap` RPC daemon is used on HP-UX version 10.20 and earlier, while `rpcbind` is used on later HP-UX versions. The names of exported file systems are listed in the `/etc/exports` file on an NFS server. These file systems are exported at boot time. File systems can also be exported using the `exportfs` command at any later stage. The `showmount` command lists all file systems that are remotely mounted by NFS clients. The `/etc/fstab` file is used on an NFS client to mount remote file systems from a server at boot time. The `mount` command can be used to mount remote file systems at any later stage. The same command is also used to list mounted file systems. Many daemon processes are used on an NFS client and server. These processes help to provide reliable file system access over a network.

The `rpcinfo` command is used for troubleshooting RPC-based services including NFS. It lists all registered RPC services on a local or remote host. The same command can be used to verify that a particular RPC service is operational and is responding to client requests. The `nfsstat` command is another useful tool for NFS troubleshooting.

▲ CHAPTER REVIEW QUESTIONS

1. How can you grant mount access to an exported file system to selected clients?

2. Which subsystems must be present in the kernel to use NFS?

3. Why is it necessary to synchronize time on all NFS clients and servers?

▲ TEST YOUR KNOWLEDGE

1. *Which NFS version is supported on HP-UX 11.00?*
   A. version 2 only
   B. version 3 only
   C. version 4 only
   D. both versions 2 and 3

2. *Which HP-UX command can be used on an NFS server to list remotely mounted file systems by NFS clients?*
   A. the `exportfs` command
   B. the `mount` command without any command-line option
   C. the `mount` command with the `-a` command-line option
   D. the `showmount` command

3. *How should the `rpcbind`, `nfsd`, and `inetd` daemons be started?*
   A. first the `rpcbind` daemon, then `nfsd`, and `inetd` last
   B. first the `inetd` daemon, then `rpcbind`, and `nfsd` last
   C. first the `inetd` daemon, then `nfsd`, and `rpcbind` last
   D. The order does not matter. These can be started in any order.

4. *Which RPC daemon is used on HP-UX 11.00?*
   A. `rpcinfo`
   B. `rpcbind`
   C. `rpcd`
   D. `portmap`

5. *What is* not *true about NFS?*

    A. A system can act as an NFS server and client at the same time.

    B. Individual files can be exported by an NFS server.

    C. An NFS server can export file systems mounted from another NFS server.

    D. A system can mount file systems exported by itself.

6. *What is the advantage of NFS version 3 over version 2?*

    A. It provides better cache management.

    B. It provides 64-bit offset for files.

    C. File sizes up to 128 GBytes are supported.

    D. All of the above.

7. *Which command is used to manually export file systems for remote mount?*

    A. `exports`

    B. `exportfs`

    C. `showmount`

    D. `init`

8. *Which command is used to list registered RPC services on a host?*

    A. `rpcinfo`

    B. `rpcbind`

    C. `netstat`

    D. `nfsstat`

HP-UX Automounter

Automounter may be considered an additional service to an NFS client. An NFS client usually mounts file systems from the NFS server at boot time and keeps these file systems mounted while the system is up. The file systems are unmounted at system shutdown time. The Automounter, on the other hand, mounts remote file systems only when needed. If a mounted file system is not accessed for a specified period of time, it is automatically unmounted. The `automount` daemon keeps this process totally transparent from the user. Automounter is a client-side service and is installed with the NFS client. All file systems and directories should be exported by NFS in the normal way as used with the NFS client.

Automounter uses map files to find mount points and server-exported file systems and directories. The maps are stored in plain text files. By default, the `automount` daemon gets its information from the *master map* file, `/etc/auto_master`, that contains a list of other map files and their locations.

659

All map files contain information about NFS servers, directories exported by NFS servers, and local mount points along with mount options. In a *direct map*, mount points for all remote file systems and directories are specified in absolute form. In an *indirect map*, a common mount point for many directories is specified. An example of an indirect map is user home directories. The reference mount point for these directories may be /home, while all directories are mounted relative to /home such that each mounted directory is visible inside the /home directory. The *special maps* are used are used for predefined purposes.

The Automounter system is very useful for load balancing when the same directories can be mounted from multiple NFS servers. An example of this is the directories containing manual pages. All NFS servers have the same copy of manual pages, and it makes no difference from which NFS server the directory is mounted. Multiple NFS servers can be listed against one local mount point inside Automounter maps. The Automounter system finds the nearest NFS server and mounts directories from this server. The system uses the ping command to send some data to all servers and calculates the distance of a particular data packet using the time taken by this packet to return. In addition to the physical distance of an NFS server from a client, this method also works well to distinguish high traffic network paths and heavily loaded servers. The same method also provides fault tolerance such that if one NFS server is not available at a particular time, the client can mount directories from another server.

This chapter starts with an introduction to Automounter maps. Here, master, direct, indirect, and special maps are explained. The effect of changing a map on the automount daemon is also presented. The next section is dedicated to the configuration of Automounter. After completing this chapter, you will be able to configure Automounter on an NFS client.

34.1 Automounter Maps

Automounter uses map files to mount a remote file system or directory using NFS. Four types of maps are used with Automounter as listed next.

1. the *Master* Automounter map
2. the *Direct* Automounter map
3. the *Indirect* Automounter map
4. the *Special* Automounter map

These maps contain lists of files and directories that are to be mounted when needed. When a user tries to access a directory listed in these maps, Automounter tries to mount that directory from the NFS server. When a server is found, the Automounter creates a temporary mount point inside `/tmp_mnt` and mounts the remote file system on this mount point. It then creates a symbolic link to this directory for the actual mount point directory. When the mounted directory is not used for a certain period of time, Automounter unmounts the remote file system, removes the temporary mount point, and removes the symbolic link.

Master Map

The master map file is `/etc/auto_master`, and it is read by Automounter at startup time. Each line in this file shows one Automounter map. A line starts with a mount point followed by the map file name that corresponds to that mount point. In the last part of the line, any mount options can be used. However, these mount options can be overridden by mount options in other map files. The general syntax of an entry in this file is shown here.

```
<mount point>    <map file name>    <mount options>
```

A sample master map file is shown below.

```
/-                /etc/auto_direct
/home             /etc/auto_home
/usr/share/man    /etc/auto_man
/net              -hosts
```

Each line starting with `/-` shows a direct map file. A line starting with an absolute directory name shows an indirect map. The last line in the file shows a special map. This is used to mount all file systems exported by a particular NFS server to a directory with the same name as the NFS server under the `/net` directory.

Direct Map

A direct map contains local mount points and corresponding file systems exported by an NFS server. The general syntax of entries in the direct map file is:

```
<local mount point>   <mount options>   <server:/directory>
```

Entries in the direct map are not related to each other. Each file system can be mounted and unmounted quite independently. When a user accesses a directory listed in the direct map, the `automount` daemon mounts the remote file system using a temporary mount point in `/tmp_mnt` and creates a symbolic link of this temporary mount point to the actual directory. A sample direct map file is shown next.

```
/apps          hp0:/apps
/opt/project   hp0:/project    myhp:/project
```

The first line mounts a directory `/apps` from an NFS server `hp0` to a local mount point `/apps`. The second line mounts the `/projects` directory from one of the two NFS servers, whichever is nearest. These two server names are `hp0` and `myhp`.

Indirect Map

The indirect map provides a reference directory for local mount points. The path to this directory is present in the master map file. All local mount points reside inside this directory. The following line in the indirect map `/etc/auto_home` mounts a directory `/home/boota` from an NFS server `hp0` to `/home/boota` on the local system.

```
boota   hp0:/home/boota
```

Mount options can be used in an indirect map after the local mount point directory.

Special Map

Automounter supports three types of special maps. These special maps are indicated in the `/etc/auto_master` file as `-hosts`, `-passwd`, and `-null`. The special map `-hosts` mounts all exported file systems from an NFS server under a directory in `/net`. This directory has the same name as the NFS server. Consider the following entry in the `/etc/auto_master` file.

```
/net              -hosts
```

When you try to access directory `/net/hp0`, your system will contact NFS server `hp0` and will try to mount all exported file systems by `hp0` under this directory. If the server has no exported file system, you will get an error message.

The `-passwd` special map uses the `/etc/passwd` file to mount user home directories. The following line can be used in the `/etc/auto_master` file.

```
/home             -passwd
```

The `-null` special map is used with the `automount` command to cancel a previously used map.

Including Maps Within Other Maps

A map file can be included in another map using a + sign followed by the map file name. The following line includes the `/etc/auto_abc` map in another map file.

```
+/etc/auto_abc
```

Modifying Automounter Maps

When you make a change to any map file, the following rules show whether the `automount` daemon should be started.

1. If you make a change to a master map, you must either reboot the system or kill the `automount` daemon and restart it. This is necessary because the `automount` daemon reads the master map only at startup time. However, when killing the `automount` daemon, don't use the `kill -9` command. Instead, use the `kill -TERM` command that causes `automount` to shut down gracefully.
2. If you modify options or the server part in a direct map, you don't need to restart the `automount` daemon. If you modify a mount point, you have to restart the `automount` daemon.
3. There is no need to restart the `automount` daemon if you make a change to an indirect map.

34.2 Configuring Automounter

Automounter is started by the `nfs.client` script in the `/sbin/init.d` directory during the system boot process at run level 2. It reads its configuration information from the `/etc/rc.config.d/nfsconf` file. The following variables are used for `automount` configuration.

```
AUTOMOUNT=1
AUTO_MASTER="/etc/auto_master"
AUTO_OPTIONS="-f $AUTO_MASTER"
```

The `AUTOMOUNT` value determines if the `automount` daemon will be started at boot time. A value of `1` enables startup and a value of `0` disables it. The `AUTO_MASTER` variable shows the file name of the master `automount` map. The default name is `/etc/auto_master`, and you are free to change this to any other file. The `AUTO_OPTIONS` variable shows the set of options that are passed to the `automount` daemon at startup time. The `-f` option passes the name of the master map file to the `automount` daemon. Other useful options that can be used with `automount` are listed in Table 34-1. Please note that the `automount` daemon can also be started at any time using the same options on the command line.

Table 34–1 *Options Used with the* `automount` *Daemon*

Option	Description
`-T`	This option is used for tracing and debugging purposes. The activity is logged in the `/var/adm/automount.log` file.
`-v`	Verbose. When this option is used with `automount`, it logs events and status messages to `syslog`. The messages can be found in the `/var/adm/syslog.log` file.
`-f`	Used to specify the master map file name.
`-M`	Used to specify the mount directory. This directory is used in place of the `/tmp_mnt` directory.
`-tl`	Used to specify time in seconds for which a directory remains mounted without any activity. The default is 300 seconds. If no file is accessed in the directory during this time, the directory is unmounted.
`-tm`	This specifies time in seconds used as the interval between mount attempts. The default is 30 seconds. If a mount attempt fails, Automounter retries the mount attempt after this time interval.
`-tw`	This is used to specify time in seconds between retries to unmount a file system. The default value is 60 seconds.

The procedure of configuring Automounter may be completed in the following steps.

1. Make sure that the required file systems are exported by the NFS server. You can use the `showmount` command with the `-e` option for this purpose.
2. Edit the `/etc/rc.config.d/nfsconf` file to set proper configuration parameter values for Automounter.
3. Create the master map file.
4. Create direct and indirect map files as listed in the master map file.
5. If the `automount` daemon and NFS clients are not started yet, start these using the `nfs.client` script as follows.

   ```
   /sbin/init.d/nfs.client start
   ```

   If `automount` is already running, kill it using `SIGTERM` (Signal 15) and then restart it. Signals are discussed in Chapter 20. You can also reboot the system to start Automounter.
6. Access a directory in the map files to verify that it is mounted.

■ Chapter Summary

Automounter is a supplemental product to an NFS client. It is used to automatically mount required file systems and unmount them when not in use. Another advantage of Automounter is that it can be used to balance the load among multiple NFS servers. It also supports fault tolerance such that if a particular NFS server is not available, it can use another NFS server. The `automount` daemon is used at boot time for this purpose. This daemon uses plain text files, called Automounter maps, for a list of mount points and file systems that can be mounted from a particular NFS file server. It reads its configuration data from the `/etc/rc.config.d/nfsconf` file and uses a master map file to locate direct and indirect map files. These files contain the local mount points, NFS server name, and exported file system along with mount options. The `automount` daemon can be started using the command line or the `nfs.client` script in the `/etc/init.d` directory at system boot time. It needs to be restarted every time you make a change to the master map file. You must also restart the daemon if you make a change to the mount points in the direct map. However, you need not restart it after any change to the indirect map.

▲ CHAPTER REVIEW QUESTIONS

1. How is Automounter used for load balancing and fault tolerance?

2. What is the difference between direct and indirect maps?

3. What rules apply to restarting the `automount` daemon after modifying different maps?

▲ TEST YOUR KNOWLEDGE

1. *Which of the following is* not *an Automounter map?*

   A. master map

   B. slave map

   C. direct map

   D. indirect map

2. *When do you need to restart the* `automount` *daemon?*

   A. after modification to the master map

   B. after modifying mount options in a direct map

   C. after modifying an indirect map

   D. all of the above

3. *What is the default interval of time after which Automounter unmounts a directory if no reference is made to a mounted file system?*

   A. 30 seconds

   B. 60 seconds

   C. 3 minutes

   D. 5 minutes

4. *The master* `automount` *map contains the following indirect map entry.*

   ```
   /home              /etc/auto_home
   ```

   The `/etc/auto_home` *file has one line as shown below.*

   ```
   boota    hp0:/home/boota
   ```

   Where will the directory `/home/boota` *on an NFS server* `hp0` *be mounted on the local system?*

A. `/boota`

B. `/home/boota`

C. It will be mounted in a temporary directory under `/tmp_mnt` and linked to `/boota`.

D. It will be mounted in a temporary directory under `/tmp_mnt` and linked to `/home/boota`.

Network Time Protocol

Network Time Protocol (NTP) is used to synchronize a system clock with a reliable time source. Clock synchronization of all hosts on a network is often needed when you are running applications over a network that uses time in calculations. A common example of this is the use of incremental backup where file modification time is compared with the time of the previous backup. If the incremental backups are performed over a network, differences in system clock time among hosts may result in a wrong file selection. Manual synchronization of time on a large network is a particularly difficult task.

The NTP daemon runs on all participating hosts. It is started at system boot time and may act as a client, server, or both simultaneously. Every system synchronizes its time with one or more of the available resources. These resources are categorized depending on the accuracy of the time. Considered the most accurate resource is time from global positioning system (GPS) satellites or a

669

radio broadcast. The least accurate is the system clock of one of the hosts on the network. Usually one or more hosts on the network use a reliable external source, while other hosts on the network use these systems as their time server.

NTP can be configured using the command line or SAM. During startup, the NTP daemon (`xntpd`) checks its configuration file and synchronizes its clock with a reliable time source provided in the configuration file. The daemon then maintains a file to track any drift in local time.

In this chapter, we will start with an introduction to Network Time Protocol and the terminology used with it. Different types of reference time sources will be discussed. Then you will see how to configure the `xntpd` daemon and the NTP server and client. In the last part of the chapter, you will use SAM to configure NTP.

35.1 Introduction to NTP

The Network Time Protocol (NTP) package comes bundled with HP-UX. The `xntpd` daemon is responsible for synchronization of time. The daemon uses a configuration file, `/etc/ntp.conf`. The synchronization process depends on a reference time source. After the initial synchronization process, NTP keeps track of any drift in the local system clock compared with the reference time and continuously synchronizes itself. Depending on the accuracy of the local clock, the frequency of consulting the reference time source decreases with the passage of time.

NTP Time Sources

There are usually three types of time sources used by `xntpd`. These are listed in the order of their reliability.

1. The clock from a global positioning system (GPS) satellite or a radio broadcast. These are the most reliable sources and you need to attach additional hardware to your system to get GPS or a radio broadcast. An example of a radio broadcast is the National Institute of Standards and Technology (NIST) radio station WWVB that broadcasts time signals at 60 KHz. This radio station does not broadcast voice announcements.

2. Some NTP servers are available on the Internet. If your system is connected to the Internet, you may use time from one or more of these servers as reference time. A list of NTP servers is available at `http://www.ntp.org`. The NTP protocols make corrections in the time synchronization information received from any of these servers by making adjustments caused by data propagation delays on the Internet.

3. If your local network is not connected to the Internet, you may use one of the machines on your LAN as your timeserver and consider its clock as standard. This is the least accurate method.

Some Definitions

Before moving further in this chapter, let's go through some basic terminology used with NTP.

SERVER

Any host that provides time to other systems is a server. The server itself gets time from one of the reference sources mentioned earlier.

CLIENT

A client is a system that gets its time information from a server. A client may direct a *polling client* where it has information about a timeserver in its configuration file and polls that server. Some servers may also broadcast time information on the network, and a client may be configured to listen to these broadcasts and synchronize its time accordingly. This type of client is called a *broadcast client*. A client may also act as a server for some other clients.

PEER

Two or more systems may act as peers if they use time sources of equal reliability or *stratum level*. If the primary source of time for a server becomes unavailable, a server may synchronize its time with its peer servers. Peer servers also synchronize their time even in the case of availability of the reference time source. If there is a time difference among peer servers, NTP employs a special algorithm to reconcile peer server time.

STRATUM LEVEL

A stratum level is an indication of the accuracy of a reference time source. Stratum levels are numbered from 1 to 15. A reference at stratum level 1 is the most accurate time source, while a source at stratum level 15 is the least accurate time source. A server at stratum level 1 receives its time from an external accurate time source such as a GPS radio signal. If your network is connected to the Internet and you are getting time from a server at stratum level 1, you will assign a stratum level greater than 1 to your local time server.

35.2 Configuring the NTP Server

The NTP daemon process is started at boot time. Startup operation of NTP is controlled by the XNTPD variable in the /etc/rc.config.d/netdaemons file. If the value of this variable is set to 1, xntpd is started at boot time. At start time, xntpd reads its configuration file /etc/ntp.conf and configures itself. It can also be started at the command line using the following command.

```
/etc/init.d/xntpd start
```

A typical /etc/ntp.conf file is shown here.

```
server navobs1.gatech.edu
server bitsy.mit.edu
peer gama
broadcast 192.168.2.255
driftfile /var/adm/ntp.drift
```

This file shows that xntpd will try the navobs1.gatech.edu and bitsy.mit.edu servers to adjust its time clock. Both of these servers are running at stratum level 1. Another peer server gama is present on the network. This daemon will also broadcast time synchronization messages on the local network for other clients. The drift file is used to track the accuracy of the local clock over time. It is maintained by xntpd and used later to send fewer time synchronization requests to the server.

Some NTP servers may also require authentication from clients. In that case, the client machine maintains the /etc/ntp.keys file for this purpose.

When making any configuration, it must be remembered that the time zone setting on your system must be correct. For example if you are in the eastern daylight time zone, the /etc/TIMEZONE file must contain the EST5EDT time setting.

The activity of NTP can be verified using the ntpq -p command at any time. This command can be run in interactive mode when used without any option and is used as a debugging tool.

Configuring a Server to Use a Radio Clock

A radio broadcast clock is used through an external device that listens to radio signals. This device is usually attached to the system through a serial port. A typical /etc/ntp.conf entry for such a system is shown next.

```
server 127.127.4.1
```

The first three octets of the server address 127.127.4 tell xntpd to use an external device as the time source. The last octet shows the port number of the serial port to which the device is connected. The device files for the time source are /dev/wwvb1 to /dev/wwvb4.

Configuring a Server to Use Another Server

Most often, an NTP server is configured to use another server at stratum level 1. In this case, you specify the server name or IP address in the /etc/ntp.conf file. The following entry in the file is used to set bitsy.mit.edu as the source of standard time.

```
server bitsy.mit.edu
```

Configuring a Server to Use a Local Clock

To configure a server to use its own clock as the standard time source, the following two lines in /etc/ntp.conf are used for the server entry.

```
server 127.127.1.1
fudge 127.127.1.1 stratum 8
```

The IP address used here is a pseudonumber that tells xntpd to use the local clock as its time source. The fudge line configures a stratum level 8 for the timeserver.

35.3 Configuring an NTP Client

NTP client configuration is also made in the /etc/ntp.conf file. An NTP client may be a polling client or a broadcast client. In the cases of a polling client, you provide the server name in the /etc/ntp.conf file.

Configuring a Client to Use Server Polling

A polling client has information about its server and contacts it for time information over a network. A typical /etc/ntp.conf file for a client that is using gama as its timeserver is as shown next.

```
server gama
driftfile /var/adm/ntp.drift
```

Multiple timeservers may be used in the configuration file. The default polling time for the timeserver is once every 64 seconds. At every poll time, drift in the local time and the server time is recorded. If the drift is high, the next polling time is scheduled to occur earlier. If the drift is low, the next polling time is later.

Configuring a Client to Use Server Broadcast

A broadcast client does not contact any server for time information but listens for broadcast time information from a broadcast timeserver. The configuration for the broadcast NTP client is like the following.

```
broadcastclient yes
driftfile /var/adm/ntp.drift
```

Using the ntpdate Command

This command can be used at startup and through cron to synchronize your clock with one or more servers at any given time. If you specify more than one server at the command line, the results are better. The following command corrects local time after consulting two servers.

```
ntpdate ben.cs.wisc.edu bigben.cac.washington.edu
```

35.4 Using SAM to Configure NTP

Like other system administration tasks, SAM can also be used to configure NTP. The SAM Time area window is shown in Figure 35-1.

Here you can add a broadcast server or client, establish a network time source, and set the system clock. Let's add an NTP server on the Internet with Network Time Sources as shown in Figure 35-2.

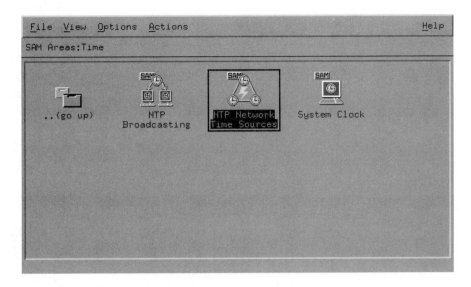

Figure 35–1 *SAM* Time *window.*

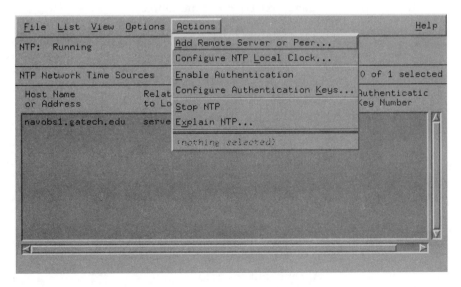

Figure 35–2 *Adding a server from the Internet as the reference time source.*

Using this window you can add, remove, or modify a network time source. This window lists current time sources and shows if NTP is running. NTP can be started or stopped using the Actions menu.

■ Chapter Summary

Network Time Protocol (NTP) is used to synchronize system time with a reference time source. Reference time sources are radio broadcasts, timeservers on the Internet, or a system's internal clock. The broadcast is the most accurate time source while the system internal clock is the least accurate. NTP activities are controlled by the xntpd daemon on HP-UX, which is started at boot time. A host may be configured as an NTP client, server, or both. Stratum levels are used to grade the accuracy of a timeserver. The NTP daemon xntpd uses a configuration file /etc/ntp.conf, which contains a list of servers. A client may be a direct polling client or a broadcast client. A broadcast client depends on time information broadcasted by a timeserver on a network. The ntpdate command is used to manually synchronize a system clock. NTP can be configured using the command line or SAM.

▲ CHAPTER REVIEW QUESTIONS

1. What are three types of time sources?

2. What is a stratum level?

3. What is the use of a drift file?

▲ TEST YOUR KNOWLEDGE

1. *What is the most accurate time source for NTP?*
    A. a broadcast radio signal
    B. an internal system clock
    C. an Internet time server
    D. a crystal oscillator card installed in the system

2. *What is the configuration file used by the* xntpd *daemon?*
    A. /etc/xntpd.conf
    B. /etc/ntp.conf
    C. /var/tmp/ntp/ntp.drift
    D. none of the above

3. *Which command is used to synchronize time with one or more NTP servers on the Internet?*

    A. `ntpdate`

    B. `ntpq`

    C. `ntpd`

    D. `ntpsync`

4. *What is the default polling time for a server?*

    A. 64 seconds

    B. 60 seconds

    C. 10 seconds

    D. 100 seconds

System and Network Administration: Final Thoughts

Computer networks provide many benefits to common users as well as system administrators. For a common user, it is very easy to use resources such as network printers and the facility of remote login. Users can also collaborate with others more conveniently through file transfer and electronic messaging. For system administrators, a network makes many system administration and trouble-shooting tasks more convenient. You can set up a central software installation server from which you can install applications and patches to other systems on the network without any need to move installation media from system to system. The remote login facilitates logging into a distant HP-UX system to carry out maintenance or trouble-shooting tasks. You can also use the syslog facility to collect system-generated messages from all hosts on a network to a central management server, where different alarms can be generated in case of any problems with the hosts on the network. Central backup and restore is another important system administration task that is done over the network to provide efficient unattended routine backup of many hosts.

You have used System Administration Manager (SAM) for many tasks related to local system administration. It can also be used for multiple system administration on a network. The Run SAM on Remote Systems area in SAM is used to configure and manage other systems that use SAM. When you go into this area for the first time, there is no entry for any other host. You can use Add System in the Actions menu to add hosts that you want to manage remotely using SAM. This is a very important feature with which you can administer any number of systems from a central management server. All this is made possible by the presence of a network.

Through the years, the use of networking has developed a new culture in the computer user community, and many users cannot think of living without being connected to a network. Business needs are growing more and more. Larger networks using high-capacity interconnection media are becoming more common in the corporate sector. Emergence of larger and faster networks and the dependence of business on network availability has made the job of network administrators more important. Today you are not only concerned with the availability of a network but also how to use it more efficiently and keep it operational. Network troubleshooting and network performance monitoring has become an important network administration task to enhance network availability. Like other network operating systems, a number of utilities are available on HP-UX that can be used for monitoring network activity and troubleshooting network problems.

To manage complex networks, where hundreds of hosts are present in each participating LAN, you need to have specially designed network management tools. One of the most important products used for network management is HP OpenView Network Node Manager. It has many advanced features, such as network discovery and event correlation that can be used to locate network problems quickly. It can inform you about network events in the initial stage and can also be used to trigger certain actions when an event occurs.

This chapter starts with a list of operations that are performed on a network on a daily basis. An introduction to `syslogd` is presented next. Then you will see how you can monitor network performance. In the last part of the chapter an introduction to routine system administration tasks is presented. The routine system administration tasks like deleting and trimming files on many hosts can be performed easily using SAM over a network.

This chapter does not contain any end questions, as the material presented here is not a part of the HP-UX certification exam.

36.1 Routine Uses of a Network

HP-UX uses the network connection to perform many useful tasks in daily routine life. You are already familiar with these tasks. Some are listed here just for a review.

SD-UX Server

In a network having several HP-UX nodes, you have to install applications and patches released by the Hewlett-Packard Company from time to time. These applications and patches are installed from a software depot. Using a network, you can create a software depot on a central software server. After creating the software depot on this server, you can use `swinstall` command to install any software from that server. The following `swinstall` command gets a software list from the `/var/spool/sw` software depot located on host `myhp`.

```
/usr/sbin/swinstall -s myhp:/var/spool/sw
```

Network Printing

Network printing is another useful way of sharing resources. Sophisticated and high-speed printers are costly. By using a network, you can share these printers among users. You have already learned how to set up remote printers in Chapter 21.

A Standard Environment for Users

Many corporate networks may need to provide a consistent environment to all users no matter which workstation or server they log into. A user should be able to use the same login name and password and get the same home directory and files everywhere. This is done by using NIS and NFS together. A central file server is set up that has all users' home directories. NIS is used to provide the same login names and passwords on a network, while NFS is used to mount home directories from the central file server. A typical example of such a system is a campus-wide network in educational institutions where students can log in anywhere on the network.

Time Synchronization

In business applications and databases, time stamps are used with many transactions. It is important that all hosts on a network have the same clock time to ensure the proper order of data records. The time synchronization is facilitated by using Network Time Protocol (NTP), where you can use one or more standard time servers on the Internet or local network to synchronize the clocks of all hosts on the network.

Network File System

The network file system (NFS) is used to share disk resources among hosts on the network. Not only does it provide convenience for sharing files among network users, it is also cost effective as data storage. If user data are located at a central place, they are more convenient to back up and restore.

Backup and Recovery

A major advantage of a network is to carry out the routine system administration task of system backup. In the absence of a network, you have to plan and implement a separate backup strategy for every host. Using a network connection, a central backup server can be set up that can use any of the backup facilities discussed in Chapter 23 to create backup and to restore data.

The backup process generates heavy network traffic. Usually network backups are scheduled for nighttime, when there is less network activity, to avoid congestion on a network. However, if the network is busy around the clock and the backup process degrades network performance, a separate network for creating backup may be installed. All hosts that take part in the backup process have an additional network interface adapter connected to the backup network segment. The backup server is also connected to the backup network segment. The backup server uses this segment for data transfer while other network segments continue to function as usual. This

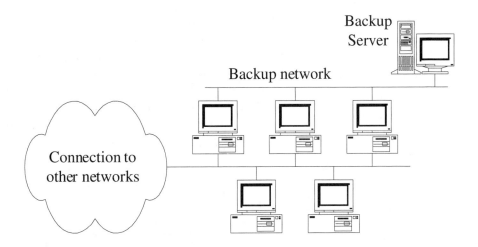

Figure 36–1   *Using a separate backup network.*

scheme is shown in Figure 36-1, where a backup server and three other hosts are connected to a backup network segment.

In the case of complex network strategies, you can use additional backup tools. One such tool is HP Omniback II.

36.2   Using syslogd Over a Network

The `syslogd` daemon is the most important daemon for logging system messages. It reads messages generated by the operating system and applications from a number of sources and logs these to different locations depending on its configuration file `/etc/syslog.conf`. It collects messages from the following resources.

- UNIX domain socket `/dev/log.un`
- Internet domain socket defined in `/etc/services`
- named pipe `/dev/log`
- kernel log device `/dev/klog`
- `syslogd` daemon on other hosts

Applications can send messages to the `syslogd` daemon using the `syslog()` function. The `syslogd` daemon can also collect messages from the `syslogd` daemon of other hosts on a network. This makes it suitable to collect messages on a central management server.

The configuration file for the `syslogd` daemon is `/etc/syslog.conf`. Each line in this file consists of a *selector* and an *action*. The selector consists of a semicolon-separated list of priority specifiers. A *specifier* consists of two fields: a *facility* that determines the subsystem that generated the message and a *level* indicating the severity of the message. The action part of the line is separated from the selector part by using one or more tab characters, and it shows what actions will be taken corresponding to a particular selector. The severity levels used by `syslogd` are listed in Table 36-1.

Table 36–1 *Severity Levels Used by* `syslogd`

Severity Level	Description
LOG_EMERG	Shows a system panic condition
LOG_ALERT	Alert, an action should be taken immediately
LOG_CRIT	Critical condition
LOG_ERR	Error
LOG_WARNING	Warning
LOG_NOTICE	Notice
LOG_INFO	Information
LOG_DEBUG	Debug

All kernel messages are considered critical by `syslogd`. The kernel panic messages are not logged. The following is a sample `/etc/syslog.conf` file.

```
mail.*          /var/adm/syslog/mail.log
*.info          /var/adm/syslog/syslog.log
*.alert         /dev/console
*.alert         root,boota
*.emerg         @myhp
```

The first line shows that all messages generated by the mail system should be logged to the `/var/adm/syslog/mail.log` file. The second line shows that all messages from all systems that have a severity level *info* or above (notice, warning, error, etc.) should be logged to the `/var/adm/syslog/syslog.log` file. The third and fourth lines show that all messages of severity level *alert* and above should be sent to the system console. In addition, if users **root** and **boota** are logged in, these messages should also be displayed on their terminal screens. The last line shows that all messages of severity level *emergency* and above should be forwarded to the `syslogd` daemon running on host `myhp`. The `syslogd` daemon on host `myhp` can then be configured to display messages to the system console or to a logged-in user for immediate action. If all hosts on a network are configured to send critical messages to a management host, errors can be detected immediately and corrective measures may be taken.

The `syslogd` daemon reads its configuration file at startup time. If you make a change to the configuration file, you have to either restart `syslogd` or send a Hangup signal to it. After receiving a Hangup signal, `syslogd` rereads its configuration file. The following command can be used to send the Hangup signal to `syslogd` using its PID stored in the `/var/run/syslog.pid` file.

```
kill -HUP `cat /var/run/syslog.pid`
```

36.3 Network Performance Monitoring

To use a network efficiently and to make plans for expansion in the network, it is important to know the current network behavior. HP-UX provides some commands that can be used for basic network performance monitoring. The `netstat` command shows some information about network activity. The `nfsstat` command shows NFS activity. You have also used the `lanadmin` command, which gives information about data packets transmitted and received on a particular network interface adapter and errors occurring on that segment. The following `lanadmin` command session shows network activity on interface `lan2`. To monitor network activity for a specified period of time, you can clear the interface statistics and display them after a desired period of time.

```
# lanadmin


          LOCAL AREA NETWORK ONLINE ADMINISTRATION, Version 1.0
                     Sat, Jan 1,2000  9:01:50

             Copyright 1994 Hewlett Packard Company.
                     All rights are reserved.


Test Selection mode.

          lan      = LAN Interface Administration
          menu     = Display this menu
          quit     = Terminate the Administration
          terse    = Do not display command menu
          verbose  = Display command menu
```

```
Enter command: lan

LAN Interface test mode. LAN Interface PPA Number = 0

        clear   = Clear statistics registers
        display = Display LAN Interface status and statistics registers
        end     = End LAN Interface Administration, return to Test
                  Selection
        menu    = Display this menu
        ppa     = PPA Number of the LAN Interface
        quit    = Terminate the Administration, return to shell
        reset   = Reset LAN Interface to execute its selftest
        specific = Go to Driver specific menu

Enter command: ppa 2
Enter PPA Number.  Currently 0: 2

LAN Interface test mode. LAN Interface PPA Number = 2

        clear   = Clear statistics registers
        display = Display LAN Interface status and statistics registers
        end     = End LAN Interface Administration, return to Test
                  Selection
        menu    = Display this menu
        ppa     = PPA Number of the LAN Interface
        quit    = Terminate the Administration, return to shell
        reset   = Reset LAN Interface to execute its selftest
        specific = Go to Driver specific menu

Enter command: display

                     LAN INTERFACE STATUS DISPLAY
                   Sat, Jan 1,2000   9:03:13

PPA Number                        = 2
Description                       = lan2 Hewlett-Packard 10/100Base-TX Half-
   Duplex Hw Rev 0
Type (value)                      = ethernet-csmacd(6)
MTU Size                          = 1497
Speed                             = 100
Station Address                   = 0x080009d50e81
Administration Status (value)     = up(1)
Operation Status (value)          = up(1)
Last Change                       = 100
Inbound Octets                    = 937224
Inbound Unicast Packets           = 12667
Inbound Non-Unicast Packets       = 1758
Inbound Discards                  = 0
```

```
Inbound Errors                     = 0
Inbound Unknown Protocols          = 18
Outbound Octets                    = 1166059
Outbound Unicast Packets           = 13748
Outbound Non-Unicast Packets       = 130
Outbound Discards                  = 0
Outbound Errors                    = 0
Outbound Queue Length              = 0
Specific                           = 655367

Press <Return> to continue


Ethernet-like Statistics Group

Index                              = 2
Alignment Errors                   = 0
FCS Errors                         = 0
Single Collision Frames            = 11
Multiple Collision Frames          = 0
Deferred Transmissions             = 10
Late Collisions                    = 0
Excessive Collisions               = 0
Internal MAC Transmit Errors       = 0
Carrier Sense Errors               = 0
Frames Too Long                    = 0
Internal MAC Receive Errors        = 0


LAN Interface test mode. LAN Interface PPA Number = 2

        clear    = Clear statistics registers
        display  = Display LAN Interface status and statistics registers
        end      = End LAN Interface Administration, return to Test
                   Selection
        menu     = Display this menu
        ppa      = PPA Number of the LAN Interface
        quit     = Terminate the Administration, return to shell
        reset    = Reset LAN Interface to execute its selftest
        specific = Go to Driver specific menu

Enter command: quit
#
```

Network monitoring tasks can also be carried out using HP GlancePlus, which can be purchased separately. To start it in GUI, use the gpm command. In the startup window, it shows multiple graphs. You can double-click on a network graph to display the network activity window shown in Figure 36-2.

It shows basic information about combined network activity on all network interfaces. The following four graphs are displayed in this figure.

1. Input packets (PktIn)
2. Output packets (PktOut)
3. Collisions
4. Errors

You can use the `Reports` menu in the main window to display different network activity graphs as shown in Figure 36-3.

Figure 36-4 shows individual graphs for each network interface adapter. Here you can see that one of the four network interface adapters has much more traffic compared with the other three. You should monitor such activity over a period of time. If the same pattern continues, you may rethink your network plan to distribute the load on all network adapters. Figure 36-5 shows a report for NFS activity taking place on the host.

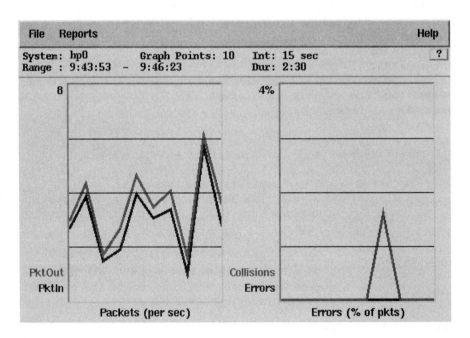

Figure 36–2 *Basic network activity graphs using HP GlancePlus.*

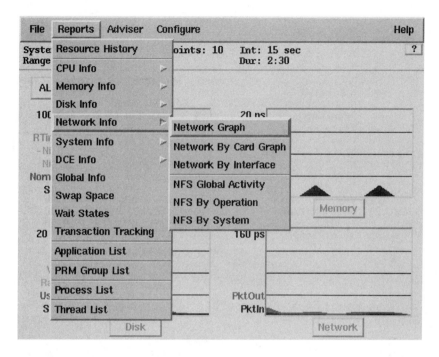

Figure 36–3   *Network reports that can be generated using HP GlancePlus.*

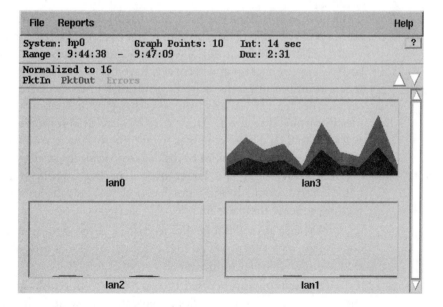

Figure 36–4   *Network activity on each network interface adapter.*

File Reports				Help
System: hp0	Last Update: 9:56:41		Int: 15 sec	?

Activity	Server (Inbound) Current	Cum	Client (Outbound) Current	Cum
Read Rate	0.0	0.0	0.0	0.0
Write Rate	0.0	0.0	0.0	0.0
Read Byte Rate	0.0	0.0	0.0	0.0
Write Byte Rate	0.0	0.0	0.0	0.0
NFS IOs	0	0	0	7
NFS Calls	0	0	0	7
Bad Calls	0	0	0	0
Service Time	0.00	0.00	0.00	0.00
Network Time			0.00	0.00
Read/Write Qlen			0.00	0.00
Idle biods			4	

Figure 36–5   *NFS activity.*

36.4 Routine Tasks

Until now in this book we have not discussed much about routine system administration tasks. These tasks may not be strictly related to the use of networks but are important for all system administrators. Some of these tasks, such as system backup and recovery, have been discussed in previous chapters. Two important tasks are to monitor disk utilization and remove or trim certain files regularly. Many programs that terminate abnormally create core files in various directories. These core files are used for debugging purposes. You have to delete these core files from time to time as some of them may be very large and consume a lot of disk space. Similarly, system and application log files grow larger and larger over a period of time if not deleted or trimmed. A system administrator has to develop strategies for deleting these files or reducing their size on a regular basis.

SAM also provides a facility to carry out these routine tasks in a more convenient way. When you go to the `Routine Tasks` area of SAM, you will find a window similar to the one shown in Figure 36-6.

This window can be used to carry out routine tasks as represented by the different icons. In this section, I have shown a window in Figure 36-7 that appears when you double-click on the `System Log Files` icon. This win-

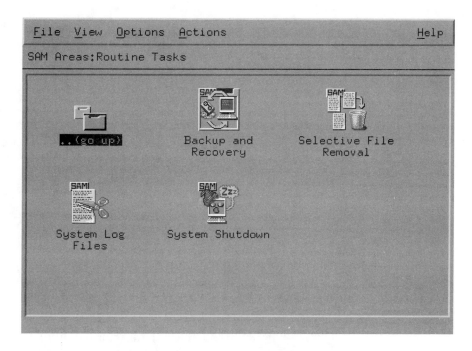

Figure 36–6 *The* Routine Tasks *area of SAM.*

dow shows a preconfigured list of system log files and their current and recommended sizes. The first column in the list shows file names with their complete paths. The last column shows the recommended maximum size of the file. This recommended size can be changed for each file using the Change Recommended Size option in the Actions menu. The third column shows current file size in bytes. If a file does not exist, NA is placed in this column. The second column shows file size as a percentage of the recommended file size. If a file size is larger than the recommended file size, its percentage of the full size will be greater than 100.

Different operations can be performed on a file using the Trim option in the Actions menu. These are as follows.

1. Trim to zero
2. Trim to recommended size
3. Trim to a line number
4. Trim to a percentage

You can use the left mouse button to select one or more files and then apply an action on the selected file(s). For example, it is very convenient to select all files and trim to 50% of the recommended size in one step.

```
 File  List  View  Options  Actions                          Help

 System Log Files                              1 of 49 selected

                               Percent    Current Size    Recommended
      File Name                  Full      (Bytes)         Size (Bytes)
   /etc/eisa/config.err           NA           NA              1024    ▲
   /etc/eisa/config.log           NA           NA              1024
   /etc/rc.log                    154        15788            10240
   /etc/rc.log.old                240        24616            10240
   /etc/shutdownlog               26          276             1024
   /var/adm/OLDmessages           NA           NA              4096
   /var/adm/OLDrld.log            NA           NA              1024
   /var/adm/OLDsulog              NA           NA              4096
   /var/adm/backuplog             NA           NA              1024
   /var/adm/btmp                  NA          180               NA
   /var/adm/cron/OLDlog           0           65              32768    ▼
```

Figure 36–7   *List of* System Log Files *and their sizes as shown by SAM.*

Files can be added to this list or removed from the list using the Actions menu. When you install applications, there may be some additional application log files. You can add these files to the list and set the recommended size for each file. Later on, you can use SAM to trim these files on a regular basis.

If you are using SAM on a network and managing many systems from a central place, it becomes even more convenient to carry out the Trim task on all systems on the network by using SAM. The management server or workstation where you use SAM can be used to trim log files on all systems.

■ Chapter Summary

Computer networks play an important role in personal and business life. Where networks have increased responsibilities of system administrators, they have also made many system administration tasks more convenient and easier. Tasks such as network printing and network backup and restore have proved very useful. Use of NFS and NIS adds many features to computer networks and provides central management for user data files and user accounts. At the same time, it is important to keep networks operational with minimum down time. Proper network monitoring and troubleshooting are musts for this purpose. HP-UX provides commands and utilities to monitor and troubleshoot network connectivity. SAM can also be used to manage many hosts on a network from a central place.

APPENDIX A: CHAPTER REVIEW ANSWERS

▲ PART ONE: FUNDAMENTALS OF THE UNIX SYSTEMS

▲ Chapter 1: Getting Started with UNIX

1. What is the role of the shell in a UNIX system?

   The shell is a command interpreter for UNIX users. It reads input from users and performs an action depending upon that input.

2. What is the difference between intrinsic and extrinsic commands?

   Intrinsic commands are built into the shell while extrinsic commands are stored as separate files.

3. What restrictions apply to an HP-UX password?

   The length of a password is between six and eight characters.

   It must be a combination of characters and numbers.

   At least two characters of the password must be letters and one must be a number or a special character such as, a dash (-), underscore (_), or asterisk (*).

   If you use a password of length greater than eight, any characters after the eighth character are ignored.

4. What are shell startup files? Is it possible for a user to have no startup file?

   There are two shell startup files: a system startup file and a user startup file. The system startup file is /etc/profile, *while the user startup file is* .profile *and it is stored in the home directory of the user.*

▲ Chapter 2: Working with Files and Directories

1. What restrictions apply to UNIX file names?

   The maximum length of a file name is 256 characters.

   A file name can be a combination of letters, numbers, or special characters.

693

All letters, both upper (A...Z) and lower case (a...z) can be used in file names.

Numbers from 0 to 9 can be used in file names.

Special characters like plus (+), minus (-), underscore (_), or dot (.) can be used in file names.

2. What is the difference between the *home directory* and the *root directory*?

   The root directory is the reference point for UNIX file systems and is represented by the / character. The home directory is particular to a user. When a user logs into a UNIX system, he or she goes into the home directory just after the login.

3. Is it possible to create multiple directories with a single command line?

   You can use the mkdir *command to create multiple directories.*

4. What is the difference between the cp and mv commands?

   The cp *command copies a file, leaving the original file in place. The* mv *command copies a file to a new location and then deletes the original file. The* mv *command can also be used to rename a file.*

5. How do absolute path names differ from relative path names?

   Absolute path names start with the / character while relative paths do not.

6. Write a command to list all files that start with my, with any characters in the third to fifth positions, and that end with the e.txt pattern.

   ```
   ls my???e.txt
   ```

▲ Chapter 3: Environment Variables

1. What is the difference between environment and shell variables?

   Environment variables are inherited by all child processes while shell variables are not.

2. What is the role of the time zone (TZ) variable in a company with offices in many countries?

   It can be used to differentiate between older and newer files.

3. Why do you export a variable?

   A variable is exported to make it visible for child processes.

4. Name any four predefined environment variables.

   `$HOME`

   `$PATH`

   `$SHELL`

   `$TERM`

▲ Chapter 4: Input/Output Redirection and Pipes

1. UNIX is a "file-based" system. What does that mean?

   All system resources (disks, printers, keyboards, etc.) are referenced using file names in UNIX.

2. What if we redirect output of a command to a file that already exists?

   The existing file will be overwritten if the redirection is made using a single greater-than sign ">". The data will be appended to the file if a double greater-than sign ">>" is used.

3. What if we pipe output of a command to another command that expects nothing as input?

   The second command will ignore the input received from the first command. Output of the second command will be printed on the screen.

4. Can we redirect both input and output to same file?

   Theoretically we can do so, but the file will be destroyed.

▲ Chapter 5: Using the vi Editor

1. What is the difference between the insert and command modes of the `vi` editor?

   In the insert mode, every typed character is inserted into a file buffer. In the command mode, every typed character is considered a command.

2. How is *cut-paste* different from *import-export*?

   Cut-paste is carried out in the opened file buffers. Import-export is done to disk files.

3. Is it possible to edit binary files with the `vi` editor?

   The `vi` editor is used for text files.

4. What is the role of the `.exrc` file?

   When this file is placed in the home directory of a user, it is used for `vi` settings.

▲ Chapter 6: Regular Expressions

1. Describe the process used by the UNIX shell for command execution.

   If the command is an intrinsic command, it is executed by the shell itself. If it is an extrinsic command, the command execution process is completed in the following steps.
   - *The shell looks for a valid command by searching all directories specified by PATH variable.*
   - *Options and arguments are parsed and arguments are expanded depending on the special characters used.*
   - *The command is invoked.*
   - *The results of the command are displayed back to the user.*

2. What is the command to find all lines in a file that start or end with the word "an"?

   Create a file with the name f2 with the following two lines.

   ```
   ^an
   an$
   ```

   Now use the following command:

   ```
   grep -f f2 filename
   ```

   where `filename` is the name of the file you want to search.

3. What is the result of the following command?
   ```
   grep ^[a-z]$ ?
   ```

   It matches all lines that have only one lowercase letter.

4. Write a command that lists all users in the `/etc/passwd` file whose name starts with a vowel and who are assigned the POSIX shell (`/usr/bin/sh`).

   ```
   grep ^[aeiou] /etc/passwd | grep "/usr/bin/sh"$
   ```

▲ Chapter 7: File Permissions

1. How many types of users are present in UNIX and what is the use of groups?

   There are basically three types of users.

   - *owner of a file*
   - *group members of the file owner*
   - *all other users*

   Groups are useful to grant additional permissions to some users of the system. Usually users working on common problems are placed in one group.

2. What is the advantage of placing a user in more than one group?

   A user may be member of more than one group depending upon his or her responsibilities. For example, a finance manager may be placed in the finance group as well as the managers group because she has both types of responsibilities.

3. What is the use of SETUID from the system administration point of view?

   *A system may use SETUID so that some programs run with **root** privileges. An example is the passwd command.*

4. Write a command to find all files in a directory with the sticky bit set and copy these files to the /tmp directory.

   ```
   find / -perm -u+s -exec cp {} /tmp \;
   ```

5. What if the SUID for a file is set but the file is not executable?

   The SUID without execute access rights shows a mandatory file lock.

6. Why are the Access Control Lists used?

   The ACLs are used to grant file access rights on an individual user basis.

▲ Chapter 8: UNIX File System Hierarchy

1. Why are static directories also called shared directories?

   Static directories can be shared across systems on a network to save disk space. For example, the manual pages may be placed on only one system on the network and used by all other systems. That is why these directories are called shared directories.

2. If you install a new application on the system, where would you like to place its files? What is the recommended place for its configuration and log files?

   The recommended place for applications is the /opt directory. The log files should go to the /var/opt directory and configuration files to the /etc directory. However this is not mandatory and you can place any application anywhere in the file system hierarchy.

3. What is the use of the /tmp directory?

   It is used to place temporary files.

4. What are spool files and where are they placed in the HP-UX file system hierarchy?

   The spool files are temporary files waiting for processing by some application. For example, the print spool files are waiting for printing and the mail spool files are waiting for transmission to the destination. These files are kept in the /var/spool directory.

5. What are device files and how are they arranged?

   Device files are used to access different devices attached to the system. These are places in the /dev directory.

6. What is the relation between physical disks and the directory structure of HP-UX?

   There is no relation of physical disks to the HP-UX directory structure.

7. What is the difference between the whereis and which commands?

   The whereis command locates source, binary, and manual pages for a program while the which command displays the path name for a program file.

▲ Chapter 9: Working with the POSIX Shell and Job Control

1. List two features that are present in the POSIX shell but not in the Bourne shell.

   history

   line editing

   file name completion

2. What types of substitutions are used in the POSIX shell? What are their advantages?

   Tilde substitution is used to substitute a directory name in the command line.

   Variable substitution is used to substitute the value of a variable in the command line.

   Command substitution is used to substitute the output of a command in the command line.

3. What is meant by job control?

   Job control is a process of managing jobs where a user is able to move jobs from the foreground to background and vice versa.

4. What are the differences between foreground and background jobs?

   The background job gives the command prompt back to the user so that another command may be issued. The foreground job does not give the command prompt back until these are finished.

▲ Chapter 10: Introduction to Shell Programming

1. What problem may arise if you don't provide the shell name inside a program?

   A program may be executed by a wrong shell. Since every shell has different control structures, the execution may not be successful.

2. Is it necessary to make a file containing a shell program executable?

   A shell program may be executed by spawning a subshell without making a shell program executable. For example, a shell program prog *may be executed as follows.*

   ```
   $ /usr/bin/sh prog
   ```

3. Create a shell program that reads three command line arguments and then prints these in reverse order.

   There may be multiple ways to write such a script. One of the choices is shown below.

   ```
   #!/usr/bin/sh
   echo $3
   echo $2
   echo $1
   ```

4. What is the importance of exit codes?

The exit codes are used to verify if a program executed successfully.

5. Write a shell program that uses the `test` command in explicit mode to check if the first and second command line arguments have the same value.

```
#!/usr/bin/sh
if test $1 -eq $2
then
    echo "The arguments are equal"
else
    echo "The arguments are NOT equal"
fi
```

6. What is the major difference between the `if` and `case` structures?

The `if` structure is used to make a choice between two options while the `case` structure makes a choice among several options.

▲ Chapter 11: Advanced Shell Programming

1. What is the difference between the `test` and `let` commands?

The `test` command performs logic operations. The `let` command is used to perform both arithmetic and logic operations.

2. Explain the unary and binary negative signs.

The binary negative sign is used for subtraction. The unary negative sign is used for negation.

3. Consider the following program. What may be the possible problem?

```
VAR=1
(($VAR=$VAR+1))
while [ $VAR -lt 10 ]
do
    echo $VAR
done
```

The loop variable is not incremented inside the loop resulting in an infinite loop.

▲ PART TWO: HP-UX SYSTEM ADMINISTRATION

    ▲ Chapter 12: The System Administration Manager

      1. List three advantages of using SAM.

       Centralized management in a network.

       Specific rights can be assigned to different users.

       Comprehensive administration tools which are uniform across all HP-9000 systems.

       Graphical User Interface.

      2. What are the major parts of the SAM window?

       Menu bar

       Functional areas

      3. Explain why SAM can't be used for system troubleshooting.

       System troubleshooting is a complex task and has no defined rules to carry out this task. That is why SAM can't be used for this purpose.

    ▲ Chapter 13: Installing HP-UX

      1. The 64-bit HP-UX version can be installed on all HP-9000 servers and workstations (Yes/No).

       No. The 64-bit version can be installed only on supported platforms.

      2. Which media can be used for HP-UX installation?

       Tape

       CD-ROM

       Network depot

      3. How would you configure a 4-GByte disk for a fresh HP-UX installation?

       A typical assignment of disk space may be like the following.

/	100
/stand	100
Swap	512
/home	200
/opt	800
/tmp	700
/usr	800
/var	800

4. What restrictions apply to the hostname for HP-UX?

   It must start with a letter.

   The maximum length is 64 characters.

   It can contain only letters, numbers, dash, and underscore characters.

5. What is the basic information you need for initial configuration of HP-UX?

   Hostname

   IP address

   Time zone

6. What is the use of PDC?

   Processor Dependent code is used for many purposes. Among these are:
   - *Selecting the primary and alternate boot paths.*
   - *Booting from a specific device.*
   - *Booting in single-user mode.*

▲ Chapter 14: System Startup and Shutdown

1. Why is understanding the startup and shutdown processes important for system administration?

   It helps in troubleshooting the startup problems. This is also necessary to boot the system in single-user mode for maintenance purposes.

2. Where does PDC store its configuration information? What potential problem may arise if this information is stored on the disk?

It is stored in flash memory. The information may be lost in case of a damaged disk if it is stored on the disk.

3. List the steps performed by PDC during the startup process.

Processor Dependent Code (PDC) executes and performs a self-test and detects any peripherals attached to the system.

PDC initializes the console to display messages.

It looks for the primary boot path for booting the system.

PDC loads and executes the Initial System Loader (ISL) from the boot path and executes it.

4. What are runlevels and what is their utility?

A runlevel is a system state. Runlevels are used to start system services in different stages during the boot process.

5. List three tasks performed by the `init` process.

Read the `initdefault` parameter from the `/etc/inittab` file.

Initialize the kernel data structures using `/sbin/ioinitrc`.

Runs `/sbin/bcheckrc`.

Runs `/sbin/rc` and bring the system in default runlevel.

6. What are sequencer directories?

These directories are named `/sbin/rcn.d` where n is a runlevel. Each of these directories contains links to startup and shutdown scripts in the `/sbin/init.d` directory which are used to start and stop system services in a defined sequence.

▲ Chapter 15: Software and Patch Management

1. What tasks are carried out using SD-UX?

Installing software

Removing software

Listing installed software

Verifying installed software

Copying and packaging software

Configuring software

2. What is a software depot? What is the difference between the `swinstall` and `swcopy` commands?

   A software depot is a place where SD-UX filesets, packages, or products are stored. It may be a directory, a CD-ROM, or a tape cartridge. The `swcopy` command is used to manipulate a software depot, while `swinstall` is used to install software from a software depot to an HP-UX system.

3. A depot is a superset of products (True/False).

   True

4. What is included in the output of the `swlist` command if you use it without any arguments or options?

   All software bundles and products that are not part of any bundle are listed.

5. Software is installed in separate directories under the /opt directory. Is it possible to remove software by deleting the directory used for a particular software? Why?

   This is not a proper way of deleting software as a record of all installed software is kept by SD-UX. This record is checked for dependency verification during the installation and removal of software. The proper way of removing software is to use the `swremove` command. Additionally, some software files may not be present under /opt.

6. Describe the purposes of patches.

   Patches are used for one of the following purposes.
   - *To add new functionality to the HP-UX operating system or its products.*
   - *To add support for new hardware.*
   - *To fix bugs in the operating system and applications.*

▲ Chapter 16: Reconfiguring the HP-UX Kernel

1. List at least three situations in which you would need to rebuild the HP-UX kernel.

   Modify system parameters.

Add new hardware drivers.

Add new subsystems.

2. Why is it important to keep your old kernel?

In case the new kernel fails to boot, you can use the old kernel to recover from this situation.

3. How can you find existing kernel configurable parameters?

Use the `sysdef` *command.*

4. What is the name of the newly created kernel?

`vmunix_test`

5. Why is it necessary to reboot the system after building the kernel? Is it possible to load a new kernel on a running system?

You must reboot the system to reload the new kernel. It is not possible to load a new kernel without rebooting.

▲ Chapter 17: Peripheral Devices

1. What is the difference between major and minor device numbers?

The major device number shows the device driver used for a device. The minor device number shows the physical location of a device in a system.

2. Write two commands to list device files.

The `ll` *command*

The `lssf` *command*

3. Describe the autoconfiguration process.

During the boot process the kernel probes all devices attached to the system

▲ Chapter 18: HP-UX File Systems and Logical Volume Manager

1. What are the differences between the whole-disk and LVM approaches?

Only one file system exists on a disk in the whole-disk approach. This file system can't be modified later on. In the LVM approach you can create multiple file systems that can be modified at a later stage.

2. Explain how physical volumes, volume groups, and logical volumes are arranged in LVM.

   A physical volume represents a disk. A volume group consists of one or more physical volumes. The combined data storage capacity of all physical volumes is the capacity of the volume group. Logical volumes are created inside a volume group and can span over multiple physical volumes.

3. What are physical and logical extents?

   A physical extent is the minimum space that can be allocated to a logical volume. A logical extent is a pointer to a physical extent in kernel memory.

4. What steps must be completed before creating logical volumes when creating a new volume group?

   Create physical volumes.

   Create a volume group consisting of the new physical volumes.

   Create logical volumes.

5. What are the differences between the HFS and the JFS file systems?

   HFS is the legacy HP-UX file system based upon blocks. JFS is an extent-based file system with fast recovery mechanisms. HFS is being replaced by JFS on HP-UX. JFS can be managed without unmounting and can create inodes dynamically on demand.

6. How are hard and soft links different from each other?

   Hard links can be created within a file system while soft links can be created across different file systems.

7. What is a mount point?

   It is a directory where a file system is mounted.

8. Can you extend a file system without extending a volume group?

   If unallocated space is available on the volume group, the file system can be extended without extending the volume group.

9. For what purpose is the `lost+found` directory used?

   It is used in the file system repair process to store damaged files.

▲ Chapter 19: User and Group Management

1. Can you create a new user with the help of an editor (without using any specific commands for this purpose or SAM)? How?

   Yes, you can do so by creating a user entry in the /etc/passwd *file using an editor.*

2. What are a user's inactivity and expiration periods?

   The inactivity period is the time during which a user does not use his or her account. The expiration period is the time limit after which the user account becomes disabled.

3. Explain the syntax of the /etc/passwd file.

   It contains seven fields:
   - *Login name*
   - *Password*
   - *User ID*
   - *Group ID*
   - *ID string, which is an optional field, the user's full name, telephone number, or other information may be stored here.*
   - *Home directory*
   - *Shell assigned to the user.*

▲ Chapter 20: Dealing with HP-UX Processes

1. What information do you get from the ps command?

   By using different command line switches, it shows information about the kernel process table.

2. Why does a process go into a sleeping state?

   A process goes into sleeping state when a needed resource is not available.

3. What are signals and how can they be sent to a process?

   Signals are software interrupts. The kill *command can be used to send a signal to a process.*

4. For what purpose is the nohup command used?

   A process is attached to a controlling terminal. When you log out from the terminal, the process dies. If the nohup *command is used on the comand line while starting the process, the process does not die when you log out.*

5. How can you execute both the `pwd` and `date` commands when a `DEBUG` signal is received?

You can use the `trap pwd;date DEBUG` *command for this purpose.*

6. A sleeping process can go to a running state directly. (True/False)

False

▲ Chapter 21: Printing on HP-UX

1. Depending on how a printer is physically connected, what are the different types of printers in an HP-UX system?

Local printer

Remote printer

Network printer

2. What are print priorities and how are these used to allow only selective requests to be serviced by a printer (using a fence priority)?

A fense priority is used to allowed only those jobs to be printed that have a priority greater than a certain value. The `lpfense` *command is used to set these priorities.*

3. What is the role of the interface program in the printing system?

Interface programs are used to format data for a particular type of printer.

4. A printer is not printing anything sent to it. What steps will you follow to troubleshoot this problem?

Check the physical connection.

For network printers use the `ping` *command to verify network connection.*

Verify that `lpsched` *is running.*

5. A network printer is physically connected to a system on the network. (True/False)

False

▲ Chapter 22: Memory and Swap Space Management

1. What are the different types of swap?

   Device swap

   Filesystem swap

   Primary swap

   Secondary swap

2. How is the swapper process used to handle thrashing?

   If a system starts thrashing, the swapper process detects the situation and temporarily swaps out some of the processes. It deactivates these processes and puts these on hold until a particular amount of memory becomes free.

3. What is the advantage of file system swap over device swap?

   File system swap space can be configured dynamically.

4. How do swap priorities affect system performance?

   You can assign a high priority for a swap space on a fast disk, thus increasing system performance.

▲ Chapter 23: System Backup and Recovery

1. What is difference between a full backup and an incremental backup?

   A full backup is used to backup all files. Incremental backup is used to backup only those files that have been modified since the last backup.

2. What is the advantage of tar over fbackup?

   The fbackup *command can be used only on HP-UX. The* tar *command is a standard UNIX command and can be used to transfer files from one type of UNIX to another.*

3. What is the role of the graph file in a backup?

   It stores a list of directories and files that are included in a backup. It plays an important role in an incremental backup.

4. Why do you use an Ignite-UX recovery tape? Isn't it sufficient to make a full backup of a system?

An Ignite-UX tape helps to recover a damaged boot disk. A full backup can be restored only after a system is running. If the boot disk is damaged, the Ignite-UX recovery tape brings the system back to the running state.

▲ Chapter 24: Automating Jobs

1. What is the difference between jobs submitted using the `crontab` and those using the `at` commands?

The jobs submitted using `crontab` are executed repeatedly. The jobs submitted using the `at` command are executed once.

2. Write a `crontab` file entry that executes the `ll` command every minute.

```
* * * * * ll
```

3. Schedule a daily backup at 2 A.M. using a graph file that creates a backup of the `/home` directory.

Create a file `/home/root/gfile` with a single line in it. This line should be `/home`. Now add this line to `crontab`.
```
0 2 * * * fbackup -g /home/root/gfile -u -f /dev/rmt/0m
```

▲ PART THREE: HP-UX NETWORK ADMINISTRATION

▲ Chapter 26: Basic Network Concepts

1. What is a protocol?

A protocol is a set of rules and regulations that govern the communication between two computers.

2. What is the advantage of a layered network model?

The complex task of network communication can be divided into different stages using a layered model.

3. What are peer protocols?

Peer protocols are used in network communications between two computers having the same layer number.

4. What is the function of the network layer?

   It is used for network addressing and routing.

▲ Chapter 27: Network Components and Topologies

1. What is an access method? Explain how CSMA/CD works.

   An access method is a procedure of accessing a physical medium and sending data over it. In case of CSMA/CD, a station first checks the network medium for any existing network traffic before sending its own data. If the network medium is free, the station starts sending its data. Otherwise, it waits for a random time and retries the transmission. If two stations check the medium and find it free and start sending data simultaneously, a collision occurs which is detected by both stations. The stations then retry transmission after a random period of time.

2. What is the difference between a hub and a switch?

   A hub is a physical layer device, while a switch also covers the data link layer.

3. Write one characteristic of each of the following network topologies.
   A. bus
   B. ring
   C. star

   A bus is inexpensive and easy to implement.

   A ring is a bus where two ends are tied together.

   All hosts are connected to a central place in a star topology.

4. What is the function of a repeater?

   It is used to extend the length of a network segment. It regenerates the electrical signal.

▲ Chapter 28: Introduction to the TCP/IP Protocol

1. What is the use of a netmask?

   A netmask is used to assign a certain number of bits to the network and host parts of an IP address.

2. What are the major differences between the TCP and UDP protocols?

   TCP is a connection-oriented protocol used for reliable data transfer. UDP is a connection-less protocol and does not guarantee reliable data transfer.

3. What is the use of sockets?

   A socket is a combination of an IP address and port number. It is used to provide a virtual connection point for client and server applications.

4. Why is ARP necessary for network communication?

   ARP maps IP addresses to MAC addresses. Without ARP it is not possible to determine to which machine a particular IP address is assigned.

▲ Chapter 29: Configuring LAN Interface Adapters

1. List the steps involved to configure a network adapter.

   Shutdown the system and install a LAN adapter.

   Install the software driver for the adapter if it is not already there.

   Use the lanscan *command to verify that the adapter is visible.*

   Either use SAM to assign an IP address to the adapter or use the ifconfig *command and manually edit the* /etc/rc.config.d/netconf *file.*

   Add a routing entry, if needed.

   Update /etc/hosts. *If you are using SAM, this part will be done by SAM.*

2. What does NamePPA mean?

   The PPA is the Physical Point of Attachment, while the name is either lan *or* snap. *The combination of the name and PPA (NamePPA) is used in network administration commands.*

3. Is it always necessary to add a default route? Why or why not?

   If you have routing entries for all connected networks, there is no need to have a default route. However if your network is connected to a public network, you should define the default route pointing to the router that connects your network to the public network.

4. What steps can you take if a network adapter is not visible with the `lan-scan` command?

   Verify that the adapter is correctly inserted into the system.

   Verify that driver for the adapter is built into the kernel.

   If both of the above conditions are met, verify that the adapter is not bad.

5. Multiple IP addresses can be assigned to a network interface (True/False).

   True

▲ Chapter 30: Configuring and Managing ARPA/Berkeley Services

1. What are the advantages and disadvantages of activating a service using `inetd`?

   If you activate a service using `inetd`, *the server process is started only when needed. The system resources are not used when a server process is not running. However, this may also slow down the response time.*

2. List four Internet services used on HP-UX.

   Remote login

   Remote file transfer

   Electronic mail

   Network time protocol

3. What rules apply to entries in the `/etc/hosts.equiv` file?

   If a remote host name is listed in the file, users of the remote host are allowed to access the local system if the local user name also matches the remote system user name.

   If the host name starts with a negative sign, access of all users on that system is denied.

   If a line contains a "+" symbol, it matches every host.

▲ Chapter 31: Host Name Resolution and Domain Name Server

1. What are the three most common host name resolution methods?

   NIS

   DNS

   Hosts

2. Give a short description of the three types of domain name servers.

   The primary name server is an authority for a domain name.

   Secondary name servers are used to back up the primary server and for load distribution.

   Caching servers don't have their own data files and are used for name resolutions on a departmental level.

3. Why is the `db.cache` file used?

   It contains a list of root name servers.

4. How are DNS data files updated on the secondary server?

   These are automatically updated at regular intervals by the secondary server. These can also be updated manually using the `sig_named_restart` *command.*

▲ Chapter 32: Configuring and Managing NIS

1. What is the function of NIS?

   It provides centralized information of network resources.

2. For what purpose are escape entries used in the `/etc/passwd` file?

   These are used to control access for selected users.

3. What is the difference between NIS and DNS?

   DNS provides only host name resolution, while NIS also provides other services.

   NIS uses a flat name space, while DNS uses a hierarchical name space.

   A host may participate in only one NIS domain, while it may be a part of multiple DNS domains.

NIS can be used on private networks, while DNS is also used on public networks.

▲ Chapter 33: Configuring and Managing the Network File System

1. How can you grant mount access to an exported file system to selected clients?

   You can use the /etc/exports file to grant mount access to selected clients.

2. Which subsystems must be present in the kernel to use NFS?

   The networking and NFS subsystems must be present.

3. Why is it necessary to synchronize time on all NFS clients and servers?

   If the time is not synchronized, a client may be confused about a file being old or new.

▲ Chapter 34: HP-UX Automounter

1. How is Automounter used for load balancing and fault tolerance?

   Automounter mounts file systems from the nearest of multiple NFS servers. In case a server is not available, it can mount a file system from another server.

2. What is the difference between direct and indirect maps?

   A direct map has an explicit mount point. Directories in an indirect map are mounted within a reference directory.

3. What rules apply to restarting the automount daemon after modifying different maps?

   If you make a change to a master map, you must restart the daemon.

   If you modify the options or server part in a direct map, you don't need to restart the automount daemon. If you modify a mount point, you have to restart the automount daemon.

   There is no need to restart the automount daemon if you make a change to an indirect map.

▲ Chapter 35: Network Time Protocol

1. What are three types of time sources?

   GPS satellites

   Radio broadcasts

   Internet time servers

2. What is a stratum level?

   It is an indication of the accuracy of a time source. A level 1 time source is the most accurate and a level 15 time source is the least accurate.

3. What is the use of a drift file?

   It is used to track any time drift in the local clock.

▲ PART ONE: FUNDAMENTALS OF UNIX SYSTEMS

▲ Chapter 1: Getting Started with UNIX

1. *The system startup file for a UNIX shell is invoked:*

   C. The system startup file for the `/etc/profile` shell is invoked when a user logs into the system.

2. *The default POSIX shell prompt for a common user is:*

   C.

3. *When a user logs into HP-UX, the initial directory is:*

   B.

4. *What is the difference between intrinsic and extrinsic UNIX commands?*

   A.

5. *What is true about the superuser?*

   C. Any user having user ID 0 is a superuser. Creating more than one user with the same user ID is another way of giving the same rights to multiple users in a system.

6. *The default shell for HP-UX users is:*

   C.

7. *To log out of the HP-UX session, you use command:*

   B. There is no logout command.

▲ Chapter 2: Working with Files and Directories

1. *The* `cat` *command is used to:*

   C. This command can be used for both creating and displaying a file.

2. *The maximum length of a file name may be:*

   C. A file name in HP-UX may be 256 characters long.

3. *The* more *command is used to:*

   A. This command is used to display text files, one page at a time.

4. *What is the function of the following command*
   grep "Mark Black" /etc/passwd

   A. Words enclosed in quotation marks are considered as one string. The find command can't be used to find text within a file.

5. *Consider a directory with five files in it. The file names are* pg.c, pg1.c, pg2.c, pg3.cpp, *and* pg10.c. *We use the command* ls pg?.?. *The files displayed are:*

   A. The question mark is used to match only one character.

6. *How can you tell the number of user accounts on a UNIX system?*

   D. Each user name is listed in one line in the /etc/passwd file. There is no number command in HP-UX.

7. *You are currently in the* /home/boota *directory. Which command will bring you the to* /etc *directory?*

   D. Option A is not correct as it will move you to /home/boota/etc (if this exists). Option B is correct as you will go back two steps to the root directory and then go to etc directory. Option C is also correct as you have specified an absolute path.

▲ Chapter 3: Environment Variables

1. *Just after login, you issue the command* echo HOME. *What will be the output of this command?*

   C. Option A is not correct because to display the value of a variable you have to use a dollar sign with the variable name. Option B is not correct because the HOME variable is set when you log in. Since you have not used a dollar sign, the command will simply display the word "HOME", so option C is correct.

2. *What is* not *true about the* PATH *variable?*

   A. The PATH variable does not show anything about the current directory.

3. *You have a variable "*ABC*" with value "*Alphabets*". You use the following command to change its value.*
ABC='All $ABC'
What will be the new value of the variable?

A. Any string specified with single quotation marks is taken as-is by HP-UX commands.

4. *To assign the output of a command to a variable, we use:*

D.

5. *The value of the* PS2 *variable on your system is ">" (greater-than symbol). You issue an incomplete command. What will be the shell's response?*

D. The shell displays the value of the PS2 variable as prompt when you issue an incomplete command.

6. *What is wrong with the shell variable name* 3Xyab2?

A. Ahell variable name can't be started with a digit.

▲ Chapter 4: Input/Output Redirection and Pipes

1. *What is the file descriptor used for stderr?*

C.

2. *The symbol used to append to a file when redirecting stdout to that file is:*

B. Option A overwrites the existing file. Option C is used for input redirection. Option D is used for stderr redirection.

3. *When you redirect both stdout and stderr to the same location, you use:*

C.

4. *A pipe is used to:*

A.

5. *Which is* not *true?*

B. A pipe can be used in a command where the stdin is redirected.

▲ Chapter 5: Using the `vi` Editor

1. *You have made changes to a file and want to quit* `vi` *without saving these changes. What command will you use?*

   C. Option A will save the changes and then quit. Option B will save the file and then quit. Option D will force saving the file.

2. *You want to replace* cat *with* dog *in your file at all locations in the* `vi` *editor. You use:*

   C.

3. *While in command mode you press "a"; what happens?*

   B.

▲ Chapter 6: Regular Expressions

1. *The purpose of the command* `grep  ^Test$` *is:*

   D.

2. *Square brackets in pattern matching are used for:*

   C.

3. *A regular expression* `\<join` *matches:*

   A.

4. *The* `grep` *command can use:*

   A.

5. *Which of these is NOT a meta character?*

   D.

▲ Chapter 7: File Permissions

1. *A file has* `rwxr-xr--` *permissions. It is owned by a user* **mark** *belonging to a group* **users**. *You are logged in as user* **jim** *belonging to group* **users**. *What permissions do you have for this file?*

   C. All group members have read and execute permissions.

2. *You are logged in as user* **jim** *and create a file* myfile *and want to give it to a user* **mark** *by changing its ownership. The command for this is:*

   B.

3. *The* id *command without any argument lists:*

   C.

4. *You want to change your group ID temporarily. Which command will you use?*

   A. The chgrp command changes the group ownership of a file. The id command is used to display the user and group IDs.

5. *The system administrator wants a command to be executed with* **superuser** *permissions no matter which user executes it. He or she will set:*

   A.

6. *A file* myfile *already exists. You use command* touch myfile. *What will be the effect of this command?*

   C.

7. *You are logged in as user* **boota** *belonging to group* **users**. *When you list files using the* ll *command, you see the following list.*

   ```
   -rwxrw-r--   1 jim    class    0 Sep  8 18:06 myfile
   ```

   What operations can you perform on this file?

   C. You are neither the owner of the file nor a group member of the owner.

8. *You use the command* chmod 764 myfile. *It provides:*

   D.

▲ Chapter 8: UNIX File System Hierarchy

1. *What can be determined about file name* /etc/named.boot?

   B. The /etc directory contains most of the configuration files.

2. *The HP-UX file system hierarchy is based on:*

   B.

3. *Mail files are kept in which directory?*

   D.

4. *What is true about the* `lost+found` *directory?*

   B.

5. *To find a command in the search path, we use the command:*

   B.

6. *Which directory contains programs needed at boot time?*

   A.

7. *The HP-UX kernel is located in:*

   D.

▲ Chapter 9: Working with the POSIX Shell and Job Control

1. *The default HP-UX shell is:*

   C.

2. *You are in a directory having three files,* `file1`, `file2`, *and* `afile`. *You type a command* `ls  f` *and then press the* `Esc` *key followed by the* `=` *key. What happens?*

   D.

3. *You use the* `date` *command to see the current system time. Just after that, you press the* `Esc` *key followed by the* `j` *key. What happens?*

   D. This key combination is used to go to the next command in the command history. Since there is no next command, nothing will happen.

4. *What does the command* `r  3` *do?*

   D.

5. *For what purpose is the* `stty` *command used?*

   D. The `stty` command is used for terminal related settings.

6. *Your home directory is* /home/boota. *You moved from your home directory to the* /etc *directory. How can you go back to your home directory?*

   B. Choices A and C seem to be correct but the $ symbol is missing in the variable name with both of the choices.

7. *A job running in the foreground can be suspended by:*

   C. No command can be used while a job is running in the foreground, so choices A, B, and D are incorrect.

8. *Background jobs are always in:*

   D. A background job may be in any state.

▲ Chapter 10: Introduction to Shell Programming

1. *You create a shell program and save it into a file with name "*more*". Your current directory name is included in the **PATH** variable at the end. When you run this program by typing "*more*", nothing happens and the cursor just stops at the next line. What may be the problem?*

   C. The more command is a standard UNIX command that expects an input from stdin. Since your current directory is at the end of the PATH variable, the standard more command gets executed instead of your own program. Choice A is incorrect because, in the case of an unrecognized command, you will get an error message. Choice B is incorrect because you will get an error message if the program is not executable.

2. *What is true about variables used in shell programs?*

   D.

3. *You use the* echo $? *command. The result is* 2. *What do you conclude from this?*

   B. The command prints the return code of the last command. Any return code other than 0 shows that the execution of the last command was not successful.

4. *You used* shift 3 *in your shell program. What will be its effect?*

   C. The shift command shifts all command line arguments to the left.

5. *What does the* echo "\a" *command do?*

   D. This is an escape character used for an alert sound.

6. *What is wrong with the command [* `"ABC" -eq "ABC"` *]?*

   A. To test string equality you use the equal sign (`=`).

7. *A shell script with the name* `myscript` *does not have the execution bit set. How can you execute it?*

   B.

8. *How can you list all command line arguments?*

   A.

9. *The true return value of the* `test` *command is:*

   C. It returns a positive integer including zero.

10. *You have a shell script as shown here. What will be the result when it is executed?*
    ```
    #!/usr/bin/sh
    ABC=aac
    case $ABC in
        a)      echo "First"
                ;;
    [aa]c)      echo "Second"
                ;;
    a*)         echo "Third"
                ;;
    *)          echo "Last"
                ;;
    esac
    ```

    C. The only matching choice is `a*`.

▲ Chapter 11: Advanced Shell Programming

1. *Which command will you use to add the values of two variables* `VAR1` *and* `VAR2`, *and store the result in* `VAR3`?

   D.

2. *You want to wait for 10 seconds at the end of the loop in each loop cycle. Which command will you use?*

   A. There is no `pause` command. The `wait` command is used to wait for a child process to terminate.

3. *Consider the following code segment. How many times does the loop execute?*

```
A=1
until [ $A < 10 ]
do
    echo $A
    (( $A=$A+1))
done
```

A.

4. *What will be the output of the program shown here?*

```
#!/usr/bin/sh
A=1
while [ $A -lt 10 ]
do
    B=1
    while [ $B -lt 10 ]
    do
        break 2
        echo "Inner loop"
    done
    echo "Outer Loop"
done
```

D. The `break` command terminates both loops before anything is printed.

5. *While writing a program, you meet a situation where you want to break the normal execution and shift control to the beginning of the loop, skipping the remaining commands in the loop. Which command will you use?*

B.

▲ PART TWO: HP-UX SYSTEM ADMINISTRATION

▲ Chapter 12: The System Administration Manager

1. *SAM can't be used for:*

B.

2. *The SAM builder is used to:*

   C.

3. *The SAM log file is:*

   C.

4. *The utility for viewing the SAM log file is:*

   A.

▲ Chapter 13: Installing HP-UX

1. *The length of the HP-UX host name may be:*

   D.

2. *The HP-UX host name may contain:*

   C.

3. *Which command is used for initial configuration of the system?*

   B.

4. *Which statement is true?*

   B.

5. *How can you change the primary boot path?*

   A. PDC decides from which path the system should be booted.

6. *Which command do you use in PDC to find the device name for a CD-ROM drive?*

   C.

7. *You use the* search *command, and a list of devices is displayed as shown below. Which command will you use to boot from the CD-ROM?*

Path Number	Device Path (dec)	Device Type
P0	10/0/6	Random Access Media
P1	10/0/5	Random Access Media
P2	10/0/4	Random Access Media
P3	10/0/3	Random Access Media
P4	10/0/2	Random Access Media
P5	10/0/1	Random Access Media

```
P6              10/4/4.2            Toshiba CD-ROM Device
P7              10/4/4.1            Sequential Access Media
```

D.

▲ Chapter 14: System Startup and Shutdown

1. *All HP-9000 systems have processor dependent code (PDC). What is true about it?*

   D.

2. *The autoboot information is stored in:*

   D.

3. *What can be used to boot HP-UX in single-user mode?*

   C.

4. *What is the function of the secondary loader?*

   B.

5. *The boot area of the primary system disk contains:*

   D.

6. *The* search *command in PDC is used to:*

   B.

7. *What is the order of execution of scripts* becheckrc, ioinitrc, *and* rc?

   B.

8. *What information is present in stable storage?*

   D.

9. *What is true about the* lifls *command?*

   A.

10. *The ID field in* /etc/inittab *file shows:*

    C.

11. *What happens if the runlevel for a program is not specified in the* /etc/inittab *file?*

    B.

12. *Which runlevel can be used for multiuser operation?*

    D.

13. *What command is used to check the current runlevel?*

    B.

▲ Chapter 15: Software and Patch Management

1. *What is* not *true about a fileset?*

   B. A fileset may belong to many products.

2. *What is the default location of software on your disk?*

   A.

3. *When the* swlist *command is used without any arguments, it lists:*

   D.

4. *When using the* swinstall *command in the text menu, you can activate the menus using the:*

   A.

5. *In which runlevel is the SD-UX software daemon started?*

   B.

6. *What is the use of the* freedisk *command?*

   B.

7. *Which SD-UX command is used to install software?*

   A.

8. *For what purpose are patches* not *used?*

   C.

9. *Every patch is a* shar *file when you download it from the Hewlett-Packard Internet site. How many files are created when you* unshar *it?*

   A.

▲ Chapter 16: Reconfiguring the HP-UX Kernel

1. *The default HP-UX kernel is:*

   C.

2. *The HP-UX kernel is:*

   A.

3. *If you don't back up the old kernel:*

   B. The only implication on not saving the old kernel is that you may not recover from a bad new kernel.

4. *A new kernel is rebuilt whenever you:*

   B.

5. *For a proper memory dump, the size of the swap space must be larger than:*

   B.

6. *What does the* sysdef *command show?*

   B.

7. *The* maxswapchunks *kernel parameter shows the value of maximum swap space:*

   A.

▲ Chapter 17: Peripheral Devices

1. *What is the usual or default target address of an SCSI controller card?*

   C.

2. *What is the interface card instance number of disk* 8/6.5.0?

   B.

3. *What is the device file name for disk* `7/3.4.0` *attached to a card having instance number 1?*

   B.

4. *Which command can't be used for creating a device file?*

   B.

5. *The device class* `disk` *includes:*

   B.

6. *A terminal is represented by how many files in the* `/dev` *directory?*

   A.

7. *What information is necessary for the* `mknod` *command on the command line?*

   D.

8. *Which command is executed automatically for new devices at boot time?*

   C.

▲ Chapter 18: HP-UX File Systems and Logical Volume Manager

1. *What is the name used for the root volume group?*

   A.

2. *Which statement is* not *true?*

   D. The name of a logical volume may start with other characters.

3. *The default physical extent size is:*

   A.

4. *The* `pvdisplay` *command uses:*

   B.

5. *What is true about space allocation to a logical volume?*

   B.

6. *By default, how many logical volumes can be created in a volume group?*

   C.

7. *Which command can be used to create a physical volume?*

   A. The `pvcreate` command always works on raw devices.

8. *Which command would you use to create a logical volume of 200-MByte size with the name* `myvol` *in volume group* `vg02`*?*

   C.

9. *Which statement is true?*

   C.

10. *What is* not *true about the JFS file system?*

    C.

11. *You use the* `pvcreate`*,* `vgextend`*,* `lvextend`*, and* `extendfs` *commands to increase the size of a file system. In which sequence would you use these?*

    C.

12. *Which command can you use to list the mounted file systems?*

    C.

▲ Chapter 19: User and Group Management

1. *To change a group ID temporarily, which command is used?*

   B.

2. *What information is a must when you use the* `useradd` *command?*

   A.

3. *How many fields are present in the* `/etc/passwd` *file?*

   C.

4. *In which directory are stored the default configuration files for a user?*

   B.

5. *What is wrong with the following* `/etc/passwd` *entry?*
   `boota:OV81GT8LCiRO.:1225:20::/home/boota:/sbin/sh:`

   B.

6. *Which command would you use to change a user ID?*

   C.

7. *For what purpose is a restricted shell used?*

   D.

▲ Chapter 20: Dealing with HP-UX Processes

1. *Which kernel tunable parameter determines the maximum size of a process table?*

   B.

2. *Which signal is sent by the* kill *command by default?*

   C.

3. *The default nice level is 20. You start a new process in the background using the "&" symbol. What will be its nice level?*

   C. The nice level is increased by 4 for background processes.

4. *A process is in a sleep state while waiting for a resource that is currently busy. It receives a stop signal (*SIGSTOP*) and goes into a stopped state. After some time it receives a continue signal (*SIGCONT*). To which state will it go?*

   B. After receiving the SIGCONT signal, the process goes into its previous state.

5. *You are logged in as user* **boota** *and want to change the nice level of the* init *process to 15. Which of the following commands will you use? Remember the PID for the* init *process is 1.*

   D. The **root** user can change the nice value for the init process.

▲ Chapter 21: Printing on HP-UX

1. *What is the result of the* lp -dLJ4 /etc/profile *command?*

   C.

2. *How are local print jobs scheduled?*

   B.

3. *How can the print priority of a job be increased when this job is waiting in the print queue?*

   B.

4. *What do you need to do to set up a remote printer, assuming DNS or NIS is not used?*

   D.

5. *What happens after you issue the following command?*

   ```
   disable -r "Printer disabled" laserjet3
   ```

   B.

6. *What is the result of the following command?*

   ```
   lpfence laserjet3 5
   ```

   A.

▲ Chapter 22: Memory and Swap Space Management

1. *Which swap area must be available at system bootup time?*

   A.

2. *Where can you create a device swap?*

   D.

3. *You have three identical disk drives. How would you like to use these for swap and file systems for the best swap performance?*

   A.

4. *You have three different swap areas in LVM. These are:*

   ```
   /dev/vg03/lvol2
   /dev/vg03/lvol8
   /dev/vg03/lvol9
   ```

   You want to stop using /dev/vg03/lvol2 as swap space. How can you do it?

   C.

5. *What information is* not *displayed by the* swapinfo *command by default?*

    D.

▲ Chapter 23: System Backup and Recovery

1. *You are using incremental backup in two levels. The levels used are 1 and 5. When restoring data, in what order will you restore the backup?*

    A.

2. *You used the* tar *command to back up your system. Which command will you use to restore it?*

    A.

3. *You are using files larger than 2 GBytes on your system. Which utility will you prefer to use to back up the system?*

    A.

4. *While creating incremental backup at level 2, you used the following command.*

    ```
    fbackup -v -g gfile -2 -f /dev/rmt/0m
    ```

    The next day you performed backup at level 3 using the following command.

    ```
    fbackup -v -g gfile -u -3 -f /dev/rmt/0m
    ```

    Which files will be backed up?

    A. Since you did not use the −u option with the first backup, the new backup will contain all files listed in the graph file.

5. *Which backup level is always a full backup, no matter how the previous backup has been performed?*

    A.

6. *Which* tar *command is used to restore data?*

    A.

7. *Why is a recovery tape made with the* make_recovery *command important?*

    C.

8. *Which statement is true?*

    B.

9. *What information is present in* Backup Scope *when using SAM?*

    B.

▲ Chapter 24: Automating Jobs

1. *At what run level is the* cron *daemon started?*

    B.

2. *On your system, file* cron.allow *exists and is empty. File* cron.deny *is also present and contains the login name of user* **boota**. *Who is allowed to use* cron?

    C.

3. *A* crontab *entry is shown below. At what time will the* trimlog *command be executed?*

    ```
    0   *   1,6   1   *   /home/root/trimlog
    ```

    C.

4. *It is exactly 12:00 noon. You want to execute a command at the same time the next day. Which of the following commands will you use?*

    D.

▲ PART THREE: HP-UX NETWORK ADMINISTRATION

▲ Chapter 26: Basic Network Concepts

1. *The order of the top four OSI layers from top to bottom is:*

    B.

2. *What is the function of the network layer?*

    A.

3. *Peer protocols are used between:*

    C.

4. *Which OSI layer is divided into Logical Link Control (LLC) and Medium Access Control (MAC)?*

D.

5. *What is not true about the OSI model?*

C.

▲ Chapter 27: Network Components and Topologies

1. *Which cable is used in 100BASE-T networks?*

D.

2. *What is not true about a bridge?*

B.

3. *Which of the following is not a physical layer device?*

D.

4. *Terminators are used in:*

A.

5. *CSMA/CD is not used in:*

D.

6. *The maximum length of a 10BASE-2 cable segment is:*

C.

7. *What is the maximum number of repeaters that can be used in an Ethernet network?*

B.

8. *Which statement is true?*

C.

▲ Chapter 28: Introduction to TCP/IP Protocol

1. *The application layer of the OSI model covers which three layers?*

B.

2. *What is the starting bit pattern of a class C IP address?*

   D.

3. *The maximum number of hosts in a class C network are:*

   C.

4. *A host on an IP network has an IP address 192.168.3.65 with a netmask 255.255.255.224. What is the broadcast address?*

   C.

5. *Given a netmask of 255.255.255.240, how many hosts can be placed in the network?*

   A.

6. *In an IP network, 18 bits are used in the network address. What is the value of the netmask?*

   A.

7. *Address resolution protocol is used to:*

   A.

8. *Which statement is true with reference to an IP address and a socket address?*

   B.

9. *Which file on HP-UX contains standard port numbers assigned to different applications?*

   B.

▲ Chapter 29: Configuring LAN Interface Adapters

1. *Which command is used to list network drivers configured into the kernel?*

   D.

2. *For what purpose is the* ifconfig *command used?*

   D.

3. *The following statements are related to the assignment of IP addresses to network interfaces. Which of these is true?*

   B.

4. *For what purpose is the* `/etc/rc.config.d/netconf` *file used?*

   B.

5. *Which command is used to display a routing table?*

   B.

6. *When creating a default route, you see a* `network unreachable` *message. What may be the cause?*

   B.

7. *Which command is used for listing installed network adapters?*

   C.

▲ Chapter 30: Configuring and Managing ARPA/Berkeley Services

1. *What port number is used for telnet service?*

   A.

2. *The telnet service is invoked using* `inetd`. *The configuration entry for this service contains the keyword* `nowait`. *What does it mean?*

   D.

3. *What is the server process for the* `rcp` *command?*

   A.

4. *Which command is used to execute a program on a remote system?*

   B.

5. *Which of the following is not a network service?*

   C. This is a restricted shell on HP-UX.

6. *An HP-UX server contains a single character + (plus) in the* `/etc/hosts.equiv` *file. Which hosts are allowed to use the network services?*

   A.

7. *You want to allow a user* **jeff** *at host* myhp *to access your account using the* rlogin *command. What should be present in the* .rhosts *file in your home directory?*

   C.

▲ Chapter 31: Host Name Resolution and Domain Name Server

1. *A system has the following* /etc/hosts *file.*
   ```
   192.168.2.1 hp01
   192.168.4.5 hp01
   ```

   You use the ping hp01 *command to send an ICMP packet to host* hp01. *To which IP address will these packets be sent?*

   A. The first matching entry in the /etc/hosts file is taken.

2. *Which file determines the order in which different services try to resolve a host name?*

   C.

3. *At which run level is* named *started?*

   B.

4. *What is the DNS port number?*

   D.

5. *The* hosts_to_named *command is run on which server?*

   A.

6. *Which file on a client machine is used for listing available name servers?*

   B.

7. *Which is the configuration file used by* named *at boot time?*

   B.

8. *You have your own domain name and want to create zones and delegate authority of these zones to a departmental name server. Which name server will delegate this authority?*

   B.

9. *For what purpose is the NS resource record used in DNS data files?*

   A.

▲ Chapter 32: Configuring and Managing NIS

1. *An NIS client can take part in how many NIS domains?*

   A.

2. *What is true about an NIS domain name?*

   A.

3. *The* ypxfr *command is used on:*

   B.

4. *Which daemon is used for an NIS password change?*

   D.

5. *What is true about NIS?*

   A.

6. *Which of the following is* not *an NIS map?*

   D.

7. *Which command is used to display the name of an NIS server bound to a host?*

   C.

▲ Chapter 33: Configuring and Managing the Network File System

1. *Which NFS version is supported on HP-UX 11.00?*

   D.

2. *Which HP-UX command can be used on an NFS server to list remotely mounted file systems by NFS clients?*

   D.

3. *How should the* rpcbind, nfsd, *and* inetd *daemons be started?*

   B.

4. *Which RPC daemon is used on HP-UX 11.00?*

   B.

5. *What is* not *true about NFS?*

   C.

6. *What is the advantage of NFS version 3 over version 2?*

   D.

7. *Which command is used to manually export file systems for remote mount?*

   B.

8. *Which command is used to list registered RPC services on a host?*

   A.

▲ Chapter 34: HP-UX Automounter

   1. *Which of the following is* not *an Automounter map?*

      B.

   2. *When do you need to restart the* automount *daemon?*

      A.

   3. *What is the default interval of time after which Automounter unmounts a directory if no reference is made to a mounted file system?*

      D.

   4. *The master* automount *map contains the following indirect map entry.*

      ```
      /home              /etc/auto_home
      ```

      The /etc/auto_home *file has one line as shown below.*

      ```
      boota    hp0:/home/boota
      ```

      Where will the directory /home/boota *on an NFS server* hp0 *be mounted on the local system?*

      D.

▲ Chapter 35: Network Time Protocol

1. *What is the most accurate time source for NTP?*

   A.

2. *What is the configuration file used by the* xntpd *daemon?*

   B.

3. *Which command is used to synchronize time with one or more NTP servers on the Internet?*

   A.

4. *What is the default polling time for a server?*

   A.

This is a list of commonly used commands and configuration files. You may find some questions about these commands and files in the HP-UX certification exam. This is an alphabetically sorted list. The description of the commands and files is taken from HP-UX manual pages with slight modification in some cases.

Commands

Command	Description
accept, reject	Allow/prevent LP printer queuing requests.
arp	Address resolution display and control.
arp	Address Resolution Protocol.
at	Execute commands immediately or at a later time.
banner	Make posters in large letters.
bdf	Report the number of free disk blocks (Berkeley version).
cal	Print calendar.
cat	Concatenate, copy, and print files.
catman	Create the cat files for the manual.
cd	Change the working directory.
chfn	Change the user information used by the finger command. This command updates the /etc/passwd file.
chmod	Change file mode access permissions.
chown, chgrp	Change the file owner or group.
chsh	Change the default login shell for a user. This command updates the /etc/passwd file.
clear	Clear the terminal screen.
cmp	Compare two files.
comm	Select or reject lines common to two sorted files.
compress, uncompress	Compress and expand data. These are standard UNIX commands for file compression and decompression.
cp	Copy files and directories.

Commands *(continued)*

Command	Description
cpio	Copy file archives in and out; duplicate directory trees. This command is used for backup and recovery on many UNIX systems.
cron	Timed job execution daemon.
crontab	User job file scheduler.
csh	User shell with C-like syntax.
cut	Cut out (extract) selected fields of each line of a file or stdin. This is often used in shell scripts.
date	Display or set the date and time.
dd	Convert, reblock, translate, and copy a (tape) file. This command dumps raw data on a device (not files).
df	Report the number of free file system disk blocks.
diff	Differential file and directory comparator.
diskinfo	Describe the characteristics of a disk device.
dmesg	Collect system diagnostic messages to or from the error log.
domainname	Set or display the name of the Network Information Service (NIS) domain.
du	Summarize disk usage.
dump, rdump	Incremental file system dump, local or across a network.
echo	Echo (print) arguments.
enable, disable	Enable/disable LP printers.
ex, edit	Extended line oriented text editor.
exportfs	Export and unexport directories to NFS clients.
expr	Evaluate arguments as an expression. Often used in shell scripts.
extendfs	Extend a file system size.
fbackup	Selectively back up files.
file	Determine the file type.
find	Find files.
finger	User information lookup program.
frecover	Selectively recover files.

Commands *(continued)*

Command	Description
freedisk	Recover disk space by finding filesets that have not been used for a certain period of time.
fsadm	A file system administration command.
fsck	File system consistency check and interactive repair.
fstyp	Determine the file system type.
ftp	File transfer program. Used to transfer files over a network.
ftpd	File Transfer Protocol server.
fuser	List processes using a file or file structure.
getty	Set terminal type, modes, speed, and line discipline.
grep, egrep, fgrep	Search a file for a pattern.
groupadd	Add a new group to the system.
groupdel	Delete a group from the system.
groupmod	Modify a group on the system.
groups	Show group memberships.
head	Print the first few lines of input.
hostname	Set or display the name of the current host system.
hpux	HP-UX bootstrap.
id	Print the user and group IDs and names.
ifconfig	Configure network interface parameters.
inetd	Internet services daemon.
init	Process control initialization.
insf	Install special (device) files.
ioinit	Test and maintain consistency between the kernel I/O data structures and /etc/ioconfig.
ioscan	Scan the I/O system.
iostat	Report I/O statistics.
isl	Initial system loader.
kill	Send a signal to a process; terminate a process.

Commands *(continued)*

Command	Description
`killall`	Kill all active processes.
`ksh, rksh`	Shell, the standard/restricted command programming language.
`lanadmin`	Local area network administration program.
`lanscan`	Display the LAN device configuration and status.
`last, lastb`	Indicate the last logins of users and ttys.
`lifcp`	Copy to or from LIF files.
`lifls`	List the contents of an LIF directory.
`lifrm`	Remove an LIF file.
`linkloop`	Verify LAN connectivity with link level loopback.
`ln`	Link files and directories.
`login`	Sign on; start a terminal session.
`logname`	Get the login name.
`lp, lpalt, cancel`	Print, alter, or cancel requests on an LP printer or plotter.
`lpadmin`	Configure the LP spooling system.
`lpsched, lpshut, lpmove, lpfence`	Start or stop the LP request scheduler, move requests, and define the minimum priority for printing.
`lpstat`	Report line printer status information.
`ls, lc, l, ll, lsf, lsr, lsx`	List the contents of directories.
`lsacl`	List the access control lists (ACLs) of files.
`lsdev`	List device drivers in the system.
`lssf`	List a special file.
`lvchange`	Change LVM logical volume characteristics.
`lvcreate`	Create a logical volume in the LVM volume group.
`lvdisplay`	Display information about LVM logical volumes.
`lvextend`	Increase space or increase mirrors for LVM logical volume.

Commands *(continued)*

Command	Description
lvlnboot	Prepare an LVM logical volume to be the root, boot, primary swap, or dump volume.
lvmerge	Merge two LVM logical volumes into one logical volume.
lvreduce	Decrease the space allocation or number of mirror copies of logical volumes.
lvremove	Remove one or more logical volumes from the LVM volume group.
lvrmboot	Remove the LVM logical volume link to the root, primary swap, or dump volume.
mail, rmail	Send mail to users or read mail.
man	Find manual information by keywords; print out a manual entry.
mediainit	Initialize disk or cartridge tape media; partition DDS tape.
mesg	Permit or deny messages to a terminal.
mkboot, rmboot	Install, update, or remove boot programs from a disk.
mkdir	Make a directory.
mkfifo	Make FIFO (named pipe) special files.
mkfs	Construct a file system.
mknod	Create special files.
mksf	Make a special (device) file.
model	Print detailed hardware model information.
more, page	File perusal filter for CRT viewing.
mount , umount	Mount and unmount file systems.
mountall, umountall	Mount and unmount multiple file systems.
mountd	NFS mount request server.
mt	Magnetic tape manipulating program.
mv	Move or rename files and directories.
named	Internet domain name server.
ndd	Network tuning.
netstat	Show the network status.
newfs	Construct a new file system.
newgrp	Switch to a new group.

Commands (*continued*)

Command	Description
nfsd, biod	NFS daemons.
nfsstat	Network File System statistics.
nice	Run a command at nondefault priority.
nohup	Run a command immune to hangups.
nslookup	Query name servers interactively.
ntpdate	Set the date and time via NTP.
ntpq	Standard Network Time Protocol query program.
passwd	Change a login password and associated attributes.
pax	Extracts, writes, and lists archive files; copies files and directory hierarchies. Can be used for backup and restore.
pcnfsd	PC-NFS authentication and print request server.
pdc	Processor Dependent Code (firmware).
ping	Send ICMP Echo Request packets to a network host.
ps	Report process status.
pvchange	Change the characteristics and access path of a physical volume in an LVM volume group.
pvck	Check or repair a physical volume in an LVM volume group.
pvcreate	Create a physical volume for use in an LVM volume group.
pvdisplay	Display information about physical volumes within an LVM volume group.
pwck, grpck	Password or group file checkers.
pwd	Working directory name.
rarpd	Reverse Address Resolution Protocol daemon.
rc	General purpose sequencer invoked upon entering a new run level.
rcp	Remote file copy over a network.
read	Read a line from stdin. Often used in shell scripts.
reboot	Reboot the system.
remsh, rexec	Execute from a remote shell.
remshd	Remote shell server.
renice	Alter the priority of running processes.

Commands *(continued)*

Command	Description
`rlogin`	Remote login.
`rlogind`	Remote login server.
`rlpdaemon`	Remote spooling line printer daemon; message write daemon.
`rm`	Remove files or directories.
`rmdir`	Remove directories.
`rmnl`	Remove extra new line characters from a file. This is used to get rid of empty lines.
`rmsf`	Remove a special (device) file.
`route`	Manually manipulate the routing tables.
`rpcbind`	Universal addresses to RPC program number mapper.
`rpcinfo`	Report RPC information.
`ruptime`	Show the status of local machines on a network.
`rusers`	Determine who is logged into machines on a local network.
`rwho`	Show who is logged into local machines.
`rwhod`	System status server.
`sam`	System administration manager.
`samlog_viewer`	A tool for viewing and saving the SAM logfile.
`sar`	System activity reporter.
`sed`	Stream text editor.
`sh, rsh`	Standard and restricted POSIX.2 conformant command shells.
`shar`	Make a shell archive package.
`showmount`	Show all remote mounts.
`shutdown`	Terminate all processing.
`sleep`	Suspend execution for an interval.
`sort`	Sort or merge files.
`strings`	Find the printable strings in an object or other binary file.
`stty`	Set the options for a terminal port.
`su`	Switch user.
`swacl`	View or modify the Access Control Lists (ACLs) which protect software products.

Commands (*continued*)

Command	Description
swagentd, swagent	Serve local or remote SD software management tasks.
swapinfo	System paging space information.
swapon	Enable the device or file system for paging.
swconfig	Configure, unconfigure, or reconfigure installed software.
swinstall, swcopy	Install and configure software products; copy software products for subsequent installation or distribution.
swlist	Display information about software products.
swmodify	Modify software products in a target root or depot.
swpackage	Package software products into a target depot or tape.
swreg	Register or unregister depots and roots.
swremove	Unconfigure and remove software products.
swverify	Verify software products.
sysdef	Display the system definition.
syslogd	Log system messages.
tail	Deliver the last part of a file.
talk	Talk to another user over a network.
tar	Tape file archiver. Used for backup and restore.
tee	Pipe fitting.
telnet	User interface to the TELNET protocol.
telnetd	TELNET protocol server.
test	Condition evaluation command. Mostly used in shell scripts.
tftp	Trivial file transfer program.
time	Time a command.
timex	Time a command; report process data and system activity.
top	Display and update information about the top processes on the system.
touch	Update the access, modification, and/or change times of file. Also creates a zero byte size file.
true, false	Return an exit status of zero or one respectively.

Commands *(continued)*

Command	Description
`tset, reset`	Terminal dependent initialization.
`tty, pty`	Get the name of the terminal.
`ttytype`	Terminal identification program.
`umask`	Set or display the file mode creation mask.
`uname`	Display information about a computer system; set a node name (system name).
`uniq`	Report repeated lines in a file.
`uptime, w`	Show how long a system has been up, and/or who is logged in and what they are doing.
`useradd`	Add a new user login to the system.
`userdel`	Delete a user login from the system.
`usermod`	Modify a user login on the system.
`users`	Compact list of users who are on the system.
`vgcfgbackup`	Create or update LVM volume group configuration backup files.
`vgcfgrestore`	Display or restore the LVM volume group configuration from a backup file.
`vgchange`	Set the LVM volume group availability.
`vgcreate`	Create an LVM volume group.
`vgdisplay`	Display information about LVM volume groups.
`vgexport`	Export an LVM volume group and its associated logical volumes.
`vgextend`	Extend an LVM volume group by adding physical volumes.
`vgimport`	Import an LVM volume group onto the system.
`vgreduce`	Remove physical volumes from an LVM volume group.
`vgremove`	Remove the LVM volume group definition from the system.
`vgscan`	Scan physical volumes for LVM volume groups.
`vi, view, vedit`	Screen oriented (visual) text editor.
`vipw`	Edit the password file.
`vmstat`	Report virtual memory statistics.
`wait`	Await process completion.

Commands (*continued*)

Command	Description
wall	Write a message to all users.
wc	Count words, lines, bytes, or characters in a file.
whereis	Locate the source, binary, and/or manual for program.
which	Locate a program file including aliases and paths.
whoami	Print the effective current user ID.
whodo	List which users are doing what.
xntpd	Network Time Protocol daemon.
ypcat	Print all values in the Network Information Service map.
ypinit	Build and install Network Information Service databases.
ypmake	Create or rebuild Network Information Service databases.
ypmatch	Print the values of selected keys in the Network Information Service map.
yppasswd	Change a login password in the Network Information System (NIS).
yppasswdd	Daemon for modifying the Network Information Service password database.
yppoll	Query the NIS server for information about the NIS map.
yppush	Force the propagation of the Network Information Service database.
ypserv, ypbind, ypxfrd	Network Information Service (NIS) server, binder, and transfer processes.
ypset	Bind to a particular Network Information Service server.
ypupdated, rpc.ypupdated	Server for changing NIS information.
ypwhich	List which host is the Network Information System server or map master.
ypxfr	Transfer an NIS database from the server to local node.

Configuration Files

File Name	Description
/etc/exports	Describes the directories that can be exported to NFS clients.
/etc/xtab	Contains entries for directories that are currently exported.
/etc/fstab	Contains a list of mountable file-system entries.
/etc/ftpuser	The ftpd daemon rejects remote logins to local user accounts that are named in /etc/ftpusers.
/etc/group	The /etc/group file exists to supply names for each group.
/etc/hosts	Associates Internet (IP) addresses with official host names and aliases.
/etc/hosts.equiv, $HOME/.rhosts	Specifies remote hosts and users that are "equivalent" to the local host or user.
/etc/inetd.conf	Configuration file for the inetd daemon.
/var/adm/inetd.sec	Optional security file for the inetd daemon.
/etc/inittab	Supplies the script to the init boot daemon.
/etc/issue	Contains the issue or project identification to be printed as a login prompt.
/etc/mnttab	Contains a table of devices mounted by the mount command.
/etc/networks	Associates Internet (IP) addresses with official network names and aliases.
/etc/nsswitch.conf	Service switch configuration file.
/etc/passwd	Contains user names, passwords, and other user information.
/etc/profile	System startup file for the user shell.
$HOME/.profile	User startup file for a shell.
$HOME/.exrc	Startup configuration file for the vi editor.
/etc/ntp.conf	Configuration file for the NTP xntpd daemon.
/etc/rpc	Contains user-readable names that can be used in place of RPC program numbers.
/etc/services	Associates official service names and aliases with the port number and protocol the services use.
/etc/shells	Contains a list of legal shells on the system.

This is a sample test paper for the HP-UX certification examination. The correct answers are written in boldface. In the actual test the number of questions may vary.

1. *On a UNIX system, the primary interaction of a user is with:*
   A. Kernel
   B. Shell
   C. device drivers
   D. file system

2. *The* rsh *command on HP-UX can be used to:*
   A. execute a remote command
   B. log in and initiate a shell on a remote system
   C. This is a restricted shell on HP-UX.
   D. grant read-only access to a system

3. *Which shell does not have history feature?*
   A. Bourne shell
   B. Korn Shell
   C. C Shell
   D. POSIX shell

4. *The* **root** *user has user ID:*
   A. 0
   B. 1
   C. 100
   D. The **root** user may have any user ID.

5. *What is the default history file in the HP-UX POSIX shell?*
   A. history
   B. $HOME/.history
   C. $HOME/.sh_history
   D. /etc/history

6. *The* alias *command in the POSIX shell is used to:*
   A. create a command alias
   B. create a mail alias

C. create shell alias

D. create a file system alias

7. *You want to add a directory to the PATH variable for all users of the POSIX shell. Which file will you modify?*

    A. `/etc/profile`

    B. `$HOME/.profile` of the root user

    C. `/home/root/profile`

    D. `/etc/default`

8. *You use a command "`cat > myfile`". What will be the result of this command?*

    A. Nothing happens and you will get the command prompt back.

    B. The file named `myfile` is overwritten and you get the command prompt back.

    C. The command waits for user input which is appended to the file named `myfile`.

    D. The command waits for user input which is written to the file named `myfile`. The original contents of the file are deleted.

9. *When you use the `ll` command, the first character of each line in the output of the command shows the type of the file. The next nine characters show file access permissions for HP-UX users. What is the order of these access permissions?*

    A. others, group, owner

    B. owner, group, others

    C. owner, others, group

    D. group, owner, others

10. *Which command do you use to list hidden files?*

    A. `ls -h`

    B. `ls -l`

    C. `ls -a`

    D. `ls`

11. *You are in the `/var/tmp` directory and want to copy file `myfile` from the `/tmp` directory to the current directory. Which command cannot be used for this purpose?*

    A. `cp /tmp/myfile .`

    B. `cp /tmp/myfile /var/tmp`

C. create shell alias

D. create a file system alias

7. *You want to add a directory to the PATH variable for all users of the POSIX shell. Which file will you modify?*

    A. `/etc/profile`

    B. `$HOME/.profile` of the root user

    C. `/home/root/profile`

    D. `/etc/default`

8. *You use a command* "`cat > myfile`". *What will be the result of this command?*

    A. Nothing happens and you will get the command prompt back.

    B. The file named `myfile` is overwritten and you get the command prompt back.

    C. The command waits for user input which is appended to the file named `myfile`.

    D. The command waits for user input which is written to the file named `myfile`. The original contents of the file are deleted.

9. *When you use the* `ll` *command, the first character of each line in the output of the command shows the type of the file. The next nine characters show file access permissions for HP-UX users. What is the order of these access permissions?*

    A. others, group, owner

    B. owner, group, others

    C. owner, others, group

    D. group, owner, others

10. *Which command do you use to list hidden files?*

    A. `ls -h`

    B. `ls -l`

    C. `ls -a`

    D. `ls`

11. *You are in the* `/var/tmp` *directory and want to copy file* `myfile` *from the* `/tmp` *directory to the current directory. Which command cannot be used for this purpose?*

    A. `cp /tmp/myfile .`

    B. `cp /tmp/myfile /var/tmp`

APPENDIX D: SAMPLE HP-UX CERTIFICATION EXAM

This is a sample test paper for the HP-UX certification examination. The correct answers are written in boldface. In the actual test the number of questions may vary.

1. *On a UNIX system, the primary interaction of a user is with:*
   A. Kernel
   B. Shell
   C. device drivers
   D. file system

2. *The* rsh *command on HP-UX can be used to:*
   A. execute a remote command
   B. log in and initiate a shell on a remote system
   C. This is a restricted shell on HP-UX.
   D. grant read-only access to a system

3. *Which shell does not have history feature?*
   A. Bourne shell
   B. Korn Shell
   C. C Shell
   D. POSIX shell

4. *The* root *user has user ID:*
   A. 0
   B. 1
   C. 100
   D. The root user may have any user ID.

5. *What is the default history file in the HP-UX POSIX shell?*
   A. history
   B. $HOME/.history
   C. $HOME/.sh_history
   D. /etc/history

6. *The* alias *command in the POSIX shell is used to:*
   A. create a command alias
   B. create a mail alias

C. `cp ../../tmp/myfile /var/tmp`

D. `cp /tmp/myfile ..`

12. *Which command will you use to count the number of lines in a text file?*

   A. `wc`

   B. `ls`

   C. `lines`

   D. `cat`

13. *Which command displays the value of the HOME variable?*

   A. `echo $HOME`

   B. `echo HOME`

   C. `echo '$HOME'`

   D. `echo ˋ$HOMEˋ`

14. *Pipes are used to:*

   A. redirect standard input

   B. redirect standard output

   C. redirect either standard input or standard output but not both simultaneously

   D. send output of one command to the input of another command.

15. *Which mode is not used in* `vi` *editor?*

   A. command mode

   B. insert mode

   C. preserve mode

   D. last line mode

16. *You want to search all lines in a file* `myfile` *that start with the word* "`boota`". *Which of the following commands will you use?*

   A. `grep $boota myfile`

   B. `grep ^boota myfile`

   C. `grep boota^ myfile`

   D. `grep boota$ myfile`

17. *Which variable in a shell program is used to determine the total number of command line arguments?*

   A. `$?`

   B. `$#`

   C. `$*`

   D. `${10}`

18. *Which of the following is* not *a shell program control structure?*

   A. while-do-done

   B. until-do-done

   C. repeat-do-done

   D. if-then-fi

19. *Which statement is* not *true?*

   A. SAM can be used in both text and graphic modes.

   B. SAM can be used to grant restricted access to users.

   C. SAM can be used for troubleshooting.

   D. SAM can be used for routine system administration tasks.

20. *The* `set_parms` *command is used to:*

   A. set the hostname.

   B. set the time zone.

   C. set the IP address.

   D. all of the above

21. *What is the secondary system loader?*

   A. the `hpux` utility

   B. the `init` process

   C. PDC

   D. the `/stand/system`

22. *HP-UX Software Distributor commands are used for:*

   A. installing and removing software

   B. distributing software packages

   C. verifying installed software

   D. all of the above

23. *A software bundle contains:*

   A. software depots

   B. filesets that may belong to different products

   C. filesets that may belong to only one product

   D. filesets that belong to subproducts of only one product

24. *What is a file descriptor?*

   A. It is a number used to reference an open file.

   B. It represents the inode number of a file.

C. It corresponds to a process table entry for a process created by a file.

D. It is the number of a directory entry for the file in a filesystem.

25. *Which of the following is* not *a label in the* `swinstall.log` *file?*

    A. ERROR

    B. WARNING

    C. CRITICAL

    D. NOTE

26. *Which command is used to build a new HP-UX kernel?*

    A. `mk_kernel`

    B. `make`

    C. `build_kernel`

    D. `make_vmunix`

27. *Three disks are attached to an SCSI adapter with device numbers 6, 1, and 15. Which of these has the highest priority?*

    A. 6

    B. 1

    C. 15

    D. All disks have the same priority.

28. *Which statement is* not *true?*

    A. A major device number represents a kernel driver used for a device.

    B. All devices of the same type have the same major number.

    C. All devices of the same type have the same minor device number.

    D. A minor device number is a six digit hexadecimal number.

29. *What is the major device number for LVM device files?*

    A. 64

    B. 32

    C. 128

    D. 1

30. *What is the default physical extent size used in LVM?*

    A. 4 Mbytes

    B. 4 Kbytes

    C. 16 Mbytes

    D. 16 Kbytes

31.   *Which step is required before adding a new disk to a volume group?*

A. **create a physical volume**

B. extend the logical volume

C. create a filesystem

D. extend the filesystem.

32.   *What is the name for the default volume group?*

A. `default`

B. **`vg00`**

C. `vgdefault`

D. There is no particular name for the default group. Any group can be configured as the default volume group.

33.   *Which information is* not *displayed when the* `pvdisplay` *command is used without any command-line options?*

A. name of the volume group to which the physical volume is related

B. total number of physical extents

C. **name of the filesystem created on the disk**

D. allocated physical extents

34.   *What is the default number of the logical volumes in a volume group?*

A. 15

B. 16

C. **255**

D. 1024

35.   *A filesystem metadata area contains:*

A. superblock

B. inodes

C. directory area

D. **all of the above**

36.   *Which statement is* true?

A. HFS keeps a record of all transactions in the intent log.

B. **JFS keeps a record of all transactions in the intent log.**

C. Both JFS and HFS keep a record of all transactions in the intent log.

D. The JFS filesystem size cannot be modified.

37. *Which command can be used to display the filesystem usage on HP-UX?*

    A. `df`

    B. `bdf`

    C. `rbdf`

    D. all of the above

38. *Which is* not *a standard state of any HP-UX process.*

    A. running

    B. sleeping

    C. zombie

    D. printing

39. *Which command is used to cancel a print job?*

    A. `cancel`

    B. `stop`

    C. `rm`

    D. `disable`

40. *Data backed up by the* `fbackup` *command is restored by:*

    A. the `frecover` command

    B. the `frestore` command

    C. the `tar` command

    D. It can be restored by any of the above commands.

41. *The* `cron` *daemon is responsible for jobs submitted by:*

    A. the `crontab` utility only

    B. the `at` utility only

    C. the `batch` utility only

    D. jobs submitted by the `at`, `batch`, and `crontab` utilities

42. *Fast Ethernet operates at which speed?*

    A. 10 Mbits per second

    B. 100 Mbits per second

    C. 155 Mbits per second

    D. One gigabyte per second

43. *The presentation layer in the OSI reference model is responsible for:*

    A. data format conversion

    B. establishing a network connection

C. Routing

D. Flow control

44. *Which statement is* not *true?*

    A. A token ring network is physically connected star topology.

    B. A token ring network is physically connected ring topology.

    C. An Ethernet network may be connected in star topology.

    D. An Ethernet network may be connected in ring topology.

45. *BNC connectors are used with:*

    A. coaxial cable

    B. category 3 coaxial cable

    C. category 5 coaxial cable

    D. fiber optic cable

46. *Which of the following devices operates in layer 3 of the OSI model?*

    A. repeater

    B. router

    C. hub

    D. bridge

47. *In which type of network is the MAC address used?*

    A. Ethernet

    B. Token Ring

    C. FDDI

    D. all of the above

48. *The application layer in TCP/IP protocol is equivalent to which three OSI layers?*

    A. transport, network, presentation

    B. presentation, application, transport

    C. application, presentation, session

    D. session, application, transport

49. *What is the default subnet mask for the IP address 172.23.15.99?*

    A. 255.255.255.0

    B. 255.0.0.0

    C. 255.255.0.0

    D. 172.23.255.255

50. *What is the loopback address for a host?*

　　A. the first address on the network

　　B. any address ending with 0

　　C. 0.0.0.0

　　D. 127.0.0.1

51. *Which protocol is used to map an IP address to a MAC address?*

　　A. ARP

　　B. RARP

　　C. ICMP

　　D. TFTP

52. *Which file on HP-UX contains a list of standard port numbers for different applications?*

　　A. /etc/hosts

　　B. /etc/ports

　　C. /etc/services

　　D. /etc/protocols

53. *The* netstat *command can be used to:*

　　A. list the IP addresses assigned to network adapters

　　B. configure routes

　　C. number the incoming and outgoing data packets

　　D. all of the above

54. *The standard telnet port address is:*

　　A. 21

　　B. 23

　　C. 25

　　D. 80

55. *The* /var/adm/inetd.sec *file is used for:*

　　A. an added layer of security to the inetd daemon.

　　B. a secondary file for the inetd daemon which is used if the primary file is not present

　　C. a backup file for /etc/inetd.conf

　　D. a secondary log file for the inetd daemon

56. *Which of the following is* not *a hostname resolution service?*

    A. DNS

    B. NIS

    C. the /etc/hosts database file

    D. the /etc/resolv.conf file

57. *Which configuration file is used by the DNS daemon* named *at startup?*

    A. /etc/named.conf

    B. /etc/named.boot

    C. /etc/resolv.conf

    D. /etc/nsswitch.conf

58. *The default location for NIS maps is under which directory?*

    A. /var/yp

    B. /etc

    C. /etc/nis

    D. /var/nis

59. *Which command is used to configure the master NIS server?*

    A. ypinit

    B. ypmake

    C. ypserv

    D. ypset

60. *What is* not *true about NFS?*

    A. A system can act as NFS client and server at the same time.

    B. A system can export a single file, a directory, or a filesystem.

    C. A system can export a filesystem mounted from another NFS server.

    D. If a directory is exported, all of the directory tree under this directory is automatically exported.

61. *Which of the following daemon is* not *an NFS daemon?*

    A. rpc.mountd

    B. biod

    C. rpc.lockd

    D. named

62. *Which command is used to export filesystems manually?*

     A. exports

     B. exportfs

     C. showmount

     D. nfsstat

63. *Which of the following is* not *an NFS Automounter map?*

     A. direct

     B. indirect

     C. master

     D. slave

64. *What is the name of the NTP server daemon?*

     A. ntpd

     B. xntpd

     C. rpc.ntpd

     D. rpc.xntpd

APPENDIX E: GLOSSARY

A complete list of glossary items can be obtained by using the `man glossary` command on HP-UX.

. (dot)	A special file name that refers to the current directory.
.. (dot-dot)	A special file name that refers to the parent directory.
Absolute Path Name	A path name beginning with a slash (/).
Access Mode	A form of access permitted to a file.
Address Space	The range of memory locations to which a process can refer.
Archive	A file comprised of the contents of other files, such as the `tar` archive.
ASCII	An acronym for American Standard Code for Information Interchange.
Background Process	Any process that gives the shell prompt back to the user.
Backup	The process of making a copy of all or part of the file system in order to preserve it, in case a system crash occurs.
Block	The fundamental unit of information HP-UX uses for the access and storage location on a mass storage medium.
Block Special File	A special file associated with a mass storage device.
Boot, Boot-up	The process of loading, initializing, and running an operating system.
Boot Area	A portion of a mass storage medium on which the volume header and a "bootstrap" program used in booting the operating system reside.
Boot ROM	A program residing in ROM (Read-Only Memory) that executes each time the computer is powered up.
Bus Address	A number which makes up part of the address HP-UX uses to locate a particular device.

Character	An element used for the organization, control, or representation of text. Characters include graphic characters and control characters.
Character Set	A set of characters used to communicate in a native or computer language.
Character Special File	A special file associated with I/O devices that transfer data byte-by-byte.
Child Process	A new process created by a pre-existing process.
Command	A directive to perform a particular task.
Command Interpreter	A program which reads lines of text from standard input (typed at the keyboard or read from a file), and interprets them as requests to execute other programs. A command interpreter for HP-UX is called a shell.
Control Character	A character other than a graphic character that affects the recording, processing, transmission, or interpretation of text.
Controlling Terminal	A terminal that is associated with a session. Each session can have at most one controlling terminal associated with it, and a controlling terminal is associated with exactly one session.
Crash	The unexpected shutdown of a program or system. If the operating system crashes, this is a "system crash" and requires the system to be rebooted.
Current Directory	See working directory.
Current Working Directory	See working directory.
Daemon	A process which runs in the background, and which is usually immune to termination instructions from a terminal.
Default Search Path	The sequence of directory prefixes that HP-UX commands apply in searching for a file known by a relative path name (that is, a path name not beginning with a slash (/)).
Device	A computer peripheral or an object that appears to an application as such.
Device Address	See bus address.
Device File	See special file.

Directory	A file that provides the mapping between the names of files and their contents, and that is manipulated by the operating system alone.
End-Of-File (EOF)	The data returned when attempting to read past the logical end of a file.
Environment	The set of defined shell variables.
EOF	See end-of-file.
Epoch	The time period beginning at 0 hours, 0 minutes, 0 seconds, Coordinated Universal Time (UTC), on January 1, 1970. Increments quantify the amount of time elapsed from the Epoch to the referenced time.
FIFO Special File	A type of file. Data written to a FIFO is read on a first-in-first-out basis.
File	A stream of bytes that can be written to and/or read from.
File Access Mode	A characteristic of an open file description that determines whether the described file is open for reading, writing, or both.
File Access Permissions	Every file in the file hierarchy has a set of access permissions. These permissions are used in determining whether a process can perform a requested operation on the file.
File Descriptor	A small, unique, per-process, nonnegative integer identifier that is used to refer to a file opened for reading and/or writing.
File Hierarchy	The collection of one or more file systems available on a system.
File Name	A string of up to 255 bytes used to refer to an ordinary file, special file, or directory.
File System	A collection of files and supporting data structures residing on a mass storage volume.
Filter	A command that reads data from the standard input, performs a transformation on the data, and writes it to the standard output.
Fork	An HP-UX system call, which, when invoked by an existing process, causes a new process to be created.
Graphic Character	A character other than a control character that has a visual representation when hand-written, printed, or displayed.
Group	See group ID.

Group ID	Associates zero or more users who must all be permitted to access the same set of files.
Home Directory	The directory name given by the value of the environment variable HOME. When you first log in, login(1) automatically sets HOME to your login directory.
Host Name	An ASCII string of at most 8 characters.
init	A system process that performs initialization.
Inode	An inode is a structure that describes a file and is identified in the system by a file serial number. Every file or directory has an inode associated with it.
Interrupt Signal	The signal sent by SIGINT.
I/O Redirection	A mechanism provided by the HP-UX shell for changing the source of data for standard input and/or the destination of data for standard output and standard error.
Job Control	Allows users to selectively stop (suspend) execution of processes and continue (resume) their execution at a later time.
Kernel	The HP-UX operating system. The kernel is the executable code responsible for managing the computer's resources, such as allocating memory, creating processes, and scheduling programs for execution.
LIF	See Logical Interchange Format.
Link	A directory entry. It is an object that associates a file name with any type of file.
Link Count	The number of directory entries that refer to a particular file.
Logical Interchange Format (LIF)	A standard format for mass storage implemented on many Hewlett-Packard computers to aid in media transportability.
Login	The process of gaining access to HP-UX.
Login Directory	The directory in which a user is placed immediately after logging in. This directory is defined for each user in the /etc/passwd file. The shell variable HOME is set automatically to the user's login directory by login.

Magic Number	The first word of an `a.out-format` or archive file. This word contains the system ID, which states what machine (hardware) the file will run on and the file type (executable, sharable executable, archive, etc.)
Major Number	A number used exclusively to create special files that enable I/O to or from specific devices. This number indicates which device driver to use for the device.
Meta Character	A character that has special meaning to the HP-UX shell, as well as to commands.
Minor Number	A number that is an attribute of special files, specified during their creation and used whenever they are accessed, to enable I/O to or from specific devices.
Newline Character	The character with an ASCII value of 10 (line feed) used to separate lines of characters.
Node Name	A string of up to 31 characters, not including control characters or spaces, that uniquely identifies a node on a Local Area Network (LAN).
Ordinary File	A type of HP-UX file containing ASCII text.
Orphan Process	A child process that is left behind when a parent process terminates for any reason. The init process inherits all orphan processes.
Owner	The owner of a file is usually the creator of that file. However, the ownership of a file can be changed by the superuser or the current owner.
Parent Directory	The directory one level above a directory in the file hierarchy.
Parent Process	Whenever a new process is created by a currently-existing process, the currently existing process is said to be the parent process of the newly created process.
Parent Process ID	A new process is created by a currently active process. The parent process ID of a process is the process ID of its creator for the lifetime of the creator.
Password	A string of ASCII characters used to verify the identity of a user.
Path name	A sequence of directory names separated by slashes and ending with any file name.

Pipe	An interprocess I/O channel used to pass data between two processes.
Process	An invocation of a program or the execution of an image. Although all commands and utilities are executed within processes, not all commands or utilities have a one-to-one correspondence with processes. Some commands (such as cd) execute within a process, but do not create any new processes.
Process ID	A positive integer less than or equal to PID_MAX by which each active process in the system is uniquely identified during its lifetime.
Program	A sequence of instructions to the computer in the form of binary code.
Prompt	The characters displayed by the shell on the terminal indicating that the system is ready for a command.
Raw Disk	The name given to a disk for which there exists a character special file that allows direct transmission between the disk and the user's read or write buffer. A single read or write call results in exactly one I/O call.
Regular Expression	A string of zero or more characters that selects text.
Regular File	A type of file that is a randomly accessible sequence of bytes, with no further structure imposed by the system.
Relative Path Name	A path name that does not begin with a slash (/).
Root Directory	The highest level directory of the hierarchical file system.
Root Volume	The mass storage volume which contains the boot area (which contains the HP-UX kernel) and the root directory of the HP-UX file system.
Secondary Prompt	One or more characters that the shell prints on the display, indicating that more input is needed.
Set-Group-ID Bit	A single bit in the mode of every file in the file system. If a file is executed whose set-group-ID bit is set, the effective group ID of the process which executed the file is set equal to the real group ID of the owner of the file. See also group ID.

Set-User-ID Bit	A single bit in the mode of every file in the file system. If a file is executed whose set-user-ID bit is set, the effective user ID of the process that executed the file is set equal to the real user ID of the owner of the file.
Shell	A user interface to the HP-UX operating system. A shell often functions as both a command interpreter and an interpretive programming language.
Shell Program	See shell script.
Shell Script	A sequence of shell commands and shell programming language constructs stored in a file and invoked as a user command (program). No compilation is needed prior to execution because the shell recognizes the commands and constructs that make up the shell programming language.
Signal	A software interrupt sent to a process, informing it of special situations or events.
Single-User State	A condition of the HP-UX operating system in which the system console provides the only communication mechanism between the system and its user.
Special File	A file associated with an I/O device. Often called a device file.
Standard Error	The destination of error and special messages from a program, intended to be used for diagnostic messages. The standard error output is often called stderr.
Standard Input	The source of input data for a program. The standard input file is often called stdin.
Standard Output	The destination of output data from a program. The standard output file is often called stdout.
stderr	See standard error.
stdin	See standard input.
stdout	See standard output.
Sticky Bit	A single bit in the mode of every file in the file system. If set on a regular file, the contents of the file stay permanently in memory instead of being swapped back out to disk when the file has finished executing.

Subdirectory	A directory that is one or more levels lower in the file system hierarchy than a given directory.
Superblock	A block on each file system's mass storage medium which describes the file system.
Superuser	The HP-UX system administrator. This user has access to all files and can perform privileged operations. The superuser has a real user ID and an effective user ID of 0, and, by convention, the user name of `root`.
Symbolic Link	A type of file that indirectly refers to a path name.
System	The HP-UX operating system.
System Call	An HP-UX operating system kernel function available to the user through a high-level language.
System Console	A keyboard and display (or terminal) given a unique status by HP-UX and associated with the special file `/dev/console`. All boot ROM error messages, HP-UX system error messages, and certain system status messages are sent to the system console.
Terminal	A character special file that obeys the specifications of `termio`.
Text File	A file that contains characters organized into one or more lines.
tty	Originally, an abbreviation for teletypewriter; now, generally, a terminal.
User ID	Each system user is identified by an integer known as a user ID, which is in the range of zero to UID_MAX, inclusive.
Utility	An executable file, which might contain executable object code (that is, a program), or a list of commands to execute in a given order (that is, a shell script).
Volume Number	Part of an address used for devices.
Whitespace	One or more characters which, when displayed, cause a movement of the cursor or print head, but do not result in the display of any visible graphic.
Working Directory	Each process has associated with it the concept of a current working directory. For a shell, this appears as the directory in which you currently "reside."

Zombie Process   The name given to a process which terminates for any reason, but whose parent process has not yet waited for it to terminate (via `wait(2)`). The process which terminated continues to occupy a slot in the process table until its parent process waits for it.

INDEX

Hewlett-Packard Computer Education and Training

Hewlett-Packard's world-class education and training offers hands on education solutions including:

- Linux
- HP-UX System and Network Administration
- Y2K HP-UX Transition
- Advanced HP-UX System Administration
- IT Service Management using advanced Internet technologies
- Microsoft Windows NT
- Internet/Intranet
- MPE/iX
- Database Administration
- Software Development

HP's new IT Professional Certification program provides rigorous technical qualification for specific IT job roles including HP-UX System Administration, Network Management, Unix/NT Servers and Applications Management, and IT Service Management. For more information, go to http://education.hp.com/hpcert.htm.

In addition, HP's IT Resource Center is the perfect knowledge source for IT professionals. Through a vibrant and rich Web environment, IT professionals working in the areas of UNIX, Microsoft, networking, or MPE/iX gain access to continually updated knowledge pools.

http://education.hp.com

In the U.S. phone 1-800-HPCLASS (472-5277)